ACKNOWLEDGEMENTS

The original idea for this project was conceived while the EU was engaged in a heated debate with the energy industry and Member States on Commission proposals for liberalization Directives on electricity and gas. The unexpected length of time that this debate took led to a first version of the book being shelved until the law had emerged in a sufficiently settled state to allow in-depth analysis. By the end of 1998 it seemed that such a study was indeed possible. The draft was commenced at the *Fundación de Estudios de Regulación* in Madrid and written mostly in Dundee in Scotland. I am grateful to my colleagues at the Centre for Energy, Petroleum and Mineral Law and Policy at the University of Dundee for their support. In addition, I wish to thank Gaspar Ariño Ortiz of the University of Madrid (Autónoma) for his support at the initial stages of this work. It is perhaps fitting that a study of law and policy in a key economic sector that ultimately raises wider questions about governance in the EU should be fine-tuned at the Robert Schuman Centre for Advanced Studies at the European University Institute in Florence, Italy.

The book would be a less satisfactory work were it not for the considerable efforts of Michael Brothwood of Denton Wilde Sapte as consultant editor. When the idea was originally conceived, Michael and I proposed to write it together and to limit its scope to natural gas market liberalization. The new version was more ambitious in scope and as a result required an input of time that academics sometimes can make available but practising lawyers only rarely. I am grateful to Michael for agreeing to this rôle and for reviewing, commenting on, and making suggestions for the final version of the work, bringing important insights to a number of issues raised in this book.

Since the book examines in places processes of deliberation and negotiation that were not always public and about which little has been published, a number of people have been consulted for opinions as to the accuracy of the accounts presented in these pages. I wish to acknowledge the contribution of Ana Aguado, Monica Baumanns, Robert de Bauw, Christian Egenhofer, Claus-Dieter Ehlermann, Leo Flynn, Margot Loudon, Jose Sierra, and Bruno de Witte. Responsibility for the final publication lies with the author entirely.

Peter Duncanson Cameron
Robert Schuman Centre for Advanced Studies
European University Institute, Florence
October 2001

COMPETITION IN ENERGY MARKETS: LAW AND REGULATION IN THE EUROPEAN UNION

COMPETITION IN ENERGY MARKETS: LAW AND REGULATION IN THE EUROPEAN UNION

PETER DUNCANSON CAMERON

Consultant Editor: Michael Brothwood, M.A. (Cantab), Solicitor

Great Clarendon Street, Oxford OX2 6DP

Oxford University Press is a department of the University of Oxford.
It furthers the University's objective of excellence in research, scholarship,
and education by publishing worldwide in

Oxford New York

Auckland Bangkok Buenos Aires Cape Town Chennai
Dar es Salaam Delhi Hong Kong Istanbul Karachi Kolkata
Kuala Lumpur Madrid Melbourne Mexico City Mumbai Nairobi
São Paulo Shanghai Taipei Tokyo Toronto

Oxford is a registered trade mark of Oxford University Press
in the UK and in certain other countries

Published in the United States
by Oxford University Press Inc., New York

First published 2002

British Library Cataloguing in Publication Data

Data available

Library of Congress Cataloging in Publication Data

Data available

ISBN 0–19–825770–8

3 5 7 9 10 8 6 4 2

Typeset in Garamond by
Cambrian Typesetters, Frimley, Surrey

Printed in Great Britain
on acid-free paper by
Biddles Ltd, *www.biddles.co.uk*

To Margaret and Stewart Cameron

FOREWORD

There is broad agreement that European energy markets should be liberalized and also that they need some degree of regulation. The question of how this should be achieved raises a problem that is both exceptionally important and exceptionally difficult.

It is important because the availability of energy at competitive prices affects us all, directly and indirectly. It is difficult because there are so many competing interests at stake, yet there is no consensus as to what those interests are, far less how they should be reconciled.

This book is probably the first in any language that seeks not only to assess the nature of the problem and the steps that have been taken so far in the European Union to resolve it, but also to point up the positive interaction and potential conflicts between primary and secondary legislation, judicial decisions, and political action.

The basic rules of the EC Treaty are designed to ensure free movement of goods and services and to promote competition for the benefit of the economy—and ultimately of the consumer. In this context, the various forms of energy are 'goods' and their supply is a form of 'services'. The primacy of the Treaty rules has been invoked in a series of judgments of the European Court of Justice removing some of the political roadblocks to deregulation of sectors and markets formerly subject to state ownership and control, including the energy sector.[1]

At the same time, the Court has recognized the importance in the energy sector of security and continuity of supply and—since the policy emphasis of the Treaties was changed by the Treaties of Maastricht and Amsterdam—protection of the environment and promotion of renewable energy sources. The conflict between all these competing objectives has recently been illustrated by the Court's judgment in *PreussenElektra*; while the earlier judgment in *Commission v France* emphasized that there are limits to the extent to which the Court can be expected to make social and economic choices and to compensate for political and legislative inaction.[2]

---

[1] eg, Case C-393/92, *Almelo* [1994] ECR I-1477.

[2] See Case C-379/98, *PreussenElektra* AG and Schleswag AG [2001] ECR I-2099, and Case 159/94, *Commission v France* [1997] ECR I-5815.

It should be recognized that the energy sector is not unique in these respects. The achievement of a fully functioning internal market in other sectors, such as telecommunications, transport, and finance, has thrown up comparable problems. Detailed legislation to supplement the basic Treaty rules is needed to give effect to political choices and to define more precisely the legal obligations of the Institutions of the Union, the Member States, and economic operators. Legislation that has been promoted by the European Commission in all these sectors has served to filled some of the gaps. But it has also drawn attention to the complex problems and deep political differences that remain.

Despite the success of the 1992 programme, a free competitive internal market is not yet a reality. It is important that policymakers, legislators, and commentators should be fully aware of what remains to be done and how difficult it will be to achieve it. They will find this book a valuable guide to the problems of the energy sector and the possible solutions.

But I hope the book will also serve as a case study of problems of governance in the twenty-first century. What kind of legislation is needed to achieve economic and social goals in complex markets? How should political choices be translated into legislative texts? What should be the respective responsibilities of legislators, administrators, and judges? In particular, how far can judges be expected to decide which of a number of conflicting objectives, defined in Treaties, Conventions and Legislation, should take precedence in any particular case?

These are questions that need to be discussed, not only by lawyers and constitutional experts, but also by citizens, since the answers affect everyone, albeit indirectly, almost as much as the availability of energy in everyday life. This book will help to stimulate the debate.

DAVID EDWARD

Court of Justice of the European Communities
Luxembourg
14 September 2001

INTRODUCTION

The subject of this book is the law and regulation of energy markets in the European Union, focusing on the markets for electricity and natural gas.

It has two main aims. First, to provide a detailed analysis of the legislation and relevant rules of law made by European Community institutions that apply to the electricity and gas industries. In doing so, it explains the EU legislative process and the institutional framework for supervision and enforcement. Secondly, it provides a detailed account of the programme of liberalization in the EU energy sector known as the Internal Energy Market programme, which began in 1988 and continues today.

The study is divided into three PARTS.

PART I comprises two chapters setting the scene for the rest of the book.

PART II examines in detail the establishment of a legal framework in the EU for the Internal Energy Market, covering its origins, policy development, the principal legislation adopted, and the rôle of primary law and jurisprudence.

PART III is concerned with the transition to a single market. Inevitably, since this process is not yet completed, these chapters highlight problems that have arisen and initial attempts at their solution, but cannot go further at this stage.

The subject of PART I is the Origins of a Single Market in Energy. Chapter 1 provides an overview of the global context of energy market liberalization, emphasizing how recent the trend is from public monopolies dominating the electricity and gas sectors to a liberalized structure with a variable degree of market regulation. The notion of 'paradigm shifts' has been used to characterize this change in policy and practice. It was also felt to be important to capture the element of 'Europe' in this wider process of change (see below). Chapter 1 concludes with an introduction to the European Commission's challenge to the segmented EU energy market structure which is preventing the integration of the EU in a way that complies with the EC Treaty requirements and especially the assumptions on which it is based.

Chapter 2 raises a question about the EU and energy market liberalization: to what extent has the process of liberalization within the EU been dependent on the continuous constitutional reorganization that has occurred over the last 15 years? The initiative for a change in the energy sector dates back to the effects of the

Single Act of 1986. Progress with secondary legislation has been linked to a succession of amendments to the EC Treaty in relation to the powers of the respective Community institutions, decision-making procedures, especially on voting and the status of services of general economic interest. A pooling of sovereignty by the Member States has been an important part of this process, one that has had important effects on energy, a sector for decades so very close to national economic policies.

This is the 'Europe' factor in energy market liberalization within the EU, which distinguishes it from experiments in energy market liberalization elsewhere in the world. The EU goal of a single, integrated market among 15 Member States is similarly a unique feature. Chapter 2 provides an introduction to the institutions, law-making procedures and key energy texts of the EU, showing how their recent growth is linked to and influenced by this process of constitutional reform. At the same time, it notes the legal implications of the wider, pan-European dimension of EU energy market reform.

PART II examines the various steps that have led to the Establishment of a Legal Framework for a more open energy sector. The axis on which this PART turns is the choice made with respect to legal reform of the energy sector and electricity and gas in particular. It was often said that if liberalization could not be achieved by means of the consensus-oriented procedure of Article 95 (formerly Article 100A), recourse could be had to the law-making powers granted to the Commission under Article 86(3) (formerly Article 90(3)) and if necessary to other powers granted to the Commission by the EC Treaty. The former approach was considered at an early stage by the Commission and abandoned. The latter (challenge by the Commission to existing laws) was initiated in 1992 in relation to the export/import monopolies in electricity and gas in a number of Member States. This led after a very lengthy process to ECJ judgments on import and export monopolies in electricity and gas. Neither proved to be a serious alternative to the legislative procedure under Article 95.

Chapter 3 examines the first stage of establishing a legal framework, involving the adoption of four Directives covering transit (electricity and gas dealt with separately), price transparency, and licensing of hydrocarbons reserves. It is seen that the legislative achievements of the period were overshadowed by the highly acrimonious exchanges between the Commission, the Member States and the energy industry, focusing mainly upon the proposals (contained in two other draft Directives) to allow network access to third parties. During this period the EC Treaty was also modified (at Maastricht) and as a result the influence of the Parliament on the Commission's proposals (as amended by the Council) increased. A new emphasis upon public service obligations was one result of this constitutional development.

Chapter 4 analyses in fairly extensive detail the various provisions of the controversial Directives providing for the introduction of common rules for the electricity and gas sectors, which are to bring about, on a staged basis, a limited liberalization of the electricity and gas markets. They introduced for the first time in these sectors ideas of network access, unbundling, and 'eligible customers'. Difficulties in providing fair and appropriate solutions to problems arising from the transition to a competitive market are discussed, including reciprocity, compensation for stranded assets, and 'take-or-pay' clauses in long-term contracts. Particular complexities are seen to arise from the gas industry's complex dependence on supplies from non-EU countries.

Chapter 5 provides an overview of the developments in the primary law during this period. For many years there had been scarcely any rulings by the ECJ on the electricity and gas sectors, but this began to change with the Commission's attempts to challenge incumbent monopolies in import, export, transmission, and distribution. A key development was the ECJ challenge to the assumption that special or exclusive rights granted to monopolies were sacrosanct. However, the slow and controversial character of reform by the legislative route made the ECJ reluctant to become involved in a highly political process, as is evident from the judgments on import and export monopolies in electricity and gas. This caution was linked to an awareness of the process of constitutional development. The balance between Council and Parliament on the one hand and ECJ on the other discouraged the latter from performing a rôle that would be perceived as having a legislative character.

PART III concerns developments that have occurred since the adoption of the two Directives on electricity and gas. The Transition to a Liberalized Energy Market has been characterized by the emergence of various obstacles to integration and by attempts to solve them by new and traditional mechanisms.

Chapter 6 explains how the implementation of the Electricity and Gas Directives in most Member States far exceeded—both in scope and speed of introduction—the minimum requirements of the Directives, creating expectations of reform that could not be met within the framework of the two Directives. In addition to problems that had been underestimated or ignored when the Directives were drafted, there was a demand from more and more market players and Member State governments for an acceleration of the liberalization process, both within and between Member States. The Commission sought mechanisms appropriate to tackling this demand for further reform and, as an alternative to promoting further legislation, established two Fora designed to encourage debate among the Member State regulators and to promote change by means of persuasion.

Chapter 7 summarizes the experience of so-called 'Florence' and 'Madrid' Regulatory Fora, and their relationship to the two other traditional instruments of reform—legislation to amend and supplement the Directives; and competition law, rapidly being reshaped to address the challenges of electricity and gas markets in transition. The Fora were sometimes described as new instruments of governance appropriate to the EU at its current stage of constitutional development. However, any results reaped by the Fora proved too limited for many Member States who, by means of summit meetings of Heads of State (European Council meetings), requested the Commission first to draft new legislative measures, and then to report back to it for further instructions. The 'activist' approach of competition policy and its efforts is explained in some detail.

Finally, Chapter 8 looks at the legislative package presented by the Commission to the Council in 2001. These measures are evidence of a dissatisfaction with the progress of competition in EU energy markets in two senses. First and foremost, they are an attempt to redress the shortcomings of the existing legal and regulatory framework and to build upon and generalize its successes across the EU. Secondly, they are evidence of reactions to the experience of liberalization among the Member States. Early experience of the recently-established regulatory structures, for example, has shown their performance has not always been optimal. Potential negative effects of liberalization have also had to be taken into account, such as falling employment, environmental considerations and security of supply. In addition, the experience of reform in non-energy network sectors of the EU economies (and indeed outside the EU itself) has shown that there are similarities in the tasks of regulators which suggest that some cross-fertilization of experiences may be beneficial.

The final shape of the proposals for reform will be influenced by this wider reappraisal of efforts at constructing a legal and regulatory framework for greater competition in network-bound markets.

This book has attempted to show how the issues arise at the EU level. It has not therefore had much to say about the individual experiences of Member States in energy market reform. It is clear from the developments since the adoption of the Directives that the single market is still a 'work-in-progress', as the transitional process continues. It is also clear that legislation continues to play a central rôle in promoting competition, while the alternative models of consensus building appear to be too embryonic to achieve this end in a sector dominated by large incumbent players.

CONTENTS—SUMMARY

CONTENTS

CONTENTS: TABLES

TABLES OF CASES

EUROPEAN COURT OF JUSTICE AND COURT OF FIRST INSTANCE

Alphabetical

Numerical

EUROPEAN COMMISSION DECISIONS

TABLES OF LEGISLATION

EUROPEAN UNION

Treaties

Decisions

Directives

Regulations

Notices

Recommendations

Council Recommendation 83/230/EEC on methods of forming natural gas prices and tariffs in the Community (OJ 1983 L123/40) 3.14
Council Recommendation 81/924/EEC on electricity tariff structures in the Community (OJ 1981 L337/12) 3.14
Commission Recommendation 1999/28/EC on TEN's authorization procedures (OJ 1999 L8/27) 2.96

Agreements

EEA Agreement 2.03, 2.97, 2.98, 2.100–2.101, 2.103, 2.106, 2.131, 2.151, 3.16, 3.46, 5.95, 6.11, 6.51, 6.90
Annex IV 2.99
point 14 . . . . .2.108
Appendix 2 . . . . .3.18
Art 2(1)(a) 3.18
Art 3(1) 3.18
Appendix 3 . . . . .2.110
Appendix 4 . . . . .3.24
Annex XXI, point 26 . . . . .3.13
Art 53(1) 2.107
EU–Switzerland Free Trade Agreement 4.54

General Agreement on Tariffs and Trade 1.18, 2.118, 6.87

INOGATE Agreement 2.149

Partnership and Co-operation Agreement between the EU and Russia (OJ 1997 L 327/3) 2.144
Art 65 . . . . .2.143

Stockholm Convention 2.98

Trade and Commercial Co-operation Agreement between the EC and the former USSR 1989 . . . . .2.143

Other Jurisdictions

Belgium
Act of 8 August 1980
Art 181 . . . . .5.35
Act of 29 July 1983 . . . . .5.35

Portugal

Spain

United Kingdom

ABBREVIATIONS

AG	*Aktiengesellschaft*
AP	Accession Partnerships
ATC	Available Transmission Capacity
Bcm	Billion cubic metres
BDI	*Bundesverband der Deutschen Industrie* (Federal Association for German Industry)
BG	British Gas
BGW	*Bundesverband der Deutschen Gas- und Wasserwirtschaft* (Federal Association for German Gas and Water Industry)
CBT	Cross-Border Transaction
CCEME	*Comité Consultatif États Membres Électricité* (Consultative Committee of Member States on Electricity, organized by the EC)
CCEMG	*Comité Consultatif États Membres Gaz* (Consultative Committee of Member States on Natural Gas, organized by the EU)
CEEC	Central and East European Countries
CEEP	*Centre européen d'enterprises public*
Ceer	Council of European Energy Regulators
CEGB	Central Electricity Generating Board
Cegedel	Central European Generators and Distributors of Electricity
Centrel	Central European Electricity Networks
Cert	Committee on Energy, Research and Technology of the European Parliament
CFI	Court of First Instance
CHP	Combined Heat and Power
CJEG	*Cahiers Juridique de l'Électricité et du Gaz*
Coreper	Committee of Permanent Representatives
CTC	*Costes de Transición a la Competencia* (Transition Costs to a Competitive Market)
DEP	*Dimitoki Etairia Pliroforissis* (Greek plaintiff in ERT case)
DG	Directorate General (European Commission)
DONG	*Dansk Olie og Naturgas* (Danish National Oil and Gas Company)
DSO	Distribution System Operator
EBH	*Energie Bedrijf Holland*
EC	European Commission
ECJ	European Court of Justice
ECT	Energy Charter Treaty

ECU	European Currency Unit
ED	Electricity Directive
EdF	*Électricité de France* (French National Electricity Utility)
EEA	European Economic Area
Efet	European Federation of Energy Traders
EG	*Europäische Gemeinschaft* (European Community)
EnBH	*Energiewerke Baden-Württemberg* (full name no longer used, only acronym)
Enel	*Ente Nazionale per l'Energia Elletrica* (Italian National Energy Utility)
ENER	European Network of Energy Research
ENI	*Ente Nazionale Idrocarburi*
E.ON	Name given to merged entity between German utilities VEBA and VIAG
ERF	Electricity Regulatory Forum
ERT	*Elleniki Radiophonia Tileorassi* (Greek National Radio and Television Utility)
Etso	European Transmission System Operators (Association)
EU	European Union
Eurelectric	European Association of Electricity Industry
Eurogas	European Industry of Natural Gas Association
Europex	Association of European Power Exchanges
Eurostat	European Union Statistics Office
EuZH	*Europäische Zeitschrift für Hirtschaftsrecht*
Fébeliec	*Fédération Belges Industriels des Consommateurs* (Federation of Belgian Industrial Consumers)
FERC	Federal Energy Regulatory Commission (USA)
FSU	Former Soviet Union
G	Generation
GATT	General Agreement on Tariffs and Trade
GCC	Gulf Co-operation Council
GD	Gas Directive
GdF	*Gaz de France* (French Gas)
GFU	*Gassforhandlings ut valget* (Norwegian Gas Negotiating Committee)
GJ	Gigajoule (equivalent to 277.8 KWh)
GRF	Gas Regulatory Forum
GSM	Global System Module (digital telephone system)
GTE	Gas Transmission Group Europe
GwH	Gigawatt per hour electricity use
IEA	International Energy Authority
IEM	International Energy Market
IFIEC	International Federation of Industrial Energy Consumers

INOGATE	Interstate Oil and Gas Transport to Europe
INPC	Irish National Petroleum Company
IPPC	Integrated Pollution Prevention and Control
IRC	Irish Refining Company
KWh	Kilowatt hour
L	Load
LNG	Liquefied Natural Gas
LPG	Liquefied Petroleum Gas
M & A	Mergers and Acquisitions
Mcm	Million cubic metres
MFM	Most Favoured Nation
Mtoe	Million tons of oil equivalent tons
MW	Megawatt = One million watts
NAM	*Nederlandse Aardolie Maatschappij* (Dutch Oil Company)
Neta	New Trading Arrangement
NIE	Northern Ireland Electricity
Nordel	Nordic Electricity Grid
NPAA	National Programmes for the Adoption of *Acquis*
NRA	National Regulatory Authority
NSO	National System Operator
NT	National Treatment
nTPA	Negotiated Third Party Access
NTS	National Transmission System (UK)
OAEPC	Organization of Arab Exporting Countries
OECD	Organization for Economic Co-operation and Development
OEW	*Zuckverband Oberschwäbische Elektrizitätswerke* (Austrian Municipalities Association)
Opec	Organization of Petroleum Exporting Countries
OPEC	Oil-producing Exporting Countries
PCA	Partnership and Co-operation Agreement
PCCE	Professional Consultative Committee on Electricity
PCCG	Professional Consultative Committee on Gas
PSOs	Public Service Obligations
QMV	Qualified Majority Voting
RdE	*Recht der Energiewirtschaft*
Redesa	*Red Eléctrica de España*
RPI-X	Retail Price Index - x%
RTE	*Reseau de Transmission d'Électricité* (French Electricity Grid Operator)
RTT	*Regie des Télégraphes et des Téléphones* (Belgian Telephone Utility)
RWE	Formerly *Rhenisch-Westfälische Elektrizitätswerke AG* (now known only by its acronym)

SEA	Single European Act
SEP	*Samenwerkende Electriciteits Productiebedrijven NV* (Dutch Electricity Generators Association)
SME	Small and Medium Sized Enterprises
SNAM	Subsidiary of EMI (acronym used only)
SOEC	Statistical Office of the European Communities
TA	Treaty of Amsterdam
TEU	Treaty on European Union ('Maastricht' Treaty)
TENs	Trans-European Networks
TPA	Third Party Access
TSO	Transmission System Operator
UCPTE	Union of Electricity Production and Transmission Companies
UCTE	*Union pour la Coordination du Transport d'Électricité* (French Union for the Co-ordination of the Transmission of Electricity)
VAT	Value Added Tax
VEAG	*Vereinigte Energiewerke AG*
VIK	*Verband der Industriellen Energie- und Kraftwirtschaft* (German Association of Industrial Energy and Power)
VKU	*Verband kommunaler Unternehmen* (German Union of Municipal Enterprises)
VV	*Verbädevereinbarung* (Association Agreement)
WETT	Water, Energy, Transport and Telecommunications (subject of EU Directive)

GLOSSARY

alternating current Electricity current that moves forwards and backwards with a frequency measured in hertz.

ancillary services All services necessary for the operation of a transmission and/or a distribution system and in the case of gas, LNG facilities, and such storage facilities and equivalent instruments providing flexibility including load balancing and blending (ED, GD new).

auctions The base mechanism for several congestion management methods. In all cases, each market participant offers a price for use of the net transfer capacity. The bids of the participants are stacked with the highest bids first until the capacity is completely used.

base load The minimum continuous load on an operating electricity system.

Chinese Wall A mechanism for the separation of transmission from supply and other functions within a vertically-integrated undertaking to preserve the confidentiality of commercially sensitive information obtained by a system operator when carrying out its business, especially with respect to taking decisions on network access.

cogeneration Generation of electricity and steam simultaneously. The steam may be used locally and the electricity may be used by local customers, sold through a pool or both.

congestion A situation in which the transmission line linking transmission networks cannot accommodate all scheduled or intended

	transactions due to a lack of capacity (adapted from ER).
contract path	A chain of contiguous transmission areas, identified without reference to the multitude of parallel flows which exist in practice on a meshed system.
cross-border transmission	The transmission service provided by a TSO, resulting from all physical flows across borders, including imports, exports, and transits.
derivatives market	A market in which financial instruments are traded, the terms of which are derived from or linked to some underlying product or other extraneous matter.
direct lines	Electricity line or gas pipeline complementary to the interconnected system (ED, GD).
dispatch	Process by which the system operator instructs generators to operate their generating plant, or to stop doing so.
distribution	Transport of electricity or gas across the medium/low-voltage integrated system or medium/low-pressure pipeline network/regional and low-voltage/local systems or networks with a view to its delivery to final customers (ED, GD).
Distribution System Operator	One or more operators of distribution systems in a Member State.
firm	Non-interruptible terms of gas supply.
first-come, first served	A method of capacity reservation in which the first reservation made for a given period of time has priority over the subsequent reservations; leaves little room for short-term trading.
generation	Production of electricity (ED).
incumbent	company holding a monopolistic position by law prior to market liberalization.
interconnectors	Equipment used to link electricity systems (ED).
interruptible	Gas supply terms which include specific rights of curtailment of supply by vendor.

line pack The quantity of gas in a network segment of a pipeline after deducting daily offtake and operational requirements have been met. This will normally include an element of storage gas. Buffer capacity within a network segment.

load factor Ratio of estimated average daily quantity of gas to be taken by a gas purchaser over a specified time period (eg, month, quarter, year) per day to the maximum permitted daily delivery schedule on any day in that period. The load factor cannot exceed one. The size of the load factor has an impact on the designed capacity of production and pipeline facilities taken on any day during the year. Reflecting pattern of future load on its system and that of the gas supply company to alter that pattern by such means as interruptible sales. The size of load factor has an impact on the amount of production and pipeline facilities.

loop flow The unscheduled power that flows inadvertently across an electricity system caused by electricity taking the path of least resistance from generation to load instead of flowing across a particular schedule or contract transmission.

market splitting A system where optimal use of an interconnection is determined on the basis of a comparison of market prices prevailing in the relevant interconnected markets. Encourages trading in so far as market participants receive *ex ante* information about the probability of congestion between some areas. Works best when there is a common market structure and organization on both sides of a constrained border.

natural monopoly Where average costs of the new entrant exceed the marginal costs of the existing supplier (ie, a situation where the market is

	most efficient economically if there is only one provider).
negotiated TPA	Third-party access in which tariffs and conditions are the result of negotiations.
nodal pricing	A method of electricity transmission pricing by location, where in the presence of competition the price at each location or node will be equal to marginal production and transportation cost.
outrage	Withdrawal from service or non-availability of a generating set, or any part of a transmission or distribution system for a period of time, either scheduled or unscheduled.
pancaking	Accumulation of tariffs to be paid by a shipper on energy transactions between two locations using two or more TSOs with their own sets of tariffs.
pools	Arrangements established to allow generating units sellers of power to bid to the TSO (mainly a single buyer) to have their power dispatched and where the TSO dispatches the generating units buyers to bid to purchase, in which the system operator dispatched the generating units in the economic order of the bids.
postage-stamp system	A system of transmission pricing in which the same unit price is charged for transmission, irrespective of how far the energy is transported.
power exchange	An entity that will establish a competitive spot market for electricity through day-and/or hour-ahead auction of generation and demand bids.
regulated TPA	Third-party access in which tariffs and conditions are approved or determined by the regulator.
secondary market	A market in which rights are traded.
shipper	A company which contracts with a transmission/distribution company for the transportation of electricity or gas that purchases gas and sells it to customers.

single buyer	Any legal person who, within the system where it is established, is responsible for the unified management of the transmission system and/or for centralized electricity purchase and sale (ED).
sink	A method of disposal of surplus electricity supply.
small fields policy	Dutch Government policy aimed at the intensive exploration for and production from small gas fields in The Netherlands, contributing to a lower rate of depletion of the large Groningen field and enhancing its balancing function.
spot market	The market (electricity or gas) in which contracts are struck for forward delivery normally where delivery is to take place within a very short period after the contract is struck.
spot price	The price quoted on a given day for delivery of a product (electricity/gas) either on that day or normally within a very short period thereafter.
stranded assets	Past investments in plant, equipment, and/or power purchases made by utilities to meet customer (or governmental) needs, rendered uncommercial as a result of a liberalization of the market.
stranded costs	Synonymous with 'stranded assets'.
supply	Delivery and/or sale of electricity to customers (ED).
swing	Flexibility of gas supply contracts, allowing the buyer to vary daily take of gas up to a specified quantity. It is the quality (expressed as a percentage) by which maximum daily quantity exceeds the estimated average daily quantity calculated as maximum daily quantity divided by daily contract quantity; expressed as a percentage (100% equals zero swing).
transit	Transport of energy from country A across country B intended for country C (Energy Charter Treaty).

transit	Transportation of electricity/gas which involves the crossing of at least one Member State border (Transit Directives).
transit	A physical flow of electricity hosted on the transmission system of a Member State, which was neither produced nor is destined for consumption in this Member State; this definition includes transit flows which are commonly denominated as 'loop-flows' (draft ER).
transmission	Transport of electricity or gas across the high-voltage interconnected system or high-pressure pipeline network (other than an upstream pipeline network) with a view to delivery to final customers or distributors.
transmission system operator	One or more of the operators of the national transmission system in the Member States.
wheeling	The movement of electricity from one system to another over transmission facilities of intervening systems. Wheeling service contracts can be established between two or more systems.

Part I

ORIGINS OF A SINGLE MARKET IN ENERGY

1

REGULATING FOR COMPETITION: A PARADIGM SHIFT

Today no-one doubts the need to adopt the new model of regulation for competition. The differences are only evident in the 'how' and the 'when'.[1]

A. Introduction

The potential for increased competition in the network-bound energy industries (electricity and gas) has attracted a great deal of attention in recent years in the context of discussions about market liberalization and privatization.[2] Until 1.01

[1] Ariño G O, *Principios de Derecho Público Económico* (1999), 607.

[2] The literature is extensive but the following are notable contributions: Henry, C, Mathey, M, and Tennemaître, A (eds) *Regulation of Network Utilities: the European Experience* (2001); OECD/IEA, *Competition in Energy Markets* (2001); Midttun, A (ed), *European Electricity Systems in Transition: A Comparative Analysis of Policy and Regulation in Western Europe* (1997); Zaccour, Georges (ed), *Deregulation of Electric Utilities* (1998); Gilbert, R J, and Kahn, E P (eds), *International Comparisons of Electricity Regulation* (1996); Hunt, S, and Shuttleworth, G, *Competition and Choice in Electricity* (1996); OECD/IEA, *Electricity Market Reform* (1999); OECD/IEA, *Regulatory Reform: European Gas* (2000); OECD/IEA, *Natural Gas Distribution: Focus on Western Europe* (1998); International Chambers of Commerce, *Liberalization and Privatization of the Energy Sector* (1998). More generally, on regulation issues see the works of Kahn, A E, *The Economics of Regulation: Principles and Institutions* (1998), and Ogus, A I, *Regulation: Legal Form and Economic Theory* (1994).

recently the physical characteristics of networks—such as fixed grids and pipelines—seemed to have constrained the scope for such liberalization and market-opening. A further constraint has been perceived in the high degree of government ownership and control in these industries—especially in much of continental Europe. Supervision by public authorities has seemed necessary to protect the large numbers of captive consumers dependent upon energy supplied through transmission and distribution networks. And the very high cost of infrastructure investment has contributed to the high profile of national governments.

However, underlying assumptions about these constraints on the scope of competition have increasingly been challenged. As a result, in most of the industrialized (and in many industrializing) countries, the structure of the electricity and gas industries, stagnant for some decades, is now being transformed by sweeping programmes of institutional reform. The core aim of these measures is generally the creation of enforceable rights of access for third parties to the transmission and distribution networks.

1.02 The drivers for this policy change are several. At an economic level, they include the familiar desire to promote national and regional competitiveness in an era of globalization. The energy industry now operates in a more interconnected and mutually dependent marketplace than ever before. The importance of energy costs as a factor in industrial competitiveness can hardly be exaggerated. Technological developments too play a rôle, especially in lowering costs and entry barriers in electricity generation. Current thinking on economies of scale has radically changed as smaller, independent operators have proven themselves able to provide cheaper energy. The increased use of information technology in the energy sector is also having an impact, showing that despite the fact that the supply chain is part of a complex system that must be balanced and managed, it is still possible to have competition.

1.03 In the context of the EU, changing perceptions of the scope for competition in network-bound industries have fed into efforts to establish a single internal market within its frontiers. Historically, the Member States have been unwilling to relinquish their extensive direct and indirect controls over their national energy businesses—presenting a serious barrier to integration of EU energy markets (although the supply of oil and oil products is an exception to this). As the process of economic liberalization has proceeded in non-energy sectors (such as telecommunications, and to a lesser extent air transport and postal services), the European institutions have moved to bring energy into line by specifying and enforcing the legal obligations on service providers under EC primary law. In so doing, they have had to find a balance between centralized and decentralized regulation in a sector in which national interest has been highly resistant to attempts at central direction. However, this internal dynamic towards the establishment of an internal market has been strongly influenced in recent years by the various processes associated with globalization. The result has been to accelerate the process of energy market liberalization in the EU, despite an attitude of continuing ambivalence in some Member States.

This chapter sketches out the wider context in which EU energy market liberalization has been taking place:

- where the impetus behind liberalization of the energy markets came from;
- what its main components have been; and
- how liberalization has been put into operation.

Some observations will also be made on features specific to the electricity and gas industries as opposed to other energy source industries, as well as non-energy industries.

B. Energy Markets and Government Intervention: Then and Now

Historical Characteristics of the Electricity and Gas Industries

In every industrialized country it has been normal practice for governments to involve themselves in the energy business, and especially in the activities of the electricity and gas industries. This has been encouraged by at least five principal characteristics of these industries: **1.04**

1. These industries necessarily involve activities that develop in successive phases (generation or production; followed by transmission, distribution and supply/retailing).[3] There are elements of *natural monopoly* in transmission and distribution activities which stimulate vertical integration of the activities within a single company. Those companies have traditionally been obliged to provide and supply electricity and gas, and have in return been granted exclusive rights of supply over a specific area or territory (*see below*).
2. The services provided by these companies have traditionally been seen as *essential* for communities, and an obligation to supply has often been imposed by governments on the companies—electricity prices normally being controlled by government and based on costs.
3. The electricity and gas sectors are *strategic* for the overall economy and for the military capability of the nation-state.

[3] Other phases can be distinguished, eg system operation and dispatch, 'spot' and contractual markets and, for gas, storage and possibly liquefaction and re-gasification. These, however, have different functional and cost characteristics and are less fundamental.

4. They are capital-intensive industries with a high degree of technical complexity, which creates entry barriers and necessitates technical co-ordination in their operation. This has led to a structure of regulation that places strong emphasis on reliability of transmission and delivery. This has been particularly evident in the electricity sector, because electricity cannot be stored; rapid changes in demand can occur throughout any given day, and each request must be linked with supply.
5. There is a measure of *integration* between the various energy subsectors, so the regulatory status of one influences the other. Electricity is a secondary form of energy that derives from various primary natural sources such as gas, oil, coal, water or uranium. Gas is commonly found in conjunction with oil. But both electricity and gas can be substituted for each other and so compete for end-use in consumer markets.

(a) The traditional paradigm

1.05 These characteristics contributed to a specific model or pattern of government–energy industry relations that, with some variations, has been dominant in all the industrialized countries for several decades. Its wide acceptance over a long period of time and its impact on the policies of governments suggest that it may be described as the 'traditional paradigm' of energy network regulation. By this it is intended to refer not only to certain ways of organizing government relations with the electricity and gas industries, but also to a set of ideas about the scope of competition and the appropriate legal and institutional methods to achieve public policy aims. Such ideas have had both a prescriptive and a constraining effect on choices in policy.

The concept of 'paradigm' has been defined in the context of the natural sciences as comprising 'universally recognised scientific achievements that for a time provide model problems and solutions to a community of practitioners'.[4] In the electricity and gas sectors the traditional paradigm comprised a wide variety of legal and institutional arrangements that were predicated on *a model of technical organization involving central control over a synchronized network*. It was assumed that these network-bound systems were strategic assets for a national economy and that the nature of their production made it economic to have a single entity construct the system facilities and operate the transmission grids. It emphasized stability, reliability of supply, and public service. This model of centrally-controlled and vertically-integrated monopoly is still to be found in various forms in some OECD countries, and in many developing countries as well as countries in transition.

[4] Kuhn, T, *The Structure of Scientific Revolutions* (1970) viii. Although Kuhn's work is primarily concerned with the natural sciences, the paradigm concept that he uses has gained a wide currency in law and the social sciences, even if not always acknowledged.

For many years most countries favoured a common technical model of an electricity system, based on central station synchronized 'AC' (alternating current). However, each system evolved its own structures for planning, decision-making, and other aspects of management. The technical feature was common but the legal and institutional arrangements varied widely according to local history, politics, and culture. **1.06**

The principal regulatory characteristics included:

- exclusive rights to build and operate networks, granted under concessions or licences;
- closure to competition;
- detailed regulation;
- vertically-integrated operations;
- remuneration on the basis of historical costs; and
- a high degree of planning with tight, centralized control.

They had another common feature: they do not allow the ultimate beneficiary—the electricity consumer—to participate in decision-making. The electricity user had 'almost no rôle in this process except to switch things on and off'.[5] The legal and financial arrangements were set up and supervised by governments, generally national governments. Technical arrangements were designed, manufactured, and installed by engineering companies. Electricity systems were operated by companies that had grown up with the systems—such as *Électricité de France* (EdF), Ontario Hydro, and Tokyo Electric Power.

The activities of all of these participants were guided by a single basic idea: large power stations generate electricity in large quantities and deliver it by wire to every user in the area, continuously adjusting the total amount being generated to match the total amount being used at any instant. A serious shortcoming of this approach was that those who planned, managed, and operated the system did not bear any of the risk, and did not suffer if it failed. The costs of incompetence or bad judgment were passed on to customers and sometimes to taxpayers. A similar approach was adopted in the transmission and supply activities of the natural gas industry.

(b) Beyond the traditional paradigm

The basic relationship between government and the electricity and gas industries has for some time been undergoing a radical, and seemingly irreversible, change. With respect to electricity markets, the current state of change has been characterized as one in which the 'comfortable old certainties have evaporated'. Indeed, the 'basic premises that everyone involved accepted without thought, which guided **1.07**

[5] Patterson, W, *Transforming Electricity* (1999), 5.

the evolution of electricity systems worldwide throughout the 20th Century, suddenly no longer apply'.[6] Throughout the 1990s, governments in countries around the world began to change the ground rules. This change has been characterized as a movement from 'traditional regulation' to 'regulation for competition'.[7]

1.08 The new idea behind this movement was that the institutional configuration of a system based on the technically-centralized model can be restructured, and monopoly rights withdrawn to permit different suppliers to compete for customers. The technical reasons for this have been discussed in the literature,[8] and include particularly the development of the combined cycle gas turbine. As a result, a new paradigm in government–energy industry relations has emerged, based on a greater reliance on markets. It seeks to introduce competition whenever possible, encouraging openness, decentralized production with network access, and remuneration on the basis of market prices, not costs. If an activity has the potential for competition, the kind of regulation implied by the new paradigm facilitates competition by (*inter alia*) encouraging and supporting new market entrants. If an activity is a natural monopoly, then regulation provides a substitute for the competitive market by introducing measures which act as a surrogate for competition (eg, publication of tariffs for transmission and distribution). Many diverse approaches result from this. Several basic characteristics of this new kind of regulation may be identified as follows:[9]

- separation of activities in order to facilitate the introduction of competition wherever possible;
- freedom of entry and freedom of investment in competitive activities, instead of a centrally-planned approach;
- freedom of contract and competitive formation of prices;
- access to networks and infrastructure;
- supervision of the model by an independent regulator; and
- adaptation to the use of information technology.

1.09 For effective regulatory oversight it is necessary that the regulators understand how the energy businesses work and how the various elements in them combine. In systems organized according to the traditional paradigm, where public sector monopolies predominated in the energy sector of many economies, problems of

---

[6] ibid, 3.

[7] Ariño, n 1 above, 605–55. There is a considerable body of literature on economic regulation and on theories such as those of the public choice and public interest schools. An overview of the arguments of the latter two schools is provided in Ogus, A, *Legal Form and Economic Theory* (1994), ch 4. An introduction to the various meanings of the concept of regulation is provided by Daintith, T, 'Regulation: Legal Form and Economic Theory', in *International Encyclopedia of Comparative Law*, vol XVII (State and Economy), ch 10. For an overview of UK experiences in energy and non-energy sectors of the economy, see Prosser, T, *Law and the Regulators* (1997).

[8] eg, OECD/IEA study, *Electricity Market Reform* (1999) 23–4.

[9] Ariño, n 1 above, 608–09.

co-ordination and cost allocation among the elements of an electricity or gas network were concealed. And in the reformed electricity markets in particular it has become of critical importance to understand how the different components work and *must work* together. New rules (including those on cost allocation) must be designed to promote the economic benefits that liberalization is supposed to bring. Some co-ordination by a regulator is necessary to support competition. However, the profile of other government bodies should decline through arrangements set up under the new paradigm, except in relation to social and environmental matters.

The new paradigm is emerging in a context that displays some of the familiar characteristics of paradigm change noted by Thomas Kuhn.[10] A radical shift involves the successful challenge by a competitor theory of the practice carried out within the traditional paradigm, and leads to a redefinition of the problems suitable for research and a change in world view. To promote this change, he notes, the proponents of a new paradigm will claim that they can solve the problems that have led the old one into its condition of crisis. In energy regulation, the advocates of a new market-oriented paradigm have successfully challenged the idea that network-bound energy industries defy the introduction of competition because of their natural monopoly characteristics. There is a new consensus organized around a belief in markets. However, its supporters are not for the most part proponents of some form of market fundamentalism in which all key issues are settled by way of reference to market principles. In challenging the traditional paradigm, it may well appear that this is being argued, but it does not necessarily follow and is expressly contradicted in some cases.[11] It is not necessarily being argued that energy should be treated as just another commodity. **1.10**

On the contrary, in at least two ways the new paradigm's supporters acknowledge flexibility and open-endedness. First, the way in which governments introduce and promote competition is and will remain highly diverse. Secondly, no-one knows much at all as yet about the medium to long-term effects of liberalization (particularly on security and continuity of supply) because experience in most cases is too recent.

(c) A three-stage evolution

The reasons for this paradigmatic shift are economic, ideological, and legal. They can perhaps best be understood in an historical context since much of the power of the new paradigm comes from its claim that the traditional paradigm in the **1.11**

[10] Kuhn, T, *The Structure of Scientific Revolutions* (1970).

[11] OECD/IEA, *Electricity Market Reform* (1999); Hogan, W F, 'Making Markets in Power', (2000) London (http://ksghome.harvard.edu/~.whogan.cbg.ksg/index.htm); Helm, D, 'Energy Markets Since 1979: From Lawson to Mandelson' (1999) (paper presented to the British Institute of Energy Economists).

electricity and gas industries had—because of technological advances and globalization of trade—outlived its usefulness. A number of recent studies of energy market reform have been at pains to explain the historical developments that have led to the present market-oriented reforms and to claim their superiority. For convenience, *three* broad stages in the evolution of government relations with the energy sector can be distinguished.

The first began with the reconstruction and expansion after the Second World War. In Europe it saw the nationalization of energy companies (electricity, gas, town gas, coal, and, to a limited extent, oil companies) and the establishment of very close relationships between government and the state-owned (or controlled) energy companies. A characteristic of this stage was the consolidation of a highly fragmented electricity industry and, in Western Europe following the introduction of natural gas, the creation of state-owned monopoly suppliers.

A second stage can be seen as commencing with the energy crises in the 1970s and is characterized by a critical reassessment of the government–energy relations that had been built up during the previous stage, particularly those that had been built up in relation to security of supply in the oil industry and the construction of nuclear power stations. The beginnings of a new market-based approach to energy policy are evident during this stage, especially in the United States.

A third stage began from around 1985 onwards. Governments loosened the ties that bound them to their energy companies, whether through strategies of commercialization or privatization or both, and moved to set up independent regulators. Despite many national variations, a clear market orientation has now become evident in the energy affairs of most industrialized countries.

This three-stage scheme provides a useful framework for a brief review of the principal linkages between governments and the energy industry over these decades.

1.12 (i) **Stage 1: Intervention** The dominant view of governments in Western Europe in 1945 was that the control by the state of the commanding heights of the economy (which included the coal, electricity, and gas industries) was essential to the reconstruction of Western Europe and the creation of the new post-War society. Accordingly, those industries were nationalized and their assets vested in state agencies or state-owned companies which were responsible, subject to tight governmental control, for running them. In this way the high cost of investment incurred in production and infrastructure could be made to meet rising demand. Abuse of this concentrated power was to be avoided in most cases by public ownership or significant public control. Examples of this approach are to be found in France with the creation of EdF and GdF (Gaz de France) in 1946 and 1949, in Italy with the creation of ENEL in 1962, and in the United Kingdom with the establishment in the late 1940s of the Central Electricity Generating Board (CEGB), the Electricity Council and the regional Electricity

Boards, and the establishment of the Gas Council and the area gas boards that were superseded by the state-owned British Gas Corporation in 1972.[12] So close was the relationship between government and industry in these cases that the term 'regulation' seems inappropriate to describe it.[13]

Further consequences of this assumption were that the operations of the industries were usually exempted from the scope of national competition law and entry of new players into the market was excluded or strictly limited by statute. Public service obligations were imposed on the industry with respect to equality of treatment and continuity of service. In return, these industries obtained exclusive rights that amounted to, in practice, a monopoly, although the exact form differed from one country to another according to institutional structure, cultural background, political style, economic policy, and of course, the energy resource base.

In the United States, a different model was in operation: that of the private monopoly regulated by a publicly-appointed state or federal regulatory commission. There were a number of federal or municipally-owned power companies in business. The nearest counterpart to this in Europe was found in West Germany, where large, privately owned electricity and gas (and oil) companies constituted the dominant force in the energy sector. There too, many smaller energy distribution companies were in municipal or mixed ownership.

The highly interventionist rôle of the state during this time appeared to be vindi- **1.13**
cated by the rapid economic growth in which the energy industry played a major part by supplying increasing quantities of energy at affordable prices. It was also promoting the investment in networks that established the modern electricity and gas businesses.

This extensive and overt rôle of the state in national energy management had a considerable impact on the first efforts at European integration. The EC Treaty addressed issues of economic integration, but energy was not expressly mentioned. Although nuclear energy and coal were treated in some detail in the two other Treaties of the period (ECSC and Euratom), the network-related problems of the electricity and gas sectors were not addressed. In practice, even the antitrust provisions of the EC Treaty were not applied to the energy sector, allowing various kinds of exclusive rights to be exercised by monopolies in most of the Member States. Indeed, it was not until the judgments of the ECJ in the *Corbeau*

---

[12] This even extended into the oil sector with the establishment of a state oil corporation which operated for several years: see Cameron, P, *Property Rights and Sovereign Rights: the Case of North Sea Oil*, (1983).

[13] Well-illustrated by the use in the UK in the 1970s and 1980s of the term 'lunch-time Directive' to describe the means by which the minister responsible for a particular nationalized undertaking communicated his requirements to the Chairman of the undertaking.

and *Genoa* cases (*see* chapter 5) that it was established that holders of exclusive or special rights could be challenged under Article 86 (ex Art 90).

1.14 (ii) **Stage 2: Uncertainty** The energy crises of the 1970s led to the high watermark of government intervention in the energy sector in the industrialized economies. This was a period in which the goal of security of supply figured largely in public policy. For oil supply, this was a matter of particular concern due to the dependence of most of the industrialized countries on imports from the OPEC countries. The energy crises called into question the reliability of that oil supply—at that time the principal input fuel to electricity generation after coal.

There were many specific government interventions in energy markets. Some of these were concerned to avoid possible politically inspired disruptions to supply, but others were aimed at encouraging fuel diversification to reduce dependence on imported oil supplies and avoid a possible future scarcity of fossil fuels. Very expensive programmes were introduced to fund the construction of nuclear power plants and subsidies made available for alternative forms of energy generation. At intergovernmental level, the International Energy Agency was established to supervise an emergency allocation scheme and encourage fuel diversification. The European Community took related measures, including the adoption of a new Directive restricting the use of gas for electricity generation.[14] A proliferation of national energy policies and plans emerged, as well as energy departments and agencies to implement them.

1.15 The results of these market-distorting interventions were on the whole mixed. On the positive side, there was reduced dependency on imported fuels, greater efficiency in oil production, and use of alternative fuels, especially nuclear energy. Indeed, much of the French nuclear energy programme resulted from policy decisions taken as a result of these interventions. However, in the United States, federal capping of wellhead gas prices had adverse and unexpected results. Moreover, the government-inspired investment in new power plant capacity subsequently proved in a number of cases to have been very costly and unnecessary. Examples of this were particularly evident in the nuclear energy sector in several countries.

The negative effects of such attempts at government direction of the energy economy led to a severe questioning of the assumptions on which the interventions had been made. This climate of doubt about the rôle of government in the energy sector in the face of considerable evidence of malfunctioning did not by itself bring about a change in thinking about the adequacy of the prevailing paradigm

[14] Council Directive 75/404/EEC of 13 February 1975 on the restriction of the use of natural gas in power stations, No L 178/24 (since repealed by Council Directive 91/148/EEC of 18 March 1991 revoking Directive 75/404/EEC on the restriction of the use of natural gas in power stations, Official Journal No L 75/52; 21 March 1991).

for government–energy industry relations. That change required another very important development—a synergy between advocates of an alternative, pro-market approach and decision makers who were able to put their ideas into practice. Such pioneers were beginning to emerge in the United Kingdom and the USA by the end of the 1970s.

Those pioneers were encouraged by several developments that occurred from the 1970s. Alternatives to vertically-integrated electricity systems appeared possible from the experience of independent generators operating on existing grids without seeing any decline in the quality of service provided through the system. Technical progress was also shifting the minimum efficient scale in power generation away from the large fossil fuel consuming units towards smaller ones, creating the possibility of easier entry for new players into energy markets. These developments were seized upon to challenge the traditional mode of thinking and replace it with the idea that some competition in energy networks was both possible and desirable. It was argued that the activities of generation/exploration, end-use supply, marketing, and billing could be unbundled and opened to competition without significant adverse effects. This laid the basis for an alternative paradigm. **1.16**

(iii) **Stage 3: Globalization** From the mid-1980s onwards, the traditional paradigm of government–energy industry relations was challenged again. There were two principal sources of this challenge. The first lies outside the energy sector—the complex of processes commonly referred to as 'globalization'. The second came from within—specific initiatives taken by states to liberalize their energy markets. **1.17**

'Globalization' refers to processes that promote economic interdependence and cut across the borders of nation-states, seeming to threaten the sovereignty of those states. These processes have been greatly assisted by changes to the GATT agreed in the Uruguay Round (1994) bringing about both the creation of the WTO and increased opportunities for international trade. One of globalization's most striking features is the expanded rôle of world financial markets which increasingly operate on a real-time basis on a global scale. Another is its relationship to the spread of information technology and transformation of everyday notions of time and space. Support for globalization has come from corporations, states, and many NGOs. Its effects have been most visible in the OECD countries. **1.18**

Economic globalization has triggered a debate on the future of the nation-state. With a few notable exceptions,[15] most writers seem to agree that there has been no decline in the nation-state but rather a transformation in its functions, some powers

[15] Ohmae, K, *The End of the Nation State: The Rise of Regional Economies* (1996).

transferred away from nations and into a depoliticized global space or to supra-national entities.[16] At the same time, there has been a trend for some decision-making to move from the centre of nation-states to sub-national level. However, the scope of government, taken overall, appears to expand rather than diminish as globalization proceeds.[17] Nation-states remain the most important agents on the international scene.

Although the phenomenon of economic globalization is not entirely new, the current globalization processes have been occurring hand-in-hand with a widespread economic liberalization in which many functions associated with the state have been transferred to the private sector and made subject to different and often unfamiliar forms of regulation, either by the state or its agencies. There has also been a change in the rôle of supra-national institutions in promoting and facilitating these economic reforms. The nation-state has become more and more involved in the implementation of those laws necessary for economic liberalization and globalization, especially those concerning deregulation and the formation of legal régimes that favour the free circulation of capital, goods, information, and services.

1.19 The second and most significant challenge of all has come from the actions taken by advocates of a new market-oriented approach to energy market organization. Their early experiments in liberalizing the electricity and gas markets first of the United States, the United Kingdom, and farther afield in Chile showed that positive results could follow from the process, and went some way to confounding predictions of inefficiency and even system collapse. Amid much debate about the virtues and shortcomings of traditional regulation, a number of experiments were initiated in the liberalization of national energy markets. The significance of these early—and in retrospect rather primitive—experiments in market reform is that they had sufficient success to persuade others that there were hardheaded arguments in favour of this paradigm. As the arguments multiplied, with the growing number of experiments, the converts grew. There was a basis in the real world for faith in the new paradigm.

Other countries soon followed this route. In doing so they showed that there was no single model to be replicated but rather a set of ideas that could be adapted to permit a liberalization tailor-made to each specific setting. In the Nordic countries, for example, an electricity pooling system was established but without the privatization that had been chosen in the United Kingdom and in Chile. Australia and New Zealand also favoured approaches that suited their own special circumstances. Other countries took measures in Latin America (Argentina and

[16] Sassen, S, *Losing Control? Sovereignty in an Age of Globalization* (1996) xii–xiii.

[17] See, for example, Giddens, A, *The Third Way: the Renewal of Social Democracy* (1998) 32; *The Third Way and its Critics* (2000) 122.

Mexico)[18] and in the federal systems of North America (eg Ontario, Quebec,[19] and California). The new paradigm became associated with 'progress', even if some stocktaking has taken place in the light of the energy shortages in California following a programme of liberalization of its electricity market.

Differences between the two industries (electricity and gas) did present liberalizers with serious challenges. Take the United States for example. There the transition to greater reliance on competition to govern the performance of the natural gas market did not raise many important structural issues[20] (in contrast to the UK). Essentially, the network of gas pipelines had reached a mature stage and when access provisions were introduced in the legal régime a very large geographical market was created. After the elimination of west-to-east constraints in transportation capacity, a continental market was created making it virtually impossible for a single seller or a combination of a few sellers to exercise market power. By contrast, the transition to competition in electricity markets has raised a host of structural questions. As one commentator observed, 'depending on the locations and effects of transmission capacity constraints, and depending on the way transmission is priced, the geographic market for electricity can be as large as a region of the country or as small as part of a single state.'[21] As a result, the idea took root in the US that it is technically possible and economically desirable to develop a model of regulation based on market principles. There was a growing pressure for reduction in gas and electricity prices, particularly from major energy users. In addition, somewhat fortuitously, this pressure coincided with a period in which oil and gas were available at historically low prices. Moreover, as consumer benefits of competition in other sectors such as telecommunications became clear, similar benefits were sought in electricity and gas. **1.20**

At a wider international level, there has been a growing acceptance of policies aimed at generating revenues for state finances from privatizations and of the benefits of international trade. An effect of globalization has been to encourage governments to accelerate experimentation in market reform at national level. The various experiences of governments committed to energy market reform showed too that the chaos predicted by some critics was avoidable. As a result of all this, the mindset of governments to competition in network-bound energy markets has changed fundamentally since the mid-1980s. **1.21**

[18] See two publications by the OECD/IEA: *Regulatory Reform in Argentina's Natural Gas Sector* (1999) and *Regulatory Reform in Mexico's Natural Gas Sector* (1996).

[19] See chs 5 and 6 of Zaccour, G (ed), *Deregulation of Electric Utilities* (1998).

[20] Pierce Jr, R J, 'The Antitrust Implications of Energy Restructuring', in *Natural Resources & Environment* (1998), 269.

[21] ibid.

(d) Postscript: Lessons from California

1.22 Against the argument in the preceding paragraphs it could be argued that the energy crisis in California that began in 2000 illustrates the risks of energy market liberalization. Some governments including those in Korea, Malaysia, Singapore, and Thailand have already slowed their electricity restructuring programmes to try to identify whether there are any lessons to be learned. The California crisis comprised a lack of supply and artificially escalating prices resulting in the largest utility filing for bankruptcy. A combination of factors led to this situation including:

- lack of new generation capacity due to an uncertain regulatory environment and unusually strict planning controls;
- rapidly increasing demand due to Silicon Valley (high-tech industry) consumption;
- existence of an obligatory pool leading to anti-competitive, oligopolistic pricing practices;
- the impossibility of off-setting risk through long-term supply agreements;
- locked retail prices and exposure to spot prices;
- impossibility of TSO launching tenders for the construction of new capacity combined with power purchase agreements;
- lack of interconnection capacity and supply arrangements with neighbouring states;
- external factors, eg drought; and
- lack of appropriate inter-state trading arrangements.

The result of this unusual combination of adverse conditions was a kind of 'perfect storm' that few, if any systems could have survived intact, unless heavily protected by state subsidies and bail-outs funded by taxpayers.

1.23 However, several of these factors could have been anticipated when designing the legal and technical structure of the liberalized régime. If new generation capacity is an objective of the régime, then incentives for new investment should be included and unduly restrictive planning or environmental laws should be either removed prior to implementation or taken into account in the régime's design. In the EU, the Commission has been keen to emphasize that the EU internal energy market régime allows Member States to take emergency action at an early stage if faced with an imbalance between demand and supply—notably by launching tenders for new capacity backed up by fixed price power purchase agreements.[22] In addition, most EU Member States have an excess of capacity that could, if necessary, provide a cushion to any disruptive effects of liberalization.

[22] European Commission, 'Communication on Completing the Internal Energy Market' (2001) 46; European Commission Press Release, 'The California Power Crisis', 14 May 2001.

(e) Unfinished business

In spite of the continued existence of systems organized according to the traditional paradigm, by the late 1990s the competition appeared to have been decisively won by the new market-oriented paradigm: 'regulation for competition' (see below) had become at least an organizing principle to which most governments aspired in those sectors of the economy characterized by networks. **1.24**

However, a paradigm is more like an open-ended framework than a model, and the triumph of the market-oriented paradigm leaves a great many issues open for development by its supporters (and its converts). These may be divided into two categories.

First, there are problems that must be addressed that arise from the introduction of competition into network-bound energy sectors, such as the so-called 'stranded asset problem' (problems of *application*). They do not involve questioning the basic assumptions of the new paradigm but lead instead to the analysis and attempted solution of what might be called 'micro problems', using techniques compatible with the basic assumptions of the new paradigm. **1.25**

Secondly, there are problems that are not directly connected with the new paradigm but which impact on it and present a possible threat to its implementation (problems of *compatibility*). They include the many environmental and public service issues that affect the energy sector and the issues concerned with the sustainable development debate. **1.26**

(i) **Problems of application** Problems of application are already apparent and are certain to increase. Three sets of problems may be noted. First, there are those concerning the transition to a liberalized market. As the IEA has noted, '[g]iven that no competitive power market has operated for more than five years, none has yet completed the stage of transition.'[23] Indeed, '[t]he impact of market liberalization on investments in long-term generating capacity and diversity of fuel inputs to power generators is not yet fully clear.'[24] The problem of stranded costs, or remuneration for sunk costs incurred in a regulated régime but not recoverable after the market has been opened to competition is only one example of such a problem of mopping-up after the basics of the new paradigm have been accepted. It has sparked off a very lively debate and interesting research into the possible solutions.[25] **1.27**

[23] OECD/IEA, *Electricity Market Reform* (1999) 93.

[24] ibid, 98.

[25] See, eg, Sidak, G, and Spulber, D, *Deregulatory Takings and the Regulatory Contract: the Competitive Transformation of Network Industries in the US* (1998).

More fundamentally however, it appears that the transitional period may be a very lengthy one, involving periodic reviews by government and regulatory authorities and further legislation. In other words, the rôle of government may well have changed but the electricity and gas industries will probably remain subject to a high degree of government interference for the foreseeable future.

1.28 Another set of problems concern the application of competition law in the context of liberalized energy markets. As the authors of a recent study note, 'many of the established notions of the energy market are open to question because of the spread of liberalization'.[26] They might have added that this is especially so when the actions of market incumbents are such as to anticipate and undermine the effects of liberalization while it is being introduced (through mergers and acquisitions, for example).

1.29 Finally, outside of the mature energy markets there are problems that affect those developing countries in seeking to liberalize their energy markets and at the same time increase investment in new networks and plant. These include markets in South-East Asia as well as Latin America, where Brazil's attempts at expanding generation capacity have been limited by an energy crisis caused by drought and poor forward planning.

1.30 (ii) **Problems of compatibility** Problems of compatibility primarily involve potentially market-distorting initiatives taken by governments. In particular they could involve measures to promote policies of sustainable development. It is early days for trying to discern how such problems will be addressed in ways that are compatible with the promotion of competitive markets. This is something of a 'black box'. The increasingly central position taken by environmental and social questions in energy law and policy is a powerful trend that has not as yet tested the market orientation that developed in the 1990s. Indeed, the new paradigm has emerged during a period of abundant supply of electricity and gas and has not had to concern itself unduly with issues of security of supply.

The significance of these historically specific conditions for its long-term continuation is not yet clear: the complex relationships between markets, regulation, and investment behaviour (often cyclical in character when left to the market) are indeed 'not properly understood'.[27]

Paradigm changes also affect the method of inquiry in problem-solving. They will have a significant impact on the way in which a problem is defined and the way in

---

[26] Devlin, B, and Levasseur, C, 'Energy', chapter 10 in Faull, J, and Nikpay, A, *EC Competition Law* (1999).

[27] Perceptive remarks by Robert Mabro underline this point: Oxford Institute for Energy Studies News, May 2001. For an assessment of the potential impact on energy of legal developments in combating climate change, see the contributions in Cameron, P D and Zillman, D (eds) *Kyoto: From Principles to Practice* (2002).

which problems are prioritized.[28] A paradigm shift will ensure that some problems are not placed on the agenda for solution, as they would have been under the preceding paradigm.

(iii) Example: unsolved problems due to 'wrong' paradigm An example may illustrate this. A recent report from a United Kingdom Royal Commission recommended the construction of many new nuclear plants as a way of solving probable long-term energy shortages.[29] Apart from the unpopularity of nuclear power as an obstacle to this course of action, the implementation of such a recommendation would probably involve the kind of large-scale intervention in energy markets that is associated with the traditional paradigm, and is no longer seen as beneficial. Instead, a likely response to such advice is inaction by government, justified on the ground that the market will provide a solution in the coming years by providing, for example, cheaper sources of renewable energy. Acceptance of the report's recommendations would seem to violate the assumptions on which energy policy is now based. Similar difficulties arise in taking action on proposals to address sustainable development issues. 1.31

C. Specifics of Gas and Electricity Supply

The dependence of electricity and gas supply on fixed networks to transport and deliver energy to users is a serious complication for any policy of market opening. In practice, the transmission/delivery system is almost always a national monopoly. By contrast, the supply of oil and coal are not affected by such transportation bottlenecks. The physical characteristics of coal and oil have led to international trade and free market practices, with a declining government rôle except in fiscal matters. Customers can readily negotiate with competing suppliers to obtain the best deal for oil or coal purchase. The price obtained by the customer may be influenced by product quality and by differing levels and structures of taxation or subsidies. However, transportation and distribution constraints in a network will not create problems of access for customers and producers in the way that they readily do in the gas and electricity sectors. 1.32

A further characteristic of both sectors, linked to the above, is the high cost of infrastructure and the element of sunk costs. This has often been used to justify anti-competitive features. Exclusive rights over a determinate period have been sought by investors to permit financing of these projects, with long-term contractual obligations, such as those involving 'take-or-pay' obligations. The rights granted

[28] Kuhn, T, *The Structure of Scientific Revolutions* (1970) 110.

[29] Royal Commission on Environmental Pollution, 'Energy: The Changing Climate', Cm 4749.

may include an exclusive right to own and operate a transmission system over a specified period and an exclusive right to import gas or electricity.

(1) Electricity

'Multiple time-differentiated products' and problems of 'peak-demand' and self-sufficiency

1.33 There are nevertheless some characteristics of electricity and gas that are not shared. Electricity has a number of characteristics that are specific to it and require mention since they impact on the design of any regulatory régime. First, electricity may not be stored in large amounts and at low cost, with the consequence that power at any point in time is not a good substitute for power at another point in time (except possibly in the case of small consumers of electricity). Power production and supply may therefore be seen as 'multiple time-differentiated products'.[30] Secondly, there is a high cost involved when load exceeds supply, or when there are so-called 'brownouts' or blackouts. These features, when taken together with a feature that electricity shares with gas—that demand varies in a daily and a seasonal pattern (with random variations superimposed, in large part due to the fact that much of it is used in weather-related uses such as heating and cooling)—create what is known as a 'peak-demand problem'. Essentially, if the entire load has to be supplied, capacity has to equal or exceed the load at all times. If not, there will be random supply interruptions in the form of brownouts or blackouts, leading to considerable economic damage.

A further notable characteristic of electricity demand is that it requires transformation of electricity into some final form before it may be met. This form may be light, heat, and cooling- or motion-power. It means that some of the input energies to electricity such as natural gas are also its competitors in final energy markets. Moreover, demand is not very 'price-elastic' in the short term since a customer's transformation equipment is generally long-lasting. Electricity supply assets such as generating capacity have an even longer working life.

1.34 Finally, in the European context import dependence is practically zero. Self-sufficiency is very high as electricity companies have been able to locate generation close to where electricity is needed. Cross-border trade represents about six to eight per cent of total UCTE electricity consumption.[31] Electricity is generated to meet immediate demand and usually travels much shorter distances, requiring closer co-ordination between generation, transmission, and distribution elements of the industry, encouraging the creation of vertically-integrated

---

[30] IEA, *Electricity Market Reform: An IEA Handbook* (1999) 11.

[31] European Commission, 'Communication on Completing the Internal Market in Energy', 13.3.2001, COM (2001) 125 final.

monopolies. Where issues of cross-border trade have arisen, their focus has largely been on how to improve the efficiency, depth, and interconnected character of the existing transmission grids to promote exchanges between incumbent players. Consumer choice across borders has arguably been less important as a result. In this context, it is unsurprising that a major objective of the European Commission has been to identify and remove obstacles to cross-border trade in electricity.[32]

(2) Gas

Gas[33] has six principal contrasting characteristics that impact significantly on the design and pricing of transmission services. **1.35**

1. *Geopolitics.* Gas supply must frequently be organized to take into account separation of the sources of production from the consumption markets. In Europe natural gas frequently travels very long distances and crosses many inter-state borders to reach its users. For many gas-consuming countries in Europe a dependence on external (non-EU) suppliers has been a fact of life for decades. More than forty per cent of EU gas supply originated from non-EU sources such as Algeria, Norway, and Russia.[34] Even with respect to the EU's own gas production, the element of cross-border trade is considerable, one in every five cubic metres of gas produced in EU countries being exported. Just as non-EU gas from Norway is transported across The Netherlands to Belgium and France, gas produced from The Netherlands crosses Germany and Switzerland to reach Italy. About fifty per cent of all internationally-traded gas in the world is imported into the EU. This geopolitical element makes energy policy links with Russia, Algeria, and Norway of great importance. At the same time, such cross-border transactions normally take the form of transit and/or supply agreements between incumbent major gas wholesalers. It is misleading to describe it as 'trade' in the generally accepted sense of the term. **1.36**

2. *Storage and timing of actions.* Gas can be stored in underground facilities, in transmission or distribution pipelines, in above-ground LNG facilities or by means of a technique known as 'line-pack'. The result is to provide gas system **1.37**

[32] See chs 7 and 8 below: European Commission, 'Proposal for a Regulation of the European Parliament and of the Council on Conditions for Access to the Network for Cross-Border Exchanges in Electricity in the Internal Electricity Market', 13 March 2001, COM (2001) 125 final. The Commission's proposal for a draft regulation on cross-border trade in electricity is likely to be followed by a similar measure to facilitate cross-border trade in gas.

[33] 'Gas' means here natural gas and not so-called 'town gas', which is manufactured from coal or oil at gasworks located very near consumption areas. It includes liquefied natural gas (LNG) but not liquefied petroleum gas (LPG).

[34] European Commission, *Next Steps Towards Completion of the Internal Market in Gas: draft strategy Paper for discussion* (2000) 2.

operators with a considerable degree of flexibility in balancing their systems over time. This contrasts quite starkly with the lot of electricity system operators who must manage the stability and reliability of the grid according to a time-frame of a few seconds. Pressure and flow management in gas pipelines may occur over much longer intervals, perhaps hours or days. This presents a rather different situation on harmonization requirements between the respective systems. In gas there is more flexibility, since the task is only to manage the balancing protocols between systems to ensure that there is adequate gas quality and timing consistency to permit each operator to maintain its system flexibility.[35] Customers have in principle more discretion in exercising their rights to utilize various receipt and delivery points.

1.38 3. *Technical ('loop-flows' and 'wheeling').* Electricity and gas share the characteristic, being network-bound energy sources. The network effects have different characteristics in either case. The flow of electricity over wires follows different physical laws to that of gas, giving rise to 'loop-flows'. These are intrinsic to electricity transmission and affect the way that access to transmission capacity is made available to buyers and the way it is controlled by the system operator. So-called 'wheeling' transactions along one part of the path can have an effect on the availability of transmission capacity along an interconnected path.[36] In the EU context, 'transit' has recently been defined as a physical flow of electricity hosted on the transmission system of a Member State, neither produced nor destined for consumption in this Member State, and including transit flows commonly denominated as loop-flows.[37] Although there are no 'loop-flows' in gas transmission, there are network effects nevertheless. The use by a consumer or third-party supplier of a receipt point into a gas network, or a delivery point out, will affect the ability of another shipper to utilize other receipt and delivery points on the network. As a result, the amount of transmission capacity that may be made available at any given time is a function of the planned utilization of the network. In electricity, however, the determination of available capacity is made considerably more difficult by the existence of loop-flows.

1.39 4. *Energy quality.* Gas produced from different fields and wells can have a very different energy content and may contain variable contaminants and water in the gas stream. A number of issues of supply quality must therefore be addressed through physical specification standards or accounting treatment (calorific value). In electricity, by contrast, the supply is generated to meet very specific characteristics.

[35] 'Methodologies for Establishing National and Cross-Border Systems of Pricing of Access to the Gas System in Europe', report for the European Commission prepared by the Brattle Group (Feb 2000), Appendix 2, 96.

[36] ibid.

[37] European Commission, 'Proposal for a Regulation of the European Parliament and Council on Conditions for Access to the Network for Cross-Border Exchanges in Electricity in the Internal Electricity Market', 2001.

5. *Safety.* If electricity is temporarily interrupted, it can be restored without risk to the consumer at a later date. This is not possible with the supply of gas. If non-interruptible gas consumers have their gas supplies unexpectedly terminated, supply cannot be resumed until safety checks have been carried out on every appliance to make sure they are switched off. This process may be costly and time-consuming, especially if it involves residential consumers. In terms of operational security of supply, it is not 'fail safe'. **1.40**

6. *Size of provider.* Historically, the players have been different between gas and electricity, with large international companies involved in gas and often also the oil business, directly or indirectly. They are often vertically integrated too. This situation arose from the fact that gas was usually found in association with oil or as an indirect result of exploration originally directed at finding oil. Conveniently, the price of gas is linked to oil, reflecting the high degree of substitutability between them. In recent years there has been a trend towards convergence of gas and electricity supply by companies that have become increasingly focused on the provision of several kinds of energy. In some cases, such companies have also been involved in the provision of water or telecommunications services as well, creating a so-called 'multi-utility'. **1.41**

D. Introducing Competition into Network-Bound Industries

There are a number of prerequisites for the introduction of competition into the gas and electricity markets. They include changes in the legal and institutional framework of regulation, as well as liberalization, industry restructuring, and ownership changes. Such changes are usually linked and are especially necessary where the industry has been vertically integrated or highly concentrated horizontally. Both of these characteristics were familiar in the traditional paradigm and have therefore had to be redesigned in the move to the new paradigm of regulated competition (see below). Various national programmes of energy reform have yielded examples of the practical mechanisms required to support change, but diverse approaches to the introduction of competition have resulted. **1.42**

(1) Regulation

The idea of 'regulated competition' may seem perverse. After all, the aim of liberalization and de-regulation is to allow competition to do the work of regulating rather than to leave it to a regulator. As competition will not naturally occur in markets where natural monopolies of transportation exist, it is necessary for regulation to provide a surrogate for competition. Essentially, a dominant network owner will control access to consumers and network access will quickly become the principal but not the sole barrier to entry. Some form of regulation will **1.43** be required to prevent the owner and operator of the networks from extracting monopoly rents at the expense of other parties in the supply chain. One of the tasks of a regulator will be to define and prioritize rights of access to the network. Another task will be to address the pricing of these rights.

The various regulatory tasks may be conveniently classified according to:

- structure (concerning unbundling and prevention of cross subsidies),
- conduct (organization of regulation and the control of market behaviour through licensing, price-capping and non-discriminatory access) and
- transitional problems (so-called 'stranded investments' and environmental matters).

Tasks affecting conduct, for example, would include the regulation of quality through safety standards and safety margins to ensure security of supply. Transitional issues have focused principally on 'stranded' investments. These can be unamortized costs of prior investments that would have been recovered through the continued charging of monopoly prices had liberalization of the market not taken place. They may include generation and transmission facilities, nuclear plant maintenance, and decommissioning costs as well as conservation measures. Other forms of stranded cost include contracts to purchase power from alternative energy sources and 'take-or-pay' obligations in long-term gas contracts. The latter impose an obligation on the buyer to pay for a percentage of the annual off-take volume even if he is unable to use or re-sell the gas.

An independent regulator

1.44 Experience has shown that a prerequisite to a successful programme of liberalization in the network-bound sector of the energy market is the establishment of an independent regulator charged with taking actions to promote competition. Independence in this context means independence of the regulator from the companies being regulated and from day-to-day interference from the government authorities. This autonomy will provide assurance to market participants and especially to potential new market entrants that the rules of the game will be applied in a non-discriminatory, stable, and transparent manner. This facilitates the creation of a 'level playing field'. The question of independence does however raise issues about accountability of the regulatory body. It has been addressed differently by various governments.

There has been much debate about the organization of regulation and especially about the horizontal and vertical allocation of authority.[38] Not surprisingly, such

[38] Some examples are: McCahery, J, Bratton, W W, Picciotto, S, and Scott, C, *International Regulatory Competition and Coordination: Perspectives on Economic Regulation in Europe and the US* (1996); the various contributions in the Journal of International Economic Law, June 2000, vol 3, no 2.

debates have been particularly intense in countries with federal systems of government. However, in the context of the EU, the interplay between the centre and Member State levels with respect to energy regulation is particularly complex, as will be seen in the following chapters.

In the network-bound energy sector, there is now a widespread acceptance that a single regulator to monitor the electricity and gas industries jointly is the most efficient solution. There is a broad consensus too that a regulatory commission is preferable to regulation by an individual since it helps to avoid a personalization of the process. A separate issue concerns the relationship to be established between the regulatory body and the competition authority, where separate institutions are to be in operation. The important issue is which body is to be responsible in cases where both have jurisdiction. The regulation involved in each case is quite different—that of a competition authority being *post facto* in character. A sector-specific regulator will be charged with applying rules irrespective of actual conduct. Key differences will turn on the specificity of the rules, the burden of proof , and the penalties for violating the rules. **1.45**

The procedures established for regulation are of great importance. Decision-making has to be transparent and the reasons should be published. The procedures should also be detailed and set out in advance.

(2) Structure

It has been said that 'structure forms the context within which regulation takes place.'[39] If an industry is structured in such a way as to give market power to a single producer or consumer, choice for other producers and consumers must inevitably be limited and regulation has to be strongly interventionist. In recent years, an appreciation of the importance of industry structure for market reform has made restructuring central to most programmes of energy market reform. The aim has usually been to dismantle the monopoly positions that were common for many years and to introduce competition. However, the natural monopoly elements in transmission and distribution networks present a challenge to such efforts. **1.46**

(a) Elements of natural monopoly in supply phases

A network owner and operator is likely to have a conflict of interest if also involved in generation or supply phases. Both the latter stages in the supply chain are actually or potentially competitive, while the transmission and distribution phases are natural monopolies, allowing the owner and operator to extract monopoly rents. In the electricity chain this also applies to dispatch and real-time balancing. There **1.47**

[39] Helm, D and Yarrow, G 'Regulation and Utilities', (1988) 4 Oxford Review of Economic Policy, vii.

is ample evidence that, if unchecked, the exercise of such monopoly rights will lead to abuses.[40] The customer could be charged anything the monopolist wishes for network access up to the cost of building an alternative system (or switching to another fuel). A policy objective is therefore to establish arm's length relationships between the owner and operator of the natural monopoly phases and the parties in the other phases of the supply chain.

(b) Solutions: 'Unbundling'

1.48 Various techniques have been developed to deal with this among countries engaged in market reform. The solutions have to take into account the continuing inter-relationship between the generation or production phases with the transmission network and between the distribution network and sales within vertically-integrated energy companies. They will involve a form of vertical separation of activities known as 'unbundling', aimed at eliminating incentives or abilities to discriminate against competitors by means of vertically-integrated companies. This may take one of three forms:

1. full structural separation by law;
2. functional separation; or
3. separation for accounting purposes.

1.49 (i) **Full structural separation by law** A full legal separation of the various operations is one possibility. In the electricity sector, for example, a separation of supply or retailing from distribution is likely to encourage competition to develop in supply. Assets from the integrated company would be divided up among several newly-formed legal entities that have no common ownership, management, control, or operations. However, vertical separation may also be effected by means of a form of corporatization rather than formal legal separation. This has been the approach favoured in Norway, Sweden, and New Zealand.

1.50 (ii) **Functional separation** Alternatively, there may be an unbundling according to functions. Functional unbundling allows for the same ownership of the elements that may be subject to competition and the monopoly infrastructure elements, but their operation is placed in the hands of separate management structures. The disaggregated entities will be managed independently but will not be legally separate companies. This kind of unbundling is designed to prevent discrimination against competitors who do not have a direct financial interest in the physical infrastructure.[41] In California an entity has been established in the electricity sector called an Independent System Operator. It has responsibility for

40 Kahn, A E, *The Economics of Regulation: Principles and Institutions* (1998), 118–20.

41 In the US a definition of functional unbundling is in FERC Order 888 (1996).

short-term co-ordination, prices for use of the transmission grid, and administers a system of tradable congestion contracts.[42]

(iii) Separation for accounting purposes Finally, there is the option of arranging unbundling by ring-fencing the accounts of the different types of businesses in the entity. The idea is that this promotes transparency and in so doing it will expose cross-subsidies and so prevent an entity from discriminating in favour of itself and against competitors. However, in practice it is hard to ensure that commercially sensitive information is not being transferred between the business units. This is probably the weakest form of unbundling and requires detailed regulation to be effective. **1.51**

So far, experience in market reform suggests that the unbundling of transportation networks from the activities that can be subjected to competition is a structural change of major importance. The means by which it is achieved and the extent to which it is adopted have, however, differed.

(3) Liberalization

Some of the general conditions for liberalization are obvious. If customers are to be able to choose suppliers, any statutory restrictions that limit their freedom to a particular supplier must be removed. Entry of new suppliers and producers should be possible, and the normal commercial consequences should apply to those companies which are unsuccessful in the market. In the EU entry barriers have often taken the form of exemptions from general competition law, frequently involving the grant of special or exclusive rights. However, competition is unlikely to develop if governments dismantle entry barriers and do little else. A level playing field for information is also important to establish. All market participants should have simultaneous and equal access to information on the price of a commodity, whether it is gas or electricity, and for capacity. **1.52**

Since transmission and distribution networks are likely to remain natural monopolies in most cases, the creation of non-discriminatory access rights to the networks is one of the most important conditions for liberalization. However, the tariffs and conditions of such access need to be transparent if competition is to develop in activities such as generation or production and supply. There are two régimes to facilitate the exercise of such rights: (i) regulated and (ii) negotiated access. In practice, the latter has proved less effective and usually involves an element of regulation too. **1.53**

The method of opening up gas and electricity markets has not been uniform but this is usually carried out in a staggered manner, the large industrial customers

[42] IEA, *Electricity Market Reform: An IEA Handbook* (1999) 40–1. Australia and Canada have similar ISOs, while the US has moved toward Regional Transmission Organizations.

being included in the first phase of market opening. Among the reasons for this approach is that the liberalization process creates problems as it develops and a staged approach allows adaptation to incorporate the lessons of previous stages. It also allows for the incorporation of lessons from the experiences of other countries with market reform. Some of the specific problems of transition that have arisen in the European setting are considered later in this work (see Part III).

(4) Ownership

1.54 The importance of ownership for the introduction of competition is complex.[43] Early experience of privatization showed that the transfer of a publicly-owned monopoly into private ownership did not produce the expected benefits in competitiveness. Other structures are possible and perhaps inevitable when one considers the range of forms of public ownership: national, federal, provincial, cantonal, or municipal ownership. Nonetheless, substantial public ownership in energy companies is likely to impede the operation of competition by encouraging their protection from adverse market developments. They will not in all probability have the 'freedom to fail'. Changes in ownership have therefore been encouraged as part of an overall reform programme, involving an unbundling of industry elements. Usually, they involve a minimum of corporatization, where a government continues to hold a substantial shareholding but ceases to have any direct control of management. A financial separation will ensure that financial and asset transfers between government and the corporatized entity are at arm's length and transparent. This is intended to facilitate a degree of competition.

Licensing and concession régimes

1.55 However, a key element in any regulatory system will be the establishment of a license or concession régime. This instrument will set down obligations with respect to the operation, maintenance, and development of transmission or distribution systems, as well as obligations to supply gas or electricity—the 'public service obligations'. With this instrument it is possible for the authorities to exercise a potentially large measure of control over the natural monopoly elements of an industry—irrespective of the form and pattern of ownership that is chosen.

E. Energy in Europe

1.56 In the context of the European Union, the paradigm shift described earlier unfolds differently because of the extensive integration of the EU that has been

[43] An IEA review notes that ownership alone is not of overwhelming importance for power sector performance *in the short term*. Instead, key factors are to subject potentially competitive parts to more competition and increasing the quality of regulation: *Electricity Market Reform: An IEA Handbook* (1999).

promoted by its 15 Member States. Here there are two considerations that are of great importance.

1. A complex allocation of authority between the EU and national bodies and resulting interplay of regulatory competence.
2. The energy sector is perhaps the most sensitive economic sector of all in relations between Member States and EU institutions.

The unique approach to energy market liberalization that has resulted is the subject of this book.

As an economic sector dear to the hearts of national policymakers, the pooling of national sovereignty in energy matters has been done only most reluctantly and in a piecemeal fashion. It is a process that is as yet far from complete. For several decades, it is not an exaggeration to say that energy simply did not figure in the EU integration process except in terms of a limited co-ordination of nuclear policy and coal restructuring and some measures aimed at improving the security of oil supply. It had *de facto* an exceptional status.

However, the acceleration of integration that began with the Single European Act **1.57** of 1986 put an end to the relative insulation of the electricity and gas industries for good. Whatever criticisms may be made about the pace of such integration in the energy sector, these industries have now joined the mainstream of market-oriented change in Europe. The legal and policy framework for government relations with the energy industry is as a result no longer largely a national one, but both national and EU in character.

Harmonization: 1986 and beyond

Until the mid-1980s, there had been hardly any harmonization of the laws or **1.58** rules in the energy sector. In electricity and gas the traditional paradigm dominated completely, based on the assumption that its monolithic style national arrangements were in the public interest. This did not mean however that a single approach was adopted by each Member State. On the contrary, diversity was the norm reflecting the different allocation of energy resources, history, policy preferences, and economic structures.[44]

In 1988 the European Commission, in the context of the creation of the Single **1.59** Market that was required to be completed by 1 January 1993, published a review of the obstacles to the creation of a single market in energy. In a Communication

[44] Overviews of the history and structure of the European electricity and gas industries include: references in n 2 in this chapter and: Cameron, P, *Gas Regulation in Europe*, (1995), Estrada, J, Moe, A, and Martinsen, K D, *The Development of European Gas Markets: Environmental, Economic and Political Perspectives* (1995), and Cross, E D, *Electric Utility Regulation in the EU: A Country by Country Guide* (1996).

entitled 'The Internal Energy Market: Commission Working Document',[45] the Commission analysed the general problems involved in the creation of a single energy market, proposed an approach to solving those problems, and in a series of Annexes set out, for each sector of the energy market, an inventory of the existing or potential obstacles to the creation of the single market, covering solid fuels, oil, natural gas, electricity, and nuclear power. It noted that a set of energy objectives had been agreed by the Member States in 1986.[46] It was subsequently invited by the Council of Ministers to draw up the inventory and submit proposals for a progressive elimination of those obstacles.[47]

The analysis carried out by the Commission led to a negative assessment. The market structures that provoked this assessment showed much variation from one Member State to another. However, they had in common specific features which hampered development towards an integrated energy market and which formed an infringement of European law on the free movement of goods and on competition. The Commission's main concerns were with the gas and electricity industries, which depended on networks in transmission and distribution for their operation. The oil sector was already subject to a large degree of competition in the Community energy sector.

1.60 Characteristics of the gas and electricity markets thought to be *obstacles to the creation of an internal market* were as follows:

1. *de iure* or *de facto* exclusive national monopolies in some Member States in the *import and export* of gas and electricity;
2. in all Member States except Germany, undertakings, whether state or privately-owned, had been granted exclusive or special rights in connection with *transmission and/or distribution* of gas and electricity at a national and/or local level, and (even in the case of Germany), some form of protection existed in the form of demarcation and concession areas;
3. a statutory *right of access* to the gas pipelines and electricity grids owned by others existed only in a few Member States. The absence of these rights militated against the creation of a single market for gas and electricity; and
4. the gas and electricity *distribution* monopolies, whether *de iure* or *de facto*, also contributed towards the creation of captive markets, having an effect on the competitive situation in Europe.

1.61 The second of these, segmentation of the EU gas and electricity markets through the existence of the statutory or *de facto* monopoly transmission companies within

[45] IEM Working Document, COM (1988), 238 final, 2 May 1988. Its aim was to implement the general conclusions of the White Paper on the Internal Market.

[46] Council Resolution of 16 September 1986 on new Community energy policy objectives for 1995 and convergence of the policies of the Member States, OJ C241: 25 July 1986.

[47] Energy Council Meeting of 2 June 1987: *Energy in Europe*, no 8, October 1987.

the individual Member States was considered to be a main obstacle towards the creation of an integrated energy market. These undertakings could restrict the through transport of energy and even where no specific legislation existed, could block the import and export of gas and electricity. Consequently, one suggested priority area in the natural gas sector was the 'de-compartmentalisation of the natural gas markets' through the mode of 'common carriage' or the provision of access rights to third parties to the grid as against payment of a reasonable charge. To achieve this aim, the following measures were proposed:[48]

- the exclusive transmission concessions should be checked to see how to facilitate the free movement of natural gas whilst maintaining a high level of security of supply and economic transmission conditions;
- transmission or distribution undertakings could be allowed direct access to the resources in question;
- the prospect of extending direct access to resources to large industrial consumers should be considered in the light of the results of the above findings.

The general problems concerning the inclusion of energy in the single market concept were examined and four sets of actions identified. These included: carrying out the provisions concerning the energy sector which were contained in the Working Document; the attainment of a satisfactory equilibrium between energy and the environment; the definition of appropriate means, to be selected on a case-by-case basis in areas specifically selected to energy policy; and, significantly, 'the determined application by the Commission of the provisions of Community Law'.[49] **1.62**

In its analysis of the position relating to energy and the application of Community law,[50] the Commission identified four main areas of concern: the free movement of goods; state monopolies of a commercial character, including exclusive rights to import and export gas and electricity, and exclusive rights of transport and distribution of gas and electricity; the rules of competition; and state aids, particularly in the coal and nuclear power industries.

The Working Document was the first step towards the development of a strategy for liberalization, which, though much amended in the coming years, would lead to a radical reform of the EU energy sector. In retrospect, it sounded the death knell for the kind of energy regulation that has been described above as the traditional paradigm. **1.63**

[48] IEM working document, COM (1988), 238 final, point 20, 66.
[49] ibid, point 38, 13.
[50] ibid, points 49–70, 18–23.

F. Conclusions

1.64 This chapter has attempted to sketch out the wider context in which a liberalization of EU energy markets was launched. It has emphasized the importance of the 'ideas' factor in energy market regulation by reference to a paradigmatic shift from a monopolist and state-interventionist approach to one in which market mechanisms are given a wide rein, checked mainly by independent regulation. The idea has taken firm root in public policy that the natural monopoly element in network industries was not such a barrier to the creation of the internal market in electricity and gas as had been asserted by the opponents of liberalization. It was accepted that the natural monopoly element could be dealt with by using regulation as a surrogate for competition and that the physical and technological problems of mass third-party access could be dealt with.

Key features of the new context such as the emphasis on markets and their creation and the impacts of globalization are not absolutely new. However, the extent of their acceptance and their effects is unprecedented. In this sense it is justified to utilize the concept of a paradigm shift. The rejection of many of the features associated with the 'traditional' paradigm is now widespread, most evidently in the developed countries but also in a growing number of developing countries and economies in transition.

1.65 However, it is important to note how recent this consensus is and how open-ended the new paradigm is. Reformers face challenges in applying its framework character and in dealing with some issues that are potentially incompatible with it, such as those concerning environmental protection and sustainability. As the liberalization of the world's electricity and gas markets gathers pace, many questions about reform remain to be answered including questions that are being generated by the reform process itself. These include factors not specific to the European situation but nonetheless essential to an understanding of it. If one recalls the words of Thomas Kuhn about the victory of a new paradigm, he notes that its success depends 'less on past achievement than on future promise'.

In practice, whoever embraces a new paradigm at an early stage must 'have faith that the new paradigm will succeed with the many large problems that confront it, knowing only that the older paradigm has failed with a few'.[51]

Diverse national models

1.66 The significance of the EU developments in electricity and gas liberalization goes beyond the 15 Member States. They will include Norway, already well-advanced along the liberalization road in its electricity sector and also all the States that have

[51] Kuhn, T, *The Structure of Scientific Revolutions* (1970), 158.

applied for membership of the EU (including Poland, the Czech Republic, Hungary, the Baltic Republics, Slovakia, and Slovenia) which, as a condition of becoming members of the EU, will be required to incorporate the EU legal and regulatory régimes for electricity and gas into their national laws. The diversity of models that is emerging provides interesting and perhaps instructive material for countries outside Europe. In particular, the interplay between centralized and decentralized regulation—the debate about subsidiarity—should yield some insights and perhaps lessons about competition and co-operation among diverse regulatory authorities and the courts in the liberalization process.

2

THE LEGAL BASIS FOR A EUROPEAN ENERGY MARKET

Since the mid-1980s [there has been] an almost continuous process of constitutional change in the EU.[1]

A. Introduction

The steps taken by the EU towards the creation of an Internal Energy Market (IEM) in the 1990s marked a watershed in Community energy law and policy. Never before had there been such a deliberate and comprehensive attempt to link energy specifically to the body of Community law and to the integration process. **2.01**

[1] Dashwood, A, 'The Constitution of the European Union after Nice: law-making procedures', (2001) 26 EL Rev 215–38.

It marked the beginning of a determined—and so far quite successful—attempt to put an end to the 'special' status of the energy sector in the process of EU integration.

However, the IEM programme established under the Single European Act is more than an ambitious attempt at energy market liberalization. It has been driven not by a belief in markets *per se* but rather by a commitment to the establishment of an internal market among the Member States of the EU. In this sense, it differs from the programmes of market liberalization elsewhere in the world, which are nearly always carried out within the framework of the nation-state. Indeed, many of the concepts discussed in chapter 1 have at least a special nuance when applied to the liberalizing activities of the EU.

2.02 This unique aspect of the IEM programme gains in importance when one appreciates that the EU has experienced almost continual constitutional reform since the mid-1980s. It is no accident that the start of this period of reform corresponds closely with the moment when the idea of the IEM emerged in its current form. The constitutional reform involved changes in the voting procedure of the Council (qualified majority voting) and significant enlargements of the law-making rôle of the Parliament. Without these changes it would have been very difficult, if not impossible, to procure the adoption of the Electricity and Gas Directives.

2.03 This chapter outlines the principal legal and institutional contours of the European energy scene that have a bearing upon the development of competition in the EU energy markets. Many of these have emerged or have been shaped by constitutional reforms occurring since the mid-1980s. Amendments to the primary law of the EU have been made through the Inter-Governmental Conferences (IGCs) and resulting Treaty revisions. During these conferences—generally initiated by Heads of States or governments—amendments and extensions of the basic EU rules were negotiated: affecting areas like decision-making procedures, institutional structures, and policy—including new fields of application of the Treaty—with consequent changes in the primary legislation. Inevitably, such processes have had an impact on the form and substance of the IEM programme of energy law and policy.

That programme of reform is still gaining momentum, as the EU considers what constitutional actions are required to meet its goal of enlargement to include many new applicant states. This chapter therefore sketches out the principal legal and institutional pillars of the energy scene in the EU relevant to the IEM programme—past, present, and future. It is divided into seven parts:

1. Origins of an EU Acquis in Energy
2. The Treaties

3. The European Commission and its institutional setting[2]
4. Trans-European Energy Networks
5. The European Economic Area Agreement
6. The Energy Charter Treaty, and
7. Enlargement of the EU and the EU *acquis* in energy.

A key feature of these seven subjects is their contemporaneousness: they all developed considerably, or—in the case of (3) to (6)—came into existence during the years in which a legal framework for the energy sector was established under the IEM. As is apparent from the chapters in Part III (dealing with issues arising from the transition to an IEM), the wider 'pan-European' dimension of the IEM programme is becoming increasingly intermeshed with the deepening of the IEM in the transition to a liberalized EU energy market.

B. Origins of an EU *Acquis* in Energy

The IEM programme was clearly intended to strengthen the framework of EU law as it applied to EU energy markets. At first, this may seem a little puzzling. Much of the law in the EC Treaty already granted the Community institutions extensive powers to achieve the objectives of such a programme, especially with respect to competition matters—such as an abuse of dominant positions by the operators of energy networks. In principle, further legislation was not a prerequisite for a liberalization of the energy sector. But it was quite clear that if the Commission was to rely on EC competition law to deal with individual cases of abuse of a dominant position by system network owners it would take many years of litigation before a body of case law could be built up which could clarify the basic legal principles to be applied in cases of abuse of dominant position in relation to networks. There was also uncertainty about the legal position in relation to abuse of dominant position where the network owner had been granted exclusive or special rights in respect of the network. In these circumstances, and having regard to the need to establish common rules applicable throughout the Community, the Commission decided to tackle the removal of obstacles to the IEM by applying the existing law and also submitting specific initiatives in the form of proposed Directives. The Council of Ministers supported this approach **2.04**

[2] For further detail, refer to general works including: Hartley, *The Foundations of European Community Law: an introduction to the constitutional and administrative law of the European Community* (4th edn, 1998); Wyatt, D, and Dashwood, A, *European Union Law* (4th edn, 2000); Kapteyn P J G and VerLoren van Themaat P, *Introduction to the Law of the European Communities: From Maastricht to Amsterdam* (3rd edn, Gormley (ed), 1998). On energy, see chapter on energy by Devlin and Levasseur in Faull, J, and Nikpay, A, *The EC Law of Competition* (1999), and Ehlermann, C D, 'The Rôle of the European Commission as Regards National Energy Policies' (1994) 12 J Energy Natural Resources L 342.

(see below). Changes made in the law-making process under the EC Treaty including the introduction of qualified majority voting in the Council and a greater involvement of the European Parliament in the law-making process were to greatly enhance the possibility that such Directives would be adopted and be transposed into law.

2.05 A new framework of EC energy law was to emerge during the 1990s, following extensive consultations with the energy industry and the Member States. The most important of the specific measures were the Directives concerning common rules for the electricity and gas industries. They took no less than five and seven years respectively to go from initial proposal stages to adoption by the Member States and the European Parliament. During that time, the context of European integration changed dramatically. A Treaty establishing the European Union and amending (*inter alia*) the EC Treaty—the Treaty on European Union (TEU) was concluded at Maastricht in 1992, and, after a review of its operation at an Inter-Governmental Conference in 1997, further amendments were subsequently included in the Treaty of Amsterdam (TA). Among the many changes were procedural ones that extended the influence of the European Parliament over a wide range of matters including energy harmonization proposals. The European Union acquired three new members from the European Economic Area (EEA). Discussions were opened to negotiate the terms of a further enlargement to the East.

2.06 Further, the collapse of the Soviet Union triggered a pan-European approach to energy policy that reflected the importance of non-EU suppliers and transit countries to the EU energy market. From the early 1990s the EU gave support to the development of international agreements to promote stability in the East and to ensure the continuation of the oil and gas supplies that many Member States relied on. These included the use of bilateral association agreements on co-operation between the EU and the countries of post-Communist Central and East Europe, as well as looser forms of partnership agreement between East and West. The EU also played a leading rôle in the negotiation and conclusion of another, more ambitious legal instrument, the Energy Charter Treaty, signed and ratified by more than 50 nation-states from East and West. All such instruments have, in addition to their political objectives, the goal of economic liberalization in which energy market reform plays a more or less important part. As EU energy law and policy was re-moulded in the 1990s, these instruments increasingly functioned as channels for the export of ideas and techniques that were being developed within the EU internal energy market programme.

2.07 In aggregate, the various legal and policy instruments constitute a pan-European legal order for the energy sector, sometimes called an '*acquis communautaire*' or

EU *acquis* for energy.[3] Essentially, this comprises all of the rights and obligations, actual and potential, which result from EC legislation and case law. Much of it is of very recent origin, dating from long after the first period of European integration. It has been constructed or has become operational during the 1990s. Although some of the instruments have a distinctly 'soft' legal character, they act as a channel for a Europe-wide dissemination of the ideas of energy market liberalization and create a system of peer group pressure among the many countries that act within this framework. To the extent that liberalization is an ongoing—and distinctly unfinished—process, they facilitate the rapid transmission of ideas and experiences around Europe. Although the instruments have diverse goals, including integration and economic co-operation, they all share, to a greater or lesser degree, a commitment to the introduction of competition in energy markets, and to 'regulation for competition'.

(1) The Treaties

(a) Should energy be afforded a special status in the Treaties?

Since the inception of what is now the EU, there has been no explicit grant of a 'special' status to the energy sector under the EC Treaty (formerly EEC Treaty; see para 2.17 below), exempting it from the ambit of some or all of its provisions. There are at least two possible interpretations of this. First, it may be argued that the intention was to treat energy no differently from any other economic sector in the integration process. Had the authors of the Treaty establishing the European Economic Community sought to set the industry apart in any way, they would have been well aware of the means by which this could have been done—but they did not.[4] After all, explicit provisions were inserted into the Treaty, especially Article 33(1),* at a time when, with the aim of stabilizing markets, actions were envisaged to ensure security of supplies (including energy products) or to guarantee access to the market to consumers at reasonable prices). **2.08**

For example, production of and trade in agricultural products was excluded from the application of the competition rules under Article 37* to the extent determined by the Council. Where special circumstances were deemed to exist—as in the sub-sectors of coal and nuclear energy—legal instruments had already been

[3] For discussion of this concept see Gialdino, C, 'Some Reflections on the *Acquis Communautaire*' (1995) 32 CML Rev 1089 and Delcourt, C, 'The *acquis communautaire*: Has the concept had its day?', (2000) 38 CML Rev 829. More recently, the abbreviated term has been preferred to reflect Treaty changes that make it an *acquis* of the EU. Parts of the Energy Charter Treaty go beyond the competence of the European Community and are based on the prerogatives of the Member States.

[4] This view is expressed in Ehlermann, see n 2 above. See also Daintith, T, and Hancher, L, *Energy Strategy in Europe: The Legal Framework*, (1986).

* The Articles of the EC Treaty were re-numbered by the Treaty of Amsterdam (TA) in 1997. For the original, pre-1997 numbering, see the Table of Derivations, Appendix 4. The consolidated version of the EC Treaty, as amended by the TA, was published at (1997) OJ C-340/173.

concluded and were in force. Moreover, the Court of Justice has expressly ruled that electricity is a 'good' and falls within the scope of the competition rules.[5] And there was no doubt about other sources of energy—such as oil and gas—that they were classifiable as goods.

2.09 Another view is that the energy sector has unique characteristics and a special importance in the EU so that provision for it should be made in the primary law itself. The absence of a systematic provision in the EC Treaty was therefore a mistake. The most important sources of energy in the EU today—oil, natural gas, and electricity—received little or no express treatment in the three fundamental legal instruments: the European Coal and Steel Community Treaty, the Euratom Treaty, and the Treaty of the European Community. Indeed, the only subjects expressly covered by law were coal, nuclear energy and, at a time of emergency in supply, oil.[6] One commentator has concluded that this situation was 'a failure of vision' on the part of the progenitors of the Community.[7] Another has described the patchwork treatment of energy policy in the EC Treaty as 'astonishing'.[8] The effect of this approach has been that measures on energy were for many years adopted on the basis of powers conferred for other purposes, such as competition matters, the environment or external relations.[9]

Whatever assessment one may make of the treatment of energy in the primary legislation of the EC Treaty, it is certainly true to say that for many years the application of those provisions relevant to the network-bound energy sector was virtually

5 Case 6/64 *Costa v Enel* [1964] ECR 1251. At a later date, this was reinforced by Case C-393/92 *Almelo Gemeente v NV Energiebedrijf Ijsselmij* [1994] ECR I-1477, and Cases C-157/94 *Commission v Netherlands*, C-158/94 *Commission v Italy* [1997] ECR I-5789, C-159/94 *Commission v France*, C-160/94 *Commission v Spain* [1997] ECR I-5699 *et seq.*

6 There have been attempts to enlarge Community competencies during crises in oil supply in the 1970s and during the Gulf War: see *Security of Supply, the Internal Market and Energy Policy*, Working Paper of the Commission of the EC, 1990: SEC (90) 1248; and later in the definition of common energy objectives.

7 Green, N, 'The Implementation of Treaty Policies: the energy dilemma' (1983) 8 ELR 186, 189.

8 Schwarze, J, 'European Energy Policy in Community Law', in Mestmaeker E J, (ed), *Natural Gas in the Internal Market*, (1992) 155.

9 The main powers are to: establish a common commercial policy (if measure relates to trade in raw materials, eg oil or coal; Art 133* and Arts 71–74 ECSC) ; adopt research and development programmes and agreements (Title XVIII (ex Title XV) EC); adopt measures relating to the environment (Title XIX (ex Title XVI) EC); take measures or conclude agreements in the area of development co-operation policy (under Title XX (ex Title XVII EC), if they are part of the Community's co-operation with less developed countries; encourage the establishment and development of trans-European networks, if measure concerns energy infrastructures (Title XV, ex Title XII EC); conclude association agreements under Art 238 EC, that provide *inter alia* for energy co-operation). Also relevant are powers under Art 100a where a proposed agreement might concern internal common rules adopted under the powers conferred by that Article, and Art 95 ECSC and Art 235 EC where no other powers can be found and where the proposed measure meets the criteria in these Articles.

non-existent—for the reasons stated above. Even for the European Commission, state monopolies of a commercial character 'were not perceived as an obstacle to the establishment of the first stages of the Common Market'.[10]

A key factor behind this state of affairs was the close relationship between Member State governments on the one hand and public undertakings in energy networks on the other. Historically, Member States have been reluctant to cede control over energy policy to the European institutions. If the absence of a systematic approach to energy constituted a flaw, it nevertheless received tacit approval from the majority of Member States, wishing to retain maximum control over their national energy régimes.[11] Moreover, given the diversity of aims of national energy policies, the instruments designed to achieve them, the industry structure as well as the resource base of each Member State, this resistance to a centralized approach to energy policy was understandable. **2.10**

(b) Coal

The first source of Community interest in energy matters can be found in the European Coal and Steel Community Treaty 1951 (ECSC Treaty).[12] The aim of the ECSC was to transfer control of national coal and steel industries from national authorities, particularly those of Germany and France, to a supra-national authority (the High Authority). The Treaty provides far-reaching competencies on market organization and some horizontal policies, such as research and development, as well as restructuring of the coal and steel industries. For example, Article 50 allows the High Authority (now the European Commission) to raise levies on coal and steel production. The Treaty expires in July 2002 at which time the provisions of the Treaty will lapse and the coal industry will be subject to the general provisions of the EC Treaty including those relating to competition (with a specific regime in respect of state aids). **2.11**

The Treaty did not seek to establish full competition in the EC coal industry. It created a system of regulated competition under which the Commission could intervene in the market in specific circumstances. However, the Treaty did contain specific régimes relating to anti-competitive agreements, abuse of a dominant

[10] Ehlermann, C D, 'The Rôle of the European Commission as Regards National Energy Policies' (1994) 12 J Energy Natural Resources L 342.

[11] The close connection between energy policies and national interests as a limit to integration in the EU energy sector at the time is explored in Daintith, T, and Williams, S, *The Legal Integration of Energy Markets* (1987).

[12] ECSC Treaty (Treaty of Paris), Paris, 18 April 1951, UKTS 2 (1973); Cmnd 5189. Signed in Paris on 18 April 1951 and entering into force on 25 July 1952, it is sometimes known as the Treaty of Paris. The Treaty term is 50 years. The Contracting Parties are the 6 original Member States: Belgium, France, Germany, Italy, Luxembourg, and The Netherlands.

position and also merger control.[13] The Treaty contained social provisions on employment, cost of living, and supply[14] (and reconversion). The ECSC Treaty is in fact the only one of the original three Treaties to deal especially with the social aspects of the energy sector.

2.12 This early attempt at integration clearly accorded great weight to energy issues. Coal was at that time responsible for about 90 per cent of all energy consumed in the countries concerned. However, the provisions lost much of their significance when cheap oil imports supplanted the pre-eminence of coal in the ECSC countries. When demand exceeded supply it could be argued that a complex and quite sophisticated body of regulation was justified, allowing the High Authority to intervene in matters of pricing policy, competition policy, commercial policy, crisis management, and matters of financial and social concern. Once the hegemonic rôle of coal in the energy sector had disappeared, these provisions lost their justification in economic reality. In practice, the development of the coal market was influenced more and more by competition from other energy sources such as oil, natural gas, and nuclear power. However, it is certainly true to say that with a liberal interpretation of its state aid rules the Treaty enabled a relatively orderly rundown of unprofitable national coal production.

(c) Nuclear energy

2.13 The second instrument of integration to be aimed at the energy sector was the European Atomic Energy Community Treaty (Euratom) concluded in 1957.[15] The task of Euratom was to create the conditions 'necessary for the speedy establishment and growth of nuclear industries' among the Member States.[16] To carry out its task the Community is required to act in areas specified in Article 2. They include the establishment of a nuclear common market as provided in the Treaty and the promotion of uniform health and safety standards to protect workers and the general public. Safeguards provisions—dealing with transfers of fissile materials—were intended as a contribution to non-proliferation.[17]

2.14 The Euratom Treaty had its origins in the Suez Crisis of 1956 in the Middle East. It aimed at reducing energy import dependence upon that region and at countering the nuclear power dominance of the United States and USSR that had been established at that time. Its success turned on the willingness of key Member States to relinquish control over their national nuclear programmes.

---

[13] ibid, Art 4.

[14] ibid, Arts 2 and 3.

[15] Euratom Treaty (Rome, 25 March 1957), UKTS 1 (1973)-Pt.II; Cmnd 5179–II. Signed at Rome on 25 March 1957. Entered into force on 1 January 1958. The Contracting Parties were the 6 Member States of the ECSC. The Treaty was concluded for an unlimited period.

[16] ibid, Art 1

[17] ibid, Title II, chap 7. Their success in implementation was limited however.

However, in the event, a failure by Member States to agree about nuclear policy left important gaps in the operation of the Treaty. The establishment of a centralized monopoly agency, charged with relating user needs to producer capacities and the availability of non-EC supplies, was fundamental to the Treaty. It was given the exclusive right to import nuclear materials into the Community and an exclusive right of purchase from producers within it. It was also given responsibility for the conclusion of contracts for the provision of such supplies. This centralized supply agency never came into being. The driving force behind such a body was clearly not the idea of an internal or common market but rather the idea that users could only receive a regular supply of ores and nuclear fuels by the establishment of a centralized monopoly supply agency.[18] Two further omissions may be noted.

First, the Euratom Treaty does not confer powers of jurisdiction with respect to the use of nuclear fuels or nuclear installations for military purposes, nor powers over the safe design, construction, or operation of Member States' nuclear facilities and installations. It confers powers only over a quite narrow sector of activity. Its 'centre of gravity' is in practice in the development of research and the dissemination of technical knowledge.[19] **2.15**

Secondly, a further limit on the operation of the Treaty arises from the adverse fortunes of the nuclear industry itself since the Treaty was concluded. Costs of nuclear power plant construction have proved greater than expected. And the climate of public opinion in Europe remains largely hostile to further development of the industry despite its advantages over the alternatives in environmental terms. **2.16**

(d) EEC Treaty

Of the three treaties the more general instrument of integration is the Treaty establishing the European Economic Community. It was entered into between the six original Member States in 1957 (the EEC Treaty), and subsequently renamed the European Community Treaty (EC Treaty). The scope of the EEC Treaty was much broader than the other two treaties. Article 2 described the task of the Community as one in which, by establishing a common market and 'progressively approximating the economic policies of the Member States', it would: **2.17**

> . . . promote throughout the Community a harmonious development of economic activities, a continuous and balanced expansion, an increase in stability, an accelerated raising of the standard of living, and closer relationships between the States belonging to it.

[18] In this respect, see Gruenwald, J, 'The Rôle of Euratom', in Cameron, P, Hancher, L and Kuhne, W (eds), *Nuclear Energy Law After Chernobyl* (1988) 32 and Allen, D, 'The Euratom Treaty, Chapter IV: New Hope or False Dawn?' (1983) 20 CML Rev 473; Daintith and Hancher, n 4 above, 15.

[19] Kapteyn, PJG, and VerLoren van Themaat, P, (eds) *Introduction to the Law of the European Communities: From Maastricht to Amsterdam*, (1998), 1218

The EEC Treaty contained specific provisions dealing with the establishment of the common market, although none specifically providing for a common energy policy.[20] Some provisions of the EC Treaty are highly relevant to energy activities, and especially to the electricity and gas businesses. The rules falling under Articles 28 to 31* (in full at Appendix 4) and those falling under Article 86* (see Appendix 4) are of particular relevance.

Articles 28 and 29 prohibit quantitative restrictions on imports and exports and all measures with an equivalent effect. The ECJ has held that 'quantitative restrictions' includes all national measures and rules capable of hindering trade, no matter what their intended result.[21] There are however two sources of exceptions, deriving from Article 30 and in particular the 'public security' exemption (see ch 5, paras 5.72–5.81) and the 'rule of reason' exception which has been developed in the case law for the application of Article 28.

2.18 (i) **Article 31 and public service obligations** Article 31 requires Member States to progressively adjust state monopolies of a commercial character through which a Member State supervises, determines, or appreciably influences imports or exports between Member States. The enforcement of this requirement is a matter for the Commission.[22] It may use its powers under Article 226* (see Appendix 4) to bring a case against a Member State before the ECJ for breach of obligations under the Treaty, subject to the Member State first being given an opportunity to submit its observations on the complaint to the Commission. In the early days, the Commission used its powers under Article 31 to pursue the dismantling of 'oil products monopolies' in France and Greece—successfully, albeit over a very long period of time (see paras 5.36 and 5.79–5.80).[23] It also had success in using the Article to persuade the Belgian Government to remove the statutory exclusive right of the then state-owned gas utility, Distrigas, to import gas (para 5.35).

2.19 Under Article 86* the Commission is required (*inter alia*) to ensure that the rules of the Treaty (including, *inter alia*, Art 31,* Art 81,* and Art 82*) are complied with. Article 86(1) imposes upon Member States the obligation not to enact or maintain in force any measures contrary to Treaty rules with respect to public

---

[20] cf *Rapport des Chefs de Delegations aux Ministères des Affaires Étrangères* (Secretariat of the Intergovernmental Conference, Brussels, 21 April 1956 (the Spaak Report)). The Report had identified energy and especially oil as an area for urgent attention but this was not taken further. A widely held view at the time, which led to non-action in this area, was that oil companies were well-equipped to deal with issues in this sector.

[21] Case 8/74 *Procureur du Roi v Dassonville* [1974] ECR 837.

[22] Note that individuals may invoke their rights independently in national courts where the provisions of the Treaty have direct effect: *Allgemene Transport en Expedetie Onderneming Van Gend en Loos v Nederlandse Administratie der Belastingen* [1963] ECR 1 (see para 2.80).

[23] Sixth Report on Competition Policy (1977), points 268–9 (France); Case C 347/88 *Commission v Greece* [1990] ECR 4747. In this context see also the judgment in *Campus Oil* Case 72/83 [1984] ECR 277.

undertakings or undertakings to which they have granted special or exclusive rights. Article 86(1) acknowledges that Member States may create public undertakings (ie state owned/controlled companies) and also grant to such undertakings or private undertakings special or exclusive rights (eg, in transmission and/or distribution) subject to the proviso that the legal measures by which they create these undertakings or grant special or exclusive rights do not contain any provisions contrary to the rules of the EC Treaty. It was not until the early 1990s that a number of cases came before the ECJ which provided it with the opportunity to clarify the relationship between the provisions of Article 86(1),* the provisions of Article 82,* and Articles 29–32.* Also the ECJ assisted in the clarification of exemptions under Article 86(2)*—see Chapter 5 for explanations of a number of these cases, including *Höfner*, *Port of Genoa* and *Corbeau* (*Belgian Postal Monopoly*).[24] Essentially, these judgments opened up to legal challenge under the competition rules of the EC Treaty any exclusive generating, transportation, distribution, and supply rights—and made it possible to begin the opening up of the electricity and gas markets to new entrants.

2.20 Article 86(2) provides an exemption, narrowly drawn, from the reach of the Treaty (particularly competition) for undertakings entrusted with the operation of services of general economic interest. Services of a general economic interest include essential services provided for the public at large. They include the provision of water, electricity, and gas. Special obligations ('public service obligations') are frequently placed on the providers of such services. Such obligations include security, including security of supply, regularity, quality and price of supplies, and environmental protection. They may also include specific obligations relating to the supply of electricity and gas to householders, the poor, and disabled people. In return for the acceptance of such obligations, Member States granted special or exclusive rights.[25] The undertakings which accept such public service obligations may be able to obtain an exemption from the application of the competition rules under the provisions of Article 86(2).

2.21 **(ii) Articles 81 and 82** There are two other Articles of the EC Treaty which were relevant to liberalization. These are: Article 82,* (see Appendix 4) which prohibits companies in a dominant position from abusing that position and is

[24] *Corbeau* Case C-320/91 [1993] I-2533; *Porto di Genova* Case, C-179/90 [1991] ECR I-1979. The Court of Justice ruled that the grant of a special or exclusive right was lawful even if it gave the undertaking concerned a dominant position in the relevant market, but that the exercise of that right was subject to the provisions of Art 82* and that the exercise of that right could in itself be held to be unlawful.

[25] See generally, Buendia Sierra, JL, *Exclusive Rights and State Monopolies under EC Law* (1999).

therefore also relevant to the energy sector (possible refusal of access to networks); and Article 81* (Appendix 4) which prohibits anti-competitive agreements. Both Articles apply to public and private undertakings equally. A number of Commission decisions applying these Articles are discussed in Chapter 5, paragraphs 5.60–5.70.

2.22 (iii) **Articles 87 to 89** Finally, mention should be made of the Articles on state aids (Arts 87–89*). These are also relevant to energy. They prohibit the provision of state aids where they threaten to distort trade, but create exceptions and are subject to EC policing.

However, despite those provisions of the EC Treaty, it was not until the decisions of the ECJ interpreting Article 86(1)* in conjunction with Article 82,* that action was taken against exclusive rights of transmission, distribution, and supply existing in the Member States that had made it impossible or futile for potential applicants to try to gain access to networks. The Commission therefore responded by making several efforts to develop a Community energy policy.

2.23 (iv) **The 1960s** As early as 1964, a Protocol of Agreement between the Member States on energy problems was drawn up.[26] This resulted from a growing awareness of the global character of energy issues, covered by three different Treaties and three different bodies of institutions in an unco-ordinated manner. It comprised a statement of objectives and principles, an agenda, and a procedural agreement. In 1967 the Council took a decision on Community policy concerning oil and gas.[27] In 1968, the Commission outlined the first guidelines of a Community energy policy in a Communication to the Council, noting that 'There are still considerable barriers in trade in energy products within the Community.'[28] If this state of affairs did not alter, it argued, and if a common energy market were not achieved in the near future, 'the degree of integration achieved in this sector may well be jeopardised.'[29] In contrast to Community policy on coal and nuclear energy, the Commission assigned considerable weight to the market mechanism as a co-ordinating instrument. Further, in 1968 an obligation was imposed upon Member States to maintain a minimum level of stocks of oil and/or petroleum products.[30]

2.24 (v) **1980s: good intentions overtaken by oil price collapse** After several failed attempts, and in spite of various emergency measures taken during and

---

[26] JO 1964, p 1009.

[27] Council doc. 1014/67.

[28] *First orientation for a common energy policy*, Communication from the Commission to the Council, 18 Dec 1968, p 9, para 4.

[29] ibid.

[30] Council Directive (EEC) 68/414 on compulsory oil stocks in the Community [1968], subsequently amended on 14 Dec 1998.

after the energy crises of the 1970s,[31] the idea of a Community energy policy gave way to a new approach to energy strategy in 1981.[32] This abandoned any attempt at a transfer of competence, a centralized decision-making process or the creation of EC rules on a common policy. A leading EC official at the time put it in this way: 'The strategy . . . accepts more that action is better taken at national level, subject always to the constraint that it contributes to a common effort but Community initiatives are advantageous . . . whenever and wherever it seems necessary or more effective'.[33] A common policy would therefore be justified only in those areas where the Community possessed specific or exclusive powers.

In 1983 the Council made a formal declaration that there was a need to identify common energy objectives to be co-ordinated across the Community and at the same time to strengthen national measures.[34] In 1986 a Council Resolution set out various energy policy objectives to be achieved by 1995.[35] Principal features were security of supply and price stability. A convergence of the energy policies of the Member States was envisaged. **2.25**

However, this strategy-oriented approach was overtaken by events. In particular, the precipitous fall in oil prices in 1986 led Member States to abandon their agreed targets to achieve energy efficiency and common goals. It also underlined the vulnerability of European economies to outside forces in the supply of their energy. This generated efforts by the Commission to secure agreement with important external suppliers, including attempts to establish a general free trade and co-operation agreement with members of the Gulf Co-operation Council (GCC; a group of countries ranking among the main suppliers of oil to the Community). These proved unsuccessful due to the inability of GCC members to agree on certain prerequisites, such as the establishment of a common customs tariff. Links were in fact established with institutions grouping various oil producing countries: OAPEC and subsequently OPEC. These led to exchanges of information but not to agreements or arrangements of a legal character.

[31] The Community measures focused on crisis management and energy saving. In the former case, Directive 73/278 was adopted, implementing the rules of the International Energy Agency. They are supplemented by an agreement between the major oil companies, exempted under Art 85(3): Decision 83/671 (1983 OJ L 376/30) *International Energy Agency*, renewed by Decision 94/153 (1994 OJ L 68/35). Energy savings measures were included in Decision 77/706 (1977 OJ L 292/9). Other measures restricting the use of natural gas and petroleum products in power stations have since been repealed.

[32] *Development of an Energy Strategy for the Community*, COM (1981) 540 final.

[33] Robert De Bauw, paper presented to EU Colloquium, Florence, Italy, September, 1982: *Legal Implementation of Energy Policy*.

[34] The Declaration was made in November 1983. Council Resolution on energy objectives were made earlier in 1974 and 1980 (OJ No C 153 of 9 July 1975, p 1 and OJ No C 149 of 18 June 1980, p 1, respectively).

[35] 1986 OJ C 241/1.

2.26 Throughout this period the energy sector had proved resistant to the integration process. However, it was not unique in this respect. Progress towards the removal of barriers to trade in other sectors of industry and commerce was also slow. The legislation and practices of Member States displayed a very considerable number of barriers to the 'four freedoms': free movement of goods, persons, services, and capital—cornerstones of the common market. This situation had improved slightly during the 1970s but it became increasingly apparent that without a new impetus the level of integration implied by the idea of a common market as envisaged by the architects of the EEC Treaty would not come into existence.

(2) The Single European Act

2.27 To make further progress in integration, modifications in the Treaty framework were required. These were made through a Treaty known as the Single European Act (SEA),[36] which amended all three Treaties establishing the European Communities. The most significant of the changes were those made to the EEC Treaty to enable the internal market to be completed by removing the remaining barriers to trade within the Community before the end of December 1992. Amendments affecting the energy sector in particular were:

(1) those on the establishment of the objective of an internal market by the end of 1992
(2) a streamlining of Council decision-making procedures on internal market matters and
(3) the enforcement of the rôle of the European Parliament in the review of legislation.

(a) An internal market by the end of 1992 (Art 8A)

2.28 A new article was added to the Treaty, providing that the Community adopt measures to progressively establish the internal market over a period expiring on 31 December 1992. It defined the concept of the internal market as comprising 'an area without internal frontiers in which the free movement of goods, persons, services and capital is ensured' in accordance with the EC Treaty.[37] Implications were elucidated by a Declaration on the Article.[38] Through this the Inter-Governmental Conference expressed its 'firm political will' to take prior to 1 January 1993 'the decisions necessary to complete the internal market defined in those provisions'. This extended to the implementation of the Commission's

---

[36] OJ L 169 June 1987. It was signed by the 12 Member States at Luxembourg on 17 Feb 1986 and The Hague on 28 Feb 1986, and entered into force on 1 July 1987.

[37] Art 8(A), second para.

[38] Declaration 3, contained in the Final Act, a document forming part of the SEA.

programme described in the White Paper on the Internal Market.[39] In fact, the idea of an internal (or common) market was not at all novel, but the setting of a deadline was, and the improvement of harmonization procedures was a useful development.

The White Paper referred to in the Declaration is the Commission's White Paper to the Council of Ministers on 'Completing the Internal Market',[40] submitted in 1985. It set out the tasks that the Commission saw as being necessary for the completion of the internal market. Among its general provisions, several were of importance to the energy industry, although energy as such was omitted from the White Paper. These included the application of the Community Law[41] and the removal of territorial barriers—in particular the approximation of indirect taxation.[42] **2.29**

(b) Streamlining decision-making procedures

The second change introduced by the SEA concerned voting procedures within the Council of Ministers. A qualified majority system of voting was to apply in relation to measures involving the achievement of the objectives of the new Article 8(A). The existing system of voting that imposed a formal requirement of unanimity remained in effect with respect to many but not all other decisions of the Council. The relevant provisions were contained in a new Article 100A* of the EC Treaty providing that: **2.30**

> The Council shall acting by way of a qualified majority on a proposal from the Commission in co-operation with the European Parliament and after consulting with the Economic and Social Committee, adopt the measures for the approximation of the provisions laid down by law, regulation, or administrative action in Member States which have as their object the establishment and functioning of the internal market.

The effect of the additions to Articles 8 and 100 was to enhance the possibility of taking legislative steps to break up the existing compartmentalized energy market. It was now only necessary to obtain a qualified majority in the Council of Ministers in relation to harmonization measures proposed under Article 8A. This supplemented the legislative routes open to the Commission under existing Treaty rules that might have provided a basis for abolishing the segmented character of the energy markets. In this context, it may be noted that the weighting of votes had changed as a result of the accession of Spain and Portugal, with the effect that whereas before 1986 only one of the larger Member States could be outvoted, afterwards two could be outvoted. **2.31**

---

[39] The Declaration concludes with the words: 'Setting the date of 31 December 1992 does not create an automatic legal effect'.

[40] COM (1985) 310 final, Brussels, 14 June 1985.

[41] White Paper paras 152–9.

[42] ibid, paras 185 *et seq*.

(c) Predecessor to co-decision: the co-operation procedure

2.32 Finally, it may be noted that the rôle of the Parliament in the legislative process expanded as a result of a new *co-operation* procedure, introduced through an amendment of Article 149 of the EEC Treaty and applied to almost all internal market legislation. This was to prove an important first step in securing additional legitimacy for the Commission's proposals for completion of the internal market in energy.

Under the co-operation procedure, a Commission proposal for legislation is sent to Parliament as well as the Council. Parliament, after a first reading, notifies the Council of its opinion. The Council then adopts a common position—taking into account the Commission's proposal, Parliament's opinion and its own deliberations—which is sent to Parliament for a second reading. Within a three-month period, Parliament may accept the common position, refrain from acting, reject it or propose amendments to the common position. If the Commission accepted those amendments, the Council can accept them by a qualified majority vote. If Parliament rejects the common position, the Council can only adopt the instrument unanimously. This procedure was, in relation to many measures including IEM ones, replaced in 1993 by the co-decision procedure (see para 2.40 below), which for the first time gave Parliament the right to block measures approved in Council.

2.33 **Articles 174 and 175** Further changes were made within the framework of environmental policy that had a bearing on the energy sector. Article 174* referred to the 'prudent and rational utilisation of natural resources', while Article 175 concerned the adoption of 'measures significantly affecting a Member State's choice between different energy sources and the general structure of its energy supply'. However, in a Declaration on this Article, the Intergovernmental Conference noted that the Community's activities in environmental matters may not interfere with national policies on the exploitation of energy resources.

2.34 **1988 inventory of obstacles to an internal energy market** The Single European Act was to prove a turning point in the integration process, especially with respect to energy. The Commission took it as a green light to initiate a study of the EU energy sector in the context of the proposed completion of the single market by 1992. The Energy Council of June 1987 authorized the Commission's proposal to draw up an inventory of existing obstacles to an internal energy market, and to submit recommendations for their progressive elimination. Extensive consultations were held. Contributions were submitted to the Commission by 'a hundred or so organizations and enterprises representing all the Member States, all the energy sources and both energy producers and energy users'.[43] The result, published the following year, was a report based on a

[43] European Commission, *Energy in Europe*: Special Issue on the Internal Energy Market, 6.

comprehensive inventory outlining the expected results of an internal energy market and the main priorities to be addressed to remove the obstacles to its creation (see ch 1, paras 1.59–1.63).[44] It favoured a parallel approach to the removal of the obstacles, applying the existing rules of EC law and submitting specific initiatives in the form of Directives. The Council gave its support to this approach.[45]

This development of primary legislation in the SEA was to have an effect in a very different context from those in which the three treaties had been concluded. The European entity to which the new provisions were to apply was much enlarged. The first enlargement saw the accession of the United Kingdom, Denmark, and Ireland on 1 January 1973,[46] Greece subsequently on 1 January 1981,[47] and Spain and Portugal on 1 January 1986.[48] The diversity of energy policies and practices within the EC grew correspondingly. In this context it would prove harder to sustain the tacit consensus among the Member States that energy matters should be kept out of the integration process. **2.35**

(3) Treaty on European Union (Maastricht)

The Treaty on European Union (TEU) made further important changes to the Treaties especially through Titles II, III, and IV.[49] It was signed in Maastricht in The Netherlands on 7 February 1992 and entered into force on 1 November 1993. It established the European Union. The EEC Treaty (as amended) became the EC Treaty. **2.36**

Among the various changes made by the Treaty, one deserves particular emphasis in the context of the Internal Energy Market programme. The notion of 'subsidiarity' was introduced as a principle of general application instead of being restricted to environmental matters as it had appeared in the SEA.[50] In Article 3B (now Art 5), it is stated that:

[44] *The Internal Energy Market*, COM (1988) 238 final, 2 May 1988.

[45] *Energy in Europe*, n 43 above, Presidency Conclusions, 59, point 4.

[46] Treaty concerning the Accession of the Kingdom of Denmark, Ireland, the Kingdom of Norway, and the United Kingdom of Great Britain and Northern Ireland to the European Economic Community and the European Atomic Energy Community, Brussels, 22 Jan 1972 (UKTS 18 (1979); Cmnd 7463; [1972] OJ L 73/5), and Declaration of Accession to the European Coal and Steel Community, ibid. Following a negative result in a referendum, Norway did not ratify the Treaty and the instruments of accession were amended accordingly: see Council Decision of 1 Jan 1973 [1973] OJ L2/1.

[47] Treaty of Accession 1979 (EC 18) (1979); Cmnd 7650; [1979] OJ L291/9.

[48] Treaty of Accession 1985 (EC 27) (1985) Cmnd 9634; [1985] OJ L302/9.

[49] UKTS 12 (1994); Cmnd 2485; [1992] OJ C191/1. Signed by the 12 Member States at Maastricht on 12 Feb 1992, it came into force on 1 Nov 1993.

[50] Art 130r(4) provided that 'the Community shall take action relating to the environment to the extent to which the objectives . . . can be attained better at Community level than at the level of the individual Member States'.

> In areas which do not fall within its exclusive competence, the Community shall take action, in accordance with the principle of subsidiarity, only if and in so far as the objectives of the proposed action cannot be sufficiently achieved by the Member States and can therefore, by reason of the scale or effects of the proposed action, be better achieved by the Community.

2.37 The application of this principle requires a delicate and case-by-case balancing of central and national authority in the law-making process. In areas where the Community does not have exclusive competence, the principle must be applied to decide whether in a given case it is appropriate for the Community (and its institutions) to take action. It may be invoked to justify Community action but also to oppose it. Since it appears in the body of the Treaty, it binds the Community institutions and can give rise to annulment under Article 230* if it is disregarded. Indeed, the Commission is obliged to provide a justification for a proposed legislative measure in terms of subsidiarity in the explanatory memorandum.[51] However, its exact scope is unclear and the ECJ has yet to provide a detailed exposition of its flexibility and meaning. In the meantime, the principle has also been the subject of criticism from various legal authorities.[52]

Subsidiarity

2.38 For the energy sector subsidiarity is a principle that has had particular significance. It has both contributed to and constrained the Commission in its attempts to promote a single market in energy. While it has facilitated the making of proposals to act in this field with respect to the distribution of powers between Member States and Community institutions—it has also made their relations more complex and open-ended by encouraging a reliance on framework Directives as the favoured instrument for change. For example, the explanatory memorandum to the proposals for Directives on common rules for electricity and gas interpreted subsidiarity to mean that:

> The Community must not impose rigid mechanisms, but rather should define a framework enabling Member States to opt for the system best suited to their natural resources, the state of their industry and their energy policies.[53]

---

[51] Inter-institutional Agreement on Procedures for Implementing the Principle of Subsidiarity, concluded between the European Parliament, Council, and Commission, 25 Oct 1993, OJ 1993, C329/135.

[52] Toth, A, 'A Legal Analysis of Subsidiarity', in O'Keeffe, D, (ed), *Legal Issues of the Maastricht Treaty* (1994) 37; Steiner, J, 'Subsidiarity under the Maastricht Treaty', in ibid, 49; Lenaerts, K, 'The Principle of Subsidiarity and the Environment in the European Union: Keeping the Balance of Federalism', (1994) 17 Fordham Int'l L J 846; Brinkhorst, L, 'Subsidiarity and EC Environmental Policy', (1993) 8 Eur Env L Rev 20.

[53] Amended Proposals for a European Parliament and Council Directive on common rules for the internal market in electricity, COM (1993) 643 final, OJ C 123/1.

This leaves much scope to national authorities when incorporating the provisions of the Directives into national law.

In addition, the TEU brought about an increase in the subjects on which legislative decisions could be taken by qualified majority voting in the Council.

No specific provisions on energy were added—with the exception of Article 3(t), which lists measures in the 'spheres of energy, civil protection and tourism' as one of the Community's common policies or activities; and Declaration No 1 annexed to the new Treaty which stated that 'the question of introducing into the Treaty Titles relating to the spheres referred to in Article 3(t) . . . on the basis of a report which the Commission will submit to the Council by 1996 at the latest'. Article 129b on Trans-European Networks also included a reference to energy. **2.39**

This was rather modest progress given the original proposals to include a separate chapter on energy in the Treaty negotiations (see paras 2.42–2.45)—caused by failure of the Member States to agree on further EU competencies going beyond those already existing in the Treaties.

Enhanced rôle for Parliament: the co-decision procedure Importantly, the Treaty further enhanced the rôle of the Parliament in the legislative process with respect to internal market legislation, especially vis-à-vis the Commission. At the second reading stage, Parliament and the Council are required to proceed in *co-decision*. Parliament has three months in which to agree with the Council's common position, refrain from reacting to it, make amendments to it, or reject it. In the latter two cases, a Conciliation Committee is set up comprising representatives of the Council and Parliament in equal proportions with the task of negotiating a compromise. This requirement to hold a direct dialogue between the two institutions to secure an agreement contrasts with the SEA régime, under which only those Parliamentary amendments supported by the Commission could be adopted by a majority in the Council. **2.40**

This co-decision procedure with the Council was applied to all Internal Market legislation and some other areas. **2.41**

(4) Proposed Energy Chapter and Beyond

The absence of any reference to an energy policy or other energy provision in the Single European Act 1986 or the Treaty on European Union is significant since there were proposals for their inclusion—which were rejected. This underlined the Member States' wish to retain their competence over energy. Subsequent to the TEU, the Commission carried out its task according to Declaration No 1, producing a proposal for an energy chapter which would either have consolidated the provisions of the three Treaties or have introduced a new chapter pursuing the completion of the single market, environmental protection, and **2.42** measures to improve security of supply.[54] Although the proposal was noted by the Council of Ministers in May 1996, no action was taken or encouraged. Two months prior to the Amsterdam Inter-Governmental Conference, the Commission issued a further document.[55] It also had no effect.

2.43 An alternative approach adopted by the Commission was to advocate a greater co-ordination of existing EU competencies.[56] The impetus to both of these initiatives was the absence of a clear competence on energy matters which led to a dependence upon a number of EU competencies that have a bearing upon energy policy: for example, the single market rules including technical and tax harmonization and public procurement; environment, regional, and competition policy; and the TENs policy. However, it is questionable whether these are so inadequate that a new chapter is required. At a later date, during the discussions on the Treaty of Nice text, the Portuguese Presidency noted that an 'issue to be addressed' was whether the repeated use of Article 308* in areas such as energy, external competence, and the establishment of decentralized agencies justified the creation in the EC Treaty of a specific legal basis requiring a qualified majority.[57] However, the proposal was dropped.

(a) 'For'

2.44 Interestingly, the European Parliament was a strong supporter of an energy chapter. In various resolutions it argued for the integration of the ECSC and all relevant competencies of the EC Treaty into a single energy chapter to be called 'Environment and Security of Supply'.[58] This may have been motivated more by a desire for further powers of co-decision. The argument was ultimately lost.[59]

(b) 'Against'

2.45 However, the introduction of a new energy chapter has had very little support among the Member States, seeming like a step towards greater management of energy markets rather than less—not exactly consistent with the aims of the single market.

The TEU[60] was modified further by the Treaty of Amsterdam (TA) in 1997 but the changes were minor. They extended further the areas for co-decision making

[54] COM (1996) 496 final of 3 April 1996. There was an earlier report by the Commission for the Reflection Group chaired by Carlos Westendorp in May 1995 prior to the EC Intergovernmental conference in 1996.

[55] European Commission, *An Overall View of Energy Policy and Actions*, COM (1997) 167, 23 April 1997.

[56] COM (1995) 682 final of 13 Dec 1995: *Towards an EU Energy Policy* (the White Paper).

[57] Conference of the Representatives of the Governments of the Member States, 22 Feb 2000, CONFER 4711/00.

[58] Resolutions of 17 May 1995; 14 Dec 1995; 13 Mar 1996; and 19 June 1996.

[59] Egenhofer, C, 'Understanding the Politics of European Energy Policy', CEPS Paper, 1997.

[60] For a copy of the Consolidated Treaty see: http://europa.eu.int/eur-lex/en/treaties/dat.ec_cons_treaty_en.pdf

between Council and Parliament, and strengthened the powers of the President of the Commission in the appointment of commissioners. In the interval between the two Treaties, the EU was enlarged further by the accession of three States from the EFTA grouping. With effect from 1 January 1995, Austria, Finland, and Sweden became members,[61] bringing the total of EU member states to 15. The Treaty of Nice (TN) attempted to continue the process of constitutional change but was primarily concerned with matters left over from the previous Inter-Governmental Conference in Amsterdam, especially concerning the impact of enlargement. It has yet to be ratified.

(5) Conclusions on the Development of an Energy *Acquis*

In sum, it may be said that in practice—if not in terms of European law—the EU energy sector was for many years accorded a special status and the markets (except oil and oil products) remained highly segmented under Member State control. **2.46**

A truly European market in energy was not a reality. With the decision by the Member States to accelerate the integration process through the SEA, this situation changed irreversibly. The European Commission was mandated to propose changes and the IEM was the result. The special status of the energy sector was eventually challenged by the introduction of secondary legislation—the six Directives that comprised the core of the Internal Energy Market Programme. In addition, some Member States broke ranks and embraced the doctrine of market liberalization that was becoming attractive to governments elsewhere in the world. The globalization process was making its impact on EC energy policy. However, without a motor to drive the process of change, it was unlikely to make much progress. **2.47**

C. European Commission in its Institutional Setting

The motor driving liberalization in the EU energy sector has been and remains the European Commission. It has been the key European institution behind the adoption and promotion of the IEM programme—frequently in the face of strong opposition from individual Member States and incumbent market players.[62] It is therefore important to have some understanding of how the Commission acts within the broad institutional framework and the law-making **2.48**

---

[61] Treaty of Accession concerning the accession of the Kingdom of Norway, the Republic of Austria, the Republic of Finland, and the Kingdom of Sweden to the European Union (EC 7 (1994); Cmnd 2606; [1994] OJ C241/1). Norway did not ratify the Treaty and it was amended accordingly: see n 46.

[62] This view of the Commission follows closely that argued for by Usher, J, in 'The Commission and the Law', in Edwards, G, and Spence, D (eds), *The European Commission*, (1994), 212.

process of the EU, and how its rôle has developed over the period since the IEM legislation was put in place in the 1990s. These institutional arrangements are under review as the EC prepares itself for a further enlargement in the early part of the twenty-first century.

(1) The Commission and Commissioners:[63] functions and powers

2.49 The Commission is composed of 20 members known as Commissioners, one of whom is nominated as President by the Heads of State or Governments of the Member States. This choice is made prior to the appointment of the other Commissioners. The governments of the Member States nominate the other persons who they intend to appoint as Members of the Commission in agreement with the nominee for Commission President. Both the nominee President and the members-designate are subject to a collective vote of approval by Parliament. After such approval, they are appointed by common accord of the governments of the Member States. The Members of the Commission are appointed for a five-year term, which may be renewed. Currently, each Member State must have at least one Commissioner but may have not more than two (Art 157 EC). The larger states that have two Commissioners are France, Germany, Italy, Spain, and the United Kingdom. A maximum of two Vice Presidents may be appointed by the Commissioners themselves from among their number.

2.50 Each Commissioner is required to be independent in the exercise of his or her duties. The Commission bears collective responsibility for its acts. It takes decisions by simple majority vote. Under the Treaties of Maastricht and Amsterdam the powers of Parliamentary scrutiny of the Commission and its legislative proposals were enhanced. Previously, it had power to force the resignation of the entire Commission through a vote of censure or no confidence.

2.51 The Commissioners are supported by 26 Directorates-General (DGs) and a body of specialized services, including a Legal Service. Each DG is headed by a Director-General, with rank equivalent to the top civil servant in a government ministry. Political and operational responsibility for one or more DGs is allocated to a Commissioner, who also has a private office or 'cabinet'. The latter consists of six officials who act as the channel between the Commissioner and the DGs. The overall work of the Commission is managed by a secretary-general.

[63] See generally, Arts 211–19* EC and Arts 249–56.*

The principal functions of the Commission are threefold. It:

(1) is the main initiator of EC policy
(2) has a wide range of executive and regulatory functions and a limited law-making rôle, and
(3) acts as the guardian of the Treaties (ensuring that Treaty obligations are observed).[64]

(a) Legislative rôle

This is an important rôle since the Council of Ministers in exercising its legislative powers under the EC Treaty can normally only act on proposals submitted to it by the Commission. However, it is the Council that makes the principal decisions on EU policies and priorities and decides on major legislation in co-decision or consultation with the Parliament. The Commission is also limited by the principle of subsidiarity, which it is obliged to take into account. It may initiate legislation only in those areas where the EU is better placed than individual Member States to take effective action (see, eg para 2.38). **2.52**

The Commission can act, basing itself on the EC Treaty, either:

- where the power is specifically granted as in Art 86* (where a Member State is making improper use of the powers provided to it by this Article); or
- under the more general power in Art 308* (to propose action to the Council to attain Community objectives; matters not specifically identified in the EC Treaty).

In addition, under Article 284* of the Treaty, the Commission may collect any information and carry out any checks required for the performance of its tasks. It can also initiate White Papers, covering matters such as energy and competition;[65] and Green Papers, such as that on Security of Energy Supply issued in 2000.[66]

When preparing draft legislation, the Commission consults widely with interested parties from all sectors and attempts to take their views into account in formulating its legislative proposals. This has been very evident in the development of legislation to promote integration in energy markets. In drawing up the proposals for the Internal Energy Market Directives, several of the 26 DGs were involved: in particular, those for Energy and Transport (formerly Energy), Competition, and the Internal Market. Once the final proposal is formulated, the **2.53**

[64] eg, the Commission's powers under Arts 31* and 86* of the EC Treaty.
[65] European Commission, *An Energy Policy for the European Union*, see n 40; *White Paper on Modernisation of the Rules Implementing Articles 85 and 86 of the EC Treaty*, COM (1999) 0000 of 28 April 1999.
[66] idem, *Towards a European Strategy for the Security of Energy Supply*, 29 Nov 2000, COM (2000) 769.

document is sent to the Council where it is discussed by the Energy Experts' Group, composed of experts from the Member States and by the High-Level Energy Group. The Committee of Permanent Representatives (Coreper) will also play a rôle at this stage (see para 2.61). The difference between the Energy Experts' Group and Coreper is that is that the former is predominantly technical, while Coreper is expected to submit political dossiers to Ministers. The document is simultaneously under consideration by the Parliament and the appropriate Parliamentary Committees. In this process, two consultative bodies—the Economic and Social Committee and the Committee of the Regions[67]—provide opinions on the Commission's proposals either on an *ex officio* or voluntary basis.

(b) Executive function

2.54 As the executive body of the EU the Commission has a duty to ensure that the rules of the Treaties are applied to the conduct of Member States and also to the conduct of undertakings and individuals. Under Article 211(1)* of the EC Treaty, the Commission has a duty to ensure the application of that Treaty and the measures taken by its institutions. The EC Treaty also contains specific expressions of this duty, including those contained in Article 85* (duty to ensure the application of Arts 81 and 82)—and in Article 86(3) by which the Commission has a duty to ensure the application of the provisions of Article 86. Also Article 88* imposes a duty on the Commission to keep under strict review the application of the provisions relating to state aids. Other executive functions include the management of the EU annual budget and its Structural Funds (aimed at evening out economic disparities between the richer and the poorer parts of the EU). Its management of the budget is monitored by a body called the Court of Auditors, whose reports are reviewed by the Parliament.[68]

2.55 The regulatory functions relate to the making of secondary legislation, particularly in relation to competition matters. The law-making powers are limited but, in the context of the internal energy market, they have been used as a threat to facilitate its policy objectives.

The rôle of the Commission as guardian of the EC Treaty is, in respect of Member States, derived primarily from the duty imposed on it by Article 226* to initiate a proceeding against a Member State that it considers to have failed to fulfil an obligation under the EC Treaty. The Commission is required to draw the attention of the Member State to the alleged breach and give it an opportunity to submit its observations. If the matter is not satisfactorily resolved, the Commission is to deliver a reasoned opinion on the matter to the Member State. If the State concerned does not comply with the opinion within the period specified by the

[67] Respectively, Arts 257–62* and Arts 263–5.*

[68] Arts 246–8.*

Commission, the latter may bring the matter before the ECJ (Art 226*). The Commission also has powers to ensure the compliance of undertakings and individuals in the public or private sectors with their EC Treaty obligations and the provisions of secondary legislation made under the Treaty. These powers are particularly important in the context of the application of the Articles of the EC Treaty relating to competition, particularly Articles 81 and 82.* It may decide that an unauthorized aid is incompatible with the EC Treaty and in these circumstances, the Commission can require the Member State concerned to require repayment of the aid.

The Commission's responsibilities have expanded through the provisions of the SEA, the TEU, and the TA. Areas where new responsibilities have been added include the environment, economic, and monetary union, the development of trans-European networks and consumer affairs.

(2) Commission and Council[69]

The relationship between the Commission and the Council of the EU (the Council) is probably the most important of all relations between the Community institutions.[70] The sensitivity of energy matters to the economic well-being of Member States has given this relationship a decisive rôle in energy market liberalization. In connection with the IEM the Council shares the rôle of law-making body of the EC with the Parliament. This partnership is exercised in the co-decision procedure for legislation. 2.56

All Member States (15 at the time of publishing) are represented at ministerial level at meetings of the Council. Each Minister is authorized to commit its own government. In practice, there are specialist meetings of Council Ministers, such as that for energy, which meets normally twice a year. The Presidency of the Council is held in turn by each Member State for a term of six months in an order decided upon by the Council. The Presidency chairs meetings but also has some limited power to set priorities during its tenure. Apart from this, it plays a key rôle in establishing a consensus among the various Member States on issues facing the EU and has responsibility for liaison with the Parliament. 2.57

Decisions are taken by simple majority voting except for those cases specifically provided for elsewhere in the EC Treaty.[71] The exceptions to this rule are requirements for unanimity or a qualified majority. As mentioned, the SEA contained

[69] See generally, Arts 202–10* EC and Arts 249–56.

[70] This is not to be confused with the European Council, a political body comprising Heads of State or Governments of the 15 Member States and the President of the European Commission. It is charged by Art 4 TEU with providing the EU with 'the necessary impetus for its development' and with defining 'the general political guidelines thereof'.

[71] Art 205,* para 1 of the EC Treaty.

provisions that amended the EEC Treaty by replacing in a number of Articles a requirement for a unanimous vote or a simple majority with a requirement for a qualified majority. The purpose of the amendment was to facilitate the creation of an internal market. Among the Articles that were enhanced was Article 100 (now Art 95) that required unanimity in relation to proposals relating to the approximation of legislation. The SEA added to the EC Treaty a new Article 100A (now Art 95). More than two-thirds of the legislation required to complete the internal market might be made by a qualified majority under this Article. Article 100A states that the Council shall, acting by a qualified majority on a proposal from the Commission in co-operation with the European Parliament, and after consulting the Economic and Social Committee, adopt the measures for the approximation of the provisions laid down by law, regulation, or administrative action in the Member States which have as their object the establishment and functioning of the internal market. Fiscal provisions, measures relating to free movement of persons, or rights or interests of employed persons are excluded from the scope of Article 100A and require approval by unanimous vote under Article 100.

(a) QMV

2.58 Voting by qualified majority is a system of weighted voting,[72] as will be modified by the Treaty of Nice (TN). Acts of the Council require for their adoption at least 169 votes in favour cast by a majority of the members[73]—see Table 2.1.

2.59 The system of qualified majority voting (QMV) makes for a more rapid and effective system of decision-making than a system based upon unanimity. The

Table 2.1 Qualified Majority Voting

Member States	No. of votes
France, Italy, the UK, Germany*	29
Spain	27
The Netherlands	13
Belgium, Greece, Portugal	12
Austria, Sweden	10
Denmark, Ireland, Finland	7
Luxembourg	4†

Notes: *The four largest States; † least populous member state

[72] This was modified by the Treaty of Nice, agreed by the European Council in December 2000. The Treaty has not yet been ratified by the Member States; and ratification is not a foregone conclusion.

[73] Treaty of Nice, Amending the Treaty on European Union, The Treaties Establishing the European Communities and certain Related Acts, OJ C 80/1, 10 March 2001.

application of the QMV system to the internal market measures has emboldened the Commission to perform, with remarkable zeal, its rôle as policy initiator in the context of the internal market, not only in the energy sector. It has also led to considerable bargaining between Member States to pass measures through the Council. If the Commission agrees, a proposal may be modified by the Council by a qualified majority, but if the Commission does not agree any modification requires unanimity. For decisions on Treaty reform and enlargement of the EU, it is the Member States that decide.

(b) New co-operation procedure

Significant changes in the exercise of the Council's powers in the law-making process, accompanied by an enhancement of Parliament's rôle initially created a new co-operation procedure involving the Parliament—used primarily in cases where Council legislation concerning harmonization measures for the establishment and functioning of the internal market is proposed. Subsequently, the co-decision procedure was established between Council and Parliament, described later (see para 2.64). **2.60**

(c) Coreper

Although it does not take decisions itself, Coreper plays an important part in the decision-making process.[74] Its main responsibility is to prepare the work of the Council and to carry out tasks assigned to it by the Council. Comprising senior diplomats, civil servants, and experts, it meets weekly and must ensure that only the most difficult and sensitive issues are dealt with at ministerial level. It co-ordinates closely with the many Council working groups of national experts. **2.61**

(3) Commission and Parliament[75]

A significant factor that emerged as the IEM programme unfolded in the 1990s was the growing rôle in the law-making process of the European Parliament. Not only was the Commission required to consult and co-operate with the Parliament on a wider range of issues under the amended primary law of the EC, but it also had an interest in acquiring the support of the Parliament for its proposals in its discussions with the Member States. **2.62**

The citizens of the Member States directly elect their national members of the Parliament for a five-year term under a system of proportional representation. Until 1975 however, they were nominated from among members of the Parliaments of the Member States. In 1976 the Member States agreed in a

[74] Art 207.

[75] See generally, Arts 189–201* and Arts 249–56*.

Table 2.2 Members of the European Parliament

Member State	No. of members*
Germany	99
France, Italy, UK	87
Spain	64
The Netherlands	31
Belgium, Greece, Portugal	25
Sweden	22
Austria	21
Denmark, Finland	16
Ireland	15
Luxembourg	6

* Roughly reflecting the population of the Member States.
Note: the turn-out in the elections remains low and there is no common electoral system.

Decision and Act relating to direct elections,[76] that direct elections should be held. The first direct elections were held in Member States in 1979. There are 626 members at present (see Table 2.2), although the TN contains revised arrangements with a higher ceiling.

(d) Co-operation procedure and power of veto

2.63 Although called a 'Parliament', the institution is not the legislature of the Community in the normally accepted sense of the term.[77] Initially, the Parliament was called the Assembly of the European Communities and was merely consulted on the proposed legislation of the Council. However, the part played by the Parliament in the legislative process was enlarged by the introduction of the *co-operation* procedure through the SEA in 1987 and applied to almost all internal market legislation (see para 2.32).

2.64 The introduction of the co-operation procedure encouraged the Parliament to take a much more active and critical interest in proposed legislation affecting rights that, under the EC Treaty, the Commission is entitled to make without the need to consult or co-operate with the Parliament. This development became apparent in the summer of 1991 in the context of the proposals made by the Commission for a Directive on Third Party Access (TPA) for energy networks based on its powers under Article 86.*

[76] 1976 OJ L 278.

[77] Dashwood argues that no institution can be identified as the legislature of the EC or the EU as a whole. The primary powers conferred by the Treaties are exercised in accordance with a set of procedures under which the Parliament, Council, and Commission interact with each other in prescribed ways: see n 1. 218.

This legislative rôle was further enhanced by changes in procedure introduced under the Maastricht Treaty. In most cases, including all internal market legislation, the Parliament has acquired a power of *co-decision* with the Council in the adoption of legislation[78] and has the right to be consulted in other areas. The key point is that legislation introduced under the co-decision procedure cannot be adopted against the will of Parliament. In the last resort, the Parliament can veto the proposal.

(e) Which procedure?

The way to determine which procedure is applicable is to examine the Treaty Article or the 'legal basis' for the particular measures that are to be presented to Parliament. Under the Euratom and ECSC Treaties (and some areas of policy under the EC Treaty), the procedure is different again, requiring the Council to consult Parliament before adopting a legislative act. Essentially, the opinion of Parliament must be sought on most important legislation. **2.65**

At present, the Commission attends all sessions of the Parliament and must explain and justify its policies if requested to do so by members of the Parliament. It is required to reply to written and oral questions put to it by members of the Parliament.

In addition, the Parliament's financial control includes the right to make alterations to certain aspects of the Community's budget. The Parliament formally adopts the budget and the Commission is charged with its implementation. In terms of democratic supervision, it holds hearings for nominee Commissioners and approves the Commission by a vote of confidence. It may also dismiss the members of the Commission as a body on a vote of censure with a two-thirds majority of votes cast—although this power has never been exercised. Finally, it has the right to bring actions for judicial review of Community acts by the ECJ, under Article 230 EC 'for the purpose of protecting their prerogatives'. The origins of this power lie in the TEU but it will be enlarged by the TN. **2.66**

(f) Committees

Much of the Parliament's legislative work takes place in specialist committees. Seventeen standing committees prepare the work of the Parliament's plenary sessions, corresponding closely to the work of the Commission's DGs. Energy matters are covered by the Committee on Industry, External Trade, Research, and Energy. Initially, the function of these committees was to prepare reports that were used by members for information purposes in connection with general debates. While the Committees do perform this function, they also act to maintain contact with the Council and the Commission and with industry and consumer bodies. **2.67**

[78] Art 251.*

(g) Procedure for adopting legislation

2.68 There are four principal stages for the adoption of resolutions by Parliament:

1. The relevant committee appoints an MEP as Rapporteur to draft a report on the Commission proposal under consideration.
2. The Rapporteur delivers his or her draft report to the committee after discussions.
3. The draft report is considered by the committee and then put to the vote and perhaps amended.
4. The report is discussed in a plenary session, amended and put to the vote.

(4) Commission and Court of Justice[79]

Emergence of an ECJ energy jurisprudence

2.69 If the Commission has been the catalyst for the IEM programme, the European Court of Justice (ECJ) is the body that it has looked to as the ultimate interpreter and enforcer of the legal measures adopted under the programme. The ECJ is of the greatest importance to the implementation of the IEM. For many years, its rôle in energy matters was almost non-existent. The advent of the IEM programme in the mid-1980s led to a re-assessment of the energy sector's status in European law, and during the 1990s the case law of the ECJ began to reflect this.[80] Particularly significant are the judgments of the ECJ in the *Corbeau* and *Port of Genoa* Cases.[81] These established that while the Treaty did not prohibit grants of exclusive or special rights, the exercise of those rights can constitute an abuse of a dominant position (see ch 5, paras 5.24–5.25, 5.29–5.31).

(a) Composition of the Court

2.70 The ECJ is composed of 15 judges—one national from each of the Member States. Appointments are made by common agreement of Member State governments. The judges hold office for a renewable term of six years. Every three years there is a partial replacement of the judges (8 and 7 being replaced alternately). They select one of their number to act as President of the ECJ for a renewable term of three years. The ECJ may sit in plenary session or in chambers of three, five, or seven judges. It may sit in plenary session when a Member State or a Community institution that is a party to the proceedings requests it, or when the proceedings have a character that is especially complex or important.

---

[79] See generally Arts 220–45* and Arts 249–56*; also http://curia.eu.int

[80] See ch 5.

[81] See n 24.

(b) Advocate-General's rôle

The Treaty provides that Advocates-General should assist the ECJ in the performance of its tasks.[82] Eight Advocates-General must be appointed. Every three years there is a partial replacement of the Advocates-General, four replaced on each occasion. The function of the Advocate-General as described in Article 222* is, in respect of hearings before the ECJ, to make reasoned submissions in open court, acting with complete impartiality and independence. An Advocate-General is appointed in respect of each case to be heard before the ECJ. He or she is required to analyse to the ECJ the relevant Community law and to propose a solution to the case. Advocate-Generals' submissions are not binding on the ECJ—although the ECJ usually follows the Advocate-General's submission. Even if the ECJ does not follow the Advocate-General's submission, it may nevertheless be useful as a dissenting view. 2.71

(c) ECJ procedure

The procedure of the ECJ is divided into a written stage and an oral stage. During the written stage pleadings are exchanged in which the arguments are set out in full. In the oral stage, at which the parties must be legally represented, the legal representatives put the arguments forward to the ECJ, and questions may be asked by the ECJ and by the Advocate-General. Subsequently, the Advocate-General delivers his Opinion in open court, proposing his or her solution to the problem. After deliberations, the judgment of the ECJ is then delivered. It is taken by majority vote and no dissenting or separate judgements are published. There is no appeal against a judgment of the ECJ. Member States are required to comply with an order of the ECJ;[83] in cases where fines are imposed against undertakings or individuals, the Courts of the relevant Member State may recover such fines without any further formalities.[84] 2.72

(d) Jurisdiction of the ECJ

The ECJ has jurisdiction under the EC Treaty to hear five principal kinds of action and may also give preliminary rulings. 2.73

(i) **Failure to fulfil an obligation**[85] The ECJ will be asked to decide on whether a Member State has fulfilled its obligations under Community law. Such actions are usually brought by the Commission, but they may also be brought by another Member State. The state is first given the opportunity by the Commission to comply with a reasoned opinion on the matter within a certain period after it has had 2.74

[82] Arts. 222–3.*
[83] Art 261.*
[84] Art 256.*
[85] Arts 226–8.*

the opportunity to submit its observations. If the ECJ finds against the Member State, then it must take measures to comply without delay. Further non-compliance may result in a fixed or periodic penalty. If the action is initiated by another Member State, it must do so through the Commission.

2.75 (ii) **Proceedings for Annulment**[86] The ECJ may review the legality of a variety of measures by Community institutions in actions brought by a Member State, the Commission, the Council and in certain circumstances the Parliament. The action may be brought on grounds of lack of competence, infringement of an essential procedural requirement, infringement of the EC Treaty or of any rule relating to its application, or misuse of powers. The result may be an annulment of all or part of a measure of Community legislation. A natural or legal person may institute proceedings to annul a legal measure that is of direct and individual concern to them. If the action is well founded, the ECJ will declare the contested act or part of the act void.

2.76 (iii) **Failure to Act**[87] The ECJ may review the legality of a failure to act by a Community institution, in infringement of the EC Treaty. An action may be brought before the ECJ by a Community institution or a Member State to have the infringement established. A natural or legal person may also complain to the ECJ about inaction by a Community institution. A failure to act will be penalized by the ECJ.

2.77 (iv) **Actions for Damages**[88] The ECJ may rule on the liability of the Community in an action for damages based on non-contractual liability. The ruling will apply to damage caused by its institutions or servants in the performance of their duties.

2.78 (v) **Appeals** The ECJ may hear appeals on points of law against judgments given by the Court of First Instance in cases within its jurisdiction.

(e) Preliminary Rulings

2.79 Many disputes involving Community law are commenced in the courts and tribunals of the Member States. They have jurisdiction to review the administrative implementation of Community law and many provisions of the Treaties and of secondary legislation which confer rights on nationals and which national courts must uphold. If doubt arises about the interpretation and validity of such law, the national court or tribunal may seek a preliminary ruling from the ECJ on the relevant question. Within two months the parties, the Member States, and the Community institutions must submit their written observations to the ECJ. After

[86] Arts 230–31, 233.*

[87] Art 232.*

[88] Arts 235 and 288.*

this, the procedure is the same as that applicable to direct action. The ruling by the ECJ is sent back to the national court or tribunal, which is bound by the result in deciding the case in which the question has arisen.

The procedure for a preliminary ruling may also be activated when citizens seek clarification of the Community rules that affect them. Such a ruling may only be sought by a national court, which will also decide if this is the appropriate course of action. All parties involved in the proceedings may participate in the proceedings before the ECJ. **2.80**

Preliminary rulings have played an important rôle in the development of Community law, particularly because of two rulings on Community law made by the ECJ . The ECJ has ruled in landmark cases that primary Community law has:

1. direct effect in the Member States; and
2. primacy over national law.

(i) **Direct effect** A provision of the Treaty or of Community legislation was held to confer rights on individuals that they may enforce before a national court, provided that certain conditions are fulfilled (the legal norm must be clear, precise, and unconditional).[89] These rights flow directly from primary Community law and are independent of national law. This is not the same as the requirement that regulations are 'directly applicable', which means that the regulations have legal effect in Member States without any national implementing legislation or similar action. **2.81**

(ii) **Primacy** A large number of preliminary rulings have affirmed the principle of supremacy of Community law over the national law of the Member States since it was first established in the 1964 case of *Costa v ENEL*.[90] This has the effect that no rule of national law can be invoked to prevent the grant of a remedy to protect a Community right. **2.82**

Court of First Instance[91]

In 1989 a new court was established to assist the ECJ in handling the growing volume of cases that came before it.[92] The Court of First Instance (CFI) was created by the Council with the aim of strengthening the judicial safeguards available to individuals by introducing a second tier of judicial authority and so enabling the **2.83**

[89] Case 26/62 *Van Gend en Loos* [1963] ECR 1 brought to the ECJ on a preliminary ruling; further developed in, eg, Case 36/74 *Walrave and Koch v Association Union Cycliste Internationale* [1974] ECR 1405; Case 9/70 *Franz Grad v Finanzamt Traunstein* [1974] 1970 ECR 825; Case 41/74 *Van Duyn v Home Office* [1974] ECR 1337.

[90] Case 6/64 *Costa v ENEL* [1964] ECR 585.

[91] Art 225.*

[92] Between 1978–85 the number of new cases brought before the ECJ in a single year increased from 200 to more than 400: see http://curia.en.int/en/pres/jeu.htm

ECJ to concentrate on its basic task—the uniform interpretation of Community law. It has authority to hear and determine certain classes of action or proceeding at first instance. It has jurisdiction to rule on all actions for annulment, failure to act, and damages brought by natural or legal persons against the Community; competition proceedings and actions brought against the Commission under the ECSC Treaty by undertakings or associations of undertakings; and disputes between the Community and its officials or servants. It is not competent to hear and determine certain questions (eg those concerning the interpretation of the EC Treaty).

2.84 The CFI is made up of one judge from each Member State selected on similar terms and conditions as those appointed to the ECJ. No permanent Advocates-General are appointed to the CFI, but judges may serve in this function from time to time. The Members of the CFI select one of their own number as President and the CFI appoints its own registrar. Its administrative needs are met by the services of the ECJ. It sits in chambers of three or five judges and may sit in plenary session in cases of particular importance. Its decisions have contributed to the discussion of the doctrine of 'essential facilities' discussed in Chapter 5.

(5) Legislative Acts

2.85 The institutions share various law-making powers under the EC Treaty.[93] Legislative acts may take three principal forms: Directives, Decisions, and Regulations. Provision is also made for recommendations and opinions. These are provided for in Article 249.* For the purposes of bringing about the internal market in energy, Directives have proved to be the more influential instruments so far. The power to issue these instruments is almost always given to the Council, acting in co-operation with the Parliament. In some cases, however, the EC Treaty gives such power to the European Commission.[94] Regulations, Directives, and Decisions must state the reasons on which they are based and refer to any proposals or opinions which may have had to have been obtained before their adoption.[95]

(a) Directives

2.86 A Directive is binding with respect to ends but not the choice of form or methods. It has usually been adopted to require Member States to harmonize national law in certain areas. A deadline for implementation will always be provided, usually of one or two years from the date of adoption by the EC to implementation by the Member State. This allows a Member State to consider and decide upon

[93] eg, Prechal, S *Directives in Community Law: A Study of Directives and their Enforcement in National Courts*, (1996).

[94] eg Art 90 EC.

[95] Art 253.*

the manner of implementation. Such measures usually have a framework character and have tended to leave Member States with more or less scope in implementing their provisions. This element of subsidiarity has been especially apparent in the Directives setting out common rules for the electricity and gas sectors. In the absence of direct effect, national courts have a duty to interpret national law, as much as possible, in conformity with EC law. Where there is a failure of this duty, an individual may be able to seek damages against the Member State.

(b) Regulations

Regulations are applied directly in all the Member States without necessarily requiring national implementing measures to bring them into force. This characteristic of direct applicability once made and published is unique to regulations. They are issued by the Commission, the Council, and the Parliament and are sources of Community law in the national legal order. In this respect they contrast with the legislative character of Directives. In practice, most Regulations require some implementing action by the Member States (eg, the Regulation on the introduction of the euro). **2.87**

(c) Decisions

A decision does not normally have general application, being instead restricted to a single Member State, undertaking or individual.[96] It is binding on those to whom it is addressed. **2.88**

(d) Recommendations and opinions

Recommendations and opinions are not binding. However, despite their 'soft law' character, they may prove influential in interpreting the national law at which the recommendation is directed.[97] **2.89**

D. Trans-European Energy Networks (TENs)

Closely related to the programme of energy market liberalization is the need to expand and extend the existing infrastructure in energy networks to promote the potential for competition and cohesion.[98] This has been the focus of a number of initiatives by the EU, gathered together under the heading of Trans-European Networks (TENs),[99] first introduced under the TEU. **2.90**

[96] Art 189 EC.

[97] See the discussion in Weatherill, S, *Law and Integration in the European Union*, (1995), 83–4.

[98] European Commission White Paper, *Towards an EU Energy Policy*, COM (1995) 682 Final of 13 Dec 1995; EC Green Paper, *For a European Union Energy Policy*, Jan 1995, 38, 104–05; *White Paper on Growth, Competitiveness and Employment*, COM (1993) 700 final, ch 3.

[99] EP and Council Decision No 1254/96/EC of 5 June 1996; OJ L 161 of 29 June 1996, amended by Decisions No 1047/1997/EC (OJ L 152 of 11 June 1997) and No 1741/1999/EC (OJ L 207 of 6 Aug 1999); Commission Decision No 761/2000/EC of 16 Nov 2000, OJ L 305 of 6 Dec 2000.

2.91 The legal basis of this programme is Title XV of the Treaty of Amsterdam (TA), incorporated into the EC Treaty as Articles 154 to 156.* Article 154 sets out the objectives of Community action as:

- contributing to the establishment and development of Trans-European networks in the areas of transport, telecommunications and energy infrastructures;
- aiming at promoting the interconnection and inter-operability of national networks as well as access to such networks; and
- taking account of the need to link island, land-locked, and peripheral regions with the central regions of the Community.

In a sense, it is intended to provide the 'missing links' in the various sectors to ensure the free movement of persons, goods, services, and capital. Article 155 refers to the means for implementing these objectives, by establishing guidelines—covering objectives, priorities, and the broad lines of measures envisaged. These guidelines seek to identify projects of common interest. Community financial support is available on a limited basis to projects falling within the guidelines. Measures may also be taken to ensure the inter-operability of networks—especially on technical standardization. Finally, Article 156 sets out the procedures for carrying out these measures. Approval from the Member State concerned is required for a specific initiative that may affect it.

(1) Funding

2.92 The funding mechanism is set out in a separate instrument.[100] Several financial instruments may be used where appropriate. These include a TENs budget line. Aid has been given for co-financing feasibility studies but may in justified cases be provided for investment by means of interest rate subsidies, contributions to fees for guarantees for loans, or direct grants. Some restrictions apply:

- aid to feasibility studies is limited to a maximum of 50% of the cost;
- the maximum period of interest rate subsidy must not generally exceed five years;
- the total amount of financial support from the TENs budget line must not exceed 10% of the total investment cost;
- and EU financial support should not distort competition.

This was amended in 1999 to introduce a mechanism for granting EU aid on the basis of indicative multi-annual programmes. It allows an EU contribution to the capital risk element of project finance, with the aim of gaining access to the long-term funding available from insurance companies and pension funds for

[100] Council Regulation (EC) No 2236/95 of 18 Sep 1995 (OJ L 228 of 23 Sep 1995, p 1) laying down general rules for the granting of Community financial aid in the field of TENs, as amended by Regulation (EC) No 1655/1999 (OJ L197, 29 July 1999, p 1–7).

the financing of public infrastructure projects. Applications for TENs financial support must be submitted to the Commission by the governments of the Member States or with their approval. Normally, in the case of energy TENs, the bodies asking for assistance with studies will be the electricity or gas undertakings in the Member States.

Eligibility for financing is restricted to projects defined as being of common interest by the Community guidelines on TENs. The selection criteria include the socio-economic effects and environmental consequences of the project. Other funds available include structural funds and EIB loans. **2.93**

The Commission has also noted the external dimension of TENs.[101] This concerns the network links between the EU and third countries such as those of the Baltic, the Balkans, Central and Eastern Europe and the Mediterranean, and Central Asian areas. Access to energy resources and diversification of supply was highlighted as a consideration. In such cases, financing is linked to whether the project is of mutual or regional interest.

(2) What the TENs initiative is trying to achieve

(a) Promoting integration in infrastructure

Despite the importance of infrastructure to the single market process, there has been evidence of a lack of co-ordination at national level which has led to missing links in the networks—albeit less so in energy than in transport. To remedy this, the Commission has attempted to build up a co-ordinating rôle and to promote integration in infrastructure (see ch 8, para 8.34). At a time of growing liberalization, this improvement in infrastructure and removal of bottlenecks could have advantages to the security of energy supply. However, in contrast to the transport sector, energy networks are often privately owned. Their operation displays few shortcomings (with the exception of a lack of ready access for third parties as yet, a need to co-ordinate their current expansion and to provide for links with cohesion countries such as Spain, Portugal, Greece, Ireland, and third countries that may otherwise experience congestion in their transmission networks). **2.94**

Utilization of the funding mechanism is not difficult but may present complications for countries with mature energy markets, because any expenditure on networks will raise questions about provisions for access to third parties on those networks. In one of the Commission's annual reports on the TENs project, it notes that 'the Treaty rules including the competition rules and procedures, are naturally applicable to the energy sector. This means in particular that TENs **2.95**

[101] COM (1997) 125 final of 23 Mar 1997: *The External Dimension of Trans-European Energy Networks*.

should not lead to any reinforcement of any dominant position of undertakings which control them.'[102]

(b) Streamlining authorization procedures

2.96 Many bottlenecks in the energy sector have nothing to do with financing problems. The fact that little substantial funding is available through the TENs programme is not important. Often private sector investments are hampered by administrative and environmental constraints resulting in limited possibilities for the construction of new energy networks. This is a particular problem for new electricity lines. In this area, the Commission plays a rôle by proposing a common approach to the issue of authorization procedures in the Member States[103] and by co-financing studies investigating and analysing the alternatives for the implementation of a given project.

E. European Economic Area Agreement

2.97 Although not a Member of the European Union, Norway is linked to the corpus of EC law by an international instrument known as the European Economic Area (EEA) Agreement, which entered into force on 1 January 1994, and to which Norway is a party.[104] As a key supplier of gas and oil to the EU and an important player in the Nordic electricity market, the Norway–EU energy link is an important element in the pan-European energy scene. In practice, the Agreement has functioned as a channel for the IEM programme and its legislation into Norway, albeit with some minor modifications.

EEA Agreement: legally-binding

2.98 The Agreement was concluded between the EEC, the ECSC, their Member States, and what were at that time the seven Member States of the European Free Trade Association (EFTA).[105] Its basic aim was to extend the Single Market to the EFTA countries. Originally, it was to include Switzerland but a negative result in the Swiss referendum in 1992 led to the withdrawal of both Switzerland and Liechtenstein (with which it had a customs union). Following the rejection of membership of the EU by Norway, the EEA remains a forum for co-operation between Norway, Iceland, Liechtenstein, and the EU.

---

[102] COM (1996) 645 final of 6 Dec 1996.

[103] Commission Recommendation No 1999/28/EC (OJ L 8 of 14 Jan 1999); Commission Draft Report on the Implementation of the Guidelines for TENs in the Period 1996–2001, 14.12.2001, 9.

[104] The text can be found on the EFTA/EEA website: www.efta.int

[105] These were Austria, Finland, Iceland, Liechtenstein, Norway, Sweden, and Switzerland. EFTA was created through the Stockholm Convention in 1960 and entered into operation in the same year.

The Agreement extends many of the rights and obligations of the EU Member States to the EFTA States that participate in the EEA. It includes the four basic freedoms of the single market but also the 'flanking policies' such as co-operation on research and environmental protection. A list of legislative acts affecting the energy sector is contained in Annex IV to the Agreement.[106] It is updated from time to time. In addition to the internal market acts, the list includes acts on energy consumption of certain equipment. Rules on labelling of energy consumption of household equipment are also included in the Agreement. Acts concerning the safety of goods and 'technical' barriers to trade have a bearing on energy policy and are also included. These may concern exhaust emissions from vehicles, safety of equipment using gas, or electricity as well as sulphur and lead content in fuels. In some cases, the Agreement is subject to adaptations, transitional periods or limited derogation. For example, a four-year transition period was agreed in December 1993 for environmental standards. An important point about this **2.99**

[106] Annex IV of the EEA Agreement notes the list of EC energy Directives that are part of the Agreement. These are: Council Regulation (EEC) 1056/72 of 18 May 1972 on notifying the Commission of investment projects of interest to the Community in the petroleum, natural gas, and electricity sectors (OJ/72/L120); Commission Decision 1999/280/EC of 22 April 1999 on a Community procedure for information and consultation on crude oil supply costs and the consumer prices of petroleum products (OJ L 110, 28 April 1999, p 8); Commission Decision 1999/566/EC of 26 July 1999 implementing Council Decision 1999/280/EC on a Community procedure for information and consultation on crude oil supply costs and the consumer prices of petroleum products (OJ L 216, 14 Aug 1999, p 8); Council Directive 78/170/EEC of 13 Feb 1978 on the performance of heat generators for space heating and the production of hot water in new or existing non-industrial buildings and on the insulation of heat and domestic hot water distribution in new non-industrial buildings, (OJ/78/L052), as amended; Council Regulation (EEC) 1893/79 of 28 August 1979 introducing registration for crude oil and/or petroleum product imports in the Community (OJ/79/L220; Norway only); Council Directive 85/536/EEC of 5 Dec 1985 on crude oil savings through the use of substitute fuel components in petrol (OJ/85/L334), as amended; Council Directive 90/377/EEC of 29 June 1990 on a Community procedure to improve the transparency of gas and electricity prices charged to industrial end-users (OJ/90/L185); Council Directive 90/547/EEC of 29 Oct 1990 on the transit of electricity through transmission grids (OJ/90/L313), as amended; Council Directive 91/296/EEC of 31 May 1991 on the transit of natural gas through grids (OJ/91/L147), as amended; Council Directive 92/42/EEC of 21 May 1992 on efficiency requirements for new hot-water boilers fired with liquid or gaseous fuels (OJ L 167, 22 June 1992, p 17), as amended; Council Directives on energy labelling (7), 1992–98; Directive 94/22/EC of the European Parliament and Council of 30 May 1994 on the conditions for granting and using authorizations for the prospection, exploration, and production of hydrocarbons (OJ L 164, 30 June 1994, p 3); Directive 96/57/EC of the European Parliament and Council of 3 Sep 1996 on energy efficiency requirements for household electric refrigerators, freezers and combinations thereof (OJ L 236, 18 Sep 1996, p 36); and Directive 96/92/EC of the European Parliament and Council of 19 Dec 1996 on common rules for the internal market in electricity (OJ L 27, 30 Jan 1997, p 20). The only major piece of legislation in the energy sector to be excluded is that on mandatory oil stocks. There are 3 principal reasons for this: EFTA countries have already made the same commitments as the EC concerning stockpiling within the framework of the IEA; this legislation does not have any great importance for the normal movement of goods; although the joint decision-making system in the EC is stricter relative to that of the IEA, the EEA does not give EFTA countries any formal say in internal EC decision-making. Nuclear legislation is also not covered by the EEA.

Agreement lies in *legal enforceability* on the parties. In contrast to the various 'Europe' and related Agreements with third countries, the judicial enforcement of the EEA Agreement is very specific.

2.100 The Agreement includes rules on competition, state aids, and state monopolies—very similar to those of the EC Treaty. With respect to state monopolies, it follows the wording of Article 31.* The rules on competition follow very closely those of the EC Treaty to ensure equal conditions of competition for economic operators throughout the Area. The central provisions in the main Agreement are therefore identical to those of Articles 81, 82, and 86.* Provisions in the ECSC as well as secondary legislation were integrated into the Agreement through Protocols and an Annex.

2.101 The Agreement has a dynamic character. A central feature is that its common rules are continuously updated through the incorporation of subsequent measures of EU law in the EEA. Each month new legislation is incorporated into the Agreement by a decision of the EEA Joint Committee. Adaptations may be negotiated in the application of EC legislation to the EEA when this appears appropriate and when agreement can be reached by both sides. The idea here is to have a parallel development of new EC rules and new EEA rules.

(a) The Institutions

2.102 The institutional structures follow a two-pillar model, with strong co-operation between the Brussels-based EFTA Surveillance Authority and the European Commission. The first pillar comprises joint bodies for decision-shaping, decision-making, and dispute settlement. The EEA states have not accepted direct decision-making by the European Commission or the ECJ.

2.103 The ongoing management of the Agreement is the responsibility of the EEA Joint Committee. It comprises ambassadors of the EFTA–EEA states and representatives of the European Commission and EU Member States. Decisions are made by consensus to incorporate EC legislation into the Agreement. Decisions adopted by the Joint Committee must in principle be transposed into national legislation, in accordance with the national system in the EEA country—since there is no transfer of legislative power to the EEA institutions. Another body, the EEA Council, provides political impetus for the development of the Agreement and guidelines for the Joint Committee. It is composed of foreign ministers of the EU and EFTA–EEA countries. There is also a Joint Parliamentary Committee and an EEA Consultative Committee.

2.104 The other pillar comprises the EFTA bodies. The Surveillance Authority is responsible for implementation and enforcement of the competition rules in EFTA States. It has the same powers as the Commission in dealing with those competition matters that fall within its competence. This means that the Surveillance Authority can issue negative clearance, individual exemptions and comfort letters, and can undertake investigations and impose fines for infringements. However, it does not have a legislative power, so block exemptions are adopted through the normal EEA decision-making rules. A system for allocation of cases between the two surveillance authorities (ie, the Surveillance Authority and the European Commission) has been created which is based upon objective criteria. Decisions by either body are valid throughout the EEA.

There is also an EFTA Court operating in parallel to the ECJ in matters relating to the EFTA–EEA states. It deals with infringement actions raised against EFTA states by the Surveillance Authority concerning implementation, application or interpretation of EEA rules, and the settlement of disputes between two or more EFTA states. There is also a Standing Committee of EFTA states that has a co-ordinating rôle in preparing for meetings of the EEA Joint Committee. **2.105**

(b) Impacts on energy

Since the Agreement came into force, the EEA states have adopted that part of the EU *acquis communautaire* that falls within the scope of the Agreement. The EEA states (primarily Norway) have also provided regular input into the shaping of such EC legislation. An example of the effects of transposition is Norway's petroleum legislation. Substantial changes were made to align it with the requirements of the EC Hydrocarbons Directive within the framework of its obligations under the EEA. Changes to the 1985 Petroleum Act included amendments to its provisions on establishment (s 8(1)), procurement (ss 8(7)), 23(1), and 54(1)), landing requirements (s 26(1)), and the power to make regulations relating to the duty of information under the EEA. **2.106**

(i) **Norwegian Gas Sales Consortium** The competition provisions (Art 81 EC and Art 53(1) EEA) were applied in connection with the joint negotiation of all sales of Norwegian gas by the Gas Sales Consortium or GFU (originally comprising the 3 Norwegian oil and gas producers, Statoil, Norske Hydro, and Saga Petroleum). The latter company was subsequently taken over by Norske Hydro and disappeared from the consortium. These companies hold very substantial licence interests in the Norwegian oil and gas reserves but non-Norwegian companies (including TotalElf and Mobil/Exxon) also have significant interests. The GFU was a creation of the Norwegian Government. The consequence of the exclusive negotiating right granted to the members of the GFU for all sales of Norwegian gas automatically precluded the non-Norwegian licence interest holders from negotiating or participating in negotiation of their own sales. In spite of this, they were entitled to refuse to accept the terms negotiated for them by the GFU, if they could obtain better terms from the buyers. In practice, the negotiations were with Statoil, the most important member of the GFU and **2.107** until recently a wholly-owned state entity. The European gas buyers were effectively negotiating with the Norwegian Government.

These arrangements became the subject of an investigation that commenced in 1996, initiated jointly by the EFTA Surveillance Authority and the European Commission. The joint negotiation of natural gas sales contracts, by fixing the price, volumes, and all other trading conditions was alleged to be contrary to Article 81(1) EC and Article 53(1) EEA. For EU consumers their choice between Norwegian producers was reduced artificially from about 30 to effectively one. The Norwegian Government contended that Norway (and the GFU members) were entitled to spread the benefits of sales of Norwegian oil and gas because of their economic implications to Norway. They claimed that Article 81 EC and Article 53(1) EEA should not apply to them. However, finally on 29 May 2001, Norway agreed to disband the GFU, with effect from 1 June 2001.[107] The Commission has indicated that it intends to pursue the matter until action is taken to remedy the objections raised by it with Statoil and Norske Hydro.[108] These included its wish to have the terms of long-term contracts previously negotiated by the GFU varied in favour of the buyers (see ch 7, para 7.117).

2.108 (ii) **Electricity Directive** The provisions of the Electricity Directive (see ch 4, paras 4.02–4.65) were incorporated into the EEA in 2000,[109] with some minor adaptations to its operation:

- the obligation to communicate information relating to final consumers to calculate the average Community share defining the degree of market opening does not apply to the EEA countries; and
- applications for a transitional period to cover stranded assets are permitted but must be notified to the EFTA Surveillance Authority no later than 6 months after the EEA Joint Committee Decision.

2.109 (iii) **Electricity Transit Directive** In implementing the Directive on Electricity Transit, a Conciliation Committee was set up to deal with power exchanges between the EU and EFTA countries (see ch 3, para 3.24). This Committee is to meet on an ad hoc basis, at the initiative of the European Commission or the Surveillance Authority. The Committee is composed of representatives from industry (1 member), authorities (2 members), high-voltage networks independent from the negotiations on transit (3 members chosen

[107] European Commission Press Release, IP/01/830, Commission Objects to GFU Joint Gas Sales in Norway.

[108] Commission Press Release, IP/01/1170, Commission Insists on Effective Access to European Pipelines for Norwegian gas. A Statement of Objections is a legal step in proceedings under Art 81 EC and Art 53 EEA It does not preclude the issuance of a Statement of Objections to other Norwegian gas producers in the context of the GFU case in the future.

[109] Annex IV EEA, point 14.

from the 18 representatives of member networks), and independent experts (2 members).

(iv) Gas Directive The Gas Directive has yet to be applied in the EEA countries, although there was EEA input into the deliberations on its text (see especially ch 4, paras 4.96–4.101). Norway has declared that it will adopt it.[110] Apart from Norway, the other member of the EEA countries linked to the European gas industry is the Duchy of Liechtenstein, dependent on gas imports from Germany. Gas was introduced in 1985 and has been supplied by Ruhrgas and Gasversorgung Süd-Deutschland since then. The distribution company is Liechtensteinische Gasversorgung, listed in Appendix 3 of Annex IV of the Agreement. **2.110**

F. Energy Charter Treaty

The overall dependence of EU countries on energy imports from third countries has made it important for the EU to create formal links with producers and transmitters of energy to contribute to the long-term stability that energy supply contracts typically require—especially in the case of supplies of natural gas. This reality encouraged an orientation not only to the Gulf region but also to the Soviet Union in the East, as an important gas and oil producer. The collapse of the Soviet Union set off a chain of events that led to the creation of new states including the Caspian Sea oil and gas producing states and more independently-minded governments along the established energy transit routes from the East to the EU—raising questions about the security of future energy supplies. The EU therefore threw its weight behind the development of a legal instrument for co-operation between East and West Europe called the Energy Charter Treaty (the Treaty).[111] This multilateral treaty was signed by some 50 states and the European Communities on 17 December 1994. Its purpose is: **2.111**

> to establish a legal framework in order to promote long-term co-operation in the energy field, based on complementaries and mutual benefits, in accordance with the objectives and principles of the [European Energy] Charter.[112]

The Treaty's scope is wide: in a geographical sense, it is essentially pan-European; in an economic sense, it includes different kinds of market or market-oriented

[110] On 26 October 2001 the EEA Joint Committee decided to include the Gas Directive in the EEA Agreement. According to Art 103 EEA, Norway will do so by Parliamentary ratification.

[111] OJ L 69 9 Mar 1998, p 1. Final Act of the European Energy Charter Conference: 69/5–69/114. The Treaty and related Protocol on Energy Efficiency and Environmental Relations entered into force on 16 April 1998, following the deposit of the 30th instrument of ratification on 16 Jan 1998; see *The Energy Charter Treaty and Related Documents* (1996). The initiative behind the Treaty lay originally with the 'Lubbers Declaration' of June 1990: see below n 114.

[112] Art 2.

systems; and in a legal sense, it incorporates a wide range of legal commitments, both of the 'hard' and the 'soft' law variety. It entered into force in April 1998, three months after ratification by the required number of 30 States. It has been ratified by all of the EU States and may be seen as part of the *acquis communautaire* or legal order in energy.[113] It has also been ratified by all the EU applicant countries, the CIS countries (except Russia), the Central Asian Republics, Azerbaijan, Georgia, and Turkey.

2.112 The Treaty creates rights and obligations in international law for all of its contracting parties.[114] It applies both to East–West transactions and West–East transactions. Its scope comprises 'energy materials and products'. It is principally concerned with the promotion and protection of investment, trade, and the transit of energy goods. Other subjects covered by the Treaty are either supportive of the provisions on these matters or have a lesser significance. The provisions on competition in energy could be placed in the latter category.

Main Treaty Provisions

(a) Investment

2.113 The Treaty distinguishes between two stages in the investment process: the 'pre-investment' stage, involving the making of investments and setting of access conditions; and the 'post-investment' stage, concerning investments already in place. It is the latter stage that is subject to a legal régime of 'hard law' obligations, similar to those common to bilateral investment treaties and enforceable by international arbitration.

2.114 **(i) Post-investment stage** For the post-investment stage, contracting parties are obliged to encourage and create stable, equitable, favourable, and transparent conditions for foreign investors to make investments in their areas. The standard of treatment to be accorded to foreign investors is the better of national (NT) or

[113] See n 3 above.

[114] The origin of the Treaty lies in a non-binding Declaration signed by 50 States and the European Community 3 years earlier on 17 Dec 1991, called the European Energy Charter, based on an initiative of Prime Minister Ruud Lubbers of The Netherlands in 1990. The primary aim of the project was 'to give political support to the democratic process in the former centrally-planned economies. The welfare of these countries' population would benefit from a properly managed supply and from an influx of Western investment attracted by a stable free market system. The resulting improvement in conditions of life would underpin the evolution towards a democratic society': Dore, Julia and De Bauw, Robert *The Energy Charter Treaty: Origins, Aims and Prospects*, (1995), 2. The aims of the Charter Declaration were to: improve security of supply; maximize efficiency of production, conversion, transport, distribution, and use of energy; enhance safety; and minimize environmental problems. For a comprehensive collection of materials on the Charter see *The Energy Charter Treaty: An East-West Gateway for Investment and Trade*, (ed Waelde, Thomas W., 1996).

Most Favoured Nation (MFN) treatment.[115] From the date of signature, each contracting party agrees to treat foreign investors at least as well as it treats its national or domestic companies or investors. The exceptions to the NT and the MFN clauses are limited in scope, number, and time while being clearly known and transparent at the time of signature. In practice, the exceptions actually claimed by economies in transition were far fewer than initially expected and most of these have since been phased out. Compensation for losses is provided for under the NT and MFN clauses and fair conditions in the event of expropriation are also provided for. This means that, for instance, freely convertible currencies will be used in designing compensation arrangements. Free movement of capital and repatriation of profits are also provided for.[116] There are no NT provisions on taxes on income or on capital.

(ii) Pre-investment phase For the pre-investment phase, the NT principle is to be implemented in two stages: **2.115**

(1) investments are to receive either NT or MFN treatment on a voluntary basis (best efforts)—whichever is the most advantageous; and
(2) all signatories are committed to work towards extending the provisions on NT to the pre-investment stage, on a legally-binding basis.[117]

(iii) Supplementary Treaty Negotiations on a 'second-phase' investment treaty were to be concluded by 1 January 1998. However, although the commitment to negotiate was fulfilled it did not result in agreement on the resulting draft instrument, the 'Supplementary Treaty'. **2.116**

The Treaty contains provisions on the settlement of any investment disputes that may arise. They provide for the use of compulsory arbitration against governments at the option of foreign investors for alleged breaches of the investment agreements, without the need to first exhaust local remedies. Moreover, binding state-to-state arbitration is provided for in Article 27. This involves the use of an ad hoc tribunal for disputes between states concerning the application or interpretation of the Treaty. It is not restricted to the resolution of disputes arising from investment issues. The dispute settlement procedures may in fact be diverse, including international arbitration, and provide for final and binding solutions to many disputes. The rules and procedures governing transit disputes in particular have been enhanced since ratification to minimize disruption when a dispute is taking place.[118]

[115] Art 10(7).
[116] Art 14.
[117] Art 10(4).
[118] Rules Concerning the Conduct of Transit Disputes ('Rules'), adopted Dec 1998.

2.117 As a general comment, the sector specific character of the Treaty provisions may weaken the legal protection it offers relative to many of the investment protection treaties in force, or indeed the EC Treaty. However, the special importance of the energy sector in the economies of many Eastern European countries may justify the treatment of investment issues in a separate legal instrument focused exclusively on this sector.

(b) Trade

2.118 A second major feature of the Treaty is that it subjects trade in energy materials and products between contracting parties to the provisions of the GATT and its related instruments, even where those contracting parties to the Treaty that are not yet parties to the GATT (eg the FSU republics). The aim is to promote access to international markets for non-GATT parties on commercial terms. A weakness here is the failure to treat the link between trade and competition—the latter being relegated to the status of a second order issue. As in the investment provisions, there was also a Treaty provision for 'second stage' negotiations on trade matters.

2.119 In April 1998 a trade amendment was adopted following a meeting of the Energy Charter Conference. A new Article 29 dealt with each of the three issues on which negotiations were mandated. It included several understandings and declarations, one in relation to trade-related intellectual property rights. This brought the Treaty into line with current World Trade Organization (WTO) rules on multilateral agreements on trade in goods. It was also aimed at encouraging the introduction of WTO-compatible rules in non-WTO countries that are parties to the Treaty. In addition, it allowed the inclusion of more than 70 categories of energy-related equipment—eg pipelines, power masts, furnaces, and transformers—into the extended WTO-based régime, and opened the way for future legally-binding tariff commitments for energy materials and products, and for energy-related equipment. The amendment is provisionally applied until it enters into force. Until then the trade régime in the Treaty will continue to be more relevant.

(c) Transit

2.120 The third major feature of the Treaty is the provision it makes for the transit of energy goods through a state that is a party to it. Article 7 establishes a legal framework for relationships between governments in relation to transit. It is to be supplemented by a Protocol on transit which is in the final stages of negotiation and is expected to be signed in 2002.[119] Article 7 sets out rules on the following:

- non-discriminatory passage with no distinction allowed as to origin, destination, or ownership of products or materials;
- non-discriminatory pricing;
- absence of unreasonable delays, restrictions, or charges;
- modernization of infrastructure;
- offer of the possible new-build infrastructure;
- non-interruption of transit in case of dispute, and clear dispute and conciliation procedures.

Article 7 requires each contracting state to take:

> . . . necessary measures to facilitate the transit of Energy Materials and Products consistent with the principle of freedom of transit and without distinction as to the origin, destination or ownership of such Energy Materials or Products or discrimination as to pricing on the basis of such distinctions, and without imposing any unreasonable delays, restrictions or charges.

An obligation is therefore imposed on the parties to facilitate transit. However, the choice of the word 'facilitate' over alternatives such as 'ensure' or 'encourage' guarantees a weaker formulation. It does not require the transit states to adopt specific legislation to improve transit access, although by implementing Treaty provisions in domestic legislation a state may include provisions on access. **2.121**

(i) 'Freedom of transit' The principle of 'freedom of transit' is referred to without any apparent legal basis for such a principle. However, the obligation of non-discrimination in transit relates to both the terms of access to the energy transport facilities and to the terms and conditions of carriage. Transit is also to be allowed 'without unreasonable delays, restrictions or charges'. The contracting parties must also secure existing flows of transit energy even in circumstances where such transit would endanger the security of supply. The proposed Transit Protocol contains provisions which will greatly clarify the rights and obligations of transit states. **2.122**

(ii) Soft law obligations Other transit requirements include an obligation to encourage the relevant entities to co-operate in the following: **2.123**

- modernizing energy transport facilities which are necessary for transit
- developing and operating energy transport facilities which serve more than one contracting party

[119] Energy Charter Secretariat, Draft Energy Charter Protocol on Transit, 18 May 2001. Art 3 states that the Protocol shall complement, supplement, extend, or amplify the Treaty provisions but not derogate from them.

- taking 'measures to mitigate supply interruptions',[120] and
- facilitating interconnection.

It is unclear how a state might seek to encourage a relevant entity that is in private ownership.

The transit state is also required to transit energy 'in no less favourable a manner than its provisions treat such materials and products originating in or destined for its own Area'.[121] It must therefore apply the more favourable of NT or MFN treatment in its approach to goods in transit.

2.124 **(iii) Dispute resolution** In the event of a dispute over transit, the contracting parties must not interrupt or reduce the existing flow of energy materials and products and not permit the introduction or reduction of transit flows by any entity subject to its control or require any entity subject to its jurisdiction to interrupt or reduce a transit flow.[122] However, this is subject to an exception in Article 24.

An important qualification to the above obligation is that contracting parties are not precluded from adopting or enforcing any measure in relation to transit as is essential to the acquisition or distribution of energy materials and products 'in conditions of short supply arising from causes outside the control of that Contracting Party'.

2.125 The dispute resolution mechanism is important since, if it is successfully applied, it could function as a means of securing the continuity of transit flows when transit disputes occur between contracting parties.[123] It is governed by a set of Rules and Procedures issued by the Secretariat in 1998.[124] These include the provision of guidance to its secretary-general on how to appoint conciliators, guidance for conciliators conducting proceedings with a view to seeking agreements between parties, and the imposition of interim tariffs for one year if agreement is not reached.

2.126 If negotiations for access to existing facilities fail, provision is made to facilitate the construction of new transit facilities. In cases where transit 'cannot be achieved on commercial terms' by means of energy transport facilities, a contracting party 'shall not place obstacles in the way of new capacity being established, except as

[120] Art 7(2).

[121] ibid.

[122] Art 7(6). For comparative experiences see Stevens, P, 'Pipelines or Pipe Dreams? Lessons from the history of Arab Transit Pipelines', (2000) 54 Middle East Journal, 224–41

[123] This seems to have been the idea behind the threat to invoke the transit dispute settlement provisions by a Russian Deputy Prime Minister over charges being levied by the Ukraine for oil transited through the Druzhba pipeline: *BBC Monitoring Survey of World Broadcasts*, 19 Feb 1996.

[124] Rules, n 118 above, and Treaty, n 111 above Art 7(7).

may be otherwise provided in applicable legislation'.[125] Although the 'commercial terms' are not defined, this is a matter that could be addressed by a court in terms of the aims of the Treaty.

This provision should be read alongside the provisions of Article 7(5), which contains a number of exceptions to the obligations of transit states. For example, the transit states are required not:

- to construct or modify existing energy transport facilities, or
- to permit new or additional transit through existing energy transport facilities.

They may do so if it can be demonstrated to the other contracting parties concerned that the granting of such permissions would 'endanger the security or efficiency of its energy systems, including the security of supply'. In practice, the burden of proof would be difficult to discharge.

(iv) **Treaty transit provisions as a 'Trojan horse'** From the foregoing, it should not be assumed that the definition of transit is so broad as to impose an obligation on states to introduce third-party access. In the Understandings that are included in the Final Act of the Conference on the Charter, it is clearly stated that 'The provisions of the Treaty do not . . . oblige any Contracting Party to introduce mandatory third-party access.'[126] This provision has its origins in the discussions within the EU at the time of the Treaty negotiations on the introduction of third-party access by means of new legislation, which subsequently became the Electricity and Gas Directives. The transit provision in the Treaty was seen as a potential 'Trojan horse' for the introduction of such access into the EU to circumvent the difficulties that the European Commission was experiencing in securing the passage of the proposed Directives. The incumbent players were successful in persuading their governments to support the inclusion of this clarification. **2.127**

(d) The Charter process: an assessment

The developmental character of the Treaty may be grasped by the notion of the 'Charter process'. This can be divided into three stages,[127] with different implications for the Treaty's relationship to the EU arising from each one. **2.128**

The first stage was the difficult one of negotiating a text that could secure agreement among a very diverse group of countries. This was completed by December 1994 when the Treaty was signed in Lisbon. The second stage was characterized mainly by the efforts to encourage signatories to ratify the Treaty so it might enter into force, on the one hand, and on the other, the conclusion

[125] Art 7(4).

[126] Final Act of the European Energy Charter Conference, Understanding 1(b)(i).

[127] See discussions by Bamberger, C S, Linehan, J and Waelde, T, 'Energy Charter Treaty in 2000: in a New Phase', in (2000) 18 J Energy Natural Resources L, 331–52; and Cameron, P, 'Het Verdrag inzake het Energiehandvest: een beoordeling na zes jaar', in (2001) SEW, 139–148.

of 'second stage' negotiations as envisaged in the Treaty . This was concluded in April 1998. The third and most recent stage involves an emphasis upon the removal of obstacles to the transit of energy materials and products and attempts to secure Russian ratification of the Treaty.

2.129 (i) **Soft law 'too soft'?** The Treaty that was concluded in the first stage is a combination of hard and soft law commitments—the latter made up of aspirations or statements of legal intention. It would be unwise to restrict an assessment purely to the former provisions. Many of its concepts are new to the countries in transition. The Treaty therefore has value as an educational device, although it is still open to differences in interpretation. It may help to break with the prevailing case-by-case approach to negotiations on these matters. However, the abundance of soft law commitments such as 'shall work to promote', 'shall encourage', and 'shall agree to promote', is not likely to inspire confidence in its relevance to large-scale investment in energy infrastructure since such assurances are unenforceable in a court of law.

2.130 (ii) **East–West Exchange** The prevailing assumption behind the Treaty's inception was that there are complementary interests which permit a kind of exchange between East and West: Russia and the FSU countries have gas and oil reserves which can be developed with Western technology and capital, to restore declining production, and to provide markets for its energy production. This requires investment protection, trade, and guarantees about energy transit. To some extent this approach was overtaken by events, as many Central European countries became candidates for entry into the EU and perceptions of the investment potential of many former FSU countries became less sanguine. However, EU dependence on imports of oil and gas from the East remains and will increase once the next round of enlargement takes place.

2.131 (iii) **Competition provisions** Competition is not a central feature of the Treaty, in contrast to the EC Treaty, the EEA Agreement, and the Europe Agreements (see below). Article 6 is characterized by a procedural approach to anti-competitive conduct in which states may take steps to address the consequences of such actions.

Two obligations are imposed: each State must work towards (i) alleviating market distortions and (ii) removing barriers to competition in energy. Article 6(2) requires States to establish and enforce laws to deal with unilateral and concerted anti-competitive conduct in energy. However, Understanding No 7 to the Treaty states that what is to be included in such laws is up to each of the contracting parties. Complaints to the competition authorities of the State concerned may include a request that they take appropriate enforcement action, but they cannot compel them to do so. The kind of action taken is also a matter for the state concerned. There is no requirement that reasons be given for the action taken or failure to take action. This is the only means available to advance complaints, apart from the diplomatic means of dispute settlement in Article 27(1). Article 6 does not give rights to firms or individuals who are injured by anti-competitive conduct in other states parties to the Treaty. This missing element is a stark contrast to the EC Treaty that confers rights on individuals and means by which they can enforce these rights. The Treaty's approach is explicable, however, in terms of the Treaty's aims, which do not include that of removing barriers to competition.

(iv) Future credibility of the Charter The Charter process will continue to matter to the EU in future years, especially given its 'third stage' focus on the important area of energy transit. The Treaty established a framework within which multilateral discussions could take place among all stakeholders but especially governments. It has established a Working Group on transit, substantially completed negotiations on a legally-binding Protocol on Transit, and developed non-binding model host government and intergovernmental agreements on cross-border energy flows—including transit. If they become effective, these instruments will constitute a significant elaboration of the Treaty's provisions on transit of energy. The Charter process will therefore remain highly relevant to all the countries involved, whether the EU grouping, applicant countries of Central Europe, or both the European and Asian states of the FSU. Most of these countries lack indigenous supplies of gas and oil and are highly dependent on imports, while all of them are more or less dependent upon the Russian Federation for a transportation system that is controlled by it. The need for Russian ratification of the Treaty is a significant challenge for its future credibility. **2.132**

G. Enlargement of the EU and the EU *Acquis* in Energy

The collapse of the Soviet Union has had a radical effect upon the programmes for economic co-operation between the EU and the countries of Central and Eastern Europe. During the 1990s the existing programmes of trade and co-operation were superseded by arrangements designed to bring many of these countries into the EU itself. These accession strategies included an important element of approximation of laws, especially with respect to internal market legislation. They have given the energy *acquis* a genuine pan-European reach. However, political choices have ensured that important differences still exist between the frameworks established by agreements set up as 'associations', 'partnerships', or 'pre-accession' arrangements. **2.133**

(1) Europe Agreements

The Europe Agreements are a form of bilateral or 'association' agreement between the EU and ten countries of Central Europe which aspire to full membership of **2.134** the EU in the foreseeable future. The countries are Bulgaria, the Czech Republic, Estonia, Hungary, Latvia, Lithuania, Poland, Romania, Slovakia, and Slovenia.[128] These are mixed agreements (signed by the EC and Member States on the one hand and the associated country on the other) based on Article 238 of the EC Treaty, and covering areas of Community and Member State competence. They envisage political and economic co-operation and aim at the possible integration of the countries concerned into the EU. They have been concluded for unlimited periods and have transition periods of around ten years. They are called 'Europe Agreements' to emphasize their importance and to distinguish them from other association agreements.

2.135 The Agreements share almost identical structures and contents. They cover the same topics as the EC Treaty. The first chapter deals with the free movement of goods, making special reference to industrial products and agriculture. The second deals with movement of workers, establishment, and supply of services. The third sets out rules for payments, movement of capital, competition, and economic, cultural, and financial co-operation. Finally, an institutional framework is provided for the co-operation and for implementation of the Agreements.

The three key instruments are:

- Association Councils, which involve bilateral meetings at ministerial level between the EU and the associated country, to discuss all matters of approximation;
- Association Committees, comprising meetings at senior official level to discuss all matters covered in the Agreement but in more detail; and finally
- Joint Parliamentary Committees, bringing together members of the Parliaments of the associated countries and members of the European Parliament.

(a) An example: Polish Agreement

2.136 The provisions on energy are similar in each Agreement. An example of a Europe Agreement provision that deals with energy is Article 78 of the Agreement with Poland. It requires that co-operation shall take place 'within the framework of the principles of the market economy and develop against a background of progressive integration of the market of Poland and that of the Community'. It states, for example, that co-operation between the parties shall

[128] Bulgaria, OJ L 368 (1994), 90/519/EEC; Czech Republic, OJ L 360 (1994), 94/910/ECSC, EC, Euratom; Estonia OJ L 373 (1994), 94/974/EC; Hungary, OJ L 347 (1993), 93/742/Euratom, ECSC, EC; Latvia, OJ L 374 (1994), 94/976/EC; Lithuania, OJ L 375 (1994) 94/978/EC; L347, 31/12/93; Poland OJ L 348 (1993), 93/743/EC, ECSC, Euratom; Romania, OJ L 357 (1994), 94/907/ECSC, EC, Euratom; Slovak Republic, OJ L 359 (1994), 94/909/ECSC, EEC, Euratom; Slovenia OJ L 287 (1993), 93/598/ECSC. Three other countries have applied for membership of the EU and have concluded association agreements: Turkey, Malta, and Cyprus.

focus upon improvement and diversification of energy supply and modernization of infrastructure, as well as giving particular attention to the gas and electricity sectors—including consideration of the possibility of interconnection of supply networks and the formulation of framework conditions for co-operation between undertakings in the sector. However, in Poland's case an ECSC Protocol applies to its coal industry.

(b) An example: Latvia Agreement

Co-operation is also encouraged by facilitating the transit of gas and electricity. In the Agreement between the EU and Latvia, co-operation is to focus especially on areas such as 'regional contribution in the energy sector among the Baltic states, particularly as an important contribution to the security of energy supply in the region'. **2.137**

(c) Areas for EU-state co-operation

Typically, the Agreements also list the following areas as appropriate for co-operation between the EU and the State concerned: **2.138**

- formulation and planning of energy policy
- management and training for the energy sector
- development of energy resources
- promotion of energy saving and energy efficiency
- environmental impact of energy production and consumption
- transfer of technology and know-how, and
- opening up the energy market to a greater degree.

Usually, there are separate articles that deal with the environment and the nuclear sector.

In practice, the Agreements quickly became frameworks for pre-accession to the EU for the countries concerned. At meetings of the European Council in 1993 and 1994 the political reorientation was made clear. In a White Paper of 1995 the Commission set out in detail the approximation measures that should be adopted by the accession countries to meet the 'market criterion' for accession to the EU.[129] This included all the other rules applicable to the *acquis* in the energy sector.[130] The White Paper emphasized that the harmonization of legislation alone is not sufficient for accession to be a workable objective. The Commission saw the main challenge for associated countries in taking over the internal market legislation as being located:

---

[129] European Commission, *Preparation of the Associated Countries of Central and Eastern Europe for Integration into the Internal Market of the Union*, 10 May 1995, COM (1995) 163 final.

[130] An early summary of the *acquis* for energy may be found in the Annex to the White Paper, 359–81.

> . . . not in the technical adaptation of their legal texts to make them identical to those of the Community but in adapting their administrative machinery and their societies to the framework conditions necessary to make the legislation work.[131]

2.139 In contrast to previous enlargements, there was an evident concern about the application and enforcement of existing legislation. The new applicants were being asked to take on a more complex *acquis* and to do so from a lower starting point. The rôle of temporary derogations and transitional arrangements for candidate countries must be seen in this context.

(d) Accession Partnerships

2.140 To deal with the challenges, the Commission has concluded an Accession Partnership (AP) with each candidate country. These are the central pre-accession strategy instruments. In December 1999 APs were adopted for candidate countries in Central and East Europe. The following year they were adopted for Cyprus, Malta, and Turkey. On this basis, they submit regular reports with short- and medium-term priorities to fulfil the accession criteria. In turn, they have drawn up National Programmes for the Adoption of the Acquis (NPAA), setting out in detail how they plan to prepare for their integration into the EU, in terms of human and financial resource allocation and the timetable required to meet the accession priorities. An assessment of the NPAA is included in each regular report.

2.141 Accession has become the goal of both parties to the various Agreements and not only an objective of the associated country. While initially the approach was to distinguish countries that appeared closest to accepting membership conditions from the rest, there has been a gradual appreciation that such distinctions may prove unrealistic or even unfair over time as the countries adapt to the requirements at varying speeds.[132] There has also been an appreciation that the adaptation requirements in the energy sector are considerable, requiring some financial outlays, and therefore justify transitional measures—even if they are limited in scope and granted on a case-by-case basis, without setting a precedent.[133] This was especially applicable to oil stocks.[134]

---

[131] ibid, Annex, 2. This applied especially to the supervisory bodies for the maintenance of oil stocks and energy efficiency.

[132] The view of the Santer Commission was different from that of the Prodi Commission: for the former see the assumptions in The European Agreements and Beyond, COM (19/94) 320 and COM (1994) 361.

[133] European Commission, *Overview Progress Report on Accession*, 8 Nov 2000: http://europa.eu.int/comm/enlargement /report_11_00; see generally, Avery, G, and Cameron, F, *The Enlargement of the European Union*, (1998).

[134] Council Directive 68/414/EEC of 20 Dec 1968 imposing an obligation on Member States of the EEC to maintain minimum stocks of crude oil and/or petroleum products, OJ L 308/4, 23 Dec 1968, as amended by OJ L 358/100, 31 Dec 1998. Other problems were encountered in the field of nuclear energy: see generally Horbach, N, *Contemporary Developments in Nuclear Energy Law* (1999), esp 89–96.

(e) A moving target

Accession to the energy *acquis* during this period has been an exercise in 're-approximation', in the sense that the *acquis* has proved a moving target. Throughout this period the energy *acquis* has become significantly more complex while at the same time permitting diverging choices in the implementation of those requirements.[135] However, the Commission takes the view that the *acquis* evolves to meet changing needs and requirements and that the new energy *acquis* builds on the existing one.[136] **2.142**

(2) Partnership and Co-operation Agreements

A distinct form of agreement has been developed between the EU and the countries that were formerly part of the Soviet Union, excluding the Baltic States. A Partnership and Co-operation Agreement (PCA) is a bilateral agreement with fairly general terms that in no way implies future membership of the EU. It is a mixed agreement based on Articles 133 and 308 of the EC Treaty. It establishes an institutional, political, and administrative framework. These have their roots in the 1989 Trade and Commercial Co-operation Agreement between the European Community and the former Union of Soviet Socialist Republics. They can be distinguished into two groups: those signed with the European states of the USSR (Russia, Ukraine, Moldova, and Belarus)—and the rest. The latter are less detailed than the former. Neither category of PCA can be compared with the terms of an association agreement. **2.143**

A PCA typically includes provisions on energy and the environmental impact of energy production, covering matters such as:

- environmental impact of energy production, supply, and consumption
- improvement of security of supply
- formulation of energy policy
- improvement of the management and regulation of the energy sector in line with a market economy
- promotion of energy saving
- modernization of energy infrastructure including interconnection of gas supply and electricity networks, and
- introduction of the institutional, legal, and fiscal conditions necessary to increase trade and investment.[137]

---

[135] For current developments see the websites of the Centre of European Policy Studies (CEPS) and affiliates: www.euractiv.com

[136] *Overview Progress Report*, see n 133, 25–6.

[137] eg, Agreement on Partnership and Co-operation between the EU and Russia, Art 65, OJ L 327, 28 Nov 1997, 3.

In terms of substance and the dispute settlement mechanism, the PCA is significantly weaker than a Europe Agreement.

2.144 The most significant of the PCAs in every sense is the one concluded between the EU and the Russian Federation. It establishes three institutional mechanisms:

- a Co-operation Council that meets at least annually at the ministerial level and monitors implementation of the PCA;
- a Co-operation Committee that brings together senior civil servants; and
- a Parliamentary Co-operation Committee, composed of representatives from the European Parliament and the Federal Assembly of the Russian Federation.

It has a ten-year duration and entered into force on 1 December 1997. Renewal at the end of this period is automatic on an annual basis. Sectoral agreements are envisaged and are part of the overall PCA framework. The PCA was strengthened by the adoption of a Common Strategy in 1999. Among its 'principal objectives', it refers to the integration of Russia into 'a common economic and social space in Europe'—not least because Russia 'provides a significant part of the Union's energy supplies'. The language remains fairly general, although both parties commit to continue consultations on a multilateral transit framework that is designed to enhance co-operation between Russia and its neighbours over access to the Russian pipeline system. A complicating factor in this process is the enclave status of the Russian region of Kaliningrad, located between Poland and Lithuania, in the context that would be created by further enlargement of the EU to the East.

2.145 Despite the considerable importance of many of these countries for the pan-European energy scene, the legal frameworks established by the EU are of a different order of significance from that established with the countries of Central Europe and the Baltic States. As one commentator has observed, the PCAs 'establish and consolidate in reality a new dividing line in Europe'.[138] They express a policy of differentiated treatment from that accorded to the candidate countries and therefore have a quite different relationship to the EU energy *acquis*. This applies also to the countries involved in the EU's Stabilization and Association process, the framework for the EU's policy in South-East Europe, including the Western Balkans.[139]

Russian gas

2.146 The long-term importance of Russian gas supplies for Europe was re-emphasized when oil prices rose steeply in mid-2000. The President of the

[138] Marc Maresceau, 'Association, Partnership, Pre-Accession and Accession', in *Enlarging the EU: Relations between Central and Eastern Europe*, (Maresceau, ed, 1997), 12.

[139] Stabilization and Association Agreements are being negotiated with Albania, Bosnia and Herzegovina, Croatia, FYROM, and the Federal Republic of Yugoslavia. Integration of energy networks with the EU is a priority in this process.

Commission proposed a 'long-term strategic partnership' for gas supply from Russia to the EU to be included as an agenda item in future bilateral talks.[140] The idea appeared to be to reduce EU import dependence on OPEC oil by encouraging gas companies to secure additional supplies of Russian gas. Given the historically close links between Russian gas suppliers and the incumbent gas utilities in the EU, such a step would not contribute positively to a more liberalized gas market. Moreover, the linkage between oil and gas in such cases is of doubtful value. Oil is a readily transported and traded fuel that is sold into mature EU markets where almost 50 per cent is used for transportation purposes. Natural gas, by contrast, is much more constrained in its transportation and tradability than oil. If new pipelines were to be constructed, a potential EU rôle might be in facilitating their financing by EU based companies by taking shares in these pipelines with Russian companies.

(3) Enlargement and the Mediterranean

While the 1990s have been dominated by questions of enlargement to the East and the creation of links with former Soviet states, another region appears likely to create interest in future external policy development in energy. This is the so-called 'southern' or Mediterranean dimension of the EU. For the Member States in the northern parts of the EU with their secure supplies of energy from the North Sea, it is easy to forget that some of the largest primary fuel suppliers to the EU are located in the Mediterranean region. This reality has helped to give momentum to the establishment of a Euro–Mediterranean Partnership,[141] involving the Mahgreb (Algeria, Morocco, and Tunisia) and Mashrak (Egypt, Jordan, Syria, and Lebanon) countries, as well as Israel and the Palestinian Territories. However, it also includes three countries which have a stake in the next phase of EU enlargement: Cyprus, Malta, and Turkey. The EU and the 12 parties above signed a Declaration on 28 November 1995 to achieve, *inter alia*, a free trade zone among themselves, setting a target date of 2010 for the removal of all tariff and non-tariff barriers to trade in manufactured goods. **2.147**

For the EU the energy objectives of such a Partnership are principally justified on security of supply grounds. A number of these countries play, or in the medium-term could play an important rôle in the transit of energy from neighbouring regions such as the Gulf and the Caspian Sea and Central Asian Republics. In addition, the volume of oil and gas reserves in these countries is an important guarantee of supplies

[140] European Commission Press Release, no 405/12779/00, Joint Declaration, 30 Oct 2000[; —3]; Communication on the Russia–EU Energy Dialogue from President Prodi, Vice President de Palacio and Commissioner Patten to the Commission, May 2001: http://europa.eu.int/comm/energy_transport/en. Commission Green Paper 'Towards a European Strategy for the Security of Energy Supply', (2001).

[141] European Commission, 'Strengthening the Mediterranean Policy of the European Union: Establishing a Euro-Mediterranean Partnership', COM (1994) 427.

to the EU. However, their links to the EU in terms of external trade in energy are so diverse that a programme of common interests in this sector is difficult to define. Some of the countries, such as Algeria and Egypt, are net exporters; others, like Syria and Tunisia, are in balance; the rest are net importers of energy (Cyprus, Israel, Jordan, Lebanon, Malta, Morocco, Palestinian Territories, and Turkey). In most cases, they are characterized by a growing energy consumption, especially in electricity, which will require additional financing in the future. It is in the latter area that the linkage with the EU is most likely to lead to substantive results.

2.148 Given the differences of interest, it is hardly surprising that there have been lengthy discussions as to the appropriate instruments for developing co-operation. The principal instruments are Euro–Mediterranean Association Agreements concluded between the EU and the Mediterranean countries individually. These are free trade agreements but also aim at the greatest possible harmonization on economic issues, including competition, state aids, and monopolies, and also at economic co-operation in the field of energy, for example. They are of unlimited duration and may be denounced with a six-month notification period. Such Agreements have been concluded with nine of the 12 Partners.[142] The other three countries, Cyprus, Malta, and Turkey, are covered by Association Agreements that have their origin in trade and co-operation agreements concluded in the 1960s and 1970s.[143] The latter envisage eventual membership of the EU and provide for, *inter alia*, customs unions with the European Community. There is also a multilateral dimension to this co-operation, with funding from the MEDA programme.[144]

A possible model for regional co-operation considered by the European Commission in this context is the Energy Charter Treaty.[145] However, such an instrument is unlikely to prove suitable to the task for at least three reasons. First, the ECT has been tailored to the situation of the economies in transition and to the rôle played by many Central and East European countries as transit routes for gas and oil to the consumer countries; most of the Mediterranean countries lack this kind of energy interdependence. Secondly, one of the fundamental components of the ECT, transit, is limited in the Mediterranean region by the underdevelopment of the network infrastructure. Finally, the ECT was negotiated in response to an absence of a framework for co-operation and of legal frameworks for trade but for

142 European Commission, 'Information Notes on the Euro-Mediterranean Partnership', January 2001, 6.

143 ibid.

144 MEDA refers to the financial and technical flanking measures for the reform of the economic and social structures within the framework of the Euro-Mediterranean Partnership: Council Regulation EC/1488/96, adopted on 23.7.1996, as amended by Council Regulation EC/2698/2000, OJ L 311, 12.12.2000.

145 Communication from the Commission to the European Parliament and Council on the Euro-Mediterranean Partnership in the Energy Sector, COM (1996) 149 final, 3 April 1996.

the Mediterranean countries accession to the ECT is unlikely to make much difference to their legal situation, since their starting point is quite different.[146]

The agenda of energy issues to be addressed in this context has been defined by the principal organ for multilateral consultation, the Euro–Mediterranean Forum, set up in 1997 as the reference body for Euro–Mediterranean co-operation. There are four priority areas:[147] **2.149**

- Reform of the legislative and regulatory framework, including a restructuring of the energy industry of the Mediterranean Partners. To attract the foreign direct investment they need, a reform process is required, taking into account the EU's experience in reforming the energy sector;
- Convergence of the energy policies of the EU and the Mediterranean Partners. Part of this is an encouragement by the EU that the Partners accede to the ECT as a reference framework for the promotion of investment and security of supply;
- Integration of the Mediterranean markets and the development of interconnections. This aim is directly linked to the EU aim of security of supply, and would involve their inclusion in an enlarged INOGATE agreement;[148]
- Sustainable Development of the Mediterranean Partners and use of renewable energy.

The common thread that runs through all of these priorities is a concern by the EU to promote security of energy supply.

H. Conclusions

The origins of the IEM programme are firmly rooted in the process of constitutional change that began in 1986. This created a context in which liberalization of the network-bound sectors, including energy and telecommunications, could be first triggered and then largely sustained throughout the 1990s. The vehicle for this programme was the sectoral legislation, discussed in the following chapters. This dynamic, even volatile, context stands in sharp contrast to that of the previous three decades in which the sector had been dominated largely by public sector monopolies. As this wider process continues to have effects upon the EU institutional framework **2.150**

[146] ibid, 11–12. Turkey ratified the ECT in May 2001.

[147] European Commission, 'Enhancing Euro-Mediterranean Co-operation on Transport and Energy', Euromed Report, Issue No 26, 22 March 2001

[148] INOGATE is the Interstate Oil and Gas Transport to Europe, an EU program to promote the construction and interconnection of oil and gas transport infrastructures between the EU and the regions of the Caspian Sea, Black Sea, Mediterranean and South-East Europe. It has given rise to a multilateral agreement, signed by 17 countries of South-East Europe, and covering the operation, maintenance and safety of the above infrastructures.

and on the priorities of the EU, it can be expected to impact upon the shape of the IEM and the pace at which barriers to liberalization are removed.

2.151 It is not only the primary legislation and the institutions that have been changing in important ways. The 'reach' of EU law and market-based concepts has extended, becoming for the first time genuinely pan-European.

As a result, the legal framework has come to correspond more closely with the energy resource map of Europe. The EEA Agreement and the Europe Agreements have established bridges for the application of EU primary and secondary legislation in more than a dozen countries that are not actual members of the EU. The countries involved are, with the exception of Norway, not important producers but are in several cases important as transporters of transit energy to the main centres of consumption in the EU.

Certainly the legal provisions of these Agreements are of differing weight. The approximation of laws implied by the Europe Agreements and pre-accession arrangements (separate documents) is a minor commitment by comparison with the requirements of the EEA Agreement. As the accession process gained momentum this difference has become less marked, despite the very different levels of economic and indeed legal development between the two groups of countries.

2.152 The development of legal frameworks for co-operation in energy relations between the EU and the Russian and Central Asian/Caspian energy producers and transit states has taken a very different form. There is no broad political orientation of potential EU membership. The principal objective has been strategic: to manage the EU's increasing dependence upon supplies of energy from the East. Elements of internal market legislation have been exported but the overall legal environment is as yet too weak to support the kind of competition that the EU aims at in its energy sector. Similarly, for the countries involved in the Euro–Mediterranean Partnership, the impetus has also been largely a security-based one and has so far had little connection with economic integration.

Basing itself upon the ideas implicit or explicit in the primary law of the EC, a new legal order for energy was developed in the 1990s—slowly and with much controversy. It was characterized principally by an elaboration of existing EC rules in the form of secondary legislation. Its principal aim was to enhance the *integration* aspects of the EC Treaty with respect to the energy sector, rather than say security of supply. Efforts to amend or elaborate the primary law itself by adding a chapter on energy proved in the event unnecessary to the achievement of these objectives.

The following chapters deal with the more specific legislative measures taken within the EU to liberalize its network-bound energy markets and to promote competition.

Part II

THE ESTABLISHMENT OF A LEGAL FRAMEWORK

3

ACHIEVING AN INTERNAL ENERGY MARKET THROUGH LEGISLATION: PHASE ONE (1988–1995)

The prime objective will be to liberalise the internal market for electricity and natural gas.

The European Commission[1]

A. Introduction

A major aim of the Commission's programme of energy market liberalization was to secure for the large industrial consumers of gas and electricity (aluminium, steel, glass, and chemical companies) the right to purchase supplies of gas and electricity from any point of sale in the European Community. The thrust of this—internal energy market—programme was to provide them with greater choice of supply, on the assumption that such freedom of choice would lead to a reduction in the prices that they pay for energy and ultimately to lower prices for end-products.[2] In terms of policy, the origin of the Commission's rôle as catalyst **3.01**

[1] 'An Energy Policy for the European Union: White Paper', COM (1995) 682, 4.2.2, para (52).

[2] See, eg, the conclusion to the Commission 1988 working document 1988 (para 17): 'The Commission's evaluation is that the major direct benefits of third-party access would accrue to very large gas users, although there is a potential for small electricity consumers to benefit indirectly from

for change lay primarily in the complaints made to the Commission by large consumers about the prices they were obliged to pay for gas supplies. An important element in the Commission's justification for taking action was that, at the national level there appeared to be significant vested interests that would discourage governments and consumers from taking action on their own initiative. The issue of consumer choice was clearly an important one, not least because energy-intensive users employed about 15 million people compared with the one million directly employed by the energy utilities.[3] Yet, for a period of almost nine years from 1988 to 1997, the Commission had to wrestle with strong opposition to concretize its proposals—falling far short of its original timetable.

3.02 This chapter examines the legislative measures proposed by the Commission during the period from 1989 to the end of 1995. It was a period characterized by intense and controversial discussions between the parties on possible compromises. The measures may be distinguished into two groups:.

1. Four Directives aimed at codifying and clarifying existing practices by the incumbent players, making only minor changes in the direction of greater transparency and non-discrimination. They were proposed and adopted during this period and addressed 3 distinct sets of issues: transparency of prices for industrial users of electricity and gas; transit of electricity and gas;, and conditions for award of licences for exploration and production of hydrocarbons resources.
2. Two Directives on common rules for an internal market in electricity and gas, also proposed during this period. The inclusion in these Directives of a requirement to provide network access to third parties was so controversial that their adoption was politically impossible during this period and they were only adopted in a very modified form in 1996–97.

3.03 This first phase of the Commission's programme of legislative change[4] was characterized above all by a single important failure: its inability to secure agreement among the Member States on a measure to bring about third-party access to EU networks in electricity and gas. The legislative procedure for all of the proposals was deliberately a consensus-building one, based upon on Article 95* of the

---

the competitive pricing of gas to combined cycle power generators. Medium-sized industrial companies which could not themselves purchase direct might nevertheless form purchasing consortia or buy through independent gas marketers or traders.'

[3] Figure cited in paper on 'Advantages of Third-party access', Balocco, F, a consumer representative, at conference on the 'European Gas Market after Third-Party Access', Maastricht, 23–4 Nov 1992.

[4] The differentiation adopted by the Commission was more elaborate. From 1991 onwards, the European Commission distinguished three stages in its strategy for the Internal Energy Market Programme: access measures comprising the second stage and a further stage envisaged with objectives shaped by the experiences of the previous two stages. This approach was dictated by political considerations below. Not only was its timetable not adhered to, but the classification of measures and events that it implied is not a helpful guide to subsequent legislative events.

Treaty. The irony of this choice is that the Commission repeatedly stated that it already had powers under the Treaty to take action to achieve its objectives, primarily under Articles 31* and 86.* However, instead of relying on its existing powers (as yet untested in the energy sector)[5], it embarked on a programme of secondary legislation. This also committed the Commission to a potentially lengthy process of consultation and negotiation with affected parties and Member States over which it had limited control. The choice did however disarm, to some extent, the widely voiced criticism that in failing to consult interested partners the Commission was acting undemocratically.

This chapter describes and analyses three distinct but interrelated processes. **3.04**

1. *Provisions of the 4 Directives adopted between 1990–1994.*[6] On the whole, these represented a consolidation or codification of existing practice at that time rather than wholly new initiatives in the direction of an internal energy market. Much, but not all, of the controversy that they created was in practice about the next steps that they prepared the way for, rather than specific measures that they sought to introduce.
2. *Evolution of 2 more ambitious instruments, aimed at the liberalization of the electricity and gas sectors*, and their networks especially. During this period the draft proposals for Directives providing common rules for the 2 sectors evolved considerably in a context of acrimony and strident opposition from the respective industries. The final versions of the two Directives are considered in Chapter 4, dealing with events after 1995.
3. *Issues of legality concerning the Commission's choices of procedure.* These concerned *inter alia* the use of Art 86 as a base for the 2 Directives and the rôle of the Commission's existing powers under primary EC law. Table 3.1 chronologically lists the principal developments.

B. The 'Consolidation' Directives

(1) Price Transparency

Transparency in energy pricing to industrial end-users is 'essential to the achievement and smooth functioning of the internal energy market'.[7] It acts to reinforce **3.05**

[5] See Chapter 5, paras 5.01–5.02.

[6] The proposals for Directives on price transparency and transit of natural gas and electricity were introduced in July 1989 (COM (1989) 332; COM (1989) 334, and COM (336) respectively). The proposal for a Directive on hydrocarbons licensing was not introduced until 1992 (COM (1992) 110). A draft regulation on the notification of investment projects in the petroleum, natural gas, and electricity sectors was withdrawn, following strong opposition (COM (1989) 335).

[7] Recital 5, Council Directive (EEC) 90/377 on a Community procedure to improve the transparency of gas and electricity prices charged to industrial end-users; [1990] OJ L 185/16.

Table 3.1 Key Events in the Evolution of the IEM 1988–1996

Date	Instrument or subject	Event
May 1988	IEM Working Paper	Published
July 1989	Package of 4 proposals on price transparency, notification of investments, and transit	Published
29 June 1990	Price Transparency Directive	Adopted
17 Sept 1990	Procurement Directive	Adopted
29 Oct 1990	Transit Directive (Electricity)	Adopted
31 May 1991	Transit Directive (Gas)	Adopted
July 1991	Common Rules for Electricity and Gas	First Proposals
Aug 1991	Import/export monopolies	Infringement proceedings commenced
14 June 1993	WETT Directive	Adopted
17 Nov 1993	Common Rules for Electricity and Gas	Counter-proposal by Parliament
Dec 1993	Common Rules for Electricity and Gas	Amended proposals presented by Commission
Jan 1994	Energy monopolies of 5 Member States	Commission refers cases to ECJ
30 May 1994	Hydrocarbons Licensing Directive	Adopted
Late 1994–1995	French Single Buyer proposal	Discussion
25 July 1996	Electricity Directive	Common position reached

the conditions that prevent the distortion of competition. The Commission therefore drew up and introduced a Directive to provide it with a legal basis to obtain access to the necessary information on prices to final consumers. The Price Transparency Directive[8]—based on Article 284* of the EEC Treaty[9]—is the result of this. It was adopted on 29 June 1990.

Amended by Council Directive (EEC) 90/653 of 4 Dec 1990 laying down amendments for the purpose of implementing in Germany certain Community Directives on statistics on carriage of goods and gas and electricity prices [1990] OJ L 353/46; and Commission Directive (EEC) 93/87 amending Directive (EEC) 90/377 on survey locations and regions of the Federal Republic of Germany [1993] OJ L 277/32. See also the Act of Accession to the EU by Austria, Finland, and Sweden.

[8] The Directive is concerned with both natural gas and manufactured gas. The latter is defined as 'a derived energy, manufactured from coal, petroleum products, or cracked, reformed, or blended natural gas'. The scope of the Directive does not extend to liquefied petroleum gas (butane, propane), coke-oven gas, or blast furnace gas.

[9] EEC Treaty, Article 213 reads: 'The Commission may, within the limits and under conditions laid down by the Council in accordance with the provisions of this Treaty, collect any information and carry out any checks required for the performance of the tasks entrusted to it.'

(a) Objectives

The Directive was considered necessary to enable industrial end-users to identify the most competitive producers and suppliers and thus to negotiate more effectively their contracts with suppliers. There is a wide variation among Member States in the pricing practices for those industrial consumers that are reliant upon pre-set tariffs or are subject to special contractual rates. Without transparency the prices may contain elements of state aid unauthorized by the Commission and may cover up anti-competitive practices by undertakings in breach of Community rules on competition.[10] The variation in transparency from one energy source and one Community country or region to another was seen to be a threat to the achievement of an internal energy market.[11] **3.06**

Member States must take whatever steps are necessary to ensure that undertakings which supply gas or electricity to industrial end-users will communicate information on the prices and terms of sale to the Statistical Office of the European Communities (SOEC) periodically.[12] Three kinds of information are required, covering prices,[13] pricing systems,[14] and breakdowns of consumers and consumption volumes by category of consumption to ensure that these categories were representative at the national level.[15] Prices must relate to specific locations such as major cities or regions.[16] The undertakings compile the data on price and pricing systems twice a year and send it to the SOEC and the competent authorities of the Member States within two months.[17] The SOEC uses the data as a basis for twice-yearly publications of prices for industrial users and the pricing systems used.[18]

There were several policy assumptions guiding the Directive. They included the following: **3.07**

- the introduction of transparency should not breach the confidentiality of contracts since the prices paid by industry for the energy it uses have an influence upon on its competitiveness[19]
- data supplied to the SOEC would be more reliable to the extent that it is compiled by the undertakings themselves,[20] and

[10] Council Directive, n 7 above, Recital 5.
[11] ibid, Recital 7.
[12] ibid, Art 1.
[13] ibid, Art 1(1).
[14] ibid, Art 1(2).
[15] ibid, Art 1(3).
[16] ibid, Annex I, Item 11; Annex II, Item 1(2).
[17] ibid, Art 2(1).
[18] ibid, Art 2(2).
[19] ibid, Recitals 8, 9, and 11.
[20] ibid, Recital 17.

- the system of standard consumers and market prices (for electricity) would provide a degree of representativeness in pricing information that would benefit consumers.[21]

In addition, some familiarity with the fiscal and para-fiscal arrangements in each State was deemed necessary to ensure the kind of price transparency as intended by the Directive. Finally, the text notes that the Treaty's competition rules still apply to undertakings that supply gas and electricity as well as industrial gas and electricity consumers, independently of the application of the Directive.[22] The Commission therefore has powers to require communication of prices and conditions of sale, independently of the Directive.

(b) Submission of data

3.08 Information on breakdowns of consumers and the corresponding volumes sold for each category of consumer must be sent every two years to the SOEC and the competent authorities of the Member States, with 1 January as the date of reporting. With these breakdowns, the SOEC is able to ensure that the end-user categories were representative at the national level for each Member State. The Directive does not call for publication of the data supplied under this heading, which is governed by rules on commercial confidentiality.[23] In this way, individual commercial transactions may not be identified.[24] For a price to be published there must be at least three consumers in a particular consumption category. In the Annex on electricity, this is expressly referred to as a 'marker price' for certain categories of consumers. The data enables the SOEC to calculate the weighted average prices and the national and Community price indices—which may be published.[25]

3.09 The SOEC may ask the national bodies to allow it to inspect the appropriate disaggregated data as well as the methods of calculation or evaluation on which the aggregated data are based. This is triggered by the detection of statistically significant anomalies or inconsistencies in data transmitted under the Directive. The aim is to assess or amend any information that is deemed irregular.[26] The Directive also requires that the rates and methods of calculating taxes, including national, regional, and local taxes levied on gas and electricity sales to the consumer must be reported to the SOEC.[27] The special circumstances of the emerging gas markets

[21] ibid, Recital 9.

[22] ibid, Recital 13.

[23] ibid, Annex I, para (20) (gas); Annex II, para (19) (electricity).

[24] 17th Report from the Select Committee on the European Communities, Session 1992–93, 'Structure of the Single Market for Energy', House of Lords Paper 56, 47 (Testimony of Argyris, N, Director, Energy Directorate, European Commission).

[25] Council Directive, n 7 above, Annex II, Part II.

[26] ibid, Art 5.

[27] ibid, Annex I, para (17); Annex II, para (9).

in Portugal and Greece were recognized by postponing application of the Directive for a five-year period after the introduction of natural gas into those national markets.[28]

In practice, prices have been broken down into seven categories of consumer, and for each category, prices are given nine times: three in national currency, three for a purchasing power standard, and three in ECUs.[29] For each series the price is indicated with tax, without VAT, and without taxes altogether. Prices, all per GJ, are given for a number of different cities in each Member State. The data indicate 'geographical price differentials' which may arise from a combination of five factors: **3.10**

(i) differences in taxation and other levies;
(ii) tariff policy;
(iii) differences in costs (fixed and variable);
(iv) other subsidies not energy-related, such as those paid to support other public services like public transport; and
(vi) efficiency of economic operation.[30]

The data also highlight specific countries and cities that have relatively high 'price ratios' between small and large industrial consumers.

Details about the form, content, and other aspects of the information to be provided under Article 1 are the subject of two Annexes to the Directive. For example, in cases where one or more regions are served by more than one gas or electricity company, the data has to be communicated by an independent statistical body.[31] Changes may be made to the Annexes in the light of specific problems identified by the Commission. However, Article 6 makes it clear that such changes may cover only the technical features of the Annexes and are not to have the effect of altering the overall structure of the system. In making such changes, the Commission must be assisted by a committee of an advisory nature composed of representatives of the Member States and chaired by the representative of the Commission.[32] Otherwise, Article 8 requires that the Commission present **3.11**

[28] ibid, Art 9 and Recital 23. The first gas was imported into Greece in November 1996 and into Portugal in January 1997.

[29] See Eurostat (Community Statistics Office) 'Rapid Reports: Energy and Industry' (1992) No. 4. The summaries are of prices in force as at 1 July 1991. This information was provided to it under the Price Transparency Directive. Since 1995, the data have appeared in the 'Statistics in Focus' series.

[30] Commission of the European Communities, 'A Report from the Commission to the Council, the European Parliament and the Economic and Social Committee on the Operation of Directive (EEC) 90/377', COM (93) 666 final.

[31] Annex I, para (19); Annex II, para (11). Annex 2, para (18) also requires that, where there is more than one electricity utility, these utilities shall each provide marker prices and related information to an independent statistical body.

[32] ibid, 7.

a summary report once a year on the operation of the Directive to the Council, the European Parliament, and the Economic and Social Committee.

(c) Implementation

3.12 Some operational difficulties have arisen in applying the provisions of the Directive.[33] A review found that the data on prices provided by Member States has been unreliable and insufficiently representative. The breakdown referred to in Article 1(3) was a new requirement for information introduced by the Directive, not sought previously. It has been a source of difficulty for some Member States which have a limited disaggregation of existing consumer data. In the electricity sector, there was difficulty in defining the demand characteristics of the notional consumer to which the marker price applies and a risk that the marker prices would not reflect the prices actually charged. In particular, the data on gas prices to the largest customers had actually become less, rather than more transparent since the Directive came into operation. The use of the exemption on the grounds of commercial confidentiality has become in many cases the rule, to the detriment of information supply. This has been especially evident in cases where liberalization of a national electricity or gas industry has produced a proliferation of suppliers and a fragmented market. In such cases, the number of transactions with different suppliers in a given region is increased, making it difficult to find three consumers supplied by the same distributor. Three consumers must be identified in a given category to lift the exemption on confidentiality grounds and publish the corresponding price. Price notifications have fallen from these locations (eg, in the UK). An official report has concluded that:

> the publication of prices provided for by the Directive . . . does not seem capable, on its own, of bringing about any significant convergence of prices until the grid-based energy markets are opened up to competition.[34]

However, it may be argued that the Directive has, by publicizing price data, encouraged consumers at border areas to shop around for supplies.

---

[33] European Commission, 'A Report from the Commission to the Council, the European Parliament and the Economic and Social Committee on the Operation of Council Directive 90/377/EEC on a Community procedure to improve the transparency of gas and electricity prices charged to industrial end-users', COM (1996) 92 final 15/3/1996. The Directive has been implemented by all Member States, either by statute or by means of an agreement between Government and the affected parties (eg, in Finland, Germany, and The Netherlands).

[34] ibid, 7.However, following the adoption and implementation of the Electricity Directive a downward trend in electricity prices became apparent in both domestic and industrial sectors: Eurostat, Statistics in Focus, Equipment and Energy, No X: 'Electricity prices for EU industry on 1 January 2000: downward trend', and No Y: 'Electricity prices for EU households on 1 January 2000: downward trend'.

(d) Comment

The Directive's requirements also apply to Norway, following adoption through the provisions of the EEA Agreement.[35] In practice, only Norway is under an obligation to submit data on energy pricing to the SOEC, since both Iceland and Liechtenstein are exempted. The Directive is also relevant to the countries of Central and Eastern Europe, since the Commission's White Paper on approximation of the legislation on energy provides for the application of the most important Community energy legislation to these countries.[36] The Price Transparency Directive is one of the key measures mentioned in that White Paper, and is a part of the *acquis communautaire* in energy. **3.13**

Council Recommendations on electricity and gas tariff structures and prices **3.14**
The Directive was not the Commission's first intervention in energy pricing. Two Council Recommendations were adopted on electricity tariff structures and natural gas prices and tariffs respectively in 1981 and 1983.[37] Both Recommendations were based on Article 308 of the EC Treaty, which allows the Council to take 'appropriate measures' if action by the Community would be necessary to attain one of the objectives of the Community and where the Treaty has not provided the necessary powers. Each recommendation confines itself to setting out common principles on which the pricing and tariff structures should be based, and to emphasizing that prices on the market should be characterized by the greatest possible degree of transparency. However, they have no binding force, and were designed only to encourage Member States to adopt a certain approach, without imposing it on them by binding acts.

(2) Energy Transit

Transit of electricity and gas between grids and systems has long been a feature of intra-Community energy trade. Gas transit in particular has been considerable due to the separation between the centres of production and consumption—with many of the former located outside the EU. However, increased transfers between systems were thought likely to minimize the cost of investment, and of fuels in the case of electricity generation and transmission. **3.15**

[35] EEA Agreement, Annex 21, point 26.

[36] European Commission, 'Preparation of the Associated Countries of Central and Eastern Europe for Integration into the Internal Market of the Union', COM (1995) 163 final.

[37] Council Recommendation (EEC) 81/924 on electricity tariff structures in the Community, and Council Recommendation 83/230/EEC on methods of forming natural gas prices and tariffs in the Community. The Recommendations were reviewed by independent consultants in 1996 and 1997 and the Council resolved in 1998 not to repeal them. The conformity of EU electricity tariff structures with the Recommendation of 1981 was examined in chapter 4 of 'Electricity tariff structures in the EU Member States', a study commissioned by Eurelectric, *Unipede*, Paris, 1996.

Intra-Community trade in electricity has been relatively modest. The Transit Directives represented first steps towards changing this situation, although neither was designed to bring about a form of third-party access. The definition of 'transit' was also narrow. It related only to transportation of electricity or gas between the owners/operators of transmission lines.

3.16 It is notable that discussions about the gas transit proposal were longer and considerably more acrimonious than discussions on the Electricity proposal. In the end, however, both Directives were adopted also with certain modifications by the contracting parties to the EEA Agreement.

(a) Electricity

3.17 The Electricity Transit Directive[38] relates to transit of electricity between Member States through the high-voltage transmission grids that contribute to the operation of European high-voltage interconnections. Its aim is to remove obstacles to the cross-border exchange of electricity through these grids. Member States must 'take the measures necessary to facilitate transit of electricity'[39] but are not obliged to take measures to *compel* transit.

3.18 (i) **The Rules** *'Transit'.* Transit consists of any transaction for the transport of electricity where transmission is carried out by the entity or entities responsible in each Member State for a high-voltage electricity grid in a Member State's territory. These entities and grids are listed in an Annex to the Directive, which can be updated from time to time by a decision of the Commission after consultation with the relevant Member State.[40] Transit covers transactions in which the grid originates, or where transactions have their final destination in the Community—if at least one intra-Community border is crossed. It expressly excludes electricity distribution grids from its scope.[41]

The Directive requires that contracts involving electricity transit should be negotiated between the entities responsible for the relevant grids and for the quality of service provided.[42] Where appropriate, contracts must be negotiated with

---

[38] Council Directive (EEC) 90/547 on the transit of electricity through transmission grids [1990] OJ L 313/30, as amended by Directives (EC) 94/559, [1994] OJ L 214, and (EC) 95/162, [1995] OJ L 107

[39] ibid, Art 1.

[40] Commission Decisions (EC) 94/559 and (EC) 95/162, [1995] OJ L 107/53; Commission Directive (EC) 98/75, OJ L 276/9 (list updated due to mergers of entities and/or creation of independent grid companies in Denmark, Finland, Germany, and Portugal as well as the request from Luxembourg to include a second high-voltage transmission grid). The list of entities and grids covered by the Directive under the EEA Agreement is contained in Annex IV, Appendix 2, of that Agreement, applicable to Norway, Iceland, and Liechtenstein.

[41] EEA Agreement, Annex IV, Appendix 2, Art 2(1)(a).

[42] ibid, Art 3(1).

the entities in the Member States responsible for importing and exporting electricity.

Conditions for transit must be non-discriminatory and fair for all parties. They should not include unfair clauses or unjustified restrictions and must endanger neither the security of supply nor the quality of service, taking fully into account the utilization of reserve production capacity and the most efficient operation of the existing systems.[43] A reporting system is set up to assist the Commission and relevant national authorities in monitoring the negotiation and conclusion (or otherwise) of transit contracts.[44] The entities listed in the Annex must notify, without delay, requests for transit to the Commission and national authorities when they involve contracts for the sale of electricity of a minimum of one year's duration.[45] This represents a significant difference from the Gas Transit Directive, which contains no such time-limit on contracts to trigger the transit obligations. **3.19**

(ii) **Implementation** Member States must take the necessary measures to ensure that the entities in their jurisdiction act without delay to open negotiations on the conditions of the electricity transit in cases of dispute over the transit terms in a request. The Commission and relevant national authorities must be informed of the conclusion of a transit contract or, alternatively, be informed of the reasons for the failure of the negotiations to result in the conclusion of a contract within 12 months following communication of the request. It may be noted that the Directive does not confer rights of access upon electricity generators, suppliers, or consumers. **3.20**

The Directive provides for optional conciliation procedures. Each entity may request that the conditions of transit be subject to conciliation by a body set up and chaired by the Commission.[46] The entities responsible for the grids must be represented bodies. The Commission may also act on a complaint from the requesting body or on its own initiative if the absence of an agreement on a transit request is supported by reasons that are 'unjustified or insufficient'. **3.21**

(a) Conciliation committee. The body specified in Article 3(4) to handle conciliation issues has since been established by a Commission Decision.[47] In March 1992 a Committee of Experts on the Transit of Electricity between Grids was set up. It is to meet in an ad hoc composition (see below) to consider any request for conciliation. The Committee's tasks are to advise the Commission on the latter's **3.22**

[43] ibid, Art 3(2).
[44] ibid, Art 3(3).
[45] ibid, Art 3(3).
[46] ibid, Art 3(4).
[47] Commission Decision (EEC) 92/167 setting up a Committee of Experts on the Transit of Electricity between Grids [1992] OJ L 74/43, amended by Decision (EC) 97/559, OJ L 230/18, and Decision (EC) 98/559, OJ L 268/39.

request and to propose conciliation compromises at the request of the negotiating parties in the event of specific requests for transit.[48]

The rôle of the Committee in conciliation matters is set out in Article 8 of the Decision. A transit matter may only be referred to it by the parties to a dispute relating to a specific request for transit. Any conciliation request must be acted upon. The composition of the Committee for conciliation purposes is to comprise a chairman and six members, from whom a Rapporteur is to be designated by the Committee. There are to be three representatives from the grids not involved in the negotiations on the specific request for transit for which conciliation has been requested. Those representatives are to be chosen by and from the 12 (now 15) representatives of the grids that are members of the Committee. Two experts chosen by and from the three experts must be members of the Committee. Finally, the Committee must include a representative from the electricity association, Eurelectric. The chairman has no voting rights. Representatives from the Member States concerned by a request for transit may take part in the conciliation procedure in the capacity of observers.

3.23 *(b) Conciliation procedure.* The first step in the conciliation proceedings is for the Chairman to invite the representatives of the grids involved in the negotiations on the specific request for transit to present their points of view. Subsequently, a discussion takes place between the Committee and the Rapporteur who will formulate a compromise which is likely to attract a consensus among the full Committee. In the event of a disagreement, the Rapporteur formulates a conciliation compromise on which there is likely to be agreement among a majority of the five other members. In such cases, the opinions of the minority are placed on record. Next, the chairman submits the compromise to the parties, along with any minority opinions, within three months of the date on which the request for conciliation by the Committee was submitted.

Most importantly, the outcome of the conciliation procedure does not have binding legal force.[49] The exact operation of these powers and procedures has not become clear in the absence of a referral of a transit contract or request for transit.

3.24 *(c) Conciliation committees: trade between EFTA States and Community.* Conciliation procedure differs if it concerns the conditions of transit of electricity between an EFTA State and the Community.[50] In such cases, when an entity

[48] ibid, Art 2.

[49] ibid, Art 8(9)

[50] EEA Agreement, Annex IV, Appendix 4 (inserted by Commission Decision 167/1999).

requests conciliation, a conciliation committee is set up on an ad hoc basis on the initiative of the European Commission or the EFTA Surveillance Authority. That committee must propose conciliation compromises at the request of the negotiating parties. The committee comprises eight members from four categories:

- three representatives of high-voltage grids not involved in the negotiations relating to the specific request for transit on which conciliation has been requested, selected from the 15 representatives of the grids that are members of the Committee of Experts established under the Commission Decision of 1992, and 3 representatives of the high-voltage grids in the EFTA States, as proposed by the EFTA Surveillance Authority;
- one representative of the European Commission and one representative of the EFTA Surveillance Authority;
- two independent experts, one from the Community and one from an EFTA State;
- one representative from Eurelectric or Nordel.

(iii) Comment The Council approved the Electricity Transit Directive in less than 12 months.[51] It had to be implemented by Member States no later than 1 July 1991 under the terms of Article 5. The preferred methods of implementation varied from statute to agreement. In the case of Great Britain (not including Northern Ireland), for example, it was implemented by amending the licences of the National Grid Company, Scottish Power and Scottish Electricity. Similarly, in Denmark, the Minister of Energy modified the licences of Elsam and Elkraft instead of amending existing legislation. 3.25

The Directive would no longer be necessary if the electricity market were fully liberalized. The Commission's proposal for amending the Electricity and Gas Directives contains a provision for repeal of the Directive (see ch 8).

(b) Natural gas

The Gas Transit Directive[52] establishes a régime similar to that set up under the Electricity Transit Directive. It requires Member States to take the measures necessary to facilitate transit of natural gas between high-pressure transmission grids in accordance with the conditions set out in the Directive.[53] Its essential features are that: 3.26

---

[51] Council Directive (EEC) 90/547 on the transit of electricity through transmission grids; [1992] OJ L 74/43, as amended by Directive (EC) 94/559, OJ L 214, and Directive (EC) 95/162, OJ L 107.

[52] Council Directive (EEC) 91/296 on the transit of natural gas through grids OJ L 147/37, as amended by Directive (EC) 94/49, OJ L 295, and Directive (EC) 95/49 OJ L 233 updating list of entities covered by Directive (EEC) 91/296 on the transit of natural gas through grids.

[53] ibid, Art 1.

- it applies to transportation of gas between and not within Member States;[54]
- limited rights are granted only to major gas companies which are themselves owners of high-pressure transmission pipelines;
- all conditions of transit must be fair and equitable; and
- the Commission and national competition authorities must be informed if the negotiations for transit fail.

3.27 The overall aim is to facilitate the free circulation of gas between the transmission system owners of the Member States. Despite these rather modest objectives, the measure took almost two years to move from proposal to adoption in a process characterized by considerable acrimony.

3.28 (i) **Rules** The core provisions are contained in Articles 2, 3, and 4. Article 2.1 defines the type of gas transmission contract to which the Directive applies. These are contracts for the 'transit of natural gas between grids' which fulfil the following conditions:

1. The transmission must be carried out by the entity or entities in each Member State with responsibility for high-pressure natural gas grids (excluding distribution grids) in a Member State's territory that contribute to the efficient operation of European high-pressure interconnections. These entities are listed in an Annex to the Directive;[55]
2. the grid of origin or final destination must be situated in the Community; and
3. the transport of gas involves the crossing of at least one intra-Community frontier.

3.29 Article 3 stipulates that the contracts for transit between grids must be negotiated between the entities listed in the Annex and, where appropriate, with the entities responsible in the Member States for importing and exporting natural gas. The financial, technical, and legal conditions of a transit contract must be worked out by the parties themselves but be based upon the rules of the EEC Treaty. The rules must be non-discriminatory and fair for all parties concerned. They must not include unfair clauses or unjustified restrictions and must not endanger security of supply or quality of service. On the latter, they should take full account of the utilization of reserve production and storage capacity as well as the most efficient operation of existing systems.

Under Article 3.3 each Member State must take the measures necessary to implement the Directive. These comprise four measures necessary to impose specified

[54] However, the Transit Directive would seem to apply that, if there are two transit undertakings, A and B, in the same state (eg, Germany), in order for A to supply gas to a transit undertaking in another Member State, the gas must be transported through B's line.

[55] Council Directive, n 52 above, Art 2.2. The Commission may update this list as necessary on consulting the relevant Member State.

obligations on the entities listed in the Annex for which the Member State is responsible, namely to:

1. notify the Commission and relevant national authorities of any request for transit;
2. open negotiations on the conditions of the natural gas transit that have been requested;
3. inform the Commission and relevant national authorities when a transit contract has been concluded; and
4. inform the Commission and relevant national authorities of the reasons for the failure of negotiations to result in the conclusion of a transit contract within 12 months following communication of the request for transit.

Either party in the negotiations is given a right to request that the conditions of transit are made the subject of a conciliation procedure. That would take place before a body set up and chaired by the Commission, and on which the entities specified in the Annex must be represented. Again, it may be noted that the result of this procedure does not produce a legally-binding effect.[56] The Committee of Experts is discussed below (paras 3.31–3.33).

Article 4 states that should the reasons for the absence (of transit) appear unjustified or insufficient, the Commission, acting either on a complaint from the entity that requested it or at its own initiative, must implement the procedures provided for by Community law (ie primarily to begin an investigation under Article 81*).[57] This provision and that in Article 3.3 are intended to facilitate the work of the Commission and the national competition authorities in pursuing investigations of possible abuses of dominant positions by the listed entities. **3.30**

(ii) Implementation The Directive was approved by the Council on 31 May 1991, and has been extended to the members of the EEA. A Committee of Experts (the Committee) was set up subsequently.[58] Its tasks are to advise the Commission, at the latter's request and propose conciliation compromises, at the request of the negotiating parties, in the event of specific requests for transit. In particular, the Committee is charged with examining the technical, financial and legal conditions of transit, taking into account economic and social factors, as well as the possibilities for co-operation on transit with entities in the Community, operating grids not interconnected as yet or not figuring on the list annexed to the Directive 91/296/EEC, and the improvement of trans-European networks. Finally, it must determine the possibilities for co-operation on transit with entities **3.31**

[56] ibid, Recital 22.
[57] ibid, Art 4.
[58] Decision (EC) 95/539 [1995] OJ L 304/57, amended by Decision (EC) 98/285 OJ L 128/7. The members' 4-year terms were renewed in Oct 2000.

in non-Member States and, when appropriate assist the Commission in the drafting of an annual report on the implementation of the above Directive and in the revision of its Annex.

3.32 *(a) Conciliation committee* Membership of the Committee comprises 15 representatives of the high-pressure natural gas transmission grids operating in the European Union (one representative per Member State); three independent experts whose professional experience and competence in the field of natural gas transit in the Community are widely recognized; one representative from Eurogas and one Commission representative. The Commission appoints the 20 members, with a term of office of four years, renewable once. The Committee has met annually since its establishment.

A dispute may only be referred to the Committee by the parties to a dispute relating to a specific request for transit. In such cases, the Committee must meet in an ad hoc composition (comprising the chairman and 6 members chosen from the members of the Committee)—to consider a request for conciliation. The six chosen are to include the Eurogas representative, two of the three experts, and three representatives of the high-pressure natural gas transmission grids not involved in the negotiations relating to the specific request for transit on which conciliation has been requested. Any conciliation request must be acted upon.

3.33 *(b) Conciliation procedure* The procedure of the transmission grids involved in the negotiations on a specific request for transit on which conciliation has been requested are invited to present their points of view. After discussion, a conciliation compromise is formulated on which there is likely to be a consensus among the members of the Committee, or failing that, among a majority of the members. The compromise must be submitted to the parties within three months of the date on which the request for conciliation was submitted. The outcome of the conciliation procedure is not binding. Indeed, both the procedure and the outcome of any conciliation are 'without prejudice to application of Community law, including in particular, the competition rules'.[59]

3.34 **(iii) Comment** The scope of application of the Directive is narrower than its title implies. In fact, the Directive provides for a system of obligation and monitoring of transit rather than a grant of transit rights. Transit relates only to transportation between high-pressure natural gas transmission grids and to the entities responsible for them, and for the quality of service they provide.[60] It is

[59] ibid, Art 8 (9).

[60] The list of entities named in the Annex has been modified twice, once in 1994 and again in 1995 by (EEC) 95/49. In the first case, the revisions took into account changes in the Italian gas industry and the impact of German unification: the number of German entities on the list was reduced from 29 to 16. The second Directive took into account a reorganization of the Spanish gas industry and added the appropriate entities from the 3 new Member States: for Austria, the entity

not concerned with transit on behalf of major industrial energy users, still less with the issue of a general third-party right of access to pipelines between and within Member States. In the case of most Member States, the entities are the company or companies that have the exclusive right of transmission of gas such as Gaz de France, Dangas and Enagas-Gas Natural.

Because of the special nature of the German gas market where a large number of companies are involved in gas transmission, the number of companies is greater there. Although the major industrial energy users have no rights under the Directive, this would not preclude such users from exercising their rights under Article 81* against an entity that is responsible for a high-pressure transmission grid for failure to allow the user access to its pipelines for purposes of transit. In this context, it may be noted that Recital 20 states that 'the conditions of transit should not bring about, directly or indirectly, conditions contrary to Community competition rules'.

The final text differs in some respects from the Commission's earlier proposals, not least due to advice tendered by the European Parliament. The most significant differences are that for the Directive to be applicable, the grid of origin or final destination must be situated within the Community and there must be transportation of the gas across one intra-Community frontier.[61] Another difference is the inclusion of a right to require conciliation in the event of failure to agree terms of transit.[62] The Energy Commissioner delivered a verbal undertaking to the Council that the measure was not envisaged as a first step towards the introduction of network access in its common carrier form.[63] This was not sufficient to prevent negative votes from Germany, The Netherlands, and Denmark but, under the QMV procedure, these votes were not sufficient to block the Directive. **3.35**

named is ÖMV Aktiengesellschaft; for Finland, Neste Oy and for Sweden, Vattenfall Naturgas AB and Sydgas. The second list came into force on 31 December 1995. The entities on the list may not be amended by the Commission until the Member States directly concerned have been consulted (see Note to the Council (n 63)). In the event of disagreement, the body referred to in Art 3(4) will be asked to deliver an opinion.

[61] Council Directive, n 52 above, Art 2.1 (b) and (c).

[62] ibid, Art 3.4.

[63] In a Note from the General Secretariat of the Council, dated 14 May 1990, on, *inter alia*, the proceedings of Permanent Representatives Meetings on this matter earlier in May, the Commission representative is recorded as stating that the draft under discussion 'concerned transit alone' and 'could in no circumstances lead to the introduction of the common carrier system'; further, the 'complementary conditions governing the procedure for administering transit' could apply to 'transit' only and 'could in no circumstances refer to the "common carrier" system'; ENER 33/6341/90. In a Protocol Declaration of the European Commission dated 20 Dec 1990, it is stated that: 'The Commission declares that the sole objective of this Directive is to facilitate transit as defined by Articles 2 and 3 and is under no circumstances to be interpreted as the legal basis for permitting free grid access' (cited by Eckert, Lutz K. in 'Natural Gas in Europe', paper presented to the International Bar Association, Business Law, 7th Biennial Conference, Oct 1993, 15).

Opposition to the Directive was based largely on the assumption that it was a first step to the introduction of TPA.[64]

3.36 The notion of 'transit' in the Directive contrasts with that found in the Energy Charter Treaty (ECT) to which the EC and its Member States are parties.[65] In essence, transit under the ECT involves the passage of Energy Materials and Products (including oil, gas, and electricity) across the area of a signatory state from or to another state at least one of which is a signatory state. Article 7 requires signatory states to facilitate transit and requires them to take measures to enable access to transit lines/pipelines for electricity and gas on non-discriminatory terms. As mentioned previously (see ch 2, paras 2.120–2.122), the provisions will be considerably strengthened as and when the Transit Protocol is signed and then ratified by the required number of states.

This Directive will no longer be necessary when the gas market is fully liberalized. The Commission's proposal for amending the Electricity and Gas Directives contains a provision for the repeal of the Directive (see ch 8).

(3) Access to Hydrocarbons Resources

3.37 The conditions for access to and management of hydrocarbons resources were identified by the Commission as a source of potential obstacles to the integration required in a single energy market. For many years there had been widespread use of discriminatory provisions to limit access by foreign companies and a lack of transparency in licensing procedures. Landing obligations and rights of first refusal were frequently enjoyed by state monopolies in exploration and production.[66] Because of the uneven distribution of hydrocarbons resources in the Community this affected only a few of the Member States—mostly in the North Sea area. Although this use of discriminatory provisions appeared to be in decline, they were nevertheless still clearly inconsistent with the framework of rules being developed for the internal market.

To remedy this, a legal measure was proposed in 1992,[67] aimed specifically at the activities of exploration for and extraction of oil and natural gas. The 'Hydrocarbons Licensing Directive'[68] provoked controversy and heated debate but was adopted, with modifications, on 30 May 1994.

---

[64] The original proposal was outlined in a document that also discussed the possible introduction of third-party access: 'Towards Completion of the Internal Market of Natural Gas: Proposal for a Council Directive on the Transit of Gas Through Major Systems', COM (1989) 334 final.

[65] [1994] OJ L 380/3–91.

[66] See 'Internal Energy Market', COM (1988) 238 final, 42–55.

[67] COM (1992) 110 final.

[68] Directive (EC) 94/22 of the European Parliament and Council of 30 May 1994 on the conditions for granting and using authorizations for the prospection, exploration and production of hydrocarbons [1994] OJ L 164/3. This followed earlier unsuccessful attempts to address these problems through the procurement legislation.

(a) The Objectives

The principal objectives of the Directive are to set up common rules to ensure that: **3.38**

- procedures for granting authorizations to prospect or explore for and produce hydrocarbons are open to all entities that possess the necessary capabilities;[69]
- authorizations are granted on the basis of objective, published criteria; and
- the conditions under which authorizations are granted are known in advance by all entities taking part in the procedure.

Transparency and non-discrimination are the keywords of the Directive's objectives.

The Directive is based upon on a careful balance between respect for the Member States' rights based on sovereignty and the Community interest in the way in which those rights are exercised. It avoids detailed regulation in favour of the establishment of a framework of general principles to which the rules made by Member States must conform. In accordance with the principle of subsidiarity, the Member States remain free to choose or to maintain the rules that they consider most appropriate to their natural and operational circumstances, as well as their national policies on resource management. The approach taken involves the establishment of common rules but resembles the focused approach followed by the Directives on public procurement contracts rather than the broader approach of the two Directives on common rules for the electricity and natural gas sectors. **3.39**

Sovereignty The sovereignty or sovereign rights of Member States over natural resources within their territory is not directly affected by the provisions of the Directive. Member States retain their rights and responsibilities with respect to management of these resources, including revenues that arise from their development. In particular, they retain the right to decide: **3.40**

- which areas must be opened for exploration and production,[70]
- the level and the rates of tax, royalties and other revenues such as those arising from state participation,[71] and to
- select the licensees and monitor their activities.

The Directive expressly gives Member States the right to be involved both in areas of public policy, including the central one of depletion policy, and in the protection of the Member State's financial interest.[72]

---

69 ibid, Recital 11.
70 ibid, Art 2(1).
71 ibid, Art 6(2).
72 ibid, Art 6(2).

(b) Common rules

3.41 (i) **Award of licences** The procedures for applying for authorizations must be publicized. Three conditions are set out to ensure that procedures are transparent and objective:[73]

1. decisions must be based on objective, pre-established criteria, published in advance,
2. all general conditions and obligations imposed on undertakings must be established and made available to entities before applications are submitted, and
3. criteria, conditions, and obligations must be applied in a non-discriminatory way.

Procedures are permitted such as the 'concession' or licensing system (authorizations granted after the Member States have published a notice in the *Official Journal*), and the 'open door' system (authorizations granted on a permanent basis for a pre-declared territory). Individual awards are also possible.

Some examples of Member States' efforts to comply with these provisions include the following:

- *Germany* made a formal declaration in accordance with Art 3(3) stating that the entire area of Germany (except where there are individual authorizations) is available for licensing within the meaning of Art 3(3);
- *Ireland* published a notice stating that all areas of the Irish offshore are permanently available for licensing (with a large number of exceptions listed by block number); and
- *France* issued a notice defining the geographical areas available for hydrocarbons prospecting and setting out the procedure to apply for a prospecting licence.

The principles of transparency, objectivity, and non-discrimination must be met in the criteria on which decisions on applications for authorizations are made.[74] The criteria must be based on the financial and technical capability of entities and the manner in which they propose to prospect, explore, and bring into operation the area in question. They must be published in the *Official Journal.* Denmark obtained a derogation from this provision.[75]

3.42 (ii) **State participation** The aim of the provisions on state participation is to ensure that the Member State is allowed to participate in licences but is restricted

[73] ibid, Arts 3 and 4.

[74] ibid, Art 5.

[75] For new authorizations granted before 31 Dec 2012 for areas which must be relinquished on 8 July 2012 on expiry of the authorization granted on 8 July 1962. ibid, Art 13.

in such a way as to ensure that the principles set out in the Directive are respected.[76] The State has the right to participate in authorizations and thereby put into practice its sovereignty and ownership rights over resources, but it must do so in accordance with the principles of the Directive such as transparency, non-discrimination, and equality of treatment. Participants other than the State should not be subject to undue pressure. The State should not take part in decisions or have information regarding sources of procurement for entities; nor exercise majority voting rights; nor prevent management decisions from being taken on the basis of normal commercial principles. Voting by the State as participant must also be based on transparent, non-discriminatory, and objective principles. Much of the above, set out in Article 6.3, paragraph 2, was designed to meet the Danish insistence on a continued State presence in the exploration and production of hydrocarbons while ensuring that the Directive's principles are respected.

Dutch concerns that the State should be able to influence depletion policy and the **3.43**
State's financial interest led to the third paragraph of Article 6.3. The State as the public authority may also impose conditions and requirements on exercise of activities based on various public interest reasons such as public health, protection of the environment, safety of installations, or planned management of hydrocarbons resources. The final paragraph of Article 6.3 was developed to meet the demands of Norway, present as an observer in anticipation of its future accession to the EU (subsequently, thwarted by a referendum result in 1994). While rejecting a proposal to divide Statoil into two separate parts, a provision to create a division or 'Chinese Wall' between its business activities, especially with respect to information flow, proved acceptable.

This provision applies to authorizations granted after the date of application of the Directive and requires Member States to abrogate legal, regulatory, and administrative provisions reserving the right to obtain authorizations in a specific geographical area within the territory of a Member State to a single entity.[77] Such exclusive rights conflict with the principle of equal access to resources and were to be abolished by 1 January 1997. Essentially, this Article addresses a specific problem faced by Italy over authorizations held by the then State-owned entity, ENI.

The Commission must monitor the treatment of EU entities in third countries to ascertain whether they receive treatment comparable to the treatment granted to entities from the same third countries in the EU.[78] The Directive lays down a procedure for evaluating this situation and, if the need arises, for initiating negotiations with third countries to establish reciprocal rights.

[76] ibid, Art 6.
[77] ibid, Art 7.
[78] ibid, Art 8.

(c) Links to other legislation: Procurement

3.44 The Directive establishes a direct link with Directive 90/531/EEC of 17 September 1990[79] on the procurement procedures of entities operating in the water, energy, transport, and telecommunications sectors, and Directive 93/38/EEC of 14 June 1993[80] co-ordinating the procurement procedures of entities operating in the water, energy, transport, and telecommunications sectors[81] (the WETT Directive). A Member State is allowed to utilize the alternative régime of Article 3 of the former Directive or of the new Directive 93/38/EEC automatically once the Member State has implemented the Hydrocarbons Licensing Directive in its national law (ie by 1 July 1995).

3.45 Article 3 of Directive 90/531/EEC establishes new arrangements, provided for in the Directive, which in their application are subject to two conditions: that the granting of authorizations on the one hand, and public procurement on the other, shall be made under first non-discriminatory, and secondly transparent conditions. Initially, to seek an exemption an application to the Commission was required under the procurement legislation, but this requirement has been removed and Directive 90/531/EEC amended. This means that there is no longer a requirement that Member States submit a request for the application of the alternative arrangements nor that they demonstrate that their régimes involve award on a non-discriminatory, transparent basis. However, Member States failing to meet their obligations under this Directive will become subject to the general rules of Directive 90/531/EEC.

(d) Implementation

3.46 The Hydrocarbons Licensing Directive was to be implemented by Member States by 1 July 1995. Its operation was the subject of some scrutiny in 1998.[82] The conclusion then seemed to be that its provisions were being implemented correctly. Four years after its implementation, no reciprocity problem had been detected, not least because the Directive was operating in a context of progressive international opening-up of exploration and production. Neither the oil companies nor the entities in the Member States reported any discriminatory treatment and no entity had complained directly to the Commission. It seemed that all of the Member States—except Finland and Luxembourg, which have no commercial hydrocarbon deposits—had transposed the Directive into national law. Norway, acting through the EEA Agreement, has also transposed its provisions into national law.

---

79 [1992] OJ C 139/12.

80 [1993] OJ C 19/12.

81 Directive (EEC) 90/531, Art 12.

82 COM (1998) 447 final: Report from the Commission to the Council on Directive 94/22/EC on the conditions for granting and using authorizations for the prospection, exploration and production of hydrocarbons.

(e) Comment

As a result of discussions on the draft text, major modifications were made from the original proposal, especially in the areas of sovereignty (more emphasis was given to sovereignty); retroactivity (deleted); and state participation in licences (limited in scope). The retroactivity aspect concerned licences that had been awarded through procedures in which there had been no competition. It had been supported by France and Belgium but was strongly opposed by other Member States and by the oil and gas industry. The Directive was adopted after the TEU entered into force and was therefore made subject to the co-decision procedure with Parliament for the last stages of its passage. The inclusion of natural gas in the Directive (being subject to similar physical, technical, and legal conditions as oil) ensured that the proposed Directive on common rules for the natural gas sector would be more limited in scope than its counterpart for electricity. The former omitted production, while the latter included generation activities. **3.47**

The passage of the Directive offered a unique opportunity for pan-European co-operation as countries linked to the EU by the EEA participated in the development of the common rules. The participation of Norway—at that time engaged in discussions about possible membership—was of great importance to the final result. **3.48**

Essentially, liberalization of the upstream sector has brought benefits to all entities established in the EU, including subsidiaries of non-EU companies. Since the Directive was adopted, the Commission has become more active in the supervision of hydrocarbon exploration and production, especially of the competition aspects of joint venturing,[83] but also in areas of environmental competence such as the decommissioning of oil and gas installations[84] and impact assessment.[85]

C. The Evolution of Directives on Common Rules for Electricity and Gas

The Directives on price transparency and energy transit were widely seen at the time as the first steps towards the creation of an EU system of energy regulation in which the Commission, rather than the energy industry, would play the leading rôle. Although Member States supported the idea of liberalization and increasing competition in energy markets—albeit with varying degrees of enthusiasm—there was much less agreement on the appropriate mechanisms and the manner **3.49**

[83] Dinnage, J D, 'Joint Activities among Gas Producers: the Competition Man Cometh' (1998) 16 J Energy Natural Resources L 249–285.

[84] COM (1998) 49 final: Communication on the Removal and Disposal of Disused Oil and Gas Installations.

[85] Directive (EC) 97/11, Annexes II and III.

and timing of their introduction. In particular, the proposal to encourage access to electricity and gas networks by third parties provoked an unusually intense and uniform opposition from both the Member States and the principal utilities responsible for transportation and distribution. For the utilities it appeared to strike at the heart of their business operations.

Recognizing this opposition at an early stage, the Commission attached a special importance to procedural aspects of its proposals. It indicated that their introduction was to be accompanied by a very extensive process of consultation. This would encompass not only the Member States and the utilities involved, but also the various consumers and the relevant Community institutions. In building a consensus on specific measures to be taken, the Parliament played a significant rôle as a result of its increased authority under the TEU and lobbying by the energy utilities. The highly sensitive character of the proposals ensured too that the Council played a key rôle in brokering the final drafts.

3.50 However, a striking feature of the many attempts at consultation with affected parties and redrafting of the proposals was the failure to secure agreement on the key issues during this period, leading to a significant change of tactics by the Commission in 1994. Since this evolutionary process played an important rôle in determining the ultimate form and content of both Directives on electricity and gas, it is examined in some detail here. Given the complexity and duration of the process, a table is provided to illustrate key developments and dates (Table 3.1).

(1) Search for a Consensus

3.51 As early as 1989, the Commission had declared its intention to consult all interested parties to examine in depth whether third-party access (TPA) should be introduced in the EU electricity and gas networks.[86] TPA was defined rather inelegantly as:

> . . . a régime providing for an obligation, to the extent that there is capacity available, on companies operating transmission and distribution networks for electricity and gas to offer terms for the use of the grid, in particular to individual consumers or to distribution companies, in return for payment.[87]

Basing itself on initial consultations and on the results of consultants' studies,[88] the Commission opened the debate by putting forward its evaluation of the benefits of

---

[86] COM (1989) 332 final; COM (1989) 334 final.

[87] COM (1991) 548 final, 'Completion of the Internal Market in Electricity and Gas', 21 January 1992.

[88] In particular, the C and L Belmont study on the 'Advantages and Drawbacks for the European Community of the Introduction of a System of "Common Carrier" for the Transport of Natural Gas': commissioned by the Directorate General for Energy and was published in Jan 1989. A follow-up study was published in May 1989, attempting a quantitative assessment of the impact of natural gas common carriage.

TPA. With respect to natural gas, it was clearly influenced by experiences of TPA in North America and the UK. Counter-studies produced different evaluations of these experiences with the TPA mechanism.[89]

For the electricity sector, the Commission sponsored two in-depth analyses that were carried out in 1990 on the production and distribution of electricity.[90] The first of these involved a cost-benefit analysis of open access in electricity by reference to the concept of natural monopoly. The second focused on ways of giving third parties access to the network. The results provided material for the development of the proposed Directive on electricity. **3.52**

In the same year four consultative committees were established. The first two of these comprised representatives of the industries, such as the integrated utilities, the electricity generators and gas producers, distributors, transmission companies, large industrial users, and domestic and other consumers. These committees were called respectively the Professional Consultative Committee on Electricity (PCCE) and the Professional Consultative Committee on Gas (PCCG). The other two committees comprised representatives of the Member States and their alternates and were called respectively the *Comité Consultatif États Membres Électricité* (CCEME) and the *Comité Consultatif États Membres Gaz* (CCEMG). The four committees met each month throughout 1990 and during the early part of 1991.[91] **3.53**

The aim was to examine in depth over a period of one year whether third-party access to the European transportation system needed to be organized and, if so, under what conditions—in order to guarantee the maintenance of the quality of service to consumers and supply security. The Commission chaired the proceedings. In May 1991 four reports were issued,[92] making it clear that the industry and most Member States remained hostile towards the Commission's proposal to introduce **3.54**

[89] eg, a study by Jensen Associates (commissioned by Ruhrgas), 'US Open Access Gas Pipeline Transportation: A Model for Europe?' (Sept 1990), which concluded that there were 'very significant differences between gas markets in the US and in Europe that make it questionable whether the design of the US system is really relevant'. Another study carried out by the German Monopoly Commission, chaired by Professor Christian von Weizsäker, concluded that the introduction of a common carrier system would jeopardize the entire system of wholesalers that had been developed in Europe. See also the references in nn 99 and 108. At that time another option (rather than to securing access) was to construct an alternative pipeline, but in practice not all Member States allowed such a freedom to construct pipelines in their legal régimes. This was frequently noted by German commentators.

[90] European Commission, 'Annual Report on Competition Policy', (1990), para (391).

[91] 'Second Commission Progress Report on the Internal Energy Market', COM (1993) 261 final, para 4 (1).

[92] For a comprehensive discussion see Reports of the Consultative Committees on Third-party access to Natural Gas Networks and Electricity, Commission of the European Communities, Directorate-General for Energy, May 1991, (on the proceedings of the consultative committee of Member States and of the professional consultative committee).

TPA. No significant changes had been made in the parties' positions in spite of these long and intense discussions. The impasse was evident in the reports and in the position papers of several participants attached as annexes.

3.55 The reports contained a summary of the various arguments for and against the introduction of TPA. There were three main subjects of contention: the impact of TPA on pricing, on competition and efficiency, and security of supply in the EU. Some differences between the two industries began to be recognized. Although it appeared technically much easier to organize a TPA system for gas than for electricity, the gas industry had certain peculiar features that had to be considered—principally in the continental European gas industry, in dependence on sources of supply from outside the EU.

3.56 In this respect, the CCEMG Report on gas[93] highlighted the agreement of the delegates on the importance of long-term supply contracts in ensuring the security of gas supply, and their agreement on the need, if TPA were to be introduced, to ensure that regulation was kept to a minimum. It also highlighted their agreement that special measures would be required to deal with take-or-pay obligations under existing contracts and that protective measures would be needed for investments made in order to introduce or expand the use of natural gas in immature or new markets.

3.57 The arguments about TPA were reviewed at hearings on the proposed Directives convened by the European Parliament's Committee on Energy, Research and Technology (CERT). Their purpose was to provide an opportunity to members of the CERT—who together represented all shades of political opinion in the Parliament—to hear the views of a number of bodies affected by the proposed Transit Directives and also the proposals for TPA. The wide differences of opinion between the Commission and the incumbent players were clear to the Parliament.

(2) Legal Basis for Internal Market Directives

3.58 At the outset the European Commission had two possible legal bases for its proposed Directives on an internal market in electricity and gas (cf ch 5, paras 5.05–5.11). The first legal basis was Article 86(3),* which obliges the Commission to ensure the application of the provisions of this Article and, where necessary, to draw up Directives and decisions addressed to the Member States. It vests the Commission with law-making powers, so that a Directive could be made in principle without consultation with the Parliament and without the unanimous support of the Council. Alternatively, a Directive could be based upon on Article 95* under

[93] 'Report of the Proceedings of the Consultative Committee of Member States: Natural Gas Comité Consultatif États Membres Gaz (CCEMG)', Commission of the European Communities, Energy DG, May, 1991.

which the Council must adopt such measures as are appropriate to approximate provisions laid down by law, regulation, or administrative action in the Member States aimed at the establishment and functioning of the internal market. It began with the former approach.

Draft Directives were drawn up by the Commission in 1991 based on its powers under Article 86(3)* and other Articles relating to exclusive rights, such as Articles 30, 34, 37, 52, and 86.[94]* They would have required Member States to remove any exclusive or special rights for the import, export, production, supply, and marketing of electricity and natural gas. In each case potentially wide derogations were permitted with respect to security of supply (draft Art 9). **3.59**

Access to existing interconnected transmission and distribution networks was also to be promoted. Member States with exclusive or special rights for their exploitation were required to take the necessary measures to allow access on the basis of public, objective, and non-discriminatory conditions. Exclusive rights were defined as: **3.60**

> rights granted by a Member State or public authority to public or private bodies by means of an instrument laid down by law, regulation or administrative action reserving it the right to supply a service or undertake a specific activity in the whole of the market covered by the exclusivity granted.

'Special rights' were defined as: **3.61**

> rights granted by a Member State or public authority to public bodies by means of an instrument laid down by law, regulation or administrative action and which without being exclusive to the whole of the market concerned reserve the right to supply a service or undertake a specific activity in a defined area or part of the said market.

The idea seems to have been that these Directives would be complemented by two further Directives providing common rules for the regulation of the electricity and natural gas markets (see ch 5, paras 5.09–5.19). Both of these would be based on Article 95, and not the simpler and shorter procedure under Article 86(3). This choice of legal basis was heavily influenced by developments in the telecommunications sector, where Article 86(3) had been successfully used as a basis for the Telecommunications Directive on the liberalization of terminal equipment[95] and for the Directive on services.[96]

Although the Commission's power to adopt the Directives was challenged, the ECJ ruled in the Commission's favour.[97] The then Commissioner for Energy **3.62**

---

[94] The following is based on the draft Directives circulated for comment in mid-1991: European Commission Competition Directorate, Commission Directive on Competition in the Markets for Electricity; European Commission Competition Directorate, Directive on Competition in the Markets for Natural Gas.

[95] Directive (EC) 88/301, [1988] OJ L 131/73.

[96] Directive (EC) 90/388, [1990] OJ L 192/10.

[97] Case C-202/88 *France v Commission* [1991] ECR I-1223; Cases C-271, C-281, and C-289/91 *Spain, Italy and Belgium v Commission* [1992] ECR.

declared that the Commission felt 'able to prepare Directives of a general nature directed at telling Member states how they should allow exclusive rights to be exercised so as not to constitute measures contrary to the Treaty'.[98]

A major difference however lay in the fact that actions in the telecommunications sector were supported by a broad consensus between Member States, industry, and the EC institutions. By contrast, in energy the Commission's competence to initiate sweeping changes in the organization and functioning of the markets was not generally acknowledged and opposition to its proposals was strong from all sides.[99]

3.63 The Parliament and most of the Member States were strongly opposed to the use of this procedure for measures of such economic and political magnitude. It had a '*carence democratique*' (democratic deficit) that was unacceptable to virtually all parties. In the weeks before the European Council was to meet at Maastricht to discuss the draft text of the TEU, the Article 86(3)* approach was postponed and then abandoned.[100] Instead, the Commission elected to base its proposed Directives on Article 95,* which required a consensus to be reached between the Parliament and the Council. However, the possibility remained open at least in principle that if this new approach failed, the approach based on Article 86(3) powers could be revived.[101]

The approach based on Article 95 was also not free from controversy. Objections to its use centred on the respective competences of the Commission and the Member States. The Article aims at the harmonization of national rules, and so it was argued that it was unsuitable as a basis for what appeared to be an extension of Community competence into new areas, such as the establishment of a Community energy policy or at least the introduction of significant measures of deregulation. In such cases, competence lay with the Member States. There was no doubt that Article 95 empowers the Council by a qualified majority to remove national legal barriers that prevent or inhibit the creation of the internal market. It could be argued that the powers of Article 95 did not go so far as to enable the Council to require the introduction of TPA and unbundling.

[98] Cardoso e Cunha, A, 'The Internal Energy Market', in (1991) 9 J Energy Natural Resources L 290, 293.

[99] Especially in Germany: see, eg discussion by Friedrich von Burchard in 'Third Party Access and European Law', in (1992) *Europäische Zeitschrift für Wirtschaftsrecht* (EuZW), 693–697, and in 'Die Kompetenzen der EG-Kommission nach Art 90 III EWGV', (1991) 11 EuZW 339–43; Mestmäker, 'Erdgas im Europäischen Binnenmarkt', in *Die Gaswirtschaft im Binnenmarkt,* 1990 (*Wirtschaftsrecht und Wirtschaftspolitiek*), vol 109, 68; Eckert, L 'Die Vorschläge der EG-Kommission zu "Third-party access" in der Gaswirtschaft', (1992) RdE, 56.

[100] Europe Energy, 'Cardoso e Cunha plans to Table Liberalisation Package to October 29 Council', No 365, 18 Oct 1991. It appears that apart from the Competition Directorate, there was ultimately no support among the Commissioners for this approach either.

[101] *Agence Europe Presse,* 15 Oct 1991.

It seems implicit in this argument that, while the import and export constraints and the national monopolies of transmission and distribution fell within the scope of Article 95, the next step towards the completion of the internal market in electricity and gas (namely the introduction of TPA and unbundling) did not. Such arguments were particularly strong in Germany. The challenge was to identify and define the scope of those measures necessary to establish an internal market but which also respected the competence of the Member States. The procedure adopted by the Commission through Article 95 created a consultative framework for the parties to clarify and specify their respective competences while moving ahead with the goal of achieving an internal market in energy. 3.64

(3) First Proposals

The first draft Directives were circulated on a limited basis in July 1991 prior to formal presentation to the Council. However, the critical response that met them led to several changes:[102] 3.65

1. a phased introduction of TPA became the preferred option
2. a number of substantive changes were made: eg the thresholds for customers eligible for TPA were raised, limiting the number of players and the wide-ranging reporting obligations were limited to transparency requirements in accounting.

The Commission conducted further consultations with Member States and professional associations in late 1991. It formally introduced its framework Directives for electricity and gas in February 1992.[103] Essentially, there were three main elements or 'agents for change' in the proposals:[104] 3.66

- *Licensing:* the generation of electricity and construction of new electricity lines and gas pipelines would in future only be allowed on the basis of a transparent and non-discriminatory licensing system, taking into account factors including environmental constraints. By establishing a transparent and non-discriminatory licensing system for these investments, the aim was to increase the potential for investment in pipeline capacity by independent operators, while permitting national authorities to reject proposals that essentially duplicate existing pipeline networks.

[102] See Stern, Jonathan, *Third-party access on European Gas Markets*, Royal Institute of International Affairs (1992).

[103] Proposals for Council Directives on common rules for the internal market in electricity and natural gas, COM (1991) 548 final. [1992] OJ C65/04 (electricity); [1992] OJ C65/13 (gas).

[104] The issue of import and export monopolies was not addressed by the draft Directives, probably because it was already being tackled by a different route: an infringement procedure under existing legal powers.

- *'Unbundling':* there would be a separation of both management and accounts in vertically integrated companies as regards their transmission and distribution activities. For electricity, this would also apply to generation. The unbundling aims to promote the transparency of operations and thereby eliminate cross-subsidies and in this sense does not affect ownership structures.
- *Third-party access (TPA) to networks:* there would be an obligation on transport and/or distribution companies to allow third parties access, subject to payment of an appropriate fee and to capacity being available. Such an obligation would only be available to certain eligible entities, at least in the first instance. In the event of a dispute, there would be a binding arbitration procedure.[105]

3.67 Although central to the proposals, eligibility to TPA was to be limited to only two categories of user identified by Member States according to criteria specified in the Directives.[106]

> *Category 1, large industrial users:* eligibility would be dependent on an annual consumption threshold of at least 100 GwH of electricity or 25 million cubic metres of gas on a site. This would have included about 500 electricity users in the Member States, mostly in the aluminium, metallurgical, chemical, building materials, and glass industries. In the case of gas users, the number would be similar but would include mostly fertilizer and electricity users.
>
> *Category 2, larger distribution companies:* eligible if they supplied at least 3 per cent of the electricity or at least 1 per cent of the gas consumed in their respective Member States. The thresholds were based on percentages in preference to volumes (rejected as permitting too much variation from one country to another, since the number and size of suppliers varies widely between the Member States). However, smaller distributors could join together in order to qualify. The idea was to avoid discrimination between distributors of differing sizes. About 100 distributors each in the electricity and gas sectors were eligible on these criteria.

3.68 In designing its TPA proposal, considerations of security of supply and reliability of operation played an important rôle. A network manager was to be appointed at distribution level, but this could, where appropriate, be the existing distribution company. This contrasted with the proposal for the electricity sector, where a network manager was to be appointed to act in an independent and non-discriminatory manner in managing and supervising the technical aspects of the network and its links with other networks. The idea was to inject an element of stability into the system. To guarantee the neutrality of the network manager, the function was separated from generation and distribution to discourage self-interested action. Network managers were to connect users to their networks, ensure the co-ordinated development of the system as a whole, and manage the order of despatching the power stations on an objective and economic basis (merit order).

[105] This provision on TPA was 'the central point' of the proposals: Communication (91) 5.
[106] The criteria are set out in sections 4, 5, and 2(1); see n 101 above.

In the gas sector, the technical considerations are different (natural gas is storable, gas pipelines permit variations in temperature), and it was therefore not thought necessary to provide a manager to run the transportation network. 3.69

The official view of the Commission was that these three elements of the proposals did not impose new or additional obligations on Member States. All they did was to 'spell out already existing obligations which result both from the fundamental freedoms [free circulation of goods and services, freedom of establishment] and the competition rules of the EEC Treaty'.[107] They identified and elaborated rights and obligations that were already there for Member States and for companies.[108] They were not therefore an attempt to create a common energy policy, nor did they imply any taking of property.

(a) Staged approach to liberalization

The Commission's approach to liberalizing the gas and electricity sectors was based on four general principles: a gradualist approach to reform; respect for subsidiarity; avoidance of excessive regulation; and full consultation. 3.70

A gradual approach was thought necessary to allow the industry to adapt, in a flexible and orderly manner, to the new environment and to avoid deterring future investment. At the time there was a fear that a 'big bang' approach might lead to disruption. This appeared to be underlined by the wide diversity of industry structures and patterns of ownership among the Member States. It was compounded by a growing appreciation of real differences between the gas and electricity sectors and some uncertainty as to their significance. The gas sector's high dependence on imports from third countries on the basis of long-term take-or-pay contracts appeared to constrain the development of competition. Within the EU, some countries had a mature gas industry while others were in the stages of building up a gas industry. Although the electricity sector was more mature, the national systems varied greatly from centralized to decentralized ones, and in the primary fuels used to generate electricity. Cross-border trade was very limited. The development of Community-wide solutions therefore seemed difficult.

The Commission's solution was to divide the liberalization programme into three distinct stages. A minimum of change was to be achieved at each stage, 3.71

[107] Ehlermann, C D, 'Establishing the Single Market in Energy' (1991) Oil Gas Taxation L Rev 295–298, 298.

[108] Ehlermann, C D, 'Rôle of the European Commission as regards National Energy Policies', (1994) J Energy Natural Resources L 342–353, 343; see also Ehlermann, CD, '*EG-Binnenmarkt für die Energiewirtschaft*', (1992) *Europäische Zeitschrift für Wirtschaftsrecht* 689–693; '*Die vorgesehene Regelung zur Strom- und Gasdurchleiting (TPA) als Verwirklichung der Wettbewerbsvorschriften des EWG-Vertäges*' (1993) *Recht der Energiewirtschaft*, 41–45; '*Grundfreiheiten und Wettbewerbsregeln des EWG-Vertäges*' (1992) *Energiewirtschaftliche Tagesfragen*, 96–101.

thereby allowing Member States to choose a faster pace of liberalization of their national markets if they so wished. In its explanatory memorandum the Commission summarized this approach to the completion of the internal market in gas and electricity,[109] adding (perhaps unwisely) the following timetable:

1. 1991–92: Implementation of the Directives on Energy Transit and Price Transparency. By this time the Directives had already been approved.
2. 1993–95: Introduction of new measures of liberalization that respect the existing structures.
3. 1996–98: Completion of the internal market for gas and electricity and widening of the criteria for eligibility for TPA to include small consumers.

The problem with the phased approach was that it carried the risks of slow progress on liberalization and uneven implementation by the Member States.

(b) Subsidiarity and avoidance of excessive *regulation*

3.72 The Commission's proposals were guided by the principle of subsidiarity. Member States would be able to choose a system that best reflected their natural resources, the state of their industry, and their energy policies, within a framework of general rules defined by the Commission but leaving the Member States to determine the precise manner in which they wished to meet the general objectives.

This approach linked up with a third principle—the avoidance of excessive regulation—with the Commission limiting its actions to those necessary to achieve the aims of liberalization. The working assumption was that any such new regulation would replace rather that supplement existing regulation. This was a rather naïve view of the kind of regulation that would be required in a liberalizing market. In practice, the regulation of competition among utilities would prove more complex than the regulation of monopolies. Different problems were implied by the Commission's decision to leave the monitoring of capacity allocation and rate design in TPA cases to the Member States. Moreover, the Commission's approach to questions of structure was weak, influenced heavily by EC Treaty considerations about property ownership rather than desired regulatory effect.

3.73 In terms of procedure, the proposals would involve a maximum of consultation with the Council and Parliament under the co-operation procedure (subsequently replaced by the co-decision procedure) and with other interested parties. This statement was accompanied by the caveat that the Commission reserved the right to use all of its powers conferred by the EC Treaty as and when appropriate.[110] The final recital of each draft Directive stated that the Directive 'does not prejudice the application of the rules of the Treaty'.

[109] See n 103 above.
[110] Communication, Explanatory Memorandum, 8.

The reaction of Member States to the proposals aired in the bilateral consultations varied.[111] In general, there was some sympathy for liberalization of the rules concerning the construction of gas pipelines and power lines, although there were concerns about the possibility in law of creating parallel networks. The real opposition came from many Member States (and virtually all of the gas utilities) to TPA in gas and electricity—if not in principle then in practice.[112]

Concerns turned above all on the security of supply aspects, protection of small consumers, and the making of new investments. On the whole those concerns appeared greater in the gas industry than in the electricity industry. Consultations with the Member States were supplemented by an informal consultation with the professional associations, Eurogas, and Eurelectric. **3.74**

By contrast, the electricity association showed interest in an increase in competition in the generation of electricity—should the TPA proposal fail to be adopted. Increasing competition for new investments, either by independent producers setting up in the territory of a Member State, or by imports of electricity from another Member State seemed the best way to proceed. Eurelectric remained sceptical, however, about the added value that a TPA system would bring. It should remain optional.[113]

(c) Comparisons with the USA

The novelty of the Commission's proposals ensured that it was involving itself in a learning process: learning especially from the US experience of network access. In its proposal on common rules for the gas sector, the Commission had initially seemed to be influenced by the recent US experience of gas market deregulation. In its Working Document, for example, it had referred to the term 'common carriage', but this was subsequently dropped from the 1992 proposals. The reason for the change in the term 'common carriage' appears to have been to avoid confusion with legal terminology used in the USA. Under a US-style common carriage régime the introduction of a new user to a pipeline would—if there were insufficient capacity in the pipeline to carry the requirements of the new user and all existing users—lead to a pro rata reduction of the rights of the existing users. **3.75**

[111] n 106, 3–4.

[112] eg, Eurelectric, 'The Outlook for Europe's Electricity Market', conference proceedings, Brussels, 17 March 1992.

[113] They argued that a generalized system of TPA would make it difficult to operate rational energy use systems. The resulting transaction costs could be higher than the increase in profits due to the increased competition; see Explanatory Memorandum, n 108.

3.76 Such a common carriage régime applies to oil pipelines in the USA but not to gas pipelines. The régime applicable to gas pipelines is known as 'open access'. Under that régime access is available on a first-come, first-served basis to all customers willing to pay the maximum tariff applicable to the pipeline.

The term 'third-party access' avoids the confusion of the terminology and also avoids identification with the US concept of open access, although it appeared that the TPA being proposed would in practice have many of the features of open access in the USA.

3.77 In addition there were a number of problems with the US model that went far beyond conceptual and linguistic considerations.[114] First, US experience was relevant, if at all, only with respect to the gas sector, since (at that stage) the electricity sector had not been the subject of any market-oriented restructuring. By contrast, the Commission was proposing to liberalize both gas and electricity markets at the same time. Secondly, the US experiment followed a period of capping of wellhead prices and the introduction by the Federal Energy Regulatory Commission (FERC) of regulation of tariffs in inter-state gas pipelines. It had therefore a very different starting point from that of the European Community, although its basic objective of bringing about a competitive gas market was the same. Thirdly, comparisons between the US and European gas markets only highlighted the very different geo-political context. While the US could rely on many suppliers located within its national frontiers, the European buyers had to rely on a handful of large-volume sellers, based mostly outside of the Community. The only other models of TPA in their gas markets at that time were the UK and Canada but both differed considerably from continental Europe in terms of industry structure, market maturity, and institutional and political arrangements.

(d) Opposition and counter-proposals

3.78 The first set of proposals met an overwhelming degree of opposition. On 30 November 1992 the Council passed a resolution urging the Commission to consider modifications to the proposed Directives.[115] Progress had been insufficient

---

[114] The literature on this was often German-inspired and argued for the most part that the US experience was irrelevant to or dangerous for the future development of EU gas markets. eg, Teece, D J, 'Structure and Organisation of the Natural Gas Industry: Differences between the US and Federal Republic of Germany and Implications for the Carrier Status of Pipelines', (1990) The Energy J 1–35; Mestmäker, E J, 'Natural Gas in the European Internal Market: a Comparative Analysis of Common Carriage and Price Transparency', (1990) Michigan J of International L 691–765; Christian von Weizsacker, C, Schneider, H K, and Schmitt, D, 'Natural Gas on the Single European Market', *Energiewirtschaftliches Institut, Universität Köln*, May 1990; Jensen, (n 89 above). An exception is the report by Hopper, R J, 'Natural Gas: Open Access: The Potential Economic Benefits to Consumers in EC Markets', prepared for the *Conseil Européen des Fédérations de l'Industrie Chimique*, Brussels, 1991.

[115] *Agence Europe Presse*, No 5869, (1992); see also House of Lords Report: *Structure of the Single Energy Market*, para 2, and evidence submitted by Mr Fremantle, 58.

and new measures were required to overcome the remaining obstacles. It asked the Commission to take into account the forthcoming opinion of the Parliament, based on its deliberations in the course of 1992. In fact, the Parliament had held a public hearing on 1 to 2 October 1992, at the end of which the Rapporteur (also the chairman of the CERT) had concluded that the Commission's proposals could be neither accepted nor rejected but that proposals had to be made to revise them. Further opposition came several months later in an opinion issued by the Economic and Social Committee on 27 January 1993.[116] The Committee expressed 'serious reservations about some aspects' of the proposals and rejected the plans and deadlines for the introduction of TPA.[117] Interestingly, for the first time in the Committee's history there were two counter-opinions tabled on a single subject, one of which was openly supportive of TPA. In its view, experience of TPA in other parts of the world, including the UK, was too recent to allow an assessment of their advantages and drawbacks.[118] The opinion was nevertheless supportive of the principles of unbundling of accounts, opening up of new capacity, and the rôle of system operators.

There was a subsequent report by the CERT[119] on which Parliament based its critical opinion on the proposals, delivered on 17 November 1993. In effect Parliament was suggesting a series of detailed counter-proposals for the revision of the draft Directives, the main elements of which were as follows: **3.79**

- monopolies in electricity generation would be maintained except for new supply needs, which could be met by means of calls for tender open to all EU operators and newcomers;
- a concession system for the distribution networks would be maintained;
- access to third parties would be permitted on the basis of free negotiations, instead of being based on TPA rights;
- unbundling would be limited to accounting aspects only, without a separation between the activities of generation and transmission; and
- future liberalization would be subject to prior harmonization in specific areas such as environment and taxation.

These proposals struck at the heart of the Commission's philosophy on liberalization of energy markets and, had they been accepted, would largely have maintained the status quo for several years. They had to be taken very seriously, not least because the Parliament's rôle had been strengthened by the amendments to the EC Treaty at Maastricht and the introduction of a new co-operation approach to decision-making. The end result of this opposition from the institutions, the **3.80**

[116] [1993] OJ C 73/31.
[117] Economic and Social Committee, 'Briefing on 302nd Plenary Session', IB 1/93, 5 Feb 1993.
[118] Opinion, 2.9.4, p 38.
[119] OJ C 259 dated 16 Feb 1993.

Member States, and industry was that in late 1993 the Commission produced an amended set of proposals in conjunction with the Parliament.[120]

(4) Import and Export Monopolies

3.81 The introduction of new secondary legislation was only one strand in the strategy pursued by the Commission in promoting the internal energy market. A second, but by no means subordinate strand in its strategy involved a more vigorous application of existing EC Treaty rules. This was evident at an early stage in its treatment of import and export monopolies.

The draft Directives were notably lacking in provisions that expressly addressed the subject of import and export monopolies. In practice, the Commission had identified such monopolies as creating important barriers to a single market in energy. These were considered 'obviously contrary to the EC Treaty' as being in breach of Article 31(1)(former Article 37(1)*).[121]

3.82 In August 1991 the Commission initiated infringement proceedings against those Member States with statutory-based exclusive rights for the import and export of electricity and natural gas. Such provisions were in breach of Article 31(1) of the EC Treaty, requiring Member States to adjust any state monopolies of a commercial character so as to ensure that no discrimination exists between nationals of Member States in relation to conditions under which goods are procured and marketed, and also to avoid breaches of Article 28* which imposes a general ban on quantitative restrictions on trade between Member States or measures having an equivalent effect.

Initially, as many as nine Member States were involved.[122] Those invited to submit their observations by early October 1991 included Belgium, Denmark, France, Greece, Ireland, Italy, The Netherlands, Spain, and the United Kingdom. It became clear that there were no exclusive rights for the import and export of electricity and gas in the legislation of Belgium and Greece so the infringement proceedings against those two Member States were dropped. The United Kingdom gave a commitment to eliminate existing exclusive rights for import and export of electricity in Northern Ireland, and in consequence, the infringement proceedings against the United Kingdom were suspended.

3.83 However, the other responses were quite negative in character. They disputed the Commission's position at the legal level, arguing, for example that Article 31 relating to the dismantling of state monopolies of a commercial character would not

[120] 'Amended Proposals for a European Parliament and Council Directive on common rules for the internal market in electricity', COM (93) 643 final, COD 384, [1993] OJ C123/1.

[121] Ehlermann, C D, 'Role of the European Commission as regards National Energy Policies', (1994) J Energy Natural Resources L, 343.

[122] European Commission, '2nd Progress Report', ch I, para 3(2).

apply to the electricity sector. They disputed the position at an economic level too, arguing that electricity was a service, not a 'good'—notwithstanding the judgment in *Costa v ENEL*. In particular, they argued that Member States had the right to impose public service obligations as they saw fit, including the supply of electricity.

In November 1992 the Commission sent six reasoned opinions to the remaining Member States, on the ground that their legislation provided for import and export monopolies in gas or electricity or both. The countries concerned were Denmark, France, Ireland, Italy, The Netherlands, and Spain. In the cases of Denmark and France, the monopolies concerned gas, while the others—including France again—concerned monopolies in electricity. The exclusive rights involved were alleged to be in violation of Articles 28,* 29,* and 31.* **3.84**

In 1993 the proceedings were suspended to give the Member States more time to review the barriers to trade in their national legislation. This move followed assurances to the Commission from France and The Netherlands in particular that they would take steps to liberalize their régimes. However, little followed from this period of grace. The French Government, in particular, appeared reluctant to take steps to adopt even the very modest proposals of the 'Mandil Report' for liberalization published in early 1994.[123] On 26 January 1994 the Commission announced its intention to press ahead by referring to the ECJ the maintenance in force of exclusive rights to import and export electricity and gas in breach of Article 31 of the Treaty.[124] This concerned legislation in France, Italy, Spain, The Netherlands, and Ireland. On 14 June the Commission lodged an application pursuant to Article 169 before the ECJ claiming that France, Ireland, Italy, The Netherlands, and Spain were in contravention of Articles 28, 29, and 31 with respect to electricity monopolies. France was also challenged in relation to monopoly rights it had granted in the gas sector.[125] The proceedings represented an escalation in the efforts of the Commission to secure acceptance of its proposals for common rules Directives on gas and electricity.

The tactical nature of this approach should not be neglected. Then Competition Commissioner, Karel van Miert, had expressly linked the proceedings to progress made on the proposed Directives.[126] This was part of its 'carrot and stick' approach to the existing, powerful combination of gas, oil, and electricity interests, whether **3.85**

[123] *Cahiers Juridiques de l'Électricité et du Gaz* (CJEG), April 1994, 155.

[124] Min (94) 1186, cit in Competition Report 1994, 133.

[125] In March 1995 the British Government lodged a statement of intervention with the ECJ in support of the actions being brought by the Commission against 5 Member States with respect to import and export monopolies. The intervention remains confidential to the Court but it describes how the gas and electricity markets work in the UK without needing import and export monopolies to achieve security of supply while meeting public service obligations.

[126] (1993) EC Energy Monthly, 56/2.

in private, public, or mixed ownership, which benefited from *inter alia* the monopolies on import and export. Some years earlier there had been a successful use of a threat to act in the case of a monopoly import franchise held by Distrigaz in Belgium, which was removed.[127]

Throughout this period, the Commission was careful to remind Member States of the powers it had under existing Treaty rules,[128] namely those falling under Article 31 and those under Article 86.

3.86 Article 31 requires Member States progressively to adjust state monopolies of a commercial character. The enforcement of this requirement is a matter for the Commission. It may use its powers under Article 226 to bring a case against a Member State before the ECJ for breach of its obligations under the Treaty, subject to the Member State first being given an opportunity to submit its observations to the Commission with respect to the complaint.

Under Article 86 the Commission must ensure that the provisions of that Article are complied with. Paragraph 1 imposes on Member States the obligation not to enact or maintain in force, with respect to public undertakings or undertakings to which they have granted special or exclusive rights, any measures contrary to Treaty rules. Paragraph 2 provides an exemption, narrowly drawn, for undertakings entrusted with the operation of services of general economic interest. Where it is considered necessary, the Commission may address Directives and decisions to Member States to ensure compliance, without necessarily engaging in a lengthy consultation process. The Commission considered both of these courses at various times (for the possible use of Article 86(3) see paras 3.58–3.62 and ch 5, paras 5.09–5.19).

By early 1994, the absence of action by the Member States concerned, coupled with the lengthy co-decision procedure with the Parliament on the proposed Directives, threatened to deliver a fatal blow to the core elements in the internal energy market programme. This background provided a renewed impetus to the infringement action. Nor did it fail to yield results. The proceedings initiated against Denmark with respect to its gas sector were terminated when the Commission was sent a copy of the Danish Government's letter of April 1994 to the state-owned utility, Dansk Naturgas A/S, which formally repealed its exclusive right over imports.[129] The Government declared that it would, in principle and

[127] 'Thirteenth Report on Competition Policy', point 291, 191.

[128] eg, Internal Energy Market White Paper, COM (1988) 238 final; '2nd Progress Report on the Internal Energy Market', 1993, ch II, para 7 (COM (1993) 261 final): 'The Commission intends to continue the application of Community law as and when appropriate'.

[129] Executive Order, Danish Official Journal, (1994) vol 69. The Danish Government also decided to abolish the monopoly rights in natural gas transportation, storage, and trading, on condition that there was a corresponding opening in other countries and transitional arrangements should be allowed under the EU Gas Directive then being negotiated: DONG Annual Report 1996, 62.

subject to certain conditions, be ready to abolish Dansk Naturgas's exclusive right of transmission, storage and trading of natural gas. Ireland too, succeeded in having the infringement action against it removed in 1994,[130] largely because the legislation in question was enabling legislation.[131] As a result, the only complaint specifically directed at the gas sector of a Member State that remained was that against France.[132]

A problem with this course of action is that the removal of import and export constraints and national monopolies of transmission and distribution would not in itself be sufficient to create an internal market in electricity and gas. It might well facilitate the development of competition and encourage new entrants. However, it would certainly not be a substitute for the introduction of an effective form of TPA and a measure of unbundling as mechanisms for the achievement of an internal market in energy. This underlined the importance of both a vigorous application of the competition rules of the Treaty (see ch 5) and adoption of the proposed Directives. **3.87**

(5) Rediscovery of Public Service

A radically modified set of proposals for the electricity and gas sectors was adopted by the Commission on 8 December 1993.[133] This marked what one observer has called a 'rehabilitation of the notion of public service'.[134] Although TPA remained central to the proposals, this was a watered-down draft which was to some extent constrained by considerations of public service (defined quite broadly). This emphasis is derived from the provisions of Article 90(2)* which permitted, on limited grounds, exemption from the rules of the Treaty, particularly competition, for undertakings entrusted with the operation of services of general economic interest (see ch 5). There were some who questioned whether such exemptions were necessary in liberalized electricity and gas markets. **3.88**

---

[130] [1994] OJ C 202/9, and Order of the President of 11 Sept 1995; [1996] OJ C 336/23.

[131] It allowed the Electricity Supply Board, a public corporation, to do certain things, but did not imply that other bodies were precluded from doing the same: Faull, J, and Nikpay, A, *EC Law of Competition* (2000), 725.

[132] The resulting decision was made in 1997: Case C-159/94 [1997] *Commission v France* ECR I-5815; see ch 5.

[133] European Commission, Amended Proposal for a European Parliament and Council Directive on common rules for the internal market in electricity: COM (1993) 643 final, OJ C123/1; for natural gas, COM (1993) 643 final, OJ C123/26 (1994).

[134] *Le Marché Interieur de l'Électricité: Chronique d'un Débat* (1987–1996), CJEG No 532, May 1997, 166–173. See also the CEEP (Centre Européen d'Entreprises Publiques) Report, 'Updating the Concept of Public Service', June 1992; Lamort, Fabien 'The Notion of Public Service in European Power Industries: A Comparative Cultural and Historical Analysis in France, Germany and England', ENER Bulletin, no 15 (1995), 10–28; Bonino, Emma 'L'Europe peut concilier libéralisation des services publics et cohesion économique et sociale', *Actualité des Services Publics en Europe*, no 24, May 1996, 1.

The Commission's proposals envisaged the following key elements:

- *negotiated* access to power grids rather than an automatic right of access to the network;
- unbundling of accounts only and not management as well;
- non-discriminatory tendering or bidding for some new generating and transmission capacity as defined by local authorities or by an independent entity charged with this task; and
- a harmonization programme, although not on Parliament's suggested model (which would have conditioned future liberalization on the success of the programme).

(a) 'Negotiated access'

3.89 The approach to TPA was based upon on a new concept of 'negotiated access', replacing the earlier concept of regulated access to the networks. Rights of access would be acquired at the end of a process of negotiation, which would be carried out within a legal framework that Member States would be required to introduce. This would provide protection to the prospective system user. By law the negotiations had to be carried out in good faith and without an abuse by the network owner of his negotiating position by preventing a successful outcome of the negotiations. Under the earlier proposals, a system user would have had a right of access to the network, subject only to capacity being available and to meeting specific technical requirements. The central point of difference was the burden of proof. Under a system of negotiated access, the prospective system users would have no right to require access unless at the end of a period of unsuccessful negotiation they could show that the network owner has not complied with the good faith and other obligations, as well as with his obligations under competition law including those relating to the abuse of a dominant position. Under the former system, the system user could require access on terms, including price, that would be established according to specific provisions in the law unless the network owner could show insufficient capacity was available or technical incompatibility. The change was therefore one with very significant practical implications.

3.90 Moreover, the revised proposals attempted to make explicit the right of Member States to impose public service obligations (PSOs) on undertakings, with respect to the security, regularity, quality, and price of supplies. It noted that 'free competition, left to itself, cannot be relied upon to fulfil'[135] such obligations. In six places in the text and recitals, it contained a direct or indirect recognition of the importance of the concept in the context of security of supply and consumer protection. However, Member States would be required to define these obligations in such a way that they became known and transparent. In specific cases,

[135] Recital 11, amended proposal, see n 101.

the performance of PSOs could constitute a reason for refusing access to the network, particularly in cases where their performance would be obstructed by the transaction in question. This would have to be proved by the refusing system operator. The non-observance of PSOs could also constitute a reason for refusing the grant of an authorization for the construction of new production and transport capacity. Without a doubt, the views of the Parliament played an important rôle in persuading the Commission of the need for this emphasis on public service, which had been mentioned only once in the previous proposals.[136]

(b) Unbundling requirements

Vertically-integrated undertakings were no longer required to unbundle their management. However, the unbundling of accounts with respect to generation, transportation, and distribution activities on a harmonized basis was retained. This implied a public availability of information and it was therefore not sufficient for the unbundled annual accounts to be made available only to national control bodies. **3.91**

The Commission also accepted the Parliament's request that the competent authorities designated by the Member States should have the right of access to internal gas company accounts to enable them to carry out their control functions, without commercial confidentiality being compromised by a wider disclosure than this. Obligations for technical reporting and capacity-use planning were also reduced for the distribution companies.

(c) Non-discriminatory trading

The modified proposals also retained provisions for a system of transparent and non-discriminatory authorizations for the construction and operation of transmission and distribution lines and storage and LNG installations. However, they omitted a provision in the previous proposals that allowed Member States to refuse authorizations for the construction of new pipelines if sufficient capacity were available in the existing interconnected system at reasonable and equitable prices. This nodded to the fact that the option of constructing a new line might be an important factor in the negotiations for access to the existing network and might strengthen the position of the requesting party, usually the weaker negotiating party. **3.92**

(d) Harmonization

A programme of harmonization was envisaged for the proper working of the internal market for electricity and gas. The Commission decided not to fix the details of this in advance but to undertake an investigation into the areas in which harmonization measures were required to avoid distortions of competition affecting trade between Member States. **3.93**

[136] Art 14(1) of the 1991 proposals.

3.94 Many of the specific recommendations made by the Parliament were rejected by the Commission on the ground that they would have compromised the aims of the Commission's proposals and also appeared to be incompatible with the Treaty. Three proposals made by the Parliament which were rejected by the Commission are worth some comment:

- *The requirement on Member States to establish a body called a Gas Council.* These control bodies, composed of representatives of gas utilities and distribution companies, industrial consumers, small and medium-sized consumers, and trade unions, would have had the task of assisting the competent Member State authorities to put the Directive into effect. In accordance with the principle of subsidiarity, the Commission considered that it was up to the Member State to decide whether or not they wished to create such a control body.
- *The proposal to impose on gas companies a set of commonly-defined PSOs.* The concept of a PSO was not known to all Member States and varied so much from one country to another that a common definition at Community level would have been difficult to establish, as would the development of a means for fulfilling these PSOs—eg some Member States viewed the supply of gas as a normal commercial activity and not as a public service.
- *Parliament's request that the supply monopolies of the distribution companies should be maintained.* Rejected since it would have limited the process of opening-up markets to more competition. Nonetheless, Member States were to be able to continue to control the setting of tariffs for all final customers who were not eligible for access to the transmission and distribution system or who did not want to have such access.

3.95 The two amended proposals were sent to the Council on 11 February 1994. Under the co-decision procedure, the Council had to adopt a 'common position' on the basis of the amended proposals. This in turn would have had to have been sent to the Parliament for a second reading, where amendments could be made. However, a consensus on either proposal proved elusive in the coming months and, as a result, the Council took the decision on 29 November 1994 to split the dossier. From that point on, the proposal for a Directive on common rules for the electricity sector would take priority over the proposed Directive on gas—which was temporarily set aside. The thinking behind this appears to have been that the proposed Gas Directive was complicated by the rôle of imports from non-EU suppliers, take-or-pay clauses in long-term contracts, and the uneven development of the gas industry itself within the EU at that time. By contrast, there was an overcapacity of electricity and an absence of dependence upon suppliers from outside the EU, ensuring that security of supply issues had a less sensitive character.

(6) Single Buyer and Beyond

The wisdom of separating out the elements in the common rules package quickly became apparent. By the end of 1994, agreement in principle had been reached in the Council on no less than *four* of the five key points in the draft Electricity Directive:[137] **3.96**

- liberalization of electricity generation;
- separation of accounts of vertically-integrated enterprises;
- provisions on the operation and management of the networks; and
- criteria for Member States in setting requirements in the general interest on electricity enterprises.

The outstanding point of difficulty was the French Government's proposal to provide a 'Single Buyer' option, advanced as an alternative to a TPA system. The Council requested the Commission to establish whether the creation of two systems alongside one another would produce equivalent economic results and a directly comparable level of market-opening and degrees of market access, in compliance with the Treaty provisions. There was a risk that such an approach would preserve most of the monopoly powers of a dominant utility like EdF or, in the gas sector, GdF.

The 'Single Buyer' concept

A system based on the Single Buyer concept would envisage a tendering procedure for new capacity requirements organized by the network operators. Essentially, this means a particular type of organizational structure used for a national electricity industry that may also be applied to a national gas industry. It has been used in countries including some Member States of the EU (notably France but also Ireland and Greece) where the state wishes to exercise central control over the planning and operation of electricity generation and supply. In France it has also been used for the gas industry. Control is thereby exercised through the state-owned electricity utility that is granted a monopoly of generation and transmission and also enjoys in practice a monopoly of supply. The state imposes PSOs on the utility. These may include both long-term and operational security of supply. It is an important part of the PSOs that the utility should be responsible for buying all the electricity produced or imported into the state and for selling all electricity exported from the state. For these purposes, it is granted a monopoly of export and import of electricity. It is the sole purchaser or Single Buyer. As such, it is the owner of all electricity that passes through the transmission lines. It follows that because under the Single Buyer system all electricity must be sold to the Single Buyer at the point of entry into the transmission lines, the parties to supply **3.97**

[137] Competition Report 1994, 133–4.

contracts cannot negotiate TPA. The same rationale lay behind the principal buyer status of GdF and also its de facto monopoly of transmission and supply.

3.98 Between March and May 1995 the Commission presented two working papers at the request of the Council covering the organization of the internal market in electricity[138] and the rôle of small and very small electricity systems in the internal electricity market.[139] The first paper examined whether the Commission's proposal of negotiated TPA could co-exist with the Single Buyer system. Its conclusion was that such a co-existence would only be acceptable if some modifications were made to the Single Buyer concept. Specific observations were also made in the paper with respect to the implications of Article 5(3) of the draft Directive. This provision required an authorization procedure for auto-producers and independent producers even in Member States that select the tendering procedure for new production and transmission capacity.

3.99 In the second working paper issued in May 1995, the Commission argued that small electricity systems, as in Ireland or in Luxembourg, should not be treated as special cases nor should they receive special protection. However, the Commission considered that a special redefinition of 'independent producer' might be justified in small isolated systems insofar as they were not interconnected, given the possibility of exporting surplus capacity to other small, interconnected systems. This report was reviewed and commented on by the Parliament.[140]

3.100 A modified version of the Single Buyer concept (see ch 4, paras 4.25–4.27) was considered by the Commission to be compatible with the Treaty and, as a result, the Spanish Presidency of the Council developed a compromise text during the second half of 1995 that integrated the modified proposal with the existing option of negotiated TPA. This proposal was well received but failed to produce a result due to disagreements on the degree of market-opening in the first phase of liberalization and on which consumers should be allowed to participate in this phase.[141]

In the first half of 1996 the Italian Presidency attempted to resolve these issues. The Italian approach was to relate market-opening to a percentage figure of between 20 and 40 per cent of consumption. Member States would be free to identify those customers that would be eligible to participate in this percentage of

[138] 'The Organisation of the Internal Electricity Market', SEC (1995) 464 final, 22 March 1995.

[139] 'Small and Very Small Electricity Systems in the Internal Electricity Market', SEC (1995) 685 final. The Commission drew on a study carried out at its request by the Energiewirtschaftsliches Institut, Universität Köln: 'TPA and Single Buyer Systems, Producers and Parallel Authorizations: Small and Very Small Systems', Köln, 1995.

[140] European Parliament, PE 215.270/def (7 Feb 1996).

[141] Faross, P, 'Neuordnung des Wettbewerbs auf den Energiemärkten' (1996) 2 VIK-Mitteilung, 32–5.

market-opening, and would be supported by safeguard and transparency measures. Despite various difficulties in agreeing on the percentages, as well as further growth in opening and the periods of transition, a political agreement was finally reached in June 1996 at an extraordinary meeting of the Energy Council, and subsequently confirmed by the legal adoption of a common position by the Council on 25 July 1996.[142]

Agreement followed the hearing in the ECJ of the import–export monopoly cases, but preceded delivery of the judgment. However, if the impending judgment acted as an incentive to reaching agreement (and it could be that the converse was more accurate)—it was at least very probable that French opposition to the draft Directive was blunted by an important development elsewhere, in the negotiations on the revisions of the EC Treaty. These resulted in the acceptance, in 1996, of a concept of public service that eventually became the new Article 7d. However, it is also probable that the Commission was eager to make a start on the process of liberalization in the face of continuing pressure from industrial consumers and generating companies wishing to export electricity. **3.101**

(7) Conclusions

The first phase of the Internal Energy Market programme was characterized by an extraordinary degree of opposition to liberalization by a combination of Member States and utilities. This was more evident in the gas sector than in electricity, leading to the proposed Directive on common rules for that sector being temporarily set aside. Frequently the debate was conducted in an atmosphere charged with predictions of disaster as a result of a too rapid liberalization process. This offset the modest legislative successes of the Commission in price transparency, transit, and hydrocarbons licensing. **3.102**

The Commission's efforts to develop suitable legal instruments to bring about a significant increase in competition were hampered as a consequence. This was evident in the shift from regulated to negotiated TPA, the extended public service obligations, very limited unbundling and the inclusion of a Single Buyer option. Perhaps more than any of the specific changes, the emphasis on public service underlined the risks attached to these compromise measures. Indeed, some notion of public service was compatible with and probably desirable for a market-oriented system of energy supply through networks. However, its scope and limits had to be very clearly defined and enforced if it were not to become a back-door way of preserving the practices that the Internal Energy Market programme was designed to abolish. **3.103**

[142] Klom, A M, 'Effects of Deregulation Policies on Electricity Competition in the EU', (1997) 15 J Energy Natural Resources L, 1–22.

3.104 The other strand in the Commission's strategy was the deployment of existing Treaty rules. In this too it had limited success. The use of infringement procedures and ultimately proceedings before the ECJ was proved to be a useful source of pressure on some Member States and utilities, even if the exact impact of these measures can only be surmised. During this time, there were several judgments in cases before the ECJ relevant directly or indirectly to the energy sector.[143] The results gave little support to the Commission's hopes for the Internal Energy Market programme and served to confirm that the ECJ was not the right forum for the development of liberalization measures if they were strongly opposed by several Member States.

3.105 By the end of this period the institutional setting had changed in ways that blunted the Commission's powers to initiate controversial measures such as these. Under the TEU the Parliament had enhanced powers of scrutiny over legislative proposals. The proposed Directives on common rules for the electricity and gas sectors could not be accepted without the development of a consensus between the Parliament and Council. Within the Council itself, it is striking how reluctant Member States were to resort to QMV in the face of strong opposition, especially from France. Instead, all efforts were made to secure consensus, in spite of the amount of time that this required. Such a context was quite different from that of the Delors Commission in which the Internal Market programme had been conceived. On the face of it, this setting was less favourable to the achievement of the Commission's programme for the energy sector.

3.106 The drivers for change lay elsewhere, among the industrial consumers of energy facing increased international competition for their products and in developments within the Member States themselves. The number of Member States that were sympathetic to energy market reform had increased to include Germany and the new members from the Nordic countries. From early 1994 the German government initiated reforms of the country's energy laws, with the aim of removing restrictions that were limiting the scope of competition. In the Nordic countries efforts at electricity market liberalization were also proceeding. All of this had the effect of adding to the models, alternatives, and experiences that could be drawn on when designing measures for the enhancement of competition. It was no longer necessary to look exclusively to the experiences of the United Kingdom or of countries outside Europe.

---

143 See ch 5.

4

ACHIEVING AN INTERNAL ENERGY MARKET THROUGH LEGISLATION: PHASE TWO (1996–1998)

A. Introduction

The most essential legislation in the Internal Energy Market programme comprised two Directives on common rules for the electricity and gas industries. The Electricity and Gas Directives took between five and seven years of negotiation to reach adoption in the face of serious opposition from industry and many Member States (see Table 3.1). These two framework Directives have considerable similarities in structure and content despite the different industries they apply to. They are examined in some detail in this chapter. Chapter 6 deals with issues arising from their implementation. 4.01

The first part of this chapter explains the principal provisions of the Electricity Directive. The second part looks at the sister Directive on Gas, which borrowed from the former a very similar structure and was adopted almost 18 months later.

B. Electricity Directive

(1) Overall Aims

4.02 On 25 July 1996 the Council adopted a Common Position or political agreement on the draft Directive.[1] In its Communication to the Parliament,[2] the Commission argued that the Common Position was 'generally in line with the amended proposal', emphasizing that increased competition would be introduced gradually and that no risk was presented to the performance of essential services in the process. It regretted, however, that distributors 'will not in all cases be eligible to participate in the new market arrangements'. The statement was an admission that the scope of the 'eligible customers' under the Directive had been defined much more narrowly than had originally been sought.[3] Significantly, it emphasized the provision in Recital 3 of the text, which states that 'the provisions of the Directive should not affect the full application of the Treaty, in particular the provisions concerning the internal market and competition'.

4.03 There were five principal areas in which the Common Position differed from the Commission's amended proposal of 1993 to 1994. They concerned the:

1. scope of public service and definition of 'related obligations';
2. provisions for the construction of new generating and transmission capacity;
3. operation of the distribution system;
4. unbundling; and
5. access.

The emphasis placed on public service was greater than in the original proposal, reflecting the Parliament's views on this. However, the new emphasis on public service had to be placed in the context of Community law and in particular of Article 86(2). The Commission proposed to monitor the result to ensure that public service obligations would be respected.

---

[1] Commission of the European Communities, Doc 8811/96 ENER 105.

[2] European Commission, 'Common Position taken by the Council of the European Union on the Proposal for a Directive of the European Parliament and of the Council on Common Rules for the Internal Market in Electricity', 26 July 1996, SEC (1996) 1409 final, COD (1996)/384.

[3] The term 'eligibility' was used in the 1991 draft of the Directive but its meaning was wider (see ch 3, para 3.67). Here eligibility is limited to the right to purchase electricity in the competitive sector of the market and to have rights relating to access as described in the Directive.

On 19 December 1996 Directive 96/92/EC on common rules for the internal market in electricity (the Electricity Directive) was adopted by the European Parliament and the Council. It entered into force two months later on 19 February 1997.[4] Member States had until 19 February 1999 to bring into force laws, regulations, and administrative provisions necessary to comply with its terms. All Member States complied with the timetable except France and those Member States which were granted extensions (Belgium and Ireland were granted an additional one year, and Greece an extra two years to transpose the Directive). **4.04**

The general aim of the Electricity Directive is to establish common rules for the generation, transmission, and distribution of electricity. It sets out rules for the organization and functioning of the electricity sector, access to the market, criteria and procedures applicable to calls for tender, the granting of authorizations, and the operation of systems.[5] **4.05**

Its adoption marked an important step for the discussions on the similar proposal for the gas sector, since many of the agreements and compromises made on electricity liberalization could be drawn on to resolve outstanding issues in the drafting of the Gas Directive. The principle of subsidiarity is followed in both Directives, which offers specific choices to Member States and lays down procedures and conditions to be followed and observed, according to the specific actions they take under the Directive.

(2) Generation

The aim of the provisions on generation is to completely open up the construction of new generating capacity to competition. The significance of this lies in the assumption that independent generators will play an important part in stimulating competition in future years. To achieve this aim, there are two procedures available to Member States under Article 4: either an authorization procedure or a tendering procedure, although a mix of the two is also permitted. Whichever procedure is chosen, it must be carried out in accordance with objective, transparent, and non-discriminatory criteria[6] and the end result of each procedure must be the same. The difference between the two procedures is that in the tendering procedure the Member State sets up an inventory of the need for future generating capacity, including the estimated demand for electricity. These estimates are proposed by the Transmission System Operator (TSO) or any other **4.06**

[4] Directive 96/92/EC of the European Parliament and of the Council of 19 December 1996 concerning common rules for the internal market in electricity, 1997 OJ L 27, 20. The legal basis for the Directive is Arts 47(2), 55, and 95 of the EC Treaty. Article 95 requires the procedure of Art 251 of the EC Treaty.

[5] ibid, Art 1.

[6] ibid, Art 4.

competent authority that has been designated by the Member State. By contrast, in the authorization procedure, applications that fit the criteria for granting an authorization must be approved. Lack of demand is not a valid reason for a refusal.

4.07 Under the authorization procedure, Member States must lay down criteria for the grant of authorizations for the construction of generating capacity in their territory.[7] These criteria must be made public and may relate to:

- safety and security of the electricity system, installations, and associated equipment
- protection of the environment
- land-use and siting
- use of public ground
- energy efficiency
- the nature of the primary sources
- characteristics particular to the applicant, eg technical, economic, and financial capabilities, or
- public service obligations.

In the event of a refusal to grant an authorization, the applicant must be informed of the reasons, which must be objective and non-discriminatory. They must be 'well-founded and duly substantiated' in the criteria for granting authorization. Such data must be forwarded to the Commission for information purposes. Appeal procedures must be made available to the applicant.

4.08 Under the tendering procedure, Member States or any competent body designated by the Member State concerned may plan for the construction of new capacity by drawing up an inventory of new capacity to be constructed, including replacement of old capacity.[8] Inventories must take account of the need for interconnection of systems. The requisite capacity must be allocated by means of a tender in accordance with transparent and non-discriminatory criteria. Details of the tendering procedure must be published in the *Official Journal* of the European Communities at least six months before the closing date for tenders. Tender specifications must contain a detailed description of the contract specifications, of the procedure to be followed for all tenderers and an exhaustive list of criteria governing the selection of tenderers and the award of the contract.

4.09 Responsibility for organizing, monitoring, and controlling the tendering procedure must be vested in an authority designated by the Member State or in a body independent of the generation, transmission, and distribution activities.[9] It must take all necessary steps to ensure confidentiality of the information contained in

[7] ibid, Art 5(1).
[8] ibid, Art 6(1).
[9] ibid, Art 6(5).

the tenders. This is intended to encourage objective and non-discriminatory decision-making. However, there is no specific régime to provide remedies in the event of a breach.

In the tendering procedure, it has to be possible for certain categories of generators, such as auto-producers and independent power producers, to obtain a parallel authorization if they fulfil the above criteria with respect to the authorization procedure.[10]

(3) Transmission

Chapter IV concerns the operation of the transmission system. 'Transmission' is defined as the transport of electricity on the high-voltage interconnected system with a view to its delivery to final customers or to distributors.[11] The focus of its three Articles is the technical issues (including dispatching) for operators of the transmission system. Organization of access to the system is dealt with separately in Chapter VII of the Directive. **4.10**

Member States must designate or require undertakings which own transmission systems to designate a system operator to be responsible for operating, ensuring the maintenance of and, if necessary, developing the transmission system in a given area to guarantee security of supply. This also includes the transmission system's interconnectors with other systems. The appointment of the Transmission System Operator (TSO) must be for a given period of time to be determined by the Member State taking into account considerations of efficiency and economic balance. **4.11**

The TSO is responsible for dispatching the generating installations in its area as well as for determining the use of interconnectors with other systems.[12] Criteria for dispatching and use of interconnectors must be objective, published, and applied in a non-discriminatory manner. In other words, the TSO is not allowed to favour those generating facilities belonging to the same company or to shareholders of the company in cases where the TSO is not totally separated from production. The criteria also have to take into account the economic precedence of electricity from available generating installations of interconnector transfers and any technical constraints on the system. This entails the application of economic merit order—but not solely on a cost basis—which means, for instance that plant could be dispatched for system security.

There are also a variety of technical and operational requirements concerning the operation of the transmission system. Technical rules must be developed and **4.12**

[10] ibid.
[11] ibid, Recital 5.
[12] ibid, Art 8(1).

published which establish the minimum technical design and operational requirements for connection to the system of generating installations, distribution systems, directly connected consumers' equipment, interconnector circuits and direct lines. The aim of these requirements is to ensure inter-operability of systems. They must be objective, non-discriminatory and must be notified to the Commission.[13]

System operators must be independent, at least in management, from other activities not concerned with the transmission system.[14] They should have responsibility for the technical operation of the system, managing energy flows and taking into account exchanges with other interconnected systems.[15] They are charged with ensuring a secure, reliable, and efficient electricity system, and with ensuring the availability of all necessary ancillary services. They must not discriminate between system users or classes of system user, especially in favour of their subsidiaries or shareholders.[16] They must also provide the operator of any other system with which their system is interconnected with sufficient information to ensure the secure and efficient operation, co-ordinated development, and inter-operability of the interconnected system.[17] The TSO has an obligation to preserve the confidentiality of commercially sensitive information that is obtained in the course of carrying out its business.[18]

4.13 On the construction of new transmission network capacity, the provisions of the Directive were amended by the Council to remove this matter from the scope of the Directive. Where mechanisms for the expansion of capacity are required, these will must be set up at the national level.

On the potential for a common transmission methodology, it appears that the Commission had considered a European Regulation on this as early as 1992, at the time of its first proposal for a Directive on electricity.[19] The issue was dropped however following the incorporation of a definition of subsidiarity into the EC Treaty (as a result of the TEU) and the shift towards negotiated TPA in 1993 following the comments by the Parliament. This important topic is discussed further in Chapters 6 and 7.

4.14 In pursuit of an environmental policy, Member States may require the TSO to give priority in dispatching electricity to those generating installations producing

[13] In accordance with Art 8 of Council Directive 83/189/EEC of 28 March 1983 setting a procedure for the provision of information in the field of technical standards and regulations: OJ L 109, 26 April 1983, 8, as amended by the 1994 Act of Accession.

[14] Electricity Directive, n 4 above, Art 7(6).

[15] ibid, Art 7(3).

[16] ibid, Art 7(5).

[17] ibid, Art 7(4).

[18] ibid, Art 9.

[19] Commission of the European Communities, 'Frequently Answered Questions', at http://europa.eu.int/en/comm/dg17/elec/faq.htm

electricity from renewable energy sources or waste or producing CHP.[20] It is permissible to design an environmental policy so as to assist these forms of electricity despite their (generally) higher cost than electricity produced from traditional sources. This is the only express mechanism in the Directive for the favourable treatment of electricity from renewable energy sources, waste, or CHP. Most Member States already used such a mechanism. Essentially, a TSO will purchase electricity from renewable energy or the other sources and will pass the cost on to its captive customers, such costs being distributed over the total consumer base. In itself, favourable dispatching is unlikely to support a policy for promoting renewables. However, the Directive does not cover schemes that provide direct or indirect support to renewable energy sources nor does it allow Member States to authorize a TSO to oblige eligible customers to purchase its share of renewable energy directly or via green certificates or the imposition of levies. For Member States seeking to go further than the favourable dispatching mechanism, the provisions of Articles 3(2) and 24 would be relevant.[21]

A priority in dispatching may also be given to electricity produced from indigenous primary fuel sources up to 15 per cent in any calendar year of the overall energy necessary to produce the electricity consumed in the Member State concerned. Under the Directive the aim is to meet concerns about security of supply but it might also help to protect the market share of ex-monopolists. **4.15**

(4) Distribution

'Distribution' is defined as the transport of electricity on medium-voltage and low-voltage distribution systems with a view to its delivery to customers. It is the subject of Chapter V of the Directive. This provision was included in the Directive text only after lengthy and difficult negotiations with the incumbent players about so-called 'final wire competition'. The result was that the distribution companies were not included in the definition of 'eligible customers' in spite of the Commission's recommendation, and much room was left in the provision for subsidiarity, thereby diluting its effect. **4.16**

In most Member States there is a single TSO and several distribution system operators (DSOs). The Directive requires Member States to designate or to require undertakings owning or responsible for distribution systems to designate a system operator.[22] As is the case with the TSOs, the DSO is charged with operating, ensuring the maintenance of, and, if necessary, developing the distribution system in **4.17**

[20] Electricity Directive, n 4 above, Art 8(3).

[21] European Commission, Report to the Council and the European Parliament on Harmonization Requirements: Directive 96/92/EC concerning common rules for internal market in electricity, 16 March 1998, COM (1998) 167 final, 6–8.

[22] Electricity Directive, n 4 above, Art 10(2).

a given area and its interconnectors with other systems. It may be subject to an obligation to supply customers located in a given area.[23] The tariff for such supplies may be regulated to achieve various objectives, such as the equal treatment of all customers in the area.

4.18 DSOs must meet various technical requirements similar to those of the TSOs. They are charged with maintaining a secure, reliable, and efficient electricity distribution system in their areas, taking the environment into account.[24] They must not discriminate between system users or classes of system users—especially in favour of their subsidiaries or shareholders.[25] They must preserve the confidentiality of commercially sensitive information obtained in the course of carrying out their businesses[26] and may be required to give priority to generating installations using renewable energy sources or waste or producing CHP, if a Member State considers this appropriate.[27] In practice, this policy concern for CHP will prove more significant at the distribution rather than transmission level.

4.19 A number of changes were made by the Council to the Commission text, whereby Member States were given powers to impose an obligation on supply undertakings (ie distributors) and to regulate tariffs for consumer groups. The definition of 'supply' as distinct from 'distribution' is also not always clear, in spite of separate definitions of the terms. Sometimes the text refers to 'distribution' when the issues of competition at which it is directed are those of a supply business rather than a wires business.

(5) Access

4.20 For electricity to be transmitted from generators to 'eligible' customers, network access has to be provided by the system owners and operators. The Directive permits three ways of organizing access to the transmission and distribution networks. Member States may choose negotiated or regulated TPA or, if they have chosen a Single Buyer régime, they could follow the Single Buyer access procedure.[28] Whatever option they chose, the procedures must operate in accordance with objective, transparent, and non-discriminatory criteria. They must also lead to equivalent economic results and therefore to a directly comparable level of opening-up of markets and to a directly comparable degree of access to electricity markets.[29]

---

23 ibid, Art 10(1).
24 ibid, Art 11(1).
25 ibid, Art 11(2).
26 ibid, Art 12.
27 ibid, Art 11(3).
28 ibid, Art 17 (negotiated and regulated access) and Art 18 (Single Buyer).
29 ibid, Art 3(1).

(a) Negotiated TPA

Under the negotiated TPA (nTPA) procedure, producers and consumers of electricity enter into contracts for supplies directly with each other, but must negotiate access to the network with their operators. These negotiations will cover matters such as transport charges and other conditions. The consumers are 'supply undertakings', ie, distributors (where Member States authorize their existence)[30] and 'eligible customers', whether inside or outside the territory covered by the system. In cases where the eligible customer is connected to the distribution system, system access must be the subject of negotiation with the relevant DSO and if necessary with the TSO concerned. **4.21**

To promote transparency and to facilitate negotiations for system access, the TSOs and DSOs must publish an indicative range of prices for use of the transmission and distribution systems. This must be done in the first year following implementation of the Directive. The indicative prices for subsequent years should be based, as far as possible, on the average price agreed in negotiations in the previous 12-month period. The use of Internet sites for publicity of available prices in all Member States is to be encouraged by the Commission.[31] **4.22**

Either the TSO or DSO may refuse access in the event of a lack of necessary capacity.[32] The burden of proof falls on the network operator, which must provide duly substantiated reasons for the refusal. This means that capacity allocation mechanisms need to set priorities that will apply during system operation. In interconnected systems, for example, long-term contracts could be given a higher priority than 'spot market' ones. Refusal of access would also be permitted if a Member State had exercised its right under Article 3.3 not to apply the provisions of Articles 17 and 18 on the grounds that the application of Articles 17 and 18 would obstruct the performance, in law or in fact, of the PSOs of the relevant system operator. Finally, refusal may be made on the grounds of reciprocity under Articles 19(5) and 26. There is no provision in the Directive for an obligation on the TSO or DSO to construct new capacity in cases where no available capacity exists. This weakness could be remedied however if the charging régime created incentives for construction of new capacity.

Negotiations are subject to a dispute settlement procedure. Member States must ensure that negotiations are conducted in good faith by all of the parties and that no party abuses its negotiating position by preventing the successful outcome of negotiations. A competent authority must be established for the settlement of disputes relating to the contracts and negotiations in question. It **4.23**

---

[30] ibid, Art 17(1).

[31] Commission of the European Communities, 'Guide to the Electricity Directive', (28 March 1999), 4: see online at www.europa.eu.int/comm/energy/en/elecsinglemarket/memor.htm/

[32] Electricity Directive, n 4 above, Art 17(5).

must be independent of the parties. Article 20 specifies that such authority shall be responsible for settling disputes relating to contracts, negotiations, and refusal of access or refusal to purchase.[33] Where cross-border disputes are involved, the authority must be the dispute settlement body covering the system of the Single Buyer, or the system operator that refuses the use of or access to the system. Activation of these procedures does not prejudice the exercise of rights of appeal under Community law.[34] Independently of this requirement, Member States are obliged to create appropriate and efficient mechanisms for regulation, control, and transparency so as to avoid any abuse of a dominant position, in particular to the detriment of consumers, and to avoid predatory behaviour.[35] These mechanisms must take account of the EC Treaty rules, especially Article 81 and the rules on state aids.

(b) Regulated TPA

4.24 An alternative to the negotiated TPA procedure is that of regulated TPA (rTPA). This also allows producers and eligible consumers to contract directly with each other for supply. Eligible customers are granted a right of access on the basis of published tariffs. This system has to be at least equivalent to the other procedures in terms of system access. For dispute settlement under this procedure, Member States are obliged (by Art 20) to designate a competent body to settle disputes in the same way as they are if they take the negotiated access option, with the same provision governing cross-border disputes.

(c) The Single Buyer

4.25 If a Member State has chosen the Single Buyer régime then it must put in place the Single Buyer access system set out in Article 18 (see ch 3, paras 3.96–3.98). The main characteristics of the Single Buyer access system are as follows:

- publication by the Single Buyer of a non-discriminatory tariff for the use of the transmission and distribution system;
- eligible customers free to conclude supply contracts to cover their own needs with producers inside and outside the territory covered by the Single Buyer;
- Single Buyer obliged to purchase the electricity contracted by an eligible customer from a producer inside or outside the territory at a price equal to the sale price offered by the Single Buyer to eligible customers minus the price of the published tariff for use of the network. Single Buyer is not to be informed of electricity price as it appears in contract between producer and eligible customer. In effect, the Single Buyer has no merchant function; only a transportation function;[36] or

[33] ibid, Art 20(3).
[34] ibid, Art 20(5).
[35] ibid, Art 22.
[36] 'Guide to the Electricity Directive', n 31 above, 5.

- combining the Single Buyer principle with the TPA model (either negotiated or regulated), no purchase obligation on the Single Buyer which then acts like a system operator in a TPA model. If negotiated TPA were applied, there would be no obligation on the Single Buyer to publish tariffs for use of the transmission and distribution system.[37]

In the Single Buyer access system independent producers have the right to negotiate access to the system with the TSOs and DSOs and to conclude supply contracts with eligible customers outside the system on the basis of a voluntary commercial agreement, in a manner analogous to a TPA arrangement.[38] Both independent producers and auto-producers also have the right in the Single Buyer system to negotiate access to supply their own premises in the same Member State or in another Member State by using the interconnected system. **4.26**

With respect to unbundling, Single Buyer activities must be managed separately from production and distribution activities and separate accounts must be kept for the activities of vertically-integrated undertakings. The flow of information between the Single Buyer and the production and distribution activities must be limited to that which is strictly necessary to carry on the Single Buyer's responsibilities (creating 'Chinese Walls'). **4.27**

Access to the system may be refused by the Single Buyer, as may the purchase of electricity from eligible customers where the Single Buyer lacks the necessary transmission or distribution capacity. Duly substantiated reasons for such a refusal must be given, especially with respect to PSOs.

(6) Direct lines

All electricity producers and suppliers have a right to supply their own premises, subsidiaries, and eligible customers through a direct line once the producers and suppliers have the necessary authorization from the Member State.[39] A 'direct line' is defined as an electricity line that is complementary to the interconnected system. **4.28**

Any eligible customer within the territory of a Member State may be supplied through a direct line by a producer and supply undertakings, where they have been authorized by the Member States to do so. The criteria for the grant of an authorization for constructing a direct line must be objective and non-discriminatory. Member States may nevertheless make the grant of such authorizations subject to conditions. These may include the refusal of system access on grounds of a lack of transmission or distribution network capacity, or the opening of a dispute settlement procedure under Article 20. Moreover, Member States may refuse

[37] Electricity Directive, n 4 above, Art 18(3).
[38] ibid, Art 18(1)(iv).
[39] ibid, Art 21.

to authorize the construction of a new direct line if it might obstruct the performance of PSOs (in which case, duly substantiated reasons must be given).

4.29 This provision was unlikely to prove of much practical significance. The definition of 'direct line' is narrow, meaning only that it would connect producers or suppliers with subsidiaries or eligible customers. Such a line would normally have only one connection point to the interconnected system, with the second point being a power plant or a consumer. The definition of 'direct line' here means that third parties cannot use the line for purposes other than direct supply contracts with the owner of the direct line. Issues of network access and remuneration are therefore of little consequence. This conclusion does not apply, however, if a direct line connects two distinct TSO systems.

4.30 **Example** The generation or sales arm of a vertically-integrated company might build a direct line to a distribution company within another TSO area. This distributor might be a subsidiary of the vertically-integrated company but still be a purchaser under Article 21 of the Electricity Directive, with a right to build a direct line. Such a line would be connected at both ends to two interconnected systems and could be used by third parties.[40]

Market-opening and eligibility

The Directive requires Member States to take steps to introduce an opening of the electricity markets in three stages over a six-year period.[41] The first stage was taken on 19 February 1999, the second on 19 February 2000, and the third is scheduled for 19 February 2003. At each stage Member States are expected to ensure at least the minimum opening of the market. Member States may go further than this minimum and many have chosen to do so. The aim is to ensure that contracts benefiting from the access provisions in Articles 17 and 18 may be concluded.

> Stage 1: the minimum market-opening corresponding to stage 1 was calculated as the share of the total EU consumption that is consumed by final consumers with an annual consumption exceeding 40 GwH (on a consumption site basis and including auto-production: ie, electricity generation for own consumption). This implied that about 26.48% of each national market was scheduled to be opened for competition in the first stage.[42]
> Stage 2: the second stage envisaged a reduction of the threshold to a level of 20 GwH. This would increase the minimum market-opening to about 28%.
> Stage 3: this was expected to reduce the threshold further to 9 GwH to equal a market-opening of 33%.

[40] European Commission, '2nd Report to the Council and the European Parliament on Harmonization Requirements', SEC (1999) 470, 13–14.

[41] Electricity Directive, n 4 above, Art 19(1) and (2).

[42] Commission of the European Communities, 'Background Briefing Paper', 18 Feb 1999.

These calculations were made by the Commission on the basis of data submitted by the Member States.

Within these common percentages the Member States themselves are allowed to define which customers inside their territory are eligible to participate in the opening of the market.[43] In the text of the Directive there is no actual definition of 'eligibility' (in contrast to earlier drafts), reflecting the major divisions of opinion among Member States on this issue during the negotiations on the Directive. The provisions of Article 19 reflect the need for a compromise among the Member States on eligibility for access under Articles 17 or 18. However, in calculating the shares, Member States must include in their definitions of eligible customers very large final consumers of over 100 GwH annually. The figure of 100 GwH must be calculated on a consumption site basis and not a group or a single site basis. It must also include auto-production. Those distributors responsible for the volume of electricity consumed through their distribution network by such final customers must also have access to the extent of the final customers' entitlement (even if those distributors are not specifically designated as eligible). The criteria for the definition of eligible customers are published by Member States by 31 January each year in the *Official Journal*.[44] **4.31**

(7) Structure

Unbundling and Transparency of Accounts

Historically, transmission networks have usually been owned by vertically-integrated monopolies.[45] Non-discriminatory access is essential to bring about competition. However, this is only partly provided for by negotiated or regulated access. It also requires an effective unbundling of transmission system interests from any other interests of the vertically-integrated company.[46] To achieve this, the Directive contains requirements on three areas: **4.32**

- for internal accounts, separate accounts for generation, transmission and distribution activities from other parts of the company (Arts 13 and 14);
- establishment by the TSO of appropriate mechanisms to prevent confidential and commercially sensitive information being passed by it within the integrated company or to third parties (Art 9); and
- management unbundling of the TSO (Art 7(6)).

[43] Electricity Directive, n 4 above, Art 19(3).

[44] ibid, Art 19(4).

[45] ibid, Art 14. A 'vertically-integrated undertaking' is defined in the Directive as 'an undertaking performing two or more of the functions of generation, transmission and distribution of electricity' (definition 18).

[46] The requirement to unbundle had been accepted earlier by the ECJ in its judgment on the telecommunications terminal equipment Directive: C-202/88 *France v Commission*, [1991] ECR I-1223, para 25.

4.33 Member States must ensure that integrated undertakings keep separate accounts for generation, transmission, distribution, and activities—for internal accounting purposes.[47] The purpose of this provision is to provide for maximum transparency, in particular by identifying possible abuses of a dominant position.[48] Examples of this would include excessively high tariffs for transmission and distribution, excessively low tariffs for generation activities, and discriminatory practices for equivalent transactions. Terms such as 'excessive' and 'discriminatory practices' are well known in competition law and will be applied by the relevant judicial bodies, whether regulators or courts, both national and EU. Moreover, these separated accounts may be consulted by Member States when carrying out their monitoring activities. Article 13 states that this right of access to the unbundled accounts of undertakings extends to any competent authority Member States designate as well as dispute settlement authorities designated under Article 20(3) of the Directive. A national regulator would therefore have access to the accounts to carry out efficiency checks.

4.34 In cases where the TSO is not already independent from activities not related to the transmission system, this should be established, at least in management terms. The aim of Article 7(6) is to ensure non-discrimination of competitors, transparency, and objectivity in the behaviour of the TSO.[49] As an alternative to the management and accounts unbundling approach, it is possible to create a legally separate TSO, making it easier to ensure non-discrimination (legal unbundling). A third option would be to create a TSO that is completely separate from other interests and owns all the transmission assets (ownership unbundling).

4.35 Electricity undertakings must draw up, submit to audit, and publish their annual accounts in accordance with the rules of national law.[50] Undertakings not legally obliged to publish their annual accounts must keep a copy of these at the disposal of the public in their head office. To avoid discrimination, cross-subsidization, or distortions of competition, integrated electricity undertakings must keep separate accounts for their generation, transmission, and distribution activities. If they are engaged in other non-electricity activities, these must be accounted for separately as if they were carried out by separate undertakings.

---

[47] Electricity Directive, n 4 above. Art 14(3) is unclear whether the trading or supply of electricity is an activity distinct from distribution which would therefore be subject to a requirement to have its accounts separated out. If they are not separated out, the possibility of cross-subsidies and distortions of competition arise.

[48] ibid, Recital 32.

[49] ibid, Recital 25.

[50] ibid, Art 14(2). Those rules are based on the 4th Council Directive 78/660/EEC of 25 July 1978 based on Art 54(3)(g) of the EC Treaty on the annual accounts of certain types of companies: 1978 OJ L 222, 11.

The Directive provides specific details on the kind of data that must be provided in the accounts. Data must be provided in the form of notes to the accounts of undertakings, explaining the rules governing the allocation of assets and liabilities. These notes should also cover the expenditure and income followed in drawing up separate accounts.[51] Similarly, the accounts must include data (in note-form) on transactions of a certain size conducted with affiliated undertakings or with associated undertakings or with undertakings that belong to the same shareholders.[52] The latter expression is to be understood as meaning those shareholders having at least a material or a major interest (percentages below 20% would not qualify).[53] The TSO must preserve the confidentiality of commercially sensitive information obtained in the course of carrying out its business.[54] 4.36

The unbundling provisions also impose requirements on Member States applying the Single Buyer access régime.[55] They must take measures to ensure that the Single Buyer operates separately from the generation and distribution activities of the integrated undertaking. They are also required to ensure that there is no flow of information between the Single Buyer activities of vertically-integrated undertakings and their generation and distribution activities. However—rather confusingly—this does not have to include information that is deemed to be necessary for the conduct of the Single Buyer tasks.

Originally, there had been a provision to require a wider unbundling of management. This was removed following a critical opinion by Parliament and greater clarification of the provisions on unbundling of accounts. In particular, measures were also introduced to ensure the full independence of the system management in Single Buyer systems (Art 15), while in a negotiated TPA system the system operator must be independent at least in management terms (Art 7). 4.37

(8) Public Service Obligations

Public service obligations (PSOs) are fairly common in the utility sectors of many Member States, especially where such industries have traditionally been state-owned. There is no Europe-wide definition of 'public service' but most Member States have adopted mechanisms in their electricity régimes designed to achieve 4.38

[51] Electricity Directive, n 4 above, Art 14(4).
[52] ibid, Art 14(5).
[53] European Commission, 'Guide to the Electricity Directive', see n 31 above.
[54] Electricity Directive, n 4 above, Art 9. A similar obligation is imposed on distribution system operators in Art 12.
[55] ibid, Art 15.

benefits or assurances to the public good. Underlying these mechanisms lies the objective of balancing the public interest in competition with the provision of an adequate level of public service—which some Member States feel is not likely to be guaranteed by the operation of market forces alone.[56]

4.39 The Directive allows Member States to impose on their electricity undertakings PSOs in the general economic interest.[57] There are five categories of PSO:

- security (including security of supply);
- regularity of supply;
- quality of supplies;
- price of supplies; and
- environmental protection factors.

4.40 The obligations must be clearly defined, transparent, non-discriminatory, and verifiable. They must be published and notified to the Commission 'without delay', where their compatibility with Community law will be assessed (see the discussion of PSOs at paras 4.122–4.124). If carrying out any of these PSOs, Member States are permitted to introduce the implementation of long-term planning.[58] However, regard must be had to the Treaty rules, especially Article 86.

4.41 The PSOs must respect the Community framework and must not be used to favour domestic electricity producers at the expense of producers in other Member States.[59] Examples of PSOs would be: an obligation for customers to purchase a certain percentage of its electricity from renewable sources; or an obligation for a distributor to supply all customers in its area at an equal price per kWh.

4.42 The reference in Article 3(2) to the Treaty rules is important (when introducing PSOs regard must be paid by the Member State to Treaty rules). This is apparent from the detailed information which the Member State must provide to the Commission when notifying its PSOs (see paras 4.123–4.124 for Gas PSOs; the same requirements apply to electricity PSOs).

4.43 However, it is important to note that in limited circumstances Member States are entitled to decide not to apply certain provisions of the Directive. These exceptions are contained in Articles 5 and 6 on authorization or competitive tendering of generation capacity, Articles 17 and 18 on refusal of access to the system in both negotiated third-party access and Single Buyer systems, and refusal of the

---

[56] ibid, Recital 13.

[57] ibid, Art 3(2); see also Recitals 13,14, and 19.

[58] 'Long-term planning' is defined in the Directive to mean 'the planning of the need for investment in generation and transmission capacity on a long-term basis, with a view to meeting the demand for electricity of the system and securing supplies to customers'.

[59] Commission of the European Communities, Guide, n 31 above.

construction of direct lines in Article 21.[60] The choice is only available to the extent that the application of the relevant provisions of the Directive 'would obstruct the performance in law or in fact of' the PSOs that are imposed on the electricity undertakings in the general economic interest. Neither must the decision not to apply affect the development of trade to an extent that it is contrary to the interests of the Community. The latter includes the Community's interest in competition with regard to eligible customers under this Directive and also Article 86 of the Treaty (which Art 3(3) effectively re-states in the context of this Directive). If the Commission considers that the application of the relevant provision would not obstruct the performance, in law or in fact, of the obligations—then it would require the Member State to apply the relevant provisions.

The ECJ has also stated that a narrow interpretation of exceptions to the Treaty rules in Article 86(2) is required.[61] This would have a bearing on any attempt by a Member State to seek an exemption under Article 86(2) from the Directive provisions, whether of a broad or a narrow character. **4.44**

An example of a broad application of an exemption would be one in which the implementation of the levels of market-opening specified in Article 19 made on the basis that the market-opening requirement would obstruct the performance in law or in fact of a PSO (eg, security of supply). This is an area that will undoubtedly be monitored closely by the Commission and the ECJ for potential abuse given the lack of clarity in the interface between the public service concept, the competition rules, and Article 86. Nevertheless, it should be noted that the notion of PSOs in the general economic interest has been confirmed by Article 16 EC Treaty (introduced by TA).[62] **4.45**

In a distinct category from the other PSOs mentioned above, but still representing a departure from the application of market conditions, the Directive allows Member States to take temporary measures to safeguard electricity supply in the event of a sudden crisis in the energy market or where the physical safety or security of persons, apparatus or installations, or system integrity is at stake.[63] **4.46**

---

[60] Electricity Directive, n 4 above, Arts 5(1)(h), 6(3), 17(5), 18(4), and 21(5).

[61] See eg Cases C-157/94 *Commission v The Netherlands*; C-158/94 *Commission v Italy*; C-159/94 *Commission v France*; and C-160/94 *Commission v Spain* [1997] ECR I-5699 et seq.

[62] 'Without prejudice to Arts 73, 86, and 87, and given the place occupied by services of general economic interest in the shared values of the Union as well as their rôle in promoting social and territorial cohesion, the Community and the Member States, each within their respective powers and within the scope of application of this Treaty, shall take care that such services operate on the basis of principles and conditions which enable them to fulfil their missions' (Art 16). Note also the text of the Declaration: 'The provisions of Article 7d of the Treaty establishing the European Community [now Art 16] on public services shall be implemented with full respect for the jurisprudence of the Court of Justice, *inter alia* as regards the principles of equality of treatment, quality and continuity of such services'.

[63] Electricity Directive, n 4 above, Art 23.

However, the freedom is narrowly formulated: the measure has to be proportionate to the crisis and is subject to review by the Commission.

4.47 Despite the above remarks on how the grant of PSOs is carefully circumscribed in the Directive, it should be noted that the origin of the PSO provision lay in efforts by the Parliament to limit the scope of the Commission's original liberalization measures. The frequency of their appearance in the Directive testifies to the influence of the Commission's critics on the text of the final draft.

(9) Reciprocity

4.48 The Directive includes some possibilities for a Member State to refuse access to suppliers from another Member State when the receiving Member State opened up a larger part of its market than the other. The reciprocity clause (Art 19) allows Member State A to refuse deliveries to certain types of customers with respect to imports from Member State B, if such customers in Member State B would not be free to choose a supplier of electricity in Member State A.[64] Member States that have elected to include such a clause in their implementing legislation include: Austria, Belgium, Germany, Luxembourg, The Netherlands, Portugal, Spain, and the United Kingdom.

4.49 According to Article 19(5), these clauses seek to avoid imbalance in the opening of the electricity markets. This is a transitional mechanism, expressly directed at the nine-year period of market-opening commencing from entry into force of the Directive to the year 2006. It must be reviewed by the Commission during the fifth year of application of the Directive on the basis of market developments. The Commission is charged with evaluating and reporting on possible imbalances in the opening of electricity markets.

4.50 Where a transaction for electricity supply cannot proceed because a customer is eligible in only one of the two Member States concerned, the Commission may oblige the refusing party to execute the requested electricity supply at the request of the Member State where the eligible customer is located.[65] However, before this provision can be activated, two preconditions must be fulfilled.

1. A higher level of market-opening (in terms of a percentage higher than the minimum) must be applied by the Member State seeking to utilize Art 19(5) against a company located in another Member State.
2. An eligible customer that seeks to contract electricity from a supplier located in the other Member State would not have the status of eligible customer in that Member State.

[64] European Commission, 'Communication on Completing the Internal Energy Market', COM (2001) 125 12 Mar 2001, 66.

[65] Electricity Directive, n 4 above, Art 19(5)(b).

However, in any determination of the possible activation of this approach, it should be borne in mind that the requirement for all Member States to liberalize a minimum of 23 per cent of domestic consumption in the initial phase has the effect that the actual threshold (in terms of GwH corresponding to the 23% figure) will not be identical in each Member State. This applies also to the different qualitative eligibility criteria. Recourse to Article 19(5) is not therefore possible to counteract the difference in quantitative or qualitative thresholds necessary to reach the principal aim of the Directive—that is, an equivalent market-opening.[66] It can only be claimed by Member States that liberalize more than the common minimum percentage. 4.51

Strictly speaking, reciprocity is not a principle of the European Community. Instead, the principle of equal treatment applies. However, the Commission took the view that the combination of the principles of progressivity, under which Member States may be allowed to follow up a stage-by-stage opening of the market, and subsidiarity—where Member States may choose to open the market more rapidly—could have the effect of creating serious imbalances in the rights and obligations among electricity companies of different Member States. In these circumstances a reciprocity rule aimed at introducing a better balance between electricity companies was thought to be compatible with the Treaty to the extent that this provision is a transitional one, is of reasonable duration, and is in keeping with a progressive pattern.[67] (However, see the subsequent development described in ch 8, at paras 8.32–8.33.) 4.52

The principle is also likely to have an impact on energy trade between the EU and third countries. With respect to the Europe Agreements, for example, the Commission has stated that 'as the reciprocity clause . . . and environmental standards form part of the Community law, application of reciprocity and conditions with regard to environmental standards seem to be compatible' with these Agreements.[68] The Commission supports the conclusion of bilateral or multilateral agreements or understandings to create a legal framework for electricity trade. Reciprocity would therefore be ensured and a level playing field established on the basis of equivalent market access. 4.53

In this respect, the joint declaration on liberalization of electricity markets by the Joint Committee EU/Switzerland may be noted as a possible example.[69] It stipulates that mutual access to the Community and Swiss electricity markets must be 4.54

[66] 'Guide to the Electricity Directive', n 31 above, 10.

[67] ibid, 11. For an extended discussion of this principle in the context of electricity liberalization, see Johnston A, 'Maintaining the Balance of Power: Liberalization, Reciprocity and Electricity in the European Community', in (1999) 17 J Energy Natural Resources L, 121–50.

[68] Communication, n 64 above, 67.

[69] ibid, 68.

organized on the basis of reciprocity as defined in the Electricity Directive and the corresponding stipulations in Swiss law. However, a curious feature of this declaration is that it interprets (for a specific good, ie electricity) a pre-existing general free trade agreement—the EU–Switzerland Free Trade Agreement—itself based on the principle of reciprocity.

(10) Transition

4.55 The Directive text declares that it represents 'a further phase of liberalization' but notes at the same time that some obstacles to trade in electricity will remain in place once it has been adopted.[70] It allows for the possibility of further proposals for improving the operation of the internal market in electricity once the Commission has had an opportunity to experience the Directive's operation (and has reported its observations to the Council and Parliament).[71] Harmonization requirements for the effective operation of the internal market in electricity are also to be the subject of reports from the Commission at specific intervals[72] (see ch 6, paras 6.53–6.58).

4.56 **Transitional arrangements and derogations** The Directive contains express provision for countries that may have difficulties with the transition to a liberalized market. For Member States in which commitments or guarantees have been given before the date of entry into force of the Directive, and where these may not be honoured because of the provisions of the Directive, it is possible to apply for a transitional régime that may be granted to them by the Commission and most have done so.[73] Subject to this requirement, Article 24 allows Member States to derogate from some provisions of the Directive, such as:

- the organization of system access (Chapter VII);
- transmission system operation (Chapter IV); or
- unbundling and transparency of accounts (Chapter VI).

4.57 The Commission's decision must take into account factors including the size of the system concerned, the level of interconnection of the system, and the structure of the electricity industry. The decision must be published in the *Official Journal*. Any such transitional régime must be limited in duration and must be linked to the expiry of commitments or guarantees that are at risk because of the new or emerging market conditions. Applications for a transitional régime were to be notified to the Commission no later than one year after the entry into force of the Directive. All Member States except two—Finland and Sweden—

---

70 Electricity Directive, n 4 above, Recital 39.

71 ibid, Art 26.

72 ibid, Art 25. See ch 7, paras 7.99–7.115.

73 ibid, Art 24.

expressed interest in operating a transitional régime. In several cases the measures notified did not fall within the scope of Article 24.[74] Six Member States proposed schemes for financial compensation while two proposed to derogate from the Directive's provisions. Several Member States agreed to indicate the details of their schemes, involving state aids, at a later date. These were: Italy, Belgium, Portugal, Ireland, and Greece.

It may also be noted that Article 24(3) allows Member States to make a case for special provision for any small isolated systems—(meaning a system with consumption of less than 2500 GwH in the year 1996 where less than 5% of the consumption is obtained through interconnection with other systems)—where those systems appeared likely to experience substantial problems in operation after the Directive has been brought into force. This derogation is of particular importance for the small Greek Islands. The Commission is required to inform Member States prior to taking any decision of this kind and to publish the decision in the *Official Journal*. **4.58**

Article 26 of the Electricity Directive envisages a review of its operation in 2006. In a Communication, the Commission stated that the Directive:

> . . . is part of the second phase of the effort of the Commission to establish the internal energy market and as such represents an intermediate phase towards the full liberalization of the electricity sector. It will be followed by further measures promoting market-opening.[75]

(11) Stranded Costs

The device of the transitional régime in the Directive represents an attempt to manage a problem familiar in liberalizing electricity markets. The costs of some prior investments, principally in generating plants, may be unrecoverable or 'stranded' in the transition to a competitive pricing régime. Generation from old coal-fired plant, for example, cannot compete with electricity generated from gas-fired power stations constructed as a result of the introduction of competition under the Directive. 'Stranded' costs or assets involve past investments in plant and equipment and power purchases made by utilities to meet estimated customer needs, stranded as a result of the liberalization process in the markets. New market entrants, which have not been subject to the same PSO to meet customer needs, have no such costs and therefore enjoy an inequitable competitive advantage. Stranded costs impose a significant financial burden on incumbent **4.59**

[74] Note in particular the Commission Decisions 1999/791/EC, 1999/792/EC, 1999/795/EC, 1999/796/EC, 1999/797/EC, and 1999/798/EC, concerning respectively the UK, France, Austria, The Netherlands, Spain and Denmark, pursuant to Art 24 of Directive 96/92/EC, OJ L 319, 11 Dec 1999.

[75] Communication, n 64 above, 2.

electricity utilities. Examples of their liabilities include long-term power purchase contracts, investment based on a guaranteed market for output, or investment beyond the scope of normal business.

4.60 Although this is a temporary problem, it has provoked considerable controversy, being described as 'a fundamental issue in electricity deregulation'.[76] In the USA for example, it has been argued that a 'regulatory contract' existed between government and the utilities.[77] Attempts to change the environment in which the contract operates have the effect of violating the terms of the contract and should lead to compensation being paid to the utilities that are parties to this contract. The EU's mechanism to address this thorny issue is the transitional régime provision in Article 24 of the Directive, although the term 'stranded assets'—(or any variation thereon)—is not expressly mentioned in the text.

There are many examples of compensation schemes that have been notified to the Commission, since 12 of the 15 Member States found it necessary to make provision for stranded assets.

Spain: stranded assets compensation schemes

4.61 In Spain there were two separate schemes, both of which were notified to the Commission (see ch 7, para 7.101). First, there was a Costs of Transition to Competition Scheme (CTC) régime, which provided compensation over a maximum of ten years to Spanish electricity generators because of the fall in electricity prices from liberalization. Most of this would accrue to 11 utilities, amounting to 1,693 billion pesetas. The remainder, comprising 295 billion pesetas, was designed to cover a fixed premium of one peseta per KWh of power from indigenous coal. The utilities would be able to sell bonds immediately to a group of banks, which would then be paid back over a period of ten years by the utilities. The utilities could pass on the costs to customers via a 4.5 per cent levy on all end-user bills. This method of calculating CTCs was dropped in favour of the 'differences method' in June 2001.

4.62 A second scheme proposed to redistribute the relatively high cost of generation and distribution in the isolated systems of the islands and extra-peninsular systems by means of a specific levy on the mainland power tariffs and transmission fees. At the time, the operators of the systems in these locations benefited from specific exemptions from the market rules applicable to the mainland power market.

---

[76] Kahn, Edward 'Introducing Competition to the Electricity Industry in Spain: the Rôle of Initial Conditions', in Zaccour, Georges (ed), *Deregulation of Electric Utilities*, (1998) 259–73.

[77] Sidak, J Gregory and Spulber, Daniel F, *Deregulatory Takings and the Regulatory Contract: the Competitive Transformation of Network Industries in the United States*, (1998). For an interesting critique of this position, see book review: Rossi, Jim 'The Irony of Deregulatory Takings', (1998) 77 Texas Law Review 297–320.

The Commission assessed these proposals and concluded that both schemes failed to qualify according to four tests that it applied to them. These were: 4.63

- that the company's viability must cease or be endangered;
- the amount of compensation must be subject to an annual review;
- costs must not be calculated globally (by including, say, all subsidiaries of a company); and
- the degree of compensation must be taken into account.

In the Spanish Government's case there was an intention to raise compensation before losses were incurred, a controversial step since it involved an element of forecasting losses that had not yet been incurred. A weakness of such systems of forecasted compensation is that the estimated losses might never occur in practice.

It is evident that Article 24 opens the door to a wide range of schemes and creates a considerable amount of work for the Commission in assessing the acceptability of compensation schemes. Inevitably, Commission decisions in this area will attract opposition from Member States and possible review by the ECJ. If so, such judgments are likely to provide guidance on the definition of a 'stranded cost', the acceptability of specific recovery mechanisms, and links to state aid. Meanwhile, the Commission itself has made efforts to provide such clarification since the adoption of the Directive[78] (for a detailed discussion of this see ch 7, paras 7.107–7.115). 4.64

(12) Enforcement

Member States must create appropriate and efficient mechanisms for regulation, control, and transparency so as to avoid any abuse of dominant position, in particular to the detriment of consumers and any predatory behaviour.[79] These are mechanisms that must take into account the provisions of the Treaty and especially Article 86 of the Treaty. However, the complexity of the issues raised by the Directive and difficulties in interpretation of its provisions suggest an important rôle for the Commission as both arbiter and enforcer. 4.65

C. Gas Directive

The Directive establishing common rules for an internal market in natural gas (the Gas Directive) was adopted by the Council in April 1998 and entered into 4.66

[78] See, eg 'Commission Communication on Methodology for Analysing State Aid linked to Stranded Costs', 26 July 2001.

[79] Electricity Directive, n 4 above, Art 22.

force on 10 August 1998.[80] Its structure and many of its provisions were based on comparable provisions in the Electricity Directive.

The aim of the Gas Directive is to establish common rules for the transmission, distribution, supply, and storage of natural gas. It lays down rules relating to the organization and functioning of the natural gas sector, including liquefied natural gas, access to the market, operation of systems, criteria and procedures applicable to the granting of authorizations for transmission, distribution, supply, and storage of natural gas.[81]

(1) Background

4.67 The Gas Directive is a compromise document based on extensive discussions with the Member States and the various players in the gas market. An impasse was reached with the 1994 draft text, leading the Energy Council to suspend its efforts to develop an acceptable draft until agreement had been reached on the content of the draft Electricity Directive. A common position on the Electricity Directive was reached in July 1996[82] and work on the draft Gas Directive was resumed in September leading to the circulation of a new draft in October for comments from the Member States.[83] This work continued under the leadership of three Presidencies of the EU: the Irish, Dutch, and Luxembourg Presidencies.

4.68 The Irish Presidency draft was based on its counterpart for the electricity sector rather than its predecessor, the 1994 draft gas Directive[84]—which was largely superseded. It provided only the basic rules and a framework for national legislation, with Member States being allowed, following the subsidiarity principle, to fill out the detail. This in itself implied the likelihood of diverse approaches to implementation by Member States.

4.69 There were two principal areas of controversy: (i) market access and (ii) take-or-pay contracts.

(i) The Directive proposed an initial minimum market-opening percentage access, unspecified in the text (Art 18), with the Commission required to publish a minimum market-opening percentage for each subsequent year.

---

[80] Directive 98/30/EC of the European Parliament and Council of 22 June 1998, [1998] OJ L 204/2.

[81] ibid, Art 1.

[82] Common Position (EC) No. 230/96 adopted by the Council on 25 July 1996, with a view to adopting Directive 96/92/EC of the European Parliament and Council on Common Rules for the Internal Market in Electricity (OJ/96/C315).

[83] Presidency Compromise Proposal, 15 Oct 1996, SN 4325/96 (General Secretariat of the Council).

[84] Amended Proposal for a European Parliament and Council Directive concerning common rules for the internal market in natural gas, OJ C 123 4.5.94, 26.

(ii) The take-or-pay provision (Art 23) provided for the granting of derogations in respect of access obligations only for contracts entered into before 25 July 1996. These transitional régimes were to be granted by the Commission on application by the relevant Member State.

Extensive negotiations on the text continued under the guidance of the Dutch Presidency in the first half of 1997. This led to the circulation of a further compromise text on 25 April 1997.

On market-opening it specified that: in the first stage, all power generators and other customers using more than 25 million cubic metres a year should qualify as 'eligible customers' who would be able to benefit from competition in the supply of gas; that this threshold should fall to 10 million cubic metres a year after five years and to one million cubic metres a year after ten years; and that the resulting market-opening should amount to at least 30 per cent initially, rising to 40 per cent after five years (2003), and 50 per cent after ten (in 2008). 4.70

On take-or-pay contracts, the text dropped the term 'transitional régime' in favour of 'derogations' that could be granted in respect of access obligations for long-term take-or-pay contracts entered into at any time. The latter meant either before or after 25 July 1996. 4.71

A subsequent draft produced by the Dutch Presidency on 6 June 1997 replaced these indicative figures with letters of the alphabet, indicating the extent of the disagreement that still remained among the parties. It also modified the proposals on take-or-pay in accordance with whether the contract was entered into before or after 25 July 1996: if the contract was entered into before that date, Member States would have the power to grant derogations without reference to the Commission; if after, they were required to notify their intention to grant a derogation to the Commission, which was able to require amendments to the derogation or to refuse permission to grant it. 4.72

After continuing discussions without agreement, a further draft was produced by the incoming Luxembourg Presidency on 18 July 1997. It proposed thresholds for eligible customers (except power generators) of 25 million cubic metres initially, 15 million cubic metres after five years, and five million cubic metres after ten years, and minimum figures for market-opening of 28, 40, and 45 per cent respectively. This text was also the first draft to include recitals.

Among the various other changes made in the draft were those concerning the grant of derogations to a transmission company from the obligation to grant access to their pipelines if in so doing it would encounter serious economic and financial difficulties because of its take-or-pay commitments accepted in one or more gas purchase contracts. This significantly enhanced the powers of the Commission. A two-stage procedure was introduced that would allow a gas undertaking which has 4.73

received an application for access to apply to the Member State concerned for a derogation, either before or after access is refused. If a Member State received a request for a derogation, it would have to take into account the terms of the contract in question, including the extent to which it allowed for changes in market conditions. Prior to any grant of a derogation, it had to notify the Commission, which had to apply the same criteria as the Member State. The Commission could request the Member State to amend or withdraw the proposed derogation within a four-week period.

4.74 Further compromise texts were issued in September and October 1997. They included an additional criterion to the list applicable to the granting of derogations. It required the Member State and the Commission to take into account 'the extent to which, when accepting the take-or-pay commitments in question, the undertaking could reasonably have foreseen, having regard to the provisions of this Directive, that serious difficulties were likely to arise'.[85] Member States were also given the right (in the October text) to choose whether an applicant for a derogation should submit the application before or after refusing access. A revised definition of 'transmission' was included, which had the effect of excluding from the scope of the Directive those production lines subject to the Hydrocarbons Licensing Directive. The texts also introduced Chinese Wall provisions to prohibit transmission or distribution undertakings from abusing 'commercially sensitive information obtained from third parties in the context of providing or negotiating access to the system'. The idea of a list of qualifying regions (to be Annexed) was dropped in favour of a definition of 'emergent regions' taken from an earlier draft text.

Despite the convening of an extraordinary Energy Council on 27 October, no political agreement was reached on the text until the Energy Council on 8 December 1997.[86] After discussion in the Committee of Permanent Representatives, it was formally adopted as a Common Position on 12 February 1998.[87]

(2) **Production**

4.75 In contrast to its sister Electricity Directive, the Gas Directive is not concerned with the provision of common rules for production operations. For gas this had been done already via the Hydrocarbons Licensing Directive, adopted in 1994 (see ch 3, paras 3.37–3.47). The only exception is a provision in the Gas Directive concerning access to facilities linked to offshore production installations for network access purposes (see below, paras 4.96–4.101). Otherwise, the provisions of

[85] Presidency Compromise Proposal for a European Parliament and Council Directive on common rules for the internal market in natural gas, Brussels, 18 July 1997.
[86] Consolidated text issued by General Secretariat, 10 Dec 1997, SN 4930/97 (OR.EN).
[87] [1998] OJ C 91/46, and *corrigendum* of [1998] OJ C 181/20.

the Hydrocarbons Licensing Directive should be referred to, since they concern similar subject matter to that of the generation-related provisions of the Electricity Directive, covering authorization procedures, non-discrimination including the abolition of exclusive rights, tendering criteria, and so on.

(3) Transmission

By contrast to the Electricity Directive, storage plays a rôle in system access and is treated together with transmission. 'Transmission' is defined as the transport of natural gas through a high-pressure pipeline network other than an upstream pipeline network with a view to its delivery to customers, and is referred to in Chapters III and VI (on access to the system).[88] **4.76**

A general duty is imposed on transmission, storage, and LNG undertakings to operate, maintain, and develop under economic conditions the secure, reliable, and efficient transmission, storage and/or LNG facilities, with due regard to the environment.[89] These undertakings must not discriminate between system users or classes of system users, especially in favour of their related undertakings. They are placed under an obligation to provide any other transmission, storage or distribution undertaking with sufficient information to ensure that the transport and storage of natural gas takes place in a manner compatible with the secure and efficient operation of the interconnected system.[90] The confidentiality of commercially sensitive information obtained in the process of carrying out the business must be preserved.[91] In particular, transmission undertakings must not abuse commercially sensitive information obtained from third parties in the context of providing or negotiating access to the system. This is especially relevant in cases of sales or purchases of natural gas by the transmission undertakings or related undertakings. This does not imply, however, that a company is under any obligation to modify its legal structure or create new companies.[92]

(4) Distribution

The provisions on distribution and supply as set out in Articles 9 to 11 of the Directive are almost identical to those applicable to Articles 6 to 8 on transmission, storage, and LNG. The definition of 'distribution' provided in Article 2(5) is given as the transport of natural gas through local or regional pipeline networks with a view to its delivery to customers. **4.77**

[88] Gas Directive, n 80 above, Art 2(3).
[89] ibid, Art 7(1).
[90] ibid, Art 7(3).
[91] ibid, Art 8(1).
[92] Statement 86/98 in Council Minutes, May 1998.

With respect to distribution and/or supply undertakings, Member States may impose on them an obligation to deliver to customers located in a given area or of a certain class or both.[93] The tariff for such deliveries may be regulated. The aim of any such regulation may be to ensure equal treatment of customers. Each distribution undertaking must operate, maintain, and develop under economic conditions a secure, reliable, and efficient system, with due regard to the environment. No discrimination may take place between system users or classes of system user, especially in favour of its related undertakings. Each distribution undertaking must provide any other distribution undertaking and/or transmission and/or storage undertaking with sufficient information to ensure that the transport of gas may take place in a manner compatible with the secure and efficient operation of the interconnected system.

4.78 Confidentiality requirements on information are imposed on distribution undertakings in Article 11. Each distribution undertaking is to preserve the confidentiality of commercially sensitive information obtained in the course of carrying out its business. Further, distribution undertakings are prohibited from abusing commercially sensitive information obtained from third parties in the course of providing or negotiating access to the system. This does not however require that the distribution undertakings modify their legal structure or create new companies.[94]

4.79 Article 4 which lays down rules for the granting of licences/approvals authorizing the construction or operation of natural gas facilities (which include production, transmission, distribution, and storage facilities) exempts Member States from the obligation to grant authorizations in relation to distribution systems in an area where such a system has already been or is proposed to be built in the area concerned or if existing or proposed capacity is still available. Two conditions apply here:

(i) distribution pipelines should already exist in the area or are scheduled to be built on the basis of an authorization granted and work commenced; and
(iii) spare capacity in existing pipelines should exist.

4.80 In the Commission's view, a Member State may only utilize the latter exemption when it is pursuing two objectives at the same time: development of newly-supplied areas and efficient operation.[95] Any such exemption is likely to be limited in time to the period covered by the term 'newly supplied areas', which is undefined in the Directive's definitions section. As a reference point for duration, the

[93] Gas Directive, n 80 above, Art 9(2). An overview of the European distribution sector is contained in 'Natural Gas Distribution: Focus on Western Europe', OECD/IEA, 1998.

[94] Statement 86/98, n 92 above.

[95] European Commission (DG XVII/A3/B3), 'Authorizations for New Distribution Pipelines' (Discussion Note prepared for the Follow-up Meeting, 22 Oct 1998). Twelve Discussion Notes on integration and application of the Gas Directive were issued by the European Commission for two 'Follow-Up' meetings with Member State and industry representatives in 1998–99. They are available on the Commission website at www.europa.eu-int/comm/energy/en/gas_single_market/discussion_notes.html

generous provision of ten years in Article 26(3) may prove attractive to Member States, although the Directive text on Article 4 provides no express guidance on this.

It may also be that the provisions of Article 4 in relation to a distribution system do not apply. This situation could occur under the provisions of Article 3(3) which states that the provisions of Article 4 need not be applied by Member States to distribution systems if this would obstruct (in law or in fact) the performance of the obligations imposed on natural gas undertakings.[96] **4.81**

The provisions on investment in distribution systems contained in Article 26 are discussed below at paras 4.162–4.165.

(5) Access

At the core of the Directive are the provisions on system access. A choice is given to Member States in the way that they organize access to their gas systems (both transmission and distribution). The choice is between one or both of the procedures set out in Articles 15 and 16: either a *negotiated* or a *regulated* system of network access. In the former case, access is based on 'the main commercial conditions for the use of the system'; while in the latter it is established by 'published tariffs and/or other terms and obligations for use of that system'. Both procedures must operate in accordance with objective, transparent, and non-discriminatory criteria. A combination of both systems may involve the use of negotiated access at the transmission level and regulated access at distribution level. Such combinations have subsequently been favoured in Denmark and The Netherlands. **4.82**

(a) Negotiated TPA (nTPA)

The option of negotiated access requires Member States to take measures necessary to allow natural gas producers, supply undertakings, and eligible customers—either inside or outside the territory covered by the system—to negotiate access to the system with a view to concluding supply contracts with each other. These must be concluded on the basis of voluntary commercial agreements and access must be negotiated with the relevant natural gas undertakings in good faith. The main commercial conditions for system use must be published by the natural gas undertakings of Member States within the first year of implementation of the Directive and annually after that (Art 15(2)). **4.83**

Questions arise as to what those published conditions should be and how the pricing of access to the gas system should be organized. The Commission has listed the following as main commercial considerations: **4.84**

[96] Art 3(3) is explained at para 4.127.

- timing of uptake of gas per day;
- point of entry of gas to be contracted;
- an example of prices usually charged for using the system;
- method by which a customer may request a price for delivery of gas;
- contractual terms and conditions on use and payment;
- technical requirements for network access; and
- time-frame within which gas company must reply to request for access.[97]

The list reflects the Commission's view and is not legally binding, although a court might use it as a guide in its interpretation. And it is not exhaustive. Information would also normally be required by a requesting party on the nature of the transmission service (whether firm or interruptible; overrun provisions); on capacity booking; balancing requirements (over what period; what charges or penalties apply); the quality of gas delivered, since this can affect the way in which gas is delivered; and/or nomination rules and settlement or reconciliation rules between forecast and actual meter readings.

4.85 Variation of the precise criteria from one Member State to another is inevitable, as is variation according to the exact circumstances of the application for access. The aim of the requirement is to ensure that the gas companies publish sufficient information to allow potential users of the negotiated access option the possibility of clearly understanding what the procedure is under which they may gain access to the network and enter into and conclude negotiations. It would seem to follow that some indication of the charges or principles of charging structure should also be provided but this is certainly not an express obligation. In practice, most operators under nTPA have published their commercial conditions on their websites.[98]

Probably the most important commercial condition of all is an indication of charges or principles of charging structure. However, the design of charges for TPA will be a new experience for many countries and companies and could therefore take some time. This is a practical obstacle to speedy implementation since gas pricing in the EU has largely been based on a bundled and market-value approach rather than a cost-plus approach—as normally used in the electricity sector due to its relatively more regulated pricing history. In the short term, this could put a brake on the development of suitable methodologies for transportation charges and for charging other services.

4.86 The charges for access may be developed on the basis of a number of different methods and assumptions[99] such as:

---

[97] European Commission (DG XVII/A3/B3), 'Publication of main commercial conditions' (Discussion Note, 22 Oct 1998, see n 95 above).

[98] eg www.gasunie.nl (Gasunie, The Netherlands); www.distrigas.be (Distrigas, Belgium), and www.gazdefrance.com (Gaz de France).

[99] 'Access charges: A First Attempt to Identify Issues in relation to Pricing of Access to the Gas System', (Discussion Note, 22 Oct 1998, see n 95 above).

- cost basis (long-run or short-run marginal costs, average costs based on historic accounts; average costs based on replacement costs);
- acceptable level of rate of return/profit and profile of depreciation; proportion of operating and other costs that can be attributed to each function in the gas chain;
- definition of 'system capacity'; calculation of attribution of costs to a particular customer based on size and load factor to the customer; and
- actual or notional distance over which the gas is transported and also charging for additional items such as gas storage for back-up.

The overriding objective is to provide appropriate incentives to market players to participate in the open gas market. This will include a provision for recovery of costs by the gas company and a suitable return on the assets involved, as well as a provision of incentives to it to maintain and further develop the transportation system, maximizing its use while providing potential customers with predictable and stable access charges to stimulate TPA. **4.87**

(b) Regulated TPA (rTPA)

Alternatively, there is a procedure for regulated access (Art 16). Under this option, Member States give natural gas producers and eligible customers either inside or outside the territory covered by the interconnected system a right of access to the system, on the basis of published tariffs and/or other terms and obligations for use of that system. The effect of this should be at least equivalent, in terms of access to the system, to the procedures for access set out in Article 15. **4.88**

(c) Tarification practices

Some general principles have since been offered to Member States and companies by the European Commission by way of guidance to access tarification.[100] The tariffs should be objective, fair, non-discriminatory, simple and transparent and predictable and stable. 'Objectivity' is defined as based on a systematic methodology applicable to all requests for access on a consistent and comparable basis, established for example on a cost-of-service tariff which places all fixed costs in a capacity charge and all variable costs in a commodity charge. **4.89**

In practice, the experiences of individual Member States will be important in determining how to proceed. Examples of transportation charges at national level are seen in Great Britain and the Spanish systems of tarification of access to pipelines.[101] **4.90**

[100] ibid.

[101] The examples given in the Discussion Note on Access Charges reflect the situation at the time. The Note also refers to Dutch experience and the tariff structure introduced by Gasunie. This was replaced in 2001 by Dte, the Dutch regulator: Office for Energy Regulation (Dte), Guidelines Gas Act for the Year 2002, 30 Aug 2001, 11–12, 39–46.

4.91 In Great Britain (but not Northern Ireland) access to the greater part of the national grid is on the tariffs and other terms established by Transco, which owns and operates nearly all of the integrated gas network and transports gas from six coastal terminals, and from small onshore fields to almost 20 million customers around the United Kingdom. All charges other than entry capacity are based on published tariffs. Entry capacity is sold by auction, some of it long term and traded on a secondary market. Transportation charges are based on a price control formula set by the industry regulator, which sets the maximum revenue that Transco may earn from each unit of gas transported through its network on the basis of a price cap for transportation business (RPI-X). The structure is separated into four categories relating to:

- National Transmission System (NTS);
- Local Distribution Zones;
- Customer Charges; and
- Storage (Transco's storage assets have been sold off).

4.92 The NTS charges are separated into capacity and commodity elements. The charging system for capacity for using the NTS is separated into a system entry charge, determined by the point of entry, and an exit charge, determined by the exit zone which contains the off-take point. The capacity charges are based on the calculated long-run marginal costs of extending the system to meet a sustained increase in demand. BG Transco publishes a Ten Year Statement containing the basis for this methodology. A uniform commodity charge is adopted for use of the NTS.

4.93 In Spain principles for the determination of tariffs for TPA have been in operation since 1997.[102] They include a guaranteed recovery of investments made, an allowance for a reasonable return on the investments, and incentives for an efficient operation and increased productivity. The latter is in part to be redistributed to users and customers. The calculated tariffs are maximum tariffs but the gas companies are under an obligation to communicate the actual tariffs to the Ministry. The tariff elements for access cover services such as re-gasification, transportation, distribution, and storage. There is no special tariff for interruptible use of the network. Interruptible gas contracts are freely negotiable by the parties. The tariff structure is a two-tier system with one part of the capacity reserved and the other part related to the volume re-gasified, transported, or stored. A commodity charge is included for use of the network.

(6) Dispute Settlement

4.94 Access may be refused on the ground of a lack of capacity, where access would prevent the system operator from carrying out PSOs or in the context of serious economic

[102] Real Decreto 1914/1997, 19 Dec 2001, establishing the conditions for TPA to facilities for receiving, regasification, supply and transport of natural gas; based on the principles in Law 34/1998 of 7 Oct 1998 on hydrocarbons.

and financial difficulties arising for the system owner in connection with its take-or-pay contracts if it were to allow access (see para 4.136).[103] The burden of proof will be on the refusing party.

A refusal of access by a pipeline owner could trigger the dispute resolution process. Clearly, if this process is deficient that factor will act as a constraint on the development of competition. The Directive requires Member States to set up a competent authority to be responsible for dispute settlement. In particular, this authority 'must settle disputes concerning negotiations and refusal of access'.[104] It must be independent of the parties. The authority must rule on the dispute without delay or if possible within 12 weeks of the introduction of the dispute. It is expressly stated that recourse to the authority will not restrict the complainant's rights of appeal under Community law. Therefore, if an authority upheld a refusal, it would still be possible for the complaining party to take the case to the ECJ. Other bodies could be involved such as the national courts, the national regulatory authorities, and the Commission's Competition Directorate. **4.95**

(7) Access to Upstream Pipeline Networks

Upstream pipeline networks were included in the scope of the Gas Directive only after much controversy.[105] Such access must be 'provided in a manner determined by the Member State in accordance with' its laws.[106] In doing so, Member States must apply the overall objectives of the Gas Directive, namely: fair and open access; achieving a competitive market in natural gas and avoiding any abuse of a dominant position—while taking into account security and regularity of supplies; capacity which is or can reasonably be made available; and environmental protection. In this respect, those other provisions of the Directive relevant to upstream pipeline networks (eg unbundling rules specifically mentioned in Recital 22) are applicable. Other areas in which the Directive's provisions may be relevant to implementation measures for upstream operations include the establishment of technical rules to ensure inter-operability and interconnections in relation to upstream gas facilities, as well as rules on information exchange and the publication of technical rules for access to these pipelines. The following specific considerations may be taken into account by Member States in their implementation procedures:[107] **4.96**

[103] Gas Directive, n 80 above, Art 17(1).

[104] ibid, Art 21(2).

[105] In practice, such networks may be operated and/or constructed as a part of an oil and/or gas production project that is licensed as part of a licence for exploration and production of hydrocarbons. In such cases, Article 3 of the Hydrocarbons Licensing Directive is applicable in place of Article 4 of the Gas Directive: ('Upstream Pipeline Networks' Discussion Note, 22 Oct 1998 see n 95 above).

[106] Gas Directive, n 80 above, Art 23(2).

[107] ibid.

(a) The need to refuse access where there is an incompatibility of technical specifications which cannot be reasonably overcome;
(b) The need to avoid difficulties which cannot be reasonably overcome and could prejudice the efficient, current and planned future production of hydrocarbons, including that from fields of marginal economic viability;
(c) The need to respect the duly substantiated reasonable needs of the owner or operator of the upstream pipeline network for the transport and processing of gas and the interests of all other users of the upstream pipeline network or relevant processing or handling facilities who may be affected; and
(d) The need to apply their laws and administrative procedures, in conformity with Community law, for the grant of authorization for production or upstream development.

These considerations will be of more relevance to gas producing companies than to eligible customers. Most of them relate to the capacity available in the upstream pipeline networks and related facilities.

4.97 When establishing the detailed rules, Member States must take into account which additional capacity can reasonably be made available in case of capacity constraints. The first consideration (a) relates to the refusal of access if it would be technically impossible; it might, for example, create serious technical problems due to incompatibility of gas qualities; (b) is designed to safeguard current and planned production against serious difficulties that could have been caused by the implementation of the Directive; operational considerations such as those that may act to hamper access to upstream pipeline networks must be fully substantiated and justified; (c) refers to existing commitments and needs of current users that must be respected in the same way as with downstream pipeline networks; the assumption here is that access must be provided only to the extent that uncommitted capacity is available; (d) refers to the need for balance between national laws and EU legislation and the interface between the Gas Directive and other legislation such as the Hydrocarbons Licensing Directive.

4.98 However, considerable scope for interpretation by Member States appears to have been left to Member States at implementation stage. For example, the text of the Directive reflects the need to meet the concerns of Member States with significant gas production and the gas producing companies themselves, which had originally sought to limit the Directive's scope to downstream pipeline networks. Specifically, Recital 25 notes that provision should be made for access to upstream pipeline networks while adding that 'separate treatment is required as respects such access . . . having regard, in particular, to the special economic, technical and operational characteristics relating to such networks'.

4.99 Upstream pipeline networks are defined in the Directive as 'any pipeline or network of pipelines operated and/or constructed as part of an oil or gas production project, or used to convey natural gas from one or more such projects to a processing plant or terminal or final coastal landing terminal.'[108] They constitute an important part of the gas chain and are therefore relevant to the general aim of achieving a competitive market in natural gas.

Article 23 sets out the general principles that Member States must follow when making specific rules for access to upstream pipeline networks and related facilities. Member States must take the necessary measures to ensure that natural gas undertakings and customers that will be eligible under Article 18 are able to obtain access to upstream pipeline networks, including facilities supplying technical services incidental to such access. The measures must be notified to the Commission. Exempted from this requirement are those parts of networks and facilities used for local production operations at the site of a field where the gas is produced. **4.100**

To deal with any possible disputes, the independent authority designated under the Directive (see para 4.95) will become involved.[109] The aim is to settle such disputes relating to access to upstream pipeline networks expeditiously, taking the above criteria into account and the number of parties that may be involved in negotiating access to such networks. Where the disputes have a cross-border character, the arrangements for settlement for the Member State with jurisdiction over the upstream pipeline network that refuses access must be applied.[110] Consultation between Member States is necessary where more than one Member State has jurisdiction over a network and a cross-border dispute arises. The aim is to ensure that the provisions of the Directive are applied consistently. **4.101**

(8) Direct Lines

The Directive facilitates the construction of direct lines. Where an authorization is required for construction or operation of direct lines, the Member State or competent authority it designates must lay down the criteria for the grant of authorizations for the construction or operation of such lines in their territory. These criteria must be objective, transparent, and non-discriminatory.[111] The authorizations for pipeline construction may be made subject to either the refusal of pipeline system access provisions (under Art 17) or to the opening of a dispute settlement procedure (Art 21).[112] **4.102**

In particular, Article 20 requires Member States to take measures necessary to enable natural gas undertakings established within their territory to supply eligible **4.103**

108 ibid, Art 2(2).
109 Art 23(3).
110 Art 23(4).
111 ibid, Art 20(2).
112 ibid, Art 20(3).

customers by means of a direct line and to ensure that any such eligible customer may be supplied through a direct line by natural gas undertakings.

(9) Market-opening and Eligibility

4.104 The Directive requires that Member States specify 'eligible customers', defined as those customers inside their territory that have the legal capacity to contract for or to be sold natural gas according to the procedures set out in Articles 15 and 16.[113] It requires that initially two categories of customer—at least—be included as eligible customers.[114] These are:

(1) all final consumers consuming more than 25 million cubic metres of gas per year on a consumption site basis; and
(2) gas-fired power generators, irrespective of their annual consumption level.

4.105 In the case of (2), Member States may introduce thresholds for the eligibility of CHP producers to safeguard the balance in their electricity market. Distribution undertakings, if not already specified in their own right as eligible customers, must have the legal capacity to contract under the conditions of Articles 15 and 16 for the volumes of natural gas being consumed by their customers designated as eligible within their distribution system to supply those customers.[115] Five years after entry into force of the Directive (2003), the threshold of 25 million cubic metres a year must be reduced to 15 million cubic metres a year, and to five million cubic metres a year ten years after that initial date (2008).

4.106 The criteria for the definition of 'eligible customers' able to conclude contracts under the access procedures must be published by 31 January of each year.[116] That information must be passed on to the Commission, together with all other appropriate information to justify the fulfilment of market-opening. Article 18(9) further states that the Commission may request a Member State to modify its specifications 'if they create obstacles to the correct application of this Directive as regards the good functioning of the internal gas market'.

The definition of 'eligible customers' must result in an opening of the market equal to at least 20 per cent of the total annual gas consumption of the national gas market—increasing to 28 per cent five years after the Directive has entered into force (2003), and 33 per cent ten years after that date (2008).[117]

[113] ibid, Art 18(1). See also n 3 above.

[114] ibid, Art 18(2).

[115] ibid, Art 18(8).

[116] ibid, Art 18(9).

[117] ibid Art 18(4). The figure of 20 in the English language text of the Directive, referring to the number of years before the 33% share of market-opening was to be reached, was erroneous and was corrected in 1998 to 10: *corrigendum*, 1998 OJ L 245/43.

Should the definition (of eligible customers) lead to a market-opening of more than 30 per cent of the total annual gas consumption of the national gas market, Member States are permitted to modify the definition so that the opening is reduced to no lower than 30 per cent of consumption. After 2003 this figure is increased to 38 per cent and after 2008 the figure is increased to 43 per cent. 4.107

(10) Storage

By contrast to electricity, the optimal functioning of a gas system is heavily dependent on the existence and use of storage facilities. The Directive therefore includes provisions that address the issue of access to storage facilities. 4.108

These apply when such access is technically necessary to provide efficient access to transmission and/or distribution networks. Access is *not* granted independent of system use.[118] This is the key test for the interpretation of the Directive's provisions on storage access. It is not the aim of the Directive to provide access to storage without access to pipelines, even though the definition of 'system' includes 'facilities supplying ancillary services'—a term that encompasses storage, load balancing, and blending.[119] The test of a grant of access to storage in a particular case is one of technical necessity and of efficient access, taking into account the fact that access to transmission and distribution networks may be technically feasible *without* access to storage but that this may not be a commercially efficient solution and could function as a barrier to efficient system access. Access to storage is therefore linked to system (or pipeline) access and in normal circumstances efficient system access will imply some access to storage facilities. The issue is an important one, since without access to storage facilities in some form or another a new market entrant will be at an immediate disadvantage vis-à-vis incumbent transmission companies that do have such access at their disposal.[120] 4.109

It may be noted that storage facilities used in connection with local production operations at the site of a gas field are excluded from the access provisions relating to upstream pipeline networks in Article 23(1) ('technical services incidental to such access'). The storage requirements of these production operations are therefore excluded from the access rights of third parties to storage facilities. 4.110

[118] Statement of Council and Commission No 81/98: 'The Council and the Commission consider that the provisions on access to the system in relation to storage facilities or activities do not cover access to such facilities/activities independent of system use. Access to such facilities should only be possible when such access is technically necessary for providing efficient access to transmission and/or distribution networks'.

[119] Statement of Council, No 80/98: the concept of 'ancillary services' 'shall include all services necessary for the operation of transmission and/or distribution networks and/or LNG facilities including storage, load balancing and blending'.

[120] Emphasized in 'Role of Storage or Similar Services in a Competitive Gas Market': Discussion Note, 22 Oct 1998, (see n 95 above): 'It is vital that the provision of the Gas Directive regarding access to storage is not being [sic] interpreted and implemented in a way that will hamper market-opening'.

4.111 Member States must adopt measures necessary to ensure that storage undertakings operate in accordance with Articles 7 and 8 of the Directive. Storage undertakings must operate, maintain, and develop under economic conditions a secure, reliable and efficient storage, taking environmental considerations into account. There must be no discrimination between system users or classes of system users, especially with regard to any related undertakings. Each storage undertaking must provide any other storage undertaking (or transmission or distribution undertaking) with sufficient information to ensure that storage of natural gas may take place in a manner compatible with the secure and efficient operation of the interconnected system. A confidentiality requirement is imposed on storage undertakings in Article 8 with respect to commercially sensitive information obtained in the course of carrying out their business.

4.112 In cases where construction of new storage facilities is permitted only after grant of an authorization, this must be made on the basis of objective and non-discriminatory criteria (made public). This is important given the potential expansion in storage facilities as a result of the opening up of the EU gas market. New players are expected to enter the gas storage and flexibility business.

Tariffs for the use of storage services must be published if a Member State chooses a system of regulated access (as in the UK), while, under nTPA systems, information on the main commercial conditions for the use of the system must be made available. This should include information on the commercial conditions for access to storage or similar services to allow customers and new players to assess the total costs of the gas supply prior to making their business decisions.

4.113 Since storage may be an important contributor to a country's strategy for security of supply, the Directive is not designed to operate in a way that limits this security —one of the main pillars of EU energy policy. Access to storage, when necessary for system use, is only to be available to the extent that storage capacity is available.

4.114 In practice, the provision of storage facilities varies widely across the EU. Six Member States have no storage of any kind. In Finland and Sweden, the geology is unsuitable for storage construction, while in Greece, Ireland, and Portugal there are sites that have potential for storage but as yet no facilities have been built. In contrast, a number of Member States, such as Austria, Denmark, France, Germany, Italy and Spain, have significant levels of strategic storage over and above that required for normal seasonal use.

4.115 Gas storage plays an important rôle in optimizing the operations of a pipeline network and in overcoming constraints in system capacity. It helps to match gas supply and demand at seasonal and daily level so that the utilization of capital-intensive gas production and transport infrastructure improves and the unit costs of gas supply decline. Without this storage capacity, production and transportation capacity would have to be built to meet the peak day demand and so have a significant over-capacity for much of the time. Availability of storage facilities (eg underground salt caverns or aquifers) or similar alternative flexibility mechanisms (eg gas production and supplies with a high 'swing factor', coming from fields close to the market or interruptibility of supplies to customers) is essential to the smooth operation of a gas system. It has been a common feature in the gas supply activities of integrated gas companies. It is also important in connection with the provision of security of supply. As a capital-intensive activity, it is normally carried out by a few transmission companies as part of their bundled gas supply activities. They have taken decisions as to the amount of storage that needs to be constructed and the storage service is then offered as part of a bundled sales service. This has the potential to act as a barrier to entry for new market players and as a limit to competition.

Experience of market liberalization in the United Kingdom and the United States shows that the availability of storage or similar services may be very important to a new market entrant as part of the system to which it is seeking access. It is therefore in the customer's interest that the services and activities are unbundled at least to the extent required by Article 13(3) so that a minimum level of transparency and comparability may be achieved. **4.116**

(11) Structure

Unbundling of Accounts

Integrated gas companies are required by Article 13 to keep internal accounts for their natural gas transmission, distribution, and storage activities as if they were separate businesses. Where appropriate, consolidated accounts for non-gas activities must be prepared, as if the activities were carried out by separate undertakings. These internal accounts must include a balance sheet and a P&L account for each activity. The aim of this requirement is to ensure non-discrimination and fair tariffs to avoid cross-subsidization and the distortion of competition. It should be noted that the Gas Directive does not impose the minimum management unbundling required by the Electricity Directive. **4.117**

Integrated natural gas undertakings are defined as vertically or horizontally integrated undertakings under Article 2(15). A vertically integrated undertaking is a natural gas undertaking that performs two or more of the tasks of production, transmission, distribution, supply or storage of natural gas.[121] A horizontally integrated undertaking is an undertaking that performs at least one of the functions of production, transmission, distribution, supply or storage of natural gas and a non-gas activity.[122] **4.118**

[121] Gas Directive, n 80 above, Art 2(16).
[122] ibid, Art 2(17).

In their internal accounting, the undertakings must specify rules for the allocation of assets and liabilities, for expenditure and income as well as for depreciation, without prejudice to nationally applicable accounting rules that are followed in drawing up the separate accounts mentioned above. These may be amended only in exceptional cases and any amendments must be mentioned and duly substantiated. Article 13 also requires that the annual accounts indicate any transaction of a certain size conducted with related undertakings, meaning affiliates and/or associated undertakings and/or undertakings that belong to the same shareholders.[123] However, an exception may be made in those cases where TPA is carried out on the basis of a single charge for both transmission and distribution, in which case the accounts for transmission and distribution activities may be combined.

4.119 Gas companies are specifically required to draw-up, submit to audit, and publish their accounts in accordance with national rules on annual accounts of limited liability companies. Such rules must be in accordance with the Fourth Council Directive 78/660/EEC of 25 July 1978, based on Article 54(3)(g) of the Treaty on the annual accounts of certain types of companies. The form of ownership is not at issue here and that is expressly stated. If there is no legal requirement to publish annual accounts then undertakings must keep a copy of those accounts at their head office at the disposal of the public.

4.120 The accounts are open to inspection by various authorities. Under Article 12 Member States or any competent authority they designate, including dispute settlement authorities, have a right of access to accounts they need to consult in carrying out their functions. However, Member States and any competent authorities designated in this way, including dispute settlement authorities, must, as always, preserve the confidentiality of commercially sensitive information. It is nevertheless permissible for Member States to introduce exceptions to the principle of confidentiality where this is deemed necessary for the authorities in carrying out their functions.

4.121 In Articles 8 and 11 (see paras 4.76 and 4.77–4.81) there are further provisions concerning confidentiality of commercially sensitive information, which establish the Chinese Wall principle. These provisions are more strict than those of the Electricity Directive. In Article 8 each transmission, storage, and/or LNG

[123] 'Affiliates', as defined by Art 41 of the 7th Council Directive, 83/349/EEC of 13 June 1983, based on Art 54(3)(g) of the Treaty on consolidated accounts; for 'associated undertakings' see Art 33(1) of the same Directive: and Art 2(18) of the Gas Directive. The wording here reflects that of Art 14(4) of the Electricity Directive. This has since been interpreted by the Follow-up Group meeting of the Electricity Directive of 30/31 Oct 1997, and is argued by the Commission to be applicable to Art 13(5) of the Gas Directive ('Unbundling of Accounts', Discussion Note, 22 Oct 1998, n 95 above).

undertaking must preserve the confidentiality of commercially sensitive information when such information is obtained in the course of carrying out its business. Transmission undertakings are further required not to abuse commercially sensitive information obtained from third parties in the context of sale or purchase of natural gas when providing or negotiating access to the system. Article 11 extends the same obligation to distribution undertakings. The aim is to prevent any flow of commercially sensitive information between the activities of 'system operators' (transmission and distribution undertakings) in deciding on network access and suppliers or purchasers of natural gas. In this way, steps are taken to avoid distortion of competition and to avoid the risk of potential discrimination. If unbundling is to promote access for third parties, the key to success is to separate the management of the transmission functions of an integrated undertaking—(which, as system operators, receive commercially sensitive information about competitors who are suppliers or purchasers of gas)—from its supply and other activities (where such information might be abused). Failure to separate these out could weaken these provisions on confidentiality.[124] In practice, it will be very difficult to detect a breach of confidentiality or a case of discrimination.

(12) Public Service Obligations

The obligations on public service are identical to those set out in the Electricity Directive. Article 3 sets out the specific obligations that may be included in the category of public service. The obligations that a Member State may impose on a natural gas undertaking relate to: **4.122**

- security, including security of supply (possibly including long-term planning);
- regularity;
- quality of supplies;
- price of supplies; and
- environmental protection.

Public service obligations (PSOs) must be clearly-defined, transparent, non-discriminatory, and verifiable; and must be published and notified to the Commission by Member States 'without delay'. The idea behind publication is to make the terms of the obligations available to third parties who may be interested. The notification to the Commission has to be separate from measures taken further to Article 29. It must also refer to any impact that such PSOs may have on the application of the Gas Directive and for the internal market in gas. This means **4.123**

[124] Other provisions affected by this approach to unbundling are those directed at obtaining the benefits of non-discriminatory access in Arts 7(2) and 10(2) and the confidentiality provision of Art 11(2).

that a Member State has to submit 'a single document which identifies, lists and sets out the PSOs, their impact and/or method of funding (if any) and references to the legal provisions concerned'.[125] On receiving notification, the Commission examines its compatibility with the Gas Directive and the Treaty and will 'verify whether it represents the least distortive measure necessary to achieve the objective in question'.[126]

4.124 Pre-existing exclusive rights and PSOs are also subject to the Directive and must be notified by Member States to the Commission. They may be applied at national or regional (ie Member State) level. The justification behind these requirements is noted in Recital 12: individual Member States perceive that 'free competition, left to itself, cannot necessarily guarantee' obligations like security of supply and consumer and environmental protection.

(a) Long-term planning and implementation

4.125 Member States can introduce the implementation of long-term planning as a means of carrying out PSOs but only those relating to security of supply. However, this does not apply to the Electricity Directive which permits long-term planning to be applied as a means of carrying out any PSOs. Specifically, Article 2(23) defines 'long-term planning' as 'the planning of supply and transportation capacity of natural gas undertakings on a long-term basis with a view to meeting the demand for natural gas of the system, diversification of sources and securing supplies to customers'. In addition, when a Member State introduces long-term planning it is expressly required to take 'into account the possibility of third parties seeking access to the system'. This latter phrase is important in acknowledging that TPA must have implications for the planning of supply and transportation capacity.

4.126 As mentioned in the section on distribution, Member States may in limited circumstances decide not to apply the provisions of Article 4 to distribution systems (Art 3(3)). There must first be obligations in the general economic interest imposed on natural gas undertakings within the framework of public service obligations in Article 3(2). It is also a requirement for the non-application of Article 4 that the development of trade must not be affected to such an extent as would be contrary to the interests of the Community, including competition with respect to eligible customers within the terms of the Gas Directive and Article 86* of the EC Treaty.[127] There should also be a direct link between obstruction to the performance of such obligations and the application of Article 4 of the Directive. The overall aim of Article 4 is relevant: to

125 'Public Service Obligations', Discussion Note, 29 Apr 1999, see n 95 above.
126 ibid.
127 Gas Directive, n 80 above, Recital 15.

ensure that eligible customers benefit from a competitive framework, the provision is designed to give gas undertakings the possibility of establishing a distribution network on the basis of Article 4. Not every customer has the right to be supplied with natural gas since there is no universal obligation to supply gas. In this Article 4 essentially supplements the market access provision of Article 18 the Directive.[128]

The narrow scope of Article 3(3) of the Gas Directive can be contrasted with the much wider scope of the corresponding Article 3(3) of the Electricity Directive, which provided that Member States could decide in specific circumstances not to apply the provisions of the Directive relating to competition in generation, access to networks, and direct lines. **4.127**

It could be argued that these differences reflect an important difference between gas and electricity. Gas is a substitutable primary source of energy. It can be replaced by alternative sources such as oil or coal. The dependence of final consumers on it is therefore less acute than on electricity supply, which is used by virtually all households.

In addition, by contrast to the Member States' powers not to apply the access provisions, a natural gas undertaking must be allowed to refuse access to its transmission/distribution system if the granting of access would prevent it from carrying out its PSOs referred to in Article 3(2). However, in that event, duly substantiated reasons must be given for such a refusal (Art 17(1)). **4.128**

When imposing PSOs on natural gas undertakings, Member States must have full regard to the Treaty provisions and especially Article 86.[129]* Recital 16 expressly refers to the need to have regard to the interpretation of the relevant rules of the Treaty by the ECJ.

(b) Derogations

Apart from the right not to apply the distribution system provisions of Article 4 on PSO grounds, Member States may have recourse to derogations. In the Gas Directive the term 'derogation' is used in two senses, describing: **4.129**

1. an act of the Commission which grants to a Member State a right not to comply with its obligations under specific provisions of the Directive (eg Art 26(3)), and

[128] In a draft EU Directive for the telecommunications sector, 'universal service' is defined as a set of services of specified quality, is available to all users in the territory of a Member State regardless of their geographical location and, in the light of specific national conditions, at an affordable price: Proposal for a Directive on universal service and users' rights relating to electronic communications networks and services, COM (2000) 392, 17 July 2000, Art 3(1). See ch 8, para 8.15.

[129] Gas Directive, n 80 above, Art 3(2).

2. a unilateral act by a Member State made under specific provisions of the Directive by which it states that specific provisions will not be applied (eg Arts 26(1) and 26(2), and Art 25 (access/take-or-pay)).

Derogation decisions taken under Article 26(2) and 26(3) could be challenged by the Commission on the grounds that conditions for making the derogation were not satisfied. Details of these derogations are set out at paras 4.138–4.151.

4.130 As in the case of electricity, Member States may apply for an exemption under Article 86(2) from the application of the Directive on the grounds of PSOs. Exemption applications are considered on a case-by-case basis. However, the intention is not to allow Member States to apply PSOs to such an extent that the market would in effect be closed indefinitely. A failure to open the market as required by the minimum requirements of Article 18 would impede the development of trade and be against the interests of the Community. In the gas industry, it is particularly important to emphasize that derogation from the provisions of the Directive on the basis of PSOs concerned with security of supply is unlikely to be permitted 'in the absence of extraordinary circumstances'.[130]

4.131 The procedure for assessing an application for an exemption under Article 86(2) is two-stage. Stage one addresses the issue of whether the exemption is justified; stage two addresses the issue of whether the proposed measure is the least restrictive one reasonably available to achieve the objective in question. A proportionality test will be applied to both and the Commission will benchmark an application against the best practice. The provisions on derogations will be applied in a restrictive manner in order to prevent a widespread proliferation of derogations. In sum, the proportionality test has at least three principal elements, comprising examinations of the:

1. legitimacy of the purpose of the exemption
2. adequacy of the measure proposed to meet the objective, and
3. necessity of the measure proposed and its scope by comparison with other possible alternative measures which might have a less distortive effect on the internal gas market.

In procedure (3) there is a benchmarking of best practice and of the least distortive measure necessary to meet the objective.

4.132 More general rules applicable to the award of derogations include the following:

[130] 'Security of Supply': Discussion Note, 29 Apr 1999 (see n 95 above).

- the derogation sought should not be wider in extent than is strictly necessary for the ends sought;
- the party applying for the derogation (and refusing access) has the burden of proof to demonstrate that a derogation is necessary;
- it must also establish that it is subject to a specific PSO that has been imposed on it by a public authority and that the performance of that obligation would be obstructed if the access applied for were granted;
- applicants for a derogation are limited to the possibilities for derogations arising from the Directive;
- further derogations than these are not granted by Art 86 of the Treaty.[131]

Like the Electricity Directive, the Gas Directive allows Member States to take temporary measures to safeguard gas supply in the event of a sudden crisis in the energy market or where the physical safety or security of persons, apparatus, installations, or system integrity is at stake.[132] But any freedom to depart from market conditions in this way is strictly limited by a narrow formulation in the Directive and is subject to review by the Commission. **4.133**

(13) Implementation

A report was to be submitted by the Commission to the Parliament and the Council on the harmonization requirements that are not linked to the provisions of the Directive, such as environmental regulations or energy taxation, before the end of the first year following the entry into force of the Directive (ie, 10 Aug 1999; see ch 6 paras 6.59–6.67). If it were considered necessary, Article 27 also empowers the Commission to attach harmonization proposals to the report if such proposals appeared necessary to bring about the effective operation of the internal gas market. **4.134**

The Commission must review the application of the Gas Directive and submit a report on the experience gained on the functioning of the internal market in natural gas and the implementation of the rules on PSOs (Art 28). This seeks to ensure that the Parliament and Council are both to consider, in the light of experience gained, what provisions are required for further *improving* the internal market in natural gas that would be operational ten years after 10 August 2008.

This provides an interesting contrast to the wording of Article 26 of the Electricity Directive. That Directive states that a review is necessary because of 'the possibility of further *opening* of the market which would be effective nine years after the **4.135**

[131] ibid.

[132] Gas Directive, n 80 above, Art 24. The wording is virtually identical to Art 23 of the Electricity Directive.

entry into force of the Directive'. The difference in the choice of words appears to be more than semantic.

(14) Transition: Take-or-Pay

4.136 The bulk of European gas supplies are contracted under long-term contracts that contain so-called 'take-or-pay' clauses. Under such arrangements, gas buyers will agree to take delivery of not less than a minimum quantity over a specified period (such as a year), or, if they do not, pay for the shortfall from the agreed minimum. In this way, the buyer bears the market risk, while the gas producer takes the production risk. By assuring a regular cash-flow over a period of many years, such contracts reduce the risk for producers and facilitate their ability to finance the infrastructure of their projects.

The duration of such contracts has typically been for between 15 and 25 years, and could cover the life of the project. They have played a key rôle in bringing the European gas market into existence. However, long-term gas contracts were concluded at a time when the Member State gas markets were organized around national and regional monopolies of supply and distribution and an absence of competition in supply.

The benefits of long-term contracts to buyers diminish with the growth of a competitive market in gas unless the contract provides for some price adjustment to reflect market changes. Specifically, natural gas purchased under existing contracts will not always be able to compete on price with gas that becomes available in the competitive gas market following from the Gas Directive.

4.137 A transitional régime is therefore included in Articles 17(1) and 25 to mitigate the effects of the transition to a liberalized gas market on the performance of take-or-pay contracts entered into by transmission or distribution system companies. If a natural gas undertaking encounters, or considers it will encounter, serious economic and financial difficulties because of the take-or-pay commitments it has accepted in one or more of its gas purchase contracts, an application may be made for a *temporary* derogation from the access provisions of Articles 15 and 16. This is intended as a last resort measure for exceptional cases in which a company may face the prospect of bankruptcy. However, it may be noted that in principle an undertaking may refuse access to an applicant company before it has experienced serious economic and financial difficulties and before it has applied for a derogation. This system of derogations in the Directive is important due to its potential for delay and frustration of the objectives of the Directive. The system is essentially equivalent to the transitional régime established for stranded assets under the Electricity Directive but the treatment of criteria for the grant of derogations is more detailed than its counterpart in the electricity sector.

(15) Procedures for Granting a Take-or-Pay Derogation

Applications for derogations are made on a case-by-case basis. There is a two-stage procedure for dealing with applications which involves: (i) submission of an application to the Member State of the applicant or to its designated competent authority (eg the *Bundeskartellamt* in Germany), and (ii) notification and review by the European Commission of any decision by a Member State or its designated competent authority to grant a derogation. The Commission has the final say. **4.138**

Member States are allowed, under Article 25(1), to give the natural gas undertaking the choice of presenting its application either before or after refusal of access to the system. In cases where a natural gas undertaking has refused access to the system, the application for a derogation must be presented 'without delay'. The Commission has stated that the maximum delay in this respect is one week, corresponding to the delay allowed for notification under the EU Merger Regulation.[133] All applications must be accompanied with information relevant to the nature and extent of the problem and also the efforts undertaken by the gas undertaking to solve the problem. If there are no reasonable alternatives available to the company, a derogation may be granted by the Member State or designated competent authority.

Once a derogation has been granted, either by the Member State or by its designated competent authority, the Commission must be notified, without delay, of the decision.[134] All relevant information must be submitted to the Commission, if appropriate in an aggregated form, so that the Commission may reach a 'well-founded decision'. Within four weeks of receiving notification, the Commission may request that the Member State or designated competent authority amend or withdraw the decision to grant a derogation. Failure to comply with the Commission's request for amendment or withdrawal within a period of four weeks will lead to a final decision being taken 'expeditiously' under procedure I of Article 2 of Decision 87/373/EEC.[135] Throughout, the Commission must preserve the confidentiality of commercially sensitive information. Derogations granted must be properly substantiated and published in the *Official Journal*. **4.139**

Decisions on requests for derogations concerning contracts concluded *before* the Directive entered into force should not create a situation in which it is not **4.140**

133 'Take-or-Pay Contracts', Discussion Note, 22 Oct 1998 (see n 95, at 5).

134 Gas Directive, n 80 above, Art 25(2).

135 Council Decision 87/373/EEC of 13 July 1987 setting out procedures for the exercise of implementing powers conferred on the Commission, 1987, OJ L 197, 33–5; subsequently repealed by Council Decision of 28 June 1999 laying down procedures for the exercise of implementing powers conferred on the Commission, 1999, OJ L 184, 23–6 (see Art 9).

possible to identify alternative outlets that are economically viable.[136] The Commission will not consider problems as 'serious difficulties' unless sales of natural gas fall below the level of minimum off-take guarantees contained in gas purchase take-or-pay contracts or if the relevant gas purchase take-or-pay contract can be adapted, or the gas undertaking is able to identify alternative outlets for the gas. This provision appears to enhance the possibility of obtaining derogations in respect of contracts in existence before the Directive entered into force, but also sets criteria which must be satisfied to obtain a derogation for such a contract.

In cases where a gas company has not been granted a derogation by the Member State under Article 25 of the Directive, the company can no longer refuse access to the system because of take-or-pay commitments that have been accepted in a gas purchase contract. Member States must ensure that the provisions on system access are then complied with. The unsuccessful applicant may then rely on the mechanisms for appeal in the Member State.

4.141 In circumstances where the Commission requests the Member State to withdraw a decision and the Member State fails to do so, a consultative committee will advise the Commission on next steps. This committee will be composed of representatives of the Member States and will be chaired by a representative of the Commission. Three steps follow from this:

1. the Commission representative submits to the Commission a draft of the measures to be taken;
2. the committee delivers its opinion on this draft within a time-limit set by the chair. That opinion is recorded in the minutes. Each Member State is entitled to ask to have its position recorded in the minutes.
3. The Commission takes its decision, drawing on the opinion and informing the committee of the decision, and how the opinion has informed it.

The operation of Article 25 is subject to a review to be carried out within five years of the Directive entering into force. The findings of this review will be reported to Parliament and Council, who may then consider whether amendments are needed.

(16) Criteria for Grant of Derogations

4.142 Derogations may not be granted unless and until nine criteria listed in Article 25 are considered by the Member State and the Commission.[137] These are as follows, the:

[136] Gas Directive, n 80 above, Art 25(3).
[137] ibid.

(a) objective of achieving a competitive gas market;
(b) need to fulfil PSO and to ensure security of supply;
(c) position of the natural gas undertaking in the gas market and the actual state of competition in this market;
(d) seriousness of the economic and financial difficulties encountered by the natural gas undertakings and transmission undertakings or eligible customers;
(e) dates of signature and terms of the contract or contracts in question, including the extent to which they allow for market changes;
(f) efforts to find a solution to the problem;
(g) extent to which, when accepting the take-or-pay commitments in question, the undertaking could reasonably have foreseen, having regard to the provisions of the Gas Directive, that serious difficulties were likely to arise;
(h) level of connection of the system with other systems and the degree of interoperability of these systems; and
(i) effects that the grant of a derogation would have on the smooth functioning of the internal natural gas market.

This is not an exhaustive list and may therefore be supplemented by criteria relevant to the specific case in question. More importantly, the criteria are not necessarily listed in order of importance (and do not indicate the weight a court might give them in the event of a dispute). A different order of priority would probably be adopted by an applicant for a derogation.[138] Such a 'practice' order of the nine criteria would probably take the following form (retaining the above numbering): beginning with criterion Article 25(3)(e), then (a), (b), (c), (h), (g), (f), (a), and finally (i).

Irrespective of their order of priority, the individual criteria require some comment, given their broad formulation in the Directive itself. They are considered below in the 'practice' order and *not* in the order presented in Article 25(3) of the Directive text.[139]

(a) Dates of signature and terms of contract(s), including extent to which they allow for market changes (e)

4.143 From a practical point of view the most important criterion will concern the dates when the contract or contracts were signed. This allows for distinctions to be made between existing and future contracts. This was designed to give market operators a clear signal that prudence should be exercised when signing future take-or-pay contracts to take account of the changing market circumstances. It was also

[138] Brothwood, M, 'The EU Gas Directive and Take or Pay Contracts' [1998] Oil Gas L Taxation Rev 318.

[139] The order specified in Art 25(3) is noted in brackets after the practice order numbering. See especially 'Take-or-Pay Contracts', Discussion Note, n 95 above.

designed to ensure that any take-or-pay contracts entered into or renewed after the entry into force of the Directive would make a prudent allowance for changes resulting from a more competitive gas market so as not to hamper a significant opening of the market.[140]

The relevance of the date of signature is that it gives an indication of the extent to which legislative changes could and should have been taken into account when signing a contract. However, no date is expressly mentioned in the Directive. In the original proposal submitted by the Commission in February 1992, only contracts signed before 1 July 1991 were covered. This date was retained in the amended proposal of early 1994 but prior to conclusion of the present text, it seems that a possible cut-off date was 25 July 1996. For contracts signed after the adoption of the Gas Directive (10 August 1998) the matter is easier.

(b) Seriousness of economic and financial difficulties encountered by natural gas undertakings and transmission undertakings or eligible customers (a)

4.144 This criterion concerns the economic and financial difficulties faced by the players. Since Article 25(1) expressly refers to derogations being considered if a company encounters 'or considers it would encounter' serious difficulties, this criterion implies that preventive action may be considered before the serious problems have in practice occurred. Such problems must of course have their origins in the entry into force of the Gas Directive and not in any other cause. The economic and financial implications for the eligible customers should be taken into account since they face their request for access being denied as a result of the grant of a derogation. The seriousness of the problem should be reflected in a proportionate manner with access refusal tailored according to a percentage of the requested TPA volumes. It appears that the Commission would take the view that a serious economic and financial difficulty would imply a major loss caused by a greater than normal business risk.[141] It seems that a comparative analysis would be carried out between the Member States when analysing a request for derogation to obtain input from concrete examples and actual experiences, if available, where serious economic and financial problems have in fact faced gas companies in take-or-pay situations.

(c) Need to fulfil public service obligations and ensure security of supply (b)

4.145 Although this criterion concerns PSOs and security of supply, the main provision for the protection of PSOs is in fact Article 3, not Article 25. Article 17(1) takes Article 3(2) into account and should therefore be seen as the principal vehicle for protection of PSOs rather than Article 25.

---

140 Gas Directive, n 80 above, Recital 30.

141 Discussion Note on Take-or-Pay, n 95 above, 7.

(d) *Position of natural gas undertaking in the gas market and actual state of competition in the market (c)*

This criterion refers to the position of the natural gas undertaking in the gas market and the actual size of competition in this market. It should be kept in mind here that the Council and the Commission have declared that this criterion must be applied equally to all natural gas undertakings.[142] The 'position' of the gas undertaking can be taken to include *inter alia*: **4.146**

- size of the company, including area of operation, balance sheet, assets, market-share, and turnover;
- rôle of the company in international gas trade;
- supply and sales portfolio of the company;
- extent of infrastructure owned, including storage; ownership in other energy/gas companies, whether upstream or downstream; and
- rights and obligations of the company, including PSOs.

The market conditions referred to in the criterion are also open to interpretation. They could be regional, national, or wider within the EU. An analysis of the state of competition would include an assessment of the level of market-opening in the area concerned in terms of both the eligible share of the market and the share of the market that actually benefits from competition. It would also include a consideration of the number of suppliers competing in the market and the impact of competition on market shares, prices, and profits. The general level of competition in the market may also be considered, not only the level of gas-to-gas competition.

(e) *Level of connection of the system with other systems and degree of inter-operability (h)*

An important criterion concerns the level of connection of the system with other systems and the extent of their inter-operability. Although the pace of network integration is fast, there remain regional and national gas networks that are not well-integrated into the European gas grid. Technical aspects may hamper inter-operability with other systems and in such areas gas companies may face difficulties to sell gas outside their traditional supply area in the event of serious take-or-pay problems. **4.147**

(f) *Extent to which, when accepting take-or-pay commitments, undertaking could reasonably have foreseen, having regard to the provisions of the Gas Directive, that serious difficulties were likely to arise (g)*

This applies to take-or-pay contracts signed after the entry into force of the Directive. It turns on the prudence that an undertaking has shown when taking **4.148**

[142] Statement 93/98 to the Minutes of the Council Meeting, May 1998.

on the take-or-pay commitments at issue and whether the resulting difficulties could reasonably have been foreseen. If they could have been foreseen or were in fact foreseen, there is no basis for an expectation that a grant of derogation may be made to solve the difficulties that have followed.

(g) Efforts to find a solution (f)

4.149 This criterion for derogation from the access provisions of the Gas Directive is focused on the efforts made to find a solution to the problem. Derogation should be adopted only as a last resort when all other attempts by the operators involved have failed to identify an alternative solution to the problem. Such efforts may include efforts to sell the gas elsewhere or attempts to re-negotiate the contract or to increase company efficiency.

(h) Achieving a competitive gas market (a)

4.150 This criterion is likely to be influential at the Commission stage. It relates to the overall objective of the Directive: market-opening, largely by means of TPA. Whatever decision is taken with respect to refusal of access must be balanced and justified against this principal objective of the Directive, which is to provide for the opposite.

(i) Effects the grant of a derogation would have on achieving smooth functioning of the internal natural gas market (i)

4.151 Finally, there is the criterion that is based on the effects of a grant of derogation on the smooth functioning of the internal gas market. By implication, this emphasizes that any grant of a derogation would have a restrictive effect on the operation of an internal gas market in the EU. The criteria should therefore be applied by Member States and the Commission in a cautious manner and balance any derogations against the overall objective of a smooth-functioning internal gas market and a significant degree of market-opening.

(17) Comparative Experiences

4.152 In Britain, the United States, and Canada, liberalization of the gas market had the effect of rendering many take-or-pay contract provisions unsustainable.[143] Nearly all agreements failed to include provisions to deal with radical market change and so the parties had to live with their take-or-pay commitments or negotiate their way out of them against a background of possible bankruptcies of the purchasers. However, the gas purchase contracts commonly found in Continental Europe contain reasonably flexible quantity provisions and price provisions that may in

[143] Pegg, G J and Waller, M R 'Take-or-Pay Provisions in Natural Gas Contracts: US Experience as a Comparator to UK Gas Industry's Problems', (1996) J Energy Natural Resources L 456–463.

appropriate circumstances permit gas buyers to pass back to producers any reductions in price in the marketplace.

If transitional problems occur, there are some mechanisms which have been tried in these countries that may be drawn on to solve the resulting problems. For example, producers may be willing to reduce take-or-pay commitments in return for access to the buyer's pipeline; new entrants may be willing to take on part of the existing take-or-pay commitment; or a levy may be imposed on gas transported to spread the costs of financing take-or-pay payments. In the event of serious problems emerging that cannot be resolved by these mechanisms, the process of liberalization can always be slowed down. **4.153**

The two conditions necessary for the development of future gas supplies by producers and suppliers are a substantial final market and flexible pricing. Provided these are met it should not be difficult to obtain take-or-pay commitments. However, in future there is likely to be a growth of short-term trading arrangements alongside traditional take-or-pay commitments with flexible pricing. The fact that new long-term take-or-pay contracts have been entered into in Great Britain and the United States since liberalization, although in much reduced numbers, shows a continuing requirement for such contracts in appropriate circumstances, and also their capacity for adaptation. **4.154**

(18) 'Ship-or-Pay' Contracts

An issue arose after the Directive's adoption in the context of accession negotiations between the EU and Slovenia concerning the relationship between possible derogations from take-or-pay commitments and 'ship-or-pay' contracts, which are not expressly referred to nor recognized in the Gas Directive, despite being widely used within the EU.[144] These contracts are transportation contracts that contain commercial commitments for the reservation of capacity through a pipeline. Their principal feature is the obligation on the gas purchasing company to pay for the capacity contracted even if that capacity is not used. They may be used, for example, when the gas buyer is neither owner nor co-owner of the transportation system up to its national border. The buyer therefore needs to conclude commercial contracts for gas transportation with the owners of these pipelines. This transportation cost may represent a significant share of the total gas supply costs since the distance between the national border of a buyer and the delivery point of the gas producer (or supplier) is often long, and in general gas transportation costs are high. **4.155**

Such agreements are essentially complementary to take-or-pay agreements. They are concluded by gas companies when the delivery point for gas in a supply contract is further upstream than the national border of the buyer. However, they may **4.156**

[144] 'Ship-or-Pay Contracts': Discussion Note, 29 Apr 1999 (see n 95).

also be concluded with a view to reserving transportation capacity to ensure transit through the pipeline of gas supplied on a different contractual basis or as part of the company's general business operations. Since they are not expressly mentioned in the Directive, they fall under the general rules of the Treaty and in particular the competition rules. In the unlikely event of a challenge under EU law, these rules would provide the basis for an evaluation of any legal issues or disputes that may arise concerning the compatibility of ship-or-pay commitments with the *acquis communautaire*.

4.157 Given the Directive's silence on this matter, there is no legal ground for justifying a specific derogation on the basis of ship-or-pay obligations but it appeared to the Commission that an economic evaluation of 'serious economic and financial difficulties' arising under Article 25 of the Directive could lead to unequal treatment.[145] It could also lead to potential discrimination between different arrangements for gas supply according to the ship-or-pay provisions on transportation services. To resolve this, the Commission has proposed that when assessing a request for a derogation on the basis of Article 25 a separate analysis of the ship-or-pay component should be carried out to avoid derogation becoming necessary. This suggests that the Commission prefers to exclude ship-or-pay liabilities from its calculation of serious difficulties.

(19) Uneven Market Development

4.158 The wide differences in the penetration of gas in the energy markets of Member States are taken into account in several places in the Directive. In particular, it makes special provision for Member States that are not yet fully linked to the European gas system and have a high degree of dependence on a single external supplier; for Member States classified as 'emergent markets'; and for those areas or regions within some Member States seeking to encourage investment in transmission infrastructure. The latter were called 'emergent regions' in much of the negotiations on the Directive. In practice, however, no definition of this term could be provided in the final text due to unresolved disagreements in the negotiating process. The term 'emergent markets', used in Article 26(2), is however defined in the Directive. It means 'a Member State in which the first commercial supply of its first long-term natural gas supply contract was made not more than ten years earlier'. It therefore applies to Greece and Portugal, where the first supply commenced in 1996 to 1997.

4.159 Article 26 provides for the grant of derogations to Member States that experience the effects of one of three categories of uneven market development.

[145] ibid.

(a) Lack of system connection

It treats those Member States that are not directly connected to the interconnected system of any other Member State and have only one main external supplier. Such a supplier should have a market share of more than 75 per cent. In those cases, Article 26(1) permits those Member States to derogate from Article 4, Article 18(1), (2), (3), (4) and (6) and/or Article 20 of the Directive. However, such derogations expire automatically from the moment that at least one of these conditions is no longer fulfilled. At the date of publication, this would apply to Finland and Greece only. **4.160**

(b) Emergent markets

The second paragraph of Article 26 provides for a similar derogation for those Member States that are 'emergent markets' and which would experience substantial problems as a result of the implementation of the Directive. They may derogate from the same provisions of the Directive as Member States in the first category but such derogations expire once they cease to be classifiable as 'emergent markets'. Substantial problems may not be associated with take-or-pay commitments. **4.161**

In both categories (*a*) and (*b*) such derogations must be notified to the Commission.

(c) Risk to investment in infrastructure

The third category is the most complex. It concerns the interplay between investment in new transmission capacity and implementation of the Directive. For a Member State that foresees that implementation of the Directive would cause substantial problems in a geographically-limited area of its territory, an application for a temporary derogation is possible. This applies especially where the development of transport infrastructure is involved and where a competitive market as envisaged by the Directive might inhibit new large-scale investment or undermine recent investment. In other words, the infrastructure investments will or would not be economically viable within the area in question without the grant of a derogation. Temporary derogations may be granted by the Commission for developments within such an area. The derogation may be from Article 4, Article 18(1), (2), (3), (4), and (6) and/or Article 20. However, such derogations may only be granted if no gas infrastructure has yet been established in the area or where it has been in operation for less than ten years. The temporary derogation may not exceed a period of ten years from the time that gas is first supplied in the area concerned. The procedure for grant of derogations in this category is different from that in the other two. Once an application for a temporary derogation has been submitted to the Commission by a Member State, it may grant a derogation only after taking into account at least six criteria. **4.162**

4.163 The list in Article 26(4) is not exhaustive but includes the following, the:

- need for infrastructure investments, which would not be economical to operate in a competitive market environment;
- level and pay-back prospects of investments required;
- size and maturity of gas system in the area;
- prospects for gas market;
- geographical size and characteristics of area or region; plus
- socio-economic and demographic factors.

4.164 It is certain that the Commission will seek to apply the above criteria in a restrictive manner, and that derogations for investments in the transport of gas through local or regional pipeline networks to final consumers are unlikely to be accepted. Indeed, it has stated 'in principle, there will be no need to grant derogations under Article 26(4) in order to facilitate investment in distribution systems, in view of the provisions in Article 4(4)'[146] (Art 4(4) has already established a procedure for exemptions for areas of recent supply by distribution undertakings in a particular area).

4.165 In designing specific tests for assessing rates of return on investments with or without a derogation some reference may be made to experience gained under the Trans-European Networks programme, which allows for a grant of limited investment subsidies in exceptional circumstances. Recital 31 makes it clear that all derogations arising from this Article should be limited in time and scope and that the Commission should have a 'significant' rôle in granting them. As a general rule, any derogation must satisfy the test of having the least distorting effect possible to achieve the desired objective. The reasons for such an approach are clear: the derogations are a potential constraint on the introduction of competition, even if they are temporary.

(20) Contrast with the Electricity Directive

4.166 There are strong similarities between the two Directives, especially in form. There are nevertheless important differences between them. With respect to the fundamental aims of the two measures, one point of difference has been noted by MEP Claude Desama. For electricity the principal objective is to stimulate competition in generation, while in the gas sector it is to diversify the distribution networks, the beginning of the supply chain being unaffected and remaining concentrated in a few hands.[147] However, with reference to the specifics of the texts themselves, four differences are noted below.

[146] Statement 95/98 in Council Minutes. The principle is restated in the Discussion Note on Emergent Regions, 22 Oct 1998 (see n 95 above). This has been contested by the industry body Eurogas, which has argued that the wording of Art 26(3) does not exclude distribution infrastructure.

[147] House of Lords Select Committee on the European Communities, *EU Gas Directive*, HL paper 35 [1997–8] 114.

The scope of the unbundling provision in the Gas Directive is narrower than that in Article 14 of the Electricity Directive. The activities covered by the unbundling of accounts obligation in Article 13(2) do not include the production of gas. Integrated natural gas undertakings must keep separate accounts in their internal accounting only for natural gas transmission, distribution, storage activities, and non-gas activities. By contrast, Article 14(3) of the Electricity Directive requires integrated electricity undertakings to keep separate accounts in their internal accounting for the activities of generation, transmission, and distribution. This despite the fact that the definitions of 'vertically' and 'horizontally integrated undertakings' in Article 2(16) and (17) of the Gas Directive expressly include production within their scope. Note that Recital 22 states: 'integrated accounts for hydrocarbon production and related activities may be produced as part of the requirement for accounts for non-gas activities required by this Directive'. The same Recital also notes that when providing information to dispute settlement authorities in connection with access to upstream pipeline networks, it: 'should include, where required, accounting information about upstream pipelines'. This may have some interpretative force for Member States in designing and enforcing their legislation to implement the Directive's provisions. **4.167A**

The provisions of the two Directives relating to the form and content of public accounts and internal accounts are similar. However the provision relating to confidentiality of commercial information in internal accounts differ. In both cases the Member State, any competent authority (eg regulators) and independent dispute settlement authorities, have the right of access to those accounts for purposes of carrying out their activities. However, in the case of internal accounts of independent gas companies the Member State and other authorities are required to preserve the confidentiality of commercial information in these accounts (Article 12). The reasons for this requirement arise from the external dimension of the gas market in the EU.[148] **4.167B**

In the case of rTPA under the Gas Directive, where a single charge is made for both transmission and distribution access, the accounts of the two activities may be combined. **4.167C**

It is notable that the Gas Directive does not require any separation of the system operator from the commercial activities, in contrast to the Electricity Directive.[149] The only attempt at 'management' unbundling are the provisions in Article 8(2) and Article 11(2) on confidentiality that imply the establishment of Chinese **4.167D**

[148] Electricity Directive, n 80 above, Art 13(2).
[149] ibid, Art 7(6).

Walls between activities inside a single company. This is likely to prove a weakness in the Directive's capacity to secure access for third parties.

D. Conclusions

4.168 In their final form, both of the Directives on Electricity and Gas represented a substantial modification of the original proposals made prior to 1995. For evidence of this, the relevant provisions would include those on the introduction of nTPA, the Single Buyer, the limited form of unbundling, and the derogations due to PSOs and take-or-pay contracts. For some, this represented a 'watering down'[150] or a 'double-tracked compromise' between on the one hand the European institutions and those Member States that had already commenced energy market liberalization like the United Kingdom and the Nordic countries, and on the other hand those Member States that had been and remained opponents of liberalization.[151]

4.169 However, the Directives committed all of the Member States to a staged programme of change with minimum objectives at each stage and a time-table in which to achieve them. Legislative responsibility was handed to the Member States to transpose the Directives into national law and to signal to potential competitors that an environment was being created in which they could thrive. The benefits of competition in energy markets were more widely accepted than ever before. This context differed greatly from that in which the original proposals had been presented.

4.170 The adoption of the Directives also brought to an end the Commission's rôle as initiator of the basic legislation required to bring about change in the EU energy markets. This had been its principal rôle for several years. After 1998, there was a new emphasis in its strategy on monitoring of the Directives and supervision of Member State actions in implementation. However important these actions were, they represented a step back from the front of the 'liberalization stage'. In future years, the Directives seemed to imply that the key steps were to be taken by the individual Member States—at least, that is the impression gained from a literal reading of the texts themselves. In practice, however, such a passive, reactive stance by the Commission was unlikely due to three important weaknesses in the Directives.

4.171 First, the Directives had indeed provided the legal framework for a single market in energy in the EU. However, for such a market to really take root, the predominantly

[150] See James Candon's remarks on the Gas Directive in relation to the Irish Presidency proposal of 1996: 'Liberalization of the Gas Market in the EU', [1998] Oil Gas L Taxation Rev, 353.

[151] Pfrang, Elvira, *Towards the Liberalization of the European Electricity Markets* (1999), 87.

national character of the EU energy markets had to be challenged. The 'common rules' approach of the Directives, with their recognition of the principle of subsidiarity, created a risk of uneven implementation. Instead of a single market in energy, 15 different markets—more or less liberalized—might emerge. This risk strongly suggested that the Commission had a continuing rôle in taking initiatives to prevent the emergence of a segmented energy market and to remove any obstacles to the integration process that became evident as the Directives took effect.

Secondly, the Directives were curiously reticent about cross-border trade in spite **4.172** of their overall aim of creating a single market in energy. There are few explicit references to cross-border trade to be found in either of the texts. Cross-border trade in electricity was a very small percentage of total trade in electricity, although it played a very important rôle in gas. The potential for increasing trade in electricity across frontiers was considerable however, and much of the gas trade was conducted on the basis of contracts that presupposed a segmented market. To remedy these limitations, a proactive rôle by the Commission appeared necessary.

Finally, the delicate balance between the provisions of the Directive and those of competition law was specified only in rather general terms in the texts. As the Directives took effect, it was not clear how that balance would be affected nor what consequences it might have for the subsequent stages of market-opening. The matter could not be ignored since it required some interplay between two distinct areas of competence within the Commission itself and within various national regulators and competition authorities.

Although not the only shortcomings of the Directives, these three were likely to **4.173** have the most direct impact on the Commission's rôle in the period after their adoption. With respect to the relationship between the Directives and competition policy, Chapter 5 examines the basic interplay between competition law and energy policy that formed a backdrop to the events considered in this and the preceding chapter. In particular, it notes the Court's rôle in this process. The constraints and potential for the Commission's rôle in developing this further are examined in Chapters 6 and 7, which also addresses the issues of Member State implementation of the Directives, various pressure points established by the Commission to promote this, and the impact of the Community institutions in the process.

5

ENERGY MARKETS AND COMPETITION LAW

The fact that the energy sector has special features cannot . . . mean that it should operate without a limited degree of competition.[1]

A. Introduction

The programme of secondary legislation introduced from 1990 to 1998 transformed the framework of European law as it applied to the energy sector. However, none of this legislation has actually replaced the rules contained in the primary legislation of the European Union, neither in the EC Treaty nor in the jurisprudence of the ECJ. **5.01**

Indeed, throughout this period the Commission was keen to argue that the IEM legislative programme merely defined the application of existing Treaty rules

[1] Ehlermann, C D (former Director-General for Competition, European Commission), 'Establishing the Single Market in Energy', (1991) Oil Gas L Taxation Rev, 295–8, at 296.

with respect to the energy sector.[2] This could be achieved not only by means of secondary legislation, but also by applying the existing Treaty rules more rigorously on competition matters and, where necessary, by encouraging attempts at clarification from the ECJ on key legal issues. The Commission's strategy was to pursue both routes whenever possible. From the late 1980s onwards, several cases came before the ECJ that were directly or indirectly relevant to the promotion of competition in the electricity and gas industries, especially the former. In addition, a number of cases which could be decided by the Commission on the basis of its powers under the EC Treaty gave it an opportunity to influence the legal and contractual arrangements governing the electricity and gas industries in a way that promoted IEM objectives.

5.02 This chapter is concerned with developments in primary law relating to competition in the electricity and gas markets that arose *during the period up to the adoption of the Electricity and Gas Directives*, and assesses their interplay with the IEM programme at this time. Developments in the application of competition law since the adoption of the Directives are considered in some detail in Chapter 7. The argument presented here is that significant progress was made towards removing some of the obstacles to the creation of an IEM at this stage. This was evident principally in the rules relating to freedom of movement of goods and the rules on competition. However, this *complemented and supported* the ongoing process of developing secondary legislation, rather than replacing it. Indeed, the limits to the development of the primary law during this period served to underline the central rôle of secondary legislation in bringing about a legal framework for the IEM.

5.03 The chapter examines five main areas in which the primary rules were developed during this period, as follows:

(1) *The ECJ began to place a more restricted interpretation on the scope of exclusive or special rights granted to undertakings by governments.* This has come about largely through judgments of the ECJ on references for preliminary rulings as to the legality of such exclusive or special rights, made by national courts of Member States and arising from legal proceedings brought by undertakings or individuals to challenge such rights. The ECJ had to consider whether the exercise of such rights would in itself lead to a breach of specific rules of the EC Treaty, such as the competition rules in Articles 81* and 82* and those relating to the free movement of goods in Articles 28, 29, 30, and 31.* The proceedings were based on Article 86(1).* Prior to these judgments there had been a widely accepted view that such exclusive and special

[2] ibid. This view can be summarized as follows: 'The proposals for Directives presented by the Commission restrict themselves essentially to specifying rights and obligations arising already today from the Treaty in order to ensure the legal safety of all the operators present on the market', 13–14; by 'operators' should be understood 'players' (not only transmission network operators). See also remarks by Devlin, B and Levasseur, C, both Commission officials, at a later date: 'parts of both Directives are either directly derived from the competition rules, or are designed to facilitate their application', in Faull, N and Nikpay, A, *EC Competition Law* (2000) 735.

rights were presumed to be compatible with EC law. The judgments changed this, and showed a trend to restrict the validity of such rights to those core activities which an undertaking is required to perform in fulfillment of its obligation to provide a service of general economic interest.

(2) *Progress made in removing import and export monopolies in electricity and gas.* Such rights might seem evidently in breach of the EC Treaty rules but were unchallenged for decades. The initiation of legal proceedings against Member States was first mooted in 1991 but action was not taken until 1994 and the ECJ delivered its judgments only in 1997. The proceedings, as well as the judgments, did much to change Member State practice in this field, but ultimately require careful assessment of their implications.

(3) *Development in thinking with respect to competition rules in Articles 81 and 82.** These Articles had by that time scarcely been applied to the energy sector at all. In particular, developments with respect to access to networks, notably in transmission and distribution, and the grounds for refusal of such access. The entry of the controversial notion of 'essential facilities' into legal discourse was also a significant development.

(4) *Significant actions by the Commission.* Contracts notified to the Commission gave it an opportunity to secure modifications in their terms to facilitate the creation of a liberalized market. Developments in competition policy examined.

(5) *Finally, the development of thinking on rules governing security of supply in the energy sector.* In particular, looking at grounds on which security of supply considerations can be used to depart from obligations in EC law , considered in relation to the ECJ case law.

Inevitably, this overview of developments affecting energy markets during the period presupposes some understanding of EC competition law and the workings of the relevant Community institutions. This wider context was sketched out in Chapter 2 and has been treated in depth by respected authorities elsewhere.[3] For reasons of space, no attempt is made here to present a more detailed picture. Although it is clear from this chapter that cases and decisions on non-energy issues are important for the development of the sector-specific law, specifically energy cases are examined more extensively. A broad approach to the cases and decisions has much to recommend it but an abbreviated form is adopted here to avoid loss of focus. The aim is to explain some important trends in jurisprudence during this period that have a bearing upon the IEM process, and which have interacted with the progress of secondary legislation. The structure of the sections reflects this aim. 5.04

B. Rolling Back Monopolies and Exclusive Rights

Historically, monopolies and exclusive/special rights have played a crucial rôle in the development of the European energy economy. For many years the norm was 5.05

[3] See in particular, Faull, J, and Nikpay, A, ibid., and Bellamy & Child, *European Law of Competition*, (2001).

to have exclusive national monopolies *de iure* or *de facto* relating to electricity generation, electricity and gas transmission, distribution and supply, and to the import and export of electricity and gas. Such monopolies were vested in undertakings that were more or less controlled by the state. In the case of transmission and distribution of electricity and gas, all Member States except Germany granted undertakings (whether state, private, or mixed in ownership), exclusive or special rights. Even in Germany's case, there were private law agreements between the undertakings that achieved the same effect. Access to networks by third parties was in most Member States not given any special legal protection. The net effect of these arrangements was, as noted by the Commission in its 1988 Working Document, to contribute to the creation of captive markets, and to undermine the creation of a single market in energy.[4]

5.06 The legal basis for such monopoly and exclusive rights has been primarily Articles 86(1) and Article 31,* although the preservation of property rights in Article 295 has also played a supporting rôle.[5] Article 86(1) implicitly recognized the rights of Member States to grant special or exclusive rights to public or private undertakings,[6] while Article 31 requires only the adjustment and not the abolition of state monopolies.[7] It may be noted, however, that Article 86(1) imposes a duty on Member States, in relation to undertakings to which they grant special or exclusive (ie monopoly) rights, not to enact or maintain in force any measures that are contrary to the rules of the EC Treaty, especially in relation to the undertakings that have monopoly or special rights—including those rules relating to discrimination, on grounds of nationality, competition, or state aids. A duty to ensure that Member States comply with their obligations under Article 86(1) is imposed on the Commission by Article 86(3).

5.07 These Treaty provisions were important for the electricity and gas industries—characterized as they were by substantial national monopolies, particularly in transmission, distribution, and supply. The existence of such monopolies was accepted, but the Member States which had granted the exclusive or special rights to the undertakings could not by legal measures protect them in the conduct of their businesses from the full impact of the Treaty rules (including competition rules). A special exemption from this provision was permitted in the

[4] Commission of the European Communities, 'An Internal Market in Energy', COM (1988) 4(9) (see ch 1, paras 1.59–1.63).

[5] 'The Treaty shall in no way prejudice the rules in Member States governing the system of property ownership' (Art 295*).

[6] For the full text of Art 86, see Appendix 4.

[7] Art 31* is quoted in full in Appendix 4, ibid (the current text: which differs in very minor respects from that in force during the period covered in this chapter).

case of undertakings entrusted with the operation of services of general economic interest.[8]

It is only in recent years that cases have been brought before the ECJ which required it to rule on the circumstances in which the dominant position created by the grant of an exclusive right could be exercised so as to constitute an abuse of a dominant position,[9] thereby opening up the possibility of challenges to the exclusive right itself.[10] The relevant litigation reflects the general context of liberalization and deregulation in the economic life of the European Community.

During the 1990s the ECJ delivered judgments in a number of cases not involving the energy industry which helped to establish the circumstances in which the exercise of a dominant position created by the grant of a monopoly could in itself be treated as an abuse of a dominant position giving rise to a breach of Article 82.* Another judgment helped to clarify the scope of monopolies which might be capable of exemption from the rules of the Treaty and especially Article 86(2). The cases brought before the ECJ were mostly referred by courts of Member States under Article 234 of the Treaty. They do not directly concern the electricity and gas sectors but their subject-matter is closely related to the kind of special and exclusive rights found in those sectors. In each case the ECJ was required to consider whether an existing special or exclusive right granted by a Member State was compatible with a particular rule or rules of the Treaty. Prior to discussion of the more important of those cases, attention is given here to a case arising from a challenge by several Member States to the Commission's legislation in the telecommunications sector, where the program of liberalization was more advanced than in energy. It concerned action by the Commission to put an end to special and exclusive rights but also the method of enforcement appropriate to achieving this objective. 5.08

(1) Choosing the Legal Instrument for Liberalization: *France v Commission (Telecoms)*

The procedure adopted by the Commission to bring about liberalization in the telecommunications sector offers an interesting contrast to its approach in the energy 5.09

[8] Wainwright, R, 'Public Undertakings Under Article 90', ch 13, [1990] Fordham Corporate Law Institute, 239–70; Brothwood, M, 'The Court of Justice on Article 90 of the EEC Treaty', (1983) CML Rev, 335–46.

[9] See generally, Buendia Sierra, JL, *Exclusive Rights and State Monopolies under EC Law* (2000).

[10] The first case decided on the Commission's powers under Art 86(3) concerned the Transparency Directive 80/723 (Treatment of Financial Relations between Public Undertakings and National Governments) 1980 OJ L 195/35: Cases 188–190/80 *France, Italy, and the UK v The Commission* [1982] ECR 2545. The ECJ interpreted the Commission's duty of surveillance as an extensive one and confirmed the competence of the Commission to act. The scope of the Directive was amended in 1984 to include the energy, water, transport, and telecommunications sectors, which had been excluded from the original draft, as happened with public procurement legislation.

sector. Telecommunications policy developed from the late 1980s onwards by relying upon Directives based on both Article 86(3) and Article 95 of the EC Treaty.[11] The relationship between Directives based on the two sets of provisions has been described as one between 'liberalization' and 'harmonization' respectively.[12] The interaction between the two legal bases was a significant feature of liberalization in the telecommunications market. Indeed, as early as its 1987 Green Paper on Telecommunications, the Commission had declared that it 'may use, as appropriate, its mandate under Article 90(3) [now 86(3)] of the Treaty to promote, synchronize and accelerate the on-going transformation'.[13] Despite this, in the energy sector, the Article 86(3) option was only briefly considered and then quickly dropped as a possible route for liberalization (see ch 3, paras 3.57–3.62).

5.10 It is important to note that the legislative procedures involved in Article 86(3) and Article 95 are quite different.

An important characteristic of Directives and decisions made under Article 86(3) is that they may be adopted by the Commission acting alone without the approval of the Council or the Parliament. This means that the procedure is potentially a faster one than the infringement proceedings under Article 226 which address problems on a case-by-case basis. Instead, the Commission can deal with sectors on a more general basis.

By contrast, the procedure under Article 95 involves consultation with a very wide range of parties. At that time, Article 95 provided for a co-operation procedure, through which the Council adopted the measure and Parliament was involved to a limited extent. Subsequently, the co-decision procedure applied and measures under Article 95 were adopted jointly by Council and Parliament. However, the key feature of Article 95 is that the Council is the motor behind the measure. Under Article 86(3) it is the Commission. Indeed, on the face of it, Article 86(3) is one of the very few instances in the EC Treaty in which a power to make laws of general application is vested in the Commission, with no express requirement to involve either the Council or the Parliament.[14]

---

[11] For an overview of developments in this sector from 1987–99, see Larouche, P, *Competition Law and Regulation in European Telecommunications*, (2000).

[12] Sauter, W, *Competition Law and Industrial Policy in the EU*, (1997), at 186 ff.

[13] 'Towards a Dynamic European Economy: Green Paper on the development of the common market for telecommunications services and equipment', COM (1987) 290 final, 30 June 1987, 186.

[14] However, it may be argued that this is not a general legislative power, but in practice limited to the adoption of Directives to spell out pre-existing obligations under other Treaty provisions, in particular Arts 81 and 82, but also the fundamental freedoms, in relation to state measures concerning legal monopolies. In that sense, it is different from, and more specific than, the general power conferred on the Council to adopt harmonization measures under Art 95 or competition law measures under Art 83: Edward, D and Hoskins, M, 'Article 90: Deregulation and EC Law. Reflections arising from the XVI FIDE Conference', 1995 CML Rev, 168, at 183.

In March 1991 the ECJ handed down its judgment in the *Telecommunications Terminal Equipment* case. The judgment confirmed the right and the duty of the Commission to address to the Member States Directives adopted under Article 86(3) to ensure the application of Treaty rules on free movement of goods and competition under Article 86. The ruling roused considerable interest among all parties involved in the ongoing debate on liberalization in the electricity and gas sectors. **5.11**

The case[15] arose from a Directive issued by the Commission under Article 86(3) as part of its plans to open up access to the EU telecommunications network.[16] The Directive required Member States to withdraw special and exclusive rights[17] granted in respect of the import, supply, installation, and maintenance of telecommunications terminal equipment. The validity of the Directive was challenged by the French Government supported by the Governments of Belgium, Germany, Greece, and Italy.[18] The ECJ was requested to annul some parts of the Directive, including those parts relating to withdrawal of special or exclusive rights granted by Member States. Although the proceedings commenced in 1988, it was not until 19 March 1991 that the ECJ delivered its judgment. More than a year had passed from the presentation of the Advocate-General's conclusions on the case to the ECJ on 13 February 1990, perhaps indicating the political sensitivity of the case. **5.12**

(a) *The Issues*

There were two issues of importance to be decided by the ECJ. First was whether the Commission should have made use of Article 226 of the EC Treaty[19] rather **5.13**

[15] Case C-202/88, *France v Commission*, ECR I-1223.

[16] Commission Directive 88/301/EEC of 16 May 1988 on Competition in the Markets in Telecommunications Terminal Equipment, [1988] OJ L 131, 73. A second Directive related primarily to the withdrawal by Member States of special and exclusive rights granted in respect of the supply of telecommunications services, other than voice telephony, and the taking by Member States of measures necessary to ensure than any operator is entitled to supply such services: Commission Directive 90/388/EEC of 28 June 1990 on competition in the markets for telecommunications services, OJ L 192/10.

[17] The Directive defined 'special or exclusive rights' as 'the rights granted by a Member State or a public authority to one or more public or private bodies through any legal, regulatory or administrative instrument reserving them the right to provide a service or undertake an activity' (Art 1).

[18] The aggregate votes of these 5 Member States would have been sufficient to block the Directive under an Art 95 legislative procedure. Larouche concludes that the Directive 'might not have been enacted with the same content under Art 95 EC, if it is assumed that Member States which went before the ECJ had reservations about the substance of the Directive as well as its legal basis': Larouche, P, see n 11, at 43, n 20.

[19] Art 226* states that: 'If the Commission considers that a Member State has failed to fulfil an obligation under this Treaty, it shall deliver a reasoned opinion on the matter after giving the State concerned the opportunity to submit its observations. If the State concerned does not comply with the opinion within the period laid down by the Commission, the latter may bring the matter before the Court of Justice'.

than Article 86(3) to attain the goal of putting to an end with immediate effect particular national measures. The second was whether the Commission had exceeded its monitoring powers under Article 86(3) by adopting a Directive that required the complete abolition of special and exclusive rights in connection with telecommunications terminal equipment.

5.14 At the time, the answer to the first question was considered a matter of great importance. It would establish what legal powers were available to the Commission to tackle constraints on the establishment of an internal market which arise from the special or exclusive rights granted not only in telecommunications, but also in other sectors such as electricity, gas, and water.

Traditionally, the transportation and distribution networks in these sectors had been dominated by entities that had been granted special or exclusive rights. The possibility was therefore raised that the Commission could, by means of a Directive issued under Article 86(3), require a Member State to withdraw exclusive rights, and thereby avoid the lengthy process under Article 226 of alleging breaches by individual Member States of EC Treaty obligations. It could also avoid the alternative procedure of requesting the Council to deal with the matter by adopting a Directive under the Article 95 procedure. Under the latter procedure, the Council may adopt 'measures for the approximation of the provisions laid down by law, regulation or administrative action in Member States which have as their object the establishment and functioning of the internal market'.[20] Since it involves consultation with the Parliament and other institutions of the Community such as the Economic and Social Committee, that process is a lengthy one. The decision of the ECJ therefore had considerable importance for the internal market strategy of the Commission.

5.15 The ECJ held, with respect to the first question, that Article 226 was required to be used in cases where a measure existed which was 'clearly and totally contrary to the Treaty'.[21] Article 86(3) gives the Commission power to specify in general terms the obligations arising under Article 86(1) by adopting Directives (see para 5.10, n 14 above). The Commission should exercise this power in cases where it defines in concrete terms the obligations imposed on the Member States under the EC Treaty. The ECJ held that 'such a power cannot be used to make a finding that a Member State has failed to fulfill a particular obligation under the Treaty'.[22] In the context of the Directive at issue, 'the Commission merely determined in general terms obligations which are binding on the Member States under the Treaty. The Directive cannot therefore be interpreted as making specific findings that particular Member States failed to fulfill their obligations under the Treaty.'[23]

[20] Art 95(1).
[21] Para 16.
[22] Paras 17–18.
[23] ibid.

In reaching this conclusion, the ECJ did not follow the opinion of the Advocate-General Giuseppe Tesauro,[24] who declared that: 5.16

> The issue of a Directive under Article 90(3) is not an appropriate way of dealing with a breach, especially in circumstances where, in the pleadings before the Court, the lawyer pleading appearing for the Commission explained the reason for preferring to use the Article 90(3) procedure rather than Article 169 was that the latter would not have the same direct and immediate effect.

He noted also that a Directive issued under Article 86(3) could not in principle provide for 'repressive' purposes in place of Article 226.

With respect to the second question, the ECJ held that even if Article 86(1) presupposed the existence of undertakings with special or exclusive rights, it did not follow that all such rights were necessarily to be considered incompatible with the EC Treaty. The ECJ held that 'the supervisory power conferred on the Commission includes the possibility of specifying, pursuant to Article 90(3), obligations arising under the Treaty. The extent of that power therefore depends upon the scope of the rules with which compliance is to be ensured.'[25] For the most part, it upheld the content of the Directive, with the notable exception of Article 12. The latter required Member States to take all necessary steps to ensure that national telecommunications monopolies made it possible for their customers to terminate, within a maximum period of notice of one year, leasing or maintenance contracts for terminal equipment which had been the subject of exclusive or special rights at the time of the conclusion of the contracts. The ECJ held that Article 86(3) was not a valid legal basis for such a measure since Article 86 did not govern anti-competitive conduct if such conduct was engaged in by undertakings at their own initiative. It conferred powers solely in relation to state measures and in this case there was no evidence that long-term contracts had been concluded under pressure from the Member States. Anti-competitive conduct of this kind was remediable only on a case-by-case basis and by means of individual decisions adopted under Articles 81 and 82.[26] 5.17

(b) Effects

The initial response of the Commission to the judgment was that its law-making powers under Article 86(3) had been significantly extended or at the very least confirmed. Moreover, the interpretation of Article 28 was wide and potentially useful for the energy sector. Because the holders of the exclusive rights could not 5.18

[24] The rôle of the Advocate-General responsible for a case is to summarize the arguments of the parties and to give the ECJ his or her views on the relevant law and the decision which the ECJ should take. The ECJ is not bound to follow the A-G's conclusions, but usually does so.

[25] Para 21.

[26] Edward and Hoskins, see n 14, at 183–4. They see this aspect of the judgment as illustrating the limited nature of the Commission's power under Art 86(3).

satisfy the market demand and since the exclusive import rights could have restricted the trade in products from other Member States, Article 28 was applicable. This included both the products and also the ancillary services necessary for the repair and maintenance of those products. Accordingly, the Commission took two distinct initiatives.

(1) First, it drafted and informally circulated among Member States Directives based on Article 86(3) to require the removal of import and export monopolies in electricity and gas (see ch 3).
(2) Secondly, it dispatched letters to several Member States which maintained exclusive import and export rights in electricity and gas. The basis for these infringement actions was Article 31 (see ch 2, para 2.18). Its use had so far been very limited with respect to its application to service monopolies. Much earlier, in the *Manghera* case[27] the ECJ had ruled that an exclusive right to import or market manufactured products constituted a form of discrimination prohibited by Article 37(1). However, the application of the Article to service monopolies had been limited by the ECJ decision in the *Saatchi* case.[28]

5.19 The first action quickly ran into difficulties. It provoked considerable opposition from the Member States. The unilateral approach by the Commission was also not proposed at a highly propitious moment since the Member States were concluding negotiations on the Treaty of European Union that would increase the consultation process between Community institutions, giving more imput, especially to the Parliament. This approach appeared to involve action in precisely the opposite direction. Moreover, the legal position was on closer inspection less clear-cut than it seemed.

This element of uncertainly was more apparent in the judgment in a second case in the telecommunications sector, involving a challenge to the validity of the Commission's Telecommunications Services Directive.[29] Significantly, the Directive had included a full explanation by the Commission of the reasons why it was using its powers under Article 86(3) to achieve the objectives of the Directive.[30]

[27] Case C-59/75 *Pubblico Ministero v Manghera* [1976] ECR 91.

[28] Case 155/73 *Saatchi* [1974] ECR 409.

[29] Joined Cases C-271, C-281, and C-289/90, *Spain, Belgium, and Italy v Commission* [1992] ECR I-5833, which challenged Commission Directive 90/388 on competition in the markets for telecommunications services: 1990 OJ L, 192/10.

[30] Recital 33 states that: 'Article 90(3) assigns clearly defined duties and powers to the Commission to monitor relations between Member States and their public undertakings and undertakings to which they have granted special or exclusive rights, particularly as regards the removal of obstacles to freedom to provide services, discrimination between nationals of the Member States and competition. A comprehensive approach is necessary in order to end the infringements that persist in certain Member States and to give clear guidelines to these Member States that are reviewing their legislation so as to avoid further infringement. A Directive within the meaning of Article 90(3) is therefore the most appropriate means of achieving this end'.

While the second of the Commission's actions (the infringement procedure under Article 169 (now Art 226) continued its course, it did so only very slowly and was clearly being used tactically by the Commission—to assist the negotiations on Directives based on Article 95.

The proposed Directives under Article 86(3) were simply dropped. Arguably, the Commission had learned from the experience of circulating draft Directives based on this Article what the limits were of this particular legal instrument in the energy sector. Without a significant level of support from the Member States it had little use. Just as important, the provision of a transitional phase to an internal energy market, which all parties considered necessary, was not feasible by this legislative route.

(2) Clarification of Monopoly Rights and their Limits

In addition to the *Telecoms* case, the ECJ clarified the legal position of monopoly rights under Article 86 in a number of cases that are explained and commented on below. 5.20

(a) *Höfner v Macrotron*[31]

This case was a reference from the *Oberlandesgericht München* (Higher Regional Court) under Article 234. The ECJ considered whether the grant of an exclusive right might inevitably lead to the abuse of a dominant position resulting from the grant of that right. The case arose from the grant of a statutory monopoly by the Federal German Republic to the *Bundesanstalt für Arbeit* (Federal Employment Office), which covered the provision of recruitment and placement services for executive positions throughout the Federal Republic. The ECJ was asked, *inter alia*, by the national court to rule on the question of whether, taking Article 86(2) into account, the monopoly of recruitment of business executives constituted an abuse of a dominant position on the market, contrary to Article 82. 5.21

The ECJ held that 'the simple fact of creating a dominant position ... by granting an exclusive right . . . is not as such incompatible with Article 82 of the Treaty'. Rather, a Member State would be in breach of its obligations under Article 86(1) in conjunction with Article 82, if the body to which it had granted an exclusive right would, by the mere exercise of its exclusive rights, be led to an abuse of its dominant position.[32] In this case, the Member State had created a situation in which the statutory monopolist (the public employment agency) was manifestly unable to satisfy the demand for its services, but private competitors (Höfner and Elser) were precluded from entering the market by a legal provision that rendered any contract for such services null and void. There was therefore a breach of Article 86(1) coupled with Article 82(b).[33]

[31] Case C-41/90, *Klaus Höfner and Fritz Elser v Macrotron GmbH* [1991] ECR I-1979.

[32] Recital 29.

[33] The same approach was adopted in the case of *La Crespelle*, where the Court held: 'The mere creating of a . . . dominant position by the granting of an exclusive right within the meaning of

(b) ERT

5.22 In this case[34] the ECJ examined an exclusive right in conjunction with alleged breaches of the EC Treaty provisions concerning the freedom of movement of goods (Arts 28–30) and the freedom to provide services (Arts 49–55). There was a clear statement in the judgment that exclusive and special rights to provide services are in breach of Article 49.

The case arose from the grant of exclusive rights to ERT, a Greek national radio and television company, for the organization, transmission, and development of radio and television in the country. In addition to the exclusive right to broadcast its own programmes, ERT had an exclusive right to re-transmit foreign television programmes in Greece. DEP had, together with another individual, established a television transmitter in Salonika, which had begun broadcasting without obtaining a prior consent from ERT as required by Greek law. As a result, ERT had taken steps to restrain DEP from broadcasting. The Greek court referred the case to the ECJ and requested a ruling on whether the exercise of exclusive rights granted to ERT was contrary to any of the rules of the EC Treaty.

5.23 The ECJ re-stated its judgment in *Saatchi*[35] to the effect that the EC Treaty does not prevent Member States from conferring exclusive rights to broadcast for non-economic reasons, based on public interest considerations. However, it added that 'the methods of organization and exercise of that monopoly must not run contrary to the rules on free movement of goods and services and the competition rules'.[36] It also examined the operation of the monopoly in relation to the provisions on free movement of goods and the freedom to provide services. With respect to the former, the ECJ ruled that a television monopoly relating to services and not goods could not in itself be contrary to the provisions relating to freedom of movement of goods.[37] With respect to the freedom to provide services, the ECJ held that the grant of the exclusive right to re-transmit foreign television broadcasts was a breach of Article 49 of the EC Treaty unless it was subject to the exemptions contained in Article 55. The latter permits an exemption from the provisions of Article 49 on the grounds specified in Article 46, such as public policy, public security, or public health.

Article 90(1) is not as such incompatible with Article 86 of the Treaty. A Member State contravenes the prohibitions contained in those two provisions only if, in merely exercising the exclusive right granted to it, the undertaking in question cannot avoid abusing its dominant position' (Case C-323/93, [1994] ECR I-5077, para 18).

[34] Case C-260/89, *Elliniki Radiophonia Tileorassi– Antonimi Erairia ('ERT') v Dimotiki Etairia Pliroforissis ('DEP')* [1991] ECR I-2951.

[35] Case 155/73 [1974] ECR 409. The judgment did not attempt to identify those instances where the grant of special or exclusive rights could infringe the Treaty rules. By contrast, judgments in subsequent cases have developed the law on this point.

[36] Recital 12.

(c) Port of Genoa[38]

The ECJ built on *Höfner* and *ERT* in its interpretation of the circumstances in which the exercise of an exclusive right granted by a Member State could then be an abuse of a dominant position under Article 82. Under Italian law Merci had been granted an exclusive right to handle at the port of Genoa all conventional goods including steel. Gabriella bought some steel from a producer in West Germany and shipped it to Genoa where it wished to unload the cargo. Gabriella was unable to unload the cargo from the boat in part because of strikes by stevedores employed by Merci, although the ship had on board equipment with which it would have been possible to unload the cargo. Gabriella claimed damages against Merci due to the delay in unloading and also claimed the return of money already paid to Merci on the ground that these payments were excessive in view of the service rendered by Merci. The Italian court referred the case to the ECJ, asking it, *inter alia*, to decide whether the exercise by Merci of its exclusive right to handle cargoes at the port of Genoa constituted an abuse of a dominant position. **5.24**

The ECJ held that the creation of a dominant position by the granting of exclusive rights is not in itself incompatible with Article 82.[39] Further, it held that a Member State commits a breach of Article 86(1), in conjunction with Article 82, if the undertaking to which the exclusive rights are granted, is led, by the simple exercise of the exclusive rights granted to it, to exploit its dominant position in an abusive way or where the grant of the exclusive rights is liable to create a situation where the undertaking exploits its dominant position in an abusive manner.[40] **5.25**

An important element in the ECJ's judgment is the reaffirmation and extension of its judgment in the *Höfner* case. The extension lay in the words 'or where the granting of the exclusive rights is liable to create a situation where the undertaking is led to exploit its dominant position in an abusive way'. The ECJ also noted in its judgment that some observations made before it to the effect that the creation of the exclusive right had led to Merci making charges for services that were not requested and to charging prices that were disproportionate to the work done and refusing to use modern technology. This resulted in increased costs and increases in the time taken to do the work. Conduct of this kind may be relevant in establishing an abuse of a dominant position by an electricity or gas transmission grid or pipeline owner. The significance of this case lies in the fact that it resulted in a successful challenge to the exclusive right. It also developed the definition of 'substantial part of the common market'.

---

[37] Recital 13.

[38] Case C-179/90 *Merci Convenzionale Porto di Genova SpA ('Merci') v Siderurgica Gabriella SpA ('Gabriella')* [1991] ECR I-5889.

[39] Recital 16.

[40] Recital 17.

(d) RTT

5.26 In this case[41] the ECJ was asked to rule on the abuse of a dominant position that arose as a result of the extension of an existing exclusive right granted by a Member State. Under Belgian law RTT held a monopoly of the provision of public telephone services. Subsequently, the monopoly had been extended by the imposition of a requirement that subscribers to the RTT telephone service could not, without the approval of RTT, attach any apparatus or line to any apparatus which they were entitled to use under their arrangement with RTT. Further, the law required that the apparatus to be attached should be approved by RTT.

5.27 GB was a merchandising company that sold subsidiary telephones to be attached to the RTT telephones in its retailing outlets. It had purchased them with a view to selling them into this market. RTT had asked for an injunction to stop sales of these telephones by GB. In turn, GB asked the ECJ to consider whether this exercise by RTT of its exclusive rights in connection with the sales of the supplementary telephones was an abuse of a dominant position under Article 82.

5.28 The ECJ did not question the legality of RTT's monopoly over the public telephone network. However, it did condemn the legislation that conferred the ancillary rights on RTT. It held that a Member State would be in breach of its obligations under Article 86(1) in conjunction with Article 82, if it granted to an undertaking which already enjoyed a dominant position as a result of a grant of exclusive rights in a particular market an exclusive right to carry on an auxiliary activity, if such auxiliary activity could be carried out by a third-party in an adjacent but separate market (Recital 21). There are links between this judgment and the so-called 'essential facilities' doctrine (see below para 5.68).

(e) Corbeau

5.29 This case concerned an exclusive right to collect, transport, and deliver mail in Belgium and was referred to the ECJ by the *Tribunel Correctionnel* of Liège.[42] It arose from a criminal prosecution brought against Mr Corbeau in respect of an alleged breach by him of the national monopoly of postal services granted to *Regie des Postes* by Belgian law. Mr Corbeau was alleged to have breached that monopoly by providing a rapid mail delivery service in the city of Liège. This involved the collection of mail from the place of business or residence of the sender and its distribution within the city before midday on the next day. The case had two relevant aspects: (1) the lawfulness of a monopoly over time, and (2) the defence of exclusive rights by reference to public service obligations.

[41] Case C-18/88 *Regie des Telegraphes et des Telephones ('RTT') v SA-GB-Inno-BM ('GB')* [1991] ECR I-5973.

[42] Case C-320/91 [1993] ECR I-2533.

In relation to the first point, at the time when the exclusive rights were granted to the Belgian postal services in 1956 and 1971 commercial demand for specialized rapid courier services did not exist. By the time the case came before the ECJ the market had changed. The question was not therefore whether the exclusive rights had conformed with Article 86(1) when the rights were granted but rather, whether such rights were in conformity with Article 86(1) in the context of the very different market that prevailed in 1993.[43] As a result, the judgment 'places an obligation on the Member States constantly to review legal monopolies in light of changing market conditions'.[44] **5.30**

The second aspect of the case concerns the relationship between exclusive rights and public service obligations. The ECJ held that the law that granted exclusive rights of collection and distribution of post in Belgium was contrary to Article 86(1) in the sense that it prohibited, with criminal sanctions, an economic operator established in Belgium from operating specific services there, even though such services were distinct from services of general economic interest, met the needs of particular economic operators, and also required certain supplementary services which a traditional postal service does not offer. However, the ECJ added that the monopoly should only be reduced to the extent that the reduction did not put in question the 'economic equilibrium' of the service of general economic interest carried out by *Regie des Postes*. By this the ECJ meant its service to core customers. In doing so, the ECJ was relying on the exemptions from the Treaty rules which may be granted under Article 86(2) to undertakings that are entrusted[45] with the operation of services of general economic interest.[46] **5.31**

---

[43] See further Edward and Hoskins (see n 14), 168.

[44] ibid.

[45] For the term 'entrusted', see Case 127/73 *BRT v SABAM* [1974] ECR 51 (it can apply to private as well as public undertakings); Case 10/71 *Ministère Public de Luxembourg v Muller* [1971] ECR 723 (the legal measure by which an undertaking is entrusted may take the form of a specific national law); Commission Decision on British Telecommunications (BT), [1982] OJ L 360/36 and [1983] 1 CML Rev 457 (UK statute constituting BT was held to have entrusted that body with services of general economic interest for the purposes of Art 86(2)); Commission Decision MAVEWA-ANSEAU, 1982 OJ L 167/39 and [1982] 2 CML Rev 193 (the act entrusting the undertaking with a service of general economic interest need not be an act of central government).

[46] For the term 'service of general economic interest', not defined in the Treaty itself, the jurisprudence of the ECJ has established that services includes goods: see Case 82/71 *Pubblico Ministero v SAIL* [1972] ECR 119 (distribution of milk constituted a service of general economic interest if it was carried out in the interest of the citizens as a whole); Case 10/71, *Ministere Public Luxembourg v Muller* [1971] ECR 723 (an authority responsible for the navigation of an important national waterway may fall within Art 86(2)); Case 155/73 *Saatchi* [1974] ECR 409 (a television company operating under statutory powers may fall within Art 86(2)) and Commission Decision 915/EEC of 16 July 1991 OJ L 28/32–IV/32 732 *Ijsselcentrale & Ors* (generators of electricity and national utility SEP operating under concession agreements were carrying out services of general economic interest). Note that Art 16 EC Treaty states:

> . . . given the place occupied by services of general economic interest in the shared values of the Union as well as their role in promoting social and territorial cohesion, the Community and the Member States . . . shall take care that such services operate on the basis of principles

C. Import and Export of Electricity and Gas

5.32 The existence of exclusive rights over imports and exports would seem to be an obvious breach of the EC Treaty rules on the free movement of goods and in particular, of Article 31 EC, which requires that state monopolies of a commercial character (whether operated on a direct or delegated basis) be operated in such a way as to eliminate all discrimination between nationals of Member States. It does not make state monopolies illegal, but requires that they be adjusted to achieve this objective.[47] The obligation to do so applies to all goods, including those such as electricity and gas that circulate through networks.

5.33 The provisions of Articles 28 to 30* require the elimination of quantitative restrictions on the import and export of goods between Member States. These obligations apply to all goods and therefore to goods that circulate through networks such as electricity and natural gas. Enforcement of these provisions is a matter for the Commission. Under Article 226, the Commission is required to enforce compliance by Member States of their obligations under the EC Treaty, including Article 31, by first delivering a reasoned opinion on the matter and then, if the Member State still does not comply, by bringing the matter before the ECJ.

(1) Early Enforcement in Energy

5.34 During the 1970s these provisions were applied to adjust state monopolies in the oil industry, and in the 1990s they were applied to electricity and gas networks. This was because state monopolies of import and export of electricity and gas or exclusive rights of transmission and distribution can by their existence frustrate the free circulation of electricity and gas within the EU and thereby frustrate the application of the rules relating to freedom of movement of goods. Prior to 1991 there had only been two challenges to such restrictions in the energy sector under Article 31.[48] They arose concerning the exclusive import of gas granted to Distrigas by the Belgian Government and the exclusive legal monopoly of the French state relating to the import and distribution of petroleum into France (see below). However, in neither case did the Commission find it necessary to take proceedings against the Member State under Article 226 to secure compliance with Article 31.

and conditions which enable them to fulfil their missions'. The provisions of this Article are to be implemented according to a Declaration in the TEU 'with full respect to the jurisprudence of the Court of Justice, *inter alia*, as regards the principles of equality of treatment, quality and continuity of service.

[47] It may be noted that there is an overlap between the powers contained in Art 31 and those contained in Art 86 which deal with public undertakings and undertakings with exclusive or special rights.

[48] 13th Report on Competition Policy, 121, point 291.

The Belgian case arose from the exclusive import concession held by Distrigas S.A. under Article 181 of the Act of 8 August 1980. The Commission informed the Belgian Government that the concession was contrary to Article 31. The Belgian Government accepted this opinion and undertook to revoke the concession, noting that the provisions of Article 181 would not be applied while new legislation was being prepared. Subsequently, Article 181 was amended by an Act of 29 July 1983 so as to restrict the exclusive concession to underground storage and to the transportation of natural gas. **5.35**

The French case involved the exclusive legal monopoly of the French state in relation to import and distribution of petroleum into France. The Commission's action was directed at the arrangements for the import and distribution of refined petroleum products based on Article 1 of a 1946 law,[49] which reserved to the State exclusive import and marketing rights in relation to petroleum products, among other things. The French Government had relied on that Law to introduce a system of special import permits. In granting such permits the Government stipulated the maximum amount of motor fuel that each permit holder was permitted to sell annually in France, irrespective of whether the product had been imported or refined in France. The Commission complained that this arrangement was contrary to the provisions relating to the free movement of goods. The exclusive rights of monopolies to import or market goods constituted discrimination against exporters from other Member States within the meaning of Article 31(1) so that the special permits scheme ought to be limited to rules laying down objective standards applicable to importers or distributors of oil products.[50] This statement was based on the judgment of the ECJ in the *Manghera* case, which ruled that Article 31 must be interpreted as meaning that as from 31 December 1969 every national monopoly of a commercial character must be adjusted so as to eliminate the exclusive right to import from other Member States.[51] **5.36**

(2) Electricity and Gas Import–Export Monopolies

In August 1991 the Commission announced that it intended to take action on the basis of Article 31 under the Article 226 procedure against several Member States on the ground that their legislation provided for import and export monopolies in electricity or gas or both. The countries concerned were Denmark, France, Greece, Ireland, Italy, the Netherlands, Spain, and the UK (with respect to Northern Ireland). Letters were sent in accordance with Article 226, setting a period of two months within which the Member States could submit observations on the Commission's opinion. Most of the Member States concerned indicated a **5.37**

[49] 12th Report on Competition Policy, point 221; Law No 46-628 of 8 April 1946.
[50] 6th Report on Competition Policy, points 268 and 269, 1977, Brussels–Luxembourg.
[51] Case C-59/75, n 63 below, p 91.

willingness to adapt their legislation to meet the Commission's objections, but in several cases no action was taken within a time-limit (see ch 3, paras 3.86–3.87). It should be noted that there was a close link between the Commission's actions and the ongoing negotiations concerning the proposed Directives on common rules for the electricity and gas sectors. This was not accidental and formed part of the Commission's strategy to establish a consensus behind its proposals.[52]

5.38 In January 1994 the Commission referred to the ECJ actions against six Member States for failure to fulfil an obligation in the infringement procedures. In each Member State there were restrictions on the import and export of electricity and, in the case of France, also of gas. In The Netherlands, final consumers were entitled to import electricity for their own needs, but for voltages exceeding 500V, only the utility *Samenwerkende Elektriciteitsproductiebedrijven* (SEP) was authorized to import electricity for public distribution. This was provided for in the Electricity Law of 16 November 1989. In Italy all of the activities of import, export, generation, transmission, distribution, and sale of electricity had been entrusted to the *Ente Nazionale per l'Energia Elletrica* (ENEL) by the nationalization law of 1962, No 1643. Further, undertakings other than ENEL were expressly prohibited from importing, exporting, or trading in electricity or transmitting electricity on behalf of third parties. The restriction was contained in Legislative Decree No 342 of 18 March 1965. Imports and exports of electricity were also subject to the grant of a licence by the Minister of Public Works. In France all activities in the import and export of electricity and gas, as well as generation, transmission, and distribution were nationalized in 1946 and management entrusted to public undertakings of an industrial and commercial nature. As a result, only *Électricité de France* (EdF) was allowed to carry out import, export, and transmission of electricity. Import and export of gas was entrusted on an exclusive basis to *Gaz de France* (GdF) under a concession agreement concluded with the State on 27 November 1958 for a period of 75 years. In Spain the national high-voltage electricity system was designated a public service by Law No 49/84 and managed as such by a state company, *Red Eléctrica de España* (Redesa).

5.39 Proceedings against Denmark in relation to its restrictions on gas imports were halted when the Commission was sent a copy of the Danish Government's letter of April 1994 to the state-owned utility, Dangas, which indicated that it would repeal the restriction. Similarly, the case against Ireland was withdrawn from the register before the hearing on the ground that the legislation in question did not expressly prohibit other companies from carrying out the same tactics as the Electricity Supply Board.[53]

[52] Schmidt, S K, 'Commission Activism: Subsuming Telecommunications and Electricity under European Competition Law', (1998) Jo of European Public Policy, 169–84. Her conclusions are largely based on extensive interviews conducted with participants in the Community institutions and Member State governments.

[53] [1994] OJ C202/9, and Order of the President of 11 Sept 1995: [1996] OJ C336/23.

The Commission's argument in each of the four remaining cases was that the national rules were liable to restrict trade between Member States and were therefore contrary to Articles 28, 30, and 31 EC. With respect to import rights, the Commission argued that a national import monopoly prevented producers in other Member States from selling electricity and, in the case of France—gas within the territory of The Netherlands, Italy, France, and Spain respectively—to customers other than the holders of the monopoly. Moreover, potential customers in one of those Member States were unable freely to choose their source of supply of electricity from other Member States. 5.40

On export rights, the Commission's argument was that holders of such rights tend to reserve national production for the national market, and so place the domestic market at a disadvantage, to the detriment of demand from other Member States.

(a) *The* Dutch *Case*

In its judgment in the case against The Netherlands,[54] the Court found that the exclusive import rights were indeed contrary to Article 31 EC, and for that reason it was unnecessary to consider whether they were contrary to Article 28, or whether they might be justified under Article 30. 5.41

It reasoned first, that it is not necessarily a requirement for illegality that the exclusive rights to import a given product relate to *all* imports. It is sufficient for these rights to relate to such a proportion that they enable the monopoly to have an appreciable influence on imports, as was shown in an earlier case, *Commission v Greece*.[55] The exclusive rights held by SEP for electricity for public distribution fall within that category.

Secondly, the Court rejected the argument that SEP could not be regarded as a monopoly of a commercial character within the meaning of Article 31. The case law of the Court applies to situations in which the national authorities are in a position to control, direct, or appreciably influence trade between Member States through a body established for that purpose or a delegated monopoly. Exclusive rights give rise to that kind of situation.

Thirdly, against the contention that only the discriminatory exercise of exclusive rights, not merely the holding of them is prohibited under Article 31, the ECJ held that the aim of Article 31(1) EC would be met if, in a Member State where a commercial monopoly exists, the free movement of goods from other Member States comparable to those with which the national monopoly is concerned were not ensured. The very existence of exclusive import rights in a Member State impedes free movement since it deprives economic operators in other Member States

[54] Case C-157/94, *Commission v The Netherlands* [1997] ECR I-5699.
[55] Case C-347/88, *Commission v Hellenic Republic* [1990] ECR I-4747, para 41.

of the possibility of offering their products to customers of their choice in the Member State concerned. In the Dutch case, all imports had to be incorporated into the plans drawn up by SEP.

5.42 The other key issue in the case concerned the possible justification of these exclusive rights under Article 86(2). The ECJ examined the Commission's main argument that Article 86(2) cannot be relied on to justify state measures that are incompatible with the Treaty rules on the free movement of goods. Taking into account the scope and combined effect of paragraphs 1 and 2 of Article 86, the ECJ considered that paragraph 2 could be relied on to justify the grant of exclusive rights by a Member State to an undertaking entrusted with the operation of services of general economic interest. This applied even where such rights were contrary to Article 31, subject to two conditions:

(1) it applied to the extent that performance of the particular tasks assigned to it could only be achieved through the grant of such rights; and
(2) the grant of such rights should not affect the development of trade to such an extent that it would be contrary to the interests of the Community.

5.43 With respect to the first point, the ECJ held that it is not necessary for there to be a threat to the financial balance or economic viability of the undertaking entrusted with the operation of a service of general economic interest. The test is whether it would not be possible for the undertaking to perform the particular tasks entrusted to it in the absence of the rights at issue. The tasks should be defined by reference to the obligations and constraints to which the undertaking is subject. Citing the judgment in *Corbeau*,[56] the ECJ noted that the conditions for the application of Article 86(2) are fulfilled if maintenance of those rights is necessary to permit the holder to perform the tasks of general economic interest assigned to it under economically acceptable conditions. It was beyond doubt that the removal of SEP's exclusive import rights would have radical effects upon the current organization of the electricity supply industry in The Netherlands. Although the Commission, in recognizing this, had outlined in general terms some alternatives in place of the rights at issue, it had not taken into account the particularities of the national electricity system nor of the question whether those alternatives would have enabled SEP to perform the tasks of general economic interest assigned to it in compliance with the obligations and constraints imposed upon it. The burden of proof here lay with the Commission and not with the Member State: the latter did not have to provide positive proof that no other measure could enable those tasks to be performed under the same conditions.

5.44 The ECJ went on to criticize the Commission's responses in the proceedings brought against The Netherlands under Article 226. It was the Commission's task

[56] See n 42 above.

to prove the allegation that the obligation had not been fulfilled and to provide the ECJ with the information required to enable it to determine whether the obligation had not been fulfilled. In the pre-litigation procedure The Netherlands had provided a justification of its position. However, when bringing proceedings before the ECJ, the Commission had specified only the legal considerations and not the factual ones on which the complaint was based. Both were required, even if only in summary form. This, the ECJ argued, had the effect of narrowing the terms of the dispute brought before it. It could base its judgment only on the merits of the pleas in law, since it could not undertake an assessment of the alternatives which a Member State might adopt to ensure electricity supply which was as inexpensive as possible, and supplied in a socially responsible manner.

The approach adopted by the Commission (failing to produce an economic assessment of the electricity market) was not accepted by the ECJ. Essentially, it was the Commission's job to provide this in an area of industrial activity which is highly regulated and economically complex. Further, on the basis of the above reasons, the ECJ declared itself unable to consider whether the rights granted to SEP went further than was necessary to enable it to perform the tasks of general economic interest assigned to it.

The second condition which had to be fulfilled for SEP's exclusive import rights to escape the application of the Treaty rules under Article 86(2) was that the development of trade must not be affected to such an extent as would be contrary to the interests of the Community. On this matter, the ECJ noted that the Commission had not provided an explanation which would demonstrate that the development of intra-Community trade in electricity had been and continues to be affected by SEP's exclusive import rights to an extent that is contrary to the interests of the Community. Yet it was the Commission's task to do so, in order to prove the alleged failure to fulfil obligations. It should have provided a definition of the Community interest in relation to which the development of trade had to be assessed. In the absence of a common policy in this area, the Commission was under an obligation to show how the development of direct trade between producers and consumers, in parallel with the development of trade between the major networks, would have been possible, taking into account the existing capacity and the transmission and distribution arrangements. The Commission's application was dismissed. **5.45**

As is clear from the above, the question of the admissibility of certain arguments was crucial. It had two aspects which defined the ECJ's later reasoning. To begin with, there had to be debate by the parties on the economic aspects of the action. This had not been done. Secondly, the well-foundedness of the action was preconditioned by its scope: that is, the import and export monopolies. Arguments which extended beyond that scope could not be considered. This meant that a **5.46** challenge to the existing régimes for transmission and distribution by the Commission was not admissible. If then a Member State were to argue that the abolition of import and export monopolies would require considerable modification of transmission and distribution systems, it could not be countered by the Commission that they also required to be changed. This point about admissibility is relevant to the other cases outlined below.

5.47 It may be noted that, by not examining Articles 28 and 30, the ECJ did not follow the reasoning of Advocate General Cosmas in his Opinion on the cases delivered on 26 November 1996. He had considered that the exclusive rights infringed Article 28 and were not justifiable on public security grounds under Article 30. It may also be noted that by the time the judgments were delivered the 1989 Electricity Law had been superseded by a new statute on electricity in The Netherlands. If the Commission were to examine the wider, extra-legal context in which the electricity supply arrangements operated, its task would be rather different, although not necessarily any easier.

(b) The Italian *Case*

5.48 In the linked case C-158/94, the ECJ adopted a similar line of reasoning with respect to the existence of exclusive rights and the interpretation of Article 86(2) as in the *Dutch* case.[57] However, it also tackled the issue of whether electricity could be classified as goods or services.

The Italian Government argued that electricity does not fall within the category of 'goods' but is rather a service, and as such does not fall within the scope of Articles 28 to 31. After all, it is an incorporeal substance that cannot be stored and has no economic existence as such, in the sense that it is not useful in itself but only through its possible applications. In this sense, it resembles a service. The Italian Government made exactly this point in its case: it followed that the import and export of electricity were therefore aspects of management of the electricity network. This argument was (unsurprisingly) rejected by the ECJ. It noted that in the *Almelo* case[58] the ECJ had observed that in Community law and also in the national laws of the Member States, electricity constituted a 'good' within the meaning of Article 28 EC. It also noted that electricity is regarded as a good under the Community's tariff nomenclature (Code CN 27.16) and that it had already been accepted that electricity may fall within the scope of Article 31 in *Costa v ENEL*.[59]

[57] [1997] ECR I-5789. The ECJ criticized the Commission for failure to take into account the particular features of the national system of electricity supply and especially those imposed by geography. The Commission had also failed to consider whether the alternative means to exclusive rights it proposed would in practice enable the electricity utility, ENEL, to perform the tasks of general economic interest entrusted to it under economically acceptable conditions. Again, it was the task of the Commission to prove that the obligation had not been fulfilled, and this had not been done.

[58] Case C-393/92, *Almelo, Gemeente v Energiebedrijf Ijsselmij* NV [1994] ECR I-1477, para 28.

[59] Case C-6/64, [1964] ECR 585.

The Government of Italy had also tried to base its case for electricity as exempt from the rules on the free movement of goods on two earlier cases decided by the ECJ. The judgments were in *HM Customs and Excise v Schindler* and *ERT v DEP*.[60] In *Schindler*, the ECJ held that the import of lottery advertisements and tickets into a Member State with a view to the participation by residents of that Member State in a lottery conducted in another Member State relates to a 'service' within the meaning of Article 49 EC. In *ERT*, it held that the grant to a single undertaking of exclusive rights in relation to television broadcasting and the grant for that purpose of an exclusive right to import, hire, or distribute material and products necessary for that broadcasting does not as such constitute a measure having an effect equivalent to a quantitative restriction within the meaning of Article 28. However, in *Schindler* the ECJ had expressly stated that the import and distribution of the documents and tickets required for the organization of a lottery are not ends in themselves, since their sole purpose was to enable residents of Member States to participate in the lottery. This judgment could not therefore be relied upon in the situation of *ENEL*, where the services required for the import or export of electricity and its transmission and distribution are only the means to supply users with goods within the meaning of the Treaty. Nor could the Italian Government rely on the *ERT* case. There, it was held that the granting of an exclusive right to import, hire, or distribute materials and products necessary for television broadcasting to an undertaking with a monopoly over television-related services, did not constitute a measure having an effect equivalent to a quantitative restriction provided that no discrimination is created between domestic products and imported ones to the detriment of the latter. There was no support for the argument that the import and export of electricity falls outside the scope of the rules of the Treaty relating to the free movement of goods. **5.49**

(c) The French *Case*[61]

The *French* case involved arrangements in both the electricity and gas sectors. The exclusive rights in question were based on a concession and not on a statute. The Commission's argument was similar to the previous cases: the national import monopoly enjoyed by *Électricité de France* (EdF) and *Gaz de France* (GdF) had the effect of preventing producers in other Member States from selling their production to customers in France other than those monopoly holders. It also prevented potential consumers in France from freely choosing their sources of supply for electricity and gas from other Member States. As measures having an effect equivalent to quantitative restrictions on imports, they were contrary to Article 28. They constituted discrimination within the meaning of Article 31 regarding exporters established in the Member States and users established in the Member **5.50**

[60] Case C-275/92, [1994] ECR I-1039, and Case C-260/89 [1991] ECR I-2925; see paras 5.22–5.23.

[61] Case C-159/94, *Commission v France* [1997] ECR I-5815.

State concerned. The Commission also argued that the same considerations applied to the exclusive export rights EdF and GdF. Holders of such rights tend to allocate national production to the national market to the detriment of demand from other Member States. They should therefore be regarded as discriminatory within the meaning of Articles 30 and 31 EC.[62]

5.51 In fact, the French Government had already conceded that available national production of both electricity and gas is reserved as a matter of priority to users within French territory. The ECJ concluded therefore that the exclusive export rights of EdF and GdF had the effect—if not the object—of specifically restricting patterns of exports. A difference of treatment was thereby established between domestic trade and export trade, in a way that gave a special advantage to the French domestic market.

With respect to exclusive import rights, the French Government's objections were not upheld. It had argued that trade in electricity is carried out under largely uniform conditions within the Community but that neither final users nor distributors anywhere enjoy the freedom to choose their suppliers. EdF is therefore not in a more favourable position than operators in other Member States and the import monopoly does not affect the conditions of competition in France, to the detriment of the latter, as compared with those found in other Member States.

The same argument can be applied to the gas industry, with the caveat that in many cases there is no statutory monopoly on imports. However, referring to the judgment in the *Manghera* case,[63] the ECJ held that the objective of Article 31(1) would not be attained if, in a Member State where a commercial monopoly exists, the free movement of goods from other Member States comparable to those with which the national monopoly is concerned, were not ensured. Exclusive import rights in a Member State do after all deprive economic operators in other Member States of the opportunity to offer their products to consumers of their choice in the Member State concerned. This applies irrespective of the conditions that they encounter in their Member State of origin or in other Member States.

5.52 In the ECJ judgment, the reasoning was similar to that adopted in the *Dutch* and *Italian* cases, concluding that the Commission had not proved its case, confining itself only to legal arguments. It was therefore incumbent upon the Commission in proceedings under Article 226 to prove that the obligation had not been fulfilled and to provide the ECJ with sufficient information to enable it to determine whether the obligation had not been fulfilled. This had not been done.

---

[62] See Case C-189/95, *Franzen* [1997] ECR I-5909, for the ECJ's further exposition on Art 31.

[63] Case C-59/75, *Public Prosecutor v Manghera* [1976] ECR 91.

However, the *French* case contained a particular emphasis on public service obligations (PSOs; discussed below (paras 5.53–5.54).

5.53 **Public service element** The ECJ paid special attention to the definition of particular tasks entrusted to EdF and GdF. These included compliance with public service obligations (PSOs) and with the implementation of national environmental and regional policies. The elimination of the exclusive rights would, the French Government argued, compromise the performance of some or all of these obligations and make it difficult or impossible to contribute to the above policies. The Commission challenged the legal basis of the PSOs as insufficient to constitute particular tasks within the meaning of Article 86(2).

However, the ECJ's decision went against the Commission. An undertaking may be entrusted with the operation of services of general economic interest through the grant of a concession governed by public law[64]—particularly when such concessions have been granted to give effect to the obligations imposed upon undertakings which by statute have been entrusted with the operation of a service of general economic interest, as is the case with EdF and GdF. Moreover, there were clear links between Articles 36 and 37 of the 1946 Law and the concessions granted to the undertakings.

5.54 The ECJ turned to the specific PSOs. For these to fall within the particular tasks entrusted to it, they had to be linked to the subject-matter of the service of general economic interest in question. They also had to be designed to make a direct contribution to satisfying that interest. This could not apply to obligations which concerned environmental and regional policy imposed on undertakings entrusted with supplying the country with electricity and gas. Even the French Government had conceded that there was no obligation specific to those undertakings and to their business imposed on EdF and GdF.

Other PSOs were more defensible. For example, the obligations of supplying all customers, ensuring continuity of supply and treating customers equally, were each included in terms and conditions annexed to the agreement under which EdF was granted a concession in respect of the general electricity supply network. However, the ECJ ruled differently with respect to the alleged obligation of EdF to seek the most competitive tariffs and the lowest possible costs for the community. Neither the limits laid down in the terms and conditions for the adjustment of tariffs nor those for upward revision were such as to guarantee that the objective of securing the most competitive tariffs and the lowest cost would be attained.

For GdF the legal basis for its PSOs was unclear in the defence, but the ECJ nonetheless concluded that, on the basis of the texts produced, it was subject to

[64] *Almelo*, n 58 above, para 47.

obligations of continuity, supply, and equal treatment as between consumers. As a result, the ECJ held it was possible to examine the necessity of maintaining EdF's and GdF's exclusive import and export rights but only in relation to the three PSOs which the French Government had proved to exist.

Note: the *Spanish* Case[64a] In contrast to the other three decisions, the ECJ found that the Commission had alleged that there was a statutory monopoly but had not proved its existence. The action was dismissed and the Commission was ordered to pay the costs.

(3) **Assessment**

5.55 In the cases involving The Netherlands, France, and Italy, the ECJ took the view that the exclusive import and export rights did indeed impede the free movement of goods and had a direct impact on the conditions regarding both outlets and supplies to operators in other Member States, contravening Article 31. However, the ECJ ruled that the Commission had not proved its case against the restrictions imposed by the Member State concerned.

5.56 These ECJ findings do not follow the Opinion of Advocate-General Darmon[65] in the *Almelo* case, who declared that import monopolies for electricity are justified particularly by considerations of security of supply. Nor do they follow the Opinion of Advocate-General Cosmas, based on Articles 28 and 31, that the import rights did not affect Community trade but the export rights were unjustified.[66] Security of supply arguments played an important rôle in the Attorney-General's argument, but not in the ECJ judgments.

5.57 There are three positive elements in the judgments that may be noted.[67]

(1) The judgments provided important guidance on matters concerning burden of proof and admissibility in relation to Art 86. This may prove useful to the Commission in any subsequent steps it may take;
(2) The ECJ held that the practices in question were indeed contrary to Art 31 (except in the case involving Spain); and
(3) The cases had a beneficial effect on the adoption of the Electricity and Gas Directives.

These three points are elaborated below.

(a) Burden of proof and Article 86 admissibility

In Cases C-157/94, C-158/94, and C-159/94, the ECJ took the view that the exclusive import and export rights did indeed impede the free movement of goods

[64a] Case C-160/94, *Commission v Spain* [1997] ECR I-5851.

[65] Case C-393/92 *Almelo/N. V. Energiebedrijf Ijsselmij*, n 58 above.

[66] 26 Nov 1996.

[67] An earlier version of these comments appeared in my note: 'Towards an Internal Market in Energy: The Carrot and Stick Approach', (1998) 23 EL Rev, 579–91.

and had a direct impact on the conditions regarding both outlets and supplies to operators in other Member States, contravening Article 31. However, the ECJ ruled that the Commission had not proved the case against the restrictions being imposed by the Member States concerned (The Netherlands, Italy, and France). The cases raise delicate issues of burden of proof. However, they also settle a key issue. Previous case law has been quite inconsistent as to whether monopolies are *legal* unless shown to be against the Community interest (ie, the Commission must so prove) or monopolies are *illegal* unless the Member States show them to be in the Community interest. The more complex the area, the more important the burden becomes. Here, it is explicitly stated that the burden of proof falls upon the Member State which invokes Article 86 to show that the conditions are fulfilled.[68] This statement may ease the task of the Commission, not only in energy but also in related fields such as telecommunications. This development is the key to an understanding of how 'conflicts over burdens of proof' can arise: in particular, the burden of proof which falls on the Commission under Article 226 and the burden of proof which falls on the Member State under Article 86.

(b) Practices contrary to Article 31

Three of the judgments turned on the application of Article 86(2), and clearly the Commission had not prepared itself for the possibility that this would provide a successful defence under Article 31. The supporting arguments presented were deemed insufficient to prove that the Member States' measures affecting imports and exports were restrictive measures not protected by Article 86(2). On the other hand, it is important to note that the ECJ did not endorse the restrictive practices adopted by the Member States concerned. On the contrary, it concluded that they were indeed in breach of Article 31. Instead, it held that the Commission had not proved its case, and by implication left the door open for it to do further research with a view to trying again.

(c) Promoting adoption of Electricity and Gas Directives

In the wider context of the IEM programme, it may be argued that the ECJ's willingness to consider the actions had important consequences for the debate on the Electricity Directive in particular.[69] It appears that all parties were eager to reach agreement on a compromise position on the Electricity Directive prior to the ECJ's judgments.[70] Above all, the proceedings contributed to the impression among energy companies and Member States that the status quo was not sustainable, an impression given already by *Höfner* and other cases mentioned above.

---

[68] Case C-159/94, n 61 above para 94. However, note the contrasting approach adopted in the *Portuguese landing fees* case: Case C-163/99 Portugal v Commission [2001] judgment of 29 Mar 2001.

[69] This is noted also by Blanchard, P, 'French Electricity Sector: ECJ Decision on Monopolies for the Import and Export of Electricity', (1999) J Energy Natural Resources L, 265–80.

[70] See Schmidt, n 52 above.

(4) Conclusions (Import and Export Monopolies)

5.58 The barriers to import and export of energy in the EU represented a very clear case of incompatibility with the idea of an internal market. Yet it was not until 1991 that a concerted attempt was made to challenge Member States to justify them. The results of the exercise have been very positive, even if the cases brought by the Commission to the ECJ are assessed less favourably. The procedure adopted led to a considerable debate and to changes in current practices by several Member States before ECJ proceedings began. However, the lack of any real challenge to these exclusive rights for many years should act as a warning against high expectations of change through this route with respect to other exclusive rights with less obviously negative effects on the energy economy.

5.59 The exclusive rights on import and export were among the few that were clearly prohibited by Article 31. For other exclusive rights concerning goods and services, the starting point was the presumption of compatibility with Community law (*Saatchi* judgment). This was reversed by the Court with respect to goods and subsequently with respect to services.

The *Corbeau* judgment went further and established the principle of the incompatibility of any exclusive right with the competition rules of the EC Treaty, unless it can be shown to be necessary for the achievement of a task of general economic interest. This development in judicial thinking is in line with the priority given to the creation of a single market from 1986 onwards. In this situation, as one author comments:

> The obstacles to the four freedoms have to be justified on a case by case basis, in accordance with the principle of proportionality, on the basis of the exemptions provided for in the Treaty and developed by case law such as the requirements envisaged in Article 36 or the tasks of general interest of Article 90(2) of the EC Treaty.[71]

D. Transmission and Distribution: Competition Issues

5.60 Despite the central importance of transmission and distribution networks for the circulation of electricity and gas, the application of the competition rules to them was for many years shrouded in doubt. This began to change in the 1980s as issues of network access came to the fore. Indeed, in a line of cases involving Dutch electricity companies, the ECJ examined the applicability of the competition law to the industry, which for long had been treated as excluded from the scope of these provisions. The applicability of Article 81 was relevant since certain agreements

[71] Ehlermann, C D, 'The Rôle of the European Commission as regards National Energy Policies', (1994) 12 J Energy Natural Resources L 342 at 348. However, note the approaches taken in the later cases of *Deutsche Post*, Joined Cases C-147/97 and C-148/97, and *Glöckner, Ambulanz v Landkreis Südwestpfalz*, Case 475–99 [2001] OJ C 369/3, para 34 in each case.

were common in the electricity sector that raised competition issues under that Article.[72] There were two principal cases: the *Ijsselcentrale* case and the *Almelo* case. The *Almelo* case was the more important of a number of Dutch electricity restructuring disputes at the time.

In the *Ijsselcentrale* case[73] the Commission prohibited an agreement concluded by electricity generating companies in The Netherlands, preventing both distribution companies and, indirectly, private, industrial consumers from using imported electricity and from exporting electricity (see para 5.92 below). Although Article 86(2) applied (the companies involved were indeed engaged in the operation of services of general economic interest), it was decided that this did not justify a monopolization of imports and exports. Also at that time DG Competition was looking at vertical agreements between coal producers and electricity generators and horizontal agreements between electricity producers). **5.61**

The *Almelo* case[74] brought before the ECJ served to highlight some of the frustrations felt by those in favour of liberalizing energy markets. It arose from proceedings brought by the Municipality of Almelo and other electricity distributors against the Ijsselmij (formerly Ijsselcentrale), an undertaking engaged in the regional distribution of electricity, concerning the interpretation of an agreement on the public supply of electricity, its conditions and especially an 'equalisation supplement', charged by Ijsselcentrale to the local distributors. The distributors argued that the exclusive purchasing obligation imposed upon them was an infringement of the Treaty since it prevented them from importing electricity. The national court referred the matter to the ECJ. **5.62**

The ECJ held that the use of an exclusive purchasing obligation by the regional electricity undertaking contained in the general conditions of sale restricted competition and also had effects on inter-state trade because the regional distributor belongs to a group of undertakings that occupy a collective dominant position in a substantial part of the common market. The competition rules in Articles 81[75] and 82[76] precluded this, and therefore were shown to be applicable to the electricity sector. Any special characteristics would have to be considered in relation to Articles 81(3) and 86(2). There were high expectations at the time that the ECJ's ruling would cast fresh light on the interpretation of Article 86(2). **5.63**

The Commission argued that Article 86(2) could not justify an exclusive purchasing agreement, but Ijsselmij claimed that the agreements were necessary to guarantee the **5.64**

[72] The text of Art 81 EC is as reproduced in Appendix 4.

[73] Commission Decision of 16 January 1991, *Ijsselcentrale & Ors* [1991] OJ L 28, 2 Feb 1991. See also the long-running *Rendo* case concerning import restrictions on electricity: *Rendo v Commission*, Case T-16/91 RV CFI, 12 Dec 1996.

[74] Case C-393/92, n 58 above.

[75] For the text of Art 81 see Appendix 4.

[76] The text of Art 82 is as reproduced in Appendix 4.

security of the electricity supply. The ECJ did not rule on these legal arguments. It held that restrictions on competition might be justified under Article 86(2) if they were necessary for the performance of tasks of general interest. This followed the line established in *Corbeau*. The task of determining whether or not such restrictions were necessary was entrusted to the national courts by the ECJ.

In practice, this interpretation of Article 86(2) was a cautious one, and omitted any consideration of the meaning of *service public*. By permitting entry barriers to the market and cross-subsidization to remain in place, based on technical considerations and the general economic interest, the ECJ 'confirmed more or less in *Almelo* the status quo with regard to the electricity market'.[77] The result was therefore a disappointing one to those who had been seeking from the ECJ evidence of support for the Commission's programme of liberalization of the electricity sector.

Refusal of Access

5.65 There are three principal competition issues concerning network access:

- who should have access and under what conditions;
- how much should the access cost; and
- what to do if congestion issues arise.

5.66 Abuse of a dominant position by an undertaking within the Common Market or a substantial part of it is prohibited by Article 82 of the EC Treaty, insofar as such abuse may affect trade between Member States. Examples of such unilateral anti-competitive conduct include the direct or indirect imposition of unfair purchase or selling prices or other unfair trading conditions, and the application of dissimilar conditions to equivalent transactions with other trading parties that place them at a competitive disadvantage.

5.67 An undertaking that has been granted, by a government body, an exclusive right to transport and/or distribute electricity or gas in a given territory may be regarded as being in a dominant position. This exclusivity usually includes the activities of marketing. The operator of such a facility de facto controls access by any other undertaking to marketing activities.

An undertaking in a dominant position as network operator is limited by Article 82 in its freedom to restrict access to a third-party. Specifically, it is limited when:

- the requesting party is willing to provide reasonable remuneration;
- there are capacities available;
- there are no technical obstacles which would make this access impossible;

[77] Pfrang, E, *Towards Liberalization of the European Electricity Markets*, (1999) 41.

- the construction of a direct line would not be an economically viable alternative; and
- the supply is carried out under a programme that permits proper planning on the part of the network operator.

On this view,[78] the transmission or distribution undertaking has an obligation to open the network to third parties and third parties have a right to obtain access to a network as a result of Article 82 EC. The only remaining condition to be fulfilled is that a possible refusal would affect trade between the Member States. The provisions on TPA in the Electricity and Gas Directives can therefore be seen less as creating a new right of access, and more as defining and clarifying the extent of a right that already exists. However, it is acknowledged that the practical application of such a right is likely to be the source of some considerable legal uncertainty since there is difficulty in defining *a priori* all the hypotheses of 'justified refusals'.

5.68 Although the prohibitions of Article 82(1) are designed to apply to all undertakings which hold or enjoy a dominant position, some of them may be exempted from it by the provisions of Article 86(2), which exempts from the scope of the competition Articles those undertakings entrusted with the provision of services of general economic interest. This is especially relevant in the electricity and gas sectors.

The provisions of Article 82 have been held by the ECJ to be directly applicable[79] and therefore individual undertakings have the right to bring proceedings before national courts alleging abuse of a dominant position by undertakings. Individual undertakings that consider themselves to have been damaged by an abuse of a dominant position as defined by Article 82(1) may also complain of the conduct to the Commission. If the Commission finds evidence of an abuse, it may impose fines on the undertaking concerned.[80]

5.69 Article 82 contrasts with the provisions of Article 81, which prohibits anti-competitive agreements. These are agreements between undertakings that may affect trade between Member States and that have as their object or effect the prevention or restriction or distortions of competition within the common market. In the context of TPA the conduct of individual grid or pipeline owners that contravenes the prohibition in Article 82 is more important since Article 81 would be limited more to cases of anti-competitive conduct of joint owners of pipelines to which third parties seek access.

[78] This is the view of Ehlermann, see n 72, at 343. See in this context the Commission's action with respect to the German distribution company, VNG: XXIst Report on Competition Policy (1991), point 31.

[79] See Case C 155/73 *Saatchi* [1974] ECR 409, where the ECJ ruled that 'Even within the framework of Article 90, therefore, the prohibitions of Article 86 have a direct effect and confer on interested parties rights which the national courts must safeguard, (point 18.a).

[80] Regulation 17/62.

(a) Cases

Case law supports the principle that a refusal to allow access may amount to an abuse of a dominant position. The first notable case is *Port of Genoa*, but a further decision of note is the decision in *Sabena*.[81] The Commission had imposed a fine on the Belgian airline on the ground that its conduct was intended to prevent a privately-owned airline from continuing its flights on the route between Brussels and Luton (UK). Sabena had refused to provide access to its computerized reservation system called 'Saphir' when this company requested it. The latter had quoted tariffs at half the standard IATA tariffs, undercutting Sabena, and had not assigned the ground handling of its tariffs to Sabena.

5.70 The Commission took the view that the computerized reservation system was an *essential facility* that air carriers required if they were to compete on this particular route. Sabena's position made it the dominant player on the route. Without access to this system a company could not compete. This use of the notion of 'essential facilities' appeared to enhance the potential for use of Article 82 to establish a right to TPA.

'Essential facilities' The doctrine of 'essential facilities' has provoked considerable discussion and controversy[82] since it was first used.[83] It was taken from American jurisprudence and applied by the Commission in the European setting. It has appeared in a number of Commission decisions on access, commencing with two interim decisions on access to the Port of Holyhead in the United Kingdom,[84] where the Commission found that there was a duty to assist competitors in certain circumstances.[85] In a robust statement, the Commission has declared that:

> . . . the owner of the essential facility, which also uses the essential facility, may not impose a competitive disadvantage on its competitor, also a user of the essential facility, by altering is own schedule to the detriment of the competitor's service, where, as in this case the construction or the features of the facility are such that it is not possible to alter one competitor's service in a way chosen without harming the others.[86]

[81] 1988 OJ L 317/47.

[82] eg Doherty, B 'Just What Are Essential Facilities?', in (2001) 38 CML Rev, 397–436; Temple-Lang, J, 'Defining Legitimate Competition: companies' duties to supply competitors and access to essential facilities', (1994) 18 Fordham International Law Journal, 437; Strothers, C 'Refusal to Supply as Abuse of a Dominant Position: Essential Facilities in the European Union', (2001) ECLR, 256–262.

[83] Although the term was not used explicitly, an early example is the *Commercial Solvents* case: Joined Cases 6/73 and 7/73, *Commercial Solvents v Commission* [1974] ECR 223.

[84] *B&I Line plc/Sealink Harbours Ltd and Sealink Stena Ltd* (1992) 5 CMLR 255; Commission Decision 94/19/EC of 21 Dec 1993, [1994] OJ L15/80; see also the *Port of Rodby* decision [1994] OJ L55/52.

[85] *B&I Line*: see n 84 above.

[86] ibid.

However, this view has attracted considerable criticism and has not yet found favour with the ECJ in its jurisprudence.[87] It is not a separate rule, apart from Article 82, and it is possible to decide most cases involving a refusal to sell (or deny access) without necessarily invoking this doctrine. It is unclear what added value lies in the use of the term since it is still necessary to show a breach of EC law.

The ECJ has never applied the doctrine and indeed neither has the US Supreme Court.[88]

E. Security of Supply

A continuing source of constraint—either actual and potential—on actions to promote competition in energy markets in the EU has been the availability of exemptions under Articles 30 and 86(2). In the energy sector, these Articles may well be invoked by Member States on the grounds of security of energy supply, which may amount to a PSO. Security of supply looms large in the oil and gas sectors due to dependence on non-EU suppliers for a significant proportion of consumption; whilst in the electricity sector security of supply derives its significance largely because of the crucial importance of continuity and regularity of supply to certain classes of consumer. These factors distinguish the energy sector from network industries such as most telecommunications services. They have implications for the way in which the energy industries are organized and encourage intervention by Member State governments. 5.71

With respect to import and export of energy, there are the obligations under Articles 28 and 29 that are subject to exemptions contained in Article 30. Article 28 prohibits quantitative restrictions on imports between Member States and also measures having equivalent effect. Article 29 prohibits restrictions on exports between Member States and all measures with equivalent effect. The prohibition is addressed to Member States. 5.72

Specific grounds for exemption to the prohibitions of quantitative restrictions and measures which have equivalent effect on the import and export of goods include public policy and public security. It is also provided that the exempted prohibitions must not constitute a means of arbitrary discrimination or a disguised restriction on trade between Member States.

There have been two important cases involving the energy industry in which the exemption of public security under Article 30 was pleaded by a Member State,

[87] eg, the judgment in *Bronner (Oscar) v Mediaprint*, Case C-7/97, [1998] ECR I-7791, and the discussion of this in Doherty, n 83 above. Also, the similar approach taken by the CFI in Joined Cases T-374/94, 375/94, 384/94 and 388/94 *European Nightservices v Commission* [1998] ECR II-3141.

[88] eg, the much-discussed *Bronner* case, n 88 above. Several illuminating contributions are to be found in Ehlermann, C D and Gosling, L (eds) *Regulating Communications Markets* (2000), 1–237; see also Flynn, L, 'Access to the Postal Networks: The Situation after *Bronner*', in Geradin, G, and Humpe, C, *Postal Services, Liberalisation and EC Competition Law* (2002).

with different outcomes. The first was *Campus Oil* (1984),[89] and the second was the *Greek Oil Monopolies* Case (1990).[90] This is an area of some sensitivity in relation to the IEM since it raises the prospect of avoidance of market-opening on the ground that this is necessary to protect security of supply.

(1) *Campus Oil*

5.73 In *Campus Oil*, the Irish Government defended a statutory requirement that Irish importers of petroleum products should purchase a percentage of their requirements through a national oil refiner. Its defence was based on grounds of public security. The ECJ upheld this defence. The facts were as follows.

The Irish Refining Company (IRC) was the owner of the only refinery in Ireland and was purchased by the Irish National Petroleum Corporation (INPC), owned by the Irish state. The Government sought to acquire the refinery to guarantee the provision of supplies of petroleum products in Ireland, and to do so by keeping refining capacity operational in Ireland, after the owners, four international oil companies, had announced their intention to close the refinery. If it had closed, all suppliers of refined petroleum products would have been obliged to obtain their supplies from abroad. The Irish market depended on them for 80 per cent of its supplies in 1981; without a refinery those supplies would have to come in future from a single external supplier, the United Kingdom. To ensure that the refinery could dispose of its products and preserve its operating capacity, the Fuels (Control of Supplies) Order 1982 was promulgated, requiring any person who imports any of the petroleum products to which it applied to purchase a certain proportion of their requirements from the INPC at a price to be determined by the Minister, who was required to take into account costs incurred by the INPC. Each importer was required to purchase up to a maximum of 35 per cent of its total requirements of petroleum products and 40 per cent of its requirements of each type of petroleum product.

5.74 Campus Oil was one of several companies trading in petroleum products that were established in Ireland and affected by this Order. They challenged the purchasing requirement under the 1982 Order before the High Court of Ireland arguing that it constituted a measure having an effect equivalent to a quantitative restriction on imports. The Irish Government maintained that it did not constitute such a restriction but that if it did, it could be justified on the grounds of public policy and public security, for which Article 30 was applicable. The High Court of Ireland referred the two questions on interpretation of EC law to the ECJ for a preliminary ruling.

---

[89] Case 72/83 *Campus Oil* [1984] ECR 2727.

[90] Case C-347/88 *Commission v Hellenic Republic* [1990] ECR I-4747.

With respect to the first question (applicability of Art 28 to the purchasing requirement of the 1982 Order), the ECJ held that the requirement constituted a measure having equivalent effect to a quantitative restriction on imports, and so fell under the scope of Article 28. The next question was whether an exception from the scope of Articles 28 and 29 was justified under Article 30 or whether such a scheme was capable of being exempt and if so, under what circumstances. The ECJ took the view that the concept of public security could include the uninterrupted supply of petroleum products, due to their fundamental importance to a country's existence. In a much-quoted passage, the ECJ ruled that: 5.75

> Petroleum products, because of their exceptional importance as an energy source in the modern economy, are of fundamental importance for a country's existence since not only is its economy but above all its institutions, its essential public services and even the survival of its inhabitants depend upon them. An interruption of supplies of petroleum products, with the resultant dangers for the country's existence, could therefore seriously affect the public security that Article 36 [now 30] of the EC Treaty allows States to protect.[91]

The ECJ noted that recourse to Article 30 of the EC Treaty is not justified if Community rules provide for the necessary measures to ensure protection of the interests set out in that Article.[92] National measures that hinder intra-Community trade cannot therefore be justified unless protection of the interests of the Member State concerned is not sufficiently guaranteed by measures taken for that purpose by the Community institutions. However, in this case, the ECJ took the view that a real danger would still occur in the event of a crisis in spite of measures brought out in response to requirements of the International Energy Agency and the existence of certain precautionary measures at the Community level,[93] since there was no 'unconditional assurance' that a particular Member State would continue to receive supplies at a level sufficient to meet its minimum needs.[94] 5.76

There was also the issue of whether the obligation to purchase was necessary to ensure that enough of the refinery's production could be marketed to guarantee a minimum supply of petroleum products to the country in the event of a crisis. A crisis may lead either to an interruption or a severe cut in supplies, and the possession of some refining capacity in such situations would allow a Member State to enter into long-term contracts with oil producers that offer better guarantees of supplies in the event of a crisis. The existence of a national refinery also offers a safeguard against the additional risk of interruption of supplies of refined products to which a state with no refinery capacity of its own is exposed. The ECJ set 5.77

---

[91] *Campus Oil*, n 90 above, para 34.
[92] *Commission v Hellenic Republic*, n 91 above, para 27.
[93] ibid, para 29.
[94] ibid, para 31.

out criteria under which such measures were necessary if the production could not be disposed of at competitive prices on the relevant market.

As to proportionality, the quantities in question should not exceed the minimum supply requirements without which the public security of the country would be affected. Nor should the minimum supply requirement exceed the level of production necessary to keep the refinery's production capacity available in the event of a crisis and to enable it to continue to refine at all times the crude oil supplies which the state has secured.

5.78 The wider relevance of this judgment is a matter of debate. At the time Ireland was almost totally dependent on imported oil products. As the ECJ noted, these were not substitutable for certain purposes. It is notable that the ECJ emphasized that Article 30 has to be interpreted in such a way that its scope is not extended any further than is necessary to protect the interests it is intended to secure. The measures taken 'must not create obstacles to imports which are disproportionate to those objectives'.[95] The measures adopted on the basis of Article 30 must not restrict intra-Community trade more than is absolutely necessary.

(2) *Greek Oil Monopolies*

5.79 In the second case, the *Commission v Hellenic Republic* (*Greek Oil Monopolies* case), the Government of Greece defended a state monopoly of the import and marketing of refined petroleum products on the grounds of public security because of the geo-political situation of the country. The ECJ held that the state right to import and market up to 25 per cent of domestic petroleum requirements breached the requirement of non-discrimination in Article 31(1) by discriminating against exporters from other Member States.

The ECJ stated that the exclusive rights guaranteed an outlet for the products of the Greek public sector refineries. They did so at the expense of product exporters established in other Member States. The ECJ also held that the annual procurement programmes and marketing quotas run by the Greek authorities were measures that were capable of hindering intra-Community trade within the meaning of Article 28.

5.80 The defence of public security based on Article 30 was pleaded by the Greek Government but was rejected. The ECJ argued that the Greek Government had failed to produce any evidence that the powers to secure supply were in fact necessary to secure a minimum supply of petroleum products at all times.[96] The public procurement programmes could also not be justified since there were two

[95] ibid, para 37.

[96] ibid, para 60.

Greek public sector refineries with a production capacity that exceeds the country's minimum requirements in the event of a crisis. Security of supply could be assured by requiring distribution companies to notify their procurement plans and any amendments to them to the Greek authorities in due time.

From the two cases above, it can be seen that the *Campus Oil* decision does not allow the conclusion that security of supply will always be considered as an objective falling within the scope of Article 30 if the measure pursuing that objective is not necessary. It is also not possible to apply it directly to import/export, transport, or generation monopolies in the electricity and gas sectors. **5.81**

Further, it would be wrong to conclude that the ECJ's decision in *Campus Oil* would be repeated in similar circumstances at the present time.[97] The considerable growth in infrastructure, especially interconnectors between Member States, has changed, and is still changing, the pattern of energy trade within the EU. The test of 'total or almost total dependence upon imports for petroleum products' as a ground for relying on the public security defence in Article 30 will apply differently in such a context of growing mutual interdependence.

The other EC Treaty provision relevant in the context of exemptions is Article 86(2). With respect to energy, the ECJ has held that security of supply considerations can justify an exemption under Article 86(2). This emerged from the *Almelo* case[97a] where a regional distribution company, Ijsselmij imposed an exclusive purchasing obligation which prohibited local distributors from importing electricity. This clause followed the then model general conditions of supply applicable throughout The Netherlands. The ECJ examined the effect of this clause in relation to Articles 81 and 82. Its conclusion was that the obligation had a restrictive effect on competition, and that it prohibited local distributors from obtaining supplies from other sources. The national market was compartmentalized as a result. **5.82**

The security of supply consideration arose in connection with Article 86(2). Ijsselmij had been given the task of ensuring the supply of electricity in its part of the national territory. All customers, whether they were local distributors or end-users, should receive uninterrupted supplies of electricity in sufficient quantities to match demand at any given time. **5.83**

F. Competition Policy

During the 1990s the powers that were vested in the Commission itself were used to facilitate the development of competition in energy markets. They were **5.84**

---

[97] eg, see the judgment against Greece in Case C-398/98, *Commission of the European Communities v Hellenic Republic*, 25 Oct 2001.

[97a] Case C-393/92 *Gemeente Almelo & Ors v Energiebedrijf Ijsselmij NV*, Judgment of 27 Apr [1994] ECR I-1477. See paras 5.62–5.64 above.

exercised differently with respect to electricity and gas, reflecting the characteristics of the two industries at the time. For the electricity sector, several cases illustrate Commission policy: the *Scottish Nuclear* case,[98] three cases on contract duration and market foreclosure, the case of the *Jahrhundertvertrag*,[99] and the *Ijsselcentrale* case.[100]

(1) Contract Duration: Scottish Nuclear

5.85 Two supply contracts were notified to the Commission in 1990 and the Commission adopted a Decision in 1991 that authorized the contracts for a period of 15 years. They were concluded between Scottish Nuclear Ltd and Scottish Power and Scottish Hydroelectric, two vertically-integrated electricity utilities that had been created at the time of electricity privatization in Scotland. The British Government wished to provide the newly privatized companies with a diversified generating capacity portfolio and include access to power generated by Scottish Nuclear, which was to remain in the public sector. The contracts had four main characteristics:

- Scottish Nuclear was not allowed to supply electricity to any other party without the consent of both electricity companies;
- a take-or-pay obligation was imposed on Scottish Power and Scottish Hydroelectric for, respectively, 74.9% and 25.1% of Scottish Nuclear's production;
- the price at which the two companies purchased nuclear generated electricity was fixed under the agreements; and
- the contracts had an initial duration of 30 years.

5.86 The Commission found that the agreements restricted competition and (surprisingly) affected trade between Member States. Although it was held to infringe Article 81(1), the Commission decided that an exemption under Article 81(3) was justified due to the need for long-term planning for production purposes, the need to guarantee security of supply and the need for an independent electricity market. It did however insist on a reduction of the duration of the contracts from 30 years (which corresponded to the expected lifetime of the power stations concerned) to 15. No reasoning was provided for this choice of number, but the aim seems to have been to free-up the market while not imposing obstacles to the domestic liberalization programme.

[98] (EEC) 91/329: Commission Decision of 30 Apr 1991 relating to a proceeding under Art 85* of the EEC Treaty (IV/33.473: *Scottish Nuclear, Nuclear Energy Agreement*).

[99] 1993 OJ L 50/14.

[100] *Ijsselcentrale* [1991] OJ L 28/32.

(2) Contract Duration and Market Foreclosure

The duration of contracts figured prominently in three cases decided by the Commission between 1993 and 1996. However, this occurred in the context of restrictions arising from market foreclosure and led the Commission to limit the contract periods. The cases were: *Electricidade de Portugal/Pego*,[101] *REN/Turbogás*,[102] and *ISAB Energy*.[103] There were four principal similarities in the cases: 5.87

- in each case a power purchase agreement had been concluded between a new electricity generator and the incumbent monopoly;
- the agreement notified to the Commission had a long duration;
- the duration was rejected by the Commission, partly because of the exclusivity of supply involved and the restriction on the generator from supplying consumers other than the incumbent monopoly; and
- Commission approval in each case was conditional on a reduction of the duration to 15 years. This period has therefore acquired the status of a 'standard' term, providing investors with sufficient security for a long-term commitment.[104]

(a) Pego

In the *Pego* case the result was to reserve the capacity and output of the coal-fired power station exclusively to *Electricidade de Portugal* for 15 years instead of the original 28 years. A so-called 'first option' system was put in place for the remaining 13 years of the project, which allowed the generator to sell to third parties should there be surplus capacity not required by the grid. Under this system the generator would compete with the grid to find an outside market for its capacity, either in Portugal or in another Member State. The favourable view taken by the Commission was influenced by 'the expected development of electricity supply conditions in Portugal stemming from Decree Law 99/91 [the pro-competition law for the electricity sector]'.[105] 5.88

(b) REN/Turbogás

The *REN/Turbogás* case concerned a power purchase agreement for the supply of electricity from a combined cycle gas turbine power station in Portugal by Turbogas to REN, the Portuguese system manager and operator of the national 5.89

[101] *Electricidade de Portugal/Pego project* (Notice pursuant to Art 19(3) of Regulation 17)[1993] OJ C265/3.

[102] *REN/Turbogas* (Notice pursuant to Art 19(3) of Regulation 17)[1996] OJ C118/7.

[103] *ISAB Energy* (Notice pursuant to Art 19(3) of Regulation 17) [1996] OJ C138/3.

[104] As Devlin and Levasseur point out, there is no apparent objective legal or economic justification for the choice of the 15-year term: Faull, N, and Nikpay, A, n 2 above, at 711.

[105] *Pego*, n 103 above, para 20. This implied that any future notification would be scrutinized more critically.

grid. It involved the same 'first option' clause but this time the Commission did not accept it. Three years after *Pego*, its thinking on market liberalization had developed. It asked the parties to allow the generator to opt to sell the capacity and the electricity to third parties after 15 years. In practice, the contract design left this possibility open. The generator received a high price for electricity generated during the first 15 years and a lower price for the remaining period. However, if the generator wished to sell to a third-party after the 15-year period had elapsed, the contract provided for the provision of compensation to the incumbent monopoly for the loss of its low-cost supply during that period covered by the contract.

(c) ISAB Energy

5.90 The *ISAB Energy* case involved a notification of a contract that had a 20-year duration. The Commission concluded that the case should be re-examined after the first 15 years of commercial operation.

(d) Jahrhundertvertrag

5.91 The agreement in question was one between the German mining industry and the German public electricity supply industry and concerned annual sales of fixed quotas of German coal to the electricity companies. Under the agreement exclusive long-term purchasing obligations were imposed on the companies. These were deemed by the Commission to be in breach of Article 81(1) The undertakings argued that they were part of the German strategy of ensuring security of supply. The application of Articles 81 and 82 was therefore precluded by Article 86(2). The Commission also held that the agreement was concluded to share markets and affected trade between Member States, even though it was an arrangement involving only parties from a single Member State. The Commission adopted a similar approach to that in the *Scottish Nuclear* decision and held that the Jahrhundertvertrag qualified for an exemption under Article 81(3).[106] It took the view that the agreement improved coal production and electricity generation in an area where production and demand had to be in constant balance, since electricity cannot be stored. The Commission refused however to apply Article 86(2) on the ground that it was not evident that the security of supply could only be maintained through this particular agreement.

(e) Ijsselcentrale

5.92 This involved a demarcation agreement between SEP, a joint venture company entrusted with the planning of electricity supply and generation in The Netherlands

[106] Commission Decision of 22 Dec 1992 on a proceeding under Art 85 of the Treaty and Art 65 of the ECSC Treaty (IV/33.151; 'Jahrhundertvertrag'; IV/33.997–VIK–GVSt), OJ L 050, 2 Mar 1993, 14.

at the time, and various generating companies. It imposed an import/export ban through the co-operation agreements. The Commission held that the agreement constituted an infringement of Article 81(1) insofar as it had as its object or effect the restriction of imports by private, industrial consumers and of exports of production outside the field of public supply.[107] The Commission also examined the possibility and scope of a public security exemption under Article 86(2). It took the view that the performance of the service did not require an absolute control over exports and imports, with respect to non-public supply of electricity. With respect to electricity imports destined for and exports from the public supply, the Commission refused to even consider the application of Article 86(2).

(f) Conclusions on Commission jurisprudence

These were not the only decisions on energy taken by the Commission during this time, but they were the most relevant to competition. They show that the Commission was willing to apply the exemption clause in Article 86(2) on a case-by-case basis. It also took particular care to limit the use of the security of supply argument by parties seeking an exemption from the application of the competition rules. **5.93**

(3) Gas and Joint Marketing

The Commission's actions in the gas market were limited, during this period at least, by the fact that interconnections between the Member States were few and the commercial practices of the oil and gas companies were supported by the Member States. As a result, its actions appear cautious by comparison with its actions in the electricity sector. **5.94**

The two cases of note are those involving joint selling by the parties to the Britannia gas field,[108] and the Interconnector between the UK and Belgium. The Commission decided that joint selling arrangements for the sale of gas from the North Sea Britannia field, which were to be negotiated before the construction of the Gas Interconnector between the UK and Belgium did not fall within the prohibition of Article 81 because they did not affect trade between Member States to an appreciable extent. The Commission added that such arrangements would be challenged as and when the Interconnector was operational. A subsequent Commission decision involving sales of gas from an Irish field, shows the current position of the Commission on joint sales arrangements from a gas field. The partnership developing the Corrib gas field, comprising Enterprise Energy Ireland, Marathon Oil, and Statoil of Norway, decided to invest IR£500 million (US$577 million) in developing the field so that gas would be delivered by 2003. In 2000

[107] Commission Decision of 16 Jan 1991 relating to a proceeding under Art 85 of the EEC Treaty (IV/32.732–*Ijsselcentrale & Ors*) OJ L 28, 2 Feb 1991, 32

[108] Dinnage, J, 'Competition in Gas Supply', (1998) J Energy Natural Resources; Devlin and Levasseur, (see Faull and Nikpay, n 2 above), 700–01.

the parties to the development applied to the Commission for an exemption to allow them to market Corrib gas jointly for the first five years of production. Their argument was that joint marketing was required to counter-balance the strong market position of Ireland's national gas utility, Bord Gais Eireann and the state-owned Electricity Supply Board. The Commission took the view that the joint marketing plans would not comply with competition law. The companies withdrew the application and agreed to market the gas individually. The Competition Commissioner declared that the decision by the partners to the field development confirmed the Commission's general policy 'not to tolerate joint selling unless compelling reasons are provided as justification'.[109] Such joint marketing can infringe Article 81(1) of the EC Treaty and may be difficult to justify as falling within the exemption criteria in Article 81(3) (see ch 7, para 7.118).

(4) EFTA states

5.95 Finally, it is worth noting that the EEA Agreement extended the provisions of EC competition law to the EFTA States including Norway. Initially, this did not have any significant effect on the EU energy sector. There have subsequently been important developments with respect to the practices of the Norwegian GFU, the gas-purchasing consortium. These developments are described elsewhere in some detail (see chs 2, paras 2.106–2.110 and 7, para 7.117).

G. Conclusions

5.96 There can be no doubt that important advances were made in the development of the primary law as it applied to competition in electricity and gas markets from the late 1980s onwards: that is, from the time the Commission launched its IEM to the adoption of the Electricity and Gas Directives. The ECJ's jurisprudence on the grant by Member States of special and exclusive rights to undertakings is a good illustration of this development. Decisions by the Commission on notifications made to it also lend support to the view that competition law was making itself felt in both the electricity and (less obviously at this time) gas sectors.

5.97 However, it is also clear that progress was not as far-reaching as had been hoped by some of the parties engaged in promoting the IEM exercise, most of all the Commission itself. For some, the judgments of the ECJ in cases directly relating to the energy sector proved to be a disappointment.[110] As one observer noted:

[109] European Commission Press Release, 'Enterprise Oil, Statoil and Marathon to market Irish Corrib gas separately', IP/01/578, 20 Apr 2001.

[110] With respect to the judgments in the import and export monopoly cases, they 'seem to herald the end of an era of progressive development towards a more market-oriented economy in the Community': Slot, P J, 'Note', (1998) 35 CML Rev, 1183, 1202.

> Within the electricity sector, the Commission has proved to be the driving force behind the European integration, whereas the ECJ has tended to take a more hesitant and cautious attitude and to pay more regard to the interests of Member States.[111]

This comment is revealing in its assumptions about governance of the EU. The challenge of bringing about liberalization in the energy sector called into question the balance between the various Community institutions. Both the abandonment of the Article 86(3) draft Directives in 1991 and the highly cautious approach adopted by the Commission in the proceedings on import and export monopolies in electricity and gas show an awareness of the delicate nature of its tasks, in the face of strident and persistent opposition on the part of several important Member States and some major industry participants. The absence of a consensus among Member States meant that cases brought before the ECJ carried the direct or indirect effect of bringing pressure on the ECJ to play a law-making rôle by interpreting Community law in a progressive way with respect to liberalization, when it was clear that such a course had no support among key Member States. The ECJ judgments are only disappointing to the extent that it was expected to play this rôle—which it refused to do.[112] In the event, the development of ECJ jurisprudence during this period is positive and encouraging but hardly revolutionary. As the judge-rapporteur in the energy import–export monopolies cases comments: 5.98

> . . . it is unrealistic to assume that a coherent Community policy for each industry can be developed by the Commission pursuing ad hoc cases before the Court of Justice. It follows therefore that there must, to some extent, be Community legislation in this field. Without a legislative framework there will be inequality between the market conditions in each Member State.[113]

The thesis advanced from the outset of the IEM programme, especially by the Commission, that the powers to bring about competition in EU energy markets already existed in the primary law independently of the legislative route under Article 95, is one that may be correct. However, it required the slow, consensus-building approach of Article 95, involving all the Community institutions. It may also be correct that the principal ideas contained in the Electricity and Gas Directives are implicit in the primary law. 5.99

[111] Pfrang, E, 'Towards Liberalization of the European Electricity Markets', (1999), 122: 'The "velvet revolution", as initiated by the Commission from the late 1980s onwards so as to promote the opening of the electricity sector by applying competition and internal market rules was thus impeded by the ECJ.'

[112] Edward, D, and Hoskins, M, n 14 above, 185–186: 'the Commission and the Council cannot expect the Court of Justice to act as the Community legislator in this field. The rôle which the Court can play is restricted by limits inherent in the nature of judicial control. Where necessary, the Commission must play its part by proposing legislation to the Council under Art 100A* or by adopting its own legislation under Art 90(3)'.*

[113] Edward and Hoskins, n 14 above, 181–2.

5.100 However, the elaboration of such detailed rules has to be reviewed by the Council and Parliament. The Article 95 procedure is the available means of ensuring that such a review of proposals for legislation in a sensitive sector takes place.

The idea that a viable alternative existed to the adoption of Directives under Article 95 is erroneous, at least with respect to this period. The early attempt to build an IEM on the basis of Directives issued under Article 86(3) was stillborn in the energy sector. Similarly, progress on the basis of Commission decisions taken on a case-by-case basis during this period was encouraging, but it also suggested an uncertain and rather piecemeal effect, hardly calculated to bring about a level playing field and an internal market in this sector. They were also taken at a time when the market was at a very early stage of liberalization.

5.101 The interplay between primary rules and the emerging secondary rules that characterized this period has continued to be of practical importance after the adoption of the Electricity and Gas Directives. The Directives' phased approach towards the liberalization of energy markets has required an adaptation of the competition rules to the circumstances of a period of transition, a subject dealt with later in the third and final PART of this book (see especially ch 7).

Part III

TRANSITION TO A LIBERALIZED ENERGY MARKET

6

IMPLEMENTATION: PROBLEMS EMERGE

Neither national regulatory action nor Community action under the competition rules is fully able to address the issues concerned.

The European Commission[1]

A. Introduction

6.01 The adoption of the Electricity and Gas Directives constituted the first real steps in the establishment of a single market for energy in the European Union. Like shots from a starting pistol, they should have been initiating a radical programmes of change in two of Europe's most conservative industrial sectors, in which monopoly rather than competition had long seemed the natural order of things. The reality was, however, more muted: their adoption and transposition into national law was signalling only the end of a long, *preparatory* stage in the process of liberalization. The difficulties in making a transition to a fully liberalized energy market had only just begun.

This chapter examines the various measures taken at the European level to promote a vigorous transition to an internal energy market, based on the requirements of

[1] European Commission, DGXVII/A3/B3, 'Second Report to the Council and the European Parliament on Harmonization Requirements: Directive 96/92/EC on common rules for the internal market in electricity', SEC (1999) final 470, 16 Apr 1999 27.

the Directives. The concept of 'implementation' is used in the widest sense, including transposition of the Directives into national legislation and also identification and elaboration of the Directives' framework provisions. The measures taken fall into two categories: those depending on voluntary co-operation by the incumbents to be effective; and those that envisage the use of existing law or law-making powers to achieve their aims. In the first category, the principal step has been the creation of a Regulatory Forum for electricity and another for gas, meeting usually on a twice-yearly basis in Florence and Madrid respectively. These consensus-driven processes have been supplemented by the application of EC law, especially the competition law, not least in areas of merger control and state aids.

6.02 However, the problems that have emerged during this transition phase have proved greater and more complex than expected. Their solution requires a firmer response than is possible through a purely consensus-based approach. This was recognized by the European Council in March 2000 when it expressed its concern at the slow pace of development of the internal market in electricity and gas. Acting in a quasi-governmental manner, it asked 'the Commission, the Council and the Member States, each in accordance with their respective powers, to speed up liberalization in such areas as gas and electricity',[2] and instructed the Commission to prepare a report on liberalization and appropriate proposals for the European Council meeting in 2001. In the event, these proposals included draft legislation.

B. The Problems

6.03 The compromises evident in the final texts of the Directives created a legacy of five main problem areas that the Commission had to monitor and address, namely the:

1. potentially distorting effects of subsidiarity; particularly the risk that liberalization would proceed *within* national markets without any significant regional integrative effect;
2. lack of specific mechanisms in the Directives to remove obstacles to cross-border trade, especially in electricity;
3. need to identify key provisions in the Directives which require elaboration to make them fully effective; especially those on TPA and unbundling;
4. need to develop a coherent EU regulatory framework based on the Directives and institutional choices made by the Member States; and
5. instigation of follow-up process to this phase of liberalization envisaged by the Directives.

[2] European Council, Presidency Conclusions No 100/1/01, Lisbon, 23–24 March 2000.

(1) Subsidiarity

The choices left to Member States by the Directives' recognition of subsidiarity led to unexpected but largely positive outcomes in transposition. Most Member States showed a willingness to take legislative steps toward liberalization more quickly than mandated by the Directives, and only a very few limited their transposition to the minimum requirements. However, this raised the prospect of an uneven playing field and drew attention to the retaliatory potential in the reciprocity provisions. It also called into question the Directives' time-tables, suggesting as it did that an accelerated schedule would have been approved by most Member States. Most seriously, the spectre arose of liberalization taking place in 15 distinct national markets with little cross-border effect. 6.04

(2) Cross-border trade

The Directives had largely ignored the implementation issues of cross-border trade. They did not provide mechanisms for making cross-border trade effective, in spite of increasing the potential for cross-border exchanges. Once the Member States had made their strategic choices as to the Directives' requirements, especially relative to TPA, this became a priority for the Commission. Electricity in particular was characterized by extremely modest levels of cross-border trade within the EU, amounting to six to eight per cent of total UCTE electricity consumption (mainly exports from France to Italy, The Netherlands, and the UK).[3] By contrast, more than 50 per cent of all gas consumed in the EU has crossed at least one national border before delivery to the consumer. If the barriers to electricity trade were to be removed, further steps were required to supplement the provisions of the Directives. This meant increased co-operation among EU energy companies to address specific problems of cross-border tarification, capacity allocation, and congestion management and was a matter for competition law as well as sector-specific legislation. 6.05

(3) Key Provisions: Identification and Elaboration

Proper implementation of the Directives was not possible before the identification of key provisions in the Directives requiring elaboration to make them fully effective. This was not a mere technical exercise. The regulatory requirements of a liberalized market were quite different to anything that most Member States had experienced before and presented the national authorities with a significant challenge. The practicalities of operating a tarification system for TPA and the appropriate röle for regulatory oversight required both technical, economic, and legal 6.06

[3] European Commission, 'Next Steps Towards Completion of the Internal Market for Gas: Draft Strategy Paper for Discussion', DGTREN/A2/KG/D (00) 28 Feb 2000, 2216.

skills and a willingness to learn from the experiences of others. To the extent that the Commission became involved in this area, its attempts to identify and elaborate on key provisions in the Directives created a battleground between those who sought to interpret the Directive texts literally (in practice, meaning restrictively) and those who saw the identification exercise as an opportunity to accelerate the transition to an internal energy market.

(4) Regulation

6.07 The Directives required Member States to establish new regulatory authorities or widen the scope of existing authorities in their territories. However, the European dimension of energy liberalization dictated that the Commission play a key rôle in co-ordinating national regulators' actions to ensure harmonization. In addition, the operation of both electricity/gas regulatory law and general legislation and competition law made an active rôle for the Commission unavoidable.

(5) Follow-up Actions

6.08 The Directives envisaged a review of their application and a possible further period of liberalization in 2006 (electricity) and 2008 (gas). However, that deadline appeared too cautious in the light of the strategic choices made by most Member States in their implementation legislation. Essentially, the willingness of most Member States to adopt measures of electricity and gas liberalization that go beyond the minimum and to accept an accelerated time-table that challenged the programme envisaged by the Directives themselves. Further, the other problems noted above (points (1)–(4)) required that action be taken sooner if the Directives' objectives were to be met.[4] The actions in practice of a clear majority of Member States also had an institutional effect. The tasks of the Commission in monitoring the Directives' implementation could hardly escape a re-assessment with a view to revision.

6.09 These five problems have dominated the implementation phase of the two Directives. Attempts by the Commission to deal with them have relied on several instruments whose emphasis has shifted from one problem area to another, as circumstances seemed to require. Although these instruments are examined separately below, it should not be assumed that the options they represent are mutually exclusive. They offered three principal options:

[4] In fact, this had been appreciated by the Commission and by industry at a very early stage. The Commission held its first Follow-up Group meetings with Member States as early as 15–16 May 1997 (electricity), and 22 Oct 1998 (gas; see ch 4 n 95). This was also a means of facilitating contact between the Commission and the Member States at a time when implementation legislation was being designed.

1. There could be voluntary harmonization of national measures and the key provisions of the Directives could be elaborated. Parties could seek to agree on further changes and implement them voluntarily. This was the idea lying behind the Florence and Madrid Processes (see ch 7, paras 7.02–7.65).
2. The existing Treaty rules could be implemented vigorously to ensure that the conduct of players was appropriate to that of a liberalizing market.
3. Further legislation could be prepared and presented to the Council and Parliament for adoption. This option was envisaged in the Electricity and Gas Directives themselves but was unlikely to have much support from Member States in the initial phase of their implementation. Nevertheless, it served as a draconian threat to parties that if the other 2 options proved inadequate, the Commission would have to activate this one.

Prior to examining these three options for achieving implementation, the following paragraphs examine the measures taken by the Member States to transpose the two Directives into national law, and the Commission's attempts to adapt its strategy in the light of their actions. However, rather than analysing actions taken by individual Member States, the Member States are treated together in order to try to identify any patterns. **6.10**

C. Implementation in the Member States

(1) Electricity Directive

The deadline for transposition of the Electricity Directive into the law of the Member States was 19 February 1999 (except for Belgium and Ireland, which had until 19 February 2000, and Greece, which had until 19 February 2001). All Member States have taken implementation measures in their primary legislation.[5] The Directive was incorporated into the EEA Agreement from 1 July 2000. **6.11**

Implementation of the Directive in France and Belgium has been particularly disappointing.

In France, the necessary legislation was not enacted until one year after the deadline, which triggered infringement proceedings by the Commission. Once adopted, the law appeared to contain provisions that were not compatible with the provisions of the Directive.[6] In June 2000, after extensive review of the French law, the Commission sent a warning letter to the French Government stating that **6.12**

[5] The range of implementation measures can be seen on the EC website: http://europa.eu.int/comm/energy/en/elec_single_market/implementation/index_en.html. For a recent overview see the European Commission Staff Working Paper, 'First Report on the Implementation of the Internal Electricity and Gas Market', SEC (2001) 3 Dec 2001, 1957.

[6] Law No 2000-108 of 10 February 2000 on the modernization and development of the public service in electricity, OJ no 35, 11 Feb 2000, 2143.

Article 22(3) of the Electricity Law 'is a clear obstacle to the free movement of electricity and the provision of electricity services'.[7] The Article provides that an eligible customer may conclude a power supply contract with a producer or a supplier of its choice from the territory of an EU Member State or, within the framework of international agreements, from the territory of a non-EU Member State. The contractual framework in which the power supply is provided may not last less than three years to ensure efficient multi-annual planning of capital expenditure on generating capacity and the performance of public service tasks, while complying with the principle of the alienability of contracts. However, the Commission took the view that the Directive does not impose any time- limit for accessing the network. Power supplies could not therefore be hindered by a piecemeal approach like this and network access could not be provided on an '*à la carte*' basis since the goal is to apply the same rules to all market participants. Subsequently, the loss of market share by EdF in 2000 (mostly comprising customers that switched to German utilities for their electricity supply), made it harder to argue that the effect of the French law was in practice highly restrictive. [8] This development made it likely that the action would be discontinued.

6.13 The circumstances surrounding Belgium's failure to implement the Electricity Directive were different. Essentially, by September 2001 it had failed to appoint a system operator. Complaints were made to the Commission by the Belgian federation of large industrial energy consumers (Fébeliec) not only about this but also about the failure of power suppliers to put out tenders in response to many requests from large energy consumers[9]—and about the fact that Belgian electricity prices were about 20 per cent higher than in neighbouring countries.[10] A Reasoned Opinion was sent by the European Commission in February 2001 to the Belgian Government,[11] and in September 2001 the Commission decided to take Belgium to the ECJ for failure to designate a TSO according to the Electricity Directive.[12]

(a) Market-opening

6.14 Some aspects of implementation have been more encouraging. Many countries elected to go beyond the minimum level of market-opening required by the

[7] European Commission Press Release, 'Opening Up the Electricity Markets to Competition: Formal Notice Served on France', 13 June 2001.

[8] Europe Energy, no 572, 'Commission Takes Action Against Belgium on Power Liberalization' 22 Dec 2000, 2.

[9] ibid.

[10] EFET Press Release, 7 May 2001.

[11] Europe Energy no 578, 'Commission to Pursue Belgium and France on Energy Liberalization', 30 Mar 2001, 9.

[12] Commission Press Release, 'Belgium's electricity market is not yet completely opened up: the Commission is referring the matter to the Court of Justice', IP/01/1319, 26 Sept 2001.

Table 6.1 EU Electricity Market-opening

Year	2000 (%)	2003 (%)	Later (%)
Member State			
Austria	32	100 (2001)	100
Belgium	35	50	100 (2007)
Denmark	90	100	100
Finland	100	100	100
France	30	35	N/A
Germany	100	100	100
Greece	30	35	N/A
Ireland	30	40	100 (2005)
Italy	35	70	70
Luxembourg	40	56 +	75 (2005)
Netherlands	33	100	100
Portugal	30	35	N/A
Spain	54	100	100
Sweden	100	100	100
UK	100	100	100
EU average	66	75	83

Source: European Commission

Directive. Table 6.1 sets out the percentage of actual and expected opening in the years 2000, 2003, and subsequently. Four Member States have already opened their markets completely: Finland, Germany, Sweden, and the United Kingdom. Six other Member States have plans to move in the short or medium term to full market-opening: Austria, Belgium, Denmark, Ireland, The Netherlands, and Spain. However, these percentages are only indicative of the level of competition since 'real competition' requires a choice of supplier in addition to eligibility status.[13] For this to occur, other conditions have to be fulfilled, such as: real supply-side competition;, ease of switching suppliers for metering or other services; and—above all—non-discriminatory network access. The latter applies not only to access within a TSO network but also to the interconnections with other networks.

(b) Construction of new generation capacity

The response of Member States to the choice offered by the Directive between either the authorization or tendering procedures, has overwhelmingly favoured **6.15**

[13] Commission Staff Working Paper: 'Completing the Internal Energy Market', SEC (2001) 438, 12 Mar 2001, 5.

the former. As many as 14 Member States have elected to open the construction of new generation capacity to competition through the authorization procedure. Under this, any person may file an application for an authorization to construct a generating plant. In this way, the market is the arbiter of whether there is room for new capacity. The level of transparency and non-discrimination is felt to be higher than under the tendering approach, which is triggered by a report by the TSO or other competent body that additional capacity is required.

6.16 That said, if a Member State chooses to adopt the authorization procedure, it is not precluded from launching a tendering procedure in addition in exceptional circumstances. For example, a tendering procedure could be triggered, for reasons of long-term planning, by the absence of sufficient generating capacity being constructed under the authorization procedure. France has retained its right to launch an additional tendering procedure in exceptional circumstances.

Portugal has adopted a hybrid system. For the market comprising eligible customers it is the authorization procedure that is applicable. The tendering procedure applies to the construction of generation plant that is built to serve that part of the market comprising 'captive customers'.

(c) Network access

6.17 Member States have chosen overwhelmingly to take the option of Regulated Third Party Access (rTPA; see ch 4, paras 4.24, 4.88). The only Member State to have chosen negotiated TPA (nTPA) is Germany. None of the Member States have adopted the Single Buyer procedure that the Directive offers for network access, in addition to the rTPA and nTPA options. However, Italy and Portugal have taken up this option in a very limited way, using it for their captive customers while electing for rTPA for their eligible customers.

6.18 The choice is an interesting one, suggesting that Member States view the requirement to re-negotiate access prices and conditions at the end of each contract as imposing an additional and unwelcome burden on companies. The result is a clear preference for a system of regulated and published prices—fixed for all parties. It would seem that it is regarded as preventing discrimination between market players on price grounds and assists companies to plan future electricity purchases with an advance knowledge of transmission tariffs.

German nTPA system The German system is based on a voluntary negotiation of prices for network access in negotiations between associations of consumers, electricity companies, and network operators. The prices that result from these negotiations are then published with the aim of providing transparency for market participants. In turn, the latter may nevertheless contest these prices since they

Table 6.2 Unbundling in EU Electricity

Unbundling of	Member States
Management	France, Germany, Austria (grid of Tiwag and Illwerke in w. Austria), UK (grids in Scotland and N Ireland), Luxembourg
Legal	Italy, Belgium,* Netherlands, Austria (main part), Portugal, Ireland, Denmark
Ownership	Finland, Sweden, UK (England & Wales), Spain

Source: European Commission
*although the TSO has not yet been nominated (2001)

are not binding, leading to possible lengthy negotiations. The prices are not subject to regulatory supervision. In practice, these association agreements, or *Verbäundevereinbarungen*, have been heavily criticized by both market participants and the European Commission (see ch 7, para 7.73). Even though amended, they have continued to attract criticism.

(d) Unbundling

The Directive contains several elements of unbundling in Articles 13, 14, and 7 (see ch 4, paras 4.32–4.37). The unbundling of accounts and the establishment of a TSO were mandatory, but the provision on the unbundling of the management of the transmission system in Article 7(6) is a *minimum* requirement. In the event, most Member States have elected to introduce measures which go beyond this minimum (see Table 6.2). They did this either by creating a legally separate transmission system company (legal unbundling) or by establishing a transmission company that is completely separate from other interests and which owns all of the transmission assets (ownership unbundling). **6.19**

One of the drivers for a more extensive form of unbundling has been the technical difficulty encountered in implementing the requirement to unbundle accounts. This included matters such as the allocation of capital structure, working capital, and corporate costs.[14] **6.20**

(e) Public service obligations

In almost all of the Member States, a common set of provisions applies to the activities of electricity companies that have a public service objective. They fall into **6.21**

[14] Eurelectric (Network of Experts for Finance and Economics), *Preliminary Report on the Tendency for Unbundling in the EU*, Dec 1999.

two categories, relating to: (1) public service obligations, particularly those relating to security of supply, regularity, quality and price of supplies; (2), protection of the environment, (a recent addition).

6.22 **Public service obligations (category 1)** The public service obligations imposed by Member States under category (1) vary greatly from state to state. The variations reflect political and social concerns of the individual states.

6.23 The methods of providing these rights, and the market players on whom the obligations are imposed vary from one Member State to another. For captive customers, it is usual for an obligation to be placed on the incumbent operator to ensure supply (eg, in Austria, Belgium, Denmark, France, Greece, Ireland, Italy, Luxembourg, The Netherlands, Portugal, and Spain). Even for eligible customers, the guarantee of competition to ensure supply of electricity to eligible customers is backed up in most Member States by provisions such as minimum obligations on suppliers and other mechanisms.

This is an area that the Commission has indicated a strong interest in developing further in the transition to a liberalized energy market (see para 6.46).[15]

(f) Reciprocity

6.24 Given the different degrees of market-opening favoured by Member States, it is hardly surprising that many of them drew on the provision in Article 19(5) of the Directive on reciprocity. The Article gives Member States the right to refuse imports to its eligible consumers if they are not considered to be eligible in the exporting Member State. As many as eight Member States have introduced this clause into their national legislation: Austria, Belgium, Germany, Italy, Luxembourg, The Netherlands, Portugal, and Spain.

6.25 Unfortunately, the provision quickly revealed its limitations. It could easily be criticized as providing a poor defence against market-opening inequalities, and it soon became clear that it also provided insufficient protection against merger and takeover bids from companies based in Member States that had elected for very limited market-opening. Such companies managed to retain a significant proportion of their customers and so enjoyed an advantageous position over companies in Member States that had opened their markets beyond the minimum required by the Directive. In particular, companies owned or controlled by a Member State

[15] See European Commission 'Communication on Completion of the Internal Energy Market', 13 Mar 2001, COM (2001) 125 final, Annex IV: 'Public Services in the Electricity Sector'; also, more generally, EC Communication on Services of General Interest in Europe OJ C17, 19 Jan 2001, 4–23.

had an advantage—due not least to the fact that they were unable to be acquired by privately-owned companies.[16]

In this context measures were taken unilaterally by some Member States in the face of attempted takeovers by the state-controlled French company, EdF, of private energy companies operating in Member States outside France. EdF attempted to acquire—directly or indirectly—stakes in Spanish, German, and Italian companies[17] (respectively Hidrocantábrico, Energie-Baden-Württemberg, and Montedison). The general aim of the measures taken by Member States was to limit the voting rights of foreign companies in the business of the Member State concerned.

***Montedison v EdF* and a loophole for M&A activities** EdF attracted considerable hostility when it bid for control of an Italian company, Montedison, resulting in a Decree being issued by the Italian Government to block this move by limiting the voting rights of foreign electricity and gas companies in Italian energy companies. A complaint was sent to the Commission by Montedison, against EdF, which holds over 20 per cent of its capital.[18] Montedison accused EdF of an abusive market position and of allying with other shareholders to take control of the company. The Commission had to decide whether the complaint was admissible by examining the rules that might have been infringed and evidence of infringement. A key part of the case made by Montedison was that there had been an abuse of a dominant position by EdF under Article 82. This issue had been raised earlier when EdF sought control of London Electricity, a UK-based utility.[19] The charge was made that EdF used revenue from its monopolistic activities, such as supplying electricity to groups of customers that were not part of a liberalized market, to fund the acquisition of companies in the liberalized sectors of the market in other Member States. On 28 August 2001 the Commission cleared a bid for Montedison by Italenergia, a subsidiary of the Fiat Group, that had a significant shareholding held by EdF. The Commission approved the bid for two main reasons. First, the voting rights of EdF were limited to two per cent in ordinary and extraordinary shareholders' meetings. The Italian electricity market is dominated by ENEL, a situation largely unaffected by this development. 6.26

[16] This coincided with actions by the Commission to investigate 'golden share' arrangements in recently privatized energy companies in Belgium, France, Italy, Portugal, Spain, and the UK. They resulted in proceedings before the ECJ: Case C-503/99 (Belgium); Case C-483/99 (France); Case C-367/98 (Portugal); Case C-463/00 (Spain). In July 2001 A-G Damaso Ruiz-Jarabo Colomer delivered his opinion that such arrangements in newly-privatized companies are acceptable as long as they do not discriminate against citizens from other Member States: Europe Energy No 585, 13 July, 2002: 'Golden Shares Not Contrary to EU Law, Says Advocate-General', 1.3–1.4.

[17] These were all cleared by the European Commission in 2001. The *Montedison* case is considered in the following para. For the clearance of the German and Spanish bids, see IP/01/175 (7 Feb 2001) and IP/01/312 (6 Mar 2001).

[18] Europe Energy no 583, 15 June 2001, 1.11–1.13. The Decree No 192 of 25 May 2001 was published in the Italian Official 'Gazette No 120 of 25 May 2001.

[19] European Commission Press Release, 'Commission clears the acquisition of London Electricity by Électricité de France', IP/99/49, 27 Jan 1999.

6.27 A similar case had arisen in 1999 in the postal services sector involving Deutsche Post and UPS. The Dutch-based company, Nedlloyd, was acquired by Deutsche Post and the acquisition authorized by the Commission in July 1999. The Commission noted that Deutsche Post 'has access to funds which were not raised in a competitive market'.[20] The concerns of competitor companies were that these funds might enable Deutsche Post to fund acquisitions and be able to operate in a market without being subject to the requirement to make a profit and hence behave in a non-competitive manner. These concerns were being examined by the Commission.[21] There were clear parallels with the EdF situation.

The Commission announced its intention in 2001 to bring forward 'temporary instruments' during a transitional period leading up to full deregulation of the electricity and gas markets. The problem was to find an acceptable legal basis for this.[22] However, it was clear that the reciprocity clause did not offer sufficient protection against planned acquisitions and mergers during this phase.

(g) Regulatory authority

6.28 The Directive requires Member States to designate an independent dispute settlement authority (Article 20(3)). They are also required to create appropriate and efficient mechanisms for regulation, control, and transparency in order to avoid abuses of dominant positions, in particular to the detriment of consumers and any predatory behaviour. These mechanisms are to take account of EC Treaty rules, especially Article 81.

6.29 Twelve Member States elected to designate a sector-specific regulator, and to rely more or less on the competition authority in cases that arise from national competition law (Belgium, Denmark, Finland, France, Greece, Ireland, Italy, The Netherlands, Portugal, Spain, Sweden, and the UK). In Austria and Germany the tasks normally carried out by regulators in other Member States are carried out by the Ministry for Economy—although Austria plans to adopt a sector-specific regulator in future. In Luxembourg the telecommunications regulator acts as regulator for the electricity sector. In some cases the regulators' powers are defined broadly, with tariff-setting powers (eg, Italy and Great Britain); in others more restrictively, advising on tariffs (Spain); or setting tariffs after receiving instructions from the competent Minister (The Netherlands).

[20] See n 21, following.

[21] 2001/354/EC Commission Decision of 20 March 2001 re a proceeding under Art 82, EC Treaty (Case COMP/35.141 *Deutsche Post AG*) Doc No C (2001) 728, in OJ L 125, 5 May 2001, at 27–44.

[22] Speech by Commissioner Loyola de Palacio, Eurelectric conference on 'Electricity and Natural Gas: Evolution and Opportunities in Two Converging Markets', June 2001.

(h) Derogation

Under Article 24 of the Electricity Directive, Member States were allowed to derogate from some provisions of the Directive, such as the organization of system access (Chapter VII), transmission system operation (Chapter IV), or unbundling and transparency of accounts (Chapter VI)—provided the Commission accepts their transitional régime. **6.30**

The idea behind the régime is to provide a mechanism for addressing issues such as 'stranded costs' or 'stranded assets' (see ch 4, paras 4.59–4.64). Within one year of the Directive entering into force, a Member State was required to submit any such scheme to the Commission for approval. All Member States except two (Finland and Sweden) expressed interest in operating a transitional scheme. However, only two Member States requested temporary derogations from specific obligations under the Directive, while the rest did not wish to delay market-opening to compensate for stranded costs and chose to grant schemes of financial compensation. **6.31**

A Decision was taken by the Commission in mid-1999 which tackled the issue of which cases fell within the provisions of Article 24 and which should be considered as state aid. It stated that national schemes involving financial compensation must be treated as state aid and dealt with according to normal procedures for grant of state aid. The schemes affected include ones developed by Spain, the United Kingdom, France, Denmark, Austria, and The Netherlands. The Commission took the view that although, 'the payment of such levies can result in economic consequences substantially similar to those resulting from a total or partial derogation from some of the obligations'[23] of the Electricity Directive, such transitional schemes would have to be examined under the rules of Article 87(3) of the Treaty. **6.32**

The two requests for temporary derogation from specific obligations under the Directive were made by Germany and Luxembourg.

Germany was asking the Commission to take into account the circumstances of the electricity utility, VEAG. The company came into existence in 1990 following unification, when the East German electricity system was sold to the three largest West German electricity utilities, RWE Energie (26.25%), Bayernwerk (22.5%), and Preussenelektra (26.25%). The four other German TSOs held the remaining 25 per cent through a holding company, EBH. The utility that resulted from this operation—VEAG—had a commitment to maintain electricity generation from lignite or brown coal and to make large investments in the modernization of generation from that source. Since 1990 this had already cost DM 13 billion. **6.33**

[23] 1999/793/EC: Commission Decision of 8 July 1999, OJ L319 11 Dec 1999, 12; 1999/794/EC: Commission Decision of 8 July 1999, OJ L319 11 Dec 1999, 18 (Germany).

Regional distributors were also committed to purchasing 70 per cent of their power consumption at a price based on the total cost over a period of 20 years. According to Commission estimates, about 30,000 people were dependent on the lignite industry in East Germany. The Commission therefore allowed the utility to derogate from the Directive until 2003, but imposed a requirement that the large electricity users with consumption of more than 100 GwH a year and per site should be liberalized. This amounted to between 15 and 20 customers. However, the Decision would not take effect for two years (from 2001).

6.34 Luxembourg in fact made three distinct requests for derogations. The first concerned the obligation of the electricity utility, Cegedel, to publish separate accounts for its activities of generation, transmission, and distribution. The Government argued that this might harm the utility's competitive position since it is 90 per cent dependent on a single supplier, RWE of Germany. By contrast, its competitors have an obligation to disclose only the average costs of purchased power, with no distinction between suppliers. The Commission took the view that protection of the confidentiality of Cegedel's power purchase costs was legitimate but that such confidentiality would not be hampered by transparency of transmission costs. The derogation was therefore limited to the obligation to publish separate accounts for Cegedel's activities of generation and distribution and was to end on 31 December 2001. Cegedel is still obliged to publish its accounts for transmission.

The Commission did not accept Luxembourg's second submission. This concerned a request for a transitional régime to protect Cegedel's exclusive supply contract with RWE. The régime would have protected the contract (due to expire at the end of 2000), until 31 December 2000. In the Commission's view, Cegedel would not have been in a position in which it would have to buy power from RWE and be unable to sell it to its customers.

6.35 The third proposal involved a request for interpretation of Article 20(1) of the Electricity Directive, which allows auto-producers or independent power producers to negotiate access to the networks to supply their subsidiaries. This was rejected on the ground that it did not fall within the terms of Article 24 of the Directive.

6.36 A number of Member States wished to introduce state aid mechanisms to allow their electricity undertakings to adapt to the transition to competition under more favourable conditions. However, these do not fall within the scope of derogations provided for in Article 24 and are therefore considered in Chapter 7 (paras 7.99–7.106).

(2) Gas Directive

6.37 The Gas Directive was adopted on 22 June 1998 and entered into force on 10 August 1998. Member States were given two years from the latter date to bring into force the laws, regulations, and administrative provisions necessary to comply with the Directive (in accordance with Art 29). In addition to primary legislation, any necessary secondary legislation (eg decrees, orders, grid codes, and regulations), as well as administrative procedures were to be in place by that date. Member States were under an obligation to notify the Commission of these measures. By the 10 August 2000 deadline, all but three Member States had taken measures to implement the Directive.[24]

The Commission sent formal notices of infringement to France, Luxembourg, and Germany in the autumn of 2000. By early 2001 this was followed up by Reasoned Opinions (a second written warning) calling upon compliance within a specified period (generally two months), sent to each government. A formal notice of infringement sent to Portugal at the same time as the other three resulted in legislative action by Portugal in early 2001 (and at about the same time also by Luxembourg). However, the absence of implementing legislation did not mean that no action had been taken at all. In practice, voluntary measures were taken by gas companies in France and Germany to publish the main commercial conditions for providing access to their networks. However, this was hardly an acceptable substitute for the legal obligation required by the Directive. On 8 May 2001 the Commission decided to refer France to the ECJ for its failure to fulfil its legal obligation to implement the Gas Directive. **6.38**

In Germany, the relevant law—the Energy Industry Act of 24 April 1998—was adopted before the Directive was approved and makes no mention of the Gas Directive, contrary to Article 29(9). Although this has been supplemented by an amendment to the law on restraints on competition on 26 August 1998, and a voluntary agreement of 4 July 2000 with the gas supply associations (see ch 7, paras 7.76–7.77), key elements of the Gas Directive remained absent from the legal framework. These included provisions on: **6.39**

- unbundling of accounts of integrated companies;
- the obligation to publish the main commercial conditions in cases where nTPA is the preferred choice;
- establishment of technical rules to ensure inter-operability;
- a clear definition of the gas system to include storage and the other ancillary facilities to allow access (to the extent that the Directive requires);
- the right to negotiate access to the system; the principle of non-discrimination; and
- the preservation of confidentiality of commercially sensitive information.

Just as seriously, the industry association agreements met with widespread criticism from market participants—who lodged complaints with the appropriate competition authorities.

[24] European Commission, 'Communication on Completing the Internal Energy Market', (see n 15 above).

Table 6.3 EU Gas Market-opening

Year	**2000** (%)	**2008** (%)
Member State		
Austria	49	100
Belgium	58.7	100
Denmark	30	43
France	20	33
Finland	90	90
Germany	100	100
Greece	0	33
Ireland	75	100
Italy	96	100
Luxembourg	51.1	83.4
Netherlands	45	100
Portugal	0	33
Spain	72	100
Sweden	47	100
United Kingdom	100	100
EU (15) average	78.9	91.5

Source: European Commission

6.40 Some patterns do emerge in relation to those Member States that adopted measures of implementation in time to meet the Gas Directive. Most of them treated the requirements of the Directive as a minimum, especially with respect to the level of market-opening and eligibility.

(a) Market-opening

6.41 The degree of market-opening in each Member State is illustrated in Table 6.3 above. On average (on a volume-weighted basis) about 79 per cent of the total EU gas demand was eligible by 10 August 2000,[25] exceeding the Directive's absolute minimum requirement of 20 per cent. Apparently, this level of market-opening is likely to increase to 92 per cent by 2008.[26] However, a distinction should be made between eligible markets and real competitive markets (the latter being markets in which all eligible customers have a real choice of suppliers). This depends not only on eligibility but also on market characteristics in a wider sense, including issues such as: supply-side competition, non-discriminatory access to transportation capacity and ancillary facilities, including storage, the removal of obstacles to the free movement of goods, and the inter-operability of networks.

[25] European Commission, Staff Working Paper, March 2001, (n 13 above) 14.
[26] ibid.

(b) Network access

6.42 A majority of Member States have chosen rTPA over nTPA, or have chosen a combination of the two systems. Eight Member States have chosen rTPA based on published tariffs (Belgium, Spain, Finland, Ireland, Italy, Luxembourg, Sweden, and the UK). Three Member States have chosen a hybrid or combination of nTPA and rTPA. In two cases, Denmark and The Netherlands, rTPA has been chosen for the distribution network and nTPA for the transmission network and storage. In just two cases, Austria and Germany, the Member States elected for the nTPA option for their entire system (and Austria subsequently changed over to the rTPA system). However, even in these cases the approach was to subject tariffs for access not only to negotiation between individual parties but also prior regulatory approval or *ex ante* intervention by the authorities. In Germany the association agreement method already tried in electricity has been extended to the gas sector, with equally controversial results. The approaches to nTPA adopted in Denmark and The Netherlands for transmission are also subject to these operational qualifications. It seems therefore unlikely that a pure access régime based on nTPA organized on an agreement-by-agreement basis will develop in the EU.

6.43 In most cases the publication of network access conditions includes publication of standard conditions and tariffs, since rTPA is so widely used. However, standard conditions may be laid down in different types of network codes or technical rules published separately from the primary law. For those Member States choosing nTPA, publication of the network code includes at least the main commercial conditions in the form of agreed indicative or maximum tariffs. Many companies typically publish conditions for TPA on their websites.[27] However, a study of the TPA conditions found that there was little on company websites by way of explanation of how these tariffs were derived either methodologically or quantitatively.[28] Moreover, fundamentally different tariff models were being applied from company-to-company and pipeline-to-pipeline, varying from distance-related models to entry-exit and postalized systems.

6.44 **Example: The Netherlands** An indication of the problems that attended the introduction of a system based on nTPA is provided by the Dutch experience. The Gas Act contains a number of provisions that require a proactive stance by the regulator. Not only do they require that indicative tariffs be published, but they also require pipeline companies to consult with users' representative organizations

[27] Examples of websites include: www.omv.com; www.gasum.fi; www.snam.it; www.beb.de; www.vng.de; www.ruhrgas.com; www.wingas.de; www.thyssengas.de; www.dong.dk; www.distrigas.be; www.gasunie.nl; www.enagas.com; www.vattenfallnaturgas.com; www.transco.uk.com; www.irlgov.ie

[28] European Commission, 'TPA conditions of major European gas transmission operators: a preliminary overview and an attempt at comparison', draft discussion document prepared by DG TREN/A2, prior to the Gas Regulatory Forum, 26–27 Oct 2000.

prior to their publication. The regulator must publish guidelines for TPA and the competition authority may set a deadline for negotiations and impose temporary tariffs. To identify a balance between the concept of nTPA and the discretion permitted to the regulator under these statutory requirements, extensive consultations with market participants took place prior to the publication of detailed Guidelines.[29]

(c) Unbundling

6.45 The Gas Directive requirements to unbundle are limited to an unbundling of accounts in Article 13, and do not require the kind of management unbundling of system operators that is found in Article 7 of the Electricity Directive. However, Commission's efforts to encourage an unbundling of transmission system operators through the Madrid Forum should not be overlooked (see ch 7, para 7.44).

The Directive's requirements indicate only a minimum standard, so the actual approaches taken by Member States have been quite mixed. Some countries have chosen a separation of transportation and commercial trading activities of integrated companies that goes beyond the Directive's requirements. Spain and Italy have elected to legislate to make the grid operator a separate legal entity, irrespective of any change in ownership. Only the United Kingdom has a legal requirement for the TSO to be independently owned. Others have preferred to comply with the minimum requirement (an unbundling of accounts), and appear to have no intention of going beyond this (Denmark, Germany, Finland, France, Luxembourg, and Spain). Such arrangements leave in place only Chinese Walls separating only the TSO from the supply arm of the same company, and often also a competitor of the TSO's customers (often located in the very same premises). This may well create problems in future since the absence of a full legal unbundling is often seen as a potential obstacle to non-discriminatory network access, potentially leading to abuse of dominant positions. Although the Directive does not require such unbundling, the alternatives necessitate vigorous surveillance of market behaviour to ensure non-discrimination.

(d) Public Service Obligations

6.46 The Gas Directive provisions on PSOs are identical to those in the Electricity Directive (see paras 6.21–6.23). Most, but not all Member States envisage some form of PSOs on their gas industries. However, the manner in which they have been developed in primary legislation has been quite general. Typically, the subjects they cover include the following:

[29] Office for Energy Regulation (DTe), 'Guidelines Gas Act: Information and Consultation Document 2001', June 2001; Brattle Group Ltd, DTe Implementation of the Gas Act, Dec 2000.

- the connection and supply of captive customers
- gas quality
- safety, security, and diversification of gas supply
- interconnections and new gas infrastructure
- development and operation of underground gas storage
- gas balancing
- gas marketing
- price equalization
- sustainability
- energy saving
- research and development in the gas sector, and
- 'small fields policy' (in The Netherlands).

(e) Reciprocity

As with the Electricity Directive a Member State is entitled to refuse imports to an eligible customer in its territory if the equivalent customer in the supplier's country is not free to choose its supplier. This provision (Art 19, Gas Directive) is subject to review no later than 2003. No less than nine Member States have included a reciprocity clause in their national legislation. This is in response to fears of losing market share in less liberalized markets. **6.47**

(f) Regulatory authority

There is considerable diversity of approach towards the establishment of regulatory authorities to meet the requirements of Articles 21 and 22. A clear majority of Member States plan to combine responsibilities for gas and electricity sectors in a single common regulator. This includes dispute settlement. Eleven countries have taken this option. In no case is there a plan to establish a sector-specific regulator for gas, but in Germany not even an energy-specific regulatory authority is planned, leaving a clear field for regulation through the Federal Cartel Office. In a number of cases, such as Spain, Austria, Ireland and Denmark, the ministry responsible for energy matters will continue to play an important rôle in energy regulation. **6.48**

(g) Access to storage

Although the Directive contains provisions on access to storage and ancillary services, the extent of the obligation on Member States is far from clear, other than requiring access to storage 'when such access is technically necessary for providing efficient access to transmission and/or distribution networks' (see ch 4, n 118). This has resulted in a slow and very diverse approach to the provision of non-discriminatory access to the necessary facilities. **6.49**

Some early experiences are to be found in the United Kingdom and Italy. The former organizes auctions for access capacity for storage while 'virtual' storage is available on the spot market. In Italy, access to storage is regulated.

6.50 In France, access is subject to the operation of competition law and certain policy priorities. Other Member States appear to accept some form of access to storage but make this subject to the availability of capacity and possibly also when it is technically necessary to permit efficient access to a system.

(h) Upstream pipeline networks

6.51 These provisions are most relevant to those Member States with significant quantities of gas in production,[30] namely: Austria, Denmark, Ireland, Italy, The Netherlands, and the United Kingdom (for relevant provisions of the Directive, see ch 4, paras 4.96–4.101). In each case (except Austria), measures have been taken to implement the Directive's provisions with respect to the upstream sector, as follows:

- The UK has amended its upstream legislation (both offshore and onshore) to ensure compatibility with the Gas Directive.[31] Formerly the procedures for offshore access were governed by a voluntary code of practice and not by means of a competent, independent authority. This was modified so that if an applicant for access and an operator failed to reach agreement, the applicant might apply to the Secretary of State, who might serve a notice on the operator. It is an offence to fail to comply with such a notice.
- In The Netherlands the Gas Law 2000 includes specific provisions for access to upstream networks, which are in practice closely related to downstream facilities.[32] The national competition law applies directly to gas transport in upstream pipelines under which upstream network operators are obliged to negotiate access to networks and not abuse their monopoly power.
- In Germany, a revision of the Energy Industry Act is due that will provide rules for access to upstream pipeline networks. But in any case, the general competition law will still govern applications for access to pipelines.[33]
- In Denmark, the Government has prepared secondary legislation providing for TPA to the country's offshore upstream pipeline network.[34]
- In Italy, a specific régime applies to upstream pipelines under which owners of upstream facilities are obliged to provide access to pipelines and related services on the basis of objective criteria.[35] It provides the criteria for authorization and technical and safety conditions for such access.[36]

---

[30] See European Commission, *Upstream Pipeline Networks* (22 Oct 1998, see ch 4, n 95).

[31] Gas (Third Party Access and Accounts) Regulations 2000 No 1937, which entered into force on 10 Aug 2000.

[32] Staatsblad 2000, No 305.

[33] Competition Act (*Gesetz gegen Wettbewerbsbeschränkungen*) (GWB), s 19 (4).

[34] Act No 291 of 10 June 1981, as amended by Act No 254 of 8 June 1983 and Act No 432 of 10 June 1997.

[35] *Decreto Legislativo di Attazione della Direttiva 98/30/CE Relativa a Norme Comuni per Il Mercato Interno del Gas*, No 164, 23 May 2000, Arts 6, 24 and 25.

[36] Italy has also initiated a gas release programme and limited the volume taken by the dominant importer/producer to 75% by 2003, 61% by 2009: see First Report (2001) n 5 above, 15.

- Norway has agreed to adopt the provisions of the Gas Directive under the EEA Agreement.[37]

(j) Derogation

Three Member States have notified the Commission that they intend to derogate under Article 26 from certain articles in the Directive (Finland, Greece, and Portugal). Their justification was that they qualified as emergent markets and/or were markets not directly connected to the networks of other Member States. **6.52**

(3) EU Monitoring of Implementation

For the Electricity and Gas Directives to work, their implementation in the Member States had to be monitored and, to the extent possible, harmonized. However, focusing on harmonization would not in itself bring about a single market. The necessity of breaking down the reality of segmented markets—especially in electricity—required a different approach. The job of proposing measures to achieve this fell naturally to the Commission. In enforcing the Directives, the Commission's rôle included harmonization, monitoring, and clarification of its aims (where the aims and requirements were unclear in the light of the various compromises reached in the Directives' texts or following on subsequent developments). **6.53**

Harmonization actions: electricity

The Commission was required to produce a report on harmonization matters within 12 months of adoption of the Electricity Directive (by Art 25(1)). This was to include proposals deemed necessary for the effective operation of the internal market in electricity. Two reports were issued on harmonization requirements in 1998[38] and in 1999[39] (see Table 6.4). **6.54**

However, the notion that a proper review could be produced within a 12-month period proved to be misconceived. It was not possible to obtain a comprehensive overview of the structural choices made by Member States to implement the Directive at such an early stage. The Commission therefore proposed that there be at least one further report drafted in the light of experience gained after full implementation at national level (after February 1999). That report would cover harmonization requirements and also the latest developments in implementation of the Directive. With Council support, the Commission proceeded to draw up a further report on harmonization published in April 1999 (despite the fact that **6.55**

[37] See ch 2, para 2.109, n 105.

[38] European Commission, 'Second Report to the Council and the European Parliament on Harmonization Requirements: Directive 96/92/EC on common rules for the internal market in electricity', (16 Mar 1998, COM (1998) 167 final).

[39] European Commission, 2nd report, 16 Apr 1999, (n 1 above).

Table 6.4 Implementation Schedules for EU Electricity and Gas Provisions

19 February 1997	Electricity Directive enters into force
19 February 1998	End date for review of electricity harmonization measures: stage 1
10 August 1998	Gas Directive enters into force
19 February 1999	Electricity Directive implemented by all (non-exempted) Member States except France and Luxembourg 40 GwH threshold applicable (approx 22% market-opening)
10 August 1999	End date for review of gas harmonization measures
19 February 2000	Electricity Directive implemented by Belgium and Ireland 20 GwH threshold applicable (approx 27% market-opening) End date for views on harmonization to be given
10 August 2000	Gas Directive implemented by all Member States except France, Germany and Luxembourg EU average market-opening: 78.9%
19 February 2001	Electricity Directive implemented by Greece
19 February 2001	End date for review of safeguard clause in Electricity Directive
19 February 2003	9 GwH threshold applicable (approx 32% market-opening)
10 August 2003	Review report on operation of Gas Directive, Art 25 (take-or-pay derogations)
19 February 2006	Adoption date for a revised Electricity Directive

Source: European Commission

one Member State (France) had failed to implement the Directive by the deadline).

6.56 The first report confined itself largely to the issue of promoting schemes for renewable-based electricity generation in the single market. The second took a bolder approach, expressly drawing attention to a wide range of existing or expected obstacles within the single market in electricity. Two issues provoked extended comment.

6.57 (i) **Segmented markets** Implementation in the Member States should not result in 15 separate and rather isolated electricity markets instead of a single market, as was the goal. The total figure of market-opening might be higher than the minimum required by the Directive, but a segmented, uneven opening might nevertheless be the result. There was a significantly higher risk of this happening in electricity than in gas, so obstacles to cross-border trade in electricity had to be actively addressed. Obstacles were identified in the availability of transmission capacity in the interconnectors between Member States; the establishment of a system of trade-facilitating cross-border transmission tarification or an EU tariff system; and the related issue of cross-border electricity transactions involving third countries.

(ii) Regulation The Commission noted that the above issues raised a further issue: was it necessary to establish a system of EU regulation of the electricity network, especially to regulate those above cross-border issues? It stated, 'Neither national regulatory action nor Community action under the competition rules is fully able to address the issues concerned.'[40] Nonetheless, it intended to enforce competition rules where necessary and would examine contracts with interconnections on a case-by-case basis. In addition, it introduced the question of whether a new Directive on open access was necessary and if so what such a Directive might cover. **6.58**

Harmonization Actions: Gas

A similar harmonization provision was included in the Gas Directive. Article 27(1) requires the Commission to submit a report on the harmonization requirements not linked to the provisions of the Directive (eg energy taxation and environmental regulation),[41] and if necessary to include any proposals required for the effective operation of the internal market in natural gas.[42] In addition, the Commission must analyse the harmonization requirements and 'if appropriate, submit proposals aiming at a more efficient inter-operability of natural gas networks'.[43] As with the Electricity Directive, the Commission limited its initial report to identification of issues that could represent obstacles to trade in the single market for natural gas. **6.59**

The report benefited from research into issues of inter-operability that had been carried out at the Commission's request.[44] As a result, it focused on the technical and commercial conditions for an efficient inter-operability of the gas networks and the interconnections between the different gas systems. The obstacles to gas transfers across national borders in a liberalizing market were a matter of special interest. Historically, the vertically-integrated gas companies had carried on cross-border transportation not as trade in the usual sense of the term but for the most part to secure their import requirements. However, as the eligible customers availed themselves of TPA, cross-border transportation patterns were expected to

[40] ibid, 27.

[41] Energy taxation matters are the subject of the Commission's proposal for a Council Directive on 'Restructuring the Community Framework for the Taxation of Energy Products', COM (1997) 30 final, 12 Mar 1997. Environmental regulations and standards are covered by the Large Combustion Plants Directive and the Directive on Integrated Pollution Prevention and Control (IPPC). This does not preclude further development in harmonization however.

[42] COM (1999) 612, 23 Nov 1999, 'Report to the Council and the European Parliament on Harmonization Requirements: Directive 98/30/EC on common rules for the internal market in natural gas'.

[43] Statement 85/98 to the Minutes of the Council.

[44] European Commission Gas Unit, *Study on Interoperability of Gas Networks in EU Countries: Final Report Executive Summary*, carried out by Pipeline Engineering GmbH (PLE), 24 June 1999.

change. The diverse technical and commercial trading rules for gas network operation would therefore become important as a potential source of constraints on this process through, for example, capacity bottlenecks and high cross-border charges. At the same time, the potential for congestion was of a different order of magnitude from the electricity sector. Given the longer distances from the source of gas to consumption, cross-border transportation had been central to the European gas business for decades.

6.60 The Commission's approach in addressing issues of inter-operability of gas markets and networks has followed that which it adopted in the electricity sector. It has not confined itself to technical aspects but has also considered the legal and commercial aspects, such as capacity booking and the design of tariffs for access including cross-border tarification. In this context, gas swaps were to be taken into account as a proven and widely-practised method of optimizing transportation and of minimizing costs.

The Commission highlighted five areas as sources of problems for the development of an internal market in gas:

1. obstacles created by technical operations
2. gas quality differences
3. balancing régime
4. capacity constraints, and
5. tarification of transmission tariffs.

6.61 However, in addition, it noted the importance of gas trade with third countries given the EU's import dependence on more than 40 per cent of its gas. This contrasted with its high degree of self-sufficiency in electricity supplies. It was therefore important to promote the implementation of upstream market rules and supply-side gas-to-gas competition among individual, producing companies.

6.62 (i) **Technical conditions** The Directive had addressed the need for technical harmonization in Article 5. Specific responsibilities were given to the Member States to ensure that the technical operational rules of the gas undertakings facilitate gas trade in the EU rather than create barriers to it. Articles 7 and 11 of the Directive also ensure an exchange of relevant information by fixing an obligation on undertakings to do so. Technical matters had therefore been provided with a sufficient legal basis to be capable of being addressed in future.

6.63 (ii) **Gas quality** There are two main categories of gas quality in the EU and which are not fully interchangeable in the absence of appropriate measures:

1. high calorific gas (H-gas), the principal gas used in the EU, and
2. low calorific gas (L-gas), mainly of Dutch and German origin and used in only 5 Member States.

Separate pipeline systems are used for the transportation of the two kinds of gas. The systems are designed to operate within a range of gas quality specifications determined primarily by reference to maximum and minimum values of the calorific value which may be introduced into the system. The gas companies themselves undertake their management. The adoption of a single convertible gas quality is not practical in the EU, although L-gas is expected to decline in use over the long term. This is of more than technical importance, since a network operator may reject a request for TPA for technical reasons, given its responsibility for safe and efficient network operation. In such cases, objective, transparent, and non-discriminatory reasons must be given for the refusal. In practice, problems relating to gas quality are much less likely to arise along traditional supply lines than along the interconnector related routes. 6.64

(iii) **Balancing régimes** Market-opening will impact on the dispatching tasks of network operators and will have safety repercussions. To ensure system balancing of input and output takes place on a non-discriminatory basis, transparent frameworks should be developed in the form of network codes for all parties involved. 6.65

(iv) **Capacity constraints** Bottlenecks to capacity represent a significant obstacle to a single market in gas. Interconnections play an important rôle as the bridges between national gas network systems and may constrain the expanded gas trade that is expected with liberalization. In future, the reservation of long-term contract capacity will compete with short-term requirements for transactions of eligible customers and traders. Rules for allocating available capacity must be harmonized or else consumers could face more refusals of access requests than would be justified if based on real physical constraints alone. More accessible information on the applicable specifications is also required. 6.66

(v) **Tarification of transmission** The Commission supported the idea of an EU-wide set of general principles that could facilitate gas trade across different access régimes. This would cover, for example, non-discrimination, cost-reflectivity, transparency, and objectivity. However, it acknowledged that the matter of access charges was one of commercial importance and complexity. Further study was therefore required. 6.67

(4) Developing a New EU Strategy for the Transition Phase

The harmonization reports highlighted issues that had been of only marginal—if any—importance during the negotiations on the Electricity and Gas Directives. Examples of such issues include the design of rules for tarification of transmission across borders and for the allocation of interconnector transmission capacity in ways which are compatible with the Directives' requirements. These may be described as 'transitional issues' because they presuppose the legal framework set out 6.68

in the Directives and need to be tackled successfully if a liberalized market is to be achieved. They are new because they could not have been properly addressed until the Member States had made strategic implementation choices based on the Directives.

At first glance, these new issues appear to be primarily technical in character but they are important, perhaps crucial, to making progress on the wider legal and commercial objectives of the Directives. They underline the extent to which the regulation of energy markets in a transitional phase requires considerable technical knowledge to be effective.

(a) Cross-border trade

6.69 Both of the Directives envisaged an increase in cross-border trade in energy—a goal which was more urgent in the case of electricity than for gas. However, neither Directive provided the necessary mechanisms to achieve this.

6.70 In the electricity sector, eligible customers still found it extremely difficult to choose a supplier situated in another Member State, especially if a third or fourth Member State had to be transited. Essentially, there was no tariff framework in place for cross-border transactions. Each transaction with a cross-border element requires negotiation on the issue of transmission fees between the contracting parties and the TSO of any network within the contractual path of the electricity. Each TSO has to be paid a transaction fee, calculated at rates and by methods that are not necessarily consistent with each other. The result is an accumulation of national fees when parties transmit over more than one TSO area—a phenomenon known as 'pancaking'. It makes cross-border trading complicated and expensive, encouraging customers to remain with the local suppliers.

6.71 Historically, cross-border trade in electricity has been very limited. Often a vertically-integrated national transmission system operator carried it out. Exchanges were carried out according to rules defined by associations of TSOs. They were limited to wholesale exchanges among the TSOs on a bilateral or multi-lateral (ie, transit) basis and constituted a form of reserve guarantee or long-term power contract between the TSOs. This system excluded distribution companies and final consumers from access to interconnections, and so from the option of securing supply from beyond the network boundaries. Even the name of the association, the Union of Electricity Production and Transmission Companies (UCPTE), reflected the bundled character of the electricity companies at the time.

6.72 With gas, cross-border transportation appears at first sight to be on an entirely different scale, with large quantities commonly being transported across several national boundaries. Transit is also much more important than in the electricity sector, with more than 60 per cent of gas consumed in the EU crossing at least one border on its way to the consumer (in 2000). However, this transportation has been conducted mainly in the form of transit and/or supply agreements between incumbent gas companies. In practice, therefore, this is not really 'trade' and has arisen only because of the uneven distribution of gas reserves in the pan-European context. This physical pattern of gas flows can be expected to be less and less a source of constraints on commercial gas flows in the future as TPA makes an impact.

(i) **Electricity** The promotion of cross-border trade by establishing a common tariff framework has been a major focus of Commission attention since 1998. The organizational challenge presented by the task should not be underestimated. It is more than a matter of creating a tarification system that encourages eligible customers to take advantage of the single market, since physical flows of electricity do not follow contract flows—especially in the highly interconnected systems of Continental Europe. An analogy may be drawn with a common lake to which some parties add water and others take water out. Such a system has to be complemented with a settlement or clearing régime among the TSOs, which allows them to redistribute the tariff revenues according to both physically-metered flows and complex intra-TSO rules. In the Commission's view, relying exclusively on national measures cannot solve the making of rules for cross-border transactions.[45] Actions by 15 different regulatory authorities are unlikely to be co-ordinated and could not support a potential single EU tarification mechanism. Nor is the instrument of competition policy likely to be sufficient either since 'almost all jurisdictions world-wide now accept that competition policy is an inadequate instrument to regulate transmission tariffs.'[46] **6.73**

Early discussions of this problem revealed that there were two very different approaches to the pricing of cross-border transactions: (1) transaction-related pricing, and (2) nodal pricing. The crux of the problem lay in the possible payments to be made by TSOs or other market players to other TSOs by way of compensation for use of the international transmission capacities, or to provide incentives to potential users. The TSOs sought in their own interest to develop exact and cost-reflective remuneration, while the interests of the customers lay rather in simple and non-transaction related tariffs. **6.74**

(1) *'Transaction-related' pricing* bases the transmission fee on the information provided by the parties about the entry and exit points of each transaction to be concluded and the theoretical path of the electricity between them. This is also known as 'point-to-point' tarification. Every TSO within the contract path of the proposed transaction can charge a fee for the hypothetical use of its system.
(2) *'Nodal' pricing* involves a recovery of transmission system costs from access or connection charges paid by consumers and generators. The access fee is the same irrespective of the supplier. The tariff is described as a 'postage-stamp' tariff (see para 6.76) and the system sometimes called 'point of connection' tarification.

[45] European Commission, 2nd Report on Harmonization, (n 1 above), at 5.
[46] ibid, 27.

6.75 Of the two approaches, (2) has secured most support within the EU (non-transaction-based or nodal tariff system). It has advantages in terms of simplicity and ease of use by customers seeking to change supplier. Its principal advantage, however, is that it better reflects the low correlation between physical flow and the flow envisaged in the individual contract. This results from the use of counter-directed transmission requests that, once superimposed, increase the contractual capacity of the system to a level higher than the physical capacity. (Returning to the analogy of the common lake, it does not matter in terms of cost if the party taking water from the lake (or grid) is located close to the party supplying water to the lake or is located on the other side of the lake.) Calculations of cost have therefore to be based not on contract flows but rather on the actual costs incurred in carrying out the physical flow. A further disadvantage of the transaction-based system lies in the difficulties of combining it with power exchanges and spot-market based systems.

6.76 (ii) Gas The development of a practical approach to cross-border tarification was a priority but the complexity of the issues involved suggested some further research was necessary. For this purpose as well as for the analysis of methodologies for access pricing in national systems, the Commission initiated a study. The consultants' report formed the basis for the Commission strategy in this area.[47]

The report concluded, *inter alia*, that no single model of access pricing could be applied across the EU and that concrete solutions required national characteristics and circumstances to be taken into account. The solution had to be justifiable in terms of the principle of non-discrimination. Currently, several methodologies are in use for pipeline tarification. The model favoured in Member States varies according to the size and type of the transmission system and of the eligible customers. There are three principal approaches:

- *distance-related tariffs*: charges based on the distance the gas has to travel from a receipt point to a delivery point;
- *postage-stamp tariffs*: charges based on the notion that every gas unit pays the same amount regardless of how far or where it is transported on the network; and
- *entry–exit tariffs*: charges applied separately for taking gas into the system and off-taking it from the system.

6.77 Hybrid approaches are possible, as in The Netherlands, where a distance-related tariff has been adopted for the high-pressure (or main) grid but a postage-stamp system adopted for the low-pressure (or regional) grid. The unit charges may be linked to capacity, to throughput, to distance, or to a combination of these.

47 The Brattle Group, Methodologies for establishing national and cross-border systems of pricing of access to the gas system of Europe, see ch 7, paras 7.55–7.58.

The risk is that such systems will develop in a segmented fashion in each Member State, with tarification systems emerging based on the technical characteristics and constraints in each national system and on the current amount of physical flows and costs. If each company has its own set of tariffs and each Member State has its dispute settlement authority (to deal with any problems that may arise), it could be argued that cross-border tarification is not an issue. However, in the case of cross-border trade, pancaking of rates (see para 6.70) between national systems may still arise. This problem has arisen in Germany in connection with the *Verbändevereinbarung* (see ch 7, paras 7.76–7.77). The Gas Directive is weaker than its electricity counterpart in its provisions on the independence of transmission system operators, which may also hinder the development of cross-border trade.

The above features, combined with the absence at that time of trading hubs and exchanges, and the limited number of suppliers of gas, favoured a consensus-based approach to the promotion of a competitive market, supplemented by political pressure when appropriate. **6.78**

(b) Capacity allocation

(i) **Electricity** Interconnectors are like bridges between national networks or regional systems but at the same time can act as potential bottlenecks (sometimes called 'flow gates') for transmission. By definition, they involve two TSOs, making co-ordination between them essential. The expanded trade in electricity involving eligible customers and traders in a liberalizing market will place strains on existing (and scarce) interconnector capacity, leading to refusals of network access in the face of congestion, and higher costs to customers. The Electricity Directive does not set out specific allocation rules for available transmission capacity, making this another gap in the framework for an internal market in energy. **6.79**

In managing cross-border transmission capacity, certain principles and techniques may provide some guidance in the transition to a liberalized market. Refusals of access due to a lack of capacity should be based on lack of *physical* capacity, not a lack of co-ordination between neighbouring TSOs or the existence of long-term reservation contracts (contractual blocking).[48] The latter are a matter of some sensitivity since the TSO may be part of a vertically-integrated company that benefits from a long-term power purchase or sale contract that requires long-term capacity reservation. Such agreements have the potential to prevent, restrict, or distort competition and are therefore vulnerable to scrutiny under Articles 81 and 82 of the Treaty. **6.80**

Otherwise, there are several established techniques to maximize available transmission capacity such as: **6.81**

[48] ibid, 7.

- re-dispatching (where TSOs change the dispatching order of power plants to create overall electricity flows that remain within the limits of transmission line constraints);
- superimposition of counter-directed transmission requests (off-setting of transmission requests in opposite directions by TSOs on both sides of the interconnector, acting together); and
- counter trading (where TSOs actively offsets trading contracts with generators and/or consumers to create a contractual flow in the opposite direction of any congestion).

6.82 Costs involved in using any of these techniques could be passed on in the form of an *ex ante* congestion fee. Similarly, there are techniques available that serve to ration limited capacity. These include a first-come, first-served approach; pro rata rationing; merit order prioritization; bidding or auctioning for scarce capacity; and prioritization for renewables.

6.83 **(ii) Gas** Similar observations could be made with respect to gas . A key difference is that the Gas Directive, in contrast to the Electricity Directive, does not require the establishment of an independent (in management terms) system operator. However, trade between the main transmission systems could not be facilitated without making rules on similar issues such as tariff régimes, capacity booking, and allocation rules for congestion management.

(c) Inter-operability

6.84 As the Gas Directive had anticipated, the degree of interoperability of Europe's diverse gas networks is a factor that could act to limit competition in EU gas markets. It appears that immediately after the adoption of the Directives the level of inter-operability in the EU was high.[49] Therefore the Commission has sought to build on this by encouraging the improvement of the interconnections and their inter-operability. Pressure on existing pipeline capacity was expected from the national and cross-border TPA practices and aspirations of eligible customers. In this context, possible technical barriers to trade included differences in gas quality; in network specifications; in load balancing; odorization practices; gas metering; accounting procedures; and in physical constraints on the system such as capacity constraints or missing links. However, the Commission had no intention of restricting itself to expressly technical matters and proposed to focus also on capacity booking and tarification of access. A number of areas were identified in an experts' report for which harmonization measures seemed necessary. The following are the principal ones:[50]

---

[49] European Commission Gas Unit, *Study on Interoperability of Gas Networks in EU Countries*, n 44 above.

[50] European Commission 2nd Report (see n 1).

- *Access to pipelines of different quality specifications.* Gas consumer groups asked for publication of the gas specifications accepted by operators for system access. Regulation of this is probably unnecessary however since this is covered by Article 5 of the Gas Directive.
- *Legal framework for metering and accounting* in the individual Member States. Harmonization is required.
- Requirements for regulation of *load balancing*, including the rôles, obligations, rights, and exchange of information of the parties in relation to system balancing. A number of parties including gas consumer interests, some Member States, and gas companies have argued for harmonization of load balancing practices. An hourly balancing of input and output of system users is, in their view, unnecessary, discriminatory, and hinders new entry and access to the network. This could be remedied by requiring harmonization across the borders of similar balancing régimes. However, the expert report concluded that at that stage, a precise definition of the regulatory framework on balancing issues could not be made (further development of the internal gas market would be required before such a definition could become possible). It did support the convergence of technical rules to avoid both barriers to trade and too frequent changes in the technical rules.
- Appropriate measures for inter-changeability of different gas qualities supplied within the EU. Such measures include the *treatment* and *blending of gas.* Normally, existing gas transmission companies carry out such operations on the basis of an array of facilities and ancillary services. The expert report supported cost/price transparency of each of these services to facilitate access to the network.
- Fair and non-discriminatory harmonized *allocation rules* will be required to facilitate cross-border trade and access. Potential barriers to trade arise from differences in national systems of *capacity booking* and priority of *allocation of scarce transportation capacity.*

(d) Energy trade with third countries

A new issue that was not primarily technical in character but nonetheless impor- **6.85**
tant concerned energy trade with neighbouring non-EU countries. Patterns of such trade were expected to change in the transition to a liberalized market. Technical obstacles to trade such as low capacity of electricity interconnectors between national systems or differing operating standards were of diminishing importance as interconnections improved between the UCTE network and Central and Eastern Europe.

(i) Electricity Until the 1990s the grid system of EU Europe was physically sepa- **6.86**
rated from those of Continental and Eastern Europe so any trade there was had a marginal importance. Exchanges took place between the former monopolists primarily

to sell electricity produced by their own production facilities, to maintain profits, and to maintain the operation of their plants. At EU level no specific rules for electricity import and export existed. Although the interconnections were growing during the early 1990s, the legal implications could not be addressed in the Electricity Directive because its legal authority was Article 95,* restricting its scope to harmonization measures. However, an intensification of such trade with neighbouring countries would have to take place on the basis of a level playing field for all economic operators. This required the establishment of new rules for trade, providing for reciprocity and for respect of comparable environmental and security standards.

6.87 The reciprocity principle is included in the Electricity Directive (Art 19(5)) and enables Member States to refuse deliveries to certain categories of consumer in relation to imports from another Member State if the consumers in that Member State would not be free to choose their supplier from the former Member State. Similarly, the principle of reciprocity would be applicable to trade between the EU and neighbouring countries.

The legal framework appropriate to a liberalizing energy market would have to be broader than that provided by Community law, encompassing also the WTO/GATT rules, the Energy Charter Treaty, and various agreements with the accession countries. The disadvantage of the WTO/GATT rules is that there is a lack of experience of their application to the energy industry. The Commission has noted this.[51]

6.88 The Commission proposes to develop such rules on energy trade with non-EU countries via bilateral agreements and understandings that would include an element of reciprocity. Such agreements would have to be founded on three main principles:

1. equivalent quantitative market-opening percentages;
2. equivalent qualitative market access conditions relating to unbundling, transmission fees, grounds for refusal of access, and dispute settlement;
3. equivalent environmental standards in electricity generation.

6.89 An interesting point arises here with respect to policing of the legal framework.[52] The assistance of the TSOs would be necessary since—faced with the scenario of any attempts to import (and dump in the EU) electricity that is not covered by these agreements—the only means of preventing the import of an intangible good such as electricity is to oblige TSOs in the EU to refuse access to interconnectors

[51] European Commission, 'Communication on Completing the Internal Market in Energy', March 2001, Annex VII (Trade in Electricity with non-EU Countries), 3 (see n 15 above).

[52] ibid, 5–6.

and national grid systems, playing in effect the rôle of customs authorities. The final legal framework may therefore involve some adaptation to the proposed amended Electricity Directive to address this new issue (see ch 7).

(ii) Gas More than 40 per cent of gas consumption in the EU is imported from non-EU suppliers. However, a significant proportion of this is delivered from Norway, which is a party to the EEA Agreement with the EU (see ch 2, paras 2.97–2.110). Norway adopted EC competition law on signing the EEA Agreement as part of the *acquis*. It is not automatically bound to accept Directives adopted after the EEA Agreement was signed but it is under strong political pressure to do so. Norway has adopted the Electricity Directive but not yet the Gas Directive.[53] But in 2001 the Norwegian Government announced that the GFU joint sales system would be abandoned and that the Gas Directive would be fully implemented in Norwegian law (see ch 2, paras 2.107 and, 2.110). **6.90**

Dependence on other, non-Norwegian sources is expected to grow in future. Therefore, concerns evident in the Commission's report on harmonization in the electricity sector are also evident in the gas sector. For example, there is an EU interest in ensuring reciprocity in market-opening and access with third countries.[54] However, there are also differences arising from the factual situation with respect to gas due to import dependency. The promotion of supply-side competition among individual gas suppliers will be difficult to achieve but is seen to be a necessary step if gas-to-gas competition were to develop within the EU.[55] **6.91**

D. Conclusions

Even after the adoption of the Electricity and Gas Directives the transmission of electricity and gas in the EU has continued to be dominated by incumbent players wielding monopoly power. Regulation is necessary to avoid possible discrimination by vertically-integrated TSOs in terms of access prices and network conditions to potential competitors; in excessive pricing; and to ensure that all reasonable steps are taken to reinforce the networks to meet customer demand. Many issues can be dealt with by the national regulatory authorities but some important ones have had to be addressed at the EU level. In particular, the cross-border tarification of electricity has forced the development of a solution at EU level. **6.92**

[53] An example of this is the action taken by the European Commission against joint gas sales through the Gas Negotiation Committee, on the grounds that it is in breach of the competition rules and the EEA Agreement: Reuters, 14 June 2001: 'EU/Competition: Warning to Norwegian Natural Gas Producers' on Harmonization (Gas).

[54] European Commission Report (see ch 2, para 2.107), 23 Nov 1999 (see n 42), at 9.

[55] ibid, 8.

In such circumstances, the European Commission concluded that the development of measures supplementary to the Directives was 'essential'.[56] It elected to proceed along a consensus-building route, supported by the application of competition law. However, this initial focus did not preclude the possibility that legislation might ultimately have to be introduced in the event of an impasse or to build on and codify the results of such consensus-building discussions on implementation of the Directives.

[56] European Commission, Communication to the Council and the European Parliament, 'Recent Progress with Building the Internal Electricity Market', COM (2000) 297 final, 16 May 2000, 11.

7

REGULATION BY CO-OPERATION—AND BY COMPETITION LAW

'Regulation by co-operation' has been a distinctive European characteristic, as opposed to 'regulation by litigation' practised in other continents.[1]

Jorge Vasconcelos

A. Introduction

7.01 The Electricity and Gas Directives have initiated a very different regulatory environment in the EU from the one that existed before their adoption. Their provisions have had far-reaching institutional consequences for the supervision of the electricity and gas sectors, leading to a proliferation of regulatory authorities in the Member States—and raising questions about the interaction between these new institutions and the EU authorities.

[1] 'The Rôle of Regulation in a Single Energy Market', delivered at conference on 'Launching a Common European Energy Market', Lisbon, 5–6 June 2001.

A complex and multi-layered regulatory framework is emerging for the EU energy sector at a time when the EU institutions are themselves in the throes of a debate on restructuring in anticipation of further enlargement. At the same time, the number of players in the energy marketplace has multiplied, to include not only new consumers and suppliers, but also energy traders and regional exchanges for spot and futures transactions. Mergers and takeovers have begun to alter the landscape of the electricity and gas industry, and convergence of the two industries has accelerated.

B. The Forum Concept: Progress by Voluntary Agreement

7.02 The transition to a fully operational IEM required close co-operation between the Member States, national regulators, industry (transporters, distributors, and producers), Community institutions, consumers, traders, and other interested parties. The Commission therefore developed the instrument of a Regulatory Forum as a means of harmonizing and co-ordinating the diverse liberalization strategies adopted by the Member States. As explained in Chapter 6 (paras 6.06–6.09), much work had still to be done to clarify and elaborate on the Directives' provisions. The Forum concept emerged as a response to this task. It has acted as a two-way channel of communication for the participants in deepening the IEM. However, if the Forum concept is evaluated as a new form of EU governance, aiming to meet those challenges, then early experience of its application has revealed its limitations. This chapter examines how the operation of this voluntary mechanism led to frustration at European Council level and eventually to the submission of new legislative proposals to bring forward the dates of full liberalization of the electricity and gas industries by the Commission at the Council's request. Alongside those developments EC competition law and policy were developed throughout this period and applied by the Commission to complement and support the IEM programme during the transition to a liberalized EU energy market. The principal steps taken, and their interface with the IEM programme are considered here.

7.03 A major concern behind the establishment of the Fora was the possibility that liberalization within the EU might lead to the creation of 15 liberalized, but largely separate, national markets in electricity and gas instead of an integrated EU energy market. Without some monitoring by the Commission, there was, and remains, a possibility that the Member States would take differing routes to the implementation of the Directives, raising the not unlikely possibility that companies would face inconsistent regulatory régimes which would in turn create obstacles to cross-border trade.

Many specific and often highly technical issues had to be addressed in order to make the Directives effective. If left entirely to the national authorities, the mixture of separate national solutions to these specific issues which would emerge—(eg rules for tarification and allocation of transmission capacity)—would undermine overall the goal of the creation of a level playing field in the EU. The Forum concept, with its wide-ranging participation and consensus approach to the development of common principles and rules, therefore appeared to present an ideal solution to the problem of harmonization in this context. It seemed to offer a form of 'regulation by co-operation'.

Legal status of the Fora

Each Forum has been accorded a status greater than that of a working group but has no law-making powers. It initiates and considers proposals made by participants on the basis of information provided on a voluntary basis. Information flow has been crucial since the movement towards an integrated market has given rise to new problems, many of which have a significant technical aspect, requiring both additional data and reflection to develop possible solutions. The widening range of participants in the successive meetings of the Fora illustrates how participation has been valued by the new national regulatory bodies and also by the associations of particular groups of market participants that have been formed. 7.04

C. 'Florence' Process and the Electricity Regulatory Forum

(1) Purpose

The Electricity Regulatory Forum (ERF) was initially convened by the European Commission to monitor and discuss implementation of the Electricity Directive. It met for the first time in autumn 1998 in Florence, Italy, and has been convened on a six-monthly basis since then. 7.05

The principal issues addressed in the meetings have been cross-border tarification, allocation of capacity, and congestion management. These discussions have been supplemented by the deliberations of a working group, which meets between the sessions of the Forum to elaborate the detail of the broad agreements reached in the Forum.[2] An important objective of the Forum was to encourage the formation of a Europe-wide association of TSOs to receive and channel views, proposals, and recommendations made in the Forum meetings. 7.06

[2] The first of the Working Groups met in Dec 1999, primarily charged with discussing ways of solving the cross-border tarification issue: European Commission, Minutes of the First Meeting of the Florence Working Group, 8 Dec 1999, ENER/A3/KO/KB D (99).

(2) Composition

7.07 The participants in what has become known as the 'Florence Process' comprise not only independent regulators from the Member States, government representatives of the Member States, the European Commission, and the EU Transmission System Operators' association (ETSO; see para 7.08), but also representatives of the European Parliament, the network users (Eurelectric), traders (EFET), consumers (IFIEC and CEFIC), and pools (Europex). The establishment of ETSO was an early result of the Florence Process itself and the association has played an important rôle in all of the meetings. The national regulators developed an association called the Council of European Energy Regulators (Ceer), which has also had an important voice in the initiation and co-ordination of proposals for change. Finally, the rôle of traders should be noted since they represent a new group of market players that are expected to grow in importance as liberalization takes hold.

(a) Creation of a European TSO Association (ETSO)

7.08 There were several reasons why the European Commission sought to have a single partner in its discussions with the TSOs. The independence of TSOs was a requirement of the Electricity Directive, and it made sense to establish an association to reflect their views. The Commission sought an independent body for four reasons:[3]

1. There was an expectation of increased cross-border trade in electricity in future. Work was required to facilitate this process to make such trade cost-reflective and efficient. This implied a close and long-term collaboration between the TSOs;
2. This work would require an exchange of confidential and commercial information, so the independence of the TSOs from other sectors of the electricity industry would have to be assured. Without independence, significant regulatory problems were likely;
3. No body existed that met this requirement (described at point 2), nor which was representative of all EU transmission systems, nor which possessed the infrastructure and resources necessary to carry out required functions, eg development of payment/settlement and flow-management systems; and
4. The TSOs have an obligation in the IEM to provide their services in a non-discriminatory manner to all customers. An association that is independent of any particular group of customers is an important element in ensuring this.

[3] European Commission, Steering Brief, Meeting of Transmission System Operators, 21 Jan 1999 (unpublished).

The TSOs established an association in 1999 in response to the European Commission's request for a single partner in its dialogue on cross-border electricity issues. Members of the European Transmission System Operators (ETSO) are: 7.09

- the Western European TSOs association
- UCTE
- NORDEL (Scandinavian grid operators), and
- British and Irish power grid owners.

The ETSO had as its first task the development of proposals for pricing of electricity transits across Europe, which include total transparency of transactions. Proposals were circulated by the newly-named European Transmission System Operators (ETSOs)[4] and by several of the national regulators in a joint document, *Transmission and Trade of Electricity in Europe*.

The formation of ETSO was an important step. In effect, it established a form of unbundling at the European level, by separating out the transmission system operators from companies involved in other activities in the electricity business. This was done irrespective of what happened at the national level. As a result, the Commission was able to conduct a dialogue about the rules on transmission and transmission services. ETSO could be relied on to draft the operational rules to implement the principles developed in the Forum. 7.10

(b) Council of European Energy Regulators (Ceer)

A further development in terms of articulating group interests within the Forum was the establishment of the Council of European Energy Regulators (Ceer) in March 2000. It comprises the national independent regulators with responsibility for electricity and/or natural gas. Initially, it had ten members, comprising the regulators of Belgium, Finland, Ireland, Italy, The Netherlands, Portugal, Spain, Sweden, and the UK. Among its stated objectives are: co-operation to achieve competitive European markets in electricity and gas; the provision of the necessary elements for the development of regulation in electricity and gas; the development of joint approaches with respect to transnational energy utilities and companies that operate in separated regulated utility markets; and the establishment of common policies among members[5] on important issues based on common regulatory principles. It provides a forum in which the national regulators can co-ordinate their work for the Florence and Madrid Processes. However, it should not be seen as a kind of supranational regulator. Regulatory policy in each Member State remains a matter for national regulators and their respective governments. 7.11

[4] International Exchanges of Electricity: Rules proposed by the European Transmission System Operators, 23 Mar 1999.

[5] Ceer, 'Practical Steps for Developing a Competitive European Gas Market', Oct 2000.

(c) Trading in electricity

7.12 The development of energy trading in Europe had long been considered a probable (and desirable) consequence of the liberalization process. In other liberalized markets, so-called 'hubs' had been set up to manage spot trading. Trading on power exchanges plays an important rôle in promoting price transparency where such exchanges operate as a secondary market in tandem with bilateral contracts. Exchanges were expected to develop on which electricity, and ultimately gas, could be bought and sold like any other commodity. Evidence of this was present in the Forum's composition.

(d) European Federation of Energy Traders (Efet)

7.13 As a counterpart to ETSO in the new and expanding area of electricity trading, a body was established in 1999 for electricity and gas traders called the European Federation of Energy Traders (Efet).[6] By 2001 it comprised 63 European electricity and natural gas traders from 15 countries. It has been involved in the consultation process started by the second harmonization report on electricity and also in the Florence and Madrid Regulators' Fora on Electricity and Gas. One of its objectives is the standardization in Europe of the contractual instruments for gas and power trading. Efet has a number of working groups and task forces to target specific issues important to its members.

(e) Europex and Neta

7.14 Separately, a body was set up to co-ordinate the interests of power exchanges, called Europex. Since the Directive had entered into force, power exchanges have been established in Amsterdam, Frankfurt, Leipzig, and Madrid. In France and Italy preparation for the establishment of power exchanges is at an advanced stage. In both the United Kingdom and the Nordic countries, electricity has been traded for several years on power exchanges or as part of pool arrangements. In the United Kingdom a system has been established called the New Electricity Trading Arrangement (Neta), in which electricity is traded largely on the basis of bilateral contracts, and generators receive the contract price (established by reference to quoted prices available online) instead of the cleared pool price.[7]

(3) **Agenda**

7.15 Transmission pricing was placed at the top of the Forum's agenda. The first meetings involved some data-gathering about systems already in operation within the Member

[6] Further details may be found at its website: www.efet.org

[7] See generally, Macatangay, Rafael E A, 'Market Definition and Dominant Position Abuse under the New Electricity Trading Arrangements in England and Wales', (2001) 29 Energy Policy 337.

States and inside the EU generally, as well as those applicable to cross-border trading. Further down the agenda were issues of congestion management, ways of regulating the TSOs, stranded costs, and the interaction between EU competition policy and national regulatory competences. Many of these issues had been addressed in the Commission's second harmonization report (see ch 6, paras 6.53–6.54).

The greatest challenge for the Forum was to provide for cross-border tarification. **7.16**
To improve knowledge of the different solutions available for tarification, the Commission commissioned research. That independent report,[8] carried out by the University of Aachen (Germany), was influential on the Commission's initial reflections on these issues. Its results were presented at the third meeting of the Electricity Regulatory Forum.[9]

(a) Aachen Report

The report identified two principal types of issues that network operators and users **7.17**
(including traders) would have to deal with: (1) network pricing and (2) congestion management. In the EU context, the latter might be a short-term, unexpected form of constraint on transmission following high demand or an 'outage'. It could also be caused by transmission capacity being too low for the transmission demand in the market. The authors of the report examined these issues in relation to two distinct approaches: a transaction-based approach and a non-transaction-based approach. With respect to transmission pricing, they recommended a non-transaction-based approach consisting of input tariffs for generators and output tariffs for consumers. The formula chosen should be one that reflects real costs, and should be both transparent and non-discriminatory. They also recommended that there should be remuneration for the TSOs that carry transits and loop-flows. This compensation should be based on physical flows and would preferably be paid to the TSOs themselves (inter-TSO payments). These payments could be passed on to the network users by various methods: implicitly as a contribution to input and output tariffs, or by introducing additional cross-border transmission charges, following the postage-stamp system, with charges related to volume, not distance. Only in exceptional circumstances should there be transaction-based surcharges and discounts.

(i) Transaction-based approach The transaction-based approach would deliver the following results. With congestion management, contractors would be required to provide network operators with information (as detailed as possible) on the source and destination of electricity. With network pricing, prices are built on each transaction, with the source and sink required in order to be able

[8] 'Cross-Border Electricity Transmission Tariffs', study carried out by Prof Dr-Ing Hans-Jürgen Haubrich, Dr-Ing Wolfgang Fritz and Dipl-Ing Hendrik Vennegeerts, Aachen University in 1999. The report is available online at http://europa.eu.int/comm/energy/en/single_market/florence/index_en.html

[9] Minutes of the 3rd Meeting of the European ERF, Florence, 20–1 May 1999; this was the first meeting held after the end of the implementation period under the Directive.

to calculate a transportation charge. The report suggested that a transaction-based approach to congestion management would allow TSOs (which usually have responsibility for evaluating and predicting congestions on transmission lines) to detect potential congestion and to refuse transactions that create congestion. However, they also concluded that the price of such a method would be a large data demand on network operators and users, with attendant uncertainty about the independence of TSOs. The method therefore made it difficult for market operators to take speedy decisions.

(ii) **Non-transaction-based approach** The alternative, the non-transaction-based approach, would deliver contrasting, and more attractive, results. Congestion management would be managed by the TSOs on the basis of aggregated load forecasts provided by the TSOs and generation patterns submitted by the generators. The TSOs would not take into account the commercial relationship between the parties. In the event of 'imminent congestion', a series of non-transaction-based countermeasures could be adopted. Network pricing, on this approach, would depend only on the location of an electricity source or a load, with no link being made between the two. This approach was, in the view of the report's authors, one that 'clearly emphasises the interests of market players'. On the other hand, it had the disadvantage that it would then be difficult to establish incentives to network users to avoid contributing to network congestion. With network pricing, however, the approach had advantages in terms of non-discrimination and the promotion of competition.

7.18 (iii) **Segmented markets** The report also examined conflicts that could arise from the operation by Member States of different types of access régimes. This scenario would arise if segmented markets were allowed to develop. The conflicts it envisaged included a lack of homogeneity in market development. There could also be negative effects on the political objective of establishing a proper internal market in electricity.

The report's conclusion was similar to that reached by the Commission in its second report on harmonization requirements, expressing a clear preference for a non-transaction based solution for tarification. Under this approach, fees should be shared among the TSOs according to the real physical network usage.

(b) Debate

7.19 The Aachen Report constituted an intervention in a debate on network pricing that had already begun. Alternative proposals were already in existence from the European TSOs, the British Electricity Association, the Swedish Electricity industry, and Swiss TSOs.[10] In addition, several national regulators had themselves begun to develop alternative proposals to solving this problem.

10 Section 5 of the Aachen study and citations there.

(i) TSOs The European TSOs had, after lengthy discussions, developed draft rules on international transmission access and pricing and circulated them for comment.[11] They argued that the system of international transmission pricing had to accommodate different pricing models within the Member States, both point-of-connection (entry–exit) in orientation and transaction-oriented. By 'transaction' they used a wide definition that could include aggregation of the net values of all transactions between countries or areas. This was intended to be a compromise between the advantages of a secure system of notification and pricing of all individual transactions at one extreme, and the advantages of unencumbered power trading—or not having to notify and price any transactions—at the other. **7.20**

This proposal by ETSO placed an emphasis on cost-reflexivity and maximization of space for subsidiary solutions. A Cost Component Method of network pricing was proposed, with three components, reflecting: **7.21**

1. network costs exclusively caused by local access of generators to the grid (G),
2. costs caused by local access to consumers (L), and
3. costs of allowing transport to/from the border and through transit countries (T), which could be direction- and distance-dependent.

The 'T' component could be related to individual transactions or to physical flows resulting from the sum of all transactions. This is a matter left to the operation of subsidiarity. In the terms of the Aachen study, there is a co-existence between transaction-based and non-transaction based pricing models. Charges for a specific transaction comprise the 'G' and 'L' components in the source and sink area, plus the 'T' components of all TSOs with networks affected physically by the transaction. Each is to be multiplied by a participation factor that reflects the proportion of power flowing through the respective network. Under this approach, few details would be provided of the TSOs' participation factors.

A disadvantage of this approach is that individual calculation of these factors per transaction would be time-consuming and would hinder the pre-calculation of charges. However, some charges below a threshold should not be imposed. Adding the 'T' components of the TSOs affected by the transaction would also result in an element of 'pancaking'. For the rest, much of the ETSO proposal addresses the technical implementation of open access, where the authors emphasize again the operation of the principle of subsidiarity.

[11] Working Group of European TSO Associations and Eurelectric, International Exchanges of Electricity: rules proposed by the European transmission system operators, 23 Mar 1999 (there were several drafts of this document).

The result of these proposals is that whatever the mechanisms for allocating capacity and setting the tariff, all third-party transactions would have to be notified to the TSOs *ex ante*. In other words, notification would be required in advance of purchase or sale of electricity for:

- precise transmission conditions (depending on subsidiarity);
- precise pricing (which may vary according to the transit country and proposed routing, contract or flow path); and
- clearing or sanctioning of the transaction to make sure it does not cause congestion.

7.22 (ii) **Regulators** Several of the regulators contributed to the debate by drawing up a paper aimed at making constructive comments on the proposal by the TSOs.[12] Its main objective was 'to contribute to better regulation of cross-border trading within the EU Internal Electricity Market, and also with agents from non-EU states that are strongly interconnected with the IEM electrical networks'. The regulators expressed a strong concern about the absence of a formally constituted association of TSOs and about the lack of complete independence of each of the TSOs.

7.23 On a number of matters the regulators were in agreement with the TSOs' proposal. They agreed as follows that:

- Implementation of cross-border trading rules must avoid the creation of barriers to trade that are not economically justified. Pancaking of transmission charges must therefore be avoided.
- Regulatory charges such as stranded costs and other charges deriving from PSOs should not be imposed in ways that set up barriers to international trade in electricity.
- Physical flows should be used in identifying and eliminating constraint violations.
- The cost-component approach to transmission pricing allows Member States to include long-term signals associated to specific network requirements that are—either partly or completely—required by international transits.
- Common guidelines for information availability and co-ordination procedures are necessary.
- Co-ordination and harmonization is recommended for those congestion management procedures that might confer some rights in the short-term markets.
- Transparency in procedures and data used in all Member States is necessary.

[12] 'Transmission and Trade of Electricity in Europe: Position Paper on Recent Developments in the Proposal of Rules', 5 Mar 1999. The authors were the offices of the Italian, Portuguese, and Spanish regulators: *Autorita per l'energia elettrica e il gas* (Italy); *Entidade Reguladora do Sector Electrico* (Portugal) and *Comision Nacional del Sistema Electrico* (Spain).

- Complete independence of the TSOs is a prerequisite for a successful internal market in electricity.
- In their treatment of the different agents, objectivity, transparency. and non-discrimination are 'critical requirements' for the implementation of cross-border trading.

Nonetheless, the regulators had a number of concerns with the TSOs' proposals. **7.24**

1. *Subsidiarity*: There was vagueness on certain matters relating to the extent that subsidiarity at national level is used, raising the possibility of misinterpretation or abuse. In particular, they were concerned that implementation of the rules may prove unnecessarily complex, leading to a loss of transparency and barriers to trade, and potentially also to excessive proportions of the total transmission costs being charged through transit fees, unless steps were taken to clearly specify what the legitimate cost components are.
2. Negotiated transmission access might lead to a non-transparent process of setting the tariffs and managing constraints.
3. Denials of network access could also lead to abuse. These should only be used as a temporary measure and with sufficient transparency to permit verification that discrimination does not exist.

There were other areas in which the regulators had concerns. **7.25**

1. *Independence*: Although the proposals emphasized the need for independence of each TSO, such independence could only be achieved by corporate unbundling and by the separation of ownership from generation or supply interests. The association of TSOs should therefore consist only of independent TSOs without the participation of other market agents.
2. *Confidentiality*: There should not be an over-emphasis of the need for confidentiality. This should be kept to a minimum to promote transparency in international trade.
3. *ATC (available transmission capacity)*: The allocation of ATCs to market agents should be done by short-term market mechanisms, instead of giving priority to long-term bilateral contracts. A complete ban on the reservation of ATCs may discourage international trade by increasing risk.
4. *Transitional arrangements*: in the transition period Member States might be permitted to reserve a maximum percentage of their interconnection capacity for contracts with priority rights.
5. *New investment:* Lack of harmonization among network users subject to charges would affect the decisions of new network users regarding location and investment.
6. *Diverging Technical Assumptions*: different definitions of the transmission network will lead to different values of connection charges and efficiency distortions.

(c) Consensus on principles for regulation of cross-border trade

7.26 By the time of the Fourth Electricity Regulatory Forum,[13] the TSOs had accepted a number of key points making a consensus possible, at least in general terms. They agreed that electricity trade should be non-transaction based, should be established on the basis of the postage-stamp system, and that only the modest physical costs actually incurred and related to cross-border trade should be allocated to and carried by those actually causing these costs.

However, the Commission and national regulators, on their part, recognized that 'the existence of cross-border transactions (CBTs) may cause individual power systems to incur some extra costs, and this fact justifies that some additional network charges could be recognized due to the existence of CBTs.'[14] Essentially, CBTs can create extra costs in the form of extra losses and congestions, and may be a reason for additional network investment. These additional costs should not be borne by the TSOs that incur them but rather by the TSOs that cause them.

(d) Inter-TSO payments

7.27 The next challenge was to develop a system for inter-TSO payments. The guiding principle behind the calculation of network costs was to be that each TSO's network costs would be recovered mainly through the 'G' and 'L' charges (see para 7.21) imposed on local network users.[15] These charges would provide access to the entire interconnected EU network and would be independent of the commercial transactions that the network users may engage in. The net credit or charge for each TSO that results from inter-TSO payments would be used to modify the revenue level from which the G and L charges of that TSO are derived, but how the individual G's and L's would be affected was to be left to the principle of subsidiarity.[16]

7.28 The specific details of calculations of CBT costs were to be finalized at working group level, based on an approach which looked at a factor of the level of losses and a component that would take into account the relevant and necessary investment to be incurred in each transmission system network due to international trade. An informal working group was established to meet regularly in the following months to develop practical rules on this approach. It was set up to achieve specific objectives, not as a permanent support mechanism to the Florence Process. It was to be composed of the Commission, national regulators, Member States, and ETSO. In the event, it held four meetings only in 1999 and 2000.

[13] Held at Florence, 25–6 Nov 1999.

[14] Minutes of the Meeting, 4th Forum, 'Towards EU Cross-Border Electricity Trade: Regulatory Remarks and Guidelines on Tariffs and Congestion (text as amended after 1st Florence Working Group of 8 Dec 1999)', para (10).

[15] ibid, para (9).

[16] ibid, para (11).

(e) Tarification formula for cross-border trade

In March 2000 the TSOs agreed in principle on a new Europe-wide formula for the calculation of cross-border tariffs to enter into force in the autumn 2000 for a test period of 11 months. The tarification formula for cross-border trade would be developed further in meetings of a working group.[17] The agreement was based on the principles of transparency, simplicity, cost-reflectiveness, and non-discrimination. It contained three principal elements: 7.29

1) TSOs would compensate each other for costs incurred through hosting transit flows of electricity on their networks;
2) the compensation fund would be £200 million for a provisional one-year period from 1 Oct 2000–30 Aug 2001 (this figure was proposed by ETSO on the basis of information provided by the national TSOs);
3) a mechanism had been developed that was applicable for a transition period of one year from 1 Oct 2000 in the UCTE countries area of the EU, taking account of the situation in Denmark and the neighbouring Centrel area. It would then be applied in a modified form one year later. It provides for compensation payments for transit flows to be collected and shared among TSOs.

The mechanism in point (3) above would be developed on the basis of the following considerations:

- it had to be based on physical flows of electricity, not on the distance between two contracting parties;
- where countries export significant net quantities of electricity, they cause physical flows and transits. These transit flows create costs in the countries hosting them. 'Host' countries should be compensated for the costs caused to their networks by the TSO responsible for them; and
- these compensations should be effected through payments made between TSOs.

(f) Compensation payments

An issue in the proposal that was to be left to subsidiarity was the way in which the TSOs would reflect the result of the compensations paid and received in their national tariff system. During the provisional one-year period this matter would be left to the discretion of the Member States. The Commission would monitor the overall co-ordination and control of the national mechanisms to ensure that the potentially different approaches at the Member State level would not result in an unreasonable distortion of the internal electricity market. In practice, France would pay most of the total compensation amount, as the largest exporter of power in the EU. Major transit countries such as Germany, Austria, and

[17] Conclusions of the 5th Meeting of the European ERF, Florence 30–1 Mar 2000.

Switzerland would receive most of the benefits. However, this provisional system did not become operative as planned due to concerns that its operation would result in unreasonable distortion of the market. The Commission noted that Member States could be divided into two groups in their approach to compensation payments: the first group would introduce an export charge; while a second would opt for a system of repartition of costs imposed on all users of the network.

The level of the export charge in the case of (1) would in some cases lead to considerably higher transaction costs than under existing national tariff systems, and in general the agreed provisional system(see above) would, if introduced in such a context, lead to a high degree of discrimination between operators and to distortions of trade.

(g) Pricing

The ETSO pricing proposals involved the separation of the pricing procedure into two stages to permit continuity and simplicity for generators and consumers, while allowing the TSOs to recover relevant costs. TSOs would identify those costs specifically related to cross-border transmission which would be translated into postage-stamp charges. These would be imposed on local network users allowing access to the complete interconnected EU network. If a TSO incurs costs additional to the income generated by these charges, it would be compensated by means of an *ex post* settlement system between the TSOs.

(h) Next steps

7.30 By autumn 2000 it had become clear that the above agreement would not be implemented as planned. German, French, and Belgian TSOs were insisting on a transaction component in cross-border tarification which if adopted would have had the effect of removing the financial incentive to trade. In effect, the Florence Process had reached an impasse.

7.31 Additionally, more work was required to harmonize, where necessary, national tarification systems for cross-border transactions, including the separation between charges on G (generation) and L (load or consumption) applied in order to achieve a level playing-field for cross-border transactions. After the Commission's proposal for a regulation on cross-border electricity trade, the Florence Process resumed in May 2001. The provisional charging mechanism that had failed to gain consensus support was not on the agenda. Instead the principles that would guide a 'definitive' mechanism were circulated by the Ceer. Other issues discussed included allocation of interconnector capacity and congestion management, where the Commission's preferred approach has been 'market splitting', a market-based solution, favoured by the Nordic countries but difficult to apply to the very different conditions that prevailed in the rest of Europe, where auctioning of capacity was more likely to succeed. Meanwhile, waiting in the wings were Commission proposals for further legislation in the shape of a new EU Regulation (see para 7.59 and ch 8, paras 8.15–8.27).

Agreement slowly emerged. By mid-2001 the only TSOs in the EU that opposed the Florence agreement were German ones.[18] The outstanding issue for the German TSOs turned on the fact that the flow of electricity between grids generated costs that had to be recovered by the networks incurring them. They felt that the countries generating such costs should pay for them. The regulators were mostly in agreement with them on the need to 'socialise' the costs of transit (ie, to spread them across all users), thereby reducing individual costs and promoting exchanges. As a result, the network charges would be similar whether the power transmission was for local consumption or for export. 7.32

In November the Commission approved a proposal by ETSO[19] for a transitional scheme, which would involve an export charge of one euro per MWh for electricity crossing in transit via the continental transmission system. This approval was subject to several conditions: that the system be introduced for a transition period of one year; that it replace the current one completely, abolishing all import and transit tariffs and so avoiding pancaking of rates or the imposition of transit charges; that there should be reciprocity; and that the payments made to TSOs as compensation for higher volumes of traffic from transit operations should not be allowed to lead to windfall profits but rather should lead to reduced charges.[20]

Guidelines for congestion management A second issue discussed at the Florence Forum was the management of congestion, a matter likely to become more pressing as electricity import and export increase. Congestion on interconnecting lines (defined in Art 2(10) of the Electricity Directive: *see* Appendix 1) was identified as an issue of particular importance. TSOs have to be kept informed by the market players about their transactions in order to predict the usage of the network. They are obliged to counteract and pay initially for measures to avoid congestions. However, private purchasing contracts are not always notified to the TSOs and so prediction of flows becomes difficult. Cross-border congestion management is even more difficult because different TSOs must co-operate, and indeed co-operate more often. Requests for transmission capacities can lead to congestion and even system failure.

An example of this occurred in Belgium on 14 July 1999 where the Belgian TSO had to take crisis measures due to very high flows on its system surpassing those predicted for that day.[21] For several hours power levels reached five times the

[18] 'ETSO Proposal for a Temporary CBT Mechanism', 3 Sep 2001.

[19] 'Commission Backs ETSO Transit Charges Plan', Europe Energy No 592, 23 Nov 2001.

[20] ibid.

[21] European Commission, 'Communication on Completing the Internal Energy Market, Annex IX: Security of Supply', March 2000.

planned day levels and breached safety requirements. The TSO was unaware of the origin of the flows and was obliged to curtail legitimately scheduled transmission.

Even a country with above-average interconnection capacity like The Netherlands can experience significant transmission constraints and problems with respect to capacity allocation.[22]

By the end of 1999 the Forum had agreed that the issue should be treated with the same urgency as the cross-border tarification issue. The first step it took was to issue a set of common guidelines on the basis of a Community-wide approach to the allocation of interconnector capacity. The Guidelines[23] require TSOs to develop market-based methods to deal with congestion management. These are mainly auctions and market splitting.

While there is experience of auctioning cross-border capacity within the EU, the schemes have yet to be made compliant with the Florence Guidelines. A possible future requirement may be to co-ordinate within the EU the timing of auctions to avoid discrimination between users in different locations. The allocation, trading, and settlement procedures in the Guidelines may also require harmonization by the Commission to ensure that the regulators and the TSOs work effectively.

Some TSOs have a keener interest in resolving these problems than others. Congestion is acute in the interconnectors linking Germany and Denmark, The Netherlands and Germany, The Netherlands and Denmark, Spain and France, France and Italy, and Italy and Austria. But the European significance of the issue is clear. Without co-ordination, the development of solutions by Member States is unlikely to lead to satisfactory congestion management, which requires a 'high degree of co-operation and standardization across borders'.[24]

The European Commission's Competition Directorate also played a rôle in the Forum discussion of this issue, submitting several papers on legal aspects.[25]

---

[22] EFET Press Release, 'Experiences from the Dutch Market Place: Lessons Learned in Winter 1999–2000, 11 Sep 2000.

[23] Congestion Management Guidelines, in 'Conclusions to the Florence Forum', Nov 2000.

[24] ETSO, 'Key Concepts and Definitions for Transmission Access Products', Apr 2001, para 63. See also Eurelectric Position Paper on Congestion Management, Nov 2000. Not all congestion problems had such wide significance, only the structural, long-term congestion identified by the Aachen study (see para 7.17).

[25] eg, 'Allocation of Interconnection Capacity on the Internal Electricity Market: Towards a Community Framework', March 2000; 'Compatibility of Long-Term Electricity Transmission Capacity Reservations with EC Competition Law', Nov 2000. For a Regulator's view see the paper submitted to the Forum by the Dutch DTe, 'Transport Capacity on International Electricity Networks'.

Between 40 and 60 per cent of the transmission capacity is reserved for long-term import contracts made by former monopolists before market opening became effective.[26] The Directorate noted the need to ensure that the reservation element was compatible with the competition rules, given the potential of these contracts to foreclose access by importers to the electricity supply market of the importing country. Such capacity reservation agreements are subject to competition law and could be contrary to Article 81 if they had as their object or effect the restriction of competition; or to Article 82 if the priority right granted to the other party by the TSO constitutes abuse of a dominant position. Dominant incumbents as well as new entrants are often allowed to compete for the remaining free capacities. These capacities are often held in addition to the capacities already held by them through the long-term agreements. An aim of the Forum was to identify ways of making this free capacity known in advance to interested importers, and then making it available by methods such as auctioning.[27]

(4) Assessment

The Florence Process has yielded various results to date but breakthroughs have proved difficult in the face of opposition from some incumbents. The exact rôle of the Commission in this has been hard to define exactly. The key issue has been the development of a single tariff for cross-border deals. There is much industry agreement on the technical and financial issues but a strong case could be made for enhancing the Commission's powers in regulating such matters (see ch 8, paras 8.17–8.32). Technical co-ordination may in future be codified and transmission tariff components harmonized in a new Directive. **7.33**

(a) Successes

The Florence Process had by 2001 demonstrated that it had both advantages as well as a number of limitations in its contribution to the completion of an internal market in electricity. The voluntary nature of the process has been beneficial in allowing the development of a common understanding of the principal issues involved in cross-border trade, as well as a large measure of consensus about possible solutions. It has also become a useful framework for sharing regulators' experiences in market liberalization and for the participation of new market **7.34**

[26] European Commission, 'Rôle of Interconnectors in the Electricity Market: A Competition Perspective', MEMO/01/76, 12 Mar 2001.

[27] ETSO submitted various papers to the Forum on this topic in April 2001: 'Co-ordinated Auctioning: a Market-Based Method for Transmission Capacity Allocation in Meshed Networks'; 'Co-ordinated Use of Power Exchanges for Congestion Management' and at an earlier meeting of the Forum, 'Evaluation of Congestion Management Methods for Cross-Border Transmission', Nov 2000: all available via www.etso-net.org. Separately, the Commission initiated studies by Aachen University (analysis of electricity network capacities and identification of congestion) and the Energiewirtschafts Institut of the University of Cologne.

entrants such as traders. The question arises as to whether the Forum can play a more tangible rôle in the decision-making processes.

Although the Commission's proposal of March 2001 for amended Directives and a Regulation on Cross-Border Trade (see Appendices 1 to 3) may be interpreted as a sign of failure of the Forum Process, the specifics of that Regulation still need to be developed since, at the date of publication, they lacked the necessary degree of implementing detail. The Forum may prove of value in providing new proposals for rules that the proposed Directive and Regulation may incorporate.

The Florence Forum has proved instrumental in providing guidance to the Commission on the application of specific provisions where they have been required and on the development of solutions for problems as they emerged from the implementation process. It has also provided a focal point for pressure from the Commission which wants to encourage participants to adopt the *spirit* of the Directive as well as its (sometimes obscure) letter, and in this way to go beyond the time-table established by its provisions.

On specific issues, the Forum allowed a challenge to the legitimacy of imposing transaction-based fees on import and export, as well as on transit—the latter largely disappearing as a result. It acted as a vehicle for work on the establishment of a compensation fund for the TSOs to compensate each other for disproportionate transits. It also provided a focus for dealing with the problems of congestion management and transparency of available transmission capacity that hindered access for eligible consumers. In this respect, it discredited the traditional method used by TSOs for allocating capacity at borders, the 'first-come, first-served' method. The auctioning of capacity has been a result of this. Even if national regulators would have acted on these issues in any case, the Forum helped to bring them into focus and accelerate action.

(b) Failures

7.35 Evidence of failure was evident in the discussions on cross-border tarification in 2000 that led to an impasse.

In particular the Florence Forum suffered from four specific shortcomings:

1. in-depth discussion of highly detailed issues was limited by the informal character of the process, based on bi-annual meetings lasting 2 days;
2. the consensus requirement made it difficult to make progress on controversial issues;
3. the absence of enforcement procedures meant that any decisions reached could be implemented only to the extent that all parties respected them; and
4. certain issues such as the calculation of the correct level of inter-TSO payments necessitated regular detailed decisions, which the Forum process was unable to accommodate.

These experiences have therefore been a source of positive and negative lessons for the Commission's strategy in implementing the Gas Directive. However, a different kind of influence on the Directive resulted from a consensus that had emerged by mid-2000 that the Electricity Directive was not leading to a sufficiently rapid pace of change in the promotion of competition. The European Council had therefore asked the Commission to forward new proposals to accelerate integration in the electricity and gas markets. 7.36

D. 'Madrid' Process and the Gas Regulatory Forum

Taking the ERF as a model, the Commission established a Gas Regulatory Forum (GRF) to assist in the detailed implementation of the Gas Directive. At the initiative of the Commission, the various national regulatory bodies responsible for the gas sector now meet twice-yearly in Madrid.[28] 7.37

(1) Purpose

The broad aim of the Madrid Process is to encourage a greater convergence of views, regulatory practices, and actions among participants as the liberalization process gains momentum. However, the specific objectives of the GRF have perhaps been harder to define than for the ERF. To begin with, the requirements of the Gas Directive are slightly different and less stringent in terms of liberalization requirements. For example, they impose different requirements with respect to unbundling of TSOs. Basing itself on the experience with ETSO, the Commission sought to encourage a separation of transmission operation from other services and to establish a gas transmission system operators association. In addition, the external dimension of EU gas—its dependence on non-EU suppliers for a significant proportion of gas—created a number of complications that were absent in the electricity sector. However, despite these considerations, there has been a strong pressure from virtually all parties involved to treat the two sectors in parallel for liberalization purposes. 7.38

(2) Composition

The participants in the GRF are similar to those in the ERF, and include representatives designated by Member State governments as having regulatory authority over the gas sector; the European Commission; representatives of the Presidency; Member State government agents; the European Parliament; and representatives from all sections of the gas industry and consumer associations. The 7.39

[28] See '4th Meeting of the Madrid Forum, 2–3 July 2001: Conclusions, Documents and Presentations', at www.europa.eu.int/comm/energy/en/gas_single_market/madrid3/madrid4.html

EEA is also represented. The Ceer has played a rôle of growing importance in its activities.

Gas Transmission Operators Group (GTE)

7.40 At the request of the European Commission the gas transmission operators established a group within Eurogas in mid-2000 to address issues on the internal gas market and also, initially, cross-border transmission. At the second meeting of the GRF the Commission had called for the creation of a new body that would bring together representatives of all those responsible for the operation of the gas transmission networks of the EU.[29] This body was to have:

> . . . the necessary degree of functional independence from or within other representative bodies to ensure that it is able to address issues concerning transmission, whilst ensuring the full respect of the provisions regarding non-discrimination and the protection of commercial information contained in the Gas Directive.[30]

7.41 The GTE (Gas Transmission Group: Eurogas) is the counterpart to the ETSO grouping in the electricity sector. It is the focal point for EC and GRF analyses of network barriers that hinder efficient cross-border flows and access to systems. The GTE has quickly become independent from Eurogas in its activities, except in its administration.

7.42 **Organization** The GTE meets in plenary session to reach decisions by way of consensus. Its inaugural meeting was held on 19 July 2000. By the end of 2001 it was developing a comprehensive set of statutes concerning its objectives, membership, and procedures for decision-making. It will be open to cross-border international pipeline companies analogous to US inter-state gas pipeline companies.

7.43 Up to five members will be allowed to join from each country, as well as a national association if one exists. Ad hoc expert groups prepare specific technical reports.

7.44 The Commission has been keen to encourage a functional separation of GTE members from those with trading interests. To assist in this aim, Eurogas has been developing a non-binding Code of Conduct between its members to ensure minimum common levels of unbundling going beyond the Gas Directive requirements.[31] Eurogas has also set up an internal group of network users, with the aim of ensuring that the views of significant customers of GTE are represented and to study issues of network access.[32]

[29] Conclusions of the 2nd Meeting of the European GRF, Madrid, 11–12 May 2000, para (2).
[30] ibid.
[31] Conclusions of the 3rd Meeting of the European GRF, 26–7 Oct 2000, point 6; Conclusions of the 4th Meeting of the European GRF (n 28 above), point 19.
[32] ibid, point 20.

(3) Issues

The first meeting of the Forum was in the autumn of 1999. Three issues emerged from the discussions.[33] 7.45

1. The Commission understood that efforts must be made to avoid clashes between the rules in the Gas Directive and primary legislation based on Treaty provisions, especially the competition provisions in Articles 81 and 82.* In practice, the primary legislation will override contradictory provisions in the Directive in the event of dispute national courts can apply such law as it has direct effect (see ch 2, paras 2.80–2.81). For example, there was some concern over the risk of conflict between provisions in the Directive on the one hand and of Treaty provisions on the other, should a company faced with a refusal of access decide to take action against an incumbent gas company. This kind of conflict is more likely to arise at national level in the first instance. The possibility of inconsistent decisions based on the competition law was noted.

2. The limits of the Gas Directive text were apparent to all parties. Even when fully transposed into national law it could function only as a starting point. The text contains loopholes: horizontal integration between energy utilities (or its impact in transforming the market structure) is not addressed, and, above all, cross-border trade in gas is scarcely mentioned—despite the fact that the kind of tarification issues that have arisen in the electricity sector will inevitably also arise in cross-border gas trade. 7.46

3. The extensive participation of government bodies and key associations from virtually all the Member States showed a real willingness on all sides to engage in debate on the issues. The Forum concept was by this time well-known, given the experience with the Florence Forum (which by then had met four times). 7.47

(4) Agenda

The agenda was organized around five main issues covering key aspects of the regulation of the internal gas market: 7.48

1. organization of access
2. access to the system, including conditions and pricing principles, the relationship between Member States, and EU regulation and competition policy
3. storage (under which conditions may access to storage be considered necessary for an efficient access to the network?)
4. harmonization, and
5. security of supply.

[33] Conclusions of the First GRF, 30 Sept–1 Oct 1999.

Again, a major concern was how to avoid the development of 15 separate liberalized markets rather than a single market in gas. Consumer groups emphasized the risks flowing from the principle of subsidiarity, as well as the need for harmonization. Inevitably, the high degree of cross-border trade in the EU gas business was noted by incumbent gas companies—more than 50 per cent of all gas trade is cross-border—but this is in practice the result of commercial co-operation between the incumbents. Such transactions can be seen as instances of companies helping each other to protect their domestic monopolies rather than instances of real trade.

7.49 The session on organization of access raised a number of complex issues such as whether the Directive gave incumbents any incentive to promote competition; whether regulation of conduct was likely to be effective instead of structural regulation; whether negotiated or regulated TPA was likely to be more effective; and how changes in the structure of the energy market might affect the operation of the Directive (mergers in the electricity sector leading to 5 dominant players and a convergence between gas and electricity making the aim of a competitive market hard to realize).

Some saw the potential outcome of all this as a growth in regulation by detail, so there would be a related need for co-ordination with the competition authorities at national and EC level. The very limited attempt by the Directive to tackle structural issues (restricted to modest provisions on unbundling), was felt likely to lead regulators to become ever more active. They could, it was thought, find themselves 'pushing water uphill'. However, the point was also made that too much weight should not be given to the differences in applying the Gas and Electricity Directives with respect to access and unbundling: nTPA being favoured more in the gas sector and rTPA more in electricity, and a more limited form of unbundling in gas. The convergence factor and the need for transfer pricing were likely to limit the significance of these differences.

7.50 On the subject of access conditions and pipelines, several national presentations were given, setting out experiences in The Netherlands, the United Kingdom, and Spain. However interesting the papers were, they conveyed a national orientation to the Directive's implementation and underscored a concern of some parties that there would be a compartmentalization of experiences. The problem at this stage was that there was little available by way of models to guide countries seeking to define key terms in the Directive such as the 'main commercial conditions' (see ch 4, paras 4.83–4.85).

(a) GRF and competition law

7.51 The interaction between the GRF process and the work of the Competition Directorate was evident. In a presentation to the Forum, the Directorate stated that with respect to the gas industry it would focus its efforts on cases leading to foreclosure of national markets and on monitoring access to cross-border pipelines: that is, cases dealing with either long-term capacity reservations on interconnecting lines or refusal of access requests from customers qualified as eligible under the Directive. With respect to the related issue of how much access should cost, the guiding rule would be that a transmission company should not charge transmission prices to third parties higher than those charged to related companies or business units. Access to scarce capacity was also identified as an important issue. In the event of congestion, such capacity had to be allocated in an objective and transparent manner.

Given the limited resources of the Directorate, it would need to focus on those cases where it could provide 'added value' to the mainstream efforts to establish an IEM. In dealing with any of the above issues, therefore, the Directorate proposed to focus on cases that have a particular Community interest and raise a new legal problem or prevent market access to operators located in other Member States. It would leave to the national authorities issues where sector-specific regulation provided more detailed rules or went beyond the requirements of competition law. Close co-operation between national authorities and the Commission was expected, with national authorities invited to consult with the Commission on cases where EC Competition rules may apply ('in order to avoid contradicting decisions and to ensure consistent application of the legislation, a close co-operation between Commission and national authorities is indispensable').[34]

(b) Storage

The GRF session on storage emphasized the changing rôle of its utilization in liberalized markets. Experience shows that the use of storage increases with liberalization, as occurred in the United Kingdom, for example. Currently, the design of storage facilities in the EU is not suitable to a single market. Many differences exist between the Member States but flexibility in access to storage facilities is crucial for TPA to be successful. If an eligible customer as a new player has no access to storage facilities, should it be made available to it? The example of the United Kingdom's auctioning of capacity was mentioned and so was the idea that the storage facility operator 'use it or lose it'. A presentation by BG Storage raised the issue that optimal use of storage facilities may be limited because of technical configurations. This could occur if the demand placed on them differed significantly from the demand they were designed to meet. In the United Kingdom adaptations seem to have been made to deal with this technical consideration. A separate issue concerned the purpose of the storage facility in relation to possible access. In some countries this seems likely to become a sensitive policy issue. In the view of some Forum participants, the purpose of a facility must be considered alongside a **7.52**

[34] A Tradacete (Competition Directorate), presentation at the First GRF, 30 Sept 1999.

possible request for access, with the French government delegate noting the importance of strategic storage.

(c) Cross-Border Trade

7.53 At the second meeting of the GRF in May 2000 the discussion focused sharply on cross-border trade in gas and related issues. A study on cross-border tarification was commissioned by the Commission. The consultants' report which was presented and discussed[35] provided several recommendations for the elements of a third-party access régime covering a wide range of issues including required services; pricing of services; balancing, storage and trading; security of supply take-or-pay contracts and public service obligations; and harmonization. In effect, it encouraged a re-interpretation of some key provisions in the Gas Directive to promote the integration process.

Non-discriminatory access to pipeline networks was a major feature of the Forum discussion, stimulated by the views in the consultants' report. The Forum participants recommended that a new body be established by the European gas industry as quickly as possible to address this and other issues of concern. This body would mirror the recently-established electricity transmission system operators association (ETSO).

7.54 In its conclusions,[36] the GRF invited that new body, subsequently designated as the GTE, to provide a detailed examination of tarification mechanisms and levels used in each Member State. These were to include the trading arrangements—such as administrative, technical, and commercial terms—which had to be respected by those responsible for providing TPA. Many other data were to be provided relevant to cross-border trade in gas, including capacity allocation mechanisms. The deadline for submission of data was 15 September 2000.

The GTE was also requested to submit, by the end of August 2000, a report on measures taken (structurally and in relation to organization) (a) to avoid discrimination in terms of network access; and (b) to guarantee the confidentiality of commercial information received by gas undertakings in the context of TPA. Again this was to be presented on a Member State-by-Member State basis. In addition, the report was to cover the range of services offered by gas companies in the context of TPA, the terms on which they are offered, measures taken to ensure appropriate transparency, and mechanisms to ensure the TPA-relevant administrative arrangements were sufficient to foster competition and market entry. All of this data would provide the basis for further action by the Commission to promote the internal market in gas.

[35] Brattle Report on Tarification Methodologies, Feb 2000.
[36] Conclusions of the 2nd GRF, May 2000, point 4.

(5) Brattle Study

To implement the Directive fully, the national systems being designed and established throughout the EU had to be coherent and not contradictory, and would ideally facilitate national and also cross-border trade. By way of contributing to this process, the Commission contracted out a study entitled 'Methodologies for establishing national and cross-border system of pricing of access to the gas system of Europe'. The lengthy and detailed study, carried out by The Brattle Group, proved influential and its analysis and recommendations viewed as providing 'the starting point for the future work [of the Commission]'.[37] It is therefore worth noting the report's principal findings. **7.55**

In providing some guidance for interpretation of the Directive in the field of price and non-price terms for transportation and cross-border trade, it argued as follows, that: **7.56**

- firms in competitive markets cannot expect to earn monopoly profits (returns above costs of capital);
- prices are necessarily cost-reflective and rule out cross-subsidies of activities;
- efficient use of all system assets must be ensured; and
- trading institutions and instruments should be present.[38]

It noted that the principle of interconnection and inter-operability of systems is inherent in the completion of the internal market and that the Gas Directive requires Member States to ensure inter-operability (under Art 5). This has significant implications for the harmonization of standards across systems and across national boundaries. Experience in mature gas markets elsewhere suggests that the required degree of harmonization can be achieved by voluntary action by industry participants in a manner that is non-discriminatory and enhances competition.

Negotiated access

The Brattle Study paid special attention to the concept of negotiated access. There were two possible interpretations of the concept: **7.57**

1. 'Negotiated access' might include some initial flexibility in designing the price and non-price terms of access, and could apply to basic services available without subsequent negotiation. The available services should be published in sufficient detail to ensure transparency and non-discrimination, and should

[37] European Commission, 'Next Steps Towards Completion of the Internal Market in Gas: a Draft Strategy Paper for Discussion', 28 Feb 2000, DG TREN/A2/KG/D(00) 2216, 6.

[38] Trading in gas has been slower to develop in continental Europe than trading in electricity. An overview of the legal issues that may arise from gas trading is contained in Brothwood's chapter in 'Gas Trading Manual: a comprehensive guide to the gas markets', D Long and G Moore eds, in 2001.

apply to all parties in a consistent and objective manner, including the TSO's own affiliates. The terms constitute 'basic services' and are available to third parties without subsequent negotiation. Only customized services should be negotiated on a case-by-case basis; or, alternatively

2. It might involve case-by-case negotiations to obtain access with indicative prices and service level further on as the subject of bargaining. Customers must then pay depending on their negotiating abilities. However, Brattle concluded that this alternative was neither compatible with the principle of non-discrimination nor with the aim of establishing competitive markets.

On unbundling, the report drew on United Kingdom experience and concluded that strong regulatory control was required. The enforcement of arrangements to separate out activities within companies such as so-called Chinese Walls was also required. The Directive does not explicitly require these steps but they would be consistent with its spirit.

On security of supply Brattle recommended that interventions were justified in exceptional circumstances but must be based on specific criteria. In general, a liberalized market would tend naturally to enhance security of supply.

On take-or-pay contracts, it recommended that there should be a temporary increase in pipeline charges rather than outright derogations on grid access. Preconditions for derogation linked to take-or-pay must be in line with the provisions of the Gas Directive and there should be no derogation for recently concluded contracts.

The report also took up the issue of inter-operability of gas networks. Some technical and commercial areas, it said, needed further harmonization. These included: gas quality; odorization; billing and metering; nomination (allocation); balancing régimes; capacity constraints; and the publication of tarification and other information.

7.58 While the report was supportive of the idea of transition periods in the Member States, it clearly provided further support for the Commission (and indeed Council) in driving accelerated progress in achieving an internal market in gas. An interesting aspect of the study was the implicit and sometimes explicit assumption that there were very clear parallels between the gas and electricity industries, especially in non-discrimination and market access. This also reflected a trend in the Commission's thinking—that the two industries should be treated in parallel rather than as distinct and requiring different treatment.

(6) Convergence of Regulation

7.59 By the time the GRF held its first meeting of July 2001 (after a gap of more than 8 months), the proposed Directive to amend the Electricity and Gas Directives and the Regulation on Cross-Border Trade had already been proposed (see ch 8, paras 8.10–8.32). If adopted, they would change the environment in which the gas industry operated. At the meeting, the agenda had been broadened considerably and a certain momentum seemed to have been injected into the process. The Commission noted that a proposal for a cross-border regulation in gas might be introduced similar to that presented for cross-border electricity trade if the Madrid Forum proved unable to tackle such issues successfully.

Among the steps taken were the development of a draft strategy paper by a Joint Working Group comprising Commission representatives, the Ceer, and interested Member States. The working group argued that no single harmonized approach to the development of a fully operational internal market was possible. Instead, it recommended, a gradual process of convergence was required in the light of the diverse national circumstances. Data and analysis sought by the Commission, regulators, and the working group then provoked further requests to GTE to forward proposals on various matters, such as capacity allocation, storage, and inter-operability. The Commission also announced plans to establish a European Gas Industry Standards Board, drawing on US experience. **7.60**

In an interesting development linked to the dependence on supplies from non-EU producers, a Commission representative from the Competition Directorate noted competition concerns over 'territorial destination clauses' in gas supply contracts, potentially contrary to EC law. Gas release programmes were being studied to ascertain the potential for releasing gas supplies from long-term contracts already signed.[39] In the Directorate's view, there were three main concerns: **7.61**

- the development of supply-side competition;
- non-discriminatory TPA; and
- transparent trading rules.

The emphasis on the supply side was a new development, broadening the Commission's focus from the access issues that had predominated in the Brattle Study, in response to complaints by prospective buyers of gas about the lack of non-contracted gas available to make competition possible.

At about the same time, a consultants' report was circulated by the Commission that surveyed the changes taking place since market opening one year earlier.[40] It identified several barriers to competition, such as restricted access to the grid, difficulties in obtaining gas and vertical integration of gas companies. It noted that three kinds of new player were emerging: producers, traders, and main gas

[39] In this respect the regulatory experience of the UK, which liberalized much earlier, is relevant; cf. Cameron, P 'Five Years of Regulating Britain's Gas Industry', (1991) *Utilities Law Review*, 70–7.

[40] DRI-WEFA Study, 'Report for the European Commission Directorate General for Transport and Energy to determine changes after opening of the Gas Market in August 2000', July 2001.

incumbents. The traders included groups of distributors, which have formed consortia, especially in Germany and Italy. The survey, to which 200 industry players responded, lent weight to the argument that several important barriers remained to the introduction of competition in the EU gas market.

The headings under which blockages to competition may remain across borders may be summarized as follows:

- *Inter-operability*: gas quality specifications differ among the Member States and for technical reasons may never be completely harmonized. This raises the possibility that the applicable gas quality standard may unnecessarily restrict sources of supply with the effect of distorting or preventing competition;
- *Storage obligations*: prospective importers of gas may be required to put in place special and onerous arrangements with respect to storage and balancing of gas, on the ground that this is necessary for security of supply, while in reality it is designed to keep importers out of the market;
- *Available capacity*: concerns were expressed at the 4th Meeting of the Forum about lack of available information to market players on available capacity, a matter on which the GTE had difficulty in persuading its members to publish data;
- *Reciprocity*: an emerging issue; and
- *Access to other services*: important for the development of new gas hubs. (Gas release programmes are important in this context).

(7) **Assessment**

(a) Successes

7.62 There have been two notable successes in the Madrid Process to date.

The first is the establishment of a group of TSOs that is—more or less—independent from the association that represents the other business interests of the gas industry. This was announced at the second meeting of the GRF and the establishment of such a body has been developing in a constructive way since that time. Given the diverse composition of the GTE, and the continuing close involvement of Member States and international oil companies in the EU gas business, the evolution of the GTE may be expected to be slower than its counterpart in the electricity sector.

7.63 A second achievement is the Forum's encouragement to market participants to prepare for a fully functioning internal market in gas by means of strategy papers and plans, even if not all participants have agreed upon their content. This has involved an (ongoing) process of data gathering, identification of the specifics of the EU gas industry, setting of priorities, and some preliminary examination of possible ways of overcoming obstacles to liberalization present in this particular industry. While a less tangible achievement than the establishment of a group of TSOs, the start made on this complex process also represents achievement. It has proved essential to gather and analyse data on the different systems in the EU for transmission tarification, capacity allocation, and balancing, gas quality and network inter-operability, with a view to ensuring their convergence.

(b) Failures

The voluntary and informal character of the process has made it vulnerable in the face of intransigence on the part of incumbent market players. If the latter insist on proceeding no farther than the minimum requirements of the Gas Directive, the GRF mechanism has no legal authority to compel them to do otherwise. In such circumstances, further legislation becomes the only alternative. There was sufficient evidence by the end of the 3rd meeting in autumn 2000 that such a point had been reached. **7.64**

The Forum process is hindered by a constraint imposed by the gas market itself. With much gas tied up at present in long-term take-or-pay contracts, it is difficult to promote competition. Increasingly, the GRF has examined ways of encouraging the release of gas already contracted to gas undertakings and reviewing the arrangements with non-EU suppliers, especially Norway. This constraint though imposed on the Forum from outside, is nonetheless real. **7.65**

E. Complementary Rôle of Competition Law

(1) Purpose

Competition policy had to be adapted to meet the specific challenges presented by the transition to a liberalized market in electricity and gas. Competition law had always been seen by the Commission as an important instrument in achieving the aims of the IEM programme, but after the Electricity and Gas Directives entered into force during 1997 and 1998 it became important to identify the precise areas in which it could be used to greatest effect, and tested in specific cases. **7.66**

It was also important to develop a rôle for the Competition Directorate of the Commission that took into account the various other bodies that now had competence in energy regulation. Apart from the Commission and the various national competition authorities, there were national energy regulatory authorities with recently granted powers over the sector. In this context, some co-ordination with the actions undertaken in the Electricity and Gas Regulatory Fora was essential.

In general terms, the broad aim of competition policy has been to complement the Directives and ensure that the market players operate on a level playing field. **7.67**

The principal instruments used have been the competition rules in Articles 81, 82, and 86 of the EC Treaty, the Merger Regulation and the state aid rules in Articles 87 and 88 EC.[41] The thrust of policy has been to prevent private arrangements or practices that restrict the emergence of competition or that foreclose national markets against new entrants. In this respect, an important consideration has been that incumbent players in the electricity and gas markets might anticipate a competitive market in ways that were potentially anti-competitive (eg, by entering into long-term supply or transportation agreements).

(2) **Policy Priorities**

7.68 The priority aim has been to ensure that effective TPA takes place, as the Directives require. Failure in this respect would almost certainly fatally undermine the attempt to create an IEM. Apart from TPA and possible discrimination, related network issues also include transmission pricing and the capacity allocation of interconnectors. The natural monopoly characteristics of networks give the TSOs a dominant position in the geographical area covered by the grid, making abuse possible and even probable.

7.69 Although several areas of competition law are relevant to the establishment of an IEM, for network issues the key rules are contained in Articles 81 and 82, rather than those concerning merger control and state aids. The former deal with concerted practices having the object to distort, or effect of distorting competition on the one hand, and with the abuse of a dominant position on the other hand. While there is a rôle for national authorities in such matters, the Community rôle in cases involving interconnectors may be more effective than that of the relevant authorities in the Member States concerned.

(a) Meaning of 'refusal of access'

In this respect, the interpretation of 'refusal of access' is important. It seems that this will be interpreted broadly by the Commission, including not only a straight refusal of access to a network by a TSO but also the imposition of excessive transmission fees or of discriminatory technical requirements.[42] The concept of available transmission capacity (ATC) will be examined not only as a technical issue but as a contractual one. In this way refusals of access motivated by a lack of transmission capacity because that capacity is reserved in the first place to another party

---

[41] M Albers (Competition Directorate) notes that these instruments, supplemented by the Commission's power of supervision of enterprises entrusted with special or exclusive rights must be used comprehensively to bring about competition in the EU electricity and gas markets, a feature that appears to be unique to this sector: 'Energy Liberalization and EC Competition Law', paper presented to 28th Annual Fordham Conference of Antitrust Law and Policy, 26 Oct 2001.

[42] Tradacete, A, (EC Competition Directorate), 'Rôle of EC Competition Policy in the Liberalization of EU Energy Markets', Apr 2000.

will lead to such a reservation clause being examined by the Commission (see ch 5, paras 5.63–5.68).

An early test of the Commission's approach to refusals of network access came in its investigation of a complaint brought by Marathon against several EU gas companies. One of the companies involved, Thyssengas AG, made proposals for rendering access more effective. The commitments concerned five areas:

- balancing,
- trade in capacity rights,
- congestion management,
- transparency, and
- the company's handling of access requests.[43]

They entered into force in December 2001 for a period of almost four years and are to be monitored by a trustee, who will report to the Commission.

(b) *'General economic interest'*

It may be noted that in enforcing the competition rules, due consideration must be given to the concept of 'services of general economic interest'. This means that enforcement has to be sensitive to the right of Member States to impose PSOs on energy undertakings or economic conditions such as long-term planning and investment and capital intensive requirements that may justify take-or-pay clauses. 7.70

There were five areas of particular interest to the Commission that required action by the competition authorities. Developments in these areas were reported regularly to the participants in the two Fora. They were:

- network issues concerning transmission pricing and access;
- merger control;
- state aid;
- joint marketing of gas; and
- long-term contracts (destination clauses).

Before examining each of the above, it is important to note that with respect to gas, the identification of priority issues differed in some respects from the above. Constraints on the development of competition arose from characteristics specific to the upstream or exploration and production aspects of that industry that the competition authorities had to address. The impact of these aspects on policy priorities is outlined in summary form below.

[43] Commission Press Release, 'Commission Settles Marathon Case with Thyssengas', IP/01/1641, 23 Nov 2001; for details of the commitments see the company website: www.thyssengas.de

Table 7.1 Gas: Constraints on competition (a) Downstream market segment

Product markets	Corresponding geographical markets
Onshore transmission	National markets and potentially markets smaller than national
Sales to regional wholesale and/or local distribution companies, power plants and other industrial users	National markets and potentially markets smaller than national
Sales to private users by local distribution companies	Regional/local markets
Storage	National markets and potentially smaller than national ones

Note: The competition characteristics of these markets is as follows: network-bound industry; number of players limited; few new market entrants.

(3) Peculiarities of the EU Gas Market

7.71 The Commission carried out some research into the European gas market as part of its investigation into the proposed merger notified by Exxon and Mobil, establishing that 'the structure of the European gas markets is currently not favourable to competition.'[44]

The analysis that led to this rather sombre conclusion included both downstream and upstream elements. Essentially, the gas markets are characterized by horizontal and vertical demarcation. This situation is brought about by the long-term supply contracts concluded by incumbents which are part of a well-established vertical supply chain, extending from gas producers to end-users.

'Vertical demarcation' means that each operator has its well-defined function and position in the supply chain and usually refrains from entering the markets of its customers and/or suppliers (eg, there will be no direct sales by producers to end-users). 'Horizontal demarcation' means that each importer or wholesaler and/or regional or local distributor has its traditional supply area and usually does not enter the neighbouring supply area (see Table 7.1).

The Commission also found that the upstream markets were for the most part characterized by various forms of co-operation between competitors. This included the activities of exploration, production, and sales to wholesalers. Downstream markets, covering transportation, distribution, and storage, are at most only national in scope and are dominated by former monopolists. The latter

[44] European Commission, 'Annual Competition Law Report 2000', 35; Commission Press Release, 'Commission clears merger between Exxon and Mobil (both USA) subject to conditions', IP/99/708, 29 Sep 1999.

Table 7.2 Gas: Constraints on Competition (b) Upstream market segment

Product markets	Corresponding geographical markets
Exploration & Development	Gas fields in EEA plus potentially Russian Federation and Algeria
Offshore Transmission Processing	Region in which the pipelines are located. Depends on geographical market defined for the offshore transmission
Production & Sales to wholesale companies	Gas fields in EEA plus potential RF and Algerian sources

Source: European Commission Competition Directorate

are usually vertically-integrated and control the pipeline network. These pipeline networks are usually, and will probably remain, natural monopolies (see Table 7.2).

This concept of the market structure in the gas industry was taken into account when the Commission set priorities for future enforcement policy.[45] Given these structural constraints, competition can only be introduced if three conditions are met:

(i) suppliers are free to compete for customers;
(ii) customers are free to change suppliers; and
(iii) a TPA régime is introduced and maintained (a régime which is also effective, non-discriminatory and cost-reflective).

As a result, the Commission set out several priorities for cases it would investigate in the transition period to a competitive gas market that would contribute to the creation of competitive market conditions. In the upstream markets, priority would be given to cases:

(i) that would contribute to ending joint marketing activities (eg joint sales);
(ii) where the buyer's ability to sell gas outside of a particular territory or to certain users was limited.

In downstream markets priority was to be given to:

- network issues, and especially the development of an effective TPA régime.

Without this, customers could not change suppliers, and suppliers could not deliver gas to customers willing to switch suppliers. Cross-border issues would be 'the main focus . . . in line with general principles of EC competition law'.[46] National authorities were encouraged to deal with cases that are national in scope.

[45] European Commission, 'Annual Report on Competition Law', 35.
[46] ibid.

(4) Network issues

(a) Transmission pricing

7.72 For competition to be effective, a transmission price had to emerge, and rules of access to the network were required—in particular to those parts of the infrastructure that were subject to congestion. The powers required to deal with this were available since network operators usually have a dominant position in the geographical area covered by the grid.

In the competition law it is clearly prohibited to impose unfair selling prices or other unfair trading conditions. An 'unfair' price could be either predatory or excessive. Prices must also be non-discriminatory. If prices appear to be unfairly high, there are three tests that may be applied:[47]

1. do the prices reflect costs related to the product sold or the service provided? (test for excessive pricing);
2. do prices charged to different customers deviate between each other without sufficient justification? (discrimination);
3. do operators' prices deviate from each other without sufficient justification? (benchmarking).

The first case in which the Commission was able to consider the calculation of transmission prices in the energy industry arose in the German electricity sector in 1998.

7.73 **(i) Electricity agreement: *Verbändevereinbarung*** Access to both the electricity and gas networks in Germany is largely governed by a system of nTPA, although electricity distribution networks are subject to rTPA. The Government had no formal rôle in the system's initial design or implementation. The TSOs and market entrants have to agree on the price and non-price terms of each request for access. To simplify matters, the German industry associations concluded a framework agreement in 1998 setting out joint principles for the calculation of prices, known as the *Verbändevereinbarung* (VV-1).[48] This framework agreement had to be approved by the Ministry of Economics, Federal Competition Office, and the European Commission. It failed to obtain EC support largely because it envisaged a transaction and distance-based price model. The Commission preferred to see transmission pricing based on the costs of actual physical flows rather than the individual generator–customer contract path. The former method reflected specific physical

[47] Schaub, A, 'Competition Policy and Liberalization of Energy Markets', paper presented at the European Utilities Circle 2000 conference, 23 Nov 2000.

[48] Competition Policy Newsletter No 3, Oct 1998: Christian Levasseur. See generally Blörner, A R 'Negotiated Third Party Access in Germany: Electricity and Gas', (2001) 19 J Energy Natural Resources L, 32; and Albers, n 41, 16–18.

characteristics of the electricity flows (which do not travel like other goods but follow the route of 'least resistance'). A TSO that charges its tariff on the basis of an erroneous parallel with other goods is not a price within the meaning of Article 82 EC since this is not related to the actual cost incurred. Other criticisms of the system said it was discriminatory in favour of generators in the vicinity of consumers.[49] A serious deficiency was identified in its lack of rules to ensure transparent and non-discriminatory access, such as rules to require the publication of available capacity and underlying transmission costs. Incumbents were granted discretion to make exceptions or depart from the guidelines of the VV-1.

7.74 As a result of these concerns, the industry associations produced a second framework agreement in December 1999. The second agreement (VV-2), concluded in January 2000, included an important step in the development of the kind of transmission pricing system appropriate to the internal market in energy. It provided for a non-transaction based tariff without any distance (point-to-point) component. This provided third-party network users with greater freedom in selecting suppliers and delivery points, and making changes to these choices as the need arose. This emphasis on network service removed the discrimination identified in the point-to-point charges in VV-1.

Unfortunately, VV-2 introduced a new form of discrimination. Its transmission tariffs included a supplementary 'T' component tariff (see below) for the transportation of gas between the two trading zones, one covering the North and the other covering the South of the country. These borders were artificially drawn so that the supra-regional incumbents could cross the zones without paying the 'T' tariff as long as they stayed within their traditional demarcation areas.

The special fee called the 'T' component would be levied on each occasion when the parties to a transaction were located in different zones or when one party operated in another Member State. It also included a balancing mechanism to allow companies to compensate their flows in opposite directions crossing those borders.

7.75 The Commission regarded this approach as incompatible with competition law and sent a warning letter to the associations concerned. There were three principal objections to the system.

1. The 'T' component did not provide for cost-reflexivity in transactions over a short distance, but had the effect of imposing an additional fee in cross-border transactions, while transmissions over long distances within a single trading zone were free of additional charges. It is a principle of EC competition law that prices lacking cost-reflexivity may be abusive.

[49] Many criticisms are summarized in Lapuerta, C, Pfaffenberger, W, and Pfeifenberger, J, 'Netzzugang in Deutschland: ein Ländervergleich (Tiel I & II)', *Energiewirtschaft*, Mar/Apr 1999.

2. The 'T' component was discriminatory because it would give large German electricity suppliers the option to balance counter-directed flows and so avoid payment of the 'T' component, even though this option was not in practice available to smaller market actors or to foreign suppliers.
3. Transmission costs were significantly higher than in Scandinavia.

The outcome was that the 'T' component ceased to be applied to transactions in Germany—but not before the Commission insisted that a merger between VEBA and VIAG could not proceed without the abandonment of the internal 'T' component (see para 7.94).

7.76 **(ii) Gas VV Agreement** To develop and apply the system of nTPA in the German gas sector, an agreement on transmission charges and conditions of access was concluded in July 2000, similar to that developed for the electricity sector. This is complicated by the fact that the gas business is split into three levels: national, regional, and local—with responsibilities divided across all three. The agreement was concluded by the associations of consumers and generators. The consumers' associations were the *Bundesverband der Deutschen Industrie* (BDI) and the *Verband der Industriellen Energie- und Kraftwirtschaft* (VIK). The generators' associations were the *Bundesverband der Deutschen Gas- und Wasserwirtschaft* (BGW) and *Verband kommunaler Unternehmen* (VKU). Like the electricity VV-1, the Gas VV agreement encountered problems.

7.77 The arrangements attracted widespread criticism from energy traders and consumers. Tariffs appeared not to be cost-related, terms for various services did not appear to be available and there was a lack of transparency regarding standard conditions and capacity availability.[50] One company, Enron, disclosed that its attempts to secure access by negotiations in a single transaction took six months to complete and cost in excess of one million Deutschmark in legal fees.[51] Negotiations among the parties began with a view to improving the arrangements for network access. Progress was assisted by the intervention of the Economics Minister, who threatened new regulation unless the participating associations created a proper framework for liberalizing the gas market.[52]

7.78 In March 2001 a supplement to the existing agreement was signed by the four participating associations. Its aim was to improve the basis for competition in the gas sector. It attempted to improve transparency, guarantee non-discriminatory treatment in transport and storage, and improve congestion management. However, there were few details available as to how these aspirations were to be made operational. The amendment contains no binding legal rules and no sanctions are provided if the

[50] European Federation of Energy Traders, 'Open Letter on Gas VV', 8 Aug 2000.

[51] Brattle Group, 'DTe Implementation of the Gas Act', Dec 2000, 9.

[52] EFET Press Release, 'German Gas Industry Increases the Chances for Regulation', 29 Jan 2001.

principles are effected. Above all, the tariff and contract arrangements remain both complex and expensive. Given the layered system that operates in Germany, the costs of gas transport when added up create an environment in which Germany has some of the highest transport costs in the EU. In this context, court action or threats of intervention by the Federal Cartel Office remain necessary to gain access to the system on reasonable terms.

Germany provides an illustration of the importance of technical considerations in the liberalization equation. Two gas qualities are supplied: low calorie or 'L' gas and high calorie or 'H' gas. The grid operators import or produce various types of gas. They then manage the qualities to ensure that customers receive the gas quality they need. Competition and especially trading are difficult if there is no blending service provided by a transportation company in accordance with predefined and transparent rules. 'L' gas can be delivered to customers by blending of 'L' gas with 'H' gas, or by adding nitrogen to 'H' gas. A blending service allows customers to have a gas that corresponds to the 'L' or 'H' limits, but transportation companies would have to provide all relevant information about blending facilities, and charges for conversion would have to be reasonable and efficiently allocated. **7.79**

(iii) Netherlands transmission tariffs A similar issue concerning the calculation of transmission tariffs arose in The Netherlands. The dominant TSO proposed to charge suppliers both for imports into The Netherlands (from Germany) and for transit transmissions of electricity through The Netherlands. The fee charged would be the same as that paid by domestic suppliers for the use of the grid. The Commission sought to have the tarification system modified so that the TSO could only charge for import and transit transmissions where these result in extra costs on lines that interconnect the Dutch grid with other grids. In practice, electricity may be traded several times across borders and the system did not envisage any precaution to avoid multiple charging of the same transmission. **7.80**

Assessment

The above cases suggest that EU competition law is flexible about the particular method adopted to calculate transmission prices, leaving this to be set by sector-specific law or regulation in a way that reflects the specific circumstances. Its aim is only to set out the parameters for the pricing conduct of the dominant network operators in individual cases. This appears to rule out the use of competition law to promote a pan-European tarification system aimed at promoting trade in electricity.[53] Such steps would have to be taken by means of a voluntary agreement or by new legislation, such as the proposed Regulation on Cross-Border Trade in Electricity (see ch 8, paras 8.17–8.32). **7.81**

[53] A Schaub, n 47 above, 6.

7.82 (b) **Interconnector access** A second network issue is interconnector access. It has become a priority area for competition policy. For both electricity and gas markets, interconnectors are crucial to the functioning of the pan-European energy network. They include both lines that cross national land borders and undersea lines that connect different countries such as the UK–Belgium gas interconnector. Access to the lines is essential if importers are to enter the markets of other Member States. They are also the only source of competition in the short-term in those Member States that have a monopolistic supply structure. However, in many cases they lack sufficient capacity to transmit all of the electricity and gas that producers, traders, and large consumers wish to import or export in a liberalizing market. In this context, two questions in particular have proved to be important to competition policy: 'how is scarce transmission capacity to be allocated in a manner compatible with the aims of the IEM?' (the method); and, 'where capacity is reserved through long-term capacity reservation agreements, are these reservations compatible with EC competition law?'.

7.83 (i) **Methods of allocating available capacity** Questions of capacity allocation are of great importance to the competition authorities since they are usually raised by potential new market entrants. An example is the Irish electricity grid which has been the subject of an informal complaint from Ireland Power Group in 2000.[54] In practice, there is no requirement in competition law to adopt a particular method of allocation of transmission rights. The aim is only to set down the parameters for dominant network operators.

The need for a method of allocation arises when demand exceeds supply. The TSOs usually choose to apply pro-rata rationing and/or auctions to deal with this. If demand does not exceed available capacity to a large extent, pro-rata rationing works well at border points and bottlenecks in some Member States. However, it may lead to the allocation of very little capacity in situations where demand greatly exceeds available capacity. The individual transaction will then lose its commercial value. This can be avoided by choosing the auction method.

7.84 In addressing this question of allocation methods and their compatibility with competition law, there have been questions about the 'first-come, first-served' method and about auctions, in the light of Commission decisions on mobile telephone licences. These are considered below.

The problem with the 'first-come, first-served' approach is that it can favour former monopolists over new market entrants. This may occur if a dominant firm has concluded long-term capacity reservation contracts before liberalization. It may also facilitate discrimination by a TSO in favour of its vertically-integrated supply business, foreclosing other traders from entering the downstream supply markets.

54 Europe Energy, 2 Feb 2001: 'Grid Access Problems in Ireland Under Commission's Scrutiny'.

Auctions: lessons from mobile phone licensing?: The problem with the auction approach is different. In Commission decisions on the grant of mobile telephone licences in Italy and Spain, it ruled that an auction relating to the allocation of a second mobile telephone licence for the operation of a GSM network is incompatible with competition law if the first mobile telephone licence was awarded free of charge to the incumbent state-owned telecommunications company. The lump sum payment raises the entry cost for the new player and creates a competitive disadvantage vis-à-vis the incumbent that did not pay an entry fee. It appears that these decisions are not to be interpreted as against the auction method of allocation but rather as underlining the requirement that no discrimination may take place.[55]

Comparisons between the GSM cases and the allocation of interconnector transmission rights for electricity are dubious. The GSM operators paid their fees as the price of entry into the market. The fees paid for electricity transmission rights are not likely to be as large nor levied as the price of market entry. Such fees will be the price of performing one or several supply contracts.[56]

(ii) Long-term reservation contracts Agreements that reserve capacity to parties over a long period have come under the scrutiny of the Commission with respect to their validity and their exclusion from normal allocation procedures. The issue is whether a long-term reservation agreement is incompatible with competition law—an important question because in the event of incompatibility, this capacity would become available for reallocation. The Commission therefore launched a number of investigations into these contracts, not least because the beneficiaries of long-term capacity reservation agreements are usually former monopolists. **7.85**

An early example of capacity booking on an electricity interconnector leading to distortions of trade was identified by the Commission at the Norwegian/Danish and Danish/German borders. The congestion on these lines was partly the result of a long-term reservation agreement for 60 per cent of the total capacity of the only cable connecting Western Denmark and Norway, called the 'Skagerrak cable'. This had a duration of around 20 years and benefited largely the dominant producers in Norway and Western Denmark, Statkraft, and Elsam. The remaining 40 per cent of the capacity on the cable was subject to a long-term reservation agreement between Statskraft and E.ON, with a duration of 25 years from 1998. It included a reservation of transit capacity through the Western Danish network and about 34 per cent of the capacity of the Danish/German interconnector towards Germany. **7.86**

[55] Schaub, n 47 above, 8.
[56] Tradacete, n 42 above, 11.

Following serious doubts expressed by the Commission about the compatibility of the reservation agreements with competition law, the Statskraft/Elsam agreement was amended to free up capacity in its entirety from 1 January 2001.[57] The German company E.ON also yielded its capacity on the Skagerrak cable and on the Danish/German interconnector.

A second case involving access to electricity interconnectors concerned the UK–French submarine interconnector.[58] Its use had been reserved exclusively for EdF exports into the UK under an agreement on management of the interconnector. Prior to the introduction of new rules on allocation of capacity, the owners sought the Commission's views. Since the TSOs are in a dominant position in the market for transmission of electricity between the continent and the UK, any restriction on the attribution of transmission rights or discriminatory treatment would have been contrary to EU competition law, under Article 82. If a priority right had been granted in favour of a particular company, this would have allowed it to circumvent the rules for capacity allocation that apply to other companies, constituting discriminatory treatment.

As a result of the Commission's observations, the two companies opened up access to the interconnector without any reserve being made in favour of any particular company, with capacity being tendered in specific blocks over the next few years. The French network operator, RTE (*Reseau de Transmission d'Électricité*) also made changes to procedures and duration of transit rights in France to ensure compatibility with the transmission rights in the UK–French interconnector.

A further example, in the gas sector, is the Commission's action against a long-term exclusive supply agreement between the Spanish gas utility, Gas Natural and Endesa, an electricity generator.[59] Under the agreement, Endesa was required to purchase its entire gas demand for new gas-fired power plants from Gas Natural for a period of more than 20 years. The interest of the Commission lay in ensuring that the supply contract did not allow the dominant gas supplier, Gas Natural, to prolong a de facto monopoly for many years and thus block new entrants into the gas market in Spain, then in the process of being liberalized. After the Commission had expressed its concerns in a warning letter,[60] the companies proposed some amendments to the contract. Essentially, the amendments proposed by the parties were to:

---

[57] Commission Press Release, 'Increased Scope for Electricity Imports Competition in Northern Europe: a step forward towards an internal market in electricity', IP/01/30, 11 Jan 2001.

[58] Commission Press Release, 'UK–French electricity interconnector opens up, increasing scope for competition', IP/01/341, 12 Mar 2001.

[59] Fernandez Salas, M, 'Long-Term Supply Agreements in the Context of Gas Market Liberalization: Commission Closes Investigation of Gas Natural', (2000) *Competition Policy Newsletter* (2000), 55.

[60] IP/00/297 of 27 Mar 2000.

- substantially reduce the gas volumes covered by the contract (around 25%) in order to free a part of Endesa's purchasing capacity and thereby ensure that it continued to exist as a customer that could attract new market entry. De facto exclusivity would disappear from the contract;
- reduce the long-term duration of the supply contract by one-third to avoid an excessively long period of dependence of the customer on the supplier. The maximum duration would therefore be 12 years during the plateau period;
- allow Endesa to resell the gas after a start-up period;[61] and
- modify other clauses of the contract that might have the effect of discriminating in favour of Endesa vis-à-vis other gas customers.

The Commission closed its investigation as a result of these commitments made by the parties.

National regulators have had to examine this problem too. In The Netherlands the regulator has reviewed long-term reservation contracts in connection with gas storage facilities and access to them. Currently, the situation is one in which the entire storage capacity of the producers, BP and NAM, has been leased to the principal transportation company, Gasunie. In the agreements BP and NAM have to ask Gasunie for permission before they may grant access to third parties. Under domestic legislation access to the storage installations may be refused if no capacity is available for the storage of the quantity of gas to which the request for access relates, or if it is not reasonable to require them to make all the capacity available. If technical research shows that not all capacity is required for Gasunie's transportation and supply activities, the fact that according to the agreement Gasunie must give its consent before access to storage installations may be granted to third parties becomes irrelevant. The domestic legislation (the Gas Act) takes precedence over civil law contracts and so the agreements do not constitute an obstacle to the grant of access to third parties. In an interesting comment, the regulator notes that if the agreements do not anticipate the introduction of the domestic legislation, this should have been done since they were entered into on 'the eve of liberalization'—defined as the period from 1986 to 1997.[62] **7.87**

(5) Merger Control

The liberalization process has encouraged energy companies to restructure by means of mergers, acquisitions and the formation of joint ventures, leading to significant changes in market structure—especially in the electricity industry. By **7.88**

[61] The Commission has accepted previously that a resale prohibition could be imposed on an electricity generator, as long as it is limited in time: see the case of Transgas–Turbogas, *Commission Report on Competition Policy* (1996), 48 and 135.

[62] Office for Energy Regulation (DEE), Guidelines Gas Act: Information and Consultation Document 2001, June 2001.

autumn 1998 the wave of mergers and acquisitions in the electricity and gas industries became a discussion point at the first meeting of the Gas Regulatory Forum. During 1998 and 1999 there were no less than 20 major mergers and acquisitions in the electricity industry, although not all of them in the EU.[63]

While these transactions may well have a pro-competitive character, leading to new entry in product or geographical markets, the converse can also be true. In the highly segregated energy markets of the EU, they could easily lead to the creation or reinforcement of a dominant position in the market. The effects of such changes in market structure on the implementation of the Electricity and Gas Directives would therefore be detrimental. The interplay between the Directives and energy market structure became a matter of some importance for the competition authorities, at both EU and national levels.

7.89 The rules applicable to mergers in the energy industry have assumed a much greater significance during this stage of the IEM. A main concern is to assess whether the transaction leads to the creation or reinforcement of a dominant position held by a former statutory monopolist in the common market. In practice, mergers in the energy industry have tended to be driven by economies of scale or by economies of scope. In the first case, companies attempt to extend their customer base by acquiring companies that operate in a different geographical market, particularly ones that are highly concentrated. Examples of these are the mergers involving EdF and London Electricity, EdF and South Western Electricity (UK), PreussenElektra and the Dutch company EZH, and Vattenfall and HEW.[64] In the second category, the acquisition is directed at companies active in other energy markets. Examples of such mergers are the Exxon/Mobil[65] and Veba/Viag[66] mergers (gas and electricity respectively).

7.90 In cases where liberalization has compelled former monopolists to become direct competitors and as a result they propose to merge, there is a risk of consolidating the strong market position of the parties in their former exclusive supply area. The Commission has in circumstances like these adopted a 'dynamic' approach, taking into account the actual and future conditions for supply competition. Factors to be taken into account include the degree of market-opening, the economic independence of TSOs, and the actual conditions for TPA. If entry into the supply area of former monopolists becomes more difficult as a result of a proposed

[63] Townsend, D, 'Mergers & Acquisitions: Leading the Merger Pack', [2000] 34 Petroleum Economist. The figure for the gas and oil industry was the same. Such increases in merger activity were also evident in the telecommunications and air transport industry when liberalization began.

[64] Commission Decision, Case IV/M 1346, 1999 *EdF/London Electricity*; Case IV/M 1606, 1999 *EdF/South Western Electricity*; Case IV/M 1659, 1999 *PreussenElektra/EZH*; and Case IV/M 1842, 2000 *Vattenfall/Hamburgische Elektricitätswerke AG (HEW)*.

[65] Commission Decision of 29 Sept 1999, case no IV/M 1383, *Exxon/Mobil*.

[66] Commission Decision, Case IV/M 1673, 2000.

merger, it is unlikely to be approved. Substantial remedies offered by the merger parties either to eliminate or to reduce the negative effects on competition are taken into account and may lead to approvals that would, on a 'static' view of existing market conditions, not have been approved.[67] This approach is illustrated by the cases discussed below (see paras 7.94–7.98).

In addition to the rules addressed to undertakings in Articles 81 and 82, the energy industry is subject to the procedural framework laid down by Regulation 17/62. This includes the merger control regulation.[68] It applies only above certain turnover thresholds of the undertakings involved, which are viewed as giving the merger a Community dimension. As a result, the transaction comes under the scrutiny of the EU authorities. **7.91**

For many years, the compartmentalization of national markets and the use of closed supply areas, with the consequent protection of energy utilities from competition acted as a disincentive to the strengthening of a corporate position through mergers. Immediately prior to and after the adoption of the Electricity and Gas Directives, this changed.[69] **7.92**

The electricity industry has been especially prominent in this increase in merger activity. It is an industry that with features such as product homogeneity that may contribute to situations of collective dominance. On the supply side, the oligopolistic structure of many generation activities may undermine effective competition.[70] **7.93**

(c) Case Studies: mergers with liberalization undertakings

(i) ***Veba/Viag***[71] A proposal to merge two German electricity companies, Veba and Viag, was referred to the Commission in 2000. Veba and Viag proposed to merge to create E.ON. Taken together with the dominant rôle of RWE/VEW in the other principal region of Germany (under investigation at the same time by the Bundeskartellamt), this would have had the effect of creating a dominant duopoly in the wholesale market for electricity throughout Germany. A combination of factors would have established a market structure conducive to co-ordinated effects. Treating the entire territory of Germany as the relevant market, the Commission noted these factors: **7.94**

- a total homogeneity of product
- market transparency

[67] See Albers, n 41 above.
[68] Reg No 4064/89, OJ 1989 L 395/1, corrigendum OJ 1990 L 257/13, amended by Reg No 1310/97, OJ 1997 L 180/1, corrigendum OJ 1998 L 40/17.
[69] Townsend: see n 63 above.
[70] Matthiesen: see n 79 above.
[71] Commission Decision, Case M 1673, 2000.

- similar cost structures due to a similarly composed stock of power stations and a few jointly-operated large power stations, plus
- various interrelationships between Veba/Viag and RWE/VEW
- the expected modest increase in demand, and
- the low price elasticity of electricity as a product.[72]

The Commission took a dynamic view of market development since a number of key requirements for the nationwide sale of electricity were already in place such as framework rules for TPA. It gave its approval when the parties provided undertakings to the respective authorities to remedy the competition problems. These consisted mainly in divestments affecting various holdings, particularly in the eastern part of Germany, thereby cutting important links between the two new groups and transforming VEAG, a major electricity generator jointly controlled by the two duopolists, into an independent competitor. The undertakings also included various improvements to the basic rules governing transmission through the network operated by the two leading interconnected entities. As a result, the incentive to peaceful parallel behaviour by the market leaders was removed and the likelihood of privileged access to information about the strategy of the other party to the duopoly was reduced.

An interesting element of the agreement was the willingness of both VEBA/VIAG and RWE/VEW to abandon the tariff for transmission known as the 'T-component', which is payable where a supplier of energy between the two German trading zones is unable to balance or 'net out' the quantities they supply against equivalent quantities in the opposite direction. This would have adversely affected competition from traders and small generators. In principle they accepted the agreement on cross-border tarification that had been worked out in the Florence Regulatory Forum (see para 7.29) in March 2000 (but which was not put into effect) in preference to the VV-2 Agreement, which had entered into force on 1 February 2000 (see paras 7.73–7.75).

The Commission also linked its competition concerns in this case to its action on the Skagerrak interconnector cable (see para 7.86). As a result, E.ON abandoned its reservation of capacity on that cable and also on the Danish/German interconnector. Finally, the parties undertook to issue in future separate bills for network charges and energy prices to promote price transparency for their customers and to limit cross-subsidies by the TSO in favour of the electricity sales units.

7.95 (ii) ***EdF/Louis Dreyfus*** EdF proposed to set up a joint venture in electricity trade with the firm of Louis Dreyfus. The Commission had concerns about the proposed merger since EdF would have become the only trader on the French market and so able to gain a competitive advantage over its competitors which

[72] Annual Competition Law Report 2000, 63.

were barred from entry. At the time of notification the market had not been liberalized and the conditions for TPA were unknown, as was the definition of eligible customers in France. During the period from the creation of EdF Trading, the joint venture, and the opening of the French market, EdF could in principle use the joint venture to provide the technical expertise and cover the risks involved in order to conclude complex structured contracts with eligible customers. It could also take advantage of this opportunity to enter into new contracts with the eligible customers and in this way delay or reduce the entry of competing suppliers.

Subsequently, approval was granted subject to undertakings by the parties to:

> implement measures to prevent the joint venture from assisting EdF in establishing prices, structuring offers or by assuming risks associated with such contracts in relation to eligible customers until the French market is legally and effectively open; ensure that there is no transfer of know-how or relevant information from EdF Trading to the departments of EdF which deal with eligible customers in France during this period.[73]

An independent observer is monitoring the performance of the undertakings.[74] However, enforcement was made more difficult by the uncertainty surrounding the entry into force of the new legal framework.

(iii) ***EdF/EnBW*** A further investigation took place with respect to EdF in relation to a proposal to take a 34 per cent stake in an electricity distributor, EnBW, the third largest in Germany. It would then share control jointly with OEW (*Zweckverband Oberschwäbische Elektrizitätswerke*) an association of nine municipalities in the south-west of Germany. The supply area of EnBW ran along the border between France and Germany, and it could be considered a potential supplier to eligible customers in the French electricity market. The acquisition could have led to the removal of a potential competitor in the French market. In the event, approval was given subject to certain conditions.[75] EdF undertook to make available to competitors 6,000 MW of generating capacity located in France. Access to this capacity is to be granted through auctions, prepared and operated by EdF under the supervision of a trustee, appointed by EdF but approved by the Commission. The aim was to open up one third of the electricity market in France. This and other undertakings, such as the severance of its connection with the French electricity generator, CNR, to make it an independent generator, have a five-year term, at the conclusion of which the Commission will review their effects and then terminate or extend EdF's obligation to grant access to generation capacities. 7.96

[73] Commission Decision of 1999, case no M 1557, *EdF/Louis Dreyfus*.

[74] Commission Press Release, 'Commission authorises EDF and Louis Dreyfus joint venture in energy trading, subject to conditions, IP/99/711, 29 Sep 1999.

[75] Commission Decision, Case No M.1853, *EdF/EnBW*, 7 Feb 2001.

(iv) ***EnBW/Hidrocantábrico*** A bid was notified to the Commission for control of *Hidroelectrica del Cantábrico* (*Hidrocantábrico*) by EnBW and a Spanish group, Villar Mir, in 2001. Given the ownership links between EnBW and EdF, the Commission was concerned about the elimination of potential competitors to EdF. In particular, there was the possibility that the existing collective dominant position of Iberdrola and Endesa on the Spanish wholesale market for electricity would be strengthened. The French–Spanish interconnector had little free capacity for commercial use, creating a barrier to imports into Spain, contributing to the market's isolation from other Member States' electricity markets. To address the Commission's competition concerns, EdF and Edf/RTE, the TSO undertook to take the necessary steps to increase the commercial capacity on this interconnector by almost four times.[76]

7.97 (v) **Convergence cases** There have also been cases before the Commission in which companies providing different forms of energy have sought to combine into a single unit. Examples are the Tractebel/Distrigaz[77] and Neste/IVO[78] mergers. If a new market entry is likely to be the result, this kind of proposal will be viewed as pro-competitive. If it is a merger between the dominant electricity undertaking and the dominant gas supplier, there is a risk that the former will take control of the cost of production of its competitors in the electricity market. In such an event, where competing electricity generators sought to enter a new geographical market on the basis of a gas-fired plant, they would probably have had to purchase the fuel from the incumbent electricity supplier. The dominant electricity supplier would also be able to influence the choice of industrial customers as to whether they should engage in auto-generation of power or to purchase from the incumbent.

The mergers were given approval only when they had provided undertakings to divest their industrial gas sales businesses to a third party.

7.98 (vi) **Comment** As a general comment, it may be noted that the Commission has been willing to make quite extensive concessions to parties in return for undertakings to take actions that will contribute to the realization of an internal energy market. The *Veba/Viag* case is a vivid example of how a large concentration may be permitted subject to the grant of such undertakings by the parties.[79] The fragility of the undertakings given can be seen in the reaction to the manner in

[76] Europe Energy, No 588, 'Conditional Authorization for EnBW's Acquisition of Hidrocantábrico', 28 Sep 2001.

[77] Commission Decision of 1 Sept 1994, case no M 493, *Tractebel/Distrigaz*.

[78] Commission Decision of 2 June 1998, case no M 931, *Neste/Ivo*.

[79] This point is discussed in some detail with reference to the *Veba/Viag* and other cases by Matthiesen, H, 'Interplay Between European Merger Control Law and the Liberalization of Electricity and Gas Markets', LLM thesis, University of Dundee, 2001.

which EdF has chosen to implement its undertakings in the EnBW case. There the auction process has been criticized by some market players as overly complex, slow, and offering inferior flexibility to the capacity retained by EdF.[80]

(6) State Aid

Transitional measures derogating temporarily from the Directive may be authorized by the Commission (Art 24, Electricity Directive; see ch 4, paras 4.59–4.64 and ch 6, paras 6.30–6.36). However, the way in which Article 24 was applied by the Commission differed from industry expectations.[81] The assumption had been that the transitional régime under Article 24 would cover any schemes intended to recover stranded costs. In the event, the Commission decided to limit the scope of the transitional régime to derogations from chapters IV, VI, and VII of the Directive. Derogations were granted to Germany and Luxembourg in 1999.[82] Most applications under Article 24 concerned the creation of financial compensation schemes under which compensation money would be levied to compensate undertakings for their stranded costs. Such schemes may constitute state aid. They were therefore examined by the Competition Directorate within the framework provided by the state aid rules in Articles 87 and 88 of the EC Treaty. Although this matter was reported on from time-to-time to GRF participants, it was handled by the Commission largely outside of the Forum framework. **7.99**

Among the cases examined separately by the Commission under the state aid rules were schemes for compensation from Spain, France, the United Kingdom, Denmark, The Netherlands, and Austria.[83] As the summaries below illustrate, the circumstances in each case were very different, creating some challenges for the application of general rules. **7.100**

(a) Stranded costs: case studies

(i) **Spain** The Spanish case concerned two separate schemes, both of which were notified to the Commission (see ch 4, paras 4.61–4.62). First, there was the Costs of Transition to Competition (CTC) régime, which provided compensation over a maximum of ten years to Spanish electricity generators because of the **7.101**

[80] EFET Press Statement, 'Present Rules of Auctions of Virtual Power Plant Capacity in France will not lead to Effective Opening of the Market', 12 Jul 2001.

[81] Union of the Electricity Industry/Eurelectric, 'Position Paper on the Further Liberalization of the Electricity Markets', Feb 2001, Annex 5: 'Stranded Costs', 23.

[82] Commission Decision 1999/794/EC of 8 July 1999; Commission Decision 1999/793/EC of 8 July 1999.

[83] See Commission Decisions 1999/791/EC, 1999/792/EC, 1999/795/EC, 1999/796/EC, 1999/797/EC, and 1999/798/EC, concerning respectively the UK, France, Austria, The Netherlands, Spain, and Denmark, pursuant to Art 24 of Directive 96/92/EC (OJ L 319, 11 Dec 1999).

fall in electricity prices from liberalization. The second scheme proposed to redistribute the relatively high cost of generation and distribution in the isolated systems of the islands and extra-peninsular systems by means of a specific levy on the mainland power tariffs and transmission fees.

In July 2001 the Commission decided that the component of aid known as the 'technological CTCs' (the premium paid for the generation of electricity from indigenous coal and the two allocations amounting to £8,664 million) were compatible with Article 87(1) EC and with the Commission's Methodology (see para 7.108). Modifications to the Methodology scheme had been made in June 2001 to comply with the Commission's interpretation of the Treaty. The premium for the generation of electricity from indigenous coal did not comply with the Methodology but might benefit from an authorization as a compensation for a service of general economic interest as regards security of supply, under Article 86(2) EC, in the light of Articles 3(2) and 8(4) of the Electricity Directive.

7.102 (ii) **France** In its submission, the French Government proposed several transitional measures to the Commission. These included:

1. contracts for electricity purchase when they concern electricity purchase by the 'peak' independent producers, amounting to 250 million Francs (FF) a year until 2012; and
2. commitments linked to the Superphoenix fast breeder reactor, amounting to 12.7 billion FF.

The government foresees a recovery method based on a fund made up of a contribution payable by all users, and based on consumption. In addition, the government proposed transitional measures for commitments linked to the financing of the special pension scheme for electricity and gas employees, for which *Électricité de France* had made neither reserve nor estimate.

7.103 (iii) **United Kingdom** In the case submitted by the United Kingdom, the Government asked for a transitional régime for the electricity sector in Northern Ireland. It concerned the power purchase agreements between Northern Ireland Electricity plc (NIE) and the four main independent power producers. The commitments entered into in power purchase agreements involve stranded capacity, amounting to up to £25 million (BPS), excess cost linked to a gas contract between NIE and Premier Power, amounting to up to BPS 25 million , cost of a gas pipeline, amounting to up to BPS 14 million, and flue gas desulphurization, amounting to up to BPS 18 million. The mechanism for recovery of eligible stranded costs proposed by the United Kingdom Government is the introduction of a surcharge on the final power consumption, known as 'Franchise Customer Excess Cost'.

(iv) **Denmark** The Danish Government notified three types of commitments for transitional régimes. They were: 7.104

1. take-or-pay gas contracts with Dangas, with a stranded cost estimated at 993 million Kroner (DKK);
2. closure of 30 or so power plants by 2025, with total stranded costs amounting to DKK 2.75 billion; and
3. pension obligations of municipal utilities, with stranded costs estimated at DKK 600–700 million.

The mechanism for recovery proposed by the Danish Government was a surcharge on electricity consumption.

(v) **The Netherlands** The Dutch Government notified four transitional measures in two stages. They comprised the following: 7.105

- recovery of the losses on some district heating projects until 2021, amounting to between 1.628 and 2.0 billion Guilder (NLG);
- recovery of extra costs of construction and operation of Demoklec (demonstration coal gasification plant) in Buggenum, with stranded costs amounting to a maximum of NLG 550 million;
- a Protocol agreement concluded between Dutch generators and distributors up to and including 2000, with no estimate of the financial consequences of repeal of the Protocol for the generators; and
- international commitments, or recovery of possible losses from power procurement contracts between SEP, the Dutch electricity utility, and EdF, PreussenElektra, and Statkraft, from investment obligations of SEP to Statnett for the NorNed cable, and from a take-or-pay gas contract between SEP and Statoil.

In the latter case, the amount of the costs depended on the evolution of gas and electricity prices in the liberalizing market, but was expected to be in the range of NLG 3.1 billion at 7 cents/kWh to NLG 4.6 billion at 5 cents/kWh. Originally, the mechanism for recovery of the stranded costs in each case, except for the Protocol scheme, was through a levy on transport tariffs. Cancellation of the Protocol might lead to a new one being imposed on the parties by the Dutch Minister of Economic Affairs, which he is entitled to do. Initially, The Netherlands had proposed two other transitional schemes, which were subsequently withdrawn. The two schemes concerned:

1. the delay of privatization of the electricity sector, where express agreement of the Minister is necessary for the sale of shares outside the circle of existing shareholders until the end of 2001; and
2. the phasing-in of corporation tax to keep pace with the liberalization process.

The Commission took the view that neither of these proposals could be seen as falling within the scope of Article 24 of the Directive. In June 2001 the Dutch Government withdrew the financing mechanism by means of a levy from its notification to the Commission, clearing the way for Commission approval of the compensation for stranded costs by the State. As a State Aid within the meaning of Article 87(1), it was in compliance with the 'Methodology' and could therefore be authorized under Article 87(3)(c) EC.

7.106 (vi) **Austria** The Austrian Government notified two schemes with a transitional régime limited until 31 December 2009. They concerned:

1. guarantees of operation given to power plants based on the authorization procedure in operation prior to liberalization, and restricted to three hydro-power plants in Freudenau, Mittlere Salzach, and Kraftwerksete Obere Drau, with stranded costs estimated at 6.27 billion Schilling (ATS); and
2. long-term procurement contracts for indigenous lignite for the Voitsberg power plant belonging to Verbundgesellschaft, amounting to estimated stranded costs of ATS 2.43 billion. The mechanism for payments is a levy on power consumption.

In July 2001 the Commission concluded that the proposed compensations for hydropower plants would comply with its Methodology and might therefore be authorized under Article 87(3)(c) EC. The notified claims for compensation for the lignite plant might benefit from an authorization as a compensation for a service of general economic interest as regards security of supply, under Article 86(2), in the light of Articles 3(2) and 8(4) of the Electricity Directive.[84]

(b) Commission response

7.107 The Commission and Member States agreed that a methodology for the examination of state aid granted to electricity companies should be prepared and that all of the schemes for financial compensation notified should be assessed according to this methodology.[85] In this way, it was hoped that all financial measures of compensation would be assessed in a coherent and equitable manner. Essentially, such a methodology would provide that aid aimed at compensating stranded costs can be authorized by a Member State, on condition that the costs result from 'well identified and quantified historical commitments that can no longer be honoured in the context of liberalisation'.[86] In such circumstances, aid could be granted since it would facilitate the transition to a competitive electricity market.

[84] Commission Press Release, 'Commission gives green light to "stranded costs" compensation by Spain, Austria and The Netherlands', IP/01/1079, 27 July 2001.

[85] Tradacete, A, 'Rôle of EC Competition Policy in the Liberalization of EU Energy Markets', n 42 above, 16.

[86] ibid, 16–17.

A Communication on the Methodology for Analysing State Aid Linked to Stranded Costs was published by the Commission in July 2001.[87] This replaced a draft memorandum on stranded costs published two years before.[88] The Communication (or Notice) was intended to clarify how the Commission intends in the light of Directive 96/92/EC to apply the rules of the EC Treaty to state aid of this kind. It is broadly in two parts: the first is concerned with the definition of eligible stranded costs and the second explains the conditions under which eligible stranded costs may be offset by aid in ways that the Commission would deem compatible with the provisions of Article 87(3)(c) of the EC Treaty. **7.108**

(c) Eligibility of stranded costs

In the Notice stranded costs are described as 'commitments or guarantees of operation . . . that it might no longer be possible to honour on account of Directive 96/92/EC'.[89] Liabilities include long-term power purchase contracts, investments undertaken with an implicit or explicit guarantee of sale, or investments undertaken outside the scope of normal activity. The Notice sets out specific criteria that would be applied for possible classification of commitments or guarantees as eligible stranded costs. The criteria are the following: **7.109**

1. Commitments or guarantees of operation must pre-date 19 February 1999, the date of entry into force of Directive 96/92/EC.[90]
2. The existence and validity of such commitments or guarantees must be substantiated in terms of the underlying legal and contractual provisions and legislative context in which they were made.
3. A risk must be created in relation to such commitments and guarantees of operation that they will not be honoured as a result of the application of Directive 96/92/EC. This applies particularly where the viability of the undertakings may be in jeopardy in the absence of aid or any transitional measures (this criterion was further elaborated by the Commission—discussed below).
4. The commitments or guarantees must be irrevocable. If, therefore, an undertaking has a possibility of revoking against payment, or of modifying such

[87] European Commission, 'Commission Communication relating to the methodology for analysing State aid linked to stranded costs', 26 July 2001. The methodology for stranded costs does not prejudice the application of the guidelines on regional aid, in the regions covered by Art 87(3)(a): OJ C 74, 10.3.1998, 9; it applies independently of whether the undertakings are in public or private ownership.

[88] European Commission, 'Methodology for the analysis of state aids linked to stranded costs', 1999.

[89] ibid, 2–3.

[90] ibid, para (3.1). The numbering in this list follows the paragraph numbering in the Commission document.

commitments or guarantees, account will be taken of this in calculating the eligible stranded costs.

5. Commitments or guarantees that link enterprises belonging to one and the same group cannot usually be eligible as stranded costs.
6. Stranded costs are economic costs that must correspond to the actual sums invested, paid, or payable because of the commitments or guarantees from which they result. This means that 'flat-rate' calculations will not be accepted unless they can be shown to reflect economic realities.
7. Stranded costs must be costs net of the income, profits, or added value associated with the commitments or guarantees from which they arise.
8. Stranded costs must be valued net of any aid that has been paid or is payable in respect of the assets to which they relate. Where a commitment or guarantee of operation corresponds to an investment that is the subject of state aid, the value of the aid must be deducted from any stranded costs resulting from the commitment or guarantee.
9. Calculation of eligible stranded costs has to take account of the actual change over time in the economic and competitive conditions prevailing on the national and EU electricity markets. This applies whenever stranded costs arise from commitments or guarantees that are difficult to honour on account of the application of the Directive. In cases where stranded costs have arisen because of a foreseeable fall in electricity prices, calculation of the stranded costs must take account of actual movements in electricity prices.
10. Stranded costs must not include costs that have been depreciated before the transposition of the Electricity Directive into national law. However, provisions or depreciation of assets that have been entered into the balance sheet of the undertaking concerned may be included, where they have the explicit aim of taking account of foreseeable effects of the Directive.
11. Eligible stranded costs must not exceed the minimum level necessary to allow the undertakings concerned to honour or secure compliance with the commitments or guarantees that have been called into question by the application of the Directive. This means that for long-term contracts of sale or purchase, the stranded costs will be calculated by comparison with the conditions on which in a liberalized market the undertaking would normally have been able to sell or purchase the relevant product. The calculation of stranded costs will have to take into account the most economic solution (in the absence of any aid) from the standpoint of the undertakings concerned. As a result, this may lead to the termination of commitments or guarantees that give rise to stranded costs or to the disposal of all or some of the assets that give rise to stranded costs.
12. Costs that have to be borne by certain undertakings after the date of full market liberalization (18 Feb 2006), are not to constitute eligible stranded costs. However, this is softened in application somewhat. The Commission may

take these commitments and guarantees of operation into account and consider them as eligible stranded costs during the next stage of market-opening. In addition, where a failure to honour commitments or guarantees after this date might give rise to major risks concerning protection of the environment, public safety, social protection of workers, or network security, such commitments or guarantees are eligible for treatment as stranded costs. Other stranded costs eligible under this methodology, which may extend beyond 2006, are not affected by the above consideration.

The criterion in point 12 above is qualified by the declaration that the Commission may agree to classify some costs as eligible stranded costs where the undertakings that have to bear them do so after 18 February 2006, if such costs follow from commitments or guarantees that meet the definitional criteria listed above and are limited to a period not extending beyond 31 December 2010. This applies only to those Member States that open up their market more quickly than the Directive requires.

For the provision in point 3 to be operational, the commitments or guarantees that run the risk of not being honoured because of the Directive's application, must subsequently become non-economic due to the Directive's effects and must 'significantly affect the competitiveness of the undertaking concerned'.[91] This means that the undertaking must make accounting entries designed to reflect the foreseeable impact of the commitment or guarantee. In addition, when assessing the effects of such commitments or guarantees on the competitiveness or viability of the undertakings concerned, the Commission will do so at what it calls the 'consolidated level'. Eligibility for stranded costs is dependent on the establishment of a cause-and-effect relationship between the entry into force of the Directive and the difficulty that the undertakings concerned may have in honouring or securing compliance with the relevant commitments or guarantees. When the Commission is attempting to establish whether such a cause-and-effect relationship exists, it will take into account any fall in electricity prices or loss of marketshare experienced by the undertakings concerned. Where commitments or guarantees could not have been honoured irrespective of the Directive entering into force, such commitments or guarantees are not to be eligible as stranded costs.

(iv) Application of state aid rules

In cases where aid is proposed to offset eligible stranded costs, the Commission will have to decide whether the aid in question is compatible with Article 87(3)(c) of the EC Treaty. In doing so, it will seek to ascertain if the aid has satisfied the following criteria: **7.110**

[91] ibid, para (3.3).

1. The aid must be used to offset eligible stranded costs that have been clearly determined and isolated. It may under no circumstances exceed the amount of eligible stranded costs.
2. The arrangements made for payment of aid must make allowance for future developments in competition—measured by the use of quantifiable factors such as prices, marketshares, or other relevant factors indicated by the Member State. The amount of aid paid will vary over time according to the development of competition. The calculation of aid paid over time must also take into account changes in the relevant factors to assess the degree of competition achieved.
3. The Member State must undertake to deliver an annual report to the Commission, describing developments in the competitive situation in its electricity market and do so by indicating *inter alia* changes observed in the relevant quantifiable factors. The report must also provide details of how the stranded costs taken into account for the relevant year have been calculated and must specify amounts paid.
4. The 'degressive' character of aid proposed is to be viewed favourably by the Commission when making its assessment, on the grounds *inter alia* that this will assist the undertaking concerned to accelerate its preparations for a liberalized market in electricity.
5. The maximum amount of aid that may be paid to an undertaking to offset stranded costs must be specified in advance. It must take account of productivity gains that may be achieved by the undertaking.
   It is also a requirement that the detailed arrangements for calculating and financing aid and the maximum period for which such aid can be granted must be clearly set out in advance. When the aid is notified it should in particular specify how the calculation of stranded costs will take account of changes in the various factors set out in (2) above.
6. The Member State must undertake in advance not to pay any rescue or restructuring aid to undertakings that are to benefit from aid for stranded costs. The idea is to avoid any accumulation of aid. The thinking behind this is that the payment of compensation linked to investments in stranded assets that offer no prospects of long-term viability will not facilitate the transition to a liberalized electricity market and so cannot qualify for a derogation under Art 87(3)(c) of the EC Treaty.

7.111 A further assessment factor (but not included in the Commission's list of criteria) is the size and level of interconnection of the network concerned and of the structure of the electricity industry. In this context, aid that is to be granted to a small network with a low degree of interconnection with the rest of the EU will be viewed more favourably since it will be less likely to give rise to substantial distortions of competition.

(v) Financing of aid to offset stranded costs

While the choice of method of financing aid designed to offset stranded costs is a matter left to the Member States, the Commission has a concern to ensure that the method chosen does not give rise to effects that conflict with the objectives of the Electricity Directive or with the Community interest. It defines the latter as taking into account *inter alia* interests relating to consumer protection, free movement of goods and services, and competition. An example of such a conflict would be aid that deterred outside undertakings or new players from entering certain national or regional markets. It would not be acceptable to finance aid to offset stranded costs from levies on electricity in transit between Member States or from levies linked to the distance between producer and consumer.[92] **7.112**

Linked to the aims of the Electricity Directive, there is also a concern that any arrangements for financing aid intended to offset stranded costs would result in fair treatment for eligible and non-eligible consumers. The Commission will therefore require that the annual report provide a breakdown by eligible and non-eligible consumers of the sources of finance that are intended to offset the stranded costs.[93] If non-eligible consumers participate in the financing of stranded costs directly through the tariff for electricity purchase, this is to be stated clearly. The contribution to the financing by either eligible or non-eligible customers must not exceed the proportion of stranded costs to be offset that corresponds to the marketshare accounted for by those customers. **7.113**

Finally, the Commission notes that where funds are raised by private undertakings to finance aid mechanisms designed to offset stranded costs, a separation is required between the management of those funds and the normal resources of the undertakings. The investments should not benefit the undertakings that manage them. **7.114**

(vi) Stranded costs and state aid

The overall aim of the Commission in approving state aid corresponding to eligible stranded costs is to facilitate the transition to a competitive electricity market. For several reasons, the Commission takes the view that aid designed to offset stranded costs: **7.115**

> . . . normally qualifies for the derogation under Article 87(3)(c) if it facilitates the development of certain economic activities without adversely affecting trading conditions to an extent contrary to the common interest.[94]

---

[92] OJ C 74, 10 Mar 1998, 9.
[93] See Albers n 41 above, 8.
[94] ibid, 6.

Among the reasons justifying this view are the following.

- If the distortion to competition that inevitably results is one that is counterbalanced by a contribution made to achieving a Community objective that could not be achieved by market forces alone, then the Commission is prepared to view it favourably.
- In addition, the aid granted for stranded costs enables electricity undertakings to reduce the risks relating to their historic commitments or investments, increasing the likelihood that they will maintain their investments in the long term.
- And without compensation for stranded costs there is a risk that the undertakings concerned might pass on the entire cost of their non-economic commitments or guarantees to their captive customers.
- Finally, aid to compensate for stranded costs in the electricity industry can be justified in relation to other sectors such as telecommunications by the fact that liberalization has not been accompanied by either a speedier technological progress or by increased demand.
- It is also not conceivable to wait until electricity undertakings encounter difficulties before taking a decision on whether to grant them support. Relevant considerations here are environmental protection, security of supply, and the smooth running of the EU economy.

(vii) State aid and renewable energy

7.116 The relationship between renewable energy, state aids and the IEM programme, points to the risks involved in balancing potentially conflicting objectives in energy and environmental policy. The methodology described above does not apply to the kind of aid commonly granted to support the development of renewable energy. The Commission's position is that 'the long-term development of new energy sources, such as the renewable ones, is only instrumental to rendering these new energy sources competitive.'[95] Its aim is to adopt a new framework for the grant of aid to renewable energy sources. There is, however, real potential for tension between this aim of including a preferential treatment for renewable energy within a competitive framework and the growing constitutional support for environmental measures from the Treaty of Amsterdam onwards.

Germany: *PreussenElektra v Schleswag* and overriding Community interests There is some evidence of this tension in a judgment delivered in March 2001 by the ECJ. It ruled that an obligation to purchase electricity generated from renewable energy sources in Northern Germany did not constitute state aid within the meaning of the Treaty merely because it was imposed by statute.[96] Priority was accorded to environmental goals over those of the internal market.

[95] Schaub, n 47 above, 15.

[96] Case C–379/98, *PreussenElektra AG and Schleswag AG*, [2001] ECR I-2099.

The German law adopted in 1990 and twice amended in 1994 and 1998 (the *Stromeinspeisungsgesetz*) requires publicly-quoted electricity supply undertakings to purchase electricity generated within their area of supply from renewable sources, including wind energy, at minimum prices that are higher than the real economic value of that form of energy. The 1998 amendment introduced a mechanism for allocating extra costs due to the fact that a purchase obligation between power suppliers and upstream electricity network operators was established. Schleswag, a regional electricity supply undertaking in the State of Schleswig-Holstein, was required to purchase electricity generated within its area of supply from renewable energy sources, involving an additional cost rising from 5.8 million Deutschmark (DEM) in 1991 to 111.5 million DEM in 1998. Under the mechanisms provided for by the statute, Schleswag applied to PreussenElektra for payment of some amounts that it had already spent in complying with its purchase obligation. PreussenElektra then brought an action for recovery of 500,000 DEM, which represented the amount paid to Schleswag in compensation for the additional costs caused by the purchase of wind electricity. PreussenElektra argued that the payment was contrary to EU law since it constituted an amended system of state aid that had not been notified to the Commission (the system established by the 1990 law had been notified to the Commission and duly approved by it). The State court of Kiel asked the ECJ for a ruling on whether the amendment to the statutory system constituted an amendment of aid within the meaning of Community law and whether the system it established was contrary to the prohibition on quantitative restrictions on trade.

In its judgment the ECJ ruled that neither the statutory restriction introduced by the 1998 amendment nor the allocation of the financial burden between private supply undertakings and private operators of upstream electricity networks involved a direct or indirect transfer of State resources and was therefore not a state aid within the meaning of Article 87(1) EC. More importantly in this context, the ECJ stated that the rules were 'capable, at least potentially, of hindering intra-Community trade' but that they are aimed in particular at 'protecting the environment in so far as it contributes to the reduction in emissions of greenhouse gases'.[97] This meant that the aim of these rules was among the priority aims of the Community. The statutory rules were not therefore contrary to the free movement of goods. The ECJ also noted the relevance of two recitals of the Electricity Directive: firstly, the 28th recital expressly states that Member States are permitted under Articles 8(3) and 11(3) to give priority to the production of electricity from renewable sources for reasons of environmental protection, and secondly, the 39th recital notes that the Directive constitutes only a further phase in electricity liberalization and leaves some obstacles to intra-Community trade in place.

[97] ibid, paras 71 and 73.

In this light, the German legislation was not incompatible with Article 30 of the EC Treaty.

The impact of this judgment has been much discussed.[98] An early consequence was to influence the Commission's decision on the Spanish and Austrian compensation schemes for stranded assets, discussed above at paras 7.101 and 7.106. The Commission was unable to decide whether or not the payments granted to the beneficiaries of the system constituted State resources.[99] The sums involved are transferred from the customers to the beneficiaries through a fund established by the State but over which the State has little control. This is analogous to the effects of the price-fixing mechanism examined by the ECJ in *PreussenElektra*. It is also analogous to the effects of the Austrian compensation scheme for stranded assets. It was not clear whether this analogy was sufficient for the Commission to conclude that the compensation scheme involved no State resources and was therefore not State aid within the meaning of the EC Treaty. The Commission reached its decision in both cases on a different basis.

(7) **Joint Marketing of Gas**

7.117 The Commission has kept under review the horizontal arrangements concluded among gas producers, on the ground that this traditional practice has artificially reduced the number of independent players through joint selling arrangements. In this connection, the Commission has taken action against the arrangements used in the sale of gas from Norway to EU gas companies (see para 2.107). The GFU, a statutory body established in Norway, entered into a number of long-term supply agreements with EU gas marketing companies that were alleged to have created rigidity in the gas markets. The Government of Norway announced that the GFU would be suspended from 1 June 2001 and that it would be abolished entirely as of 1 January 2002. However, the effects of this measure were unlikely to be felt for many years due to the fact that most of the gas sold by the GFU is already contracted under arrangements that have up to 25 years to run.

The Commission took proceedings further and issued a statement of objections to all 21 current contract sellers explaining that their contracts may be in breach of competition rules and that they may therefore be liable to the imposition of major fines. A statement by the Commission called for the remedy of 'the long-term, adverse effects of the past and present misbehaviour', suggesting that retrospective action is being sought. Under the statement of objections procedure, the companies concerned may ask for a hearing and may submit oral and written

[98] eg, Keppenne, J-P, 'National Environmental Policies: Uncharted Waters for EC State Aid Control', (2001) Nederlands Tijdschrift voor Europees recht no 7/8 193–9.

[99] Allibert, Brice, 'A Methodology for Analysing State Aid Linked to Stranded Costs', *Competition Policy Newsletter*, Oct 2001, 25–7.

arguments. The Commission then makes an assessment as to whether further action should be taken. While it is clear that the Government has taken a positive step, the focus of Commission attention has shifted to the companies and the actions they might take to increase the supplies available.

Another instance in which joint marketing was reviewed turned on plans for the marketing of gas from the Corrib gas field in Ireland, a new discovery. The licensee companies, Enterprise Energy Ireland Limited, Statoil, and Marathon, applied for an exemption to market the gas jointly for the first five years of production. They argued that joint marketing was necessary to balance the countervailing purchasing power of the incumbent Irish energy companies, Bord Gais Eirean, the state-owned gas company and the Electricity Supply Board, the state-owned electricity company. The companies withdrew their application after the Commission raised objections on competition grounds. The ongoing liberalization process would create an increasing number of 'eligible' customers, including power generators and energy-intensive industrial consumers. The net effect would be to expand the customer-base in the power market and offer potential sales outlets to gas suppliers. In the Commissioner's view, the case confirmed the Commission's general policy 'not to tolerate joint selling, unless compelling reasons are provided as a justification'.[100] 7.118

The outcome of the *Corrib* case provides an interesting contrast to the *Britannia* case of only a few years earlier (see para 5.94). The Commission cleared an Agreement notified to it by the companies participating in the development of the Britannia gas field in the UK.[101] The Agreement did not affect trade between Member States and so was outside the scope of the EC's competition rules. It affected joint selling operations between February 1992 and the end of 1994. However, the conclusion was based on the absence of any pipeline system between the UK and any other Member State that could have managed the volumes of gas to be produced by this field. At the end of 1994 the interconnector pipeline agreement between the UK and the Continent was signed, and this argument was no longer justified. Joint selling (for many years the normal way of selling gas from a field) after that date was likely to be discouraged, or prohibited. That appears to have been the case in *Corrib*.

(8) Long-term Contracts: Destination Clauses

In 2001 the Commission began a series of investigations into so-called 'destination clauses' in long-term gas sales contracts concluded by non-EU producers and EU importers. These are provisions that prohibit the resale of purchased gas to consumers outside of the traditional supply area of the importer, being usually the 7.119

[100] European Commission Press Release, 'Enterprise Oil, Statoil and Marathon to market Irish Corrib gas separately', IP/01/578, 20 Apr 2001.
[101] European Commission Press Release, IP/96/1214.

Member State in which the importer is located. Apparently, they have been included in contracts concluded between the Russian gas utility, Gazprom, and Italian companies, SNAM (the gas distribution unit of ENI), Enel, and Edison,[102] but are also found in contracts with Sonatrach of Algeria. In the former case, they also prohibit Gazprom from selling to other companies in Italy. Such clauses appear to hinder the creation of a single market in energy.

The origin of this clause appears to lie in an attempt to protect the 'market value principle' in the pricing of gas. In this way, gas is priced differently according to the alternative energy sources that are available to gas buyers in each Member State.[103] The practice is for the producers to discount from the market value price the costs of transporting their gas to the country of consumption (the 'net-back' principle), the producers have an interest in maintaining the market value principle.

The initial step of the Commission has been to send a statement of objections to the parties, including Gazprom, noting its incompatibility with Article 81 EC. In recent years, the practice has been to impose fines on companies in the car industry that have attempted the same practices, in accordance with Article 15 of Regulation 17. The cases involving automobile distributors Volkswagen and Opel and more recently, Daimler-Chrysler are thought to lend support to this approach.[104] Ultimately, the Commission may impose a sanction of a fine amounting to 10 per cent of the companies' global revenues. In this context it may be noted that indirect measures such as the refusal or reduction of bonuses or discounts are prohibited, if the aim is to induce a gas purchaser not to resell to customers outside his traditional supply territory.

The wider policy context is, as indicated above (see Tables 7.1 and 7.2) that there are already too few suppliers of gas on the market so that efforts should be made by the Commission to ensure that the suppliers are not further reduced. Such actions therefore fit with the overall aim of increasing the amount of gas available on the EU market. If SNAM, for example, is prevented by a non-EU supplier from exporting the gas it purchases, then a consumer based in another EU Member State cannot approach SNAM as a potential supplier. Such practices are targeted

---

[102] Gazprom increased its exports to Europe by 18.3% between 1990 and 1999, selling gas to no less than 19 countries, with the largest increases evident in Germany, Italy, and Turkey: Fleming UCB Research: Russia Oil and Gas, 'Gazprom: Time is Up for the Ring Fence', Oct 2001, 27–8.

[103] *Exxon/Mobil*, paras 52, 62; see Albers n 41 above.

[104] Commission Press Release, 'Commission imposes fine of nearly 72 million on Daimler-Chrysler for infringing the EC competition rules in the area of car distribution', IP/01/1394, 10 Oct 2001; Commission Decision of 28 Jan 1998 against Volkswagen AG OJ L 124, 25 Apr 1998, 60; Commission Decision of 20 Sep 2000 against Opel Nederland BV/General Motors Nederland BV, OJ L 59, 28 Feb 2001, 1; Case No. COMP/36.693 30 May 2001 (Volkswagen), OJ L 262, 2 Oct 2001, 14–37.

for removal. The fact that the Commission is raising this matter with non-EU and non-EEA suppliers is a novel development.[105]

(9) Assessment

The Florence and Madrid Processes were the most obvious expressions of the Commission's need to investigate in detail what was required to make the provisions of the two Directives workable. There were related consultants' studies, harmonization reports, strategy documents, and other communications that were officially produced or inspired. However, much of this had the character of a data-gathering exercise and a preliminary manoeuvring among the stakeholders on the new energy scene created by the Directives. At some point agreements had to be struck on ways of overcoming the remaining barriers to a single energy market or the process had to be supplemented by proposals for action backed by law. By the end of 1999 it appeared that the Florence Forum was not able to deliver the results sought by the Commission and by most of the regulators. There was no reason to suppose that the Madrid Forum, begun at a later stage, would be any more successful. A legislative package to accelerate the IEM became inevitable. **7.120**

The interplay between the enforcement of competition law rules and the implementation of the Electricity and Gas Directives has clearly been very important in the period since their adoption. The enforcement of competition law in the energy sector has never been so strong in the history of the Community. The particular decisions taken by the Commission illustrate the extent to which the authorities have given serious thought to the issues involved in the electricity and gas sectors before taking action. For example, key differences have been identified by the competition authorities between gas and electricity in terms of liberalization potential. The Competition Directorate conducted an analysis of the product and geographical markets for gas and concluded that liberalization presents special challenges, especially with respect to network access. The regular participation of this Directorate in the Electricity and Gas Forum Processes ensured that such conclusions have provided input into their deliberations. With respect to gas, the conclusion can only be that additional efforts will be required to make significant progress in that sector. In particular, the horizontal demarcations that exist on the gas market will have to be monitored to promote competition on the supply side. **7.121**

Overall, the rôle of the competition law has been to support the actions begun by the Electricity and Gas Directives. The timetable for market opening in stages envisaged by these Directives and their omission of specific dates for full market **7.122**

[105] 'The Commission will deal with all major restrictions of competition irrespective of whether the companies are located inside or outside the European Union': remarks by Competition Commissioner Mario Monti in Commission Press Release, IP/01/1641, n 43.

opening has limited the room for manoeuvre of the competition authorities, which have in many cases sought to extract undertakings from incumbents that contribute to this gradual process of liberalization of energy markets. These commitments have been obtained in return for approval of incumbents' plans for mergers and acquisitions that have impacts on the structure of energy markets. The momentum for change in the sense of a 'deepening' of the IEM has had to come either from the Forum Processes, or from new legislative proposals.

8

ACCELERATING PROGRESS TOWARDS AN INTERNAL ENERGY MARKET: A NEW EUROPEAN MODEL OF REGULATION STRUGGLES TO EMERGE

Until recently, European integration had been a largely economic process. From now on it will be an increasingly political process.
Loyola de Palacio, Vice-President, European Commission*

A. Introduction

The gradualist approach to energy market liberalization favoured by the EU has quickly led to the tabling of new legislative proposals, and a further round of debate on the future of EU energy law and policy. These developments are examined in the first part of this chapter. The second part reflects on three themes that have persisted throughout this book. They are: 8.01

1. the impact of continual constitutional reform in the EU upon the process of energy market liberalization;
2. the emerging European model of energy regulation; and

* Speech delivered at London School of Economics, 22 Nov 2001, Commission Press Release, 23 Nov 2001, DN: SPEECH/01/568.

3. the impact on legislation and regulation of the EU's concerns about regularity, quality, and price of supplier and security of energy supply in emergencies, and in the medium/long term.

The first of these themes is of fundamental importance since the impetus for legislation on electricity and gas market liberalization in the EU stemmed from the programme of accelerating the creation of an internal market within the EU that began in the mid-1980s. The wider context has been one of institutional and procedural reforms of the Treaty to facilitate closer economic integration and also, more recently, major constitutional reforms to meet the challenges arising from enlargement. The institutional and procedural reforms analysed in the earlier chapters of this book constitute some insights into this.

The second theme, the emerging system of European energy regulation has its origins in the inability of the Forum procedure to reach definitive agreement on cross-border tariffing and on congestion management. This has caused the Commission to propose for itself the principal rôle in the settling of cross-border transportation charges (after advisory consultations with the national energy regulators), and the principal role in the establishment and operation of the régime to deal with cross-border congestion (with the national regulatory bodies acting again in an advisory capacity) in respect of the Commission's proposals. The emerging model and some of the issues it raises are commented on and discussed later.

The third theme is the concern of the Commission and some of the Member States that liberalization with its resulting competition will lead to cost cutting and consequently to a reduction in public service standards, and also possible redundancies in the electricity and gas industries. This is evident in the Commission's proposals on the Directives, which require an improved standard of public service and, in the case of electricity, the provision of electricity as a universal service. The Commission also sponsored research into the consequences for employees of energy market liberalization. These issues are commented on later.

B. Mandate for Further Reform

8.02 During 1999 and 2000 the Commission began to lay the basis for a new legislative option to take the additional measures many believed were necessary to achieve further progress in establishing a single market in energy. This involved three steps:

1. Securing political support from the key institutions that would be involved in such renewed effort to accelerate the liberalization process, namely the Council and Parliament.
2. Testing the views of the diverse stakeholders in the electricity and gas markets and, if positive, transforming them into some kind of mandate the

Commission could use. (In principle, the aim was to gauge the opinion of the stakeholders in the context of ongoing market developments. In practice, the views of the parties were already well known, but their fragmented character diluted their impact significantly).

3. Developing legislation to supplement and extend the provisions in the Electricity and Gas Directives.

At the Lisbon Summit on 23–24 March 2000 the European Council gave the signal that an acceleration of economic liberalization was desirable in the electricity, gas, postal services, and transport sectors. It concluded, 'the aim is to achieve a fully operational internal market in these areas.'[1] This was justified by reference to the promotion of competitiveness in the EU. The Council asked the Commission to develop proposals for an acceleration of energy market liberalization to implement what might be described as the 'Lisbon strategy'. **8.03**

Subsequently in May, the Energy Council invited the Commission to draw up proposals for further action in energy liberalization. As a first step, it asked the Commission to provide a report for the next Council meeting covering 'the state of play and experience with regard to the functioning of the internal market for gas and electricity; the development of a real playing field and the continued development and monitoring of indicators demonstrating true and effective competition'.[2] This was further boosted by a Resolution from Parliament in July supporting the trend towards an acceleration of energy market liberalization, as shown by the liberalization legislation of the large number of Member States which opened their electricity and gas markets to competition much more rapidly than the Directives require.[3] **8.04**

C. Channelling the Views of Stakeholders

The Commission initiated a process of consultation on the progress made towards the liberalization of electricity and gas markets required by the two Directives. This included the organization of a public hearing on 14 September 2000 to obtain the views of all interested parties on the liberalization process. **8.05**

---

[1] Minutes of the Meeting of the European Council, 23–24 Mar 2000. It is the duty of the European Council 'to provide the Union with the necessary impetus for its development' and 'to define the general political guidelines thereof': see ch 2, n 70 and paras 2.56–2.61.

[2] Council Conclusions, Internal Electricity and Gas Markets, 30 May 2000, 9 (8855/00, presse 186). Relevant documents here are the Communication of 16 May 2000 setting out the Commission's preliminary thinking on the way in which electricity liberalization could be completed, and 'Recent Progress with Building the Internal Energy Market', Communication COM (2000) 297, in which the Commission provided an initial analysis of the state of play on the electricity market-opening and examined actions required to facilitate the functioning of the internal energy market.

[3] European Parliament Resolution on the Commission's 2nd report to the Council and the European Parliament on the state of liberalization of the energy markets, A5-0180/2000, 6 July 2000.

Nearly 120 associations and companies participated in the hearing, including social partners, generators, gas producers, TSOs, distributors, and consumers.[4] Oral and written contributions were taken from 70 of these parties and their views on four main areas concerning implementation of the two Directives are summarized below.

(1) Market-opening

8.06 A large percentage of respondents were in favour of full market-opening in the short or medium term (80%) instead of the staged approach which required 33 per cent for electricity (with a threshold of 9GW consumption a year), and implementation by 2003; and for gas 33 per cent liberalization by 2008 (with a threshold of five million cubic metres consumption a year). In particular, the fact that distributors were eligible customers in some Member States but not in others was regarded as being especially discriminatory. The minority view (that the current provisions were sufficient and no acceleration in market-opening was required) was held, *inter alia* by representatives of employee organizations as well as the majority of responding gas companies.

(2) Network Access

8.07 A similarly high proportion of respondents were in favour of at least published tariffs for access to gas and electricity networks (80%). Most favoured regulated tariffs. However, a minority favoured a system of negotiated access leading to published prices after industry-wide negotiations, believing such a system creates a sufficiently transparent basis for non-discriminatory market access (the views of a group from Germany comprising electricity companies, TSOs, and the VIK, representing German consumers). It should be noted, however, that this system differs from a system of negotiated access on a case-by-case basis, as envisaged in the Gas Directive.

(3) Unbundling

8.08 Over 70 per cent of respondents were in favour of a significant strengthening of the Directives' provisions on unbundling. A minimum requirement should be, in their view, a legal unbundling of the TSO. However, a clear unbundling of all of the different activities was a minimum requirement for competition. Some argued that legal unbundling of the TSOs was not enough to be effective, but rather there should be complete financial independence of the TSO; others argued for ownership unbundling of the TSO.

[4] Communication COM (2000) 297, (see n 2 above). A detailed summary of all presentations made at the hearing and the contributions submitted in electronic form is available on the EC website at: http://europa.eu.int/comm/energy/en/elec_single_market/index_en.htm

(4) Public Service Obligations

There appeared to be little concern among the participants that PSOs could be met in a liberalized market, provided the regulatory framework were appropriate and that the PSOs were clear and transparent. However, and importantly, EdF noted that a reformed and reinforced public service obligations was the key to ensuring further liberalization in France. **8.09**

D. The Acceleration Package

In March 2001 the EC circulated new proposals for an acceleration of the internal energy market process. The initiative was instigated by the Council and Parliament. The legal instruments were both based upon Article 95 (requiring only a qualified majority for adoption) and comprised a draft Directive that would amend the Electricity and Gas Directives[5] (the 'Acceleration Directive') and a draft Regulation on cross-border trade in electricity[6] (see also ch 7). The overall aim of the proposals was declared to be the completion of the IEM in order to reap full benefits from participation in it.[7] The texts of the two Directives and those texts as amended by the proposed Acceleration Directive are contained in Appendices 1 and 2. **8.10**

The measures concern the degree of market-opening ('quantitative proposals') and the minimum obligations regarding network access, regulation, and the unbundling of the transmission function in vertically-integrated electricity and gas companies ('qualitative proposals').

(1) The Acceleration Directive

The measures are directed at amending two provisions in particular in the Directives that have proved to be unsatisfactory, namely the: **8.11**

1. pace and level of market-opening and
2. guarantees for fair and non-discriminatory network access.

With respect to (1), most Member States have opened their markets further than required by the Directives, but those who have not done so have created market

[5] Proposal for a Directive of the European Parliament and of the Council amending Directives 96/92/EC and 98/30/EC on common rules for the internal market in electricity and natural gas. This was also based upon Arts 47(2) and 55.

[6] Proposal for a Regulation of the European Parliament and of the Council on Conditions for Access to the Network for Cross-Border Exchanges in Electricity in the Internal Electricity Market. The Commission has indicated that it proposes to put forward a draft Regulation for the gas industry following with appropriate changes the text of the Electricity Regulation.

[7] COM (2001) 125, 13 Mar 2001.

distortions—between electricity companies and users of electricity. The distortions had proved difficult to deal with adequately through the Directives' provisions on reciprocity.

On (2), the standards applicable to network access vary considerably from one Member State to another, accentuating distortions in the market. The Commission has received complaints that some current procedures for network access are inadequate. Without clear and effective unbundling, together with standard and published TPA tariffs (ie regulated TPA), entry by new players would be difficult because they will not believe that non-discriminatory access could exist.

(a) Electricity Directive amendments

8.12 The principal amendments proposed to the Electricity Directive are summarized in Table 8.1.[8]

(b) Gas Directive amendments

8.13 The principal amendments proposed to the Gas Directive are similar in many respects to those proposed for the electricity sector.[9] They are summarized in Table 8.2.

8.14 The two Directives, even in amended form, will need to be complemented by an additional measure in order to make appropriate new rules on:

- pricing of cross-border trade;
- allocation of scarce capacity to interconnectors that reduce distortion of trade to the minimum possible; and
- increasing existing physical interconnection capacity, where deemed to be economically justified.

8.15 The protection of public service and the social dimension (employment impacts of liberalization)[10] is an important part of the Commission's proposals. (Although the Commission is keen to emphasize that market-opening has not so far resulted in any decline in public service standards.[11]) Measures proposed would reinforce current PSOs in two principal ways:

1. Member States would also be required to introduce appropriate measures to protect final customers (eg, protection of vulnerable customers, elderly, unemployed) from unjustified disconnection and to protect final customers' basic rights (eg, by requiring a minimum set of conditions for sale contracts, transparency of information, and a low cost and transparent dispute resolution procedure).

---

[8] The amendments to Directive 96/92/EC are contained in Art 1 of the proposed Directive. This list does not follow the order in the proposed Directive.

[9] Art 2.

[10] Annex VI, Communication.

[11] ibid.

Table 8.1 Electricity Directive: Summary of provisions in amended draft

	Proposed
Market-opening	Member States are to take action to ensure that all non-domestic customers are free to purchase electricity from their supplier of choice no later than 1 January 2003. All customers are to be free to choose their supplier no later than 1 January 2005.
Access/Tariffs	TPA to transmission and distribution systems is to be based on published tariffs, applicable to all eligible customers and applied objectively and without discrimination between system users. Tariffs are to be fixed or approved by a national regulatory authority prior to their entry into force. Note: The proposed Electricity Regulation requires the imposition of a harmonized methodology for calculating charges for access to national networks (see para 8.20) Electricity Transit Directive to be repealed. TSOs will have access on non-discriminatory terms and conditions to the networks of other TSOs if necessary and for the purpose of carrying out their functions, including those in relation to transit.
Authorization for new capacity	The authorization procedure for the construction of new electricity generation capacity is to be made the norm; tendering is to be used only in exceptional cases on the basis of published criteria and in the interests of security of supply.
Single Buyer	The single buyer option is to be deleted.
Unbundling	TSOs are to be independent in legal form, organization, and decision-making from other activities not related to transmission. A corresponding provision applies to DSOs. Integrated electricity undertakings are required, in their internal accounting, to keep separate accounts for their generation, distribution and supply activities and, where appropriate, consolidated accounts for other non-electricity activities.
PSOs	To be expanded to require a higher standard of public service Also, electricity is to be provided as a 'universal service'.
Regulation	Member States must establish a national regulatory body wholly independent from the interests of the electricity industry with, at least, sole responsibility to fix or approve terms and conditions relating to connection and access to national networks including transmission and distribution tariffs; to fix or approve tariffs, or changes in tariffs at national level, to reflect costs or revenues related to cross-border transmission of electricity, and will be responsible for defining rules on management and allocation of interconnection capacity, in conjunction with the national regulators of countries with which interconnections exist; and to fix or approve mechanisms to deal with congested capacity within the national electricity system. The regulatory body is to be responsible for the implementation of PSOs.
Security of supply	A body must be designated by Member States to monitor security of electricity supply issues (including supply/demand balance in the national market, the level of expected future demand and envisaged additional capacity planned or under construction) and the level of competition in the market. Annual reports on these issues are to be published. Member States must implement appropriate measures to achieve security of supply.

Table 8.2 Gas Directive: Summary of provisions in amended draft

	Proposed
Market-Opening	Member States are to take action to ensure that all non-domestic customers are free to purchase gas from their supplier of choice no later than 1 January 2004. All customers are to be free to choose their supplier no later than 1 January 2005.
Access/Tariffs	TPA to transmission, distribution and LNG facilities is to be based on published tariffs applicable to all eligible customers; and applicable objectively and without discrimination between system/facility users. Tariffs are to be fixed or approved by a national regulatory authority prior to their entry into force. TPA for storage and equivalent flexibility instruments may be organized according to nTPA or rTPA (or both). Member States have the choice. Gas Transit Directive to be repealed. TSOs will have access on non-discriminatory terms and conditions to the networks of other TSOs if necessary and for the purpose of carrying out their functions including those in relation to transit.
Unbundling	TSOs are to be independent in legal form, organization and decision-making from other activities not related to transmission. A corresponding provision applies to DSOs. The unbundling requirements for the accounts of integrated gas companies are similar to those applied for in the case of integrated electricity companies.
PSOs	A similar PSO requirement to that in the electricity sector but with the addition of long-term planning as a means of carrying out PSOs in relation to security of supply. There is no universal service obligation.
Regulation	Member States must establish a national regulatory body wholly independent of the interests of the gas industry with, at least, sole responsibility to fix or approve terms and conditions relating to connection and access to national networks including transmission and distribution tariffs; to define the rules on management and allocation of interconnection capacity in conjunction with national regulatory authorities with which interconnection exists, and to fix or approve mechanisms to deal with congested capacity within the national gas system. The regulatory body is to be responsible for the implementation of PSOs.
Security of supply	A body must be designated by Member States to monitor security of gas supply issues. The relevant issues for gas security of supply monitoring are the supply demand balance on the gas market, the level of expected future demand and available supplies and the level of competition on the market. Member States or owners of transmission, storage or LNG facilities are required to designate system operator(s) to be responsible for ensuring the maintenance, development of transmission, storage and LNG facilities in a given area and their interconnections with other systems in order to guarantee security of supply. Member States must implement appropriate measures to achieve security of supply.

2. Member States would also be required to take appropriate measures to ensure that essential PSO objectives were met: in the following areas: social and economic cohesion; environmental protection; and security of supply notably through the maintenance and construction of necessary framework infrastructure including interconnection capacity.

The provision in the Acceleration Directive that would require electricity to be provided as universal service is unusually wide. It states that Member States have an obligation to 'ensure that all customers enjoy universal service, that is, the right to be supplied with electricity of a specified quality within their territory at affordable and reasonable prices'. The latter term is capable of a wide and subjective interpretation with respect to different income groups (eg, wealthy, poor, or in some way disadvantaged). It is not clear who will bear this cost, whether schemes may be established to pay for these costs, how such arrangements would fit in with existing PSOs in respect of supply to the poor or disadvantaged,[12] nor is it clear whether this means average costs or constitutes a form of 'social pricing'. It may be noted that in subsequent draft amended texts the scope of the obligation has been limited to 'domestic and SME [small and medium-sized enterprise] customers'. This reduces the number of problems but the ones above remain.

The proposals also include a recognition of wholesale markets and intermediaries which was absent in the earlier Directives. The intention is to avoid possible discrimination by Member States of this category of market player. Wholesale customers (ie, entities who buy electricity/gas for resale and who do not consume electricity/gas) are to be entitled as from 1 January 2003 (electricity) and as from 1 January 2004 (gas) to purchase gas from suppliers of their choice. **8.16**

(2) Cross-Border Electricity Exchanges

The second instrument proposed by the European Commission is a Regulation on Conditions for Access to the Network for Cross-Border Exchanges in Electricity in the Internal Electricity Market (see Annex 3).[13] In contrast to the proposed Directive, which must be transposed into the legislation of Member States, permitting them some margin for interpretation and a time-lag of up to two years, the proposed Regulation would, on adoption, be directly applicable in all Member States. **8.17**

The Regulation is directed at the increasing cross-border trade in electricity that currently amounts to a modest eight per cent in the EU. This increase is to be

[12] There is some experience of this in the proposed Directive on universal service and users' rights relating to electronic communication materials and services: COM 2000/0392 final—COD 2000/0183 (see ch 4, n 131).

[13] See n 7.

achieved by the establishment of a compensatory mechanism for transit flows of electricity, the setting of harmonized principles on cross-border transmission charges, and procedures for the allocation of available interconnection capacity by TSOs in the event of network congestion problems.[14] The proposed cost-reflective methodology for transit flow charges means that the costs incurred as a result of hosting transit flows would be established 'on the basis of the forward-looking long-run average incremental costs (reflecting costs and benefits that a network bears from hosting transit flows compared to the costs it would bear in the absence of such flows)'. The aim is to provide host operators with suitable incentives to make the necessary investments to host transits, based on an adequate return but avoiding windfall profits. This would reflect the costs and benefits a network bears from hosting transit flows, compared with costs it would bear in the absence of such flows. Benefits occur when, for example, transit flows contribute to the overall stabilization of a national network.

8.18 Although the Commission stated that these measures in the Regulation simply formalize progress that had already taken place in the Florence Forum, it also noted that they would not have been necessary if agreement on these matters could have been secured voluntarily in that context. It candidly noted several shortcomings inherent in the Florence Process (see ch 7, para 7.35).

8.19 Perhaps tellingly, there is in the draft Regulation a vigorous approach to the Commission's future powers in this field. A key feature is its grant of wide powers to the Commission to require information for the purpose of determining compensation levels for the TSOs and stringent provisions for the imposition of fines if the information is either incomplete or misleading.

8.20 The provisions of the draft Regulation should also be read in conjunction with the proposals to amend the Electricity and Gas Directives, discussed above. For instance, the latter would require Member States to appoint national regulatory authorities (NRAs).[15] The respective responsibilities of these bodies are summarized in Table 8.1 (Electricity) and Table 8.2 (Gas) under the heading 'Regulation' above.

8.21 The proposed Regulation for electricity provides for the creation of two committees; one committee will have an advisory role as to the amounts of compensation payable to TSOs for hosting transit flows. The Commission need not accept the Committee's opinion but is required to take the utmost account of it. The advisory procedure laid down in Article 3 of Decision 1999/468/EC shall apply to the committee in compliance with Article 7 and Article 8 of the Decision. The other committee will have a regulatory role in connection with

[14] Draft Regulation, Art 1.

[15] Draft Acceleration Directive, Art 22.

the Guidelines to be adopted (and subsequent amendments to them) on the management and allocation of available transfer capacity of interconnections between related systems. The regulatory procedure laid down in Article 5 of Decision 1999/468 EC shall apply to the Committee in compliance with Article 7 and Article 8 of the Decision. In both cases, the Member States propose a representative to sit on the committee who will almost certainly be a member of the national Electricity Regulatory Authority. There are no formal links between the Commission and the NRAs, but operational links will arise, especially in connection with the activities of the committees and the performance of duties under Article 4 of the Regulation.

Subsidiarity

The terms of the proposed Acceleration Directive and Regulation give rise to considerations of subsidiarity. In this context, the proposed Directive contains the statement: **8.22**

> In accordance with the principles of subsidiarity and proportionality, as set out in Article 5 of the Treaty, the objectives of the proposed action namely the creation of fully operational electricity and gas markets, in which fair competition prevails, cannot be sufficiently achieved by the Member States and can therefore by reason of the scale and effect of the action, be better achieved by the Community. This Directive confines itself to the minimum required to achieve these objectives and does not go beyond what is necessary for that purpose (Recital 22).

The Regulation has a similar Recital but with some differences. It states:

> In accordance with the principles of subsidiarity and proportionality, as set out in Article 5 of the Treaty, the objectives of the proposed action, *namely the provision of a harmonized framework for cross border exchanges of electricity cannot be achieved by the Member States, and can therefore, by reason of the scale and effect of the action, be better achieved by the Community.* This Regulation confines itself to the minimum required in order to achieve those objectives and does not go beyond what is necessary for that purpose (*emphasis added to show differences between the two texts*).

There are five main elements in the draft regulation concerning: **8.23**

- compensation for transit flows of electricity;
- cross-border tariffs (guidelines on details for principles and methodologies);
- national network charges;
- congestion management (allocation of interconnection capacity); and
- provision of information and confidentiality.

(a) Compensation for transit flows of electricity

This had been a major source of contention in the Florence Process and had ultimately appeared to be irresolvable within that framework (see paras 7.30–7.32). **8.24**

Essentially, a basis had to be found for compensating TSOs for costs incurred by 'transit' or 'loop-flows' of electricity, created indirectly by export transactions in countries that are not on the direct path of the electricity being exported. If TSOs are not compensated for these extra costs, the local network users would have to pay instead, despite the fact that the electricity flows are caused by market players in different transmission areas.

8.25 The Regulation proposes a system of compensation comprising three elements:

1. TSOs receive compensation for costs incurred by hosting electricity flows on their networks (Art 3(1));
2. Rules are set on how costs incurred from transits are to be determined. The priority is to ensure that such costs are compensated on a cost-reflective basis. Costs must be determined accurately to identify costs actually incurred, avoiding 'windfall profits' and excessive transaction costs. Windfall profits for the TSOs hosting transits are to be prevented by means of a model of the 'forward-looking long-run average incremental costs that a network bears from hosting transits' (see para 8.31).
3. *Compensation payments*: operators of transmission systems from which transits originate and/or operators of systems where these flows end—(including exporting and/or importing TSOs)—pay compensation on a pro rata basis. However, the Regulation does not foresee a mechanism whereby individual exporters or importers are directly held responsible for payment for transit flows (while a payment mechanism is necessary, it is not possible for technical reasons to identify whether and to what extent an individual exporter or importer causes transits).

8.26 The Regulation attaches great importance to the making of rapid and accurate decisions on the amounts of the level of compensations to be paid and received between TSOs. It stipulates that the Commission is to make, on a regular basis, decisions on the compensation payments (Art 3(3)). The regulatory authorities of Member States are to be involved in this process through an advisory committee comprising national representatives created in accordance with Council Decision 1999/468 laying down procedures for the exercise of implementing powers conferred on the Commission. The Commission is required to consult with an advisory committee (see para 8.16).

National regulatory authorities would have to ensure that national tariffs and procedures for congestion management are set and applied in compliance with the principles laid down in the Regulation and the guidelines drafted by the Commission.[16]

[16] Draft Regulation, Art 8.

(b) Cross-border tariffs: Guidelines on details of principles and methodologies

Two Articles of the Regulation expressly address cross-border tarification (Arts 3 and 4). However, their provisions are not very detailed. Instead, Article 7 provides for the determination of technical details, which are continually being refined and improved, to come later in the form of guidelines. The guidelines must comply with the principles laid down in the Regulation. They must be adopted and amended by the Commission after consultation with a regulatory committee comprising experts designated by the Member States, and created in accordance with Council Decision 1999/468. The aim would be to ensure involvement of the regulatory authorities of Member States in the process of drafting the guidelines, especially the national regulatory authority. **8.27**

The guidelines would cover two principal sets of issues: **8.28**

1. With respect to the inter-TSO compensation mechanism (Regulation, Art 3):
   - precise details of methodologies to determine the amount of transits hosted and exports/imports of electricity made (in accordance with principles in Art 3(3));
   - methodology to determine costs incurred by hosting transits of electricity (in accordance with Art 3(5) principles);
   - details on determination of which TSOs have to pay compensations for transit flows (in accordance with Art 3(2) principles);
   - details of payment procedures to be followed, including determination of first period of time for which compensations will be made (Art 3(6));
   - details on participation of national systems which are interconnected through direct current lines in inter-TSO compensation mechanism.
2. With respect to national tariff systems (Regulation, Art 4):
   - details of harmonization of levels of tariffs applied to generators and consumers (in other words, the 'load') under national tariff systems (in accordance with Art 4(2)).

(c) National network charges

The draft Regulation does not propose complete harmonization of national access charges. The methodology for establishing surcharges is required to be harmonized (Art 4). It requires that access charges should reflect actual costs incurred. The charges must be transparent, approximated to those of an efficient network operator, and not distance-related. National network charges are to be recovered largely through charges imposed on consumers (Art 4(2)). A smaller proportion of the total network costs may be recovered, however, through charges imposed on generators. In this way the national authorities can include locational signals in the tariff structure, indicating the most appropriate or inappropriate zones in which to locate new generation. The Regulation stipulates that, where appropriate, charges shall contain elements providing for such locational signals. **8.29**

(d) Congestion management: allocation of interconnector capacity

8.30 The Regulation sets out the main principles for dealing with congestion management (Arts 5 and 6). This includes an obligation in Article 5(1) to implement co-ordination and information exchange mechanisms. In particular, information concerning the capacity actually available must be made public to market players. There is also an obligation upon TSOs to publish their security standards and their operational and planning standards in open and public documents, in order to ensure full transparency of the methodologies used by TSOs when establishing the amount of available capacity (Art 5(2)). The TSOs already have at their disposal mechanisms to underestimate their capacity by way of long-term contracts. The Competition Directorate has already reviewed this area for possible abuses.

The Regulation requires that the maximum capacity of the interconnections that complies with the safety standards of secure network operation be made available to market operators. Any allocated capacity that is not used by a market operator should be reattributed to the market.

The Commission recognizes that emphasis in the Regulation on capacity allocation and the need for new interconnector capacity may be contested. In practice, it may be more efficient in the medium term to optimize the use of existing capacity and rely on market-based mechanisms and published prices for the use of that capacity.

8.31 In cases of congestion, the allocation of interconnector capacity by TSOs is to be made in accordance with market-based solutions that convey efficient economic signals to market operators and TSOs (Art 6(1)). As regards the methods for making such allocations, the favoured approach is market-splitting rather than auctions, although there is as yet insufficient experience of market-splitting in practice (see ch 7, paras 7.83–7.85). The general principles for rules on congestion management are set out in Article 6. They include the principles that: network congestion problems are to be addressed with non-discriminatory, market-based solutions; and the maximum interconnector capacity possible must be made available to market operators that is consistent with safety standards.

Revenues from congestion management are, under the Regulation, to be used for three purposes: to guarantee reliability of allocated capacity; towards investment into network maintenance or to increase capacity of the interconnector; or towards a reduction in the network tariffs. The key point is that revenues should not constitute a source of additional profit (Art 6(6)).

(e) Provision of information and confidentiality

8.32 The Regulation provides for access by the Commission to information and data relevant to the guidelines and to help it decide compensations for transit between

TSOs.[17] The Member States and national regulatory authorities must provide data on request by the Commission. The Commission may also require all necessary information directly from the undertakings concerned, where necessary to fulfil its tasks under the draft Regulation.

Subsidiarity and the Proposed Regulation

It is clear that if the Regulation were to be adopted the Commission would acquire a very substantial and long-term regulatory rôle in the operation of the internal electricity market. This raises the question of 'whether the objectives could not be sufficiently achieved by Member States themselves'.[18] In the Commission's view, the draft Regulation is 'a key instrument to promote the creation of a real internal electricity market, as opposed to a situation characterised by 15 more or less liberalised but largely national markets'. Arguably, the goals of establishing a compensatory mechanism for transit flows and procedures for congestion management could not be achieved by the Member States themselves. The same cannot so readily be said about some aspects of the Regulation relating to national network charges. The possibility that the compatibility of the Commission's proposed powers in relation to these changes might be challenged cannot be ruled out. **8.33**

(3) Infrastructure Measures

Some further legislative measures are proposed, largely to address congestion and inadequate links in the EU electricity transmission networks. In some Member States levels of interconnection capacity are too low to support the expansion in trade that the liberalization measures seeks to encourage. Seven principal bottlenecks have been identified in the electricity sector: the borders between France and Spain; West Denmark and Germany; the borders of Benelux and Italy; the interconnection between the UK and continental Europe, Greece and Ireland. **8.34**

In December 2001 the Commission published an action plan for discussion.[19] This was linked to the TENs programme, where a proposed Decision sets out a list of 12 electricity and gas projects to be designated as 'priority projects of European interest'.[20] The TENs energy policy is to be supplemented by two additional priorities: support in implementing the IEM, and connection of renewable energy production to the interconnected energy networks.

[17] Draft Regulation, Art 9.

[18] Brothwood, M, 'EC wants larger say in trade', Utility Europe, July 2001.

[19] European Commission, 'European Energy Infrastructure', COM (2001) final 20 Dec 2001.

[20] European Commission, 'Proposal for a European Parliament and Council Decision, amending Decision No 1254/96/EC laying down a series of Guidelines for trans-European energy networks', 18 Dec 2001.

The action programme contains 13 steps and is interesting *inter alia* because of the rôle it accords to regulatory players that have come into existence since the adoption of the Electricity and Gas Directives. In addition to the NRAs, the Ceer will play an important rôle in the development of guidelines for regulatory control and financial reward for gas and electricity infrastructure. Both TSO bodies for electricity and gas are expected to play rôles in this process, which will also be co-ordinated with the Forum processes. The outcome of these deliberations will determine in a number of cases whether the Commission will propose further regulations. This approach is in line with the Commission's White Paper on Governance,[21] which recommends that actions be taken at a level most appropriate to achieving flexible and practical results quickly. To the extent that these informal mechanisms deliver a result, the requirement for legal measures is correspondingly reduced.

E. Initial Reactions to the Proposals

8.35 The first formal occasion in which the Commission's proposals were discussed was the European Council meeting in Stockholm in March 2001. Reactions from political leaders were mixed and no clear body of support emerged for the proposals in their initial form. As for a time-table for further progress, the conclusions of the Council meeting (drawn up by the Presidency) cautiously state that 'the question of time-tables for the electricity and gas markets will be considered in order to implement the objective of market-opening in these sectors as soon as possible.'[22] In general, the Council endorsed 'the objective of opening markets in these sectors, taking into account the requirement to satisfy user needs and the need for transparency in the market through appropriate regulatory instruments'[23]. The Commission was invited, a prerequisite to taking any new measures, to assess the gas and electricity sectors and present its findings in a report to the Council in 2002. It appeared that the proposals had failed to receive the sort of political support that would have given them momentum. However, it could be argued that the aim was not to seek unanimous approval in Council but to prepare the ground for a decision based on a qualified majority, with the support of Parliament.

8.36 The principal opposition to the package came from France and Germany.

The French arguments were largely based on a perception that liberalization of markets implied a move away from public service. Deregulation is viewed not as

[21] European Commission, 'White Paper on European Governance', COM (2000) 428.

[22] Europe Report, 'Member States at Odds over Deregulation', no 2580, 28 Mar 2001.

[23] ibid.

an end in itself but rather as 'an instrument for taking account more effectively of users' expectations'[24] (see para 8.09). The effect of this opposition would be likely to be seen in an amended version of the Directive leaning towards these social and public service considerations, rather than any fundamental substantive change. Behind the formal positions taken, there were considerations of possible unemployment arising from liberalization, especially in the French electricity sector, and a broader lack of enthusiasm among the electorate for the changes implied by the Directives.

German opposition was based on resistance to the idea of a national independent regulatory authority for electricity and gas markets, with authority to fix, publish, and approve network tariffs. The form of regulation that was favoured in Germany was the 'ex post' regulation carried out by the federal competition authority (*Bundeskartellamt*) for industry as a whole, including the energy industries. The German authorities considered a lighter, non-sectoral form of regulation more appropriate to its fragmented energy sector.

8.37 It appears likely that the above opposition to the Acceleration Package will not affect its momentum in the medium to long term. Compromises can be developed to meet such criticisms. For example, it appeared by early 2002 that the objectives to be achieved by an independent regulatory authority could be met, in Germany's case, by reliance on a new division of the *Bundeskartellamt*:[25] modified wording to Article 22 of the Acceleration Directive suggests that with respect to both electricity and gas, the status quo could be adapted to meet the requirements of the Directive in this respect, in this way retaining its status as the only Member State without a sector-specific authority. With respect to the French emphasis on public service, there has been a marked emphasis on this in the discussion of the proposal since it was first launched (see below).

In addition, the energy industry's customers and the smaller players will continue to press regulators for greater choice. A response from the regulators is also likely. An early indication of industry reactions came from the association of electricity companies, Eurelectric. It was broadly in favour of the measures but made a number of criticisms of the electricity proposal, notably with respect to the absence of any amendment of Article 24 on stranded costs and lack of clarity on the independence of the regulatory authority.[26] Eurelectric was particularly critical of the lack of measures to promote cross-border trade in gas, similar to those contained

[24] Europe Energy, 'Member States at Odds Over Deregulation', no 578, 30 Mar 2001.

[25] Amended Proposals to Directive and Regulation produced by Council Working Group (internal documents), Sept –Oct 2001.

[26] Eurelectric, 'Position Paper on the Proposal of the Commission for a Directive of the European Parliament and of the Council amending Directives 96/92/EC and 98/30/EC on Common Rules for the Internal Market in Electricity and Natural Gas', May 2001.

in the Regulation proposed for the electricity sector.[27] Indications of support came from other industry associations.[28]

There is nevertheless room for doubt as to whether the regulatory powers that the Commission would be taking on as a result of this package are in each case necessary for the completion of the internal energy market, especially with respect to national network tariffs.[29]

8.38 The proposals to accelerate liberalization are attempting to tackle a situation that is increasingly recognized as being characterized by a distortion of competition due to the uneven pace of liberalization among Member States. Companies from some Member States are perceived as being 'free riders', triggering an interest in the use of reciprocity provisions by way of protective action—a course of conduct which has even gained approval from the Energy Commissioner.[30] This negative assessment received official support from a report published by the Commission in December 2001.[31] Based on several studies carried out on the Commission's instructions, the report concluded that asymmetries in implementation were widespread, leading to 'considerable distortions of the internal market'.[32]

8.39 An alternative legal procedure to combat such companies and their host governments lies in the competition law. Interestingly, the Council's conclusions on the draft Directive and Regulation also included a request to the Commission that it ensure that the provisions of the Treaty and in particular Articles 81 and 82, 'will be fully observed and the implementation of those decisions could create no distortions of competition'.[33] It added that the Commission should 'also ensure that those enterprises which still benefit from a monopoly situation on their national market will not benefit unduly from that situation'. In the event of a delay in the adoption of the draft Acceleration Directive and Regulation leading to a distortion of competition, the Commission subsequently agreed to consider the adoption of legislation addressed to the Member States under Article 86(3) (see ch 3, paras 3.57–3.62; and ch 5, paras 5.09–5.18).[34] Such an approach has been adopted in the

[27] Eurelectric, 'Position Paper on Parallel Opening of Gas and Electricity Markets: comments on proposed Directive amending the Gas Directive', June 2001.

[28] eg, EFET Press Release, 4 May 2001; GEODE Press Release, 12 Feb 2001.

[29] Brothwood, n 18 above.

[30] 'Electricity and Natural Gas: Evolution and Opportunities in Two Converging Markets', speech delivered at conference, 11 June, 2001. For the response, see amended ED Art 19(2) and amended GD Art 19.

[31] European Commission, 'First Report on the Implementation of the Electricity and Gas Directives', SEC (2001) 1957, 3 Dec 2001.

[32] ibid, Executive Summary, vi.

[33] Europe Energy, see n 24.

[34] Commission Press Release, 'Commission confirms need to tackle cross-border investment restrictions and energy market distortions', IP/01/872, 20 June 2001; see also First Report, n 31 above at 32.

telecommunications sector in the past, but never used with respect to the electricity and gas industries in the EU.

A consequence of the European Council's response to the legislative proposals was a renewed effort to extract benefits from the voluntary processes of the Florence and Madrid Forums. This was evident in both meetings held in May and July 2001 respectively. The limits of these informal mechanisms has been clearly established (see ch 7, Parts A and B). This did not mean that the Forum mechanism was likely to be abandoned altogether, only that expectations of what could be achieved by its use had been lowered. The next stage in the IEM process now lies with the established Community institutions and the legislative procedures normally used. **8.40**

F. Internal Energy Market: An Assessment

(1) Impact of Institutional Reform

The IEM process has its roots in the attempts by the EU to accelerate the creation of an internal market beginning with the Single European Act (SEA) of 1986. Earlier attempts to achieve the same objective in the history of the Community were not successful. The SEA created the potential for a majority of Member States to out-vote a minority through the Qualified Majority Voting system. Yet the SEA contributed largely a timetable and a programme rather than new legal powers to Community institutions. It provided a momentum to the internal market that made it impossible for the energy sector to remain outside the mainstream of European integration. **8.41**

The adoption of a comprehensive body of legal rules for the electricity and gas sectors was a very lengthy process, and the further development of that body of law appears to be characterized by a similar degree of complexity. However, it is useful to draw a distinction between the two phases in order to examine the impact of the changes in law-making processes upon this legal framework. The first phase, examined in Part II, is the 'preparation' phase, in which a legal framework was established for the internal market in electricity and gas. The second stage, examined in Part III, can be characterized as the 'transitional' stage from monopoly dominated markets to one in which competition will play the crucial rôle in these energy markets.

The features of legislation in the preparation phase have already been noted. The legal basis for the measures proposed and ultimately adopted was the harmonization provision of the EC Treaty. An alternative route, drawing on powers granted to the Commission under Article 86(3) was rejected and played no further rôle at this stage. Other enforcement powers were used by the Commission but did not play a major part. The length of time from proposal to adoption of the final text was in the case of both Electricity and Gas Directives remarkably long: respectively, five and six years. The debate among the participants was often quite acrimonious, in private and in public. What is striking about this process however is the extent to which Community institutions and Member States strove to identify a consensus that all parties could live with.

The Directives cannot seriously be understood as 'watered down' versions of the original proposals but rather as outcomes of complex negotiations that permitted transitional periods, opt-outs, or derogations and other mechanisms that recognized the particular circumstances of certain Member States. The possibility that a solution could have been reached on the basis of a QMV decision was surely influential but in the sense that the 'possibility of breaking deadlocks by voting drives the negotiators to break the deadlocks without actually resorting to the vote'.[35] It was rather the influence of 'the consensus norm' that reinforced the choice of legislative route, with the harmonization procedure taking precedence over the alternatives (in particular, by excluding the adoption of Directives issued under Art 86(3) but also limiting the scope for instruments such as infringement proceedings under Art 226 and the application of competition law, especially Arts 81 and 82 EC).[36] This was preferred in spite of the lengthy process it clearly implied, and encouraged a process of continuous revisions of drafts over a long period.

8.42 It may be concluded that, with respect to the preparatory stage of establishing a legal framework for the internal market in electricity and gas, the potential for outvoting one or more Member States that the changes in law-making procedures served at most to facilitate agreement on a set of legal rules.

There are therefore significant differences between the regulatory setting in the current (transitional) phase and the previous (preparation) one. They raise the question as to whether the treatment of the legislative package proposed by the Commission in 2001 will be subject to the consensus norm in decision-making to the same degree. Given the highly complex environment and the transparently negative impact of non-compliant Member States, it may well be that the QMV approach is more appropriate at this stage of Community development. It may also be an appropriate moment to utilize other legislative options such as that of Article 86(3).

8.43 The present, transitional phase can be sub-divided into two: the initial stage of adoption and implementation of the Electricity and Gas Directives, and the second

[35] Weiler, J, The Transformation of Europe, (1991) 100 Yale Law J 2403 at 2461–62.

[36] Eising R, 'Strategic Action and Policy Learning in Embedded Negotiations: the liberalization of the EU electricity supply industry', (2002) 56 International Organization, 1; see also Hayes-Renshaw, F and H Wallace, 'Executive Power in the European Union: functions and limits of the Council of Ministers', (1995) J of European Public Policy 2, 559–82.

acceleration of liberalization stage, with new legislative proposals as a driver for change. During the second stage, the institutional constitutional setting is again in flux, with discussions on Treaty revisions and major institutional constitutional reform to meet the challenge of a significant enlargement of the EU. Among the proposals under discussion were ones designed to achieve a new form of governance. In this context, attempts were made by the Community institutions to accelerate the completion of the IEM.

There are some important differences in the development of the legal framework at that stage which require comment.

- 1. There has been a significant increase in regulatory complexity at Member State and Community level. In (almost) every Member State there are sector-specific regulatory authorities as well as competition authorities with responsibility for the energy sector. The scope for action by the European Commission competition authorities has been de facto increased, with the appearance of 'transitional' problems such as stranded assets and congestion at interconnected electricity lines. The need for a hierarchy of authority in the face of possible jurisdictional overlap and conflict is clear. The Forum mechanism discussed in Chapter 7 has also added an important (and probably lasting) element to the informal decision-making structures, but it is the Acceleration proposals that address the sensitive issue of a hierarchy of authority in EU energy regulation.
- 2. There has been a considerable increase in transparency and information flow since the adoption of the Directives. Incumbent players remain highly influential but their operations are more visible and their abuses more open to challenge. Most importantly of all, there has been an increase in the visibility of non-compliant behaviour by Member States. The negative impact of such behaviour on other Member States is highly apparent, and may encourage a decline or avoidance in such behaviour.

(2) Emerging Energy Regulatory System

At the time of publication, a system of European energy regulation is only beginning to emerge in the face of opposition from incumbent players and from some Member States. The principal source for guidance as to how such a system might ultimately develop is not so much the Forum mechanism but rather the draft Regulation on Cross Border Electricity Trade. The approach adopted in this measure implies that complex issues involving trade between Member States at Community level are emerging in the liberalizing electricity market that require a response in accordance with the principle of subsidiarity. Examples would include the approach to the management of congestion and to national network charges. The 'comitology' or procedures for the exercise of powers conferred on the Commission is designed to resolve these and other difficult and 8.44

complex problems, while allowing the Commission to initiate the necessary measures but also to co-operate with the NRAs in various committees.

Although the Regulation is in draft form only, it does provide an indication of the kind of hierarchy of authority that could emerge to address the complex problems of a liberalizing energy market. There are inevitably questions about the trend towards the Commission becoming a kind of EU energy regulator. However, most commentators are agreed that the new market-oriented regulation that emerged in the 1990s for network industries requires an active rôle by the national regulatory authorities. This has more complex implications for a body such as the EU than for a nation-state. The liberalization of energy markets in North America, Australia, Latin America, and other parts of the world has been so far driven by a different political model. In the EU context, the liberalization goal is ultimately subordinate to the goal of creating a single market in energy. As several commentators have noted, the liberalization process in the EU has led to an increasingly complex, multi-level form of economic regulation.[37]

8.45 The parties involved in the regulatory process for electricity and gas currently include the Community institutions, national regulatory authorities, national competition authorities, and other national supervisory bodies, transmission system operators, market operators, market agents such as producers, suppliers and traders, consumer associations, and the association of EU energy regulators (Ceer). In this context, co-ordination of and co-operation among the regulators and the regulated is not an option but a necessity. The term 'regulation by co-operation' is therefore not inappropriate as a description of the kind of effort required to develop and enforce the principles, if not necessarily the rules, that apply to the game.[38]

As a vehicle for the development of co-operation the Madrid and Florence Fora have proved a novel and useful innovation, despite their limited effectiveness in the IEM process. They suggest the need for new forms of governance at the EU level, especially ones that co-opt national regulators, with the Commission playing a role of co-ordinator.

Currently, the aim is to establish a dialogue between the Commission and the national regulators with a view to developing common solutions and a dialogue with other players such as the Parliament. As a decision-making body however, the Forum concept is not developed enough to deal with the challenges it faces, and

[37] Eberlein, B 'Configurations of Economic Regulation in the European Union: the case of electricity in comparative perspective', in *Current Politics and Economics of Europe*, (eds Coen, D and Thatcher, M) (2000), 407–25; Coen, D and Doyle, C, 'Designing Economic Regulatory Institutions for European Network Industries', in ibid, 455–76.

[38] Vasconcelos, J 'The Rôle of Regulation in a Single Energy Market', presentation delivered at the conference on 'Launching a Common European Energy Market', Lisbon, 5–6 June 2000.

the practical implications of the 'associated' role of the Parliament are unclear. Given the high degree of complexity involved in energy regulatory issues, the practical (as opposed to the formal) rôle of Parliament also becomes problematic.

It is in this context that a more assertive regulatory role for the Commission assumes importance. As outlined in chapters 6 and 7, the number of problems that require an EU rather than a national response has grown rapidly, from cross-border tarification and congestion management to interconnector access and access, to non-EU gas supplies. There is also a growing awareness among regulators of the advantages of learning from the experiences of regulators in other Member States. Among companies too there is a growing demand for European solutions to regulatory problems. The uneven levels of market opening are a vivid illustration of this. **8.46**

In this context of a growing demand for EU regulatory solutions, it is appropriate to consider the solutions available from the Community institutions. The European Commission in particular has not only sought to respond to the demands for regulation but to expand its sphere of action and authority, a phenomenon already seen in telecommunications.[39] This is particularly evident in the Acceleration Package of measures for energy proposed in 2001. The outcome of the debate on these proposals will have a significant impact upon the EU's capacity to develop a form of regulation that can address the problems that are already visible. Yet there is nothing in this book that suggests that Member States would accept the establishment of an EU regulator with the Commission adopting a rôle analogous to that of the FERC in the United States in regulating interstate energy transmission. What has been accepted by Member States is a significant transfer of powers from Member State governments to national regulatory authorities (NRAs) voluntarily set up at the time of the two Directives. The accountability of the NRAs is as yet unclear in many cases, but they will be a part of the regulatory landscape for energy for some time to come. Some mechanism for improved EU co-ordination among them seems therefore highly desirable. The Ceer and the Forum concept may be seen as early and potentially dynamic responses to the need for a new form of governance. **8.47**

(3) Security of Supply

Security of supply of electricity and gas is concerned with ensuring the continuous and regular flow of electricity/gas in such quantities and of such a quality that meets the requirements of consumers. Such security is of fundamental importance to the functioning of modern industrialized economies. Elements that **8.48**

[39] Natalicchi, G, *Wiring Europe: reshaping the European telecommunications régime*, (2001), 181–210.

contribute to the security of supply of electricity are ensuring that existing/planned facilities (properly maintained) for generation, transmission and distribution are available at the relevant time to meet present and foreseeable demands. The same requirements apply in the case of natural gas except that in place of generating capacity, adequate gas supplies must be available to meet present and foreseeable demands.

Prior to the adoption of the Electricity and Gas Directives the Member States ensured security of supply by the imposition of public service obligations of security of supply and their right to do so was expressly incorporated into the Directives. This recognition, which enabled Member States to claim in appropriate circumstances, an exemption under Article 86(2) from (*inter alia*) the competition rules of the Treaty, was an important factor in ensuring the eventual acceptance of the Directives. The object of a secure and continuous supply of energy, especially electricity, is 'an essential public service obligation', and 'probably the most important public service obligation'.[40] The Directives have expressly included provisions to ensure that all the safeguards available to Member States to guarantee security of energy supplies are not undermined by the introduction of competition.

8.49 The implementation of liberalization has raised questions about the adequacy of the protections provided by the Electricity and Gas Directives on security of supply, not least because of some negative experiences with energy market liberalization in other jurisdictions (eg, California, USA). In the electricity sector, for example, the continental EU systems have to be adapted to meet the challenge of an integrated market across the EU. The provision of guidelines for congestion management and methods of allocating scarce capacity in interconnected lines are among the instruments designed to achieve this. In this connection the Acceleration Directive includes provisions incorporating into both the Electricity and Gas Directives major new obligations in respect of security of supply. Member States are required to implement appropriate measures to achieve specific objectives including security of supply (see para 8.15). They are also required to establish a body to monitor security of supply issues (see Table 8.1 for electricity and Table 8.2 for gas).[41] In the case of gas, security of supply issues are particularly important in view of the heavy dependence of the EU on imported gas. In this connection the actions taken as a result of the Commission Green Paper on Security of Supply will be particularly important.

8.50 Security of supply may be threatened by the imposition of onerous public service obligations on electricity and gas undertakings. This will occur if the performance

[40] Respectively, the quotations are from the Commission Green Paper, 'Towards a European Strategy for the Security of Energy Supply' (2001) and the Commission's Communication on Completion of the Internal Market (2001).

[41] New Art 6A to the Electricity Directive as proposed by the draft Acceleration Directive.

of the obligations is so financially onerous that generators and/or TSOs/DSOs (electricity or gas) are placed in a position where their rate of return on investment is insufficient to attract investment finance. In this connection the proposal to require electricity to be provided as a universal service at 'affordable and reasonable prices' may give rise to difficulties.

It seems likely that attempts to deepen the IEM will require corresponding efforts to ensure that the security of supply will not be reduced as a result. At the same time, the potential for tensions with the Community's environmental priorities should not be underestimated.[42]

The IEM remains very much a 'work in progress' and a regulatory model for the energy sector is embryonic. It is tempting to seek a term that would describe the European model of energy regulation that is struggling to emerge. The term 'social market paradigm' appears to be a candidate. Whatever form of regulation eventually prevails, it will have to balance market considerations with those of public service, particularly with respect to the electricity industry with its universal service obligation. This has been evident in the annexes to the Commission's communication on completion of the IEM and in the studies conducted at the Commission's request dealing with *inter alia* employment issues and other social impacts of liberalization. The term 'social market' has a long historical pedigree in Europe, especially in Germany in the years following the Second World War: *Soziale Marktwirtschaft*.[43] As the EU Competition Commissioner has noted, the word 'market' takes the central position in this concept.[44] However, with respect to the operation of the market in the energy sector, it implies that some limits on the freedom of market operation are desirable for public policy reasons, a nuance that would be less readily encountered in, say, North American energy markets. However, the word 'emerging' is very apt in this context, given the highly dynamic context in which the liberalization process is currently operating. What is new, however, is that as the benefits of energy market integration become ever clearer, the challenge has become one of convincing a diminishing number of Member States that the benefits from this process are ones that will accrue to them as well as to the EU as a whole. **8.51**

[42] Especially with respect to renewable energy sources: the Directive on the promotion of electricity produced from renewable energy sources in the internal electricity market, OJ L 283/33, 27 Oct 2001.

[43] See Von Wogau, K, *Soziale Marktwirstschaft: Ein Modell für Europa: vom Euro zum Europäischen Heimatmarkt* (1999).

[44] 'Competition in a Social Market Economy', speech delivered by Commissioner M Monti at the Conference of the European Parliament and the European Commission on 'Reform of European Competition Law' in Freiburg, 9–10 Nov 2000.

APPENDICES

APPENDICES 1 AND 2

Comparative Tables for Proposed Amendments to the Electricity and the Gas Directives (2001)

Compiled by Andreas Gunst*

The comparative tables are based on the version of the proposals published in the Official Journal in 2001. This text will be amended as a result of the legislative process before adoption by the Council and Parliament.
Footnotes to the Directives are omitted, and the recitals to the proposed amended Directive are not displayed.

APPENDIX 1

Proposed Amendments to the Electricity Directive (2001)

Directive 96/92/EC of the European Parliament and of the Council of 19 December 1996 concerning common rules for the internal market in electricity	**Directive 96/92/EC of the European Parliament and of the Council of 19 December 1996 concerning common rules for the internal market in electricity** (as amended)
THE EUROPEAN PARLIAMENT AND THE COUNCIL OF THE EUROPEAN UNION,	THE EUROPEAN PARLIAMENT AND THE COUNCIL OF THE EUROPEAN UNION,
Having regard to the Treaty establishing the European Community, and in particular Article 57 (2), Article 66 and Article 100a thereof, Having regard to the proposal from the Commission, Having regard to the opinion of the Economic and Social Committee, Acting in accordance with the procedure laid down in Article 189b of the Treaty,	Having regard to the Treaty establishing the European Community, and in particular Article 57 (2), Article 66 and Article 100a thereof, Having regard to the proposal from the Commission, Having regard to the opinion of the Economic and Social Committee, Acting in accordance with the procedure laid down in Article 189b of the Treaty,
(1) Whereas it is important to adopt measures to ensure the smooth running of the internal market; whereas the internal market is to comprise an area without internal frontiers in which the free movement of goods, persons, services and capital is ensured;	(1) Whereas it is important to adopt measures to ensure the smooth running of the internal market; whereas the internal market is to comprise an area without internal frontiers in which the free movement of goods, persons, services and capital is ensured;

*A J Gunst, Research Fellow, CEPMLP, University of Dundee

(2) Whereas the completion of a competitive electricity market is an important step towards completion of the internal energy market;

(3) Whereas the provisions of this Directive should not affect the full application of the Treaty, in particular the provisions concerning the internal market and competition;

(4) Whereas establishment of the internal market in electricity is particularly important in order to increase efficiency in the production, transmission and distribution of this product, while reinforcing security of supply and the competitiveness of the European economy and respecting environmental protection;

(5) Whereas the internal market in electricity needs to be established gradually, in order to enable the industry to adjust in a flexible and ordered manner to its new environment and to take account of the different ways in which electricity systems are organized at present;

(6) Whereas the establishment of the internal market in the electricity sector must favour the interconnection and interoperability of systems;

(7) Whereas Council Directive 90/547/EEC of 29 October 1990 on the transit of electricity through transmission grids and Council Directive 90/377/EEC of 29 June 1990 concerning a Community procedure to improve the transparency of gas and electricity prices charged to industrial end-users, provide for a first phase for the completion of the internal market in electricity;

(8) Whereas it is now necessary to take further measures with a view to establishing the internal market in electricity;

(9) Whereas, in the internal market, electricity undertakings must be able to operate, without prejudice to compliance with public service obligations, with a view to achieving a competitive market in electricity;

(10) Whereas Member States, because of the structural differences in the Member States, currently have different systems for regulating the electricity sector;

(11) Whereas, in accordance with the principle of subsidiarity, general principles providing for a framework must be established at Community level, but their detailed implementation should be left to Member States, thus allowing each Member State to choose the regime which corresponds best to its particular situation;

(2) Whereas the completion of a competitive electricity market is an important step towards completion of the internal energy market;

(3) Whereas the provisions of this Directive should not affect the full application of the Treaty, in particular the provisions concerning the internal market and competition;

(4) Whereas establishment of the internal market in electricity is particularly important in order to increase efficiency in the production, transmission and distribution of this product, while reinforcing security of supply and the competitiveness of the European economy and respecting environmental protection;

(5) Whereas the internal market in electricity needs to be established gradually, in order to enable the industry to adjust in a flexible and ordered manner to its new environment and to take account of the different ways in which electricity systems are organized at present;

(6) Whereas the establishment of the internal market in the electricity sector must favour the interconnection and interoperability of systems;

(7) Whereas Council Directive 90/547/EEC of 29 October 1990 on the transit of electricity through transmission grids and Council Directive 90/377/EEC of 29 June 1990 concerning a Community procedure to improve the transparency of gas and electricity prices charged to industrial end-users, provide for a first phase for the completion of the internal market in electricity;

(8) Whereas it is now necessary to take further measures with a view to establishing the internal market in electricity;

(9) Whereas, in the internal market, electricity undertakings must be able to operate, without prejudice to compliance with public service obligations, with a view to achieving a competitive market in electricity;

(10) Whereas Member States, because of the structural differences in the Member States, currently have different systems for regulating the electricity sector;

(11) Whereas, in accordance with the principle of subsidiarity, general principles providing for a framework must be established at Community level, but their detailed implementation should be left to Member States, thus allowing each Member State to choose the regime which corresponds best to its particular situation;

(12) Whereas, whatever the nature of the prevailing market organization, access to the system must be open in accordance with this Directive and must lead to equivalent economic results in the States and hence to a directly comparable level of opening-up of markets and to a directly comparable degree of access to electricity markets;	(12) Whereas, whatever the nature of the prevailing market organization, access to the system must be open in accordance with this Directive and must lead to equivalent economic results in the States and hence to a directly comparable level of opening-up of markets and to a directly comparable degree of access to electricity markets;
(13) Whereas for some Member States the imposition of public service obligations may be necessary to ensure security of supply and consumer and environmental protection, which, in their view, free competition, left to itself, cannot necessarily guarantee;	(13) Whereas for some Member States the imposition of public service obligations may be necessary to ensure security of supply and consumer and environmental protection, which, in their view, free competition, left to itself, cannot necessarily guarantee;
(14) Whereas long-term planning may be one means of carrying out those public service obligations;	(14) Whereas long-term planning may be one means of carrying out those public service obligations;
(15) Whereas the Treaty lays down specific rules with regard to restrictions on the free movement of goods and on competition;	(15) Whereas the Treaty lays down specific rules with regard to restrictions on the free movement of goods and on competition;
(16) Whereas Article 90 (1) of the Treaty, in particular, obliges the Member States to respect these rules with regard to public undertakings and undertakings which have been granted special or exclusive rights;	(16) Whereas Article 90 (1) of the Treaty, in particular, obliges the Member States to respect these rules with regard to public undertakings and undertakings which have been granted special or exclusive rights;
(17) Whereas Article 90 (2) of the Treaty subjects undertakings entrusted with the operation of services of general economic interest to these rules, under specific conditions;	(17) Whereas Article 90 (2) of the Treaty subjects undertakings entrusted with the operation of services of general economic interest to these rules, under specific conditions;
(18) Whereas the implementation of this Directive will have an impact on the activities of such undertakings;	(18) Whereas the implementation of this Directive will have an impact on the activities of such undertakings;
(19) Whereas the Member States, when imposing public service obligations on the undertakings of the electricity sector, must therefore respect the relevant rules of the Treaty as interpreted by the Court of Justice;	(19) Whereas the Member States, when imposing public service obligations on the undertakings of the electricity sector, must therefore respect the relevant rules of the Treaty as interpreted by the Court of Justice;
(20) Whereas, in establishing the internal market in electricity, full account should be taken of the Community objective of economic and social cohesion, particularly in sectors such as the infrastructures, national or intra-Community, which are used for the transmission of electricity;	(20) Whereas, in establishing the internal market in electricity, full account should be taken of the Community objective of economic and social cohesion, particularly in sectors such as the infrastructures, national or intra-Community, which are used for the transmission of electricity;
(21) Whereas Decision No 1254/96/EC of the European Parliament and of the Council of 5 June 1996 laying down a series of guidelines for trans-European energy networks has contributed to the development of integrated infrastructures for the transmission of electricity;	(21) Whereas Decision No 1254/96/EC of the European Parliament and of the Council of 5 June 1996 laying down a series of guidelines for trans-European energy networks has contributed to the development of integrated infrastructures for the transmission of electricity;

(22) Whereas it is therefore necessary to establish common rules for the production of electricity and the operation of electricity transmission and distribution systems;

(23) Whereas there are two systems which may be applied for opening up the production market, an authorization procedure or a tendering procedure, and these must operate in accordance with objective, transparent and non-discriminatory criteria;

(24) Whereas the position of autoproducers and independent producers needs to be taken into consideration within this framework;

(25) Whereas each transmission system must be subject to central management and control in order to ensure the security, reliability and efficiency of the system in the interests of producers and their customers; whereas a transmission system operator should therefore be designated and entrusted with the operation, maintenance, and, if necessary, development of the system; whereas the transmission system operator must behave in an objective, transparent and non-discriminatory manner;

(26) Whereas the technical rules for the operation of transmission systems and direct lines must be transparent and must ensure interoperability;

(27) Whereas objective and non-discriminatory criteria must be established for the dispatching of power stations;

(28) Whereas, for reasons of environmental protection, priority may be given to the production of electricity from renewable sources;

(29) Whereas, at the distribution level, customers located in a given area may be granted supply rights and a manager must be designated to manage, maintain and, if necessary, develop each distribution system;

(30) Whereas, in order to ensure transparency and non-discrimination, the transmission function of vertically integrated undertakings should be operated independently from the other activities;

(31) Whereas a single buyer must operate separately from the generation and distribution activities of vertically integrated undertakings; whereas the flow of information between the single buyer activities and these generation and distribution activities needs to be restricted;

(32) Whereas the accounts of all integrated electricity undertakings should provide for maximum

(22) Whereas it is therefore necessary to establish common rules for the production of electricity and the operation of electricity transmission and distribution systems;

(23) Whereas there are two systems which may be applied for opening up the production market, an authorization procedure or a tendering procedure, and these must operate in accordance with objective, transparent and non-discriminatory criteria;

(24) Whereas the position of autoproducers and independent producers needs to be taken into consideration within this framework;

(25) Whereas each transmission system must be subject to central management and control in order to ensure the security, reliability and efficiency of the system in the interests of producers and their customers; whereas a transmission system operator should therefore be designated and entrusted with the operation, maintenance, and, if necessary, development of the system; whereas the transmission system operator must behave in an objective, transparent and non-discriminatory manner;

(26) Whereas the technical rules for the operation of transmission systems and direct lines must be transparent and must ensure interoperability;

(27) Whereas objective and non-discriminatory criteria must be established for the dispatching of power stations;

(28) Whereas, for reasons of environmental protection, priority may be given to the production of electricity from renewable sources;

(29) Whereas, at the distribution level, customers located in a given area may be granted supply rights and a manager must be designated to manage, maintain and, if necessary, develop each distribution system;

(30) Whereas, in order to ensure transparency and non-discrimination, the transmission function of vertically integrated undertakings should be operated independently from the other activities;

(31) Whereas a single buyer must operate separately from the generation and distribution activities of vertically integrated undertakings; whereas the flow of information between the single buyer activities and these generation and distribution activities needs to be restricted;

(32) Whereas the accounts of all integrated electricity undertakings should provide for maximum

transparency, in particular to identify possible abuses of a dominant position, consisting for example in abnormally high or low tariffs or in discriminatory practices relating to equivalent transactions; whereas, to this end, the accounts must be separate for each activity;

(33) Whereas it is also necessary to provide for access by the competent authorities to the internal accounts of undertakings with due regard for confidentiality;

(34) Whereas, owing to the diversity of structures and the special characteristics of systems in Member States, there should be different options for system access operating in accordance with objective, transparent and non-discriminatory criteria;

(35) Whereas provision should be made for authorizing the construction and use of direct lines;

(36) Whereas provision must be made for safeguards and dispute settlement procedures;

(37) Whereas any abuse of a dominant position or any predatory behaviour should be avoided;

(38) Whereas, as some Member States are liable to experience special difficulties in adjusting their systems, provision should be made for recourse to transitional regimes or derogations, especially for the operation of small isolated systems;

(39) Whereas this Directive constitutes a further phase of liberalization; whereas, once it has been put into effect, some obstacles to trade in electricity between Member States will nevertheless remain in place; whereas, therefore, proposals for improving the operation of the internal market in electricity may be made in the light of experience; whereas the Commission should therefore report to the Council and the European Parliament on the application of this Directive,

HAVE ADOPTED THIS DIRECTIVE:

CHAPTER I SCOPE AND DEFINITIONS

Article 1

This Directive establishes common rules for the generation, transmission and distribution of electricity. It lays down the rules relating to the organization and functioning of the electricity sector, access to the market, the criteria and procedures applicable to calls for tender and the granting of authorizations and the operation of systems.

transparency, in particular to identify possible abuses of a dominant position, consisting for example in abnormally high or low tariffs or in discriminatory practices relating to equivalent transactions; whereas, to this end, the accounts must be separate for each activity;

(33) Whereas it is also necessary to provide for access by the competent authorities to the internal accounts of undertakings with due regard for confidentiality;

(34) Whereas, owing to the diversity of structures and the special characteristics of systems in Member States, there should be different options for system access operating in accordance with objective, transparent and non-discriminatory criteria;

(35) Whereas provision should be made for authorizing the construction and use of direct lines;

(36) Whereas provision must be made for safeguards and dispute settlement procedures;

(37) Whereas any abuse of a dominant position or any predatory behaviour should be avoided;

(38) Whereas, as some Member States are liable to experience special difficulties in adjusting their systems, provision should be made for recourse to transitional regimes or derogations, especially for the operation of small isolated systems;

(39) Whereas this Directive constitutes a further phase of liberalization; whereas, once it has been put into effect, some obstacles to trade in electricity between Member States will nevertheless remain in place; whereas, therefore, proposals for improving the operation of the internal market in electricity may be made in the light of experience; whereas the Commission should therefore report to the Council and the European Parliament on the application of this Directive,

HAVE ADOPTED THIS DIRECTIVE:

CHAPTER I SCOPE AND DEFINITIONS

Article 1

This Directive establishes common rules for the generation, transmission and distribution of electricity. It lays down the rules relating to the organization and functioning of the electricity sector, access to the market, the criteria and procedures applicable to calls for tender and the granting of authorizations and the operation of systems.

Article 2

For the purposes of this Directive:

1. 'generation' shall mean the production of electricity;

2. 'producer' shall mean a natural or legal person generating electricity;

3. 'autoproducer' shall mean a natural or legal person generating electricity essentially for his own use;

4. 'independent producer' shall mean:
   (a) a producer who does not carry out electricity transmission or distribution functions in the territory covered by the system where he is established;
   (b) in Member States in which vertically integrated undertakings do not exist and where a tendering procedure is used, a producer corresponding to the definition of point (a), who may not be exclusively subject to the economic precedence of the interconnected system;

5. 'transmission' shall mean the transport of electricity on the high-voltage interconnected system with a view to its delivery to final customers or to distributors;

6. 'distribution' shall mean the transport of electricity on medium-voltage and low-voltage distribution systems with a view to its delivery to customers;

7. 'customers' shall mean wholesale or final customers of electricity and distribution companies;

8. 'wholesale customers' shall mean any natural or legal persons, if the Member States recognize their existence, who purchase or sell electricity and who do not carry out transmission, generation or distribution functions inside or outside the system where they are established;

9. 'final customer' shall mean a customer buying electricity for his own use;

10. 'interconnectors' shall mean equipment used to link electricity systems;

11. 'interconnected system' shall mean a number of transmission and distribution systems linked together by means of one or more interconnectors;

12. 'direct line' shall mean an electricity line complementary to the interconnected system;

13. 'economic precedence' shall mean the ranking of sources of electricity supply in accordance with economic criteria;

Article 2

For the purposes of this Directive:

1. 'generation' shall mean the production of electricity;

2. 'producer' shall mean a natural or legal person generating electricity;

3. 'autoproducer' shall mean a natural or legal person generating electricity essentially for his own use;

4. 'independent producer' shall mean:
   (a) a producer who does not carry out electricity transmission or distribution functions in the territory covered by the system where he is established;
   (b) in Member States in which vertically integrated undertakings do not exist and where a tendering procedure is used, a producer corresponding to the definition of point (a), who may not be exclusively subject to the economic precedence of the interconnected system;

5. 'transmission' shall mean the transport of electricity on the high-voltage interconnected system with a view to its delivery to final customers or to distributors;

6. 'distribution' shall mean the transport of electricity on medium-voltage and low-voltage distribution systems with a view to its delivery to customers;

7. 'customers' shall mean wholesale or final customers of electricity and distribution companies;

8. 'wholesale customers' shall mean any natural or legal persons, if the Member States recognize their existence, who purchase or sell electricity and who do not carry out transmission, generation or distribution functions inside or outside the system where they are established;

9. 'final customer' shall mean a consumer buying electricity for his own use;

10. 'interconnectors' shall mean equipment used to link electricity systems;

11. 'interconnected system' shall mean a number of transmission and distribution systems linked together by means of one or more interconnectors;

12. 'direct line' shall mean an electricity line complementary to the interconnected system;

13. 'economic precedence' shall mean the ranking of sources of electricity supply in accordance with economic criteria;

14. 'ancillary services' shall mean all services necessary for the operation of a transmission or distribution system;

15. 'system user' shall mean any natural or legal person supplying to, or being supplied by, a transmission or distribution system;

16. 'supply' shall mean the delivery and/or sale of electricity to customers;

17. 'integrated electricity undertaking' shall mean a vertically or horizontally integrated undertaking;

18. 'vertically integrated undertaking' shall mean an undertaking performing two or more of the functions of generation, transmission and distribution of electricity;

19. 'horizontally integrated undertaking' shall mean an undertaking performing at least one of the functions of generation for sale, or transmission or distribution of electricity, and another non-electricity activity;

20. 'tendering procedure' shall mean the procedure through which planned additional requirements and replacement capacity are covered by supplies from new or existing generating capacity;

21. 'long-term planning' shall mean the planning of the need for investment in generation and transmission capacity on a long-term basis, with a view to meeting the demand for electricity of the system and securing supplies to customers;

22. 'single buyer' shall mean any legal person who, within the system where he is established, is responsible for the unified management of the transmission system and/or for centralized electricity purchasing and selling;

23. 'small isolated system' shall mean any system with consumption of less than 2500 GWh in the year 1996, where less than 5 % of annual consumption is obtained through interconnection with other systems.

CHAPTER II GENERAL RULES FOR THE ORGANIZATION OF THE SECTOR

Article 3

1. Member States shall ensure, on the basis of their institutional organization and with due regard for the principle of subsidiarity, that, without prejudice to paragraph 2, electricity undertakings are operated in accordance with the principles of this Directive, with a view to achieving a competitive

14. 'ancillary services' shall mean all services necessary for the operation of a transmission or distribution system;

15. 'system user' shall mean any natural or legal person supplying to, or being supplied by, a transmission or distribution system;

16. 'supply' shall mean the delivery and/or sale of electricity to customers;

17. 'integrated electricity undertaking' shall mean a vertically or horizontally integrated undertaking;

18. 'vertically integrated undertaking' shall mean an undertaking performing two or more of the functions of generation, transmission and distribution of electricity;

19. 'horizontally integrated undertaking' shall mean an undertaking performing at least one of the functions of generation for sale, or transmission or distribution of electricity, and another non-electricity activity;

20. 'tendering procedure' shall mean the procedure through which planned additional requirements and replacement capacity are covered by supplies from new or existing generating capacity;

21. 'long-term planning' shall mean the planning of the need for investment in generation and transmission capacity on a long-term basis, with a view to meeting the demand for electricity of the system and securing supplies to customers;

22. 'non-domestic customer' shall mean a consumer purchasing electricity which is not for his own household use and shall include producers, transmission and distribution undertakings and wholesale customers.

23. 'small isolated system' shall mean any system with consumption of less than 2500 GWh in the year 1996, where less than 5 % of annual consumption is obtained through interconnection with other systems.

CHAPTER II GENERAL RULES FOR THE ORGANIZATION OF THE SECTOR

Article 3

1. Member States shall ensure, on the basis of their institutional organisation and with due regard for the principle of subsidiarity, that, without prejudice to paragraph 2, electricity undertakings are operated in accordance with the principles of this Directive, with a view to achieving a competitive

market in electricity, and shall not discriminate between these undertakings as regards either rights or obligations. The two approaches to system access referred to in Articles 17 and 18 must lead to equivalent economic results and hence to a directly comparable level of opening-up of markets and to a directly comparable degree of access to electricity markets.

2. Having full regard to the relevant provisions of the Treaty, in particular Article 90, Member States may impose on undertakings operating in the electricity sector, in the general economic interest, public service obligations which may relate to security, including security of supply, regularity, quality and price of supplies and to environmental protection. Such obligations must be clearly defined, transparent, non-discriminatory and verifiable; they, and any revision thereof, shall be published and notified to the Commission by Member States without delay. As a means of carrying out the above-mentioned public service obligations, Member States which so wish may introduce the implementation of long-term planning.

3. Member States may decide not to apply the provisions of Articles 5, 6, 17, 18 and 21 insofar as the application of these provisions would obstruct the performance, in law or in fact, of the obligations imposed on electricity undertakings in the general economic interest and insofar as the development of trade would not be affected to such an extent as would be contrary to the interests of the Community. The interests of the Community include, inter alia, competition with regard to eligible customers in accordance with this Directive and Article 90 of the Treaty.

market in electricity. Member States shall not discriminate between these undertakings as regards either rights or obligations.

2. Having regard to the relevant provisions of the Treaty, in particular Article 86, Member States may impose on undertakings operating in the electricity sector, in the general economic interest, public service obligations which may relate to security, including security of supply, regularity, quality and price of supplies and to environmental protection. Such obligations shall be clearly defined, transparent, non-discriminatory and verifiable. As a means of carrying out public service obligations in relation to security of supply, Member States may introduce the implementation of long-term planning, taking into account the possibility of third parties seeking access to the system.

3. Member States shall ensure that all customers enjoy universal service, that is the right to be supplied with electricity of a specified quality within their territory at affordable and reasonable prices. They shall take appropriate measures to protect final customers and to ensure high levels of consumer protection, particularly with respect to transparency regarding contractual terms and conditions, general information and dispute settlement mechanisms. These measures shall include, in particular, those set out in the Annex.

4. Member States shall implement appropriate measures to achieve the objectives of social and economic cohesion, environmental protection and security of supply, notably through the maintenance and construction of necessary network infrastructure including interconnection capacity.

5. Member States may decide not to apply the provisions of Articles 5, 6, 16 and 21 in so far as their application would obstruct the performance, in law or in fact, of the obligations imposed on electricity undertakings in the general economic interest and in so far as the development of trade would not be affected to such an extent as would be contrary to the interests of the Community. The interests of the

Community include, *inter alia*, competition with regard to eligible customers in accordance with this Directive and Article 86 of the Treaty.

Article 3a

1. Member States shall, every two years, notify the Commission of all measures adopted to fulfill universal service and public service obligations, whether or not such measures require a derogation from the provisions of this Directive. This notification shall relate, *inter alia*, to the requirements of Article 3(4) and the maintenance of service standards.

2. The Commission shall publish, every two years, a report analysing the different measures taken in the Member States to meet high public service standards, together with an examination of the effectiveness of those measures.

Where appropriate, the Commission shall make recommendations as to measures to be taken at national level to achieve high public service standards.

CHAPTER III GENERATION	CHAPTER III GENERATION
Article 4 For the construction of new generating capacity, Member States may choose between an authorization procedure and/or a tendering procedure. Authorization and tendering must be conducted in accordance with objective, transparent and non-discriminatory criteria.	Article 4 (deleted)
Article 5 1. Where they opt for the authorization procedure, Member States shall lay down the criteria for the grant of authorizations for the construction of generating capacity in their territory. These criteria may relate to: (a) the safety and security of the electricity system, installations and associated equipment; (b) protection of the environment; (c) land use and siting; (d) use of public ground; (e) energy efficiency; (f) the nature of the primary sources; (g) characteristics particular to the applicant, such as technical, economic and financial capabilities; (h) the provisions of Article 3.	Article 5 1. For the construction of new generating capacity, Member States shall adopt an authorisation procedure, which shall be conducted in accordance with objective, transparent and non-discriminatory criteria.

2. The detailed criteria and procedures shall be made public	2. Member States shall lay down the criteria for the grant of authorisations for the construction of generating capacity in their territory. These criteria may relate to: (a) the safety and security of the electricity system, installations and associated equipment; (b) protection of public health and safety; (c) protection of the environment; (d) land use and siting; (e) use of public ground; (f) energy efficiency; (g) the nature of the primary sources; (h) characteristics particular to the applicant, such as technical, economic and financial capabilities; (i) compliance with measures adopted pursuant to Article 3.
3. Applicants shall be informed of the reasons, which must be objective and non-discriminatory, for any refusal to grant an authorization; the reasons must be well founded and duly substantiated; they shall be forwarded to the Commission for information. Appeal procedures must be made available to the applicant.	3. The authorisation procedures and criteria shall be made public.
	4. Applicants shall be informed of the reasons for any refusal to grant an authorisation. The reasons must be objective, non-discriminatory, well founded and duly substantiated. Appeal procedures shall be made available to the applicant.
Article 6	**Article 6**
1. Where they opt for the tendering procedure, Member States or any competent body designated by the Member State concerned shall draw up an inventory of new means of production, including replacement capacity, on the basis of the regular estimate referred to in paragraph 2. The inventory shall take account of the need for interconnection of systems. The requisite capacity shall be allocated by means of a tendering procedure in accordance with the procedure laid down in this Article.	1. Member States shall ensure the possibility, in the interests of security of supply, to tender for new capacity on the basis of published criteria. A tendering procedure can, however, only be launched if on the basis of the authorisation procedure the capacity being built is not sufficient to ensure security of supply.
2. The transmission system operator or any other competent authority designated by the Member State concerned shall draw up and publish under State supervision, at least every two years, a regular estimate of the generating and transmission capacity which is likely to be connected to the system, of the need for interconnectors with other systems, of potential transmission capacity and of the demand for electricity. The estimate shall cover a period defined by each Member State.	2. (deleted)

3. Details of the tendering procedure for means of production shall be published in the Official Journal of the European Communities at least six months prior to the closing date for tenders. The tender specifications shall be made available to any interested undertaking established in the territory of a Member State so that it has sufficient time in which to submit a tender. The tender specifications shall contain a detailed description of the contract specifications and of the procedure to be followed by all tenderers and an exhaustive list of criteria governing the selection of tenderers and the award of the contract. These specifications may also relate to the fields referred to in Articles 5 (1).

4. In invitations to tender for the requisite generating capacity, consideration must also be given to electricity supply offers with long-term guarantees from existing generating units, provided that additional requirements can be met in this way.

5. Member States shall designate an authority or a public body or a private body independent of electricity generation, transmission and distribution activities to be responsible for the organization, monitoring and control of the tendering procedure. This authority or body shall take all necessary steps to ensure confidentiality of the information contained in the tenders.

6. However, it must be possible for autoproducers and independent producers to obtain authorization, on the basis of objective, transparent and non-discriminatory criteria as laid down in Articles 4 and 5, in Member States which have opted for the tendering procedure.

3. Details of the tendering procedure for means of production shall be published in the Official Journal of the European Communities at least six months prior to the closing date for tenders. The tender specifications shall be made available to any interested undertaking established in the territory of a Member State so that it has sufficient time in which to submit a tender. The tender specifications shall contain a detailed description of the contract specifications and of the procedure to be followed by all tenderers and an exhaustive list of criteria governing the selection of tenderers and the award of the contract. These specifications may also relate to the fields referred to in Articles 5 (1).

4. In invitations to tender for the requisite generating capacity, consideration must also be given to electricity supply offers with long-term guarantees from existing generating units, provided that additional requirements can be met in this way.

5. Member States shall designate an authority or a public body or a private body independent of electricity generation, transmission and distribution activities to be responsible for the organization, monitoring and control of the tendering procedure. This authority or body shall take all necessary steps to ensure confidentiality of the information contained in the tenders.

6. (deleted)

Article 6a

1. Member States shall designate a body, which may be the independent regulatory authority referred to in Article 22, to monitor security of supply issues. This body shall monitor, in particular, the supply/demand balance on the national market, the level of expected future demand and envisaged additional capacity planned or under construction, and the level of competition on the market. The body shall publish, by 31 July each year at the latest a report outlining its findings on these issues, as well as any measures taken or envisaged to address them and forward this report to the Commission forthwith.

2. On the basis of the report referred to in paragraph 1 the Commission shall, on an annual basis, forward a Communication to the European Parliament and

the Council examining issues relating to security of supply of electricity in the Community, and in particular the existing and projected balance between demand and supply. Where appropriate, the Commission shall issue recommendations.

CHAPTER IV TRANSMISSION SYSTEM OPERATION

Article 7

1. Member States shall designate or shall require undertakings which own transmission systems to designate, for a period of time to be determined by Member States having regard to considerations of efficiency and economic balance, a system operator to be responsible for operating, ensuring the maintenance of, and, if necessary, developing the transmission system in a given area and its interconnectors with other systems, in order to guarantee security of supply.

2. Member States shall ensure that technical rules establishing the minimum technical design and operational requirements for the connection to the system of generating installations, distribution systems, directly connected consumers' equipment, interconnector circuits and direct lines are developed and published. These requirements shall ensure the interoperability of systems and shall be objective and non-discriminatory. They shall be notified to the Commission in accordance with Article 8 of Council Directive 83/189/EEC of 28 March 1983 laying down a procedure for the provision of information in the field of technical standards and regulations.

3. The system operator shall be responsible for managing energy flows on the system, taking into account exchanges with other interconnected systems. To that end, the system operator shall be responsible for ensuring a secure, reliable and efficient electricity system and, in that context, for ensuring the availability of all necessary ancillary services.

4. The system operator shall provide to the operator of any other system with which its system is interconnected sufficient information to ensure the secure and efficient operation, co-ordinated development and interoperability of the interconnected system.

5. The system operator shall not discriminate between system users or classes of system users, particularly in favour of its subsidiaries or shareholders.

CHAPTER IV TRANSMISSION SYSTEM OPERATION

Article 7

1. Member States shall designate or shall require undertakings which own transmission systems to designate, for a period of time to be determined by Member States having regard to considerations of efficiency and economic balance, a system operator to be responsible for operating, ensuring the maintenance of, and, if necessary, developing the transmission system in a given area and its interconnectors with other systems, in order to guarantee security of supply.

2. Member States shall ensure that technical rules establishing the minimum technical design and operational requirements for the connection to the system of generating installations, distribution systems, directly connected consumers' equipment, interconnector circuits and direct lines are developed and published. These requirements shall ensure the interoperability of systems and shall be objective and non-discriminatory. They shall be notified to the Commission in accordance with Article 8 of Council Directive 83/189/EEC of 28 March 1983 laying down a procedure for the provision of information in the field of technical standards and regulations.

3. The system operator shall be responsible for managing energy flows on the system, taking into account exchanges with other interconnected systems. To that end, the system operator shall be responsible for ensuring a secure, reliable and efficient electricity system and, in that context, for ensuring the availability of all necessary ancillary services.

4. The system operator shall provide to the operator of any other system with which its system is interconnected sufficient information to ensure the secure and efficient operation, co-ordinated development and interoperability of the interconnected system.

5. The system operator shall not discriminate between system users or classes of system users, particularly in favour of its subsidiaries or shareholders.

6. Unless the transmission system is already independent from generation and distribution activities, the system operator shall be independent at least in management terms from other activities not relating to the transmission system.

6. Unless the system operator is already fully independent from other activities not relating to the transmission system in terms of ownership, the system operator shall be independent at least in terms of its legal form, organisation and decision making from other activities not relating to transmission.

In order to ensure the independence of the system operator, the following criteria shall apply:

(a) those persons responsible for the management of the transmission system may not participate in company structures of the integrated electricity undertaking responsible, directly or indirectly, for the day-to-day operation of the generation, distribution and supply of electricity;
(b) appropriate measures must be taken to ensure that the personal interests of the persons responsible for the management of the transmission system are taken into account in a manner that ensures that they are capable of acting independently;
(c) the system operator must exercise full control over all assets necessary to maintain and develop the network;
(d) the system operator must establish a compliance programme, which sets out measures taken to ensure that discriminatory conduct is excluded. The programme must set out the specific obligations of employees to meet this objective. It must be drawn up and its respect monitored by a compliance officer appointed by and reporting to the President/Chief Executive of the integrated electricity undertaking to which the system operator belongs. An annual report, setting out the measures taken, must be submitted by the compliance officer to the national regulatory authority and published.

Article 7a
Transmission system operators shall procure the energy they use for the carrying out of their functions according to transparent, non-discriminatory and market based procedures.

Article 8
1. The transmission system operator shall be responsible for dispatching the generating installations

Article 8
1. The transmission system operator shall be responsible for dispatching the generating installations

in its area and for determining the use of interconnectors with other systems.

2. Without prejudice to the supply of electricity on the basis of contractual obligations, including those which derive from the tendering specifications, the dispatching of generating installations and the use of interconnectors shall be determined on the basis of criteria which may be approved by the Member State and which must be objective, published and applied in a non-discriminatory manner which ensures the proper functioning of the internal market in electricity. They shall take into account the economic precedence of electricity from available generating installations of interconnector transfers and the technical constraints on the system.

3. A Member State may require the system operator, when dispatching generating installations, to give priority to generating installations using renewable energy sources or waste or producing combined heat and power.

4. A Member State may, for reasons of security of supply, direct that priority be given to the dispatch of generating installations using indigenous primary energy fuel sources, to an extent not exceeding in any calendar year 15 % of the overall primary energy necessary to produce the electricity consumed in the Member State concerned.

Article 9

The transmission system operator must preserve the confidentiality of commercially sensitive information obtained in the course of carrying out its business.

in its area and for determining the use of interconnectors with other systems.

2. Without prejudice to the supply of electricity on the basis of contractual obligations, including those which derive from the tendering specifications, the dispatching of generating installations and the use of interconnectors shall be determined on the basis of criteria which may be approved by the Member State and which must be objective, published and applied in a non-discriminatory manner which ensures the proper functioning of the internal market in electricity. They shall take into account the economic precedence of electricity from available generating installations of interconnector transfers and the technical constraints on the system.

3. A Member State may require the system operator, when dispatching generating installations, to give priority to generating installations using renewable energy sources or waste or producing combined heat and power.

4. A Member State may, for reasons of security of supply, direct that priority be given to the dispatch of generating installations using indigenous primary energy fuel sources, to an extent not exceeding in any calendar year 15 % of the overall primary energy necessary to produce the electricity consumed in the Member State concerned.

5. Member States may require transmission system operators to meet minimum levels of investment for the maintenance and development of the transmission system, including interconnection capacity.

6. Rules adopted by transmission and distribution system operators for balancing, in real time, generation and consumption of electricity shall be transparent and non-discriminatory. Tariffs and terms and conditions for the provision of such services by system operators shall be established in a non-discriminatory way reflecting prevailing market prices and shall be fixed or approved by the national regulatory authority prior to their entry into force.

Article 9

The transmission system operator must preserve the confidentiality of commercially sensitive information obtained in the course of carrying out its business.

CHAPTER V DISTRIBUTION SYSTEM OPERATION

Article 10

1. Member States may impose on distribution companies an obligation to supply customers located in a given area. The tariff for such supplies may be regulated, for instance to ensure equal treatment of the customers concerned.

2. Member States shall designate or shall require undertakings which own or are responsible for distribution systems to designate a system operator to be responsible for operating, ensuring the maintenance of and, if necessary, developing the distribution system in a given area and its interconnectors with other systems.

3. Member States shall ensure that the system operator acts in accordance with Articles 11 and 12.

CHAPTER V DISTRIBUTION SYSTEM OPERATION

Article 10

1. Member States may impose on distribution companies an obligation to supply customers located in a given area. The tariff for such supplies may be regulated, for instance to ensure equal treatment of the customers concerned.

2. Member States shall designate or shall require undertakings which own or are responsible for distribution systems to designate a system operator to be responsible for operating, ensuring the maintenance of and, if necessary, developing the distribution system in a given area and its interconnectors with other systems.

3. Member States shall ensure that the system operator acts in accordance with Articles 11 and 12.

4. Unless the system operator is already fully independent from other activities not relating to the distribution system in terms of ownership, the system operator shall be independent at least in terms of its legal form, organisation and decision making from other activities not relating to distribution.

In order to ensure the independence of the system operator, the following criteria shall apply:

(a) those persons responsible for the management of the distribution system may not participate in company structures of the integrated electricity undertaking responsible, directly or indirectly, for the day-to-day operation of the generation, transmission and supply of electricity;
(b) appropriate measures must be taken to ensure that the personal interests of the persons responsible for the management of the distribution system are taken into account in a manner that ensures that they are capable of acting independently;
(c) the system operator must exercise full control over all assets necessary to maintain and develop the network;
(d) the system operator must establish a compliance programme, which sets out measures taken to ensure that discriminatory conduct is excluded. The programme must set out the specific obligations of employees to meet this objective. It must be drawn up and its respect monitored by a compliance officer appointed

Article 11

1. The distribution system operator shall maintain a secure, reliable and efficient electricity distribution system in its area, with due regard for the environment.

2. In any event, it must not discriminate between system users or classes of system users, particularly in favour of its subsidiaries or shareholders.

3. A Member State may require the distribution system operator, when dispatching generating installations, to give priority to generating installations using renewable energy sources or waste or producing combined heat and power.

Article 12

The distribution system operator must preserve the confidentiality of commercially sensitive information obtained in the course of carrying out its business.

CHAPTER IV UNBUNDLING AND TRANSPARENCY OF ACCOUNTS

Article 13

Member States or any competent authority they designate as well as the dispute settlement authorities referred to in Article 20 (3) shall have right of

by and reporting to the President/Chief Executive of the integrated electricity undertaking to which the system operator belongs. An annual report, setting out the measures taken, must be submitted by the compliance officer to the national regulatory authority and published.

The provisions of the first and second subparagraphs shall apply from 1 January 2003. Member States may decide not to apply those provisions to integrated electricity undertakings serving less than 100 000 customers at that date.

Article 11

1. The distribution system operator shall maintain a secure, reliable and efficient electricity distribution system in its area, with due regard for the environment.

2. In any event, it must not discriminate between system users or classes of system users, particularly in favour of its subsidiaries or shareholders.

3. A Member State may require the distribution system operator, when dispatching generating installations, to give priority to generating installations using renewable energy sources or waste or producing combined heat and power.

Article 12

The distribution system operator must preserve the confidentiality of commercially sensitive information obtained in the course of carrying out its business.

Article 12a

The rules in Articles 7(6) and 10(4) do not prevent the operation of a combined transmission and distribution system operator, which is fully independent in terms of its legal form, organisation and decision making from other activities not relating to transmission or distribution system operation and which meets the requirements of Article 7 (6).

CHAPTER IV UNBUNDLING AND TRANSPARENCY OF ACCOUNTS

Article 13

Member States or any competent authority they designate as well as the dispute settlement authorities referred to in Article 20 (3) shall have right of access to the accounts of generation, transmission or distribution undertakings which they need to consult in carrying out their checks.

Article 14

1. Member States shall take the necessary steps to ensure that the accounts of electricity undertakings are kept in accordance with paragraphs 2 to 5.

2. Electricity undertakings, whatever their system of ownership or legal form, shall draw up, submit to audit and publish their annual accounts in accordance with the rules of national law concerning the annual accounts of limited liability companies adopted pursuant to the fourth Council Directive 78/660/EEC of 25 July 1978 based on Article 54 (3) (g) of the Treaty on the annual accounts of certain types of companies. Undertakings which are not legally obliged to publish their annual accounts shall keep a copy of these at the disposal of the public in their head office.

3. Integrated electricity undertakings shall, in their internal accounting, keep separate accounts for their generation, transmission and distribution activities, and, where appropriate, consolidated accounts for other, non-electricity activities, as they would be required to do if the activities in question were carried out by separate undertakings, with a view to avoiding discrimination, cross-subsidization and distortion of competition. They shall include a balance sheet and a profit and loss account for each activity in notes to their accounts.

4. Undertakings shall specify in notes to the annual accounts the rules for the allocation of assets and liabilities and expenditure and income which they follow in drawing up the separate accounts referred to in paragraph 3. These rules may be amended only in exceptional cases. Such amendments must be mentioned in the notes and must be duly substantiated.

5. The annual accounts shall indicate in notes any transaction of a certain size conducted with affiliated undertakings, within the meaning of Article 41 of the seventh Council Directive 83/349/EEC of 13 June 1983 based on Article 54 (3) (g) of the Treaty on consolidated accounts, or with associated undertakings, within, the meaning of Article 33 (1) thereof, or, with undertakings which belong to the same shareholders.

access to the accounts of generation, transmission or distribution undertakings which they need to consult in carrying out their checks.

Article 14

1. Member States shall take the necessary steps to ensure that the accounts of electricity undertakings are kept in accordance with paragraphs 2 to 5.

2. Electricity undertakings, whatever their system of ownership or legal form, shall draw up, submit to audit and publish their annual accounts in accordance with the rules of national law concerning the annual accounts of limited liability companies adopted pursuant to the fourth Council Directive 78/660/EEC of 25 July 1978 based on Article 54 (3) (g) of the Treaty on the annual accounts of certain types of companies. Undertakings which are not legally obliged to publish their annual accounts shall keep a copy of these at the disposal of the public in their head office.

3. Integrated electricity undertakings shall, in their internal accounting, keep separate accounts for their generation, distribution and supply activities, and, where appropriate, consolidated accounts for other, non-electricity activities, as they would be required to do if the activities in question were carried out by separate undertakings, with a view to avoiding discrimination, cross-subsidisation and distortion of competition. The internal accounts shall include a balance sheet and a profit and loss account for each activity.

4. Undertakings shall specify in notes to the annual accounts the rules for the allocation of assets and liabilities and expenditure and income which they follow in drawing up the separate accounts referred to in paragraph 3. These rules may be amended only in exceptional cases. Such amendments must be mentioned in the notes and must be duly substantiated.

5. The annual accounts shall indicate in notes any transaction of a certain size conducted with affiliated undertakings, within the meaning of Article 41 of the seventh Council Directive 83/349/EEC of 13 June 1983 based on Article 54 (3) (g) of the Treaty on consolidated accounts, or with associated undertakings, within, the meaning of Article 33 (1) thereof, or, with undertakings which belong to the same shareholders.

Article 15

1. Member States which designate as a single buyer a vertically integrated electricity undertaking or part of a vertically integrated electricity undertaking shall lay down provisions requiring the single buyer to operate separately from the generation and distribution activities of the integrated undertaking.

2. Member States shall ensure that there is no flow of information between the single buyer activities of vertically integrated electricity undertakings and their generation and distribution activities, except for the information necessary to conduct the single buyer responsibilities.

Article 15

(deleted)

CHAPTER VII ORGANIZATION OF ACCESS TO THE SYSTEM

Article 16

For the organization of access to the system, Member States may choose between the procedures referred to in Article 17 and/or in Article 18. Both sets of procedure shall operate in accordance with objective, transparent and non-discriminatory criteria.

Article 17

1. In the case of negotiated access to the system, Member States shall take the necessary measures for electricity producers and, where Member States authorize their existence, supply undertakings and eligible customers either inside or outside the territory covered by the system to be able to negotiate access to the system so as to conclude supply contracts with each other on the basis of voluntary commercial agreements.

2. Where an eligible customer is connected to the distribution system, access to the system must be the subject of negotiation with the relevant distribution system operator and, if necessary, with the transmission system operator concerned.

3. To promote transparency and facilitate negotiations for access to the system, system operators

CHAPTER VII ORGANIZATION OF ACCESS TO THE SYSTEM

Article 16

1. Member States shall ensure the implementation of a system of third party access to the transmission and distribution systems based on published tariffs, applicable to all eligible customers and applied objectively and without discrimination between system users. These tariffs shall be approved prior to their entry into force by a national regulatory authority established in conformity with Article 22.

2. The operator of a transmission or distribution system may refuse access where it lacks the necessary capacity. Duly substantiated reasons must be given for such refusal, in particular having regard to Article 3.

Article 17

(deleted)

must publish, in the first year following implementation of this Directive, an indicative range of prices for use of the transmission and distribution systems. As far as possible, the indicative prices published for subsequent years should be based on the average price agreed in negotiations in the previous 12-month period.

4. Member States may also opt for a regulated system of access procedure, giving eligible customers a right of access, on the basis of published tariffs for the use of transmission and distribution systems, that is at least equivalent, in terms of access to the system, to the other procedures for access referred to in this Chapter.

5. The operator of the transmission or distribution system concerned may refuse access where he lacks the necessary capacity. Duly substantiated reasons must be given for such refusal, in particular having regard to Article 3.

Article 18

1. In the case of the single buyer procedure, Member States shall designate a legal person to be the single buyer within the territory covered by the system operator. Member States shall take the necessary measures for:

(i) the publication of a non-discriminatory tariff for the use of the transmission and distribution system;

(ii) eligible customers to be free to conclude supply contracts to cover their own needs with producers and, where Member States authorize their existence, with supply undertakings outside the territory covered by the system;

(iii) eligible customers to be free to conclude supply contracts to cover their own needs with producers inside the territory covered by the system;

(iv) independent producers to negotiate access to the system with the transmission and distribution systems operators so as to conclude supply contracts with eligible customers outside the system, on the basis of a voluntary commercial agreement.

2. The single buyer may be obliged to purchase the electricity contracted by an eligible customer from a producer inside or outside the territory covered by the system at a price which is equal to the sale price offered, by the single buyer to eligible customers

Article 18
(deleted)

minus the price of the published tariff referred to in paragraph 1 (i).

3. If the purchase obligation under paragraph 2 is not imposed on the single buyer, Member States shall take the necessary measures to ensure that the supply contracts referred to in paragraph 1 (ii) and (iii) are implemented either via access to the system on the basis of the published tariff referred to in paragraph 1 (i) or via negotiated access to the system according to the conditions of Article 17. In the latter case, there would be no obligation for the single buyer to publish a non-discriminatory tariff for the use of the transmission and distribution system.

4. The single buyer may refuse access to the system and may refuse to purchase electricity from eligible customers where he lacks the necessary transmission or distribution capacity. Duly substantiated reasons must be given for such refusal, in particular having regard to Article 3.

Article 19

1. Member States shall take the necessary measures to ensure an opening of their electricity markets, so that contracts under the conditions stated in Articles 17 and 18 can be concluded at least up to a significant level, to be notified to the Commission on an annual basis. The share of the national market shall be calculated on the basis of the Community share of electricity consumed by final consumers consuming more than 40 GWh per year (on a consumption site basis and including autoproduction). The average Community share shall be calculated by the Commission on the basis of information regularly provided to it by Member States. The Commission shall publish this average Community share defining the degree of market opening in the Official Journal of the European Communities before November each year, with all appropriate information clarifying the calculation.

2. The share of the national market referred to in paragraph 1 will be increased progressively over a period of six years. This increase will be calculated by reducing the Community consumption threshold of 40 GWh, referred to in paragraph 1 from 40 GWh to a level of 20 GWh annual electricity consumption three years after the entry into force of this Directive and to a level of 9 GWh annual electricity consumption six years after the entry into force of this Directive.

Article 19

1. Member States shall ensure that all non-domestic customers are free to purchase electricity from the supplier of their choice from 1 January 2003 at the latest. They shall ensure that all customers are free to choose their supplier from 1 January 2005 at the latest.

2. To avoid imbalance in the opening of electricity markets:

(a) contracts for the supply of electricity with an eligible customer in the system of another Member State shall not be prohibited if the customer is considered as eligible in both systems involved;

(b) in cases where transactions as described in subparagraph (a) are refused because of the customer being eligible only in one of the two systems, the Commission may oblige, taking into account the situation in the market and the common interest, the refusing party to execute the requested electricity supply at the request of the Member State where the eligible customer is located.

3. Member States shall specify those customers inside their territory representing the shares as specified in paragraphs 1 and 2 which have the legal capacity to contract electricity in accordance with Articles 17 and 18, given that all final consumers consuming more than 100 GWh per year (on a consumption site basis and including autoproduction) must be included in the above category. Distribution companies, if not already specified as eligible customers under this paragraph, shall have the legal capacity to contract under the conditions of Articles 17 and 18 for the volume of electricity being consumed by their customers designated as eligible within their distribution system, in order to supply those customers.

4. Member States shall publish by 31 January each year the criteria for the definition of eligible customers which are able to conclude contracts under the conditions stated in Articles 17 and 18. This information, together with all other appropriate information to justify the fulfilment of market opening under paragraph 1, shall be sent to the Commission to be published in the Official Journal of the European Communities. The Commission may request a Member State to modify its specifications, as mentioned in paragraph 3, if they create obstacles to the correct application of this Directive as regards the smooth functioning of the internal market in electricity. If the Member State concerned does not comply with this request within a period of three months, a final decision shall be taken in accordance with Procedure I of Article 2 of Council Decision 87/373/EEC of 13 July 1987 laying down the procedures for the exercise of implementing powers conferred on the Commission.

5. To avoid imbalance in the opening of electricity markets during the period referred to in Article 26:

(a) contracts for the supply of electricity under the provisions of Articles 17 and 18 with an eligible customer in the system of another Member State shall not be prohibited if the customer is considered as eligible in both systems involved;

(b) in cases where transactions as described in subparagraph (a) are refused because of the customer being eligible only in one of the two systems, the Commission may oblige, taking into account the situation in the market and the common interest, the refusing party to execute the requested electricity supply at the request of the Member State where the eligible customer is located. In parallel with the procedure and the timetable provided for in Article 26, and not later than after half of the period provided for in that Article, the Commission shall review the application of subparagraph (b) of the first subparagraph on the basis of market developments taking into account the common interest. In the light of experience gained, the Commission shall evaluate this situation and report on possible imbalance in the opening of electricity markets with regard to this paragraph.

Article 20

1. Member States shall take the necessary measures to enable:

(i) independent producers and autoproducers to negotiate access to the system so as to supply their own premises and subsidiaries in the same Member State or in another Member State by means of the interconnected system;

(ii) producers located outside the territory covered by the system to conclude a supply contract following a call for tender for new generating capacity, and to have access to the system to perform the contract.

2. Member States shall ensure that the parties negotiate in good faith and that none of them abuses its negotiating position by preventing the successful outcome of negotiations.

3. Member States shall designate a competent authority, which must be independent of the parties, to settle disputes relating to the contracts and negotiations in question. In particular, this authority must settle disputes concerning contracts, negotiations and refusal of access or refusal to purchase.

4. In the event of cross-border disputes, the dispute settlement authority shall be the dispute settlement authority covering the system of the single buyer or the system operator which refuses use of, or access to, the system.

Article 20

1. Member States shall take the necessary measures to enable:

(i) independent producers and autoproducers to negotiate access to the system so as to supply their own premises and subsidiaries in the same Member State or in another Member State by means of the interconnected system;

(ii) producers located outside the territory covered by the system to conclude a supply contract following a call for tender for new generating capacity, and to have access to the system to perform the contract.

2. Member States shall ensure that the parties negotiate in good faith and that none of them abuses its negotiating position by preventing the successful outcome of negotiations.

3. Member States shall designate a competent authority, which must be independent of the parties, to settle disputes relating to the contracts and negotiations in question. In particular, this authority must settle disputes concerning contracts, negotiations and refusal of access or refusal to purchase.

4. In the event of cross-border disputes, the dispute settlement authority shall be the dispute settlement authority covering the system operator which refuses use of, or access to, the system.

5. Recourse to this authority shall be without prejudice to the exercise of rights of appeal under Community law.

Article 21

1. Member States shall take measures under the procedures and rights referred to in Articles 17 and 18 to enable:

- all electricity producers and electricity supply undertakings, where Member States authorize their existence, established within their territory to supply their own premises, subsidiaries and eligible customers through a direct line;
- any eligible customer within their territory to be supplied through a direct line by a producer and supply undertakings, where such suppliers are authorized by Member States.

2. Member States shall lay down the criteria for the grant of authorizations for the construction of direct lines in their territory. These criteria must be objective and non-discriminatory.

3. The possibility of supplying electricity through a direct line as referred to in paragraph 1 shall not affect the possibility of contracting electricity in accordance with Articles 17 and 18.

4. Member States may make authorization to construct a direct line subject either to the refusal of system access on the basis, as appropriate, of Article 17 (5) or Article 18 (4) or to the opening of a dispute settlement procedure under Article 20.

5. Member States may refuse to authorize a direct line if the granting of such an authorization would obstruct the provisions of Article 3. Duly substantiated reasons must be given for such refusal.

Article 22

Member States shall create appropriate and efficient mechanisms for regulation, control and transparency so as to avoid any abuse of dominant position, in particular to the detriment of consumers, and any predatory behaviour. These mechanisms shall take account of the provisions of the Treaty, and in particular Article 86 thereof.

5. Recourse to this authority shall be without prejudice to the exercise of rights of appeal under Community law.

Article 21

1. Member States shall take measures under the procedures and rights referred to in Articles 17 and 18 to enable:

- all electricity producers and electricity supply undertakings, where Member States authorize their existence, established within their territory to supply their own premises, subsidiaries and eligible customers through a direct line;
- any eligible customer within their territory to be supplied through a direct line by a producer and supply undertakings, where such suppliers are authorized by Member States.

2. Member States shall lay down the criteria for the grant of authorizations for the construction of direct lines in their territory. These criteria must be objective and non-discriminatory.

3. The possibility of supplying electricity through a direct line as referred to in paragraph 1 shall not affect the possibility of contracting electricity in accordance with Articles 17 and 18.

4. Member States may make authorization to construct a direct line subject either to the refusal of system access on the basis, as appropriate, of Article 17 (5) or Article 18 (4) or to the opening of a dispute settlement procedure under Article 20.

5. Member States may refuse to authorize a direct line if the granting of such an authorization would obstruct the provisions of Article 3. Duly substantiated reasons must be given for such refusal.

Article 22

1. Member States shall establish national regulatory authorities. These authorities shall be wholly independent of interests of the electricity industry. They shall at least have the sole responsibility:

(a) to fix or approve terms and conditions for connection and access to national networks, including transmission and distribution tariffs;

(b) to fix or approve tariffs, or changes in tariffs at national level, to reflect costs or revenues related to cross border transmission of electricity;

(c) to define the rules on the management and allocation of interconnection capacity, in

CHAPTER VIII FINAL PROVISIONS

Article 23

In the event of a sudden crisis in the energy market and where the physical safety or security of persons, apparatus or installations or system integrity is threatened, a Member State may temporarily take the necessary safeguard measures. Such measures must cause the least possible disturbance in the functioning of the internal market and must not be wider in scope than is strictly necessary to remedy the sudden difficulties which have arisen. The Member State concerned shall without delay notify these measures to the other Member States, and to the Commission, which may decide that the Member State concerned must amend or abolish such measures, insofar as they distort competition and adversely affect trade in a manner which is at variance with the common interest.

conjunction with the national regulatory authority or authorities of those Member States with which interconnection exists;

(d) to fix or approve any mechanisms to deal with congested capacity within the national electricity system;

(e) to ensure the respect of the requirements set out in Article 3(3) and (4) of this Directive.

2. Member States shall create appropriate and efficient mechanisms for regulation, control and transparency so as to avoid any abuse of dominant position, in particular to the detriment of consumers, and any predatory behaviour. These mechanisms shall take account of the provisions of the Treaty, and in particular Article 82 thereof.

3. Member States shall ensure that the appropriate measures be taken, including administrative action or criminal proceedings in conformity with their national law, against the natural or legal persons responsible where confidentiality rules imposed by this Directive have not been respected.

CHAPTER VIII FINAL PROVISIONS

Article 23

In the event of a sudden crisis in the energy market and where the physical safety or security of persons, apparatus or installations or system integrity is threatened, a Member State may temporarily take the necessary safeguard measures. Such measures must cause the least possible disturbance in the functioning of the internal market and must not be wider in scope than is strictly necessary to remedy the sudden difficulties which have arisen. The Member State concerned shall without delay notify these measures to the other Member States, and to the Commission, which may decide that the Member State concerned must amend or abolish such measures, insofar as they distort competition and adversely affect trade in a manner which is at variance with the common interest.

Article 23a

Member States shall inform the Commission by 31 March of each year at the latest of imports of electricity that have taken place during the previous calendar year from third countries.

Article 24

1. Those Member States in which commitments or guarantees of operation given before the entry into force of this Directive may not be honoured on account of the provisions of this Directive may apply for a transitional regime which may be granted to them by the Commission, taking into account, amongst other things, the size of the system concerned, the level of interconnection of the system and the structure of its electricity industry. The Commission shall inform the Member States of those applications before it takes a decision, taking into account respect for confidentiality. This decision shall be published in the Official Journal of the European Communities.

2. The transitional regime shall be of limited duration and shall be linked to expiry of the commitments or guarantees referred to in paragraph 1. The transitional regime may cover derogations from Chapter IV, VI and VII of this Directive. Applications for a transitional regime must be notified to the Commission no later than one year after the entry into force of this Directive.

3. Member States which can demonstrate, after the Directive has been brought into force, that there are substantial problems for the operation of their small isolated systems, may apply for derogations from the relevant provisions of Chapter IV, V, VI, VII, which may be granted to them by the Commission. The latter shall inform the Member States of those applications prior to taking a decision, taking into account respect for confidentiality. This decision shall be published in the Official Journal of the European Communities. This paragraph shall also be applicable to Luxembourg.

Article 25

1. The Commission shall submit a report to the Council and the European Parliament, before the end of the first year following entry into force of this Directive, on harmonization requirements which are not linked to the provisions of this Directive. If necessary, the Commission shall attach to the report any harmonization proposals necessary for the effective operation of the internal market in electricity.

2. The Council and the European Parliament shall give their views on such proposals within two years of their submission.

Article 24

1. Those Member States in which commitments or guarantees of operation given before the entry into force of this Directive may not be honoured on account of the provisions of this Directive may apply for a transitional regime which may be granted to them by the Commission, taking into account, amongst other things, the size of the system concerned, the level of interconnection of the system and the structure of its electricity industry. The Commission shall inform the Member States of those applications before it takes a decision, taking into account respect for confidentiality. This decision shall be published in the Official Journal of the European Communities.

2. The transitional regime shall be of limited duration and shall be linked to expiry of the commitments or guarantees referred to in paragraph 1. The transitional regime may cover derogations from Chapter IV, VI and VII of this Directive. Applications for a transitional regime must be notified to the Commission no later than one year after the entry into force of this Directive.

3. Member States which can demonstrate, after the Directive has been brought into force, that there are substantial problems for the operation of their small isolated systems, may apply for derogations from the relevant provisions of Chapter IV, V, VI, VII, which may be granted to them by the Commission. The latter shall inform the Member States of those applications prior to taking a decision, taking into account respect for confidentiality. This decision shall be published in the Official Journal of the European Communities. This paragraph shall also be applicable to Luxembourg.

Article 25

1. The Commission shall submit a report to the Council and the European Parliament, before the end of the first year following entry into force of this Directive, on harmonization requirements which are not linked to the provisions of this Directive. If necessary, the Commission shall attach to the report any harmonization proposals necessary for the effective operation of the internal market in electricity.

2. The Council and the European Parliament shall give their views on such proposals within two years of their submission.

Article 26 The Commission shall review the application of this Directive and submit a report on the experience gained on the functioning of the internal market in electricity and the implementation of the general rules mentioned in Article 3 in order to allow the European Parliament and the Council, in the light of experience gained, to consider, in due time, the possibility of a further opening of the market which would be effective nine years after the entry into force of the Directive taking into account the coexistence of systems referred to in Articles 17 and 18.	**Article 26** The Commission shall review the application of this Directive and submit a report to the European Parliament and the Council, by [indicate a date] at the latest and by [indicate a date] at the latest, on the experience gained and progress made in creating a complete and fully operational internal market in electricity in order to allow the European Parliament and the Council to consider, in due time, the possibility of provisions for further improving the internal market in electricity. In particular, the report shall examine the extent to which the unbundling and tarification requirements of this Directive have been successful in ensuring fair and non-discriminatory access to the Community's electricity system. The report shall also examine possible necessary harmonisation requirements that are not linked to the provisions of this Directive.
Article 27 1. Member States shall bring into force the laws, regulations and administrative provisions necessary to comply with this Directive not later than 19 February 1999. They shall forthwith inform the Commission thereof. 2. Belgium, Greece and Ireland may, due to the specific technical characteristics of their electricity systems, have an additional period of respectively 1 year, 2 years and 1 year to apply the obligations ensuing from this Directive. These Member States, when making use of this option, shall inform the Commission thereof. 3. When Member States adopt these provisions, they shall contain a reference to this Directive or shall be accompanied by such reference on the occasion of their official publication. The methods of making such reference shall be laid down by Member States.	**Article 27** 1. Member States shall bring into force the laws, regulations and administrative provisions necessary to comply with this Directive not later than 19 February 1999. They shall forthwith inform the Commission thereof. 2. Belgium, Greece and Ireland may, due to the specific technical characteristics of their electricity systems, have an additional period of respectively 1 year, 2 years and 1 year to apply the obligations ensuing from this Directive. These Member States, when making use of this option, shall inform the Commission thereof. 3. When Member States adopt these provisions, they shall contain a reference to this Directive or shall be accompanied by such reference on the occasion of their official publication. The methods of making such reference shall be laid down by Member States.
Article 28 This Directive shall enter into force on the 20th day following that of its publication in the Official Journal of the European Communities.	**Article 28** This Directive shall enter into force on the 20th day following that of its publication in the Official Journal of the European Communities.
Article 29 This Directive is addressed to the Member States. Done at Brussels, 19 December 1996. For the European Parliament The President K. HÄNSCH For the Council The President S. BARRETT	**Article 29** This Directive is addressed to the Member States. Done at Brussels, 19 December 1996. For the European Parliament The President K. HÄNSCH For the Council The President S. BARRETT

ANNEX

(Article 3)

Without prejudice to Community rules on consumer protection, in particular Directive 97/7/EC of the European Parliament and of the Council and Council Directive 93/13/EC:

(a) Member States shall ensure that final customers have a right to a contract with their electricity service provider that specifies:
   - the identity and address of the supplier;
   - services provided, the service quality levels offered, as well as the time for the initial connection;
   - the types of maintenance service offered;
   - the means by which up-to-date information on all applicable tariffs and maintenance charges may be obtained;
   - the duration of the contract, the conditions for renewal and termination of services and of the contract;
   - any compensation and the refund arrangements which apply if contracted service quality levels are not met; and
   - the method of initiating procedures for settlement of disputes in accordance with point (f).

(b) Member States shall ensure that final customers shall be given adequate notice of any intention to modify contractual conditions and shall be free to withdraw from contracts if they do not accept the new conditions.

(c) Member States shall ensure that transparent information on applicable prices and tariffs, and on standard terms and conditions, in respect of access to and use of electricity services is available to the public, and particularly to final customers.

(d) Member States shall ensure that electricity suppliers specify in the bills sent to each final consumer, the composition of the fuel mix used to generate the electricity that is consumed by the final consumers they supply. The relative costs of the different fuels used to generate a unit of electricity supplied to the final consumers shall be specified and the relative importance of each energy source with respect to the production of greenhouse gases.

(e) Member States shall also implement appropriate measures to protect vulnerable customers.

(f) Member States shall ensure that transparent, simple and inexpensive procedures are available for dealing with final customer complaints. Member States shall adopt measures to ensure that such procedures enable disputes to be settled fairly and promptly with provision, where warranted, for a system of reimbursement and/or compensation. They should follow, wherever possible, the principles set out in Commission Recommendation 98/257/EC.

APPENDIX 2

Proposed Amendments to the Gas Directive (2001)

Directive 98/30/EC of the European Parliament and of the Council of 22 June 1998 concerning common rules for the internal market in natural gas

THE EUROPEAN PARLIAMENT AND THE COUNCIL OF THE EUROPEAN UNION,

Having regard to the Treaty establishing the European Community, and in particular Articles 57(2), 66 and 100a thereof,
Having regard to the proposal from the Commission,
Having regard to the opinion of the Economic and Social Committee,
Acting in accordance with the procedure laid down in Article 189b of the Treaty,

(1) Whereas, according to Article 7a of the Treaty, the internal market shall comprise an area without internal frontiers in which the free movement of goods, persons, services and capital is ensured; whereas it is important to adopt measures to continue the completion of the internal market;

(2) Whereas, under Article 7c of the Treaty, differences in development of certain economies have to be taken into account, but derogations must be of a temporary nature and cause the least possible disturbance to the functioning of the common market;

(3) Whereas the establishment of a competitive natural gas market is an important element of the completion of the internal energy market;

(4) Whereas Council Directive 91/296/EEC of 31 May 1991 on the transit of natural gas through grids and Council Directive 90/377/EEC of 29 June 1990 concerning a Community procedure to improve the transparency of gas and electricity prices charged to industrial end-users constitute a first phase of the completion of the internal market in natural gas;

Directive 98/30/EC of the European Parliament and of the Council of 22 June 1998 concerning common rules for the internal market in natural gas (as amended)

THE EUROPEAN PARLIAMENT AND THE COUNCIL OF THE EUROPEAN UNION,

Having regard to the Treaty establishing the European Community, and in particular Articles 57(2), 66 and 100a thereof,
Having regard to the proposal from the Commission,
Having regard to the opinion of the Economic and Social Committee,
Acting in accordance with the procedure laid down in Article 189b of the Treaty,

(1) Whereas, according to Article 7a of the Treaty, the internal market shall comprise an area without internal frontiers in which the free movement of goods, persons, services and capital is ensured; whereas it is important to adopt measures to continue the completion of the internal market;

(2) Whereas, under Article 7c of the Treaty, differences in development of certain economies have to be taken into account, but derogations must be of a temporary nature and cause the least possible disturbance to the functioning of the common market;

(3) Whereas the establishment of a competitive natural gas market is an important element of the completion of the internal energy market;

(4) Whereas Council Directive 91/296/EEC of 31 May 1991 on the transit of natural gas through grids and Council Directive 90/377/EEC of 29 June 1990 concerning a Community procedure to improve the transparency of gas and electricity prices charged to industrial end-users constitute a first phase of the completion of the internal market in natural gas;

(5) Whereas it is now necessary to take further measures with a view to establishing the internal market in natural gas;

(6) Whereas the provisions of this Directive should not affect the full application of the Treaty, in particular the provisions concerning the free movement of goods in the internal market and the rules on competition, and do not affect the powers of the Commission under the Treaty;

(7) Whereas the internal market in natural gas needs to be established gradually, in order to enable the industry to adjust in a flexible and ordered manner to its new environment and in order to take account of the different market structures in the Member States;

(8) Whereas the establishment of the internal market in the natural gas sector should favour the interconnection and interoperability of systems, for example through compatible qualities of gas;

(9) Whereas a certain number of common rules should be established for the organisation and operation of the natural gas sector; whereas, in accordance with the principle of subsidiarity, these rules are no more than general principles providing for a framework, the detailed implementation of which should be left to Member States, thus allowing each Member State to maintain or choose the regime which corresponds best to a particular situation, in particular with regard to authorisations and the supervision of supply contracts;

(10) Whereas the external supply of natural gas is of particular importance for the purchase of natural gas in Member States highly dependent on gas imports;

(11) Whereas, as a general rule, undertakings in the natural gas sector should be able to operate without being discriminated against;

(12) Whereas for some Member States the imposition of public service obligations may be necessary to ensure security of supply and consumer and environmental protection, which, in their view, free competition, left to itself, cannot necessarily guarantee;

(13) Whereas long-term planning may be one means of carrying out those public service obligations, taking into account the possibility of third parties seeking access to the system; whereas Member States may monitor take-or-pay contracts undertaken in order to keep up to date with the situation on supply;

(5) Whereas it is now necessary to take further measures with a view to establishing the internal market in natural gas;

(6) Whereas the provisions of this Directive should not affect the full application of the Treaty, in particular the provisions concerning the free movement of goods in the internal market and the rules on competition, and do not affect the powers of the Commission under the Treaty;

(7) Whereas the internal market in natural gas needs to be established gradually, in order to enable the industry to adjust in a flexible and ordered manner to its new environment and in order to take account of the different market structures in the Member States;

(8) Whereas the establishment of the internal market in the natural gas sector should favour the interconnection and interoperability of systems, for example through compatible qualities of gas;

(9) Whereas a certain number of common rules should be established for the organisation and operation of the natural gas sector; whereas, in accordance with the principle of subsidiarity, these rules are no more than general principles providing for a framework, the detailed implementation of which should be left to Member States, thus allowing each Member State to maintain or choose the regime which corresponds best to a particular situation, in particular with regard to authorisations and the supervision of supply contracts;

(10) Whereas the external supply of natural gas is of particular importance for the purchase of natural gas in Member States highly dependent on gas imports;

(11) Whereas, as a general rule, undertakings in the natural gas sector should be able to operate without being discriminated against;

(12) Whereas for some Member States the imposition of public service obligations may be necessary to ensure security of supply and consumer and environmental protection, which, in their view, free competition, left to itself, cannot necessarily guarantee;

(13) Whereas long-term planning may be one means of carrying out those public service obligations, taking into account the possibility of third parties seeking access to the system; whereas Member States may monitor take-or-pay contracts undertaken in order to keep up to date with the situation on supply;

(14) Whereas Article 90(1) of the Treaty obliges the Member States to respect the rules on competition with regard to public undertakings and undertakings which have been granted special or exclusive rights;

(15) Whereas Article 90(2) of the Treaty subjects undertakings entrusted with the operation of services of general economic interest to these rules under specific conditions; whereas the implementation of this Directive will have an impact on the activities of such undertakings; whereas, as referred to in Article 3(3), Member States need not apply Article 4, in particular, to their distribution infrastructure in order not to obstruct in law or in fact the fulfilment of obligations of general economic interest imposed on gas undertakings;

(16) Whereas, when imposing public service obligations on undertakings of the natural gas sector, Member States must therefore respect the relevant rules of the Treaty as interpreted by the Court of Justice of the European Communities;

(17) Whereas basic criteria and procedures should be laid down concerning the authorisations which Member States may grant for the construction or operation of relevant facilities under their national system; whereas these provisions should not affect the relevant rules of national legislation subjecting the construction or operation of relevant facilities to an authorisation requirement; whereas, however, such requirement should not have the effect of restricting competition among the undertakings of the sector;

(18) Whereas Decision No 1254/96/EC of the European Parliament and of the Council of 5 June 1996 laying down a series of guidelines for trans-European energy networks, contributes to the development of integrated infrastructures for the natural gas sector;

(19) Whereas the technical rules for the operation of systems and direct lines must be transparent and must ensure interoperability of systems;

(20) Whereas basic rules must be laid down with regard to transmission, storage and liquefied natural gas undertakings, as well as to distribution and supply undertakings;

(21) Whereas it is necessary to provide for access by the competent authorities to the internal accounts of undertakings, with due regard for confidentiality;

(14) Whereas Article 90(1) of the Treaty obliges the Member States to respect the rules on competition with regard to public undertakings and undertakings which have been granted special or exclusive rights;

(15) Whereas Article 90(2) of the Treaty subjects undertakings entrusted with the operation of services of general economic interest to these rules under specific conditions; whereas the implementation of this Directive will have an impact on the activities of such undertakings; whereas, as referred to in Article 3(3), Member States need not apply Article 4, in particular, to their distribution infrastructure in order not to obstruct in law or in fact the fulfilment of obligations of general economic interest imposed on gas undertakings;

(16) Whereas, when imposing public service obligations on undertakings of the natural gas sector, Member States must therefore respect the relevant rules of the Treaty as interpreted by the Court of Justice of the European Communities;

(17) Whereas basic criteria and procedures should be laid down concerning the authorisations which Member States may grant for the construction or operation of relevant facilities under their national system; whereas these provisions should not affect the relevant rules of national legislation subjecting the construction or operation of relevant facilities to an authorisation requirement; whereas, however, such requirement should not have the effect of restricting competition among the undertakings of the sector;

(18) Whereas Decision No 1254/96/EC of the European Parliament and of the Council of 5 June 1996 laying down a series of guidelines for trans-European energy networks, contributes to the development of integrated infrastructures for the natural gas sector;

(19) Whereas the technical rules for the operation of systems and direct lines must be transparent and must ensure interoperability of systems;

(20) Whereas basic rules must be laid down with regard to transmission, storage and liquefied natural gas undertakings, as well as to distribution and supply undertakings;

(21) Whereas it is necessary to provide for access by the competent authorities to the internal accounts of undertakings, with due regard for confidentiality;

(22) Whereas the accounts of all integrated natural gas undertakings should provide for a high degree of transparency; whereas the accounts should be separate for different activities when this is necessary in order to avoid discrimination, cross-subsidisation and other distortions of competition, taking into account in relevant cases that transmission for accounting purposes includes regasification; whereas separate accounts should not be required for legal entities, such as stock or futures exchanges, which do not, other than in this trading capacity, perform any of the functions of a natural gas undertaking; whereas integrated accounts for hydrocarbon production and related activities may be produced as part of the requirement for accounts for non-gas activities required by this Directive; whereas the relevant information in Article 23(3) should include, where required, accounting information about upstream pipelines;

(23) Whereas access to the system should be open in accordance with this Directive and should lead to a sufficient and, where appropriate, a comparable level of opening-up of markets in different Member States; whereas, at the same time, the opening-up of markets should not create unnecessary disequilibrium in the competitive situation of undertakings in the different Member States;

(24) Whereas, owing to the diversity of structures and the special characteristics of systems in Member States, there should be different procedures for system access operating in accordance with objective, transparent and non-discriminatory criteria;

(25) Whereas, in order to achieve a competitive market in natural gas, provision should be made for access to upstream pipeline networks; whereas separate treatment is required as respects such access to upstream pipeline networks, having regard, in particular, to the special economic, technical and operational characteristics relating to such networks; whereas the provisions of this Directive do not in any event affect national taxation rules;

(26) Whereas provision should be made regarding authorisation, construction and use of direct lines;

(27) Whereas provision should be made for safeguards and dispute settlement procedures;

(28) Whereas any abuse of a dominant position or any predatory behaviour should be avoided;

(22) Whereas the accounts of all integrated natural gas undertakings should provide for a high degree of transparency; whereas the accounts should be separate for different activities when this is necessary in order to avoid discrimination, cross-subsidisation and other distortions of competition, taking into account in relevant cases that transmission for accounting purposes includes regasification; whereas separate accounts should not be required for legal entities, such as stock or futures exchanges, which do not, other than in this trading capacity, perform any of the functions of a natural gas undertaking; whereas integrated accounts for hydrocarbon production and related activities may be produced as part of the requirement for accounts for non-gas activities required by this Directive; whereas the relevant information in Article 23(3) should include, where required, accounting information about upstream pipelines;

(23) Whereas access to the system should be open in accordance with this Directive and should lead to a sufficient and, where appropriate, a comparable level of opening-up of markets in different Member States; whereas, at the same time, the opening-up of markets should not create unnecessary disequilibrium in the competitive situation of undertakings in the different Member States;

(24) Whereas, owing to the diversity of structures and the special characteristics of systems in Member States, there should be different procedures for system access operating in accordance with objective, transparent and non-discriminatory criteria;

(25) Whereas, in order to achieve a competitive market in natural gas, provision should be made for access to upstream pipeline networks; whereas separate treatment is required as respects such access to upstream pipeline networks, having regard, in particular, to the special economic, technical and operational characteristics relating to such networks; whereas the provisions of this Directive do not in any event affect national taxation rules;

(26) Whereas provision should be made regarding authorisation, construction and use of direct lines;

(27) Whereas provision should be made for safeguards and dispute settlement procedures;

(28) Whereas any abuse of a dominant position or any predatory behaviour should be avoided;

(29) Whereas, as some Member States are liable to experience special difficulties in adjusting their systems, provision should be made for temporary derogations;

(30) Whereas long-term take-or-pay contracts are a market reality for securing Member States' gas supply; whereas, in particular, provision should be made for derogations from certain provisions of this Directive in the case of a natural gas undertaking which is or would be in serious economic difficulties because of its take-or-pay obligations; whereas these derogations should not undermine the purpose of this Directive to liberalise the internal market in natural gas; whereas any take-or-pay contracts entered into or renewed after the entry into force of this Directive should be concluded prudently in order not to hamper a significant opening of the market; whereas, therefore, such derogations should be limited in time and scope and granted in a transparent manner, under the supervision of the Commission;

(31) Whereas specific provisions are needed for markets and investments in other areas which have not yet reached a developed stage; whereas derogations for such markets and areas should be limited in time and scope; whereas, for the sake of transparency and uniformity, the Commission should have a significant role in the granting of these derogations;

(32) Whereas this Directive constitutes a further phase of liberalisation; whereas, once it has been put into effect, some obstacles to trade in natural gas between Member States will nevertheless remain in place; whereas proposals for improving the operation of the internal market in natural gas should be made in the light of experience; whereas the Commission should therefore report to the European Parliament and the Council on the application of this Directive,

HAVE ADOPTED THIS DIRECTIVE:

CHAPTER I SCOPE AND DEFINITIONS

Article 1

This Directive establishes common rules for the transmission, distribution, supply and storage of natural gas. It lays down the rules relating to the organisation and functioning of the natural gas sector, including liquefied natural gas (LNG), access to the

(29) Whereas, as some Member States are liable to experience special difficulties in adjusting their systems, provision should be made for temporary derogations;

(30) Whereas long-term take-or-pay contracts are a market reality for securing Member States' gas supply; whereas, in particular, provision should be made for derogations from certain provisions of this Directive in the case of a natural gas undertaking which is or would be in serious economic difficulties because of its take-or-pay obligations; whereas these derogations should not undermine the purpose of this Directive to liberalise the internal market in natural gas; whereas any take-or-pay contracts entered into or renewed after the entry into force of this Directive should be concluded prudently in order not to hamper a significant opening of the market; whereas, therefore, such derogations should be limited in time and scope and granted in a transparent manner, under the supervision of the Commission;

(31) Whereas specific provisions are needed for markets and investments in other areas which have not yet reached a developed stage; whereas derogations for such markets and areas should be limited in time and scope; whereas, for the sake of transparency and uniformity, the Commission should have a significant role in the granting of these derogations;

(32) Whereas this Directive constitutes a further phase of liberalisation; whereas, once it has been put into effect, some obstacles to trade in natural gas between Member States will nevertheless remain in place; whereas proposals for improving the operation of the internal market in natural gas should be made in the light of experience; whereas the Commission should therefore report to the European Parliament and the Council on the application of this Directive,

HAVE ADOPTED THIS DIRECTIVE:

CHAPTER I SCOPE AND DEFINITIONS

Article 1

This Directive establishes common rules for the transmission, distribution, supply and storage of natural gas. It lays down the rules relating to the organisation and functioning of the natural gas sector, including liquefied natural gas (LNG), access to the market, the operation of systems, and the criteria and procedures applicable to the granting of authorisations for transmission, distribution, supply and storage of natural gas.

Article 2

For the purposes of this Directive:

1. 'natural gas undertaking' means any natural or legal person carrying out at least one of the following functions: production, transmission, distribution, supply, purchase or storage of natural gas, including LNG, which is responsible for the commercial, technical and/or maintenance tasks related to those functions, but shall not include final customers;

2. 'upstream pipeline network' means any pipeline or network of pipelines operated and/or constructed as part of an oil or gas production project, or used to convey natural gas from one or more such projects to a processing plant or terminal or final coastal landing terminal;

3. 'transmission' means the transport of natural gas through a high pressure pipeline network other than an upstream pipeline network with a view to its delivery to customers;

4. 'transmission undertaking' means any natural or legal person who carries out the function of transmission;

5. 'distribution' means the transport of natural gas through local or regional pipeline networks with a view to its delivery to customers;

6. 'distribution undertaking' means any natural or legal person who carries out the function of distribution;

7. 'supply' means the delivery and/or sale of natural gas, including LNG, to customers;

8. 'supply undertaking' means any natural or legal person who carries out the function of supply;

9. 'storage facility' means a facility used for the stocking of natural gas and owned and/or operated by a natural gas undertaking, excluding the portion used for production operations;

10. 'storage undertaking' means any natural or legal person who carries out the function of storage;

11. 'LNG facility' means a terminal which is used for the liquefaction of natural gas or the offloading, storage and re-gasification of LNG;

market, the operation of systems, and the criteria and procedures applicable to the granting of authorisations for transmission, distribution, supply and storage of natural gas.

Article 2

For the purposes of this Directive:

1. 'natural gas undertaking' means any natural or legal person carrying out at least one of the following functions: production, transmission, distribution, supply, purchase or storage of natural gas, including LNG, which is responsible for the commercial, technical and/or maintenance tasks related to those functions, but shall not include final customers;

2. 'upstream pipeline network' means any pipeline or network of pipelines operated and/or constructed as part of an oil or gas production project, or used to convey natural gas from one or more such projects to a processing plant or terminal or final coastal landing terminal;

3. 'transmission' means the transport of natural gas through a high pressure pipeline network other than an upstream pipeline network with a view to its delivery to customers;

4. 'transmission undertaking' means any natural or legal person who carries out the function of transmission;

5. 'distribution' means the transport of natural gas through local or regional pipeline networks with a view to its delivery to customers;

6. 'distribution undertaking' means any natural or legal person who carries out the function of distribution;

7. 'supply' means the delivery and/or sale of natural gas, including LNG, to customers;

8. 'supply undertaking' means any natural or legal person who carries out the function of supply;

9. 'storage facility' means a facility used for the stocking of natural gas and owned and/or operated by a natural gas undertaking, excluding the portion used for production operations;

10. 'storage undertaking' means any natural or legal person who carries out the function of storage;

11. 'LNG facility' means a terminal which is used for the liquefaction of natural gas or the offloading, storage and re-gasification of LNG;

12. 'system' means any transmission networks and/or distribution networks and/or LNG facilities owned and/or operated by a natural gas undertaking, including its facilities supplying ancillary services and those of related undertakings necessary for providing access to transmission and distribution;

13. 'interconnected system' means a number of systems which are linked with each other;

14. 'direct line' means a natural gas pipeline complementary to the interconnected system;

15. 'integrated natural gas undertaking' means a vertically or horizontally integrated undertaking;

16. 'vertically integrated undertaking' means a natural gas undertaking performing two or more of the tasks of production, transmission, distribution, supply or storage of natural gas;

17. 'horizontally integrated undertaking' means an undertaking performing at least one of the functions of production, transmission, distribution, supply or storage of natural gas, and a non-gas activity;

18. 'related undertaking' means affiliated undertakings, within the meaning of Article 41 of the Seventh Council Directive, 83/349/EEC, of 13 June 1983 based on Article 54(3)(g) of the Treaty on consolidated accounts, and/or associated undertakings, within the meaning of Article 33(1) thereof, and/or undertakings which belong to the same shareholders;

19. 'system user' means any natural or legal person supplying to, or being supplied by, the system;

20. 'customers' means wholesale or final customers of natural gas and natural gas undertakings which purchase natural gas;

21. 'final customer' means a consumer purchasing natural gas for his own use;

22. 'wholesale customers', where Member States recognise their existence, means any natural or legal

12. 'system' means any transmission networks and/or distribution networks and/or LNG facilities owned and/or operated by a natural gas undertaking, including its facilities supplying ancillary services and those of related undertakings necessary for providing access to transmission and distribution;

12a. 'ancillary services' shall mean all services necessary for the operation of transmission and/or distribution networks and/or LNG facilities including storage facilities and equivalent flexibility instruments, load balancing and blending;

13. 'interconnected system' means a number of systems which are linked with each other;

14. 'direct line' means a natural gas pipeline complementary to the interconnected system;

15. 'integrated natural gas undertaking' means a vertically or horizontally integrated undertaking;

16. 'vertically integrated undertaking' means a natural gas undertaking performing two or more of the tasks of production, transmission, distribution, supply or storage of natural gas;

17. 'horizontally integrated undertaking' means an undertaking performing at least one of the functions of production, transmission, distribution, supply or storage of natural gas, and a non-gas activity;

18. 'related undertaking' means affiliated undertakings, within the meaning of Article 41 of the Seventh Council Directive, 83/349/EEC, of 13 June 1983 based on Article 54(3)(g) of the Treaty on consolidated accounts, and/or associated undertakings, within the meaning of Article 33(1) thereof, and/or undertakings which belong to the same shareholders;

19. 'system user' means any natural or legal person supplying to, or being supplied by, the system;

20. 'customers' means wholesale or final customers of natural gas and natural gas undertakings which purchase natural gas;

20a. 'non-domestic customer' shall mean a consumer purchasing natural gas which is not for his own household use and shall include power generators, natural gas undertakings and wholesale customers;

21. 'final customer' means a consumer purchasing natural gas for his own use;

22. 'wholesale customers', where Member States recognise their existence, means any natural or legal

persons who purchase and sell natural gas and who do not carry out transmission or distribution functions inside or outside the system where they are established;

23. 'long-term planning' means the planning of supply and transportation capacity of natural gas undertakings on a long-term basis with a view to meeting the demand for natural gas of the system, diversification of sources and securing supplies to customers;

24. 'emergent market' means a Member State in which the first commercial supply of its first long-term natural gas supply contract was made not more than 10 years earlier;

25. 'security' means both security of supply and provision, and technical safety.

CHAPTER II GENERAL RULES FOR THE ORGANISATION OF THE SECTOR

Article 3

1. Member States shall ensure, on the basis of their institutional organisation and with due regard for the principle of subsidiarity, that, without prejudice to paragraph 2, natural gas undertakings are operated in accordance with the principles of this Directive with a view to achieving a competitive market in natural gas, and shall not discriminate between such undertakings as regards either rights or obligations.

2. Having full regard to the relevant provisions of the Treaty, in particular Article 90 thereof, Member States may impose on natural gas undertakings, in the general economic interest, public-service obligations which may relate to security, including security of supply, regularity, quality and price of supplies, and to environmental protection. Such obligations shall be clearly defined, transparent, non-discriminatory and verifiable; they, and any revision thereof, shall be published and notified to the Commission by Member States without delay. As a means of carrying out public-service obligations in relation to security of supply, Member States which so wish may introduce the implementation of long-term planning, taking into account the possibility of third parties seeking access to the system.

3. Member States may decide not to apply the provisions of Article 4 with respect to distribution insofar as the application of these provisions would obstruct, in law or in fact, the performance of the obligations imposed on natural gas undertakings in

persons who purchase and sell natural gas and who do not carry out transmission or distribution functions inside or outside the system where they are established;

23. 'long-term planning' means the planning of supply and transportation capacity of natural gas undertakings on a long-term basis with a view to meeting the demand for natural gas of the system, diversification of sources and securing supplies to customers;

24. 'emergent market' means a Member State in which the first commercial supply of its first long-term natural gas supply contract was made not more than 10 years earlier;

25. 'security' means both security of supply and provision, and technical safety.

CHAPTER II GENERAL RULES FOR THE ORGANISATION OF THE SECTOR

Article 3

1. Member States shall ensure, on the basis of their institutional organisation and with due regard for the principle of subsidiarity, that, without prejudice to paragraph 2, natural gas undertakings are operated in accordance with the principles of this Directive with a view to achieving a competitive market in natural gas. Member States shall not discriminate between such undertakings as regards either rights or obligations.

2. Having regard to the relevant provisions of the Treaty, in particular Article 86 thereof, Member States may impose on natural gas undertakings, in the general economic interest, public-service obligations which may relate to security, including security of supply, regularity, quality and price of supplies, and to environmental protection. Such obligations shall be clearly defined, transparent, non-discriminatory and verifiable. As a means of carrying out public-service obligations in relation to security of supply, Member States may introduce the implementation of long-term planning, taking into account the possibility of third parties seeking access to the system.

3. Member States shall take appropriate measures to protect final customers and to ensure high levels of consumer protection, particularly with respect to transparency regarding contractual terms and conditions, general information and dispute settlement

the general economic interest and insofar as the development of trade would not be affected to such an extent as would be contrary to the interests of the Community. The interests of the Community include, inter alia, competition with regard to eligible customers in accordance with this Directive and Article 90 of the Treaty.

mechanisms. These measures shall include, in particular, those set out in the Annex.

4. Member States shall implement appropriate measures to achieve the objectives of social and economic cohesion, environmental protection and security of supply, notably through the maintenance and construction of necessary network infrastructure including interconnection capacity.

5. Member States may decide not to apply the provisions of Article 4 with respect to distribution in so far as their application would obstruct, in law or in fact, the performance of the obligations imposed on natural gas undertakings in the general economic interest and in so far as the development of trade would not be affected to such an extent as would be contrary to the interests of the Community. The interests of the Community include, *inter alia*, competition with regard to eligible customers in accordance with this Directive and Article 86 of the Treaty.

Article 3a

1. Member States shall, every two years, notify the Commission of all measures adopted to fulfil public service obligations, whether or not such measures require a derogation from the provisions of this Directive. This notification shall relate, *inter alia*, to measures regarding environmental protection, security of supply, protection of customers, including final customers, social and regional cohesion, and the maintenance of service standards.

2. The Commission shall publish, every two years, a report analysing the different measures taken in the Member States to meet high public service standards, together with an examination of the effectiveness of those measures. Where appropriate, the Commission shall make recommendations as to measures to be taken at national level to achieve high public service standards.

Article 4

1. In circumstances where an authorisation (e. g. licence, permission, concession, consent or approval) is required for the construction or operation of natural gas facilities, the Member States or any competent authority they designate shall grant authorisations to build and/or operate such facilities,

Article 4

1. In circumstances where an authorisation (e. g. licence, permission, concession, consent or approval) is required for the construction or operation of natural gas facilities, the Member States or any competent authority they designate shall grant authorisations to build and/or operate such facilities,

pipelines and associated equipment on their territory, in accordance with paragraphs 2 to 4. Member States or any competent authority they designate may also grant authorisations on the same basis for the supply of natural gas and for wholesale customers.

2. Where Member States have a system of authorisation, they shall lay down objective and non-discriminatory criteria which shall be met by an undertaking applying for an authorisation to build and/or operate natural gas facilities or applying for an authorisation to supply natural gas. The non-discriminatory criteria and procedures for the granting of authorisations shall be made public.

3. Member States shall ensure that the reasons for any refusal to grant an authorisation are objective and non-discriminatory and are given to the applicant. Reasons for such refusals shall be forwarded to the Commission for information. Member States shall establish a procedure enabling the applicant to appeal against such refusals.

4. For the development of newly supplied areas and efficient operation generally, and without prejudice to Article 20, Member States may decline to grant a further authorisation to build and operate distribution pipeline systems in any particular area once such pipeline systems have been or are proposed to be built in that area and if existing or proposed capacity is not saturated.

pipelines and associated equipment on their territory, in accordance with paragraphs 2 to 4. Member States or any competent authority they designate may also grant authorisations on the same basis for the supply of natural gas and for wholesale customers.

2. Where Member States have a system of authorisation, they shall lay down objective and non-discriminatory criteria which shall be met by an undertaking applying for an authorisation to build and/or operate natural gas facilities or applying for an authorisation to supply natural gas. The non-discriminatory criteria and procedures for the granting of authorisations shall be made public.

3. Member States shall ensure that the reasons for any refusal to grant an authorisation are objective and non-discriminatory and are given to the applicant. Reasons for such refusals shall be forwarded to the Commission for information. Member States shall establish a procedure enabling the applicant to appeal against such refusals.

4. For the development of newly supplied areas and efficient operation generally, and without prejudice to Article 20, Member States may decline to grant a further authorisation to build and operate distribution pipeline systems in any particular area once such pipeline systems have been or are proposed to be built in that area and if existing or proposed capacity is not saturated.

Article 4a

1. Member States shall designate a body, which may be the independent regulatory authority referred to in Article 22, to monitor security of supply issues. This body shall monitor, in particular, the supply/demand balance on the national market, the level of expected future demand and available supplies, and the level of competition on the market. The body shall publish, by 31 July each year at the latest, a report outlining its findings on these issues, as well as any measures taken or envisaged to address them, and shall forward this report to the Commission forthwith.

2. On the basis of the report referred to in paragraph 1, the Commission shall forward a Communication to the European Parliament and the Council each year examining issues relating to security of supply of natural gas in the Community, and in particular the existing and projected balance between demand and supply. Where appropriate, the Commission shall issue recommendations.

Article 5
Member States shall ensure that technical rules establishing the minimum technical design and operational requirements for the connection to the system of LNG facilities, storage facilities, other transmission or distribution systems, and direct lines, are developed and made available. These technical rules shall ensure the inter-operability of systems and shall be objective and non-discriminatory. They shall be notified to the Commission in accordance with Article 8 of Council Directive 83/189/EEC of 28 March 1983 laying down a procedure for the provision of information in the field of technical standards and regulations.

CHAPTER III TRANSMISSION, STORAGE AND LNG

Article 6
Member States shall take the measures necessary to ensure that transmission, storage and LNG undertakings act in accordance with Articles 7 and 8.

Article 7
1. Each transmission, storage and/or LNG undertaking shall operate, maintain and develop under economic conditions secure, reliable and efficient transmission, storage and/or LNG facilities, with due regard to the environment.

2. In any event, the transmission, storage and/or LNG undertaking shall not discriminate between system users or classes of system users, particularly in favour of its related undertakings.

Article 5
Member States shall ensure that technical rules establishing the minimum technical design and operational requirements for the connection to the system of LNG facilities, storage facilities, other transmission or distribution systems, and direct lines, are developed and made available. These technical rules shall ensure the inter-operability of systems and shall be objective and non-discriminatory. They shall be notified to the Commission in accordance with Article 8 of Council Directive 83/189/EEC of 28 March 1983 laying down a procedure for the provision of information in the field of technical standards and regulations.

CHAPTER III TRANSMISSION, STORAGE AND LNG

Article 6
Member States shall take the measures necessary to ensure that transmission, storage and LNG undertakings act in accordance with Articles 7 and 8.

Article 7
1. Member States shall designate or shall require undertakings which own transmission, storage or LNG facilities to designate, for a period of time to be determined by Member States having regard to considerations of efficiency and economic balance, one or more system operators to be responsible for operating, ensuring the maintenance of, and developing the transmission, storage and LNG facilities in a given area and its interconnections with other systems, in order to guarantee security of supply.

2. Each transmission, storage and/or LNG system operator:

(a) shall operate, maintain and develop under economic conditions secure, reliable and efficient transmission, storage and/or LNG facilities, with due regard to the environment;
(b) shall not discriminate between system users or classes of system users, particularly in favour of its related undertakings;
(c) shall provide any other transmission undertaking, any other storage undertaking, any other LNG undertaking and/or any distribution undertaking, sufficient information to ensure that the transport and storage of natural gas may take place in a manner compatible with the secure and efficient operation of the interconnected system.

3. Each transmission, storage and/or LNG undertaking shall provide any other transmission undertaking, any other storage undertaking and/or any distribution undertaking with sufficient information to ensure that the transport and storage of natural gas may take place in a manner compatible with the secure and efficient operation of the interconnected system.

3. Rules for balancing the gas system adopted by transmission and distribution system operators shall be transparent and non-discriminatory. Tariffs and terms and conditions for the provision of such services by system operators shall be established in a non-discriminatory way reflecting prevailing market prices and shall be fixed or approved by the national regulatory authority prior to their entry into force.

Article 7a

1. Member States may require transmission system operators to meet minimum levels of investment for the maintenance and development of the transmission system, including interconnection capacity.

2. Unless the transmission system operator is already fully independent from other activities not relating to the transmission system in terms of ownership, the transmission system operator shall be independent at least in terms of its legal form, organisation and decision making from other activities not relating to system operation.

In order to ensure the independence of the transmission system operator, the following criteria shall apply:

(a) those persons responsible for the management of the transmission system may not participate in company structures of the integrated natural gas undertaking responsible, directly or indirectly, for the day-to-day operation of the production, distribution and supply of gas;
(b) appropriate measures must be taken to ensure that the personal interests of persons responsible for the management of the transmission system are taken into account in a manner that ensures that they are capable of acting independently;
(c) the transmission system operator must exercise full control over all assets necessary to maintain and develop the network;
(d) the transmission system operator must establish a compliance programme, which sets out measures taken to ensure that discriminatory conduct is excluded. The programme must set out the specific obligations of employees to meet this objective. It must be drawn up and its respect monitored by a compliance officer appointed by and reporting to the President/Chief Executive of the

Article 8

1. Without prejudice to Article 12 or any other legal duty to disclose information, each transmission, storage and/or LNG undertaking shall preserve the confidentiality of commercially sensitive information obtained in the course of carrying out its business.

2. Transmission undertakings shall not, in the context of sales or purchases of natural gas by the transmission undertakings or related undertakings, abuse commercially sensitive information obtained from third parties in the context of providing or negotiating access to the system.

CHAPTER IV DISTRIBUTION AND SUPPLY

Article 9

1. Member States shall ensure that distribution undertakings act in accordance with Articles 10 and 11.

2. Member States may impose on distribution undertakings and/or supply undertakings, an obligation to deliver to customers located in a given area or of a certain class or both. The tariff for such deliveries may be regulated, for instance to ensure equal treatment of the customers concerned.

Article 10

1. Each distribution undertaking shall operate, maintain and develop under economic conditions a secure, reliable and efficient system, with due regard to the environment.

2. In any event, the distribution undertaking must not discriminate between system users or classes of system users, particularly in favour of its related undertakings.

integrated natural gas undertaking to which the transmission system operator belongs. An annual report, setting out the measures taken, must be submitted by the compliance officer to the national regulatory authority and published.

Article 7b

Transmission system operators shall procure the energy they use for the carrying out of their functions according to transparent, non-discriminatory and market based procedures.

Article 8

1. Without prejudice to Article 12 or any other legal duty to disclose information, each transmission, storage and/or LNG undertaking shall preserve the confidentiality of commercially sensitive information obtained in the course of carrying out its business.

2. Transmission undertakings shall not, in the context of sales or purchases of natural gas by the transmission undertakings or related undertakings, abuse commercially sensitive information obtained from third parties in the context of providing or negotiating access to the system.

CHAPTER IV DISTRIBUTION AND SUPPLY

Article 9

1. Member States shall ensure that distribution undertakings act in accordance with Articles 10 and 11.

2. Member States may impose on distribution undertakings and/or supply undertakings, an obligation to deliver to customers located in a given area or of a certain class or both. The tariff for such deliveries may be regulated, for instance to ensure equal treatment of the customers concerned.

Article 10

1. Each distribution undertaking shall operate, maintain and develop under economic conditions a secure, reliable and efficient system, with due regard to the environment.

2. In any event, the distribution undertaking must not discriminate between system users or classes of system users, particularly in favour of its related undertakings.

3. Each distribution undertaking shall provide any other distribution undertaking, and/or any transmission and/or storage undertaking with sufficient information to ensure that the transport of gas may take place in a manner compatible with the secure and efficient operation of the interconnected system.

3. Each distribution undertaking shall provide any other distribution undertaking, and/or any transmission and/or storage undertaking with sufficient information to ensure that the transport of gas may take place in a manner compatible with the secure and efficient operation of the interconnected system.

4. Unless the distribution system operator is already fully independent from other activities not relating to the distribution system in terms of ownership, the distribution system operator shall be independent at least in terms of its legal form, organisation and decision making from other activities not relating to system operation.

In order to ensure the independence of the distribution system operator, the following criteria shall apply:

(a) those persons responsible for the management of the distribution system may not participate in company structures of the integrated natural gas undertaking responsible, directly or indirectly, for the day-to-day operation of the production, transmission and supply of gas;

(b) appropriate measures must be taken to ensure that the personal interests of persons responsible for the management of the distribution system are taken into account in a manner that ensures that they are capable of acting independently;

(c) the distribution system operator must exercise full control over all assets necessary to maintain and develop the network;

(d) the distribution system operator must establish a compliance programme, which sets out measures taken to ensure that discriminatory conduct is excluded. The programme must set out the specific obligations of employees to meet this objective. It must be drawn up and its respect monitored by a compliance officer appointed by and reporting to the President/Chief Executive of the integrated natural gas undertaking to which the distribution system operator belongs. An annual report, setting out the measures taken, must be submitted by the compliance officer to the national regulatory authority and published.

The provisions of the first and second subparagraphs shall apply from 1 January 2004. Member States may decide not to apply those provisions to integrated natural gas undertakings serving less than 100 000 customers at that date.

Article 11

1. Without prejudice to Article 12 or any other legal duty to disclose information, each distribution undertaking shall preserve the confidentiality of commercially sensitive information obtained in the course of carrying out its business.

2. Distribution undertakings shall not, in the context of sales or purchases of natural gas by the distribution undertakings or related undertakings, abuse commercially sensitive information obtained from third parties in the context of providing or negotiating access to the system.

CHAPTER V UNBUNDLING AND TRANSPARENCY OF ACCOUNTS

Article 12

Member States or any competent authority they designate, including the dispute settlement authorities referred to in Article 21(2) and Article 23(3), shall have right of access to the accounts of natural gas undertakings as set out in Article 13 which they need to consult in carrying out their functions. Member States and any designated competent authority, including the dispute settlement authorities, shall preserve the confidentiality of commercially sensitive information. Member States may introduce exceptions to the principle of confidentiality where this is necessary in order for the competent authorities to carry out their functions.

Article 13

1. Member States shall take the necessary steps to ensure that the accounts of natural gas undertakings are kept in accordance with paragraphs 2 to 5 of this Article.

2. Natural gas undertakings, whatever their system of ownership or legal form, shall draw up, submit to audit and publish their annual accounts in accordance with the rules of national law concerning the annual accounts of limited liability companies

Article 11

1. Without prejudice to Article 12 or any other legal duty to disclose information, each distribution undertaking shall preserve the confidentiality of commercially sensitive information obtained in the course of carrying out its business.

2. Distribution undertakings shall not, in the context of sales or purchases of natural gas by the distribution undertakings or related undertakings, abuse commercially sensitive information obtained from third parties in the context of providing or negotiating access to the system.

Article 11a

The rules in Article 7a(2) and Article10(4) do not prevent the operation of a combined transmission and distribution system operator, which is fully independent in terms of its legal form, organisation and decision making from other activities not relating to transmission or distribution system operation and meets the requirements of Article 7a(2).

CHAPTER V UNBUNDLING AND TRANSPARENCY OF ACCOUNTS

Article 12

Member States or any competent authority they designate, including the dispute settlement authorities referred to in Article 21(2) and Article 23(3), shall have right of access to the accounts of natural gas undertakings as set out in Article 13 which they need to consult in carrying out their functions. Member States and any designated competent authority, including the dispute settlement authorities, shall preserve the confidentiality of commercially sensitive information. Member States may introduce exceptions to the principle of confidentiality where this is necessary in order for the competent authorities to carry out their functions.

Article 13

1. Member States shall take the necessary steps to ensure that the accounts of natural gas undertakings are kept in accordance with paragraphs 2 to 5 of this Article.

2. Natural gas undertakings, whatever their system of ownership or legal form, shall draw up, submit to audit and publish their annual accounts in accordance with the rules of national law concerning the annual accounts of limited liability companies

adopted pursuant to the Fourth Council Directive 78/660/EEC of 25 July 1978 based on Article 54(3)(g) of the Treaty on the annual accounts of certain types of companies. Undertakings which are not legally obliged to publish their annual accounts shall keep a copy of these at the disposal of the public at their head office.

3. Integrated natural gas undertakings shall, in their internal accounting, keep separate accounts for their natural gas transmission, distribution and storage activities, and, where appropriate, consolidated accounts for non-gas activities, as they would be required to do if the activities in question were carried out by separate undertakings, with a view to avoiding discrimination, cross-subsidisation and distortion of competition. These internal accounts shall include a balance sheet and a profit and loss account for each activity. Where Article 16 applies and access to the system is on the basis of a single charge for both transmission and distribution, the accounts for transmission and distribution activities may be combined.

4. Undertakings shall specify in their internal accounting the rules for the allocation of assets and liabilities, expenditure and income as well as for depreciation, without prejudice to nationally applicable accounting rules, which they follow in drawing up the separate accounts referred to in paragraph 3. These rules may be amended only in exceptional cases. Such amendments shall be mentioned and duly substantiated.

5. The annual accounts shall indicate in notes any transaction of a certain size conducted with related undertakings.

CHAPTER VI ACCESS TO THE SYSTEM

Article 14

For the organisation of access to the system, Member States may choose either or both procedures referred to in Article 15 and in Article 16. These procedures shall operate in accordance with objective, transparent and non-discriminatory criteria.

adopted pursuant to the Fourth Council Directive 78/660/EEC of 25 July 1978 based on Article 54(3)(g) of the Treaty on the annual accounts of certain types of companies. Undertakings which are not legally obliged to publish their annual accounts shall keep a copy of these at the disposal of the public at their head office.

3. Integrated natural gas undertakings shall, in their internal accounting, keep separate accounts for their natural gas transmission, distribution, supply, LNG and storage activities, and, where appropriate, consolidated accounts for non-gas activities, as they would be required to do if the activities in question were carried out by separate undertakings, with a view to avoiding discrimination, cross-subsidisation and distortion of competition. The internal accounts shall include a balance sheet and a profit and loss account for each activity.

4. Undertakings shall specify in their internal accounting the rules for the allocation of assets and liabilities, expenditure and income as well as for depreciation, without prejudice to nationally applicable accounting rules, which they follow in drawing up the separate accounts referred to in paragraph 3. These rules may be amended only in exceptional cases. Such amendments shall be mentioned and duly substantiated.

5. The annual accounts shall indicate in notes any transaction of a certain size conducted with related undertakings.

CHAPTER VI ACCESS TO THE SYSTEM

Article 14

1. Member States shall ensure the implementation of a system of third party access to the transmission and distribution system and LNG facilities based on published tariffs, applicable to all eligible customers and applied objectively and without discrimination between system users. These tariffs shall be approved prior to their entry into force by a national regulatory authority established in conformity with Article 22.

2. Transmission system operators shall, if necessary and for the purpose of carrying out their functions including in relation to cross-border

transmission, have access to the network of other transmission system operators based on the same conditions and principles as set out in paragraph 1.

Article 15

1. In the case of negotiated access, Member States shall take the necessary measures for natural gas undertakings and eligible customers either inside or outside the territory covered by the interconnected system to be able to negotiate access to the system so as to conclude supply contracts with each other on the basis of voluntary commercial agreements. The parties shall be obliged to negotiate access to the system in good faith.

2. The contracts for access to the system shall be negotiated with the relevant natural gas undertakings. Member States shall require natural gas undertakings to publish their main commercial conditions for the use of the system within the first year following implementation of this Directive and on an annual basis every year thereafter.

Article 15

1. For the organisation of access to storage and equivalent flexibility instruments when technically and/or economically necessary for providing efficient access to the system for the supply of customers, as well as for the organisation of access to other ancillary services, Member States may choose either or both procedures referred to in paragraphs 2 and 3. These procedures shall operate in accordance with objective, transparent and non-discriminatory criteria.

2. In the case of negotiated access, Member States shall take the necessary measures for natural gas undertakings and eligible customers either inside or outside the territory covered by the interconnected system to be able to negotiate access to the system so as to conclude supply contracts with each other on the basis of voluntary commercial agreements. The parties shall be obliged to negotiate access to the system in good faith.

Contracts for access to the system shall be negotiated with the relevant system operator or natural gas undertakings. Member States shall require natural gas undertakings to publish their main commercial conditions for the use of the system by [indicate date] at the latest and every year thereafter.

3. Member States opting for a procedure of regulated access shall take the necessary measures to give natural gas undertakings and eligible customers either inside or outside the territory covered by the interconnected system a right of access to the system, on the basis of published tariffs and/or other terms and obligations for use of that system. This right of access for eligible customers may be given by enabling them to enter into supply contracts with competing natural gas undertakings other than the owner and/or operator of the system or a related undertaking.

Article 16

Member States opting for a procedure of regulated access shall take the necessary measures to give natural gas undertakings and eligible customers either inside or outside the territory covered by the inter-

Article 16

(deleted)

connected system a right of access to the system, on the basis of published tariffs and/or other terms and obligations for use of that system. This right of access for eligible customers may be given by enabling them to enter into supply contracts with competing natural gas undertakings other than the owner and/or operator of the system or a related undertaking.

Article 17

1. Natural gas undertakings may refuse access to the system on the basis of lack of capacity or where the access to the system would prevent them from carrying out the public-service obligations referred to in Article 3(2) which are assigned to them or on the basis of serious economic and financial difficulties with take-or-pay contracts having regard to the criteria and procedures set out in Article 25 and the alternative chosen by the Member State according to paragraph 1 of that Article. Duly substantiated reasons shall be given for such a refusal.

2. Member States may take the measures necessary to ensure that the natural gas undertaking refusing access to the system on the basis of lack of capacity or a lack of connection shall make the necessary enhancements as far as it is economical to do so or when a potential customer is willing to pay for them. In circumstances where Member States apply Article 4(4), Member States shall take such measures.

Article 18

1. Member States shall specify eligible customers, meaning those customers inside their territory which have the legal capacity to contract for, or to be sold, natural gas in accordance with Articles 15 and 16, given that all customers mentioned in paragraph 2 of this Article must be included.

2. Member States shall take the necessary measures to ensure that at least the following customers are designated as eligible customers:

- gas-fired power generators, irrespective of their annual consumption level; however, and in order to safeguard the balance of their electricity market, the Member States may introduce a threshold, which may not exceed the level envisaged for other final customers, for the eligibility of combined heat and power producers. Such thresholds shall be notified to the Commission,

Article 17

1. Natural gas undertakings may refuse access to the system on the basis of lack of capacity or where the access to the system would prevent them from carrying out the public-service obligations referred to in Article 3(2) which are assigned to them or on the basis of serious economic and financial difficulties with take-or-pay contracts having regard to the criteria and procedures set out in Article 25 and the alternative chosen by the Member State according to paragraph 1 of that Article. Duly substantiated reasons shall be given for such a refusal.

2. Member States may take the measures necessary to ensure that the natural gas undertaking refusing access to the system on the basis of lack of capacity or a lack of connection shall make the necessary enhancements as far as it is economical to do so or when a potential customer is willing to pay for them. In circumstances where Member States apply Article 4(4), Member States shall take such measures.

Article 18

1. Member States shall ensure that all non-domestic customers are free to purchase gas from the supplier of their choice and shall have the rights of eligible customers for third party access in order to execute such supplies in accordance with Articles 14 and 15 from 1 January 2004 at the latest.

2. Member States shall ensure that all customers are free to purchase gas from the supplier of their choice and have the rights of eligible customers for third party access in order to execute such supplies in accordance with Articles 14 and 15 from 1 January 2005 at the latest.

- other final customers consuming more than 25 million cubic metres of gas per year on a consumption-site basis.

3. Member States shall ensure that the definition of eligible customers referred to in paragraph 1 will result in an opening of the market equal to at least 20 % of the total annual gas consumption of the national gas market.

4. The percentage mentioned in paragraph 3 shall increase to 28 % of the total annual gas consumption of the national gas market five years after the entry into force of this Directive, and to 33 % thereof 10 years after the entry into force of this Directive.

5. If the definition of eligible customers as referred to in paragraph 1 results in a market opening of more than 30 % of the total annual gas consumption of the national gas market, the Member State concerned may modify the definition of eligible customers to the extent that the opening of the market is reduced to no lower than 30 % of such consumption. Member States shall modify the definition of eligible customers in a balanced manner, not creating specific disadvantages for certain types or classes of eligible customers, but taking into account existing market structures.

6. Member States shall take the following measures to ensure that the opening of their natural gas market is increased over a period of 10 years:

- the threshold set in the second indent of paragraph 2 for eligible customers other than gas-fired power generators, shall be reduced to 15 million cubic metres per year on a consumption-site basis five years after the entry into force of this Directive, and to 5 million cubic metres per year on such basis 10 years after the entry into force of this Directive,
- the percentage mentioned in paragraph 5 shall increase to 38 % of the total annual gas consumption of the national gas market five years after the entry into force of this Directive, and to 43 % of such consumption 10 years after the entry into force of this Directive.

7. In respect of emergent markets, the gradual market opening provided for by this Article shall start to apply from the expiry of the derogation referred to in Article 26(2).

8. Distribution undertakings, if not already specified as eligible customers under paragraph 1, shall have the legal capacity to contract for natural gas in

accordance with Articles 15 and 16 for the volume of natural gas being consumed by their customers designated as eligible within their distribution system, in order to supply those customers.

9. Member States shall publish by 31 January of each year the criteria for the definition of eligible customers referred to in paragraph 1. This information, together with all other appropriate information to justify the fulfilment of market opening under this Article, shall be sent to the Commission to be published in the Official Journal of the European Communities. The Commission may request a Member State to modify its specifications if they create obstacles to the correct application of this Directive as regards the smooth functioning of the internal market in natural gas. If the Member State concerned does not comply with this request within a period of three months, a final decision shall be taken in accordance with procedure I of Article 2 of Council Decision 87/373/EEC of 13 July 1987 laying down the procedures for the exercise of implementing powers conferred on the Commission.

Article 19

1. To avoid imbalance in the opening of gas markets during the period referred to in Article 28:

(a) contracts for the supply of gas under the provisions of Articles 15, 16 and 17 with an eligible customer in the system of another Member State shall not be prohibited if the customer is considered as eligible in both systems involved;

(b) in cases where transactions as described in subparagraph (a) are refused because the customer is eligible in only one of the two systems, the Commission may oblige, taking into account the situation in the market and the common interest, the refusing party to execute the requested gas supply, at the request of the Member State where the eligible customer is located.

2. In parallel with the procedure and the timetable provided for in Article 28, and not later than after half of the period provided for in that Article, the Commission shall review the application of paragraph 1(b) of this Article on the basis of market developments taking into account the common interest. In the light of experience, the Commission shall evaluate this situation and report on any possible imbalance in the opening of gas markets with regard to paragraph 1(b).

Article 19

1. To avoid imbalance in the opening of gas markets:

(a) contracts for the supply of gas with an eligible customer in the system of another Member State shall not be prohibited if the customer is considered as eligible in both systems involved;

(b) in cases where transactions as described in subparagraph (a) are refused because the customer is eligible in only one of the two systems, the Commission may oblige, taking into account the situation in the market and the common interest, the refusing party to execute the requested gas supply, at the request of the Member State where the eligible customer is located.

Article 20

1. Member States shall take the necessary measures to enable:
   - natural gas undertakings established within their territory to supply the customers described in Article 18 of this Directive through a direct line,
   - any such eligible customer with their territory to be supplied through a direct line by natural gas undertakings.

2. In circumstances where an authorisation (e. g. licence, permission, concession, consent or approval) is required for the construction or operation of direct lines, the Member States or any competent authority they designate shall lay down the criteria for the grant of authorisations for the construction or operation of such lines in their territory. These criteria shall be objective, transparent and non-discriminatory.

3. Member States may make authorisations to construct a direct line subject either to the refusal of system access on the basis of Article 17 or to the opening of a dispute settlement procedure under Article 21.

Article 21

1. Member States shall ensure that the parties negotiate access to the system in good faith and that none of them abuses its negotiating position to prevent the successful outcome of such negotiations.

2. Member States shall designate a competent authority, which must be independent of the parties, to settle expeditiously disputes relating to the negotiations in question. In particular, this authority shall settle disputes concerning negotiations and refusal of access within the scope of this Directive. The competent authority shall present its conclusions without delay or if possible within 12 weeks of the introduction of the dispute. Recourse to this authority shall be without prejudice to the exercise of rights of appeal under Community law.

3. In the event of cross-border disputes, the dispute settlement authority shall be the dispute settlement authority covering the system of the natural gas undertaking which refuses use of, or access to, the system. Where, in cross-border disputes, more than one such authority covers the system concerned, the authorities shall consult with a view to ensuring that the provisions of this Directive are applied consistently.

Article 20

1. Member States shall take the necessary measures to enable:
   - natural gas undertakings established within their territory to supply the customers described in Article 18 of this Directive through a direct line,
   - any such eligible customer with their territory to be supplied through a direct line by natural gas undertakings.

2. In circumstances where an authorisation (e. g. licence, permission, concession, consent or approval) is required for the construction or operation of direct lines, the Member States or any competent authority they designate shall lay down the criteria for the grant of authorisations for the construction or operation of such lines in their territory. These criteria shall be objective, transparent and non-discriminatory.

3. Member States may make authorisations to construct a direct line subject either to the refusal of system access on the basis of Article 17 or to the opening of a dispute settlement procedure under Article 21.

Article 21

1. Member States shall ensure that the parties negotiate access to the system in good faith and that none of them abuses its negotiating position to prevent the successful outcome of such negotiations.

2. Member States shall designate a competent authority, which must be independent of the parties, to settle expeditiously disputes relating to the negotiations in question. In particular, this authority shall settle disputes concerning negotiations and refusal of access within the scope of this Directive. The competent authority shall present its conclusions without delay or if possible within 12 weeks of the introduction of the dispute. Recourse to this authority shall be without prejudice to the exercise of rights of appeal under Community law.

3. In the event of cross-border disputes, the dispute settlement authority shall be the dispute settlement authority covering the system of the natural gas undertaking which refuses use of, or access to, the system. Where, in cross-border disputes, more than one such authority covers the system concerned, the authorities shall consult with a view to ensuring that the provisions of this Directive are applied consistently.

Article 22
Member States shall create appropriate and efficient mechanisms for regulation, control and transparency so as to avoid any abuse of a dominant position, in particular to the detriment of consumers, and any predatory behaviour. These mechanisms shall take account of the provisions of the Treaty, and in particular Article 86 thereof.

Article 22
1. Member States shall establish national regulatory authorities. These authorities shall be wholly independent of the interests of the gas industry. They shall at least have the sole responsibility:

(a) to fix or approve terms and conditions for connection and access to national networks, including transmission and distribution tariffs, and terms, conditions and tariffs for access to LNG facilities;
(b) to define the rules on the management and allocation of interconnection capacity, in conjunction with the national regulatory authority or authorities of those Member States with which interconnection exists;
(c) to fix or approve any mechanisms to deal with congested capacity within the national gas system;
(d) to ensure the respect of the requirements set out in Article 3(3) and (4).

2. Member States shall create appropriate and efficient mechanisms for regulation, control and transparency so as to avoid any abuse of dominant position, in particular to the detriment of consumers, and any predatory behaviour. These mechanisms shall take account of the provisions of the Treaty, and in particular Article 82 thereof.

3. Member States shall ensure that the appropriate measures be taken, including administrative action or criminal proceedings in conformity with their national law, against the natural or legal persons responsible where confidentiality rules imposed by this Directive have not been respected.

Article 23
1. Member States shall take the necessary measures to ensure that natural gas undertakings and customers required to be eligible under Article 18, wherever they are located, are able to obtain access to upstream pipeline networks, including facilities supplying technical services incidental to such access, in accordance with this Article, except for the parts of such networks and facilities which are used for local production operations at the site of a field where the gas is produced. The measures shall be notified to the Commission in accordance with the provisions of Article 29.

2. The access referred to in paragraph 1 shall be provided in a manner determined by the Member

Article 23
1. Member States shall take the necessary measures to ensure that natural gas undertakings and customers required to be eligible under Article 18, wherever they are located, are able to obtain access to upstream pipeline networks, including facilities supplying technical services incidental to such access, in accordance with this Article, except for the parts of such networks and facilities which are used for local production operations at the site of a field where the gas is produced. The measures shall be notified to the Commission in accordance with the provisions of Article 29.

2. The access referred to in paragraph 1 shall be provided in a manner determined by the Member

State in accordance with the relevant legal instruments. Member States shall apply the objectives of fair and open access, achieving a competitive market in natural gas and avoiding any abuse of a dominant position, taking into account security and regularity of supplies, capacity which is or can reasonably be made available, and environmental protection. The following may be taken into account:

(a) the need to refuse access where there is an incompatibility of technical specifications which cannot be reasonably overcome;
(b) the need to avoid difficulties which cannot be reasonably overcome and could prejudice the efficient, current and planned future production of hydrocarbons, including that from fields of marginal economic viability;
(c) the need to respect the duly substantiated reasonable needs of the owner or operator of the upstream pipeline network for the transport and processing of gas and the interests of all other users of the upstream pipeline network or relevant processing or handling facilities who may be affected; and
(d) the need to apply their laws and administrative procedures, in conformity with Community law, for the grant of authorisation for production or upstream development.

3. Member States shall ensure that they have in place dispute settlement arrangements, including an authority independent of the parties with access to all relevant information, to enable disputes relating to access to upstream pipeline networks to be settled expeditiously, taking into account the criteria in paragraph 2 and the number of parties which may be involved in negotiating access to such networks.

4. In the event of cross-border disputes, the dispute settlement arrangements for the Member State having jurisdiction over the upstream pipeline network which refuses access shall be applied. Where, in cross-border disputes, more than one Member State covers the network concerned, the Member State concerned shall consult with a view to ensuring that the provisions of this Directive are applied consistently.

State in accordance with the relevant legal instruments. Member States shall apply the objectives of fair and open access, achieving a competitive market in natural gas and avoiding any abuse of a dominant position, taking into account security and regularity of supplies, capacity which is or can reasonably be made available, and environmental protection. The following may be taken into account:

(a) the need to refuse access where there is an incompatibility of technical specifications which cannot be reasonably overcome;
(b) the need to avoid difficulties which cannot be reasonably overcome and could prejudice the efficient, current and planned future production of hydrocarbons, including that from fields of marginal economic viability;
(c) the need to respect the duly substantiated reasonable needs of the owner or operator of the upstream pipeline network for the transport and processing of gas and the interests of all other users of the upstream pipeline network or relevant processing or handling facilities who may be affected; and
(d) the need to apply their laws and administrative procedures, in conformity with Community law, for the grant of authorisation for production or upstream development.

3. Member States shall ensure that they have in place dispute settlement arrangements, including an authority independent of the parties with access to all relevant information, to enable disputes relating to access to upstream pipeline networks to be settled expeditiously, taking into account the criteria in paragraph 2 and the number of parties which may be involved in negotiating access to such networks.

4. In the event of cross-border disputes, the dispute settlement arrangements for the Member State having jurisdiction over the upstream pipeline network which refuses access shall be applied. Where, in cross-border disputes, more than one Member State covers the network concerned, the Member State concerned shall consult with a view to ensuring that the provisions of this Directive are applied consistently.

CHAPTER VII FINAL PROVISIONS

Article 24

1. In the event of a sudden crisis in the energy market or where the physical safety or security of persons, apparatus or installations or system integrity is threatened, a Member State may temporarily take the necessary safeguard measures.

2. Such measures shall cause the least possible disturbance to the functioning of the internal market and shall not be wider in scope than is strictly necessary to remedy the sudden difficulties which have arisen.

3. The Member State concerned shall without delay notify these measures to the other Member States, and to the Commission, which may decide that the Member State concerned must amend or abolish such measures, insofar as they distort competition and adversely affect trade in a manner which is at variance with the common interest.

Article 25

1. If a natural gas undertaking encounters, or considers it would encounter, serious economic and financial difficulties because of its take-or-pay commitments accepted in one or more gas-purchase contracts, an application for a temporary derogation from Article 15 and/or Article 16 may be sent to the Member State concerned or the designated competent authority. Applications shall, according to the choice of Member States, be presented on a case-by-case basis either before or after refusal of access to the system. Member States may also give the natural gas undertaking the choice to present an application either before or after refusal of access to the system. Where a natural gas undertaking has refused access, the application shall be presented without delay. The applications shall be accompanied by all relevant information on the nature and extent of the problem and on the efforts undertaken by the gas undertaking to solve the problem.

If alternative solutions are not reasonably available, and taking into account the provisions of paragraph 3, the Member State or the designated competent authority may decide to grant a derogation.

2. The Member State, or the designated competent authority, shall notify the Commission without delay of its decision to grant a derogation, together with all the relevant information with respect to the

CHAPTER VII FINAL PROVISIONS

Article 24

1. In the event of a sudden crisis in the energy market or where the physical safety or security of persons, apparatus or installations or system integrity is threatened, a Member State may temporarily take the necessary safeguard measures.

2. Such measures shall cause the least possible disturbance to the functioning of the internal market and shall not be wider in scope than is strictly necessary to remedy the sudden difficulties which have arisen.

3. The Member State concerned shall without delay notify these measures to the other Member States, and to the Commission, which may decide that the Member State concerned must amend or abolish such measures, insofar as they distort competition and adversely affect trade in a manner which is at variance with the common interest.

Article 25

1. If a natural gas undertaking encounters, or considers it would encounter, serious economic and financial difficulties because of its take-or-pay commitments accepted in one or more gas-purchase contracts, an application for a temporary derogation from Article 15 and/or Article 16 may be sent to the Member State concerned or the designated competent authority. Applications shall, according to the choice of Member States, be presented on a case-by-case basis either before or after refusal of access to the system. Member States may also give the natural gas undertaking the choice to present an application either before or after refusal of access to the system. Where a natural gas undertaking has refused access, the application shall be presented without delay. The applications shall be accompanied by all relevant information on the nature and extent of the problem and on the efforts undertaken by the gas undertaking to solve the problem.

If alternative solutions are not reasonably available, and taking into account the provisions of paragraph 3, the Member State or the designated competent authority may decide to grant a derogation.

2. The Member State, or the designated competent authority, shall notify the Commission without delay of its decision to grant a derogation, together with all the relevant information with respect to the

derogation. This information may be submitted to the Commission in an aggregated form, enabling the Commission to reach a well-founded decision. Within four weeks of its receipt of this notification, the Commission may request that the Member State or the designated competent authority concerned amend or withdraw the decision to grant a derogation. If the Member State or the designated competent authority concerned does not comply with this request within a period of four weeks, a final decision shall be taken expeditiously in accordance with procedure I of Article 2 of Decision 87/373/EEC. The Commission shall preserve the confidentiality of commercially sensitive information.

3. When deciding on the derogations referred to in paragraph 1, the Member State, or the designated competent authority, and the Commission shall take into account, in particular, the following criteria:

(a) the objective to achieve a competitive gas market;
(b) the need to fulfil public-service obligations and to ensure security of supply;
(c) the position of the natural gas undertaking in the gas market and the actual state of competition in this market;
(d) the seriousness of the economic and financial difficulties encountered by natural gas undertakings and transmission undertakings or eligible customers;
(e) the dates of signature and terms of the contract in question, including the extent to which they allow for market changes;
(f) the efforts made to find a solution to the problem;
(g) the extent to which, when accepting the take-or-pay commitments in question, the undertaking could reasonably have foreseen, having regard to the provisions of this Directive, that serious difficulties were likely to arise;
(h) the level of connection of the system with other systems and the degree of interoperability of these systems; and
(i) the effects the granting of a derogation would have on the correct application of this Directive as regards the smooth functioning of the internal natural gas market.

A decision on a request for a derogation concerning take-or-pay contracts concluded before the entry

derogation. This information may be submitted to the Commission in an aggregated form, enabling the Commission to reach a well-founded decision. Within four weeks of its receipt of this notification, the Commission may request that the Member State or the designated competent authority concerned amend or withdraw the decision to grant a derogation. If the Member State or the designated competent authority concerned does not comply with this request within a period of four weeks, a final decision shall be taken expeditiously in accordance with procedure I of Article 2 of Decision 87/373/EEC. The Commission shall preserve the confidentiality of commercially sensitive information.

3. When deciding on the derogations referred to in paragraph 1, the Member State, or the designated competent authority, and the Commission shall take into account, in particular, the following criteria:

(a) the objective to achieve a competitive gas market;
(b) the need to fulfil public-service obligations and to ensure security of supply;
(c) the position of the natural gas undertaking in the gas market and the actual state of competition in this market;
(d) the seriousness of the economic and financial difficulties encountered by natural gas undertakings and transmission undertakings or eligible customers;
(e) the dates of signature and terms of the contract in question, including the extent to which they allow for market changes;
(f) the efforts made to find a solution to the problem;
(g) the extent to which, when accepting the take-or-pay commitments in question, the undertaking could reasonably have foreseen, having regard to the provisions of this Directive, that serious difficulties were likely to arise;
(h) the level of connection of the system with other systems and the degree of interoperability of these systems; and
(i) the effects the granting of a derogation would have on the correct application of this Directive as regards the smooth functioning of the internal natural gas market.

A decision on a request for a derogation concerning take-or-pay contracts concluded before the entry into force of this Directive should not lead to a situation in which it is impossible to find economically viable alternative outlets. Serious difficulties shall in any case be deemed not to exist when the sales of natural gas do not fall below the level of minimum off-take guarantees contained in gas-purchase take-or-pay contracts or in so far as the relevant gas-purchase take-or-pay contract can be adapted or the natural gas undertaking is able to find alternative outlets.

4. Natural gas undertakings which have not been granted a derogation as referred to in paragraph 1 shall not refuse, or shall no longer refuse, access to the system because of take-or-pay commitments accepted in a gas purchase contract. Member States shall ensure that the relevant provisions of Chapter VI are complied with.

5. Any derogation granted under the above provisions shall be duly substantiated. The Commission shall publish the decision in the Official Journal of the European Communities.

6. The Commission shall, within five years of the entry into force of this Directive, submit a review report on the experience gained from the application of this Article, so as to allow the European Parliament and the Council to consider, in due course, the need to adjust it.

Article 26

1. Member States not directly connected to the interconnected system of any other Member State and having only one main external supplier may derogate from Article 4, Article 18(1), (2), (3), (4) and (6) and/or Article 20 of this Directive. A supplier having a market share of more than 75 % shall be considered to be a main supplier. This derogation shall automatically expire from the moment when at least one of these conditions no longer applies. Any such derogation shall be notified to the Commission.

2. A Member State, qualifying as an emergent market, which because of the implementation of this Directive would experience substantial problems, not associated with the contractual take-or-pay commitments referred to in Article 25, may derogate from Article 4, Article 18(1), (2), (3), (4) and (6) and/or Article 20 of this Directive. This derogation shall automatically expire from the moment when the Member State no longer qualifies as an emergent market. Any such derogation shall be notified to the Commission.

into force of this Directive should not lead to a situation in which it is impossible to find economically viable alternative outlets. Serious difficulties shall in any case be deemed not to exist when the sales of natural gas do not fall below the level of minimum off-take guarantees contained in gas-purchase take-or-pay contracts or in so far as the relevant gas-purchase take-or-pay contract can be adapted or the natural gas undertaking is able to find alternative outlets.

4. Natural gas undertakings which have not been granted a derogation as referred to in paragraph 1 shall not refuse, or shall no longer refuse, access to the system because of take-or-pay commitments accepted in a gas purchase contract. Member States shall ensure that the relevant provisions of Chapter VI are complied with.

5. Any derogation granted under the above provisions shall be duly substantiated. The Commission shall publish the decision in the Official Journal of the European Communities.

6. The Commission shall, within five years of the entry into force of this Directive, submit a review report on the experience gained from the application of this Article, so as to allow the European Parliament and the Council to consider, in due course, the need to adjust it.

Article 26

1. Member States not directly connected to the interconnected system of any other Member State and having only one main external supplier may derogate from Article 4, Article 18(1), (2), (3), (4) and (6) and/or Article 20 of this Directive. A supplier having a market share of more than 75 % shall be considered to be a main supplier. This derogation shall automatically expire from the moment when at least one of these conditions no longer applies. Any such derogation shall be notified to the Commission.

2. A Member State, qualifying as an emergent market, which because of the implementation of this Directive would experience substantial problems, not associated with the contractual take-or-pay commitments referred to in Article 25, may derogate from Article 4, Article 18(1), (2), (3), (4) and (6) and/or Article 20 of this Directive. This derogation shall automatically expire from the moment when the Member State no longer qualifies as an emergent market. Any such derogation shall be notified to the Commission.

3. Where implementation of this Directive would cause substantial problems in a geographically limited area of a Member State, in particular concerning the development of the transmission infrastructure, and with a view to encouraging investments, the Member State may apply to the Commission for a temporary derogation from Article 4, Article 18(1), (2), (3), (4) and (6) and/or Article 20 for developments within this area.

4. The Commission may grant the derogation referred to in paragraph 3, taking into account, in particular, the following criteria:

- the need for infrastructure investments, which would not be economical to operate in a competitive market environment,
- the level and pay-back prospects of investments required,
- the size and maturity of the gas system in the area concerned,
- the prospects for the gas market concerned,
- the geographical size and characteristics of the area or region concerned, and
- socio-economic and demographic factors.

A derogation may be granted only if no gas infrastructure has been established in this area, or has been so established for less than 10 years. The temporary derogation may not exceed 10 years from the time gas is first supplied in the area.

5. The Commission shall inform the Member States of applications made under paragraphs 3 prior to taking a decision pursuant to paragraph 4, taking into account respect for confidentiality. This decision, as well as the derogations referred to in paragraphs 1 and 2, shall be published in the Official Journal of the European Communities.

Article 27

1. Before the end of the first year following the entry into force of this Directive, the Commission shall submit a report to the European Parliament and the Council on harmonisation requirements which are not linked to the provisions of this Directive. If necessary, the Commission shall attach to the report any harmonisation proposals necessary for the effective operation of the internal natural gas market.

2. The European Parliament and the Council shall give their views on such proposals within two years of their submission.

3. Where implementation of this Directive would cause substantial problems in a geographically limited area of a Member State, in particular concerning the development of the transmission infrastructure, and with a view to encouraging investments, the Member State may apply to the Commission for a temporary derogation from Article 4, Article 18(1), (2), (3), (4) and (6) and/or Article 20 for developments within this area.

4. The Commission may grant the derogation referred to in paragraph 3, taking into account, in particular, the following criteria:

- the need for infrastructure investments, which would not be economical to operate in a competitive market environment,
- the level and pay-back prospects of investments required,
- the size and maturity of the gas system in the area concerned,
- the prospects for the gas market concerned,
- the geographical size and characteristics of the area or region concerned, and
- socio-economic and demographic factors.

A derogation may be granted only if no gas infrastructure has been established in this area, or has been so established for less than 10 years. The temporary derogation may not exceed 10 years from the time gas is first supplied in the area.

5. The Commission shall inform the Member States of applications made under paragraphs 3 prior to taking a decision pursuant to paragraph 4, taking into account respect for confidentiality. This decision, as well as the derogations referred to in paragraphs 1 and 2, shall be published in the Official Journal of the European Communities.

Article 27

1. Before the end of the first year following the entry into force of this Directive, the Commission shall submit a report to the European Parliament and the Council on harmonisation requirements which are not linked to the provisions of this Directive. If necessary, the Commission shall attach to the report any harmonisation proposals necessary for the effective operation of the internal natural gas market.

2. The European Parliament and the Council shall give their views on such proposals within two years of their submission.

Article 28
The Commission shall review the application of this Directive and submit a report on the experience gained on the functioning of the internal market in natural gas and the implementation of the general rules mentioned in Article 3 in order to allow the European Parliament and the Council, in the light of experience gained, to consider, in due time, the possibility of provisions for further improving the internal market in natural gas, which would be effective 10 years after the entry into force of the Directive.

Article 28
The Commission shall review the application of this Directive and submit a report to the European Parliament and the Council, by [indicate date] at the latest and by [indicate date] at the latest, on the experience gained and progress made in creating a complete and fully operational internal market in natural gas in order to allow the European Parliament and the Council to consider, in due time, the possibility of provisions for further improving the internal market in natural gas. In particular, the report shall examine the extent to which the unbundling and tarification requirements of this Directive have been successful in ensuring fair and non-discriminatory access to the Community's gas system The report shall also examine possible necessary harmonisation requirements which are not linked to the provisions of this Directive.

Article 29
Member States shall bring into force the laws, regulations and administrative provisions necessary to comply with this Directive no later than two years from the date specified in Article 30. They shall forthwith inform the Commission thereof. When Member States adopt these provisions, they shall contain a reference to this Directive or shall be accompanied by such reference on the occasion of their official publication. The methods of making such reference shall be laid down by the Member States.

Article 30
This Directive shall enter into force on the 20th day following that of its publication in the Official Journal of the European Communities.

Article 31
This Directive is addressed to the Member States.

Done at Luxembourg, 22 June 1998.
For the European Parliament
The President
J. M. GIL-ROBLES
For the Council
The President
J. CUNNINGHAM

Article 29
Member States shall bring into force the laws, regulations and administrative provisions necessary to comply with this Directive no later than two years from the date specified in Article 30. They shall forthwith inform the Commission thereof. When Member States adopt these provisions, they shall contain a reference to this Directive or shall be accompanied by such reference on the occasion of their official publication. The methods of making such reference shall be laid down by the Member States.

Article 30
This Directive shall enter into force on the 20th day following that of its publication in the Official Journal of the European Communities.

Article 31
This Directive is addressed to the Member States.

Done at Luxembourg, 22 June 1998.
For the European Parliament
The President
J. M. GIL-ROBLES
For the Council
The President
J. CUNNINGHAM

ANNEX

(ARTICLE 3)

Without prejudice to Community rules on consumer protection, in particular Directive 97/7/EC of the European Parliament and of the Council and Council Directive 93/13/EC:

(a) Member States shall ensure that final customers have a right to a contract with their gas service provider that specifies:
- the identity and address of the supplier;
- services provided, the service quality levels offered, as well as the time for the initial connection;
- the types of maintenance service offered;
- the means by which up-to-date information on all applicable tariffs and maintenance charges may be obtained;
- the duration of the contract, the conditions for renewal and termination of services and of the contract;
- any compensation and the refund arrangements which apply if contracted service quality levels are not met; and
- the method of initiating procedures for settlement of disputes in accordance with point (e).

(b) Member States shall ensure that final customers shall be given adequate notice of any intention to modify contractual conditions and shall be free to withdraw from contracts if they do not accept the new conditions.

(c) Member States shall ensure that transparent information on applicable prices and tariffs, and on standard terms and conditions, in respect of access to and use of gas services is available to the public, and particularly to final customers.

(d) Member States shall also implement appropriate measures to protect vulnerable customers.

(e) Member States shall ensure that transparent, simple and in-expensive procedures are available for dealing with final customer complaints. Member States shall adopt measures to ensure that such procedures enable disputes to be settled fairly and promptly with provision, where warranted, for a system of reimbursement and/or compensation. They should follow, wherever possible, the principles set out in Commission Recommendation 98/257/EC.

APPENDIX 3

Proposed Regulation on Network Access for Cross-Border Trade in Electricity (2001)

PROPOSAL FOR A REGULATION OF THE EUROPEAN PARLIAMENT AND OF THE COUNCIL ON THE CONDITIONS FOR ACCESS TO THE NETWORK FOR CROSS-BORDER EXCHANGES IN ELECTRICITY

THE EUROPEAN PARLIAMENT AND THE COUNCIL OF THE EUROPEAN UNION,

Having regard to the Treaty establishing the European Community, and in particular Article 95 thereof,
Having regard to the proposal from the Commission,
Having regard to the opinion of the Economic and Social Committee,
Having regard to the opinion of the Committee of the Regions,
Acting in accordance with the procedure laid down in Article 251 of the Treaty,
Whereas:

1. Directive 96/92/EC of the European Parliament and of the Council of 19 December 1996 concerning common rules for the internal market in electricity constituted an important step in the completion of the internal market in electricity.

2. At its meeting in Lisbon on 23 and 24 March 2000, the European Council called for rapid work to be undertaken to complete the internal market in both the electricity and gas sectors and to speed up liberalisation in these sectors with a view to achieving a fully operational internal market in these areas.

3. The creation of a real internal electricity market should be promoted through an intensification of trade in electricity, which is currently underdeveloped compared to other sectors of the economy.

4. Fair, cost-reflective, transparent and directly applicable rules, completing the provisions of Directive 96/92/EC, should be introduced with regard to cross-border tarification and the allocation of available interconnection capacities, in order to ensure efficient access to transmission systems for the purpose of cross-border transactions.

5. In its Conclusions, the Energy Council of 30 May 2000 invited the Commission, Member States and national regulatory authorities/administrations to ensure a rapid introduction of a robust tarification system and methodology to allocate available *interconnection* capacity for the longer term.

6. The European Parliament, in its Resolution of 6 July 2000 on the Commission's second report on the state of liberalisation of energy markets, called for conditions for using networks in Member States that do not hamper cross-border trade in electricity and called on the Commission to submit specific proposals geared to overcoming all the existing barriers to intra-Community trade.

7. This Regulation should lay down basic principles with regard to tarification and capacity allocation, whilst providing for the adoption of guidelines detailing further relevant principles and methodologies, in order to allow rapid adaptation to changed circumstances.

8. In an open, competitive market, transmission system operators should be compensated for costs incurred as a result of hosting transit flows of electricity on their networks by the operators of the transmission systems from which transits originate or for which they are destined.
9. Payments and receipts resulting from compensation between transmission system operators should be taken into account when setting national network tariffs.
10. The actual amount payable for cross-border access to the system can vary considerably, depending on the transmission system operators involved and as a result of differences in the structure of the tarification systems applied in Member States. A certain degree of harmonisation is therefore necessary in order to avoid distortions of trade.
11. It would not be appropriate to apply distance-related tariffs, or a specific tariff to be paid only by exporters or importers.
12. Competition on the internal market can only truly develop if access to the lines interconnecting the different national systems is granted in a non-discriminatory and transparent way. The available capacities of these lines should be set at the maximum complying with the safety standards of secure network operation. Any discrimination in the allocation of available capacities should be shown not to unreasonably distort or hinder the development of trade.
13. There should be transparency for market actors concerning available transfer capacities and the security, planning and operational standards that affect the available transfer capacities.
14. Any revenues flowing from congestion-management procedures should not constitute a source of extra profit for the transmission system operators.
15. It should be possible to deal with congestion problems in various ways as long as the methods used provide correct economic signals to transmission system operators and market parties and are based on market mechanisms.
16. To ensure the smooth functioning of the internal market, provision should be made for procedures which allow the adoption of decisions and guidelines with regard to tarification and capacity allocation by the Commission whilst ensuring the involvement of Member States' regulatory authorities in this process.
17. National authorities should be required to provide relevant information to the Commission. Such information should be treated confidentially by the Commission. Where necessary, the Commission should have the possibility to request relevant information directly from undertakings concerned.
18. National regulatory authorities should ensure compliance with the rules contained in this Regulation and the guidelines adopted on the basis of this Regulation.
19. Member States should lay down rules on penalties applicable to infringements of the provisions of this Regulation and ensure that they are implemented. Those penalties must be effective, proportionate and dissuasive.
20. In accordance with the principles of subsidiarity and proportionality as set out in Article 5 of the Treaty, the objectives of the proposed action, namely the provision of a harmonised framework for cross-border exchanges of electricity, cannot be achieved by the Member States and can therefore, by reason of the scale and effect of the action, be better achieved by the Community. This Regulation confines itself to the minimum required in order to achieve those objectives and does not go beyond what is necessary for that purpose.
21. In accordance with Article 2 of Council Decision 1999/468/EC of 28 June 1999 laying down the procedures for the exercise of implementing powers conferred on the Commission, measures for the implementation of this Regulation should be adopted by use of the regulatory procedure provided for in Article 5 of Decision 1999/468/EC, or by use of the advisory procedure provided for in Article 3 of that Decision, according to the nature of the measures to be adopted,

HAVE ADOPTED THIS REGULATION:

Article 1
Subject-matter and Scope

This Regulation aims at stimulating cross-border exchanges in electricity and thus competition within the internal electricity market, through the establishment of a compensation mechanism for transit flows of electricity and the setting of harmonised principles on cross-border transmission charges and the allocation of available capacities of interconnections between national transmission systems.

Article 2
Definitions

1. For the purpose of this Regulation, the definitions contained in Article 2 of Directive 96/92/EC shall apply.
2. The following definitions shall also apply:
   (a) 'transit' means a physical flow of electricity hosted on the transmission system of a Member State, which was neither produced nor is destined for consumption in that Member State, including transit flows which are commonly denominated as 'loop-flows' or 'parallel-flows',
   (b) 'congestion' means a situation in which an interconnection linking national transmission networks cannot accommodate all transactions resulting from international trade by market operators due to a lack of capacity.

Article 3
Inter-transmission System Operator Compensation Mechanism

1. Transmission system operators shall receive compensation for costs incurred as a result of hosting transit flows of electricity on their network.
2. The compensation referred to in paragraph 1 shall be paid by the operators of national transmission systems from which transit flows originate and/or the systems where those flows end.
3. Compensation payments shall be made on a regular basis with regard to a given period of time in the past. *Ex-post* adjustments of compensation paid shall be made where necessary to reflect actual costs incurred.
4. The first period of time with regard to which compensation payments shall be made shall be determined in the guidelines referred to in Article 7.
5. Acting in accordance with the procedure referred to in Article 13(2), the Commission shall decide on the amounts of compensation payments payable.
6. The amounts of transit hosted and the amounts of transit flows originating and/or ending in national transmission systems shall be determined on the basis of the physical flows of electricity actually measured in a given period of time. The costs incurred as a result of hosting transit flows shall be established on the basis of the forward looking long-run average incremental costs (reflecting costs and benefits that a network bears from hosting transit flows compared to the costs it would bear in the absence of such flows).

Article 4
Charges for Access to Networks

1. Charges applied by national network-operators for access to national networks shall reflect actual costs incurred, and shall be transparent, approximated to those of an efficient network operator and applied in a non-discriminatory manner. They shall not be distance-related.

2. Generators and consumers (load) may be charged a tariff for access to national networks. The proportion of the total amount of the network charges borne by generators shall be lower than the proportion borne by consumers. Where appropriate, the level of the tariffs applied to generators and/or consumers shall provide locational signals, and take into account the amount of network losses and congestion caused.
3. Payments and receipts resulting from the inter-transmission system operator compensation mechanism shall be taken into account when setting the charges for network access. Actual payments made and received as well as payments expected for future periods of time, estimated on the basis of past periods, shall be taken into account.
4. Subject to paragraph 2, charges for access to national networks applied to generators and consumers shall be applied independently of the country of destination and respectively origin of the electricity, as specified in the underlying commercial arrangement. Exporters and importers shall not be charged any specific charge in addition to the general charge for access to national networks.
5. There shall be no specific network charge on individual transactions for transits of electricity covered by the inter-transmission system operator compensation mechanism.

Article 5
Provision Of Information on Interconnection Capacities

1. Coordination and information exchange mechanisms shall be put in place by transmission system operators to ensure the security of the networks in the context of congestion management.
2. The safety, operational and planning standards used by transmission system operators shall be made public. This publication shall include a general scheme for the calculation of the total transfer capacity and the transmission reliability margin based upon the electrical and physical features of the network. Such schemes shall be subject to the approval of the national regulatory authority.
3. Transmission system operators shall publish estimates of available transfer capacity for each day, indicating any available transfer capacity already reserved. These publications shall be made at specified time intervals before the day of transport and shall include, in any case, week-ahead and month-ahead estimates.

The data published shall include a quantitative indication of the expected reliability of the available capacity.

Article 6
General Principles on Congestion Management

1. Network congestion problems shall be addressed with non-discriminatory market based solutions which give efficient economic signals to the market participants and transmission system operators involved.
2. Transaction curtailment procedures shall only be used in emergency situations where the transmission system operator must act in an expeditious manner and redispatching or countertrading is not possible. Market participants who have been allocated capacity shall be compensated for any curtailment of this capacity.
3. The maximum capacity of the interconnections shall be made available to market participants, complying with safety standards of secure network operation.
4. Any allocated capacity that will not be used shall be reattributed to the market.
5. Transmission system operators shall, as far as technically possible, net the capacity requirements of any power flows in opposite direction over the congested interconnection line in order to use this line to its maximum capacity. In any event, transactions that relieve the congestion shall never be denied.
6. Any rents resulting from the allocation of interconnection capacities shall be used for one or more of the following purposes:

(a) guaranteeing the actual availability of the allocated capacity;
(b) network investments maintaining or increasing interconnection capacities;
(c) reduction of network charges.

These rents may be put into a fund that is managed by transmission system operators. They shall not constitute a source of extra profit to the transmission system operators.

Article 7
Guidelines

1. Where appropriate, the Commission shall, acting in accordance with the procedure referred to in Article 12(2), adopt and amend guidelines on the following issues with regard to the inter-transmission system operator compensation mechanism:
   (a) details of the determination of the transmission system operators liable to pay compensations for transit flows, in accordance with Article 3(2);
   (b) details of the payment procedure to be followed, including the determination of the first period of time for which compensations are to be paid, in accordance with the second subparagraph of Article 3(3);
   (c) details of methodologies to determine the amount of transits hosted and exports/imports of electricity made, in accordance with Article 3(5);
   (d) details of the methodology to determine the costs incurred as a result of hosting transits of electricity, in accordance with Article 3(6);
   (e) the participation of national systems which are interconnected through direct current lines, in accordance with Article 3.
2. The guidelines shall also determine details of the harmonisation of the charges applied to generators and consumers (load) under national tariff systems, in accordance with the principles set out in Article 4(2).
3. Where appropriate, the Commission shall, acting in accordance with the procedure referred to in Article 12(2), amend the guidelines on the management and allocation of available transfer capacity of interconnections between national systems set out in the Annex, in accordance with the principles set out in Articles 5 and 6. Where appropriate, in the course of such amendments common rules on minimum safety and operational standards for the use and operation of the network, as referred to in Article 5(2) shall be set.

Article 8
National Regulatory Authorities

National regulatory authorities shall ensure that national tariffs and methodologies for congestion management are set and applied in accordance with this Regulation and the guidelines adopted pursuant to Article 7.

Article 9
Provision of Information and Confidentiality

1. Member States and national regulatory authorities shall, on request, provide to the Commission all information necessary for the purpose of Articles 3(4) and 7.

   In particular, for the purpose of Article 3(4), national regulatory authorities shall provide on a regular basis, costs actually incurred by national transmission system operators associated with hosting transit flows as well as the amount of exports and imports made in a given period. They shall also provide the relevant data and information used for the calculation of those figures.
2. Member States shall ensure that national regulatory authorities and administrations are able and entitled to provide the information required pursuant to paragraph 1.

3. The Commission may also request all information necessary for the purpose of Article 3(4) and Article 7 directly from undertakings and associations of undertakings.

   When sending a request for information to an undertaking or an association of undertakings, the Commission shall at the same time forward a copy of the request to the regulatory authority, established pursuant to Article 22 of Directive 96/92/EC of the Member State in whose territory the seat of the undertaking or the association of undertakings is situated.

4. In its request for information, the Commission shall state the legal basis of the request, the time-limit within which the information is to be provided, the purpose of the request, and also the penalties provided for in Article 11(2) for supplying incorrect, incomplete and misleading information.

5. The owners of the undertakings or their representatives and, in the case of legal persons, companies of firms, or of associations having no legal personality, the persons authorised to represent them by law or by their constitution, shall supply the information requested. Lawyers duly authorised to act may supply the information on behalf of their clients, in which case the client shall remain fully responsible if the information supplied is incomplete, incorrect or misleading.

6. Where an undertaking or association of undertakings does not provide the information requested within the time-limit fixed by the Commission or supplies incomplete information, the Commission shall by decision require the information to be provided. The decision shall specify what information is required and fix an appropriate time-limit within which it is to be supplied. It shall indicate the penalties provided for in Article 11(2). It shall also indicate the right to have the decision reviewed by the Court of Justice of the European Communities.

   The Commission shall at the same time send a copy of its decision to the regulatory authority referred to in the second subparagraph of paragraph 3 of the Member State within the territory of which the residence of the person or the seat of the undertaking or the association of undertakings is situated.

7. Information collected pursuant to this Regulation shall be used only for the purposes of Articles 3(4) and 7.

   The Commission shall not disclose information acquired pursuant to this Regulation of the kind covered by the obligation of professional secrecy.

Article 10
Right of Member States to Provide for More Detailed Measures

This Regulation is without prejudice to the rights of Member States to maintain or introduce measures that contain more detailed provisions than those set out in this Regulation and the guidelines referred to in Article 7.

Article 11
Penalties

1. The Member States shall lay down the rules on penalties applicable to infringements of the provisions of this Regulation and shall take all measures necessary to ensure that they are implemented. The penalties provided for must be effective, proportionate and dissuasive. The Member States shall notify those provisions to the Commission by [indicate date] at the latest and shall notify it without delay of any subsequent amendment affecting them.

2. The Commission may by decision impose on undertakings or associations of undertakings fines not exceeding 1% of the total turnover in the preceding business year where, intentionally or negligently, they supply incorrect, incomplete or misleading information in response to a request made pursuant to Article 9(3) or fail to supply information within the time-limit fixed by a decision adopted pursuant to the first subparagraph of Article 9(6).

3. In setting the amount of a fine, regard shall be had both to the gravity and to the duration of the infringement.
4. Penalties provided for pursuant to paragraph 1 and decisions taken pursuant to paragraph 2 shall not be of criminal law nature.

Article 12
Regulatory Committee

1. The Commission shall be assisted by a committee composed of the representatives of the Member States and chaired by the representative of the Commission.
2. Where reference is made to this paragraph, the regulatory procedure laid down in Article 5 of Decision 1999/468/EC shall apply, in compliance with Article 7 and Article 8 thereof.
3. The period provided for in Article 5(6) of Decision 1999/468/EC shall be two months.

Article 13
Advisory Committee

1. The Commission shall be assisted by a committee composed of the representatives of the Member States and chaired by the representative of the Commission.
2. Where reference is made to this paragraph, the advisory procedure laid down in Article 3 of Decision 1999/468/EC shall apply, in compliance with Article 7 and Article 8 thereof.

Article 14
Entry into Force

This Regulation shall enter into force on the twentieth day following that of its publication in the *Official Journal of the European Communities.*

It shall apply from [indicate date].

This Regulation shall be binding in its entirety and directly applicable in all Member States.

ANNEX

GUIDELINES ON THE MANAGEMENT AND ALLOCATION OF AVAILABLE TRANSFER CAPACITY OF INTERCONNECTIONS BETWEEN NATIONAL SYSTEMS

General

1. Congestion management method(s) implemented by Member States should deal with short-run congestion in an economically efficient manner whilst simultaneously providing signals or incentives for efficient network and generation investment in the right locations.
2. In order to minimise the negative impact of congestion on trade, the current network should be used at the maximum capacity that complies with the safety standards of secure network operation.
3. The TSOs should provide non-discriminatory and transparent standards, which describe which congestion management methods they will apply under which circumstances. These standards, together with the security standards, should be described in open and publicly available documents.
4. Different treatment of the different types of cross-border transactions, whether they are physical bilateral contracts or bids into foreign organised markets, should be kept to a minimum when designing the rules of specific methods for congestion management. The method for allocating scarce

transmission capacity must be transparent. Any differences in how transactions are treated must be shown not to distort or hinder the development of competition.

5. Price signals that result from congestion management systems should be directional.
6. Every effort should be made to net the capacity requirements of any power flows in opposite direction over the congested tie line in order to use the congested tie line to its maximum capacity. In any adopted congestion management scheme, transactions that relieve the congestion should never be denied.
7. Any unused capacity must become available to other agents (the *use-it-or-lose-it* principle). This may be implemented by devising notification procedures.
8. Any rents resulting from the allocation of interconnection capacities may be used for redispatching or counter trading in order to comply with the firmness of the capacity that was allocated to market parties. In principle, any remaining rents should be spent on network investments for relieving the congestion or on reducing the total network tariff. TSOs may manage these funds, but cannot retain them.
9. TSOs should offer transmission capacity to the market as 'firm' as possible. A reasonable fraction of the capacity may be offered to the market under condition of decreased firmness, but at all times the exact conditions for transport over cross-border lines should be made known to market parties.
10. Considering the fact that the European continental network is a highly meshed network and that the use of interconnection lines has an effect on the power flows on at least two sides of a national border, national regulators shall ensure that no congestion management procedure with significant effects on power flows in other networks, be devised unilaterally.

Position of long-term contracts

1. Priority access rights to an interconnection capacity can not be assigned to those contracts which violate Articles 81 and 82 of the EC Treaty.
2. Existing long-term contracts shall have no pre-emption rights when they come up for renewal.

Provision of information

1. TSOs should implement appropriate coordination and information exchange mechanisms to guarantee security of the network.
2. TSOs should publish all relevant data concerning the cross-border total transfer capacities. In addition to the winter and summer ATC values, estimates of transfer capacity for each day should be published by the TSOs at several time intervals before the day of transport. At least accurate week-ahead estimates should be made available to the market and the TSOs should also endeavour to provide month-ahead information. A description of the firmness of the data should be included.
3. The TSOs should publish a general scheme for calculation of the total transfer capacity and the transmission reliability margin based upon the electrical and physical realities of the network. Such a scheme should be subject to approval by the regulators of the involved Member States concerned. The safety standards and the operational and planning standards should form an integral part of the information that TSOs should publish in open and public documents.

Preferred methods for congestion management

1. Network congestion problems should in principle be addressed with market-based solutions. More specifically, congestion management solutions are preferred which give appropriate price signals to the market parties and the TSOs involved.
2. Network congestion problems should preferentially be solved with non-transaction based methods, i.e. methods that do not involve a selection between the contracts of individual market parties.
3. The system of market splitting, as used in the Nordpool area, is the congestion management procedure that, in principle, best meets this requirement.
4. In the short term, however, methods for congestion management in Continental Europe that may be used are implicit and explicit auctions and cross-border coordinated redispatching.

5. Cross-border coordinated redispatching or counter trading may be used jointly by the concerned TSOs. The costs that TSOs incur in counter-trading and redispatching must, however, be at an efficient level.
6. Transaction curtailment, following pre-established priority rules, should be left only for emergency situations where the TSOs must act in an expeditious manner and redispatching is not possible.
7. The possible merits of a combination of market splitting for solving 'permanent' congestion and counter trading for solving temporary congestion should be immediately explored as a more permanent approach to congestion management.

Guidelines for explicit auctions

1. The auction system must be designed in such a way that all available capacity is being offered to the market. This may be done by organising a composite auction in which capacities are auctioned for differing duration and with different characteristics (e.g. with respect to the expected reliability of the available capacity in question).
2. Total interconnection capacity should be offered in a series of auctions, which, for instance, might be held on a yearly, monthly, weekly, daily and intra-daily basis, according to the needs of the markets involved. Each of these auctions should allocate a prescribed fraction of the available transfer capacity plus any remaining capacity that was not allocated in previous auctions.
3. The explicit auction procedures should be prepared in close collaboration between the national regulatory and the TSO concerned and designed in such a way as to allow bidders to participate also in the daily sessions of any organised market (i.e. power exchange) in the countries involved.
4. The power flows in both directions over congested tie lines should in principle be netted in order to maximise the transport capacity in the direction of the congestion. However, the procedure for netting of flows should comply with safe operation of the power system.
5. In order to offer as much capacity to the market as possible, the financial risks related to the netting of flows, should be attributed to those parties causing those risks to materialise.
6. Any auction procedure adopted should be capable of sending directional price signals to market participants. Transports in a direction opposite the dominant power flow relieve the congestion and should therefore result in additional transport capacity over the congested tie line.
7. In order not to risk creating or aggravating problems related to any dominant position of market player(s), capping of the amount of capacity that can be bought/possessed/used by any single market player in an auction should be seriously considered by the competent regulatory authorities in the design of an auction mechanism.
8. To promote the creation of liquid electricity markets, capacity bought at an auction should be freely tradeable before the moment of notification.

APPENDIX 4

Table of Derivations: EC Treaty, and Articles 28–31, 81, 82, 86 and 226

The Articles of the EC Treaty were re-numbered by the Treaty of Amsterdam in 1997. The wording was also modified in some cases.

Throughout this work, references are to the post-1997 numbering system. This Table shows the original numbering.

Post-1997 numbering Article	EC Treaty equivalent Article
14	7
16	7D
28	30
29	34
30	36
31	37
43	52
49	59
81	85
82	86
83	87
84	88
85	89
86	90
87	92
88	93
89	94
95	100A
133	113
154	129b
155	129c
156	129d
174	130r
175	130s
189–201	137–144
202–210	145–154
205	148
211–219	155–163

Post-1997 numbering Article	EC Treaty equivalent Article
220–245	164–188
222	166
223	167
225	168a
226	169
227	170
228	171
230	173
231	174
232	175
233	176
234	177
235	178
238	181
246–248	188a–188c
249–256	189–192
251	189b
256	192
261	197
284	213
288	215
295	222
308	235

Articles 28–31, 81, 82, 86 and 226

Article 28

Quantitative restrictions on imports and all measures having equivalent effect shall be prohibited between Member States.

Article 29

Quantitative restrictions on exports, and all measures having equivalent effect, shall be prohibited between Member States.

Article 30

The provisions of Articles 28 and 29 shall not preclude prohibitions or restrictions on imports, exports or goods in transit justified on grounds of public morality, public policy or public security; the protection of health and life of humans, animals or plants; the protection of national treasures possessing artistic, historic or archaeological value; or the protection of industrial and commercial property. Such prohibitions or restrictions shall not, however, constitute a means of arbitrary discrimination or a disguised restriction on trade between Member States.

Article 31*

1. Member States shall adjust any State monopolies of a commercial character so as to ensure that no discrimination regarding the conditions under which goods are procured and marketed exists between nationals of Member States.

   The provisions of this Article shall apply to any body through which a Member State, in law or in fact, either directly or indirectly supervises, determines or appreciably influences imports or exports between Member States. These provisions shall likewise apply to monopolies delegated by the State to others.

2. Member States shall refrain from introducing any new measure which is contrary to the principles laid down in paragraph 1 or which restricts the scope of the Articles dealing with the prohibition of customs duties and quantitative restrictions between Member States.

3. If a State monopoly of a commercial character has rules which are designed to make it easier to dispose of agricultural products or obtain for them the best return, steps should be taken in applying the rules contained in this Article to ensure equivalent safeguards for the employment and standard of living of the producers concerned.

**Note: this is the current text which differs in very minor respects from that in force during the period covered in ch 5.*

Article 81

1. The following shall be prohibited as incompatible with the common market: all agreements between undertakings, decisions by associations of undertakings and concerted practices which may affect trade between Member States and which have as their object or effect the prevention, restriction or distortion of competition within the common market, and in particular those which:

   (a) directly or indirectly fix purchase or selling prices or any other trading conditions;
   (b) limit or control production, markets, technical development, or investment;
   (c) share markets or sources of supply;
   (d) apply dissimilar conditions to equivalent transactions with other trading parties, thereby placing them at a competitive disadvantage;
   (e) make the conclusion of contracts subject to acceptance by the other parties of supplementary obligations which, by their nature or according to commercial usage, have no connection with the subject of such contract.

2. Any agreements or decisions prohibited pursuant to this Article shall be automatically void.

3. The provisions of paragraph 1 may, however, be declared inapplicable in the case of:

   – any agreement or category of agreements between undertakings;
   – any decision or category of decisions by associations of undertakings;
   – any concerted practice or category of concerted practices;

   which contributes to improving the production or distribution of goods or to promoting technical or economic progress, while allowing consumers a fair share of the resulting benefit, and which does not:

   (a) impose on the undertakings concerned restrictions which are not indispensable to the attainment of these objectives;
   (b) afford such undertakings the possibility of eliminating competition in respect of a substantial part of the products in question.

Article 82

Any abuse by one or more undertakings of a dominant position within the common market or in a substantial part of it shall be prohibited as incompatible with the common market in so far as it may affect trade between Member States.

Such abuse may, in particular, consist in:

(a) directly or indirectly imposing unfair purchase or selling prices or other unfair trading conditions;
(b) limiting production, markets or technical development to the prejudice of consumers;
(c) applying dissimilar conditions to equivalent transactions with other trading parties, thereby placing them at a competitive disadvantage;
(d) making the conclusion of contracts subject to acceptance by the other parties of supplementary obligations which, by their nature or according to commercial usage, have no connection with the subject of such contracts.

Article 86

1. In the case of public undertakings and undertakings to which Member States grant special or exclusive rights, Member States shall neither enact nor maintain in force any measure contrary to the rules contained in this Treaty, in particular to those rules provided for in Article 12 and Articles 81 to 89.
2. Undertakings entrusted with the operation of services of general economic interest or having the character of a revenue-producing monopoly shall be subject to the rules contained in this Treaty, in particular to the rules on competition, insofar as the application of such rules does not obstruct the performance, in law or in fact, of the particular tasks assigned to them. The development of trade must not be affected to such an extent as would be contrary to the interests of the Community.
3. The Commission shall ensure the application of the provisions of this Article and shall, where necessary, address appropriate directives or decisions to Member States.

Article 226

If the Commission considers that a Member State has failed to fulfil an obligation under this Treaty, it shall deliver a reasoned opinion on the matter after giving the State concerned the opportunity to submit its observations.

If the State concerned does not comply with the opinion within the period laid down by the Commission, the latter may bring the matter before the Court of Justice.

SELECT BIBLIOGRAPHY

Books

Ariño, G O Ortiz, *Principios de Derecho Público Económico* (Comares Editorial, 1999)

Avery, G, and Cameron, F, *The Enlargement of the European Union* (Sheffield Academic Press, 1998)

Bellamy and Child, *European Law of Competition* (5th edn, Roth, A (ed), Sweet and Maxwell, 2001)

Buendia Sierra, J L, *Exclusive Rights and State Monopolies under EC Law* (OUP, 2000)

Cameron, P, *Property Rights and Sovereign Rights: the Case of North Sea Oil* (Academic Press, 1982)

—— *Gas Regulation in Europe* (two vols) (Financial Times, 1998)

—— Hancher, L, and Iuhne, G, *Nuclear Energy Law After Chernobyl* (Graeme and Trotman, 1989)

—— and Zillman, D (eds), *Kyoto: From Principles to Practice* (Kluwer, 2002)

Cross, E D, *Electric Utility Regulation in the European Union: A Country by Country Guide* (Wiley, 1996)

Daintith, T, and Hancher, L, *Energy Strategy in Europe: the Legal Framework* (Walter de Gruyter, 1986)

—— and Williams, S, *The Legal Integration of Energy Markets* (Walter de Gruyter, 1987)

Dore, J, and De Bauw, R, *The Energy Charter Treaty: Origins, Aims and Prospects* (The Royal Institute of International Affairs, 1995)

Ehlermann, C D, and Gosling, L (eds), *Regulating Common Markets* (Hart Publishing, 2000)

Estrada, J, Moe, A, and Martinsen, K D (eds), *The Development of European Gas Markets: Environmental, Economic and Political Perspectives* (Wiley, 1995)

Faull, J and Nikpay, A, *Competition Law* (OUP, 2000)

Giddens, A, *The Third Way and Its Critics* (Polity Press, 2000)

—— *The Third Way: the Renewal of Social Democracy* (Polity Press, 1998)

Gilbert, R J, and Kahn, E P (eds), *International Comparisons of Electricity Regulation* (Cambridge University Press, 1996)

Hartley, *The Foundations of European Community Law: an introduction to the constitutional and administrative law of the European Community* (4th edn, OUP 1998)

Henry, C, Mathey, M, and Jeunemaître, A (eds), *Regulation of Network Utilities: the European Experience* (OUP, 2001)

Horslaach, N (ed), *Contemporary Developments in Nuclear Energy Law: Harmonising Legislation in CEEC/NIS* (Kluwer, 1999)

Hunt, S, and Shuttleworth, G, *Competition and Choice in Electricity* (Wiley, 1996)

Kahn, A E, *The Economics of Regulation: Principles and Institutions* (MIT Press, 1998)

Kapteyn, P J G, and VerLoren van Themaat, P, *Introduction to the Law of the European Communities: From Maastricht to Amsterdam* (3rd edn, Gormley, (ed), Kluwer 1998)

Kuhn, T, *The Structure of Scientific Revolutions* (University of Chicago Press, 1970)

Larouche, P, *Competition Law and Regulation in European Telecommunications* (Hart Publishing, 2000)

Maresceau, M (ed), *Enlarging the European Union: Relations between the EU and Central and Eastern Europe* (Longman, 1997)

McCahery, J, Bratton, W W, Picciotto, S, and Scott, C (eds), *International Regulatory Competition and Co-ordination: Perspectives on Economic Regulation in Europe and the United States* (OUP, 1996)

Mestmäcker, E J, *Natural Gas in the Internal Market: A Review of Energy Policy* (Kluwer, 1992)

Middtun, A (ed), *European Electricity Systems in Transition: A Comparative Analysis of Policy and Regulation in Western Europe* (Elsevier, 1997)

Natallicchi, G, *Wiring Europe: reshaping the European telecommunications regime* (Rowman and Littlefield, 2001)

OECD/IEA, *Regulatory Reform in Mexico's Natural Gas Sector* (OECD, 1996)

—— *Natural Gas Distribution: Focus on Western Europe* (OECD, 1998)

—— *Regulatory Reform in Argentina's Natural Gas Sector* (OECD, 1999)

—— *Electricity Market Reform* (OECD, 1999)

—— *Regulatory Reform: European Gas* (OECD, 2000)

—— *Competition in electricity Markets* (OECD, 2001)

Ognus, A I, *Regulation: Legal Reform in Mexico's Natural Gas Sector* (OECD, 1994)

Ohmae, K, *The End of the Nation State: The Rise of Regional Economies* (Harper-Collins, 1996)

Patterson, W, *Transforming Electricity* (Earthscan/RIIA, 1999)

Pfang, E, *Towards Liberalization of the European Electricity Markets* (Peter Lang, 1999)

Prechal, S, *Directives in Community Law: A Study of Directives and their Enforcement in National Courts* (OUP, 1996)

Prosser, T, *Law and the Regulators* (OUP, 1997)

Sassen, S, *Losing Control: Sovereignty in an Age of Globalization* (Columbia University Press, 1996)

Sauter, W, *Competition Law in Industrial Policy in the EU* (OUP, 1997)

Sidak, J G, and Spulber, D F, *Deregulatory Takings and the Regulatory Contract: The Competitive Transformation of Network Industries in the United States* (Cambridge University Press, 1998)

Stern, J, *Third Party Access on European Gas Markets* (Royal Institute of International Affairs, 1992)

Waelde, T W (ed), *The Energy Charter Treaty: An East–West Gateway for Investment and Trade* (Kluwer, 1996)

Weatherill, *Law and Integration in the European Union* (OUP, 1995)

Wogau, K von, *Soziale Marktwirtschaft—Modell für Europa: vom Euro zum Europäischen Heimatmarkt* (Europa Union Verlag, 1999)

Wyatt, D, and Dashwood, A, *European Union Law* (4th edn, Sweet and Maxwell, 2000)

Zaccour, Georges (ed), *Deregulation of Electric Utilities* (Kluwer, 1998)

Articles in Books

Brothwood, M, 'Contract Issues in Gas Trading', in Long, D, and Moore, G, *Gas Trading Manual: a Comprehensive Guide to the Gas Markets* (Woodhead Publishing, 2001)

Coen, D, and Doyle, C, 'Designing Economic Regulatory Institutions for European Network Industries', in Coen, D and Thatcher, M, *Current Politics and Economics of Europe* (2000), 407–425

Devlin, B, and Levasseur, C, 'Energy' (chapter 10), in Faull and Nikpay *Competition Law*
Eberlein, B, 'Configurations of Economic Regulation in the European Union: the Case of Electricity in Comparative Perspective', in Coen, D and Thatcher, M, *Current Politics and Economics of Europe*, 407–254
Flynn, 'Access to the Postal Network', in Geradin, G, and Humpe, C, *Postal Services, Liberalisation and EC Competition Law* (Kluwer, 2002)
Gruenwald, E, 'The Role of Euratom', in Cameron, P, Haucher, l, and Kuhn, G, *Nuclear Energy after Chernobyl* (Kluwer, 1988), 33–48
Steiner, J, 'Subsidiarity under the Maastricht Treaty', in O'Keeffe, D, (ed), *Legal Issues of the Maastricht Treaty* (Kluwer 1994)
Schwarze, J, 'European Energy Policy in 'Community law', in Mestmaeker, E J (ed), *Natural Gas and the Internal Market* (1992)
Toth, A, 'A Legal Analysis of Subsidiarity', in O'Keeffe, D, (ed), *Legal Issues of the Maastricht Treaty* (Kluwer, 1994)
Usher, J, 'The Commission and the Law', in Edwards, D, and Spence, D (eds), *The European Commission* (Cartermill, 1994), 212–234

Articles and Papers

Albers, M, 'Energy Liberalization and EC Competition Law', paper presented at 28th Annual Fordham Conference on Antitrust Law and Policy, 26 Oct 2001
Allen, D, 'The Euratom Treaty, Chapter IV: New Hope or False Dawn?' (1983) 20 CML Rev, 473
Allibert, B, 'A Methodology for Analysing State Aid Linked to Stranded Costs', Competition Policy Newsletter, Oct 2001, 25–27
Bamberger, C S, Linehan, J and Waelde, T, 'Energy Charter Treaty in 2000: in a New Phase', (2000) 18 J Energy Natural Resources L, 331–352
Blanchard, P, 'French Electricity Sector: ECJ Decision on Monopolis for the Import and Export of Electricity', [1999] J Energy Natural Resources L, 256–280
Boerner, A R, 'Negotiated Third Party Access in Germany: Electricity and Gas', (2001) 19 J Energy Natural Resources L, 32
Brinkhorst, L, 'Subsidiarity and EC ENvironmental Policy', (1993) 8 European Environmental L Rev, 20
Brothwood, M, 'The Court of Justice on Article 90 of the EEC Treaty', [1983] CML Rev
—— 'EC Wants Larger Say in Trade', Utility Europe, July 2001
Burchard, F von, 'Third Party Access and European Law', Europäisches Zeitschrift für Wirtschaftsrecht, 693–697
Cameron, P, 'Five Years of Regulating Britain's Gas Industry', [1991] Utilities Law Rev, 70–77
—— 'Towards an Internal Market in Energy: The Carrot and Stick Approach', (1998) 23 EL Rev, 579–591
—— 'Het Verdrag inzake het Energiehandvest: een beoordeling na zes jaar', [2001] SEW, 139–145
Cardoso e Cunha, 'The Internal Energy Market', (1991) 9 J Energy Natural Resources, 290
Daintith, T, 'Regulation', International Encyclopedia of Comparative Law, vol XVII (State and Economy), ch 10
Dashwood, A, 'The Constitution of the European Union after Nice: law-making procedures', (2001) 26 EL Rev, 215–238

Delcourt, C, 'The *Acquis Communautaire*: Has the Concept Had its Day?' (2000) 38 CML Rev, 829

Dinnage, J 'Competition in Gas Supply: The Competition Man Cometh', (1998) 16 J Natural Energy Resources L, 249–285

Doherty, B, 'Just What are Essential Facilities?' (2001) 38 CML Rev, 397–436

Edward, D, and Hoskins, M, 'Article 90: Deregulation and EC law: Reflections arising from the XVI FIDE Conference', [1995] CML Rev, 168

Ehlermann, C D, 'Establishing the Single Market in Energy', [1991] Oil Gas Law Taxation Rev 295–298

—— 'EG-Binnenmarkt für die Energiewirtschaft', [1992] Europäische Zeitschrift für Wirtschaftsrecht, 689–693

—— 'The Role of the European Commission as regards National Energy Policies', (1994) 12 J Energy Natural Resources L, 342

Eising, R, 'Strategic Action and Policy Learning in 'Embedded Negotiations: the Liberalization of the Electricity Supply Industry', (2002) 56 International Organization, 1

Fernandez Salas, M, 'Long-term Supply Agreements in the Context of Gas Market Liberalization: Commission Closes Investigation of Gas Natural', [2000] Competition Policy Newsletter, 55

Gialdino, C, 'Some Reflections on the *Acquis Communautaire*', (1995) 32 CML Rev, 1079–1088

Green, N, 'The Implementation of Treaty Policies: the Energy Dilemma', (1983) 8 EL Rev, 186

Hayes-Renshaw, F and Wallace, H, 'Executive Power in the European Union: functions and limits of the Council of Ministers', [1995] J of European Public Policy, 559–582

Hogan, W, 'Making Markets in Power', Cantor Lecture Series 2000: Energy and Society, London

Johnston, A, 'Maintaining the Balance of Power: Liberalization, Reciprocity and electricity in the European Community', (1999) 17 J Energy Natural Resources L, 121–150

Kepenne, J-P, 'National Environmental Policies: Uncharted Waters for EC State Aid Control', [2001] Nederlands Tijdschrift voor Europees Recht, 193–199

Klom, A M, 'Effects of Deregulation Policies on Electricity Competition in the EU', [1997] J Energy Natural Resources L, 1–22

Lapuerta, C, Pfaffenberger, W, and Pfeifenberger, J, 'Netzzugang in Deutschland: ein Ländervergleich', Energiewirtschaft, Mr/Apr 1999

Lenaerts, K, 'The Principle of Subsidiarity and the Environment in the European Union: Keeping the Balance of Federalism', 17 Fordham International L J, 846

Macatangay, R E A, 'Market Definition and Dominant Position Abuse under the New Electricity Trading Arrangements in England and Wales', (2001) 29 Energy Policy, 337

Pegg, G J, and Waller, M R, 'Take-or-Pay Provisions in Natural Gas Contracts; US Experience as a Comparator to UK Gas Industry's Problems', (1996) 14 J Energy Natural Resources L, 456–463

Pierce, Jr, R J, 'The Antitrust Implications of Energy Restructuring', [1998] Natural Resources & Environment, 269

Schaub, A, 'Competition Policy and Liberalization of Energy Markets', paper presented at European Utilities Circle Conference, 23 Nov 2000

Schmidt, S K, 'Commission Activiem: Subsuming Telecommunication and Electricity under European Competition Law', [1998] J of European Public Policy, 169–184

Slot, P J, 'Note', (1998) 35 CML Rev, 1183

Stevens, P, 'Pipelines or Pipe-Dreams? Lessons from the history of Arab Transit Pipelines', (2000) 54 Middle East J, 224–241
Strothers, C, 'Refusal to Supply as Abuse of a Dominant Position: Essential Facilities in the European Union', [2001] ECL Rev, 256–262
Temple-Lang, J, 'Defining Legitimate Competition: companies' duties to supply competitors and access to essential facilities', (1994) 18 Fordham International L J, 437
Tradacete, A, 'Role of EC Competition Policy in the Liberalization of EU Energy Markets', April 2000
Vasconcelos, J, 'The Role of Regulation in a Single Energy Market', paper presented at Conference on Launching a Common European Energy Market, 5–6 June 2000
Wainright, R, 'Public Undertakings under Article 90', Fordham Corporate Law Institute Proceedings, 1990
Weiler, J, 'The Transformation of Europe', (1991) 100 Yale Law J, 2403

Reports

Aachen University (Haubrich, H-J, Fritz, W, and Vennegeerts, H), *Cross-Border Electricity Transmission Tariffs*, April 1999
Brattle Group, *Methodologies for Establishing National and Cross-Border Systems of Pricing of Access to the Gas System in Europe* (2000)
DRI-WEFA, Report for the European Commission Directorate General for Transport and Energy to determine changes after opening of the Gas Market, in August 2000, July 2001
Egenhofer, C, 'Understanding the Politics of European Energy Policy', Centre for European Policy Studies (1997)
Eurelectric, *Preliminary Report on the Tendency for Unbundling in the EU*, Dec 1999
European Commission, 'Towards a Dynamic European Economy: Green Paper on the Development of the Common Makret for Telecommunications Services and Equipment', COM (1987) 290 final, 30 June 1987
—— 'The External Dimension of Trans-European Energy Networks', COM (1997) 125 final, 23 Mar 1997
—— 'An Overall View of Energy Policy and Actions', COM (1997) 167, 23 April 1997
—— 'Second Report to the Council and the European Parliament on Harmonization Requirements: Directive 96/92/EC on common rules for the internal market in electricity', COM (1998) final, 167
—— 'Study on Interoperability of Gas Networks in EU Countries: Final Report Executive Summary, carried out by Pipeline Engineering GmbH', June 1999
—— 'Report to the Council and the European Parliament on Harmonization Requirements: Directive 98/30/EC on common rules for the internal market in natural gas', COM (1999) 612
—— 'Recent Progress with Building the Internal Electricity Market', COM (2000) 297 final
—— 'An Internal Market in Energy', COM (2000) 4 (9)
—— 'Communication on Completion of the Internal Market in Energy', COMM (2001) 125 final
—— 'European Energy Infrastructure', COM (2001)
Fleming UCB Research, *Russia Oil and Gas, Gazprom: Time is Up for the Ring-fence*, October 2001

HL *Select Committee on the European Communities, EU Gas Directive,* (HL Paper [1997–98] no 35)

International Chambers of Commerce, *Liberalization and Privatization of the Energy Sector* (ICC, 1998)

Royal Commission on Environmental Pollution, *Energy: The Changing Climate*, Cm 4749

INDEX